The Papers of James Iredell

James Iredell, ca. 1790

Courtesy of the James Iredell Association

The Papers of James Iredell

Volume III

1784-1789

Edited by
Donna Kelly
and
Lang Baradell

Office of Archives and History
North Carolina Department of Cultural Resources
Raleigh
2003

ISBN 0-86526-310-8

Contents

List of Illustrations

Foreword

Almost a century and a half has passed since the first publication of the papers of Justice James Iredell. Griffith McRee's mid-nineteenth-century endeavor served a valuable purpose at the time, but his compilation was by no means complete. McRee omitted important letters, excessively trimmed documents, and distorted others. By contrast, Don Higginbotham's two-volume *Papers of James Iredell*, now more than a quarter of a century old and covering Iredell's life and work through 1783, is thorough and accurate. Students of Iredell and his time will benefit from Higginbotham's scholarly notes and commentary for years to come.

Publication of the remaining papers has been too long delayed, however. Now we are treated to Donna Kelly and Lang Baradell's work on documents from the remainder of Iredell's pre-Supreme Court years. Although we could well have used it sooner, the new tome is timely for two reasons. First, the years subsequent to the publication of the Higginbotham volumes have witnessed a change in the conventional wisdom that the United States Supreme Court acquired significance only with John Marshall's tenure as chief justice and his opinion in *Marbury v. Madison*. Recent works on the pre-Marshall Court, including Scott Gerber's *Seriatum: The Supreme Court Before John Marshall* and Maeva Marcus's *The Documentary History of the Supreme Court of the United States, 1789-1800*, have increased interest in the earlier Court and the men who served it, as well as creating an enlarged sense of the importance of both. Second, Iredell is arguably foremost among those early jurists in stimulating this enhanced interest and perception of significance. Editors of the documentary history of the early Supreme Court, mentioned above, readily acknowledge that their work would have been impossible without Iredell's writings. In addition, the hearings on the nomination of Judge Robert Bork and the proceedings to impeach President William Clinton both contained quotations from Iredell. He has also received renewed attention from the Supreme Court's conclusion in *Alden v. Maine* (1999) that his *Chisholm* dissent accorded with the original understanding of the Constitution and that the majority decision in that case was "discredited," thus rendering the Eleventh Amendment superfluous.

This Kelly-Baradell volume covers significant years in the Iredell saga. During this period he practiced his profession, served on the North Carolina Council of State, and commenced the revisal of his state's statutes. His friend William R. Davie launched the University of North

Carolina, the new nation's first operative public institution of higher education, and Iredell supported and assisted him. Most important, at the Hillsborough ratification convention he demonstrated his profound grasp of constitutional questions. This expertise was the primary reason for his ensuing appointment to the United States Supreme Court. While the initial failure of ratification was the greatest disappointment of his public life, his efforts on behalf of ratification became his principal source of honor and remembrance, as demonstrated in the naming of a county for him and the opportunity he received to serve on his adopted country's highest Court.

Thus, this volume covering these crucial years is a most welcome addition to the Iredell literature. It is ably crafted and will, like the earlier Higginbotham series, greatly assist scholars of Iredell, the Court, and the era for a significant period yet to come. Upon perusing this one, they will eagerly await the volumes covering the remaining years of Iredell's life and public service.

WILLIS P. WHICHARD

MAY 2003

Willis P. Whichard retired as an associate justice of the North Carolina Supreme Court and serves as dean and professor of law at the Norman Adrian Wiggins School of Law, Campbell University. He is the author of Justice James Iredell *(Durham, N.C.: Carolina Academic Press, 2000), the only full-length modern biography of Iredell.*

Acknowledgments

Though the names of only two editors appear on the title page, many other individuals have participated in the production of this volume. An extraordinary group of interns—Abigail Rovner, Amanda Daniel, Lisa Coston, Walt Evans, Jennifer Krause, Julianna Boucher, Alison Thurman, and Elizabeth Crowder— has made significant contributions to this and a fourth volume that is in progress. We hope they benefited from their internships as much as we did.

We are grateful to Justice Willis Whichard for writing the foreword for this volume and for what we have learned from his excellent biography of Iredell, *Justice James Iredell*. We would also like to thank Don Higginbotham, the editor of the first two volumes of the Iredell papers. His work set a high standard for us to follow and provided thorough background information for this volume.

William A. Owens Jr. translated many of the foreign phrases in these letters, and we appreciate his willingness to lend his linguistic skills to the project.

Last but not least we would like to thank two of our fellow editors in the Historical Publications Section for their contributions. Lisa Bailey read the page proofs. Her keen eye and sound judgment improved the final product and saved the editors from embarrassment. In addition, Susan Trimble did a masterful job in typesetting the volume. They both have added much to this book and to other works published by the Historical Publications Section.

Calendar of Iredell Papers, 1784–1789

Documents in italics are not included in this volume. An explanation of abbreviations and shortened titles is provided at the end of the calendar.

Date	Correspondents	Location	Subject
	1784		
Jan 3	To Conygham, Nesbitt & Co.	PC 67	legal business
Jan 4	From William Hooper	Duke	T. Burke's death, treaty
Jan 11	From Nathaniel Dukinfield	PC 67	power of attorney
Jan 16	*From William J. Dawson*	*Duke*	*civility, pleasantries*
Jan 28	*From Nathaniel Dukinfield*	*SHC 324*	*power of attorney*
Feb 4	From Pierce Butler	McRee	Loyalists, finances
Feb 7	From William Hooper	Duke	legal business, politics
Feb 11	To Thomas Iredell Sr.	PC 67	principles
Feb 16	To Arthur Iredell	PC 67	principles, family
Feb 18	From Arthur Iredell	PC 67	family
Feb 20, 25, Mar 12	From Henry E. McCulloh	Duke	compensation
Feb 25	A. Iredell to H. Iredell	Duke	inheritance
Mar 3	To Henry E. McCulloh	AO	legal business
Mar 14	To Pierce Butler	PC 67	Loyalists, elections
Mar 15	From William Hooper	Duke	elections, writings
Mar 16	*From James Hogg*	*Duke*	*political writings*
Mar 18	From William Hooper	Duke	court, society
Mar 26	From John Stokes	PC 67	law practice, friendship
Mar 28	To Hannah Iredell	PC 67	society, elections
Apr 8	To Hannah Iredell	PC 67	health, legal business
Apr 9	A. Iredell to H. Iredell	PC 67	family, politics
Apr 14	From Samuel Johnston	PC 67	Assembly members
Apr 14	From Nelly Blair	PC 67	move, society
Apr 17	To Hannah Iredell	PC 67	travel, health, finances
Apr 17	To Nelly Blair	PC 67	society
Apr 18	*To Hannah Iredell*	*PC 67*	*writing, health, move*
Apr 21	From Samuel Johnston	PC 67	Assembly
Apr 22	From Baron de Poellnitz	Duke	property, friendship
Apr 23	To Hannah Iredell	PC 67	health, finances
Apr 28	From Henry E. McCulloh	Duke	Geo. McCulloh, accounts
May 1	From Samuel Johnston	PC 67	treaty, Assembly
May 1	From William Hooper	PC 67	treaty, Assembly

May 15, 17	S. Johnston to H. Iredell	PC 67	confiscated property
May 20	To Hannah Iredell	PC 67	health, court
May 28	To Thomas Iredell Sr.	PC 67	profession, principles
Jun 15	To Catharine Macartney	PC 67	gratitude
Jun 15	To Archibald Neilson	PC 67	refugees, court, politics
Jun 15	To Henry E. McCulloh	PC 67/ AO	petition, confiscation
Jun 21	*From Edward Rice*	*Duke*	*legal business*
Jun 27	From Edward Rice	Duke	legal business
Jun 30	*From William Blair*	*PC 67*	*mail delivery*
July 8	From William Hooper	Duke	health, Assembly
Aug 20	James Iredell's will	NCSA- Chowan	will
Sep 3	From Alexander Diack	Duke	Tom Iredell
Sep 6	To Conygham, Nesbitt &c	PC 67	legal business
Sep 7	From Nathaniel Dukinfield	SHC 479	family, legal business
Sep 7	From Arthur Iredell	PC 67	family, society
Sep 8	From William Hooper	Duke	health, legal business
Sep 10, Oct 20	From Henry E. McCulloh	Duke	Geo. McCulloh, petition
Sep 14	From James Hogg	Duke	move, legal business
Sep 26	To Henry E. McCulloh	PC 67	resignation, business
Oct 15	To Hannah Iredell	PC 67	son's death
Oct 17	P. Dawson to H. Iredell	Duke	concern, praise
Oct 17/18	*To Hannah Iredell*	*PC 67*	*concern, health*
Oct 19	To Hannah Iredell	PC 67	deaths
Oct 22	From Michael Payne	Duke	Nath. Greene, business
Oct 24	To Hannah Iredell	PC 67	court, mourning
Nov 18	To Hannah Iredell	PC 67	health, travel, politics
Nov 19	From Thomas Iredell Jr.	PC 67	Assembly
Nov 20	To Hannah Iredell	PC 67	elections, Assembly
Nov 24	Petition of Benjamin McCulloch	NCSA-GA	confiscation
Nov 27	From Arthur Iredell	PC 67	politics, family
Dec 13	To Nelly Blair	PC 67	writing, visits
Dec 15	From Nelly Blair	PC 67	friends, family
Dec 24	Jean Blair to Hannah Iredell	PC 67	funeral, provisions
1784	List of Taxable Property	NCSA- Chowan	land, slaves

1785

Jan 6	To Henry E. McCulloh	Duke/AO	petition, accounts
Jan 9	To Nathaniel Dukinfield	Duke	Mrs. Pearson's estate
Jan 22	To Arthur Iredell	PC 67	family, finances
Jan 22	To Margaret Iredell	PC 67	family, finances
Feb 19	To Thomas Iredell Sr.	PC 67	family, finances
Feb 28	From Arthur Iredell	PC 67	mail, politics
Mar 6	To Arthur Iredell	PC 67	family
Mar 7	From Archibald Maclaine	Duke	health, business
Mar 10	From Richard D. Spaight	Duke	legal business, politics
Apr 22	To Hannah Iredell	PC 67	court, society
Apr 24	*To Hannah Iredell*	*PC 67*	*health, schedule*
Apr 30	From Arthur Iredell	PC 67	finances, family
May 15	From Henry E. McCulloh	Duke	confiscation acts
May 17	To Nelly Blair	PC 67	family, business
May 20	To Hannah Iredell	PC 67	travel, health
May 26	To Richard Caswell	GP 11	Tom Iredell
May 27	To Hannah Iredell	PC 67	health, court
May 28	*To Hannah Iredell*	*PC 67*	*health, schedule*
May 28	*To Jean Blair*	*PC 67*	*health, pleasantries*
Jun 10	From Nathaniel Dukinfield	McRee	Mrs. Pearson's estate
July 2	Smith's Academy minutes	PC 67	officers, subscription
July 4	From Tristrim Lowther	Duke	introduction
July 6	From William Hooper	NYPL/ PC 38	court, society
July 25	*To Amanda Felton*	*PC 67*	*pleasantries*
July 25	From Henry E. McCulloh	Duke	confiscation acts
July 31	From Arthur Iredell	PC 67	finances, family
Aug 5	*From Arthur Iredell*	*McRee*	*profession, politics*
Aug 7	From Samuel Cutler	Duke	friendship, religion
Sep 15	To Nelly Blair	PC 67	health, forgetfulness
Sep 17	*To Rob. & John Murray*	*PC 67*	*legal business*
Sep 28	*To Hannah Iredell*	*PC 67*	*finances*
Sep 29	To Hannah Iredell	PC 67	health, forgetfulness
Sep/Oct	*To Hannah Iredell*	*PC 67*	*health, finance*
Oct 1	To Hannah Iredell	PC 67	lodging, provisions
Oct 5	To Hannah Iredell	PC 67	lodging, travel

Oct 14	From Nelly Blair	PC 67	reading
Oct 18	To Nelly Blair	Duke	society
Oct 19	To Hannah Iredell	PC 67	health, court
Oct 22	*To Hannah Iredell*	*PC 67*	*health, society*
Oct 22	*To Nelly Blair*	*PC 67*	*homesickness*
Oct 24	From Archibald Maclaine	Duke	legal business
Oct 25	*To Hannah Iredell*	*PC 67*	*homecoming*
Oct 31	From Archibald Maclaine	Duke	legal business
Nov 4	Smith's Academy Minutes	PC 67	location
Nov 24	To Hannah Iredell	PC 67	lodging, entertainment
Dec 13	From Samuel Cutler	Duke	health, friendship
Dec 16	To James Gordon	PC 67	legal business
Dec 24	A. Maclaine to S. Johnston	SHC 324	Assembly
Dec 26	To Henry E. McCulloh	PC 67	legal business, Geo. McCulloh

1786

Jan 14	From John Burgwin	Duke	confiscation
Jan 19	From James Hogg	PC 67	confiscation
Jan 29	To James Hogg	PC 67	legal business
Jan 29	*To William Hooper*	*PC 67*	*legal business, family*
Jan 29	From Arthur Iredell	PC 67	inheritance, politics
Feb 6	To John Burgwin	PC 67	confiscation
Feb 7	From Samuel Johnston	SHC 324	legal business
Feb 7	To Samuel Johnston	SHC 324	legal business
Feb 8	1786 Tax List	PC 67	family, slaves
Feb 12	From William Hooper	Duke	society, legal business
Feb 21	From Arthur Iredell	PC 67	finances, politics
Feb 23	To Thomas Iredell Sr.	PC 67	principles
Mar 6	From Archibald Maclaine	PC 67	confiscation, court
Mar 30	From John Burgwin	PC 67	confiscation
Apr 6	*To Hannah Iredell*	*PC 67*	*travel, health, child*
Apr 18, 20	To Hannah Iredell	PC 67	society, finances
Apr 21	To Hannah Iredell	PC 67	entertainment, court
Apr 22	*To Hannah Iredell*	*PC 67*	*writing, finances*
April	From Nelly Blair	PC 67	writing
May 1	From Arthur Iredell	PC 67	family
May 19	To Hannah Iredell	PC 67	travel, forgetfulness
May 23	From John Burgwin	Duke	confiscation, business
May 23	*To Hannah Iredell*	*PC 67*	*health, travel, business*
May 24	To Hannah Iredell	PC 67	court
May 26	*From Nelly Blair*	*PC 67*	*travel, writing*
May 27	*To Hannah Iredell*	*PC 67*	*writing, pleasantries*

Aug 1	From William Hooper	Duke	elections, court
Aug 3	From Archibald Maclaine	Duke	elections, court
Aug 17	"To the Public"	Duke/ newspaper	judicial review
Aug 24	From Archibald Maclaine	McRee	elections
Sep 5	From Arthur Iredell	PC 67	finances, politics
Sep 26	*James Iredell's opinion*	*SHC 2987*	*legal business*
Sep 29, 30	To Hannah Iredell	Duke	society, travel
Oct 10	To Hannah Iredell	PC 67	health, court
Oct 17	To Hannah Iredell	PC 67	travel, finances
Oct 22	*To Hannah Iredell*	*PC 67*	*health, finances*
Oct 23	*To Hannah Iredell*	*Duke*	*health, pleasantries*
Nov 7	To Mr. Hamilton	PC 67	bar certification
Nov 10	From Richard Caswell	SHC 324	legal business
Dec 5	From Arthur Iredell	PC 67	finances, politics
Dec 14	From Alfred Moore	PC 67	court, Assembly
Dec 21	To Hannah Iredell	PC 67	Annie Iredell

1787

Jan 8	From John Witherspoon	Duke	education
Jan 11	*From William R. Davie*	*Duke*	*politics*
Jan 22	From William Hooper	NYPL/ PC 38	Assembly
ca. Jan 25	To Hannah Iredell	PC 67	travel, weather
Jan 31	To Hannah Iredell	PC 67	B. McCulloch, business
Feb 3	*From Nelly Blair*	*Duke*	*family, society*
Feb 4	*To Hannah Iredell*	*PC 67*	*legal business*
Feb 13	To Hannah Iredell	PC 67	court, B. McCulloch
Feb 15	*From Alexander McCulloch*	*PC 67*	*B. McCulloch*
Feb 19	To Hannah Iredell	PC 67	B. McCulloch
Feb 19	From John Witherspoon	Princeton	education, finances
Feb	To Richard Caswell	PC 67	B. McCulloch
Mar 1	From William Hooper	McRee	Thos. Clarke, judicial attire
Mar 27	From John Stokes	Duke	B. McCulloch
Mar 31	To Hannah Iredell	PC 67	travel
Apr 6	To Hannah Iredell	PC 67	court, society
Apr 10	From Henry E. McCulloh	PC 67	confiscation, business
Apr 14	To Hannah Iredell	PC 67	court
Apr 15	*From Nelly Blair*	*Duke*	*travel*
Apr 21	To Hannah Iredell	PC 67	horse

Apr 22	To Hannah Iredell	PC 67	B. McCulloch, entertainment
Apr 22	*To Hannah Iredell*	*PC 67*	*legal business*
Apr 24	*To Hannah Iredell*	*PC 67*	*homecoming*
Apr 25	From Nelly Blair	PC 67	accident
Apr 29	From Alexander McCulloch	Duke	B. McCulloch
Apr 30	*From William R. Davie*	*Princeton/ SHC 1793*	*political writings*
May 1	From John Burgwin	Duke	character
May 11	W. Hill to JI & S. Johnston	PC 67	legal business
May 21	*To Hannah Iredell*	*PC 67*	*travel, health*
May 23	To Hannah Iredell	PC 67	entertainment
May 25	*To Hannah Iredell*	*PC 67*	*court business, judges*
May 27	To Hannah Iredell	PC 67	health, entertainment
May 30	*To Hannah Iredell*	*PC 67*	*health, homecoming*
May 30	From William R. Davie	Duke	Constitution
May	To Whitmell Hill	PC 67	legal business
Jun 19	From William R. Davie	Duke	court, Constitution
Jun 26	To William McCleod & Co.	PC 67	legal business
July 2	From Arthur Iredell	PC 67	inheritance, family
July 3	From Richard D. Spaight	Duke	legal business, finances
July 6	*To Samuel Johnston*	*SHC 324*	*legal business*
July 8	From Hugh Williamson	McRee	legal business, politics
July 11, 12	From Archibald Maclaine	PC 67	court, judges
July 17	From William R. Davie	Duke	political writings
July 19	To William R. Davie	PC 67/ SHC 1793	English politics
July 22	From Hugh Williamson	McRee	Constitution
July 25	*From William Cumming*	*PC 67*	*legal business*
July	From Fred Ramcke	Duke	scandal, legal business
Aug 3	*To William Cumming*	*PC 67*	*legal business*
Aug 6	From William R. Davie	Duke	political writings
Aug 12	From Richard D. Spaight	Duke	judges, Constitution
Aug 18	To Mr. Littlejohn	PC 67	candidacy
Aug 18	To Stephen Cabarrus	PC 67	candidacy
Aug 18	From Stephen Cabarrus	PC 67	candidacy
Aug 20	To James Cotton	PC 67	candidacy
Aug 20	From James Cotton	PC 67	candidacy
Aug 21	To Stephen Cabarrus	PC 67	candidacy
Aug 21	*To Mr. Martin*	*PC 67*	*legal business*
Aug 23	From Samuel Johnston	PC 67	elections
Aug 24	From Nathaniel Dukinfield	Duke	family, legal business
Aug 26	To Richard D. Spaight	PC 67	judicial review

ca. Aug. 27	To the Editor of the *State Gazette*	McRee	politics, civility
Aug 29	From Archibald Maclaine	Duke	elections, politics
Aug 30	To John Moore	Duke	legal business
Sep 1	*To John Cameron*	*PC 67*	*legal business*
Sep 7	To Henry E. McCulloh	PC 67	legal business, Geo. McCulloh
Sep 20, 21	From Arthur Iredell	PC 67	books, family
Oct 6	From John Burgwin	Duke	legal business, gratitude
Oct 10	From Archibald Maclaine	Duke	business, Sam. Ashe
Oct 17	*To Hannah Iredell*	*PC 67*	*family, society*
Oct 21	To Hannah Iredell	PC 67	Constitution, society
Oct 23	To Hannah Iredell	PC 67	family, court
Nov 12	Grand Jury to Edenton Dist Ct.	McRee	Constitution
Nov 17	*From Archibald Maclaine*	*Duke*	*legal business*
Nov 22	To Hannah Iredell	PC 67	scandal
Nov 26	From a New Bern Newspaper	newspaper	Sam. Ashe
Nov 27	To Hannah Iredell	PC 67	legal business, family
Nov 27	*To Hannah Iredell*	*PC 67*	*health, schedule*
Nov 28	To Hannah Iredell	PC 67	provisions, schedule
Dec 4	From Arthur Iredell	PC 67	finances, family
Dec 13	From William R. Davie	Duke	politics, legislation
Dec 25	From Archibald Maclaine	Duke	ratification convention, judges
Dec 31	From William Hooper	McRee	ratification convention, court
1787	*To Hannah Iredell*	*PC 67*	*weather, travel*
1787	1787 Tax List	PC 67	land, slaves

1788

Jan 8	To Mr. Mason	McRee	Constitution
Jan 11	From William R. Davie	Duke	election
Jan 14	From Charles Johnson	McRee	Constitution
Jan 15	From Archibald Maclaine	Duke	Constitution, election
Jan 22	From William R. Davie	Duke	Constitution
Jan 31	H. Iredell to M. Iredell	McRee	family, society
Feb 9	*From Elizabeth Williams*	*McRee*	*friendship*
Feb 13	From Nathaniel Dukinfield	Duke	economics, slave trade
Feb 15	From John McLean	Duke	political writings
Feb 20	From Baron de Poellnitz	Duke	scandal, finances
Feb 25	To Maurice Murphy	Duke	revisal

Mar 4	From Archibald Maclaine	McRee	Constitution
ca. Mar 30	To the Freemen of Edenton	McRee	ratification convention
Apr 2	From Archibald Maclaine	Duke	elections
Apr 3	From David Witherspoon	Duke	Constitution, elections
Apr 15	From William Hooper	Duke	Constitution, business
Apr 15	To Baron de Poellnitz	PC 67	scandal, Constitution
Apr 26	To Hannah Iredell	PC 67	family, finances
Apr 29	From Archibald Maclaine	LC	patronage, elections
May 10	From William R. Davie	Duke	political writings
May 22	From Thomas Iredell Jr.	McRee	G. Washington
May 23	*To Hannah Iredell*	*McRee*	*Mrs. Huske's death*
May 27	*From Thomas Iredell Jr.*	*McRee*	*entertainment*
May 27	To Hannah Iredell	PC 67	court, finances
May 29	*To Hannah Iredell*	*PC 67*	*travel, schedule, finance*
May 29	*From Nelly Blair*	*PC 67*	*writing, society*
Jun 4	From Archibald Maclaine	PC 625	S.C.'s ratification
Jun 11	From Hugh Williamson	Duke	Congress
Jun 13	*From John Burgwin*	*PC 67*	*introduction*
Jun 29	To John G. Blount	PC 193	Va.'s ratification
Jul 2	From William Hooper	PC 67	Constitution, deaths
Jul 7	From Hugh Williamson	Duke	R.I. & N.Y. politics
Jul 7	From John Swann	NYPL/ PC 38	Constitution
Jul 9	From William R. Davie	Duke	Constitution
Jul 16	*From Henry E. McCulloh*	*McRee*	*N.C.'s ratification*
Jul 16	*To Hannah Iredell*	*PC 67*	*travel, health*
Jul 18	To Hannah Iredell	PC 67	wedding anniversary
Jul 25	To Hannah Iredell	McRee	ratification convention
Jul 26	From Hugh Williamson	Duke	Congress, Constitution
Jul 26	From Hugh Williamson	NYPL	N.Y.'s ratification
Aug 3	To Hannah Iredell	Duke	ratification convention
Aug 5	From Arthur Iredell	PC 67	family, politics
Aug 15	To Electors of Edenton	PC 67	candidacy
Aug 18	To the People of N.C.	Plea/ newspaper	Constitution
Aug 23	From Hugh Williamson	Duke	Congress
Sep 2	From William Hooper	Duke	elections, provisions
Sep 4	*From John Johnston*	*Duke*	*legal business, health*
Sep 8	From William R. Davie	Duke	political writings
Sep 10	To unknown	PC 625	Congress
Sep 12	From James Glasgow	Duke	Assembly

Sep 13	From Archibald Maclaine	Duke	elections, political writings
Sep 13	*To John G. Blount*	*PC 193*	*power of attorney*
Sep 21	From John Swann	McRee	Constitution, Congress
Sep 22	From Hugh Williamson	Duke	Constitution, Congress
Oct 15	From W. Falkener	PC 67	espionage
Oct 18	To Hannah Iredell	PC 67	health
Oct 18	*From Jonas Prentice*	*Duke*	*Mr. Maury's death, society*
Oct 21	*To Hannah Iredell*	*PC 67*	*health, finance*
Oct 27	From Archibald Maclaine	Duke	politics, legal business
Nov 8	From Samuel Johnston	PC 67	Assembly, Indians
Nov 14	From Samuel Johnston	PC 68	Assembly, son's birth
Nov 14	From Charles Johnson	McRee	Assembly, son's birth
Nov 17	From Archibald Maclaine	Duke	Assembly
Nov 17	W. J. Dawson to N. Blair	Duke	Fayetteville, society
Nov 19	*To Hannah Iredell*	*McRee*	*elections*
Nov 20	From Samuel Johnston	PC 67	Iredell County, Assembly
Nov 22	*To Hannah Iredell*	*PC 67*	*writing*
Nov 23	To Hannah Iredell	PC 67	health, society
Nov	From William R. Davie	Duke	debates, Va. politics
Dec 1	*To Hannah Iredell*	*PC 67*	*homesickness*
Dec 2	From Arthur Iredell	PC 67	mother's health
Dec 19	To Hannah Iredell	PC 67	schedule
Dec 19	From William R. Davie	Duke	debates
Dec 23	From Samuel Johnston	PC 67	Council meeting
1788	List of Taxable Property	PC 67	land, slaves

1789

Jan 5	From Hugh Williamson	McRee/ Letters	candidacy, Constitution
Jan 5/6	*From John Johnston*	*Duke*	*Mrs. Johnston's death*
Jan 6	To William Cumming	PC 67	legal questions
Jan 20	From Archibald Maclaine	PC 67	capital, court
Jan 22	To Hugh Williamson	PC 67	candidacy, debates
Jan 23	From William R. Davie	NYPL/ PC 38	debates
Jan 24	From Hugh Williamson	Duke	Assembly, candidacy
Feb 4,7,21	From Nathaniel Dukinfield	McRee	confiscation, king's health
Feb 12	From Hugh Williamson	PC 67	candidacy
Feb 16	To James Glasgow	NCSA-Sec. of State	revisal

Feb 17	To John Steele	Duke/ PC 5	Iredell County, debates
Feb 17	*From Samuel Johnston*	*PC 67*	*Council meeting*
Feb 18	From Henry E. McCulloh	Duke	finances, legal business
Feb 22	From Archibald Maclaine	Duke	debates, politics
Feb 25	To Robert Hudson	PC 67	legal business
Mar 2	From Hugh Williamson	McRee/ Letters	N.Y. politics
Mar 10	*From Penelope Dawson*	*PC 67*	*health, society*
Mar 15	To the Misses Blair	McRee	Mrs. Blair's death
Mar 29	To Hannah Iredell	PC 67	forgetfulness
Mar	From John Hamilton	PC 67	legal business
Apr 11	To Hannah Iredell	PC 67	court, health
Apr 20	To Hannah Iredell	PC 67	court, finances
Apr 20	*From Nelly Blair*	*Duke*	*family, society*
Apr 22	From John Rutherford	Duke	pardon
Apr 25	*To Hannah Iredell*	*PC 67*	*pleasantries, health*
Apr 28	To Hannah Iredell	PC 67	homecoming
May 5	From Samuel Johnston	Duke	Council meeting
May 5	From Arthur Iredell	PC 67	family, politics
May 9	From Tristrim Lowther	PC 67	Congress
May 24	To Hannah Iredell	PC 67	health, pleasantries
May	*To John Goelet*	*Duke*	*legal business*
Jun 2	From Anne Hooper	McRee	health, friendship
Jun 4	From William R. Davie	Duke	debates, amendments
Jun 6	To John G. Blount	PC 193	legal business
Jun 11	*Receipt*	*NYPL*	*Diack, MacKnight*
Jun 13	*From Nelly Blair*	*Duke*	*homesickness*
Jun 20	*From Patrick Parker*	*Duke*	*introduction*
Jun [27]	*To John Hamilton*	*PC 67*	*legal business*
Jun 27	*Certificate*	*PC 67*	*legal business*
Jun	To Anne Hooper	PC 67	friendship
Jul 1	From William R. Davie	Duke	debates
Jul 1	To John G. Blount	PC 193	debates, Indians
Jul 1	From Tristrim Lowther	PC 67	trade, judiciary
Jul 8	From Baron de Poellnitz	Duke	political writings
Jul 11	To Henry E. McCulloh	PC 67	legal business, family
Jul 15	To George Macartney	McRee	gratitude
Jul 22	From Samuel Johnston	Duke	Council meeting
Jul 25	To Pierce Butler	PC 67	ratification convention
Jul 25	To Baron de Poellnitz	Duke	politics, family
Aug 4	From William R. Davie	Duke	family, political writings
Aug 7	*To Messrs. Buchanan and Robbs*	*PC 67*	*legal business*

Aug 11	From Pierce Butler	McRee	Congress
Aug 11	From Archibald Maclaine	Duke	debates, property
Aug 12	From Hugh Williamson	PC 67	debates, judgeship
Aug 29	To Hugh Williamson	PC 67	judgeship, elections
Sep 7	From William R. Davie	Duke	elections
Sep 9	To John G. Blount	PC 193	revisal, Congress
Sep 11	From John Williams	Duke	politics, health
Sep 15	From Archibald Maclaine	Duke	elections
Sep 18	*From John Brownrigg*	*Duke*	*power of attorney*
Sep 25	To Hannah Iredell	PC 67	finances
Sep 26	From John Steele	Duke	ratification convention
Oct 6	From Arthur Iredell	PC 67	pride, family
Oct 11	*From Mrs. Hogg*	*McRee*	*legal business*
Oct 16	To House/Senate Speakers	PC 67	revisal
Oct 20	*To Hannah Iredell*	*PC 67*	*health, pleasantries*
Oct 22	To Hannah Iredell	PC 67	Constitution, business
Oct 25	To Hannah Iredell	Duke	finances, court
Oct 27	To Hannah Iredell	Duke	society, Indians
Nov 2	*From Samuel Johnston*	*PC 67*	*travel, convention*
Nov 3	From Arthur Iredell	PC 67	politics, family
Nov 13	From Samuel Johnston	PC 67	Assembly, Constitution
Nov 14	*From Samuel Johnston*	*PC 67*	*health, Caswell's death*
Nov 16	From William R. Davie	Duke	Assembly, Constitution
Nov 20	From Moses Coleman	NCSA-NB Ct.	legal business
Nov 22	From William J. Dawson	Duke	Constitution
Nov 22	From William R. Davie	Duke	Constitution
Nov 23	From Samuel Johnston	Duke	Constitution
Nov 23	From Charles Johnson	PC 67	politics, Constitution
Nov 26	From Richard D. Spaight	McRee	Constitution
Nov 26	To Hannah Iredell	PC 67	Constitution, family
Nov 26	From Archibald Maclaine	PC 67	Constitution, elections
Nov 27	*From Elizabeth Williams*	*Duke*	*invitation, friendship*
Nov 29	To Hannah Iredell	PC 67	finances, family
Nov 29	From Samuel Johnston	PC 67	politics, health
Dec 1	From Arthur Iredell	McRee	Duke of Orleans
Dec 1	From Samuel Johnston	PC 67	judgeship, election
Dec 9	From Archibald Maclaine	Duke	judgeship
Dec 21	From William R. Davie	Duke	debates
Dec 22, 23	From Archibald Maclaine	Duke	Assembly, elections
Dec 22	From John Haywood	McRee	Assembly
1789	List of Taxable Property	PC 67	land, slaves

Abbreviations and Shortened References Used in the Calendar

AO	English Records, Audit Office Papers, Loyalist Claims, North Carolina State Archives, Raleigh
Chowan	Chowan County Records, North Carolina State Archives, Raleigh
Duke	Papers of James Iredell Sr. and James Iredell Jr., Rare Book, Manuscript, and Special Collections Library, Duke University, Durham
GA	General Assembly Session Records, North Carolina State Archives, Raleigh
GP	Governors Papers, North Carolina State Archives, Raleigh
LC	Library of Congress
Letters	Paul H. Smith, ed. *Letters of Delegates to Congress, 1774-1789.* Vol. 25. Washington: Library of Congress, 1998.
McRee	Griffith J. McRee. *Life and Correspondence of James Iredell.* 2 vols. New York: D. Appleton, 1857.
NB Ct.	New Bern Superior Court Records, North Carolina State Archives, Raleigh
NCSA	North Carolina State Archives, Raleigh
NYPL	New York Public Library
PC	Private Collections, North Carolina State Archives, Raleigh. Followed by the collection's identifying number.
Plea	*A Plea for Federal Union, 1788.* Charlottesville, Va.: Tracy W. McGregor Library, University of Virginia, 1947.
Princeton	Rare Books and Special Collections, Princeton University Library, Princeton, N.J.
Sec. of State	Records of the Office of the Secretary of State, North Carolina State Archives, Raleigh
SHC	Southern Historical Collection, Wilson Library, University of North Carolina Library at Chapel Hill. Followed by the collection's identifying number.

Introduction

The years following the Revolutionary War brought great change for the nation and for James Iredell. At war's end the country was a collection of states loosely joined under a weak central government and floundering in the throes of an economic depression. By the end of 1789, a more effective political system was in place as the Constitution superseded the Articles of Confederation, and with the increasing stability of the new nation, the economy was prospering. Iredell, too, experienced a transformation during the postbellum years. When the war ended he was thirty-two years old and honing his legal skills. During the ensuing years, he emerged as a leading advocate for causes ranging from the fair treatment of Loyalists to ratification of the Constitution. Though troubled by financial woes, family problems, professional demands, and poor health, Iredell grew from a young man with a modest statewide reputation to a mature statesman of national prominence. These formative years were the prelude to the pinnacle of his professional career, his 1790 appointment to the United States Supreme Court.

Iredell came to America in 1768, at the age of seventeen, because of a family financial crisis. His father, a marginally successful merchant in Bristol, England, suffered a stroke in 1766 and could no longer work. James, the oldest child, left school and England to become a royal customs official at Edenton, a position he obtained through influential family connections. These ties of kinship also enabled Iredell to mingle with Chowan County's most prominent families. Because of his personal attributes Iredell became well-liked and respected, which was unusual for royal customs officers in America at this time. In 1773, he became a member of one of those distinguished families when he married Hannah Johnston, the niece of former royal governor Gabriel Johnston and sister of Samuel Johnston, a future governor and U.S. senator. The latter became one of Iredell's closest friends as well as his law instructor.

As tensions between the colonies and England increased, Iredell's sympathies, like those of Samuel Johnston, were with the colonies despite his employment by the British government. Iredell even wrote pseudonymous essays espousing the Patriot cause. During the Revolutionary War, Iredell did not take up arms but received his legal training by riding the court circuit with Johnston. As they traveled Iredell met many of his brother-in-law's powerful colleagues. Iredell apparently made a favorable impression, since he was selected as a superior court judge in 1777 and as attorney general in 1779. In 1781, he left public office and returned to his legal practice.

Thus during the fifteen years from his arrival in America until the end of the Revolutionary War, Iredell acquired a wife, an extended family, a profession, a mentor, and a home. But during the same period the financial problems that had brought him to America, though mitigated, had not disappeared. To his mother in January 1785, he wrote, "I owe considerable debts contracted during the war, & collect those due me very slowly."[1] A month later, he declared to his uncle, "I receive no more in ready money than is barely sufficient to defray my necessary expenses . . . & have some old debts yet to pay, tho' I have taken care to contract no new ones."[2] And to his cousin, also in early 1785, he exclaimed, "I trust you must be sufficiently sensible of the distress & embarrassment of my circumstances, occasioned by a war which annihilated all my resources. . . . I have the utmost difficulty . . . in procuring money enough for my Family's common support."[3]

Iredell's personal financial difficulties were exacerbated by a nationwide depression. The fledgling United States, adjusting from an economy based on the trade of thirteen separate colonies with Great Britain to a cohesive national economy with new markets and domestic industry, was still feeling its way. The effort was hampered by the Articles of Confederation, under which the central government lacked such basic economic powers as levying taxes and regulating interstate commerce.[4] In many ways the individual states were independent economic entities with powers superior to those of the national government. The result was a myriad of conflicting and counterproductive economic measures that produced instability and uncertainty. One of the states' prerogatives that significantly contributed to the financial gloom was the freedom to issue currency. Emissions of paper money in North Carolina in 1783 and 1785 generated inflation that caused the devaluing of debts owed to creditors, such as James Iredell.

Iredell sustained another financial blow when he was disinherited by his uncle because of his support of the colonies during the war. Thomas Iredell Sr. was a wealthy planter in Jamaica and fiercely loyal to England. He would have found his nephew's disloyalty to the Crown objectionable

---

[1] James Iredell (JI) to Margaret Iredell, January 22, 1785, in this volume.

[2] JI to Thomas Iredell Sr., February 19, 1785, in this volume.

[3] JI to Henry E. McCulloh, January 6, 1785, in this volume.

[4] Alfred H. Kelly and Winfred A. Harbison, *The American Constitution: Its Origins and Development*, 5th ed. (New York: W. W. Norton, 1976), 99.

under any circumstances, but in light of Iredell's position as a royal official, he viewed his heir's actions as unpardonable treachery.

In 1775, when the differences between the colonies and mother country seemed irreconcilable, Thomas told his nephew that the Americans were "certainly Mad" and that he "would rather live in Turkey than in N. America where a man is obliged to give up his free agency—must think with the mob or have his Person and Property torn to pieces." He advised his young nephew to "Keep yourself perfectly Neuter in those disputes both in Words and Actions unless you choose to see yourself adrift with it."[5] James, in his youthful enthusiasm, disregarded his uncle's stern warning and stayed the Patriot's course.

After the war, Iredell tried to fawn his way back into his uncle's favor. He wrote a series of gushing letters recalling the "great gratitude & pleasure the satisfaction I derived from the correspondence you honoured me with before the war, and earnestly wishing for a renewal of it."[6] After several of these letters went unanswered, a tone of desperation crept into his correspondence as he told his rich uncle, "It is now the first wish of my heart to be restored to your former kind opinion & regard."[7]

Mingled with this mercenary truckling were some substantive explanations for Iredell's actions. At no point did Iredell offer any false regrets about his course of action, and he insisted that he had acted on principle, just as James II's opponents had done during the Glorious Revolution of 1688. Iredell declared to his uncle that when a king acted contrary to the "safety & liberties of the People" then "it was <u>absolutely necessary</u>" to repudiate the monarch and that this could be done "without any imputation of dishonour."[8] Uncle Thomas was not swayed by Iredell's professions of principle nor by his historical references.

Iredell's attempts to restore his relationship with his uncle were impaired by his younger brother Arthur, who sought to displace him as Thomas's heir. Arthur, who lived in England and, like James, was in financial straits, tried to ingratiate himself to the elderly uncle, even to the point of allowing Thomas to determine what profession he should pursue. Arthur's sycophancy must have had its charms, for when Uncle Thomas died in 1796, Arthur was his heir and James did not receive a farthing.

---

[5]Don Higginbotham, ed., *The Papers of James Iredell*, 2 vols. (Raleigh: Division of Archives and History, Department of Cultural Resources, 1976), 1:280, hereafter cited as *PJI*.

[6]JI to Thomas Iredell Sr., May 28, 1784, in this volume.

[7]JI to Thomas Iredell Sr., February 19, 1785, in this volume.

[8]JI to Thomas Iredell Sr., February 11, 1784, in this volume.

Iredell's immediate family was also in a state of flux in the postwar years. The Iredells' financial worries were eclipsed in 1784 by the death of their first child. After eleven years of marriage, Hannah gave birth to a son on October 1, but the baby, called Thomas, lived only two days. The difficult delivery also placed Hannah's life in jeopardy. She soon recovered physically, but emotionally Hannah and her husband were shattered. To make matters worse, Iredell had to leave Hannah to attend court less than two weeks after the baby's death. The frequent letters that followed reflect their grief as well as a desperate need to try to find something positive in the tragedy. "The enjoyments of life are so fleeting & transitory," Iredell wrote in his first letter after the child's death, "so continually dashed with disappointment & distress, that upon our dear little Infant's own account we have reason to be satisfied with so sudden & so shocking a removal from us. He is gone to enjoy happiness without going through the usual gradations of misery."[9]

The Iredells' own misery was relieved considerably the following year by the birth of a daughter. Annie Isabella Iredell was born on December 22, 1785. Iredell was understandably concerned about the health of the baby and her mother, but as he told William Hooper with perceptible relief, "Thank God both Mother and child have been remarkably well." Annie was followed by a son, James, in 1788 and another daughter, Helen, in 1792. Thomas's death had left its mark, however. Iredell obsessively worried about the children's health while he was away from home, but despite their father's anxiety, all three children lived to adulthood.

Even before his own children were born, Iredell had shown his paternal instincts by helping with the education of his sister-in-law's daughters. Jean Johnston Blair, sister of Hannah Iredell, was left to raise five children when her husband, George Blair, died in 1772. Iredell became almost like a father to one of the daughters, Helen "Nelly" Blair. They were devoted friends for the remainder of Iredell's life and corresponded regularly.[10]

Iredell's familial responsibilities extended beyond the Atlantic to his mother and two brothers in England. With his father's death in 1773, Iredell, as the oldest child, became the de facto head of the family. After the Revolution, Arthur received an annuity from his uncle in Jamaica, though over time this became an unreliable source of income.[11] Thomas, the second brother, served in the Royal Marines but was a reckless

[9]JI to Hannah Iredell, October 15, 1784, in this volume.

[10]*PJI*, 1:100n.

[11]Willis P. Whichard, *Justice James Iredell* (Durham, N.C.: Carolina Academic Press, 2000), 238.

spendthrift. He incurred large debts, though precisely how is not revealed in the family correspondence. Iredell's mother, despite receiving assistance from wealthier relatives, was also financially hard pressed. Her maternal instincts induced her to try to save Thomas from himself, but this effort to help her extravagant son only increased her own financial burdens. Iredell worried intensely about both of them. In December 1783, he wrote his mother: "I have been extremely uneasy about my Brother Tom. I know how ruinous and dangerous his present situation is."[12] Iredell proposed that his mother and Thomas move to North Carolina, and he would train his brother to be a lawyer. While Mrs. Iredell waited until 1790 to immigrate, Thomas arrived in the late summer of 1784, and with him came yet another responsibility for Iredell.

With his increasing obligations and insufficient revenue, Iredell focused on his legal practice immediately after the war and, at least for a while, eschewed public life. His practice was in many ways typical of his time and locale. He represented clients in county courts and provided out-of-court services, such as drafting wills and contracts. He often argued civil cases before the North Carolina Superior Court, which entailed riding a circuit. The superior court was divided into six districts, but Iredell limited his practice to those closest to his home.[13] "I make a Circuit twice a year from Hillsborough by way of Halifax and this Town [Edenton] to Newbern," he explained in June 1784. "A County Court or two forms an episode, and this is my whole present history."[14] He avoided the Salisbury court, which was the most distant, and as his case load increased, he traveled less frequently to Wilmington and Hillsborough.[15]

The superior court was established under a law drafted by Iredell and passed by the General Assembly in 1777.[16] The measure provided for two annual sessions of court in each town on the circuit and three superior court judges. In the same year, the legislature appointed Iredell as one of the judges. He loathed the experience, particularly the travel, and on June 13, 1778, he resigned after only one session. The other two judges appointed at that time, Samuel Ashe and Samuel Spencer, were still on the bench

---

[12] *PJI*, 2:474.

[13] Walter Clark, ed., *The State Records of North Carolina*, 16 vols. (11-26) (Raleigh: State of North Carolina, 1895-1906), 24:48; John Charles Waldrup, "James Iredell and the Practice of Law in Revolutionary Era North Carolina" (Ph.D. diss., University of North Carolina at Chapel Hill, 1985), 91.

[14] JI to Archibald Neilson, June 15, 1784, in this volume.

[15] Waldrup, "James Iredell," 108.

[16] Whichard, *Justice James Iredell*, 19; Clark, *State Records*, 48-75.

when Iredell represented clients before the court after the war. John Williams replaced Iredell as the third judge.[17]

When riding the circuit, Iredell traveled from court to court on horseback or stage, often in the company of other lawyers. In 1784, the General Assembly authorized the improvement of roads, ferries, and bridges, but progress was slow.[18] Iredell and his colleagues usually had to make their way on narrow, muddy roads and cross rivers by ferry or canoe. While enroute Iredell found food and lodging with friends, relatives, and at taverns. Despite the discomfort, Iredell took a positive view, and the phrase "agreeable journey" appears more often than complaints in letters to his wife.

The rigors of circuit riding did, however, affect Iredell's health, which was fragile under the best of circumstances. His numerous illnesses at times kept him from attending court and thus deprived him of fees. "My very ill health had . . . prevented my attending some courts on my former Circuit, which greatly injured my affairs, and prejudiced many of my Clients," he once lamented.[19] Iredell's maladies were often minor, but even these could diminish his income. In November 1784, he missed a day of court in New Bern because of a cold, "in spite of a thousand teezing solicitations."[20] At times, Iredell's afflictions were far worse, as he explained in a letter to his wife: "Upon the road from Booth here [Elk Marsh] on Sunday afternoon I was seized with a most violent vomiting and purging, which increased after my arrival and in the night attacked me so severly that in a few hours I was reduced almost to a mere Skeleton, and was so weak and had such spasms in my thighs and legs that but for the kindest assistance from this Family, particularly Mr. B. McCulloch and Mr. Stokes, I probably should have died."[21]

Iredell's friend William Hooper of Hillsborough attributed his frequent illnesses to living in the unhealthy climate of Chowan County. "It is a melancholy consideration," Hooper wrote, "that once in every year you run the gauntlet for your lives notwithstanding the utmost regularity and temperance in your manner of living."[22] Hooper tried repeatedly to

---

[17] Whichard, *Justice James Iredell*, 20.

[18] Louise Irby Trenholme, *The Ratification of the Federal Constitution in North Carolina* (New York: AMS Press, 1967), 19; Clark, *State Records*, 24:674-678.

[19] JI to Henry E. McCulloh, June 15, 1784, in this volume.

[20] JI to Hannah Iredell, November 20, 1784, in this volume.

[21] *PJI*, 2:452.

[22] William Hooper to JI, September 8, 1784, in this volume.

persuade Iredell to move to Hillsborough. Apparently even the health-giving benefits of Orange County were no match for Iredell's sickly constitution, however. After a trip there in the spring of 1784 Iredell complained to his wife that "the water at Hillsborough affected me a good deal."[23] A week later he wrote, "I am nearly as well as before and a great deal better than I was at Hillsborough."[24]

Among Iredell's most prominent and controversial legal clients were Loyalists whose property had been confiscated by the state. Historians have called the war for American independence a civil war because of the fighting between Loyalists and Patriots, and as in any civil war, animosity ran deep. With their homes and fortunes at stake, Patriots and Loyalists fought with particular intensity and at times used the war as an excuse to settle scores and commit crimes. The resulting bitterness left little room for reconciliation and bred an implacable desire, not simply for victory, but for complete vanquishment of the enemy.

In this atmosphere, the North Carolina General Assembly, like legislative bodies in other states, passed laws to punish Loyalists in various ways, including seizing their property. The punitive measures became harsher as the war continued and resentment increased. In 1777, the assembly approved a measure requiring North Carolinians who had been out of the state on July 4, 1776, to return and establish their citizenship by October 1, 1778, or lose their property.[25] The provisions of this statute were so broad that innocent individuals were ensnared, such as John Burgwin, who eventually recovered his property. In 1779, the General Assembly refined the earlier legislation by listing individuals whose property was declared confiscated.[26] In negotiating an end to the war, the British felt compelled to aid those who had been loyal. They insisted that the treaty of peace prohibit further confiscation and require Congress to "recommend" to state legislatures that confiscated property belonging to "real British subjects" be returned.[27] In 1784, a bill in the North Carolina

---

[23]JI to Hannah Iredell, April 17, 1784, in this volume.

[24]JI to Hannah Iredell, April 23, 1784, in this volume.

[25]Clark, *State Records*, 24:123-124.

[26]Clark, *State Records*, 24:263-268.

[27]"Treaty of Peace," September 3, 1783, in *U.S. Department of State, Treaties and Other International Agreements of the United States of America, 1776-1949*, 13 vols. (Washington: Department of State, 1968-1976), 12:8-12.

legislature that would have repealed any law inconsistent with the treaty was defeated.[28]

Though Iredell was not alone in representing Loyalists—his brother-in-law, Samuel Johnston, for example, shared his views—he was part of a small and unpopular minority. Fellow attorney Archibald Maclaine was physically attacked in Bladen County in 1782 because of his advocacy for Loyalists.[29] Iredell told Pierce Butler of South Carolina that he and Samuel Johnston were looked upon with "a very hated eye," but added that he had learned "to despise that sort of popularity which is to be gained by flattering the passions of the multitude."[30] In a letter to Archibald Neilson, a Loyalist who had been an aide to Gov. Josiah Martin, Iredell reported that he and Johnston had "lost in this part of the Country at least much of our weight and influence" because of their opposition to violence against Loyalist refugees.[31]

One reason why Iredell helped Loyalists was that a number of them were old friends and relations. Iredell had known Nathaniel Dukinfield before the Revolution, when he had lived on a plantation in Bertie County near the Chowan River. Dukinfield, who owned 3,600 acres of land in North Carolina, counted the wealthy and powerful among his friends, including the Johnstons. He had once vied with Iredell for Hannah Johnston's hand. His wealth and rank led to service on the Royal Council before he returned to England in 1772. During the war he was a British army officer, though he did not fight in the American colonies. Dukinfield's past made the seizure of his property inevitable, though he had deeded his property to his mother and stepfather before leaving North Carolina. In 1784, Dukinfield gave Iredell and Samuel Johnston power of attorney with instructions to take care of his mother and save his property. Their best efforts, however, were not enough to recover Dukinfield's land.[32]

Henry Eustace McCulloh was another of Iredell's Loyalist clients as well as being his cousin and a frequent source of irritation. He had been the royal customs collector for the Port of Roanoke, which was administered from Edenton, and manager of his family's large landholdings in North Carolina. McCulloh's father in England had helped Iredell get the job as

---

[28] Clark, *State Records*, 19:800.

[29] *Dictionary of North Carolina Biography*, s.v. "Maclaine, Archibald," hereafter cited as *DNCB*, with specific entry.

[30] JI to Pierce Butler, March 14, 1784, in this volume.

[31] JI to Archibald Neilson, June 15, 1784, in this volume.

[32] *DNCB*, s.v. "Duckenfield, Nathaniel"; *PJI*, 1:52n; Nathaniel Dukinfield to JI, January 11, 1784, in this volume.

McCulloh's underling that had enabled Iredell to come to America. The McCullohs also lent money to Iredell, gave him letters of credit, and eased his entry into Edenton society.[33]

Iredell was acutely aware of what he called his "debt of honor" to the family. In 1784, he provided £300 in his will to Henry Eustace McCulloh in recognition of this debt, but the obligation went far beyond money in the minds of both men. Exploiting Iredell's conscience, McCulloh made innumerable demands on him over a period of decades. Iredell, in turn, tried to strike an honorable balance between fulfilling his perceived obligations and guarding against excessive demands.

McCulloh began imposing on his cousin as soon as Iredell reached Edenton in 1768. McCulloh, who had returned to England just before Iredell's arrival, left the seventeen-year-old to perform both of their jobs, while he continued to collect his salary. McCulloh did not return to North Carolina until 1772, only to leave again the following year. Yet Iredell did not officially fill McCulloh's position, and draw the accompanying higher wage, until 1774. McCulloh also had his young cousin perform countless tasks related to managing his family's property.[34]

While in North Carolina, Henry Eustace McCulloh indulged in a variety of vices, one of which resulted in the fathering of a child with a woman called Molly. It was just before the birth of his son, who was given the name George McCulloh, that McCulloh returned to England in 1768. McCulloh, while acknowledging paternity, was a reluctant parent and shamelessly tried to push the boy off on others. Iredell, with his debt of honor, was a vulnerable target. "When you recollect my Father's & my wishes to serve you in days past, I hope you will return them, by being a friend to this young man,"[35] McCulloh reminded Iredell. When the boy reached adolescence, he was shuffled back and forth across the Atlantic with both Iredell and McCulloh experiencing the surprise of finding him on their doorstep. In all of this, George, of course, is the one to be pitied. Eventually he became an attorney and in 1792 tried unsuccessfully to regain his father's confiscated property in North Carolina.

That property, 800,000 acres that produced £1,000 annually, according to McCulloh, was seized in 1779. McCulloh enlisted Iredell's assistance in petitioning the General Assembly to return his unsold land and to provide monetary compensation for the property that the state had sold.

---

[33] *DNCB*, s.v. "McCulloh, Henry," "McCulloh, Henry Eustace"; *PJI*, 1:xxxvii, xlvii.

[34] *PJI*, 1:xlviii–xlix, lv.

[35] Henry E. McCulloh to JI, July 25, 1785, in this volume.

Predictably, even with Iredell's help McCulloh was unable to extract sympathy, money, or property from the General Assembly. McCulloh also insisted that Iredell provide documents that he needed to prepare his appeal to the Loyalist claims commission in England. Here he had some success. That body generously compensated McCulloh for his losses but stopped short of giving him all that he had requested. Finally, McCulloh, treating his cousin as if he were still seventeen, sent Iredell power of attorney to attend to his personal affairs in the state, such as collecting debts. Because this would have required Iredell to neglect his own practice to travel to far-flung regions of the state, he refused.

Historian Don Higginbotham, who edited the first two volumes of Iredell's papers, characterized McCulloh as "a shrewd and calculating man who put his immediate interests above all else."[36] This is evident in his letters to Iredell after the war, in which he is demanding—"I beseech you to write me fully in answer to every matter contd. in my letters"; impatient—"I beg you to be informed & assured that nothing can be more distressing & injurious to me, than any further delay"; and carping—"To prove the ultimate loss of the Property, the law of Nov. 1784 for its final Sale, you as a Lawyer might have recollected, was essentially necessary for me to produce, God grant you had attended to this Idea, ..."[37]

The legal wrangling of Dukinfield, McCulloh, and other Loyalists generated a backlash in the General Assembly. In 1785, the legislature prohibited Loyalists from trying to recover their confiscated property by filing lawsuits against current owners.[38] This act violated Section 14 of the declaration of rights in the 1776 state constitution, in which the right to a jury trial in property disputes is described as "one of the best securities of the rights of the people" and one that should "remain sacred and inviolable."[39] The legislature's actions in 1785 thus transcended the issue of confiscated property and raised basic questions about how the people were to be governed, the relationship between the constitution and the legislature, and the means of resolving fundamental conflicts within the nascent government.

These questions were addressed in one of the nation's earliest examples of judicial review, that is the judiciary's prerogative to declare legislation

---

[36] *PJI*, 1:xlviii.

[37] Henry E. McCulloh to JI, February 20, 1784, May 15, 1785, in this volume.

[38] Clark, *State Records*, 24:730-731.

[39] "Constitution of North Carolina of 1776," in John L. Cheney Jr., ed., *North Carolina Government, 1585-1979: A Narrative and Statistical History* (Raleigh: North Carolina Department of the Secretary of State, 1981), 809.

unconstitutional. The case, *Bayard v. Singleton*, centered on property that had once belonged to Samuel Cornell, a wealthy merchant of New Bern. Cornell had traveled to England in 1775 and upon his return two years later was denied permission to disembark at New Bern unless he, as required by law, swore allegiance to the state. Cornell, a Loyalist, refused. Understanding the ramifications of his actions, he attempted to prevent confiscation of his substantial assets by deeding his property to his wife and daughters before sailing to New York. Despite this precaution, his property was seized, and part of it was eventually sold to Spyers Singleton, a New Bern merchant and member of the General Assembly. In 1784, members of the Cornell family attempted to regain the family property by filing a series of lawsuits against the purchasers. One of the suits was filed by Cornell's daughter Elizabeth Cornell Bayard against Spyers Singleton.[40]

The 1785 statute required the superior court, upon a motion by the defense, to dismiss cases such as Bayard's and to require plaintiffs to pay court costs.[41] Accordingly, in May 1786 Singleton's lawyers asked the court to reject Bayard's claim. The judges, rather than adhere to the law, refused to issue a ruling, and the case was continued for two court terms. Apparently the judges were hoping that the assembly would modify the law so that a confrontation between the court and legislature could be avoided. The General Assembly did make some changes, but they were insufficient to alter the situation before the court.[42]

Iredell's interest in these developments stemmed not only from his own advocacy of judicial review and his disapproval of the ill-treatment of Loyalists, but also from an earlier connection with the Cornell property. Ironically, Iredell's initial involvement with the Cornells was as an advocate of confiscation. In 1779, when Iredell was state attorney general, he acted against his own beliefs and successfully argued that the Cornell holdings could be taken by the state, contrary to the assertions of one of the occupants of the property, Spyers Singleton.[43]

When Bayard sued in 1784, Singleton, who had since purchased the property, hired a battery of North Carolina's most accomplished lawyers, including William Hooper, Archibald Maclaine, and James Iredell. Singleton did not intend for all of these legal notables to actually represent

---

[40]Whichard, *Justice James Iredell*, 10; Waldrup, "James Iredell," 258, 262, 272; Blackwell P. Robinson, *William R. Davie* (Chapel Hill: University of North Carolina Press, 1957), 166.

[41]Clark, *State Records*, 24:731.

[42]Waldrup, "James Iredell," 272-274.

[43]Waldrup, "James Iredell," 261.

him in court but hired them so that they would be unavailable to his opponent.[44] Bayard was represented by Iredell's brother-in-law Samuel Johnston and William R. Davie.

Iredell faced an ethical dilemma. He believed judicial review to be a necessary check against legislative excesses, but his acceptance of payment from Singleton seemingly prevented him from advocating that principle in Bayard's case. The records are incomplete and contradictory as to Iredell's specific role in *Bayard v. Singleton*. The official printed report of the case indicates that Iredell represented Bayard. But, as historian John Charles Waldrup has pointed out, the court dockets do not list Iredell as an attorney for the plaintiffs and there is no mention of the case in Iredell's account books.[45]

What is certain, however, is that outside of the courtroom Iredell was an effective proponent of judicial review. Iredell proffered his arguments in a letter "To the Public," which appeared in a New Bern newspaper on August 17, 1786, as the superior court judges were pondering the *Bayard* case. Conscious of his awkward position in offering arguments that would aid Bayard after he had accepted a retainer from Singleton, Iredell begins his letter on a defensive note: "As the Question concerning the Power of the Assembly deeply concerns every Man in the state, I shall make no apology for delivering my Sentiments upon it." He then proceeds to concisely define the issue, describe and defend his solution, and dismantle opposing arguments. The essence of his argument is that the constitution is "the <u>fundamental Law</u>" and the legislature is its offspring. As such, a legislative "act inconsistent with the Constitution is <u>void</u>," and the court is obligated to rule accordingly.[46]

During the May 1787 superior court term, the judges sanctioned judicial review by denying Singleton's motion for dismissal. This ruling and similar decisions by courts in other states prepared the way for the U.S. Supreme Court's endorsement of judicial review in *Marbury v. Madison* in 1803. Despite the superior court's ruling, Bayard and her siblings did not recover their father's holdings. The jury decided that when Cornell transferred his property to his family he was not a North Carolina citizen and therefore was not eligible to own property. Consequently, the state's seizure of his

---

[44]Waldrup, "James Iredell," 264.

[45]Waldrup, "James Iredell," 268.

[46]See "To the Public," August 17, 1786, in this volume.

holdings was valid, and Singleton was permitted to maintain ownership. In light of this decision, the other Cornell descendants dropped their suits.[47]

After continuing the case for two terms and refusing to issue a ruling on the motion for dismissal, what had emboldened the judges to defy the General Assembly and strike down the 1785 law? It is probably not a coincidence that the court's pronouncement came less than five months after the General Assembly had cleared the superior court judges of charges of malfeasance. These accusations had been made by lawyers who were also members of the assembly. Despite the fact that their colleagues were the source of the complaints, the legislators not only exonerated the members of the bench but passed a resolution expressing gratitude for the splendid job they were doing. This endorsement possibly gave the heretofore reluctant justices the confidence to test new ground.

The General Assembly's investigation of the judges was the climax of a battle between the bar and bench that had been raging in the superior court for years. After the Revolution, the number of court cases increased dramatically, and the work load overwhelmed the court. As cases backed up, the judges and lawyers blamed each other. The lawyers complained that the judges were incompetent, while the judges characterized the attorneys as fee chasers who harangued the court to make their clients believe that they were getting their money's worth.[48] Political differences and personality clashes added to the conflict, and at times even the judges turned on each other. Archibald Maclaine, one of the most hostile critics of the bench, described a court session to Iredell: "At the Superior Court, we did business as usual—Tried about half a dozen jury causes, wrangled with the Judges, & they with each other—at least Spencer and Williams—The latter has sworn solemnly and openly, never to sit with the former again."[49]

Maclaine and the equally fiery John Hay, both lawyers and assembly members, carried their war against the judges to the legislature. At their urging, the General Assembly during the 1786-1787 session investigated seven accusations against the superior court bench, the majority of which involved fiscal peccadilloes. Judges Williams and Spencer appeared before the assembly in their own defense, while Ashe sent a vitriolic letter.[50]

---

[47] Waldrup, "James Iredell," 278.

[48] See William Hooper to JI, January 22, 1787, n. 6, in this volume.

[49] Archibald Maclaine to JI, August 3, 1786, in this volume.

[50] Waldrup, "James Iredell," 311-319; Robinson, *William R. Davie*, 176; "Committee of the Whole of two Houses in Conferences, Jan. 1 & 2, re administration of justice," Joint Resolutions, 1786-1787, General Assembly Session Records, State Archives, Office of Archives and History, Raleigh.

Iredell, like other attorneys, was frustrated at the court's inefficiency, and he too held the judges in low regard. Iredell, however, was more discreet than some of his associates. His public statements focused on the need for systemic reform. Disparaging remarks about individuals were expressed only to his wife and close friends, and even those comments were temperate.

A notable exception to Iredell's pattern of restraint was his reaction to Samuel Ashe's letter to the General Assembly. Ashe's statement so maligned the legal profession that Iredell and his colleagues thought that it could not go unanswered. The group selected Iredell to draft their rebuttal, and eight of his associates joined him in signing it. Ashe subsequently explained to Iredell personally and in the written response to the lawyers' letter that his condemnation was not meant to include him. Iredell was not appeased, however. He wrote a second letter in defense of his profession, this time bearing only his signature. It was published in a New Bern newspaper on November 26, 1787.[51]

Iredell's selection to write the lawyers' response to Ashe's letter was a testament to his high standing among his colleagues. This was also evident in the General Assembly's appointment of Iredell in 1787 to compile the laws of North Carolina for publication. In addition to the colonial and state laws, the volume was to include such documents as the Carolina Charter, the state constitution, and the peace treaty between the United States and Great Britain. The compilation, known as "Iredell's Revisal," was published in 1791.[52]

Iredell's rise to prominence during the period covered in this volume culminated with his role as an advocate for the ratification of the U.S. Constitution. Since 1781, the country had struggled under the Articles of Confederation. These were written as the country was waging war against perceived tyrannical authority, and the authors were careful to avoid creating a domestic equivalent of the British Parliament. They were too careful, however. By bestowing excessive powers upon the individual states, they created an ineffective central government that lacked the authority to address the new nation's complex problems. For example, the national government, which could not levy taxes, had to depend upon the states' largesse for funding. In addition, state trade regulations took precedence

[51]The text of Ashe's letter to the General Assembly is in Clark, *State Records*, 18:137-142. The lawyers' letter to Judge Ashe has not been found. An excerpt of Ashe's response to that letter appears in Griffith J. McRee, *Life and Correspondence of James Iredell*, 2 vols. (New York: D. Appleton, 1857) 2:601, n. 1. JI's letter of November 26, 1787, is included in this volume.

[52]Whichard, *Justice James Iredell*, 23; Clark, *State Records*, 24:888-889.

over national policies, thus preventing the creation of a cohesive national economic program.

The Articles' shortcomings were soon evident, and even before they were put into effect movement was afoot to change them. Significant revisions were difficult, however, because amendments had to be approved by all of the states. Amid the resulting governmental and economic stagnation, delegates from five states met in Annapolis, Maryland, in September 1786 ostensibly to discuss stimulating commerce. The Virginia legislature had proposed the meeting, and every state had been invited to send representatives. Only New Jersey, New York, Virginia, Delaware, and Pennsylvania complied in a timely manner, however. Gov. Richard Caswell of North Carolina appointed five delegates, but Hugh Williamson, a physician and merchant of Chowan County, was the only appointee to make the journey, and he reached Annapolis after the convention had ended. The delegates at Annapolis were too few in number to achieve sweeping changes, but they did set the stage for such changes. They agreed to ask all of the states to send delegates to a second convention, which was to be held in Philadelphia in May 1787.

Though assembled to consider revisions to the Articles of Confederation, the delegates who gathered in Philadelphia scrapped that document and drafted the Constitution. The North Carolina General Assembly sent five delegates to the Philadelphia convention. Though Iredell was not among them, he frequently corresponded with three who were: Hugh Williamson, Richard Dobbs Spaight, and William R. Davie. They shared Iredell's views on the need for a stronger central government and kept him abreast of progress toward that goal. Davie, early in the convention, asked Iredell's opinion on key issues that were certain to arise: "Be so good as to favor me, by the next post, with your opinion how far the introduction of Judicial and executive powers derived from Congress would be politic or practicable in the States? And whether absolute or limited powers for the regulation of trade both as to exports and imports &c. I [shall tr]ouble you frequently and I [shall] expect your opinion without reserve."[53] The convention became a clearinghouse of information on developments around the country, and Iredell's friends sent him the latest news. Iredell, in turn, kept them informed about events in North Carolina, particularly regarding lawsuits in which they were involved.

On September 17, 1787, the convention concluded its business, and the campaign for ratification began. Upon approval by conventions in nine states, the Constitution would go into effect, but only in the ratifying

[53] William R. Davie to JI, May 30, 1787, in this volume.

states. Iredell quickly became a leader in the fight for ratification in North Carolina, and as in the past, his pen was his favorite weapon. At a meeting on November 8, 1787, a group of Chowan County citizens endorsed a resolution written by Iredell calling for a state ratification convention. Four days later the grand jury in the Edenton District presented a declaration supporting ratification, also drafted by Iredell, to the district court. In the latter document Iredell lamented "the disordered and distracted state" of affairs and called the nation "a union in nothing but in name." He listed the wretched consequences of the current political system—"our public debts unpaid, the treaty of peace unfulfilled on both sides, our commerce at the very verge of ruin, and all private industry at a stand"—and deplored the weakness of the national government.[54]

On December 6, 1787, the General Assembly approved an election for delegates to a ratification convention. Balloting was to occur on the last Friday and Saturday in the following March, and the convention would convene the third Monday in July. This measure passed despite Antifederalist objections and the absence of Federalist leaders Samuel Johnston and James Iredell. Johnston had chosen not to run for an assembly seat, and Iredell had been defeated. Iredell's name, to his surprise, had been put in nomination the day before the election.[55]

Some aspects of the campaign for seats in the ratification convention would be familiar to modern voters. The tone was intense, and the rhetoric bitter. The candidates' remarks and actions of the distant past were fair game, and mudslinging was common. The Federalists employed what in modern parlance would be called a media blitz. In the eighteenth century that meant using newspapers and pamphlets to lay methodical arguments before the voters. The Antifederalist approach was more visceral. Relying on face-to-face encounters with voters, the Antifederalists spread fear of the cataclysmic events that were sure to occur should the stronger central government come into being, specifically the loss of individual rights, heavy taxes, and the abolition of states' rights.[56]

Iredell was, according to historian Albert Ray Newsome, "the most active supporter and the ablest publicist of ratification."[57] Iredell's writings

---

[54]See "Grand Jury to the Edenton District Court," November 12, 1787, in this volume.

[55]Trenholme, *Ratification*, 101-102.

[56]Trenholme, *Ratification*, 107-108; Albert Ray Newsome, "North Carolina's Ratification of the Federal Constitution," *North Carolina Historical Review* 17 (October 1940): 289-290.

[57]Newsome, "North Carolina's Ratification," 290.

prior to the General Assembly's call for a convention contain general endorsements of the Constitution with limited specifics. Once the election and convention were scheduled, however, his arguments became more precise. Iredell's most comprehensive and detailed defense of the Constitution was published in January 1788. Using the pseudonym Marcus, Iredell wrote a lengthy, point-by-point refutation of George Mason's widely read "Objections to the Constitution."[58] This Antifederalist tract contained an explanation of the eleven reasons why Mason, a Virginia delegate to the constitutional convention, had refused to sign the finished document.

Paramount among Mason's complaints was the absence of a bill of rights. Antifederalists feared that the omission of explicit provisions protecting individual liberties would enable the stronger central government to deprive citizens of their rights. Mason had introduced a resolution calling for a bill of rights at the convention in Philadelphia, but it was soundly defeated. Opponents argued that because state constitutions contained such guarantees, adding them to the federal Constitution would be superfluous.[59] But for many, the fact that state constitutions, including North Carolina's, contained such provisions made the absence of similar language in the proposed U.S. Constitution conspicuous and troubling. Mason felt so strongly about this issue that the first words in his "Objections to the Constitution" are "There is no declaration of rights." Iredell countered that a written Constitution that unequivocally states what powers the government can exercise made the listing of powers that the government could not exercise "nugatory and ridiculous." In an odd analogy, Iredell compared the inclusion of a declaration of rights to a judge, who having sentenced a man to be hanged, then instructs the sheriff not to behead the condemned.

Throughout his objections, Mason reiterates the fear that the federal government under the proposed Constitution would be a threat to state prerogatives and individual liberties, while Iredell consistently contends that safeguards within the Constitution would prevent abuses of power. Mason and Iredell provide in their respective treatises a concise summary of the arguments on both sides of the ratification controversy.

---

[58] See "To Mr. Mason," January 8, 1788, in this volume.

[59] Kelly and Harbison, *American Constitution*, 142.

In the balloting for delegates to the ratification convention, Iredell was unanimously chosen to represent Edenton.[60] Like Iredell, many of the Federalists elected to the convention were from the northeastern part of the state. In addition, a number of them were among North Carolina's wealthiest citizens. While Iredell himself did not possess great riches, he was related by marriage to the prosperous Johnston family. Thus, Iredell was at least matrimonially connected to what detractors called the Federalist eastern elite. Iredell's Federalist colleagues at the convention included his brother-in-law Samuel Johnston and two of his correspondents from the Philadelphia convention, William R. Davie and Richard Dobbs Spaight.

The Antifederalists, led by Willie Jones of Halifax County, enjoyed overwhelming numerical superiority in the convention when it convened in Hillsborough on July 21, 1788. Though more numerous, the Antifederalist delegates were on the whole less eminent than their Federalist counterparts. Antifederalist notables included Samuel Spencer, the fractious superior court judge disdained by Iredell; Timothy Bloodworth, who had resigned from Congress to return to North Carolina to oppose the Constitution; and Thomas Person, a veteran legislator of Granville County.[61]

The existence of an Antifederalist majority at the North Carolina convention did not reflect the sentiments of the nation. By the time the delegates gathered in Hillsborough, ten states, including neighboring Virginia and South Carolina, had ratified the Constitution. North Carolina Federalists hoped in vain that the actions of these states would influence their opponents.

Soon after the opening gavel, Antifederalist leader Willie Jones, bristling with confidence, called for an immediate vote on ratification. The Federalists were taken aback by Jones's proposal and argued for time to debate and reflect on this serious decision. Jones countered that the issue had been debated in the arena of public opinion for months and that prolonging the convention for still more discussion would be a waste of public money. With the numbers seeming to be immutably in his favor, however, Jones could afford to be magnanimous, and he withdrew his call for a vote.

The ensuing debate was a one-sided affair, as the burden fell on the Federalists to convert their adversaries. In addition, the Antifederalists, lacking orators to match those in the Federalist ranks but enjoying a

---

[60]See "To the Freemen of the Town of Edenton," ca. March 30, 1788, in this volume.

[61]Trenholme, *Ratification*, 148-149; Whichard, *Justice James Iredell*, 20; *DNCB*, s.v. "Bloodworth, Timothy," "Person, Thomas."

majority, had nothing to gain by engaging in the discussions. Iredell, as a veteran lawyer and superb speaker, played a key role as the Federalists painstakingly explained and defended each clause of the Constitution. Their efforts were futile, however, for on August 2 the delegates voted by more than a two-to-one margin to neither reject nor ratify the Constitution. Instead the convention proposed a declaration of rights with twenty-seven provisions "asserting and securing from incroachment the great Principles of civil and religious Liberty and the unalienable rights of the People" and thirteen amendments "to the most ambiguous and exceptional parts of the said Constitution" to be presented to Congress or to a second national convention to amend the Constitution.[62] The Antifederalists thought that by withholding ratification they would gain leverage in securing these objectives. Iredell had proposed a compromise calling for ratification with a recommendation for amendments, but this was defeated.[63]

During the course of the convention, New York became the eleventh state to ratify, leaving only North Carolina and Rhode Island outside of the union. Because of the near unanimity of the states, North Carolina, instead of gaining leverage, found itself an isolated, independent country. Questions arose as to how North Carolina would defend itself against the British, Spanish, and Indians.[64] Under a graduated tariff established by Congress in 1789, North Carolina, like other foreign nations, was expected to pay the highest rate.[65]

The convention in Hillsborough had scarcely ended when Federalists began campaigning for a second convention, and once again Iredell played a leading role. On August 18, a lengthy letter appeared in the *State Gazette of North Carolina* warning readers, "Perhaps at no period since your ancestors first settled in this country has your condition been more awful and affecting." The author condemned the convention's outcome and presented a detailed defense of the Constitution.[66] Signed "A Citizen of North Carolina," the letter has been attributed to Iredell.[67] Along with William R. Davie, Iredell also sponsored the publication and distribution

---

[62]Clark, *State Records*, 22:16-31.

[63]For information on the first North Carolina ratification convention, see Newsome, "North Carolina's Ratification," 292-295, and Trenholme, *Ratification*, 146-191.

[64]Newsome, "North Carolina's Ratification," 297.

[65]See Pierce Butler to JI, August 11, 1789, n. 6, in this volume.

[66]See "To the People of the State of North Carolina," August 18, 1788, in this volume.

[67]Trenholme, *Ratification*, 199n; Whichard, *Justice James Iredell*, 80.

of a thousand copies of the debates from the Hillsborough convention. Because of the Antifederalists' reticence at the convention, the published debates were, in effect, a Federalist pamphlet, and because of Iredell's prominence in the debates, a testament to his eloquence.[68]

The first step toward a second convention was the election of General Assembly members, which occurred in August, shortly after the Hillsborough convention adjourned. Iredell, despite his fervor, did not run. Because legislators often missed the opening of the annual legislative session, the General Assembly in 1787 authorized levying fines against those who were late. The November 1788 assembly session conflicted with superior court dates, and Iredell, because of commitments to clients and financial concerns, did not want to forego attending court nor risk being fined.[69]

Despite the absence of Iredell's leadership, the Federalists elected to the assembly won approval for a second convention in a closely contested legislative battle. The date of the convention was a particularly contentious issue. Antifederalists, hoping for a second federal convention to consider proposed amendments, wanted to delay the state convention, while Federalists argued for the earliest date possible.[70] Assembly members finally agreed to hold the convention in November 1789 in Fayetteville to coincide with the next meeting of the General Assembly. Since most of those elected to one would likely be elected to the other, holding both gatherings at the same time and place would be convenient and economical.[71] The General Assembly also appointed delegates to an anticipated second federal convention. Iredell was chosen but declined the honor. In any event, that convention never occurred.[72]

Between the close of the Hillsborough convention in August 1788 and the election of delegates to the second convention a year later, public opinion in North Carolina shifted in favor of ratification. Two important reasons for this were the election of the revered George Washington as president and the successful establishment of the new national government in the spring of 1789. Despite dire warnings, the catastrophes that Antifederalists had predicted had yet to materialize. In fact, the economy had significantly improved. To what degree this financial upswing was

---

[68]Trenholme, *Ratification*, 197.

[69]See "To the Electors of Edenton," August 15, 1788, in this volume.

[70]Newsome, "North Carolina's Ratification," 204.

[71]See Samuel Johnston to JI, November 20, 1788, n. 1, in this volume.

[72]Whichard, *Justice James Iredell*, 82.

attributable to the adoption of the Constitution is questionable, but the Federalists made the most of the situation. Antifederalists had hoped that North Carolina's failure to ratify would prompt coaxing from other states. Instead, it generated in some quarters contempt and criticism. The association of North Carolina with Rhode Island, the only other state that had failed to ratify, troubled many North Carolinians because of that state's reputation for immoderate views, particularly its dubious policies regarding paper money and payment of debts.[73] Perhaps the most influential factor, however, was Congress's willingness to consider amendments to the Constitution. James Madison assuaged the fears of many Antifederalists when he raised the issue of amendments in the House of Representatives in June.[74]

The body of delegates who met in Fayetteville on November 17, 1789, was collectively a mirror image of the Hillsborough convention. At the first convention the majority was overwhelmingly Antifederalist, and the chances of ratification were virtually nil. In Fayetteville, the Federalists dominated and ratification seemed inevitable. Willie Jones, the Antifederalist leader at Hillsborough, did not seek election to the Fayetteville convention. This may have been because the Antifederalists' prospects were so dismal, or, as Federalists reported, because of a falling out with his followers.[75] Another conspicuous absentee was James Iredell. Though a popular and effective Federalist leader, Iredell was defeated by another Federalist, John Mare, a native of New York and a successful merchant engaged in trade in the West Indies.[76]

The Federalists in Fayetteville ratified the Constitution by an even larger margin than that enjoyed by the Antifederalists in Hillsborough. Iredell, though not present, must be given some credit for this outcome. As a writer and orator, Iredell was in the vanguard of the Federalist campaign offering reasoned arguments against the fearful rhetoric of the Antifederalists.

Iredell's endeavors enhanced his reputation not only within North Carolina but across the nation. Leaders around the country read the published debates from the first convention, in which Iredell figured so

---

[73]See Richard D. Spaight to JI, July 3, 1787, and Hugh Williamson to JI, July 22, 1787, in this volume.

[74]Newsome, "North Carolina's Ratification," 296-298; Trenholme, *Ratification*, 195-196, 226-227.

[75]Whichard, *Justice James Iredell*, 84; Trenholme, *Ratification*, 215; Robinson, *William R. Davie*, 215.

[76]See JI to Hugh Williamson, August 29, 1789, in this volume.

prominently, as well as his various writings on the Constitution. The eminence Iredell attained with his pen no doubt facilitated his subsequent appointment to the U.S. Supreme Court.

Nomination to the high court was the most conspicuous change among many that Iredell experienced following the war. He probably would have cited becoming a father as the most significant of these. There was also the reunification with his brother Thomas, his appointment as compiler of the state statutes, and his rise to national prominence during the struggle for ratification. There was one thing, however, that did not change. Six years after deciding to focus on his legal practice because of financial need, Iredell told Hugh Williamson that the appointment to the Supreme Court would be "very agreeable" provided that the salary "would be a sufficient compensation."[77]

[77]JI to Hugh Williamson, August 29, 1789, in this volume.

Editorial Method

The editors selected the documents contained in this volume to provide a comprehensive view of James Iredell's professional and personal life from 1784 through 1789. Most of the original papers are in the North Carolina State Archives, Raleigh; the Rare Book, Manuscript, and Special Collections Library, Duke University; and the Southern Historical Collection at the University of North Carolina at Chapel Hill. Some of the documents are included in Griffith J. McRee's two-volume *Life and Correspondence of James Iredell*, published in 1857-1858. McRee's publication contains documents that have otherwise been lost, though unfortunately some are not printed in their entirety.

This is the third volume of a projected six-volume collection of James Iredell's papers. The first two volumes, covering 1767 through 1783, were edited by Don Higginbotham and published in 1976. The fourth volume will contain documents from the last years of Iredell's life, 1790 to 1799, when he served as a justice on the U.S. Supreme Court. The final two volumes will be a collection of Iredell's legal papers edited by Anthony Joseph of Eastern University.

The Iredell papers in volume three have been transcribed and printed as closely as possible to the original text, with a few exceptions. Spelling, underlining, punctuation, indention, and capitalization are maintained, though the reader should be mindful that in some instances such determinations are highly subjective. The difference between a period, comma, and stray mark can be slight.

Headings have been inserted at the top of each document indicating the writer or recipient of the letter, or the title of the document. The place, date, and salutation in letters are arranged as they appear on the original document with the exception of dates that have been moved from the bottom or back of letters. These dates are italicized and placed in brackets. Characters in superscript have been lowered and printed in regular font throughout the documents.

Some of the original letters are torn with pieces missing, and in places Iredell's handwriting is no more than a scrawl. The context of some missing or illegible words has enabled the editors to infer what was intended. Such inferences are indicated by brackets and italics. Otherwise an explanation for missing words, such as "torn," "blot," or "illegible," is given.

When a word has been inadvertently repeated in the original the repetition is retained, with one exception. Some correspondents, in order to help readers keep the pages of a letter in order, placed at the bottom of a page the first word appearing on the following page. These redundancies have been omitted. In addition, words crossed out by a writer have been enclosed in angle brackets (< >), and interlinear insertions have been enclosed in solidi (/ /).

Closings have been placed on a single line, above the writer's name, to save space. Extra spaces have been inserted to indicate breaks in the closings.

The source and form of each document are given in small type following the writer's name. Explanations of the abbreviations used in the provenance notes can be found in "Abbreviations and Shortened References Used in the Annotations." All endorsements, which usually appear on the back of letters, are labeled "Endorsed" and are also included in small print at the end of the letter.

Notes identifying individuals, places, and events appear immediately following the document to which they refer. The editors have taken an inclusive approach in determining topics for annotation. Because readers are likely to include genealogists and local historians, notes have been provided explaining familial relationships, describing geographical locations, and citing births, marriages, and deaths. While the Iredell papers offer insight into the political events of the day, they also reveal much about late-eighteenth-century social and cultural history. Thus, in addition to notes explaining governmental developments, annotations are provided on books, plays, medicine, contemporary terminology, and other non-political subjects referred to in the documents.

In regard to political matters, the documents include frequent references to state and national legislative bodies. To distinguish between the two in the notes, house and senate are lowercased when referring to the state General Assembly and capitalized in reference to the U.S. Congress.

As is customary, citations in the notes are shortened after the first reference and abbreviations are used for some sources. For the readers' convenience, an explanation of the abbreviations and full bibliographical information for the shortened references has been provided in "Abbreviations and Shortened References Used in the Annotations."

Abbreviations and Shortened References Used in the Annotations

Abbreviations

BDC	*Biographical Directory of the United States Congress, 1774-1989.* Bicentennial Edition. Washington, D.C.: United States Government Printing Office, 1988.
DAB	Allen Johnson and Dumas Malone, eds. *Dictionary of American Biography.* 20 vols. New York: Charles Scribner's Sons, 1928-1936.
DNB	Leslie Stephen and Sidney Lee, eds. *Dictionary of National Biography.* 63 vols. New York: Macmillan, 1885-1900.
DNCB	William S. Powell, ed. *Dictionary of North Carolina Biography.* 6 vols. Chapel Hill: University of North Carolina Press, 1979-1996.
FC	File copy
NYPL	New York Public Library
OED	J. A. Simpson and E. S. C. Weiner. *The Oxford English Dictionary.* 2d ed. 20 vols. Oxford: Clarendon Press, 1989.
PJI	Don Higginbotham, ed. *The Papers of James Iredell.* 2 vols. Raleigh: Division of Archives and History, Department of Cultural Resources, 1976.
RC	Recipient's copy
SHC	Southern Historical Collection. University of North Carolina Library, Chapel Hill
TSS	Typescript

Shortened References

Achtemeier, *Harper's Bible Dictionary.*

Paul J. Achtemeier, ed. *Harper's Bible Dictionary.* San Francisco: Harper and Row, 1985.

Ashe, Weeks, and Van Noppen, *Biographical History.*

Ashe, Samuel A., Stephen B. Weeks, and Charles L. Van Noppen, eds. *Biographical History of North Carolina.* 8 vols. Greensboro: Charles L. Van Noppen, 1905-1917.

Babits and Howard, *"Fortitude and Forbearance."*

Laurence E. Babits and Joshua B. Howard. *"Fortitude and Forbearance": The North Carolina Continental Line in the Revolutionary War, 1775-1783.* Raleigh: Office of Archives and History, North Carolina Department of Cultural Resources, forthcoming.

Bailey, *Diplomatic History.*

Thomas A. Bailey. *A Diplomatic History of the American People.* New York: Appleton, Century, Crofts, 1964.

Barrett, *Old Merchants.*

Walter Barrett. *The Old Merchants of New York City.* 5 vols. 1870. Reprint, New York: Greenwood Press, 1968.

Bartholomew, *Survey Gazetteer.*

John Bartholomew. *The Survey Gazetteer of the British Isles.* Edinburgh: John Bartholomew and Son, Geographical Institute, 1932.

Brewer's Dictionary of Phrase and Fable.

Brewer's Dictionary of Phrase and Fable. 15th ed. New York: HarperCollins, 1995.

Burke's Peerage, 76th ed.

Bernard Burke and Ashworth P. Burke. *A Genealogical and Heraldic History of the Peerage and Barontage, The Privy Council, Knightage and Companiage.* 76th ed. London: Harrison and Sons, 1914.

Burke's Peerage, 104th ed.

Peter Towned, ed. *Burke's Genealogical and Heraldic History of the Peerage, Barontage and Knightage.* 104th ed. London: Burke's Peerage, 1967.

Campbell, *Patrick Henry.*

Norine Dickson Campbell. *Patrick Henry: Patriot and Statesman.* New York: Devin-Adair, 1969.

Cheney, *North Carolina Government.*

Cheney, John L., ed. *North Carolina Government, 1585-1979: A Narrative and Statistical History.* Raleigh: North Carolina Department of Secretary of State, 1981.

Clark, *State Records.*

Clark, Walter, ed. *The State Records of North Carolina*, 16 vols. Raleigh: State of North Carolina, 1895-1906.

Constitution.

The Constitution of the United States of America with a Summary of the Actions by the States in Ratification of the Provisions Thereof. 3d ed.

Richmond: Virginia Commission of Constitutional Government, 1965.

Cooke, *France, 1789-1962.*

James J. Cooke. *France, 1789-1962.* Hamden, Conn.: Archon Books, 1975.

Corbitt, *North Carolina Counties.*

David Leroy Corbitt. *The Formation of the North Carolina Counties, 1663-1943.* Raleigh: State Department of Archives and History, 1950.

Crabtree, *North Carolina Governors.*

Beth G. Crabtree. *North Carolina Governors, 1585-1974: Brief Sketches.* Rev. ed. Raleigh: Division of Archives and History, Department of Cultural Resources, 1974.

DeMond, *Loyalists in North Carolina.*

Robert O. DeMond. *The Loyalists in North Carolina during the Revolution.* Baltimore: Genealogical Publishing, 1979.

De Pauw et al., *Documentary History of the First Federal Congress.*

Linda Grant De Pauw et al. *Documentary History of the First Federal Congress of the United States of America.* 14 vols. to date. Baltimore: Johns Hopkins Press, 1972-.

Drabble, *Oxford Companion to English Literature.*

Margaret Drabble, ed. The *Oxford Companion to English Literature.* Rev. ed. Oxford: Oxford University Press, 1998.

Elliot's Debates.

Jonathan Elliot, ed. *The Debates in the Several State Conventions on the Adoption of the Federal Constitution, ...* 2d ed. 5 vols. Philadelphia: J. B. Lippincott; Washington: Taylor and Murray, 1861-1863.

Ferguson, et al., *Papers of Robert Morris.*

E. James Ferguson, et al., eds. *The Papers of Robert Morris, 1781-1784.* 9 vols. Pittsburgh: University of Pittsburgh Press, 1983-1999.

Fouts, *Abstracts from Newspapers of Wilmington.*

Raymond Parker Fouts. *Abstracts from Newspapers of Wilmington, North Carolina.* Vol. 1. *1765-1775, 1788-1797.* Cocoa, Fla.: GenRec Books, 1984.

Fouts, *Abstracts from the Edenton Gazette.*

Raymond Parker Fouts. *Abstracts from the Edenton Gazette and North Carolina General Advertiser.* 4 vols. Cocoa, Fla.: GenRec Books, 1990-1996.

Fouts, *State Gazette of North-Carolina.*

Raymond Parker Fouts. *Abstracts from the State Gazette of North-Carolina.* 3 vols. Cocoa, Fla.: GenRec Books, 1982.

Garner, *Black's Law Dictionary*, 7th ed.

Bryan A. Garner, ed. *Black's Law Dictionary.* 7th ed. St. Paul, Minn.: West Group, 1999.

Goodwin, *New Cambridge Modern History.*

A. Goodwin. *The New Cambridge Modern History.* Vol. 8. *The American and French Revolutions, 1763-1793.* Cambridge: University Press, 1965.

Gregory and Stevenson, *Longman Companion to Britain in the Eighteenth Century.*

Jeremy Gregory and John Stevenson. *The Longman Companion to Britain in the Eighteenth Century, 1688-1820.* London: Longman, 2000.

Grimes, *North Carolina Wills.*

J. Bryan Grimes. *North Carolina Wills and Inventories.* Baltimore: Genealogical Publishing, 1967.

Hagy, *People and Professions of Charleston.*

James W. Hagy. *People and Professions of Charleston, South Carolina, 1782-1802.* Baltimore: Genealogical Publishing, 1992.

Heads of Families, 1790 Census.

Heads of Families at the First Census of the United States Taken in the Year 1790: North Carolina. Washington, D.C.: Government Printing Office, 1908; Baltimore: Genealogical Publishing, 1978.

Hofmann, *Wills, 1758-1824, Halifax County.*

Margaret M. Hofmann, comp. *Genealogical Abstract of Wills, 1758-1824, Halifax County, North Carolina.* Weldon, N.C.: Roanoke News, 1970.

Holcomb, *Marriages of Granville County.*

Brent H. Holcomb, comp. *Marriages of Granville County, North Carolina, 1753-1868.* Baltimore: Genealogical Publishing, 1981.

Howatson, *Classical Literature.*

M. C. Howatson, ed. *The Oxford Companion to Classical Literature.* 2d. ed. Oxford: Oxford University Press, 1989.

Howell, *Book of Wilmington.*

Andrew J. Howell. *The Book of Wilmington.* N.p.: n.d.

Jensen et al., *Documentary History of the Ratification.*

Merrill Jensen et al. *The Documentary History of the Ratification of the Constitution.* 18 vols. to date. Madison: State Historical Society of Wisconsin, 1976-.

Journals of the Continental Congress.

Journals of the Continental Congress, 1774-1789. Edited by Worthington C. Ford et al. 34 vols. Washington, D.C.: Government Printing Office, 1904-1937.

Keith, *John Gray Blount Papers.*

Alice Barnwell Keith, ed. *The John Gray Blount Papers.* Vol. 1. *1764-1789.* Raleigh: State Department of Archives and History, 1952.

Kellam and McKoy, *St. James Church.*

Ida Brooks Kellam and Elizabeth Francenia McKoy. *St. James Church, Wilmington, North Carolina, Historical Records, 1737-1852.* Wilmington: n.p., 1965.

Kelly and Harbison, *American Constitution.*

Alfred H. Kelly and Winfred A. Harbison. *The American Constitution: Its Origins and Development.* New York: W. W. Norton, 1976.

Lefler and Wager, *Orange County.*

Hugh Lefler and Paul Wager, eds. *Orange County–1752-1952.* Chapel Hill: n.p., 1953.

Lennon and Kellam, *Wilmington Town Book.*

Donald R. Lennon and Ida Brooks Kellam, eds. *The Wilmington Town Book, 1743-1778.* Raleigh: Division of Archives and History, North Carolina Department of Cultural Resources, 1973.

Life and Times of James Hogg.

The Life and Times of James Hogg, 1729-1804. N.p.: Hogg Historical Committee, [1988].

Littlejohn and Littlejohn, *William Littlejohn.*

William Harris Littlejohn and F. S. Littlejohn. *William Littlejohn Descendants.* N.p, n.d.

London and Lemmon, *Episcopal Church in North Carolina.*

Lawrence Foushee London and Sarah McCulloh Lemmon, eds. *The Episcopal Church in North Carolina, 1701-1959.* Raleigh: Episcopal Diocese of North Carolina, 1987.

Massengill, *North Carolina Votes.*

Stephen E. Massengill. *North Carolina Votes on the Constitution: A Roster of Delegates to the State Ratification Conventions of 1788 and 1789.* Raleigh: Division of Archives and History, North Carolina Department of Cultural Resources, 1988.

McRee, *Life and Correspondence.*

Griffith J. McRee. *Life and Correspondence of James Iredell.* 2 vols. New York: D. Appleton, 1857.

Miller, *George Mason.*

Helen Hill Miller. *George Mason: Gentleman Revolutionary.* Chapel Hill: University of North Carolina Press, 1975.

Mitchell, *North Carolina Wills.*

Thornton W. Mitchell. *North Carolina Wills: A Testator Index, 1665-1900.* Rev. ed. Baltimore: Genealogical Publishing, 1992.

Morris, *Forging the Union.*

Richard B. Morris. *The Forging of the Union, 1781-1789.* New York: Harper and Row, 1987.

Namier and Brooke, *House of Commons.*

Lewis Namier and John Brooke. *The House of Commons, 1754-1790.* 3 vols. London: Her Majesty's Stationary Office, 1964.

Neal, *Abstracts of Vital Records.*

Lois Smather Neal, comp. *Abstracts of Vital Records from Raleigh, North Carolina, Newspapers.* Vol. 1. *1799-1819.* Spartanburg, S.C.: Reprint Company, 1979.

Newman, *Britain in the Hanoverian Age.*

Gerald Newman, ed. *Britain in the Hanoverian Age, 1714-1837: An Encyclopedia.* New York: Garland Publishing, 1997.

Oates, *Story of Fayetteville.*

John A. Oates. *The Story of Fayetteville and the Upper Cape Fear.* N.p., n.d.

Palmer, *Biographical Sketches.*

Gregory Palmer. *Biographical Sketches of Loyalists in the American Revolution.* Westport, Conn.: Meckler Press, 1984.

Polishook, *Rhode Island and the Union.*

Irwin H. Polishook. *Rhode Island and the Union, 1774-1795.* Evanston, Ill.: Northwestern University Press, 1969.

Pool, "Economic Interpretation."

William C. Pool. "An Economic Interpretation of the Ratification of the Federal Constitution in North Carolina." Parts 1-3. *North Carolina Historical Review* 27 (April-October 1950): 119-141, 289-313, 437-461.

Powell, *Gazetteer.*

William S. Powell. *The North Carolina Gazetteer.* Chapel Hill: University of North Carolina Press, 1968.

Pruitt, *Abstracts of Sales of Confiscated Land.*

A. B. Pruitt. *Abstracts of Sales of Confiscated Loyalist Land and Property in North Carolina.* N.p.: A. B. Pruitt, 1989.

Ray, *Colonial Granville.*

Worth S. Ray, comp. and ed. *Colonial Granville and its People.* Baltimore: Genealogical Publishing, 1973.

Reader's Digest Complete Atlas.

The Reader's Digest Complete Atlas of the British Isles. London: Reader's Digest Association, 1965.

Robinson, *William R. Davie.*

Blackwell P. Robinson. *William R. Davie.* Chapel Hill: University of North Carolina Press, 1957.

Smith and Gephart, *Letters.*

Paul H. Smith and Ronald M. Gephart, eds. *Letters of Delegates to Congress, 1774-1789.* Vol. 25. Washington: Library of Congress, 1998.

Thorne, *Heritage of Craven County.*

Barbara M. Howard Thorne, ed. *The Heritage of Craven County, North Carolina.* New Bern: Eastern North Carolina Genealogical Society, in cooperation with Hunter Publishing, Winston-Salem, 1984.

Topographical Dictionary of England, 3d ed.

A Topographical Dictionary of England. 3d ed. 5 vols. London: S. Lewis, 1835.

Treaties and Other International Agreements.

U.S. Department of State. "Treaty of Peace," September 3, 1783. *Treaties and Other International Agreements of the United States of America, 1776-1949.* 13 vols. Washington: Department of State, 1968-1976.

Trenholme, *Ratification.*

Louise Irby Trenholme. *The Ratification of the Federal Constitution in North Carolina.* New York: AMS Press, 1967.

Waddell, *New Hanover County.*

Alfred Moore Waddell. *A History of New Hanover County and the Lower Cape Fear.* Vol. 1. *1723-1800.* N.p., 1909.

Wagstaff, *Papers of John Steele.*

H. M. Wagstaff, ed. *The Papers of John Steele.* 2 vols. Raleigh: North Carolina Historical Commission, 1924.

Waldrup, "James Iredell."

Waldrup, John Charles. "James Iredell and the Practice of Law in Revolutionary Era North Carolina." Ph.D. diss. University of North Carolina at Chapel Hill, 1985.

Walker, *New Hanover County Court Minutes.*

Alexander McDonald Walker, comp. *New Hanover County Court Minutes.* Part 3. *1786-1793.* Bethesda, Md.: Alexander M. Walker, 1960.

Watson, *Index to North Carolina Newspapers.*

Alan D. Watson. *An Index to North Carolina Newspapers, 1784-1789.* Raleigh: North Carolina Department of Cultural Resources, Division of Archives and History, 1992.

Watson, *Money and Monetary Problems.*

Alan D. Watson. *Money and Monetary Problems in Early North Carolina.* Raleigh: Department of Cultural Resources, Division of Archives and History, 1980.

Watson, *Onslow County.*

Alan D. Watson. *Onslow County: A Brief History.* Raleigh: Division of Archives and History, North Carolina Department of Cultural Resources, 1995.

Whichard, *Justice James Iredell.*

Whichard, Willis P. *Justice James Iredell.* Durham: Carolina Academic Press, 2000.

WPA, Grave Index.

Works Progress Administration, Pre-1914 Graves Index. State Archives.

1784

To Mess. Conyngham, Nesbitt & Co.[1]

Edenton, N. Carolina, Jan. 3d. 1784.

Gentlemen,

We think it proper to inform you, that <Mr. John Cooper on the 27th. of last month> the suit of Mr. John Cooper upon the Attachment against Mr. Morris's, /estate/, and wherein we were summoned as Garnishees, came to a hearing at our County Court on the 27 Ulto., and that the Jury /(which was a special one)/ brought in a verdict in Mr. Cooper's favour for the Sum of [*blank*], a sum which very much surprised us, as it /so/ far exceeded Mr. Cooper's demand. <We understand Mr. Johnston> /Mr. J. appeared on Mr. M's behalf, & we understand he/ intends at the next Court (which [*torn*] be held on the fourth Monday in March next), to make a motion in arrers of Judgme[*nt,*] conceiving the proceedings <to have been irregular> in the conduct of the suit to have been irregular, and that Judgment cannot rightfully be given upon it; but for this and further particulars we beg leave to refer to his letter to Mr. Swannick.[2]

We thought it proper to give you this information, at the same time assuring you, as we sincerely do, of our desire to have the accounts depending between us ascertained, and the ballance paid whenever it can be done with safety, <a measure now becane> to effect which we are very desirous of a meeting with some Person properly authorised, and the propriety of this measure is rendered still more urgent as one of Smith's Brothers is now here who has brought full powers of settlement from his [*pri*]ncipal Legatees.[3]

FC, Charles E. Johnson Collection, NCSA. Endorsed "Copy of a Letter to Mess. Conyngham, Nesbitt & Co. Jan. 3d. 1784."

---

[1]David Hayfield Conyngham (ca. 1750-1834) and John Maxwell Nesbitt (1730-1802) were partners in a mercantile business in Philadelphia. Nesbitt was also the director and first president of the Bank of North America. During the Revolution, Conyngham, Nesbitt, and Robert Morris were involved in the operation of privateers. E. James Ferguson et al., eds., *The Papers of Robert Morris, 1781-1784*, 9 vols. (Pittsburgh: University of Pittsburgh Press, 1983-1999), 5:497n; *Dictionary of American Biography*, s.v. "Nesbitt, John Maxwell," hereafter cited as *DAB*; Clarence L. Ver Steeg, *Robert Morris: Revolutionary Financier* (Philadelphia: University of Pennsylvania Press, 1954), 35.

[2]John Cooper was a merchant in Northampton County, N.C., and Philadelphia. Robert Morris (1734-1806) of Pennsylvania was a merchant and the national superintendent of finance (1781-1784). Morris gained a reputation as the

"financier of the Revolution" for his role in managing fiscal matters related to the procurement of arms and other supplies. The case of *Cooper v. Morris* stemmed from disputes about accounts of the *Livingston*, a schooner owned by Morris and others that had been captured by the British in 1781 near Hispaniola. A "Jury of Merchants," summoned in Edenton on Friday, December 26, 1783, awarded Cooper £9,727.2.6¼. The case was discontinued in December of 1784, but a letter from Morris to Samuel Johnston dated February 8, 1785, indicates that the case was still unresolved. The matter was eventually settled out of court. *Biographical Directory of the United States Congress, 1774-1989, Bicentennial Edition*, s.v. "Morris, Robert," hereafter cited as *BDC*; *DAB*, s.v. "Morris, Robert"; *John Cooper v. Robert Morris*, December 24, 1783, Chowan County Court Minutes, State Archives, Office of Archives and History, Raleigh; *John Cooper v. Robert Morris*, December 1783, Trial, Appearance, and Reference Docket, Court of Pleas and Quarter Sessions, Chowan County, State Archives; Ferguson et al., *Papers of Robert Morris*, 1:346, 9:621n; Robert Morris to Samuel Johnston, February 8, 1785, in Walter Clark, ed., *The State Records of North Carolina*, 16 vols. (11-26) (Raleigh: State of North Carolina, 1895-1906), 22:631-632. For more information about the case, see Chowan County Civil Action Papers, 1782, State Archives.

Samuel Johnston (1733-1816), a native of Scotland and a Chowan County planter, was JI's brother-in-law, friend, and law instructor. One of Edenton's most influential citizens, Johnston held numerous public offices, including serving as governor and U.S. senator. In *Cooper v. Morris*, Johnston represented Robert Morris. *Dictionary of North Carolina Biography*, s.v. "Johnston, Samuel," hereafter cited as *DNCB*; Willis P. Whichard, *Justice James Iredell* (Durham: Carolina Academic Press, 2000), 3; Don Higginbotham, ed., *The Papers of James Iredell*, 2 vols. (Raleigh: Division of Archives and History, Department of Cultural Resources, 1976), 1:xlix-li, hereafter cited as *PJI*; Ferguson et al., *Papers of Robert Morris*, 9:621n.

The "fourth Monday in March next" was March 22, 1784.

John Swanwick (1740-1798), a Philadelphia merchant and congressman (1795-1798), was a partner in the firm of Willing, Morris, and Swanwick. *BDC*, s.v. "Swanwick, John"; Ferguson et al., *Papers of Robert Morris*, 9:297n.

[3]Robert Smith (d. 1782) represented Edenton in the General Assembly (1780-1782) and was a partner in the mercantile firm of Hewes and Smith, later Hewes, Smith, and Allen. During the Revolution, he and his company provided numerous services for the Patriot cause, from equipping privateers to providing wine for General Washington. Robert Morris often conducted business with Smith's firm, both in his role as Patriot financier and as a private merchant. When Smith died in March 1782, he left £500 for the establishment of a public academy in Edenton, which was named in his honor. John L. Cheney, ed., *North Carolina Government, 1585-1979: A Narrative and Statistical History* (Raleigh: North Carolina Department of the Secretary of State, 1981), 207-208; *PJI*, 2:263n-264n; Ferguson et al., *Papers of Robert Morris*, 9:621n; Elizabeth G. McPherson, ed., "Unpublished Letters from North Carolinians to Washington," *North Carolina Historical Review* 12 (April 1935): 153n; Will of Robert Smith, 1782, Chowan County Wills, State Archives. See also Conyngham, Nesbitt, &c to JI, September 6, 1784, in this volume.

From William Hooper[1]

Hillsboro Jany. 4th. 1784

My dear Sir

Your very obliging letters which were handed to me when I was at Newbern and announced to me your perfect recovery from a dangerous and distressing malady relieved me from the most painful suspence respecting your Situation.[2] The Severe attack which you have had will render you more Susceptible of Similar disorders, & the Shock which I fear your constitution has received from it will excite what the physicians call a predisposition of habit to that particular Species of complaint. Let me intreat of you to guard against it with particular caution & avail of the able advice you have had from Ramckey to prevent a necessity of calling him again to your aid.[3]

Our Stay at Newbern was much more agreeable than I expected. Mrs. James Ellis as well as him self were Singularly attentive to the Girls.[4] They saw the little variety that Town afforded & the new faces & new fashions supplied them with subject of new comment & Served them as matter of conversation here in discussing the comparative tast[*e*] of the ladies in the different towns they passed thro Nothing however but suffers in the competition with Edenton. Their feelings are interested there, and they have formed attachments which are very near their hearts. Your friends at Newbern enquired for you with real concern. Mrs. Gordon poor woman is hastening fast to a better world.[5] She talks with great philosophy of her approaching dissolution & seems to regret her separation from an existence which has been marked with such Scenes of Sorrow and affliction, only as she leaves her son behind her. Now and then her disorder presents a flattering appearance, but the dangerous Symptoms soon again recur and blast every hope of the return of health. It was the wish of Some one to die Suddenly and away from his friends. God Send that I and those I love may not linger out life in the habit of seeing death constantly before their eyes without availing of his fatal but friendly offices.

Doctor Burke died about fortnight ago and fell in Some measure a Sacrifice to the obstinacy which marked his character thro life.[6] Had he declined his Journey to Edenton, he might yet have been alive. It would however be a question with his friends whether life upon the terms he had it would not have been a curse in the extreme. Labouring under a complication of disorder, oppressed with the most agonizing pains which for months had deprived him of his natural rest, his whole mass of blood dissolved, his temper soured with disappointments and to Sum up his misery—No domestick prop to lean upon—No friend or companion at his own home to Sooth the anguish of his mind or mitigate his pain of body—Was not death to him "a comforter friend and Physician![''] He has carried his indifference to his wife to the grave with him.[7] By his will he has left nothing at her absolute disposal. He has devised to her an estate for life in part, not half of his estate & upon her marriage has restrained and curtailed that in some degree. Upon the death of his daughter; to whom he has given the whole upon the death of her Mother; provided the daughter dies under 21 or without Issue the whole goes to the Children of James Hogg and Wiley Jones.[8] These Gentlemen are Sole executors and Guardians to his daughter. No confidence reposed in the wife. Burke's debts I fear will Swallow up the whole. Mr. Hogg the Exe. requests that you and Mr. Johnson or Mr. Diack would as soon as possible inform him upon what terms or conditions Burke held the negroes that were purchased under Mrs. Aitchesons Execution.[9] Did Burke purchase for himself, for her, or for whom. Has he paid? or what is his estate liable for? Burke has devised all the negroes /but one/ as his own property. Mr. Hogg is Solicitous to know how this matter is circumstanced before he enters upon the Office of Exr.[10]

Sincerely do I congratulate you upon the finishing stroke being put to the treaty of peace. I am yet however /not/ without some apprehensions for the honour and faith of the united States in carrying the articles of peace into Strict & punctual execution. Col Stephen Moore who is here from New York immediately; informs us that the sending the negroes from New York to Port Romnay is considered by Congress as an infraction of the peace and will justify an infringement on the part of the States in another respect.[11] The Virginians have Seized (Mr. Moore informs us) the favourable occasion and have passed a law to prevent carrying into Execution the article for the payment of British debts.[12] Is it So? The example will soon pervade this State

Rivington holds his Station in New York Col Moore assigns the cause of his Security.[13] It has come out as there is now no longer any reason to conceal it that Rivington has been very useful to Genl. Washington by furnishing him with intelligence. The unreserved confidence which the British placed in him owing in a great measure to his liberal abuse of the Americans gave him ample opportunities to obtain information which he has bountifully communicated to our friends. Several others whom the British considered as their devoted friends have availed of the same kind of merit—A certain Black Sam has been thanked for his Service by a letter wrote by Genl. Washingtons order[14]

We have no domestick news here my family enjoys their usual Stock of health. Mr. Hogg & all well except Mrs. Hogg who continues in the old State—Entre nous. Betsy Hogg will probably change her name before you see her, and for the sake of a pun & it is the first I ever made, will Substitute the food for the animal. The young Gentleman is well known to & beloved by us both.[15]

I have Seen Marmaduke Jones. He is the greatest coxcomb alive[16]

Adieu my dear Sir. Pray make the compliments of Mrs. Hooper & her daughter & mine acceptable to Mrs. Iredell & the others of your worthy family[17] Accept them yourself & believe me

Dear Sir Ever Unalterably & Affectionately Yours

Will Hooper

RC, Iredell Papers, Duke. Printed, McRee, 2:82-85. Addressed "James Iredell esqe, Edenton." Endorsed "Hillsborough Jan. 4. 1784. Wm. Hooper. Ansd. Feb. 26th."

---

[1]William Hooper (1742-1790), an attorney of Hillsborough, was a signer of the Declaration of Independence, a noted orator, and a legislator. *DNCB*, s.v. "Hooper, William." See also *PJI*, 1:233n.

[2]JI suffered various maladies through much of his life. For a discussion of JI's health, see Whichard, *Justice James Iredell*, 279-285.

[3]Frederick Ramcke (Raunsche) (ca. 1760-1800) was a surgeon in Armand's Legion during the American Revolution and after the war a Chowan County physician. *DNCB*, s.v. "Ramcke, Frederick"; Lawrence E. Babits and Joshua B. Howard, *"Fortitude and Forbearance": The North Carolina Continental Line in the Revolutionary War, 1775-1783* (Raleigh: Office of Archives and History, North Carolina Department of Cultural Resources, forthcoming).

[4]James Ellis (d. ca. 1794) and his wife, Ann (d. before 1810). The "Girls" may refer to Hooper's wife, Anne Clark Hooper (d. 1795), and their daughter, Elizabeth (b. 1770), who would marry Henry Hyrn Watters. *Heads of Families at the First Census of the United States Taken in the Year 1790: North Carolina* (Washington, D.C.: Government Printing Office, 1908; Baltimore: Genealogical Publishing, 1978), 130, hereafter cited as *Heads of Families, 1790 Census*; Estate of James Ellis, 1796, Craven County Estates, State Archives; Thornton W. Mitchell, *North Carolina Wills: A Testator Index, 1665-1900*, rev. ed. (Baltimore: Genealogical Publishing, 1992), 247; *DNCB*, s.v. "Hooper, William."

[5]Mary Duff Gordon (d. 1784) of New Bern was the widow of Patrick Gordon (d. 1773). Mitchell, *North Carolina Wills*, 193.

[6]Thomas Burke (b. ca. 1744) of Hillsborough died December 2, 1783. He was a lawyer, physician, and poet, who served as a member of the Continental Congress and as governor (1781-1782). While governor he was taken prisoner by Tories led by David Fanning. *DNCB*, s.v. "Burke, Thomas." See also *PJI*, 1:95n.

[7]Burke married Mary "Polly" Freeman (1752-1836) of Norfolk, Va., in March 1770. *DNCB*, s.v. "Burke, Thomas."

[8]Mary Williams Burke, the daughter of Thomas and Mary Burke, was only an infant at the time of Burke's death. She never married and died in Alabama sometime after the Civil War. James Hogg (1729-1804), a native of Scotland and resident of Hillsborough, was a merchant and planter. Willie Jones (1741-1801), who owned a plantation and a large number of slaves in Halifax County, served in the General Assembly and as a delegate to the 1788 state ratification convention. Samuel A. Ashe, Stephen B. Weeks, and Charles L. Van Noppen, eds., *Biographical History of North Carolina*, 8 vols. (Greensboro: Charles L. Van Noppen, 1905-1917), 2:27; *DNCB*, s.v. "Burke, Thomas," "Hogg, James," "Jones, Willie." See also *PJI*, 2:199n, 1:130n. For more information on the Burke estate, see Will of Thomas Burke, 1784, Orange County Wills, State Archives, and Estate of Thomas Burke, 1786, Orange County Estates, State Archives.

[9]Charles Johnson (1755-1802) of Chowan County was a state senator (1781-1784, 1788-1792) and political ally of JI and Samuel Johnston. Johnson also served in the U.S. Congress (1801-1802). Alexander Diack, a Norfolk, Va., merchant, received Tom, JI's younger brother, when he arrived from England in late summer 1784. *DNCB*, s.v. "Johnson, Charles"; JI to Arthur Iredell, February 16, 1784, January 22, 1785, and Alexander Diack to JI, September 3, 1784, in this volume.

[10]Diack, executor of William Aitcheson's estate, had employed Burke to recover a debt owed to Aitcheson by Thomas McKnight of Norfolk. Fifteen slaves were obtained to pay the debt, and Burke arranged to purchase two of them. Upon Burke's death, Diack argued that Burke had never made restitution to Aitcheson's estate for the two slaves and demanded payment or return of the slaves. By June, Aitcheson's estate had been paid. Estate of Thomas Burke, 1786, Orange County Estates, State Archives; Montague Collection, Manuscripts and Archives Division, New York Public Library.

[11]Stephen Moore (1734-1799), a native of New York, lived on a plantation in Caswell County. He was deputy quartermaster general of the army (1783-1792) and a member of Congress (1793). Article seven of the Treaty of Peace of 1783 prohibited the British military from carrying "away any Negroes or other property of the American inhabitants" when withdrawing from the former colonies. *DNCB*, s.v. "Moore, Stephen"; "Treaty of Peace," September 3, 1783, in U.S. Department of State, *Treaties and Other International Agreements of the United States of America, 1776-1949,* 13 vols. (Washington: Department of State, 1968-1976), 12:8-12.

New Romney is a port located on the Strait of Dover, sixty-eight miles ESE of London. John Bartholomew, *The Survey Gazetteer of the British Isles* (Edinburgh: John Bartholomew and Son, Geographical Institute, 1932), 580; *The Reader's Digest Complete Atlas of the British Isles* (London: Reader's Digest Association, 1965), 29.

[12]Article four of the peace treaty reads: "It is agreed that creditors on either side shall meet with no lawful impediment to the recovery of the full value in sterling money of all bona fide debts heretofore contracted." In May 1782, the Virginia assembly had passed a law, to stay in effect until December 1, 1783, denying British

merchants the right to collect debts in state courts. In November 1783, the Virginia legislature renewed this statute, despite its inconsistency with the treaty. *Treaties and Other International Agreements,* 12:11; Isaac Samuel Harrell, *Loyalism in Virginia: Chapters in the Economic History of the Revolution* (Durham: Duke University Press, 1926), 125, 144.

[13]James Rivington (1724-1803), a newspaper publisher of New York, held Loyalist sympathies during the Revolution. He was allowed to remain in America after the war, in part, because he was said to have aided the spies of George Washington. *DAB*, s.v. "Rivington, James."

[14]The letter from George Washington to Samuel Fraunces, dated August 18, 1783, was written by Jonathan Trumbull Jr. Washington's headquarters were located at Fraunces's tavern in New York from November 26, 1783, to December 4, 1783. Fraunces had provided Washington with secret intelligence under the alias "Black Sam." George Washington to Samuel Fraunces, August 18, 1783, George Washington Papers at the Library of Congress, 1741-1799, February 16, 1999, *http://memory.loc.gov/cgi-bin/query/r?ammem/mgw:@field(DOCID+@lit(gw270136))* (August 5, 2002).

[15]Elizabeth "Betsy" Hogg, daughter of James Hogg, married John Huske of New Hanover County. Huske had been Gov. Thomas Burke's secretary. JI to Hannah Iredell, April 23, 1784, in this volume; *The Life and Times of James Hogg, 1729-1804* (n.p.: Hogg Historical Committee, [1988]), 17, 21.

[16]Marmaduke Jones (1724-1787) of New Hanover County held numerous colonial offices, including attorney general of the colony. After the Revolution he was an attorney in Wilmington. Jones had recently returned from England and had brought back letters for JI and a number of his associates. *DNCB*, s.v. "Jones, Marmaduke"; *PJI*, 1:225n, 2:394, 445.

A coxcomb is a vain, foolish person. The term originally applied to the type of hat worn by jesters, which resembled a cock's comb. *Oxford English Dictionary*, 2d ed., s.v. "coxcomb," hereafter cited as *OED*.

[17]Hannah Johnston Iredell (1748-1826) of Edenton, sister of Samuel Johnston, married JI on July 18, 1773. Works Progress Administration, Pre-1914 Graves Index, State Archives, hereafter cited as WPA, Grave Index; *PJI*, 1:liv.

From Nathaniel Dukinfield[1]

Sulham near Reading[2]
11th. Jany. 1784.

My dear Sir,

With great pleasure I received your Letter of the 10th. of August, & this pleasure was much inhanced by the friendship you continue for me. Your attention to my Mother deserves my Thanks much more than that to my Interest, & I am very sensible of the Part you & Mr. Johnston have taken in standing up as her Protector.[3] Since my Marriage I have not enjoyed the

Idea of Country Quarters, which I did formerly like very well, but, on considering the many Inconveniences that might arise to a dear Wife, by being moved at times when it might be most desirable to remain quiet, & then probably getting bad Accommodations, I have quitted the Service, in a manner, viz. have made an Exchange with a Captain in the 82d. regiment of Foot which will be reduced as soon as it returns from Nova Scotia, & I shall be on Half Pay, & no more Duty. I have taken a House in Berkshire about Six Miles from Reading, & am busy getting it furnished which I wish to complete as soon as possible as I expect my Kitty will be brought to Bed next Month.[4] Altho' you have no Children, I hope you are not the less happy. I assure you it would have given me no Concern, if it had been my Case, nor shall it affect my happiness, tho' I have, but I can't help wishing for a very few, as the Pasture won't bear a great Stock, two or three may live, but if more, I must begin to look about. As my Wife is past 28 & I'm near 38, I am in hopes we shall not have many.

When I was last in London, I met Mr. Dawson at Mr. Elmsly's, twice, the first time he had a slight Cold, but was better afterwards.[5] I flatter myself with the hopes of his Company at Sulham when he can make it convenient to relax from his Studies. I am very greatly obliged to you for kindly informing me, by your Brother, of my Mother's health. I have received two Letters from him, one from Oxford in 1779 & the other in July last. I did not know his Situation in Mr. Crewe's family.[6] I wish he was nearer than Cheshire that I might be acquainted with him. I shall write and acquaint him with my Habitation & invite him to see me whenever it may suit him. I can't imagine how you think I shall come over to Carolina. I said, or meant to have said, that if I had not been married I fully determined to do it, but I hope it will be quite unnecessary for me now as it would be attended with, not only, great Inconvenience, but Distress. I could not leave my dear Wife, & she is not of the strongest Constitution & therefore I could not think of risquing her, tho' I know she would venture every thing rather than be left behind, & what is to become of the Piccininny? No, my dear Friend, I give up all thoughts of revisiting Carolina.

In consequence of the Friendship I have received from you & Mr. Johnston I have ordered a Power of Attorney to be made to you, & which I shall go to Town to execute on Tuesday. I have directed it to give you the fullest Power, as I have the greatest Confidence, to transact my Affairs as you see proper.[7] I'm certain I shall approve whatever you do. I wish in the first place that my Mother be taken Care of, & next to save the Estate for the benefit of my Family. Before I came from Carolina, I executed a Deed to Mr. Pearson & my Mother, conveying <pow> to them for their joint Lives & the Survivor, a Part of the Plantation, including all the Land from the large Hiccory between my House & the Point of Salmon Creek, thro' the Swamp to the Cashie road & then down to the Creek. the Ferry was in this & Mr. Pearson meant to build a House, near his Store if I had returned.[8] <You> This was in Consideration of her giving up her Interest in the Cheshire Estate. I inclose to you Copies of Cases with Mr. Holliday's (a great Conveyancer) Opinion which I took before I went to Carolina.[9] there is also one numbered (3) twas copied by my Attorney from Mr. Holliday's Papers & before Mr. Holliday signed the second Opinion he consulted with my Attorney whether that should not be inserted when it was concluded to be omitted, for what Reason, I can't recollect at this distance of Time. I hope to see Mr. Black, on Wednesday, & shall leave this with him. I understand he will be returning soon to Carolina.[10]

I have written to my Mother & expressed my Wish to have the Plantation sold, should it avoid the confiscating Acts, & that she should return & live near us in England.[11] Could that fetch 3000£ Sterling, I could manage, <to> to allow her, out of my Income, to make her comfortable, but as my Fortune requires Aconomy, I could not maintain her to my Wishes without that Assistance, & tho' it is one of my first wishes to have her near me now I'm settled I fear it will not be practicable, unless by this Means. how far an Exchange of Climate at her Years may be adviseable I don't know, but hope for the best as I have no doubt but, as this is her <natur> native One, & less liable to fatal disorders than yours, she would not suffer more than a trifling Cold or such like, but altho' I have so anxious a Wish for her to be near me, yet at the same time I'm not ashamed to confess I had rather give up that Pleasure & hear that she is well, than, for my satisfaction have her return here, & see her suffer by the Change. I'm setting out upon a Plan of strict (but necessary) Aconomy, & hope to keep within Bounds. I have an Expectation of Increase of my Fortune but tis at a great Distance. An Estate of near 300£ a Year is intailed upon me by Sir Samuel, but there are five Lives to depart before I touch a farthing.[12] I received a letter lately from Mr. Brimage acquainting me that Mr. Pollock was dead, & supposing Mrs. P. would return immediately to England.[13]

You are mistaken in imagining my Brother was killed in a Duel unless in a Duel of Venus. his connections with the fair Sex had been unfortunate, & he had a sore throat in consequence, to which he applied a fumigation of Cinnabar, which immediately took such an effect that he never recovered.[14] this circumstance, among others, induced me, perhaps, to think /more/ seriously than I had done of late Years, of marrying, for there is no possibility of living alone, & I am most perfectly happy; & tho' married above ten Months I'm perfectly happy & much fonder of my Wife than when I married. she is not at all handsome, but what you may call a devilish good One

Whatever you do, my dear Iredell, respecting the Powers I now lodge with you let your first care be to my dear Mother, & her happiness your primary consideration. whatever afterwards can be done for my Interest, I can have no objection to. I give no Directions nor do I wish to be consulted upon any Point. My best respects to Mrs. Iredell & Mrs. & Miss Blair, & to Mrs. & Miss Dawson.[15] I fear this destructive War has carried off many young Men from the Province who might have made good Husbands. I never heard whether Peggy Cathcart was married or not.[16] Sometime ago I met with a Captain Kinloch who had served in Tarleton's Corps[17] <speek> /he spoke/ with great respect of Wilie Jones's genteel behaviour. Kinlock had got possession of a famous Mare of Wilie's which was sometime afterwards strained in the Shoulder, upon which Wilie sent a Card to Kinloch wishing as the Mare was a fav'rite & rendered useless to him, he would return her & any Horse in his Stable was at his Service in return. Kinloch told me he was so much pleased with him that he sent the Mare back. Tarleton has, by his imprudent Conduct here, lost all the Laurels he got in America.[18] His extravagance & folly has been beyond Bounds & his best friends condemn him. mais treve de la Guerre & des Guerriers.[19] adieu, my dear Iredell, & believe me,

Your much obliged & affectionate friend

N Dukinfield

I see by the Papers this evening that the 82d. is embarked for England to be <reduced> /disbanded/. I shall then have short Pay only to be sure, but no Duty but <u>family duty</u>.

25th. January. <I have just> When I went to London the week before last Mr. Black was not returned from Scotland, but I have just heard he is now come, & shall therefore go up some day this Week, & return as soon as possible, for I don't wish to be absent from home longer than Business absolutely requires at this time. I don't know what you may think of the Opinions I send you. Mr. Elmsly told /me/ he heard that several Persons had cast a longing Eye upon my Plantation, if it shod. come to Market, & he concludes they will not be dissatisfied to purchase it whenever & however the Opportunity offers. If my Mother has not burnt all my Letters there are some which I fancy, she might turn to advantage, wherein I gave her /the Plantation &/ those Negroes, which I deemed mine, to use for her Life. ask her. Nothing has occurred since I first began this Letter except my having strained my Foot, which I feared might turn to the Gout (I had a slight Fit two years ago) but tis now quite well.[20]

RC, Johnson Collection, NCSA. Printed, McRee, 2:85-87. Addressed "James Iredell Esqr. Edenton North Carolina." Endorsed "Sulham near Reading 11 Jan. 1784. Sir N. Dukinfield —Ansd. —."

---

[1]Nathaniel Dukinfield (Duckenfield) (1746-1824), a resident of Bertie County before the Revolution, was JI's friend and a rival for the hand of Hannah Johnston. A royal councilor and British army officer, Dukinfield returned to England in 1772. Because he was a Loyalist the state confiscated his land in North Carolina, though JI tried unsuccessfully to help him retain his property. *PJI*, 1:52n. See also JI to Nathaniel Dukinfield, January 9, 1785, in this volume.

[2]Sulham, Berkshire, is about six miles west of Reading, which is approximately thirty-five miles west of London. *Reader's Digest Complete Atlas*, 27, 28.

[3]Margaret Dukinfield Pearson (d. 1784) of Bertie County was the widow of Nathaniel Dukinfield (d. 1749) and John Pearson (d. 1777). Mitchell, *North Carolina Wills*, 400; Jean Blair to Hannah Iredell, December 24, 1784, in this volume; *DNCB*, s.v. "Duckenfield, Nathaniel." See also *PJI*, 1:52n.

[4]Katherine "Kitty" Warde Dukinfield gave birth to a boy, probably in June. *DNCB*, s.v. "Duckenfield, Nathaniel"; Nathaniel Dukinfield to JI, September 7, 1784, in this volume.

[5]William Johnston Dawson (1765-1796) of Bertie County was the son of John and Penelope Johnston Dawson and the grandson of Gov. Gabriel Johnston. He served in the General Assembly (1791-1792) and the U.S. House of Representatives (1793-1795). Alexander Elmsley (1730-1797) of Halifax and Craven Counties served in the colonial assembly and as an attorney for the Crown. By 1768, he was living in London. There he represented the business interests of Samuel Johnston and other North Carolinians and eventually became an official agent for North Carolina in England. Cheney, *North Carolina Government*, 226, 765, 768, 663; *DNCB*, s.v. "Dawson, William Johnston," "Elmsley, Alexander." See also *PJI*, 1:104n.

[6]John Crewe (1742-1829) of Crewe Hall, Cheshire, served in the House of Commons representing Staffordshire (1765-1768) and Cheshire (1768-1802). Arthur Iredell was employed as a tutor for the Crewe's only son. *Members of Parliament*, 2 pts. (London: House of Commons, 1878), 2:131, 137, 149, 162, 175, 188, 200; Lewis Namier and John Brooke, *The House of Commons, 1754-1790*, 3 vols. (London: Her Majesty's Stationary Office, 1964), 2:276-277; *PJI*, 2:411, 413n, 460-463.

[7]Dukinfield's "Letter of Attorney" states: ". . . I Sir Nathaniel Dukinfield of Sulham in the County of Berks Baronet . . . appoint Samuel Johnston of Hayes near Edenton in North Carolina in America Esquire and James Iredell of Edenton aforesaid Esquire jointly or either of them seperately my true and lawfull Attornies . . . to take care or manage and look after all and every the Plantations Messuages Lands, Tenements and Hereditaments whatsoever situate lying and being in North Carolina . . . And to transact do perform and execute All such Affairs, matters and Things which may arise or occur about or any ways concern the same . . . by virtue of those presents I do hereby agree to ratify and confirm In Witness whereof I the said Sir Nathaniel Dukinfield have to these presents set my hand and Seal this

twenty eighth day of January One thousand, Seven hundred and eighty four. Nal. Dukinfield." Hayes Collection, Southern Historical Collection, Wilson Library, University of North Carolina at Chapel Hill.

[8]The area described, including Salmon Creek, is in Bertie County. For a detailed map, see Loyalist Claim of Nathaniel Dukinfield, English Records, Audit Office Papers, State Archives.

[9]Enclosures not found. John Holliday (ca. 1730-1801) of London was an attorney who specialized in the conveyancing of property. *Dictionary of National Biography*, s.v. "Holliday, John," hereafter cited as *DNB*.

[10]Alexander Black (d. 1790) of Edenton was a merchant who traveled to Virginia and England transacting business and transporting mail. He served as a witness to Dukinfield's power of attorney excerpted above. Estate of Alexander Black, 1791, Chowan County Estates, State Archives; *PJI*, 2:215n.

[11]The "confiscating Acts" were a series of laws passed by the General Assembly between 1777 and 1782 enabling the state to confiscate and sell property in North Carolina belonging to Loyalists. See Clark, *State Records*, 24:123-429 passim.

[12]Sir Samuel died in 1768 without issue, thus making Nathaniel an heir. *DNCB*, s.v. "Duckenfield, Nathaniel." For an explanation of Nathaniel Dukinfield's relationship to Sir Samuel, see *PJI*, 1:80.

[13]William Brimage (d. 1799) of New Bern had been a vice-admiralty court judge. During the Revolution he was accused of being a Loyalist and expelled from the state. *PJI*, 1:52n.

[14]Cinnabar is crystal mercuric sulfide. The danger of using it medicinally was known long before Dunkinfield's brother's death. As early as 1622, a surgical publication called it "deadly . . . made half of quicksilver and half of Brimstone by Art of Fire." *OED*, s.v. "Cinnabar." For additional information on the death of Dukinfield's brother, see *PJI*, 2:442-443.

[15]Jean Johnston Blair (1729-1789) of Edenton was JI's sister-in-law and friend. Helen "Nelly" Blair (1763-1802) of Edenton was JI's niece and later Samuel Tredwell's wife. Penelope Johnston Dawson (1744-1797) of Bertie County, a cousin of Hannah Iredell and Jean Blair, was the daughter of Gov. Gabriel Johnston, the wife of John Dawson, and a signer of the "Edenton Tea Party" declaration. Penny Dawson was the daughter of Penelope, a cousin of Nelly, and the future wife of Tristrim Lowther (d. 1795). WPA, Grave Index; *PJI*, 1:100n, 88n; *DNCB*, s.v. "Dawson, John."

[16]Margaret "Peggy" Cathcart married William McKenzie (1755-1810) between April 20 and July 4, 1781, based on correspondence for those dates in volume two of *PJI*. See also *PJI*, 1:97n.

[17]Capt. David Kinloch served in the Seventy-first Regiment of Sir Banastre Tarleton's Corps. Robert D. Bass, *The Green Dragoon: The Lives of Banastre Tarleton and Mary Robinson* (New York: Henry Holt and Company, 1957), 47.

[18]Banastre Tarleton was a British officer and protégé of Lord Cornwallis. During the American Revolution, Tarleton fought in numerous engagements from South Carolina to New York. After returning to England in 1782, Tarleton led a dissolute life that included gambling, drinking, and a lengthy affair with Mary

Robinson, an actress and former mistress of the Prince of Wales, later George IV. Tarleton's extravagance resulted in debts and pursuit by creditors. Despite his wastrel ways, Tarleton became active in Whig politics and served in the House of Commons (1790-1806, 1807-1812). *DNB*, s.v. "Tarleton, Sir Banastre," "Robinson, Mary"; Holley Calmes, "Banastre Tarleton: A Biography," Oatmeal for the Foxhounds, 2001, *http://banastretarleton.org/* (October 25, 2001).

[19]Translated from French as "but no more of war and of warriors."

[20]Gout, which causes painful swelling of the joints, was frequently diagnosed in the eighteenth century, often inaccurately. Roy Porter and G. S. Rousseau, *Gout: The Patrician Malady* (New Haven: Yale University Press, 1998), 3, 49.

From Pierce Butler[1]

Charleston, February 4th, 1784.

My Dear Sir:

I was favored with your very acceptable and obliging letter of the 31st of December, some days ago; by it I learn with exceeding great concern of your indisposition. I ardently hope that the cool weather may have braced you up. I well know the strictest temperance cannot insure health in the sickly place you have fixed on for your residence, otherwise I am sure you would enjoy it. Edenton appeared to me, from its situation—the number of fens of stagnant water—the too little motion of the great body of water in front of the town,—to be more liable to putrid disorders than almost any other spot I ever saw. I often wished some circumstance might turn up to induce you to leave it.

Mrs. Butler and myself are much indebted to you for the warm interest you take in every thing that relates to our welfare and happiness. I thank God she is pretty well recovered. I am sometimes well, sometimes otherwise.

I rejoice, my dear sir, exceedingly, that our sentiments so entirely accord respecting the treatment of the wretched, deluded refugees. Your sentiments paint in strong colors, that greatness of mind, generosity, and general philanthropy that so eminently distinguish you; and confirms me that I am not a bad reader of mankind. Such as I conceived you, you prove to be—the sincere and warm friend—the generous and forgiving enemy. I have, for some time, had my apprehensions with you, that honesty and true greatness would have an ardent struggle in America; and much do I fear that the early pages of our history will be sullied by an unbecoming greediness for property,—that property that, as a great and generous people, we should disdain to touch. Here is lately arrived a Dr. Bancroft from France, whom you must have heard of as an appendage of Dr. Franklin.[2] He is an exceedingly sensible man. I had a visit from him yesterday. He took an early opportunity of assuring me that the character of America suffers much in Europe by the persecuting spirit manifested to the miserable refugees, and the too frequent infringements of the definitive treaty.[3] He says it is inconceivable to a person not present, the effect such conduct has on the different courts of Europe. How mortifying! how distressing to hear that brilliancy of character with which we established our independence, so shamefully sullied! Our Legislature have been sitting some time, and as yet have shown great liberality respecting those wretched people that went off with the enemy. Numbers have already been taken off the confiscation list. <u>All</u> are allowed to return, to try to vindicate themselves if they can: so that none may be condemned unheard. I hope we shall close the session as we began, with acts of mercy and forgiveness. As an individual, I do all in my power to instil into the minds of the back-country members, that mercy and forgiveness are Godlike virtues. I hope and think we shall restore and establish our credit. I have proposed to the Legislature to negotiate a loan in Europe, and establish a public bank.[4] I think they will agree to my proposal; if they do, I will risk my reputation on it, that we will discharge our Continental and State debt in less than ten years, and establish our bank on as good a footing as any on earth. A few of the adherents to Robert Morris are against the measure, because they think it will take up more out of his power, and lessen his consequence here; but I think I shall carry it through. The propriety of the measure will speak for itself. The footing I propose to put the bank on, is exactly the same as that of Venice; to keep constantly in bank a large sum in real specie. If your State does not shortly fall on some plan of finance to restore her lost credit, she must suffer much, and the citizens feel great distress.

Mrs. Butler joins in warm and sincere regards to Mrs. Iredell, and the ladies of your family.

Believe me to be, my dear Sir, very truly, Your affectionate friend,

P. Butler

Printed, McRee, 2:87-88.

---

[1]Pierce Butler (1744-1822), a longtime friend of JI, was a planter who lived in Charleston, S.C. He served in the South Carolina legislature (1778-1782, 1784-1789) and the U.S. Senate (1789-1796, 1802-1804). He was also a delegate to the 1787 Constitutional Convention. *PJI*, 2:215n; *BDC*, s.v. "Butler, Pierce"; *DAB*, s.v. "Butler, Pierce."

[2]Edward Bancroft (1744-1821) was an inventor who through his scientific interests came to know Benjamin Franklin. During the Revolutionary War, Bancroft, who was a native of Massachusetts and resident of England, worked as a double agent. He provided secret information to Franklin and other Americans,

while giving intelligence, in return for payment, to the British. *DAB*, s.v. "Bancroft, Edward."

[3]In the negotiations ending the American Revolution, problems related to the treatment of Loyalists were some of the most difficult to resolve. The British felt compelled to help Loyalists recover their lost property, while many Americans bitterly resented those who had supported the Crown. Feelings were so strong that the peace treaty was placed in jeopardy over this issue. The resulting compromise, expressed in articles four, five, and six of the treaty, states that no obstacles will be placed to prevent collection of debts, that Congress will "earnestly recommend" to state legislatures that property confiscated from "real British subjects" be returned, and that "future confiscations" and "prosecutions" against individuals because of their role in the war will be prohibited. Thomas A. Bailey, *A Diplomatic History of the American People* (New York: Appleton, Century, Crofts, 1964), 49; "Treaty of Peace," *Treaties and Other International Agreements,* 12:11-12.

[4]With South Carolina facing a debt of almost three million dollars, Butler proposed borrowing money in Europe and founding a state bank to reestablish South Carolina's credit. The bank measure failed, and South Carolina's financial situation worsened. Lewright B. Sikes, *The Public Life of Pierce Butler, South Carolina Statesman* (Washington, D.C.: University Press of America, 1979), 12.

From William Hooper

Hillsb. 7th. Feby. 1784—

Dear Sir

I wrote you Some time ago by a Mr. Bevan a carpenter of your town, and inclosed you Several letters for my other friends in and near Edenton.[1]

This I let off at a venture, it goes by way of Halifax & if it ever hits you it is to be noted in the chapter of accidents. Mr. Maclaine in a letter which I received from him a few days ago informs me that you are well & that he has Mr. Johnstons authority for saying so.[2] I Sincerely rejoice as I have not heard a Syllable of you Since I left Newbern

The Weather here has been Severe beyond all experience. I have been so thoroughly frozen that /it/ will require an extraordinary length of Summer and Sunshine to thaw me. While I now write before a good fire the ink condenses in my pen & my hand is So benumbed that with difficulty I shape my letters.

I have received the most extraordinary letter from our Client Walker that was ever penned. It is addressed in the usual form but begins thus, David Walker to William Hooper, and after a number of false frivolous disingenuous pretences for not Sending us his notes according to his promise he very generously promises not to avail of the late regulations made by our assembly as to Lawyers fees, but will when we have finished the business pay us according to his first engagements—and then most affectionately Supscripes himself my friend.[3] I keep the letter for your perusal as a first rate Specimen of Virginia genius—formed at Williamsburgh Alma Mater, & perfected under the auspices of a first rate Virginia Lawyer. I will not answer it until I see you.

Hay's Tiberius Gracchus is here, he has most liberally abused the New bern committee who in a body called upon Keith for the Author and threatned that unless he gave him up, He must himself be considered as such & punished accordingly.[4] Keith's fears prevailed & Hay was Surrendered to their Mercy. Sitgreaves Jas. Ellis & Ogden I hear were delegated to perform this adventurous business[5] Great I am told are the menaces, and Scandalum Magnatum is the Sin to be attoned for.[6]

Entre nous, I think Hay's piece appears worse from the press than in Manuscript. In the latter perhaps I viewed it as a production that was for the perusal only of his intimate friends, but when given to the world I consider it as intended for an exhibition of parts that bids defiance to censure and criticism. The Stile is dull & in many parts ungrammatical. I earnestly wish that for Hay's /sake/ it had "prematur, not only ad Nonum but ad nonagesimum annum."[7]

Ashe & Hay had a terrible squabble at Wilmington; Ashe from the bench told Hay that his conduct in the Admiralty to the judge there of ought to have been answered with a <cane> cane & directed the Attorney Genl to indite him & Speller for champerty.[8] Judge how Hay felt. He behaved with becoming temper & decency, but nourishes I fancy a flame in his bosom that will burn furiously when it vents itself

I have not Seen a paper or Magazine Since I came hither. We hold no more intercourse with the publick & political world than if we were no part of it. When Oppty. offers pray send us all your cast papers

Inclosed in my former letter to you were letters for Mr. Johnston, Mr. Dawson, Mr. Pollok Mr. Allen and by accident a letter for T Gilchrist[9] Pray inform them of this lest the letters should miscarry

My Wife daughter & myself unite our best acknowledgments & regards to Mrs. Iredell Mrs. Blair Miss Blair Miss Peggy & the young gentlemen. Accept them yourself & believe me ever under all possible circumstances

Yours. truly & Affecly.

Will Hooper

RC, Iredell Papers, Duke. Printed, McRee, 2:88-90.

---

[1]This is possibly a reference to a letter of November 23, 1783, but there is no mention of enclosed letters therein. Mr. Bevan is probably George Beving (d. 1790) of Chowan County. Carpenter's tools are listed in the inventory of his estate. *PJI*,

2:463-466; Estate of George Biving (Beving), 1790, Chowan County Estates, State Archives.

[2]Archibald Maclaine (1728-1790), after failing as a merchant in Wilmington, studied law and became one of the leading attorneys in North Carolina. Maclaine, whose political views were similar to those held by Hooper and JI, served in the General Assembly (1780-1781, 1783-1787). *DNCB*, s.v. "Maclaine, Archibald"; *PJI*, 1:470n-471n.

[3]The most recent state law regulating attorneys' fees was passed in 1778. Clark, *State Records*, 24:204-209.

[4]John Hay (ca. 1757-1809) was a native of Ireland who came to North Carolina in 1780. He began practicing law in 1783 and the following year was embroiled in an effort to remove Judge Samuel Ashe from the bench. Hay and Archibald Maclaine were leaders in an ongoing conflict between attorneys and judges in the 1780s.

Hay published a pamphlet under the name Tiberius Gracchus apparently attacking the General Assembly and superior court. He and other attorneys were disgruntled over the assembly's passage of an act suspending suits to collect debts for a year. Hay succeeded in offending a number of people in New Bern sufficiently that they pressured the printer Keith to divulge the author's identity and then sought him out. Robert Keith (fl. 1782-1785) of New Bern was a printer, journalist, and bookstore proprietor. In August 1783, he began publishing the *North Carolina Gazette, or Impartial Intelligencer and Weekly General Advertiser*. *DNCB*, s.v. "Hay, John," "Keith, Robert"; Clark, *State Records*, 24:490-491; S. A. Ashe, "Social Conditions in North Carolina in 1783," North Carolina Booklet, 10 (April 1911): 214-215; *PJI*, 2:362n, 466n. For more information on the conflict between attorneys and judges, see John Charles Waldrup, "James Iredell and the Practice of Law in Revolutionary Era North Carolina" (Ph.D. diss., University of North Carolina at Chapel Hill, 1985), 300-323.

[5]John Sitgreaves (1757-1802), a lawyer, represented New Bern in the house of commons (1784, 1786-1788) and was Speaker for two sessions (1787-1788). In 1785, he was a member of the Continental Congress. From December 20, 1790, until his death, he was the federal district judge of North Carolina. Titus Ogden (d. 1794) of New Bern was a merchant and auctioneer. *DNCB*, s.v. "Sitgreaves, John"; Cheney, *North Carolina Government*, 659, 753; Estate of Titus Ogden, 1801, Craven County Estates, State Archives; Mitchell, *North Carolina Wills*, 386; Clark, *State Records*, 21:19.

[6]*Scandalum magnatum* is slander against a high official. Bryan A. Garner, ed., *Black's Law Dictionary*, 7th ed. (St. Paul, Minn.: West Group, 1999), 1345.

[7]The phrase "*prematur, not only ad Nonum but ad nonagesimum annum*" means "been stopped not only at the ninth hour but at the ninetieth year."

[8]Samuel Ashe (1725-1813) of Wilmington served as a superior court judge (1778-1795) and as governor (1795-1798). Griffith J. McRee, in his biography of JI, describes Ashe as a "man of strong will and violent prejudices." According to McRee, Ashe was "moderate in nothing:—he loved ardently; he hated intensely." James Spiller (d. ca. 1798), a Sampson County attorney, was a member of the

General Assembly (1789) and a delegate to the 1789 state ratification convention. *DNCB*, s.v. "Ashe, Samuel"; Cheney, *North Carolina Government*, 160, 223, 360; Griffith J. McRee, *Life and Correspondence of James Iredell*, 2 vols. (New York: D. Appleton, 1857), 1:368; Stephen E. Massengill, *North Carolina Votes on the Constitution: A Roster of Delegates to the State Ratification Conventions of 1788 and 1789* (Raleigh: Division of Archives and History, North Carolina Department of Cultural Resources, 1988), 56. See also *PJI*, 1:444n.

Champerty is unlawful assistance given to a party in a lawsuit by a non-participant in the suit in return for a share of the award. *OED*, s.v. "champerty."

[9]See William Hooper to JI, January 4, 1784, in this volume. Cullen Pollock (1731-1795) of Chowan County was a wealthy planter and merchant, and a friend of JI. He owned Balgray plantation on the Chowan River and a home in Edenton. In 1790, he held 204 slaves, more than anyone else in North Carolina. Nathaniel Allen (ca. 1755-1805) of Edenton was a planter and legislator. Beginning in 1785, he and business partners developed the area around Lake Phelps, near Edenton. Allen was a partner in the firm of Hewes, Smith, and Allen. Thomas Gilchrist (ca. 1735-1789) of Edgecombe and Halifax Counties was a merchant, land developer, Halifax town commissioner (1785), and Willie Jones's brother-in-law. *PJI*, 1:219n-220n, 225n; Ashe, "Social Conditions," 217; *DNCB*, s.v. "Allen, Nathaniel," "Gilchrist, Thomas"; Ferguson et al., *Papers of Robert Morris*, 9:621n.

To Thomas Iredell Sr.[1]

Edenton Feb. 11th. 1784.

My dear & hond. Sir,

I wrote you [*a*] letter in the month of Dec which I hope <before> you have before this received, as it went by a Vessel directly from this Country to Jamaica.[2] <I have just received several letters from England, which have given me great satisfaction, tho' of an earlier date than some I had received before, as they contained many particulars,> I flatter myself one of the great blessings of the peace will be my having the satisfaction to hear frequently from you, & being indulged in the honour of an intimate correspondence, which I should highly value, <as it is impossible for any Man to feel greater respect or more tenderness of affection than I do, my dear Sir, for you, whom I reverence not> and by every possible means study to deserve. Some late letters from England, which in other respects have made me very happy, have informed me much to my concern that you thought unfavourably of my conduct in joining the American side of the question, after taking an oath of allegiance to the King.[3] <as I consider it my duty to take every occasion in my power to vindicate my conduct to you in any respect where it may appear exceptionable,> I had some reason before to apprehend you were displeased with me, but did not /particularly/ know the cause, and it gave me very great uneasiness, for permit me, my dear Sir, /to say that/ the uncommon respect & tenderness of affection I had for my Father makes me feel a much more than common share of both for you, and that the goodness you have uniformly shewn me makes me extremely anxious that I should appear to you not unworthy of it. Allow me therefore to state my principles to you on this subject, & <tho'>, /as/ I know, considering every thing, it is delicate in respect to you & me, <yet> I shall avoid as much as possible saying any thing offensive.

I imbibed then from my infancy almost a strong attachment to Whig Revolution Principles, and indeed I considered that it was almost universally every Man's opinion in modern times, that no oath of Allegiance bound a Man absolutely in all circumstances, but that if so unhappy case should arrive as that obedience to the King did not consist with the safety & liberties of the People, but that it was absolutely necessary in order to secure the same that the former Gov. should be renounced, & a new one chosen, this might be done <with> /without/ any imputation of dishonour since otherwise People could enjoy no liberty, & all limitations of the regal authority would be ridiculous—This therefore was an implied reservation, which the very nature of the Government suffered; although such an express reservation might be dangerous, as avowing the doctrine of resistance too frequently might dispose the People too much, & unnecessarily to it. I know no other <reason> /principle/ upon which the Revolution in 1688 can be defended, for no reasonable Man can doubt that James 2d. abdication was in fact an expulsion, and the same principles which led to the steps then taken against the Royal Authority would justify any others that seemed equally necessary with them[4]—

I considered these principles as justly operated in America, supposing (as was generally supposed, and as I supposed) that the American Claims were just, & that at the time of American Independence a new settlement was necessary. I shall not for many reasons trouble you with my particular principles on this subject, but I can assure you that I entertained them upon deliberation & with great sincerity, and that to my knowledge, excepting only a few Mad People (& I believe a very few) no measure was ever undertaken with greater reluctance than the Decl. of Ind., or with a stronger or more painful conviction of its necessity. I considered myself as living in America, entitled as well as any other to vindicate what I thought were the Rights of it, and to go in the last extremity to the ultima ratio.[5] But I did not do this until <the B> /long after/ the exercise of my Office was any longer impossible, and I thought /a/ side might be fairly chosen, and I thank God I have always had firmness enough to act according to my real opinion and to oppose any violent or unjust measure however popular—

I flatter myself this exposition of my Principles will at least serve to clear me of any thing that is dishonourable, since if I really entertained such principles (and I can lay my hand upon my heart & solemnly Declare I did) I cannot be culpable for having obeyed their influence. It is certainly a strong proof of my sincerity, that I acted a disinterested part, and plunging into a hazardous & most doubtful contest, with the risque of even wanting present support, and the imminent danger of life and all my permanent property, (to be separated too perhaps forever from Relations I most dearly loved) gave way to the impulse of feelings too powerful to be resisted—I thank God, <that> I can honestly say my Conscience does not reproach me.

I hear with joy and gratitude of <the> your extreme goodness to my Mother.[6] Permit me, my dear Sir, to offer you my most fervent thanks for it. I have had the deepest affliction about her situation, not knowing until [*torn*] now in what manner for so many years she has been supported. How great & generous has been the conduct of Lord Macartney, & Mrs. C. Macartney![7] Never shall I forget their goodness, or cease to think of it with the deepest gratitude. <For the future, I hope to be able to assure my Mother as I before wrote you myself> </I hope my own situation for the future will enable me/> /I wrote you particularly about my situation, & my present hopes of being able to serve my Mother in the letter I referred to above./[8] I have wrote for Tom if he chuses to come.[9] If I can prevail on him to apply to my profession, he may do extremely well here, and he can live with me till he is qualified to act in it. I am happy to hear you regularly correspond with Arthur, who is an honour & ornament to the Family I am highly proud of. God grant you, my dear Sir, all possible happiness. I <shall be unhappy> /cannot enjoy much myself/ until I hear, if I can be so fortunate, of my having recovered your good opinion, which to me is of the highest moment.

FC, Johnson Collection, NCSA. Endorsed "Copy of a Letter to my Uncle Iredell Feb. 11th. 1784."

---

[1]Thomas Iredell Sr. (d. 1796), JI's uncle, was a planter in Jamaica and president of the colony's royal council. He strongly disapproved of JI's disloyalty to England during the Revolutionary War, particularly in light of JI's position as a royal customs collector. In January 1775, Thomas Iredell chided his nephew for his interest in the growing conflict and warned him to stay "perfectly Neuter in those disputes." JI's failure to heed his uncle's advice resulted in Thomas Iredell disinheriting his nephew. After the Revolution, JI unsuccessfully sought a reconciliation with his uncle. *PJI*, 1:30n, 280; Whichard, *Justice James Iredell*, 40.

[2]See JI to Thomas Iredell Sr., ca. November, 1783. The letter was probably written on December 31, when he wrote several other letters going abroad. *PJI*, 2:469-472.

[3]JI is referring to a letter from his brother dated November 17, 1783 (*PJI*, 2:458-460) and one from his mother of October 2, 1783. The latter has not been found but was referred to in a letter of December 31, 1783 (*PJI*, 2:473-476). See also *PJI*, 1:235-236 for JI's commission as collector of customs for Port Roanoke and a record of his oath of office.

[4]JI repeatedly argued in defense of his conduct during the Revolution that he acted on principles similar to those held by the opponents of James II during the "Glorious Revolution" of 1688. At that time, Whigs and Tories who opposed James II and his Catholic sympathies asked William of Orange, the Protestant son-in-law of the king, to come to England to replace him. JI reasoned that just as James's adversaries were justified in rebelling against the monarch, he too acted responsibly in standing against George III. For other examples of JI's use of this argument, see his letters of May 28, 1784, and February 23, 1786.

[5]The phrase "ultima ratio" means final consideration.

[6]JI's mother, Margaret McCulloh Iredell, was living in London. JI's brother Arthur had notified him in 1783 that Thomas Iredell Sr. had "of late made some very acceptable remittances" to their mother and planned to leave her a small annuity in his will. *PJI*, 2:410, 470, 459.

[7]Sir George Macartney (1736-1806), an Irish peer, was JI's cousin. He held numerous positions in the Empire, serving as governor of Grenada and Madras and as an envoy to China. He married Jane Stuart, daughter of Lord Bute. The familial relationship between Catherine (d. ca. 1789) and George is unclear, but the two of them gave JI's mother £40 a year. The Macartneys had a long history of helping the Iredells. Catherine secured a position for JI's brother Arthur as a tutor for the son of John Crewe, an influential member of Parliament. Sir George was instrumental in JI's appointment as a customs official, which allowed JI to come to America. Sir George also helped another brother, Francis Iredell Jr. (1752-1773), to become a clerk with the Royal Africa Company, and had promised to assist still another brother, Charles, to get a commission in the navy. The last two examples of Macartney goodwill had unfortunate consequences. Francis died soon after arriving in Africa, and Charles, some years later, was killed in action. *PJI*, 1:xxxvii, 3n, 28n, 65; 2:410, 411, 413n, 432; JI to George Macartney, July 15, 1789, in this volume.

[8]JI to Thomas Iredell Sr., ca. November 1783, *PJI*, 2:469-472.

[9]Thomas Iredell (1761-after 1796), brother of JI, was living in England at this time but would move to North Carolina later in the year. *PJI*, 1:72n; McRee, *Life and Correspondence*, 1:5. See also JI to Thomas Iredell Jr., December 31, 1783, *PJI*, 2:477-478.

To Arthur Iredell[1]

Edenton Feb. 16th. 1784.

My dear Brother,

I had the inexpressible pleasure a few days ago to receive /all at once/ three most charming letters from you, <which came all at once, tho' of so

old dates as May, June, & July.> which gave me great satisfaction, though of such old dates as May, June, & July. A letter of my Mother's dated in July also, which pleased me greatly, accompanied them.[2] They gave me the first intelligence I had received of the manner in which my Mother had been supported during the war—How I admire & love the great goodness of my Lord, & Mrs. C. Macartney. God grant it may be ever in my power to express my gratitude to them. My uncle's goodness also affected me very sensibly. I thank you for your particularity in acquainting me with the cause of his displeasure. Never could I have dreamt that a Man of such a Whig Family could have thought my conduct inexcusable for adopting principles of resistance, <tho' th> merely because I had taken an oath of allegiance. Is this any other, than the old idle exploded doctrine of Passive Obedience and which I dare say my Uncle would think very unjustifiably applied by a Jacobite against the 1688 Revolution?[3] But it is not the first instance of the same principles serving one Party, & not serving <any> another, though there be no other difference but that the passions are pro on one side, & contra on the other. I have taken your kind advice, & wrote to my Uncle on this subject; not to be sure exactly in this stile, but to the same purport tho' in a more serious manner, & have assured him that however my head erred, my heart did not, and that I in my conscience thought I was acting right. I thank God, I am not apprehensive, my dear Arthur, of your censure.

It is impossible for me to say how much I am obliged to you for the kind particularity with which you have wrote upon every subject. I thank you for it with my whole Soul. Your situation & prospects (which I think are flattering) please me infinitely. That dear Lady you have been so good as to introduce to me engages a great deal of my admiration & attention.[4] I rejoice in your having found such a one, and God grant you may not be long separated. Engage for me her affection as a Sister. I shall be most proud & happy in such a one. Your Sister also bespeaks an interest in her favour, participating with me in all my anxiety for the happiness of you both—Would to God I could be blest with a sight of you;—but cursed poverty & business confines me to this Country, so as to deny me so great an indulgence.

I wrote you the beginning of Jany., as also my Mother and Tom.[5] I therein proposed Tom's coming immediately to me, if it was approved of, and if he thought he could devote few years study to my profession under me, in which case with proper application he might be sure hereafter of a very comfortable & independent Settlement. I mentioned, that in case this scheme should be approved of, he must entirely quit his station in the army, & that I would wish him if possible to sail in the month of April, but that if this was not practicable that he should leave England so as to be on <this> /the American/ Coast the latter end of Oct., or beginning of Nov., and come to Norfolk in Virginia, which is about 80 miles from here, and whereupon applying to Mr. Alex Diack a Merchant there he would meet with all possible assistance to get to me. He could <leave> /live/ with me, much to my <situation> satisfaction & Mrs. Iredell's, who would shew him all possible affection until he was in a way to provide for himself, & in the mean time might render me some useful services, which would more than compensate for the additional expence (which would not be much) of his support. But he must by no means come, until he has entirely got rid of the army, & let him leave all his Regimentals behind him, as it will require a good while to reconcile the People here to a British Officer in <his Canments (Pardon me the Expression)> /Uniform/.[6]

My letter by Mr. Black <called> contained an epitome of my History during the war, and all at present worth imparting to you.[7] It might be filled up with some Episodes of private distress, but as my lot has been better than thousands it would be ungrateful in me now to dwell on it. I have a curiosity to know, if it will not be too troublesome, your conversations with Mr. M. both in regard to yourself & me. I have long had reason to know him pretty well, & am extremely concerned that his present unfortunate condition as to this Country obliges me [*torn*] be upon terms with him, that I might not appear to be wanting in humanity, Except as to his debts, he is altogether at the mercy of this State, for the Treaty of Peace puts it fully in the power of the Assembly to be either rigorous or indulgent.

Let me request you, my dear <Arthur> to make it a rule to write to me at least once a month. I will observe the same, and have a Letter ready, whether I know of an immediate opportunity or not. You can scarcely imagine what delight your letters give me, & it is impossible to express the extreme anxiety of my heart for your welfare. Be good enough to procure for me an Interest with all your Friends, who ever must be most dearly mine. Mr. Crewe's Family, Mrs. Kemp, Mrs. Catherine Macartney, have my constant & most anxious wishes for their welfare.[8] I shall do myself the honour to /write to/ Lord Macartney when I hear of his arrival, or find a good opportunity to England. Mrs. Iredell desires her most affectionate remembrance, and joining in a request of the most respectful Compliments to that lovely Lady who I doubt not is so deserving of your admiration, adds her tenderest wishes to those of, my dear Brother,

Your extremely affectionate

Ja. Iredell

FC, Johnson Collection, NCSA. Printed, McRee, 2:91-93. Endorsed "Copy of a Letter to my Brother Arthur Feb. 16th. 1784. (with some variation.)"

---

[1]Arthur Iredell (1758-1804), JI's brother, studied law, attended Oxford, and was ordained a minister in the Church of England. The two brothers corresponded regularly following the Revolution. Arthur replaced James as heir to their uncle's estate in Jamaica. *PJI*, 1:36n, 78n; Whichard, *Justice James Iredell*, 237-241.

[2]Letter of May 30, 1783, *PJI*, 2:409-413; letter of June not found; letter of July 28, 1783, *PJI*, 2:422-423; mother's letter not found.

[3]Jacobites believed that the right of royal succession, which they thought to be divine and hereditary, had been violated by the displacement of James II in the Glorious Revolution. JI is again trying to draw parallels between his support for the American Revolution and the removal of James II. He had made this same argument only a few days earlier in a letter to his uncle, Thomas Iredell Sr. Gerald Newman, ed., *Britain in the Hanoverian Age, 1714-1837: An Encyclopedia* (New York: Garland Publishing, 1997), 371; JI to Thomas Iredell Sr., February 11, 1784, in this volume.

[4]Amanda Felton was Arthur Iredell's fiancée.

[5]He actually wrote the letters on December 31, 1783. *PJI*, 2:473-478.

[6]Thomas Iredell Jr. had served in the Royal Marines but had never been stationed outside of England. Whichard, *Justice James Iredell*, 235-236.

[7]JI to Arthur Iredell, July 30, 1783, *PJI*, 2:424-428.

[8]Mrs. Kemp was the wife of a serjeant—a lawyer who appeared in common law courts—who became Arthur's law instructor. PJI, 1:78n.

From Arthur Iredell

Crewe Hall[1] Feby. 18th. 1784

Your Letter of Decr. 4th. reached me this Morning. It very justly upbraids me with Neglect; for tho' I have actually written to you several Times since the Peace, you tell me you have received but one of my Letters.[2] Acquit me however now, my dear Brother, of Negligence & Disregard, & sail as much as you please at faithless Seas & Winds, & every other Impediment to our Correspondence. I shall in future, I trust, be more wise & successful in the Dispatch of my Letters, which you may be sure will be as frequent & as much in detail as you are kind enough to desire they maybe. Your request that I would always write at large of myself is a very flattering one; & the more so, as I had feared you were before this disgusted with a Subject which I never fail to introduce & swell out to whomsoever, & upon whatsoever Occasion I am writing. In Truth it is a very barren one, & can afford even you, with all your Partiality, but very little Entertainment—The Life I lead has so much Sameness in It that when I have told you I enjoy a large Share of Health, that my Business &

Pleasures are confined almost within the Boundary of my own Parish, & that, in short, I vegetate in Cheshire, I have nearly exhausted the Subject. I have certainly given you the great outline of It. Your reflections on Tom's Situation are very just ones.[3] I had always a dislike to a Red Coat, & I am now more than ever convinced that it always does harm to the Wearer—With regard to It's Effect upon him, his Heart, I believe, is as untainted as ever it was; but his Manners are not, I fear, equally so—He had naturally a Liveliness & Propension to Gaiety which a Military Life has indulged, & how far he will be able to turn his Mind to any serious Pursuit, much less to habituate himself to severe Application, may well be made a Question. I wish however, at all Events, he was comfortably settled on the other Side of the Atlantic—He would derive many Advantages under your Eye & Authority which he can never find here. And if it should ever be in my Power to do any thing for him, he might easily return. At present, neither his own Prospects or mine are so flattering as to encourage his Continuance in the Marines, which after all, I imagine, is not a very desireable Service. I shall acquaint him with what you have written, & advise him to accept your Invitation—You enquire how my Mother is supported—I can only tell you, that for every thing but the Annuity, which You know She receives jointly from Lord M. & Mrs. C. M. She depends entirely upon the Chapter of Accidents. I had a few months since a present of Sugars from my Uncle—they sold for about 100£ & She has had part of the Money—but her Generosity to Tom, who is perpetually applying to her for Relief, leaves her often, I fear, in the greatest Distress. I almost wish She too was with you in America. You will observe I throw all the Burthens upon your Shoulders. Would to God, My dear Brother, I could bear the whole, or any part of Them—But I cannot. I have no Preferment whatever—Indeed I am not as yet in full Orders, as I wait for my Uncle's Fiat, who, I told you in my last Letter, seemed Disaffected to my Continuance in the Church. I have left the Choice of my Profession Therefore to him. The Mail by which I expect his Answer is not yet arrived. You know I am to be his Heir, at least, that he has assured me so.[4] Oh! my dear James, if I should, & if his Property should prove sufficient to gratify my Wishes, with what Joy shall I restore You to Your native Country; & pass with you the Remainder of my Life! I have already formed my Plan, &, if Your Mind be, as I imagine it is, formed for Contemplation & Retirement You would not disapprove of It—I should then see a Sister whom already, & at the Distance of many Thousand Miles I tenderly love—& I should then introduce to you a Sister as deserving of your Regard. Such Felicity is perhaps too compleat to be realized; but I often indulge in the Anticipation of What I will still hope for!—Poor Charles! I had made him of the Party!—but; why that Tear?—He is happier, he is infinitely happy—&, as you say, we alone are the Sufferers by what we must still think a severe Fate. You ask me for the Particulars of It—I do not know them—the same Delicacy which restrained you from applying to my Mother for them, restrained me. And I was at the time they arrived too much out of the way to procure them by other Means.[5]

I shall write to my Sister, so that I need not commission You to deliver any Message.[6] I trust you are both perfectly well & happy—May you ever be so!—I am ever,

My dear Brother, Your's most affectionately

AI

I hope soon to send Your Books, which, if I shall not be able to go to London myself, I will purchase by means of a Friend—

RC, Johnson Collection, NCSA.

---

[1]Built between 1615 and 1636, Crewe Hall in Cheshire was the home of John Crewe. *PJI*, 2:413n; "Crewe Hall," 2001, *http://www.thisiscreweandnautwhich.co.uk/history/hall.html* (October 10, 2001).

[2]Arthur Iredell is probably referring to his letter to JI dated May 30, 1783, *PJI*, 2:409-413. Letters of August 18 and November 17 were probably received after JI's letter of December 4, 1783. *PJI*, 2:436-439, 458-460.

[3]See JI to Arthur Iredell, February 16, 1784, in this volume.

[4]Arthur Iredell, who was of limited fiscal means, hoped for financial assistance from his uncle, Thomas Iredell Sr. of Jamaica, and to become the elderly relative's heir. To please his benefactor-to-be, Arthur allowed his uncle to select his occupation. Whichard, *Justice James Iredell*, 237-238; Arthur Iredell to JI, November 17, 1783, *PJI*, 2:458-460.

[5]Charles Iredell (1756- ca. 1782), JI's brother, was a midshipman in the British navy. He was killed fighting against the French in India. *PJI*, 1:36n; 2:439n; Whichard, *Justice James Iredell*, 228.

[6]See Arthur Iredell to Hannah Iredell, February 25, 1784, in this volume.

From Henry E. McCulloh[1]

Triplicate.

London. 20th. Feb. 1784

My dear Sir

My last to you, was under date of the 1t. of Nov. I have since recd. yrs. of the 26. Sept. & 28t. of Nov. & am concern'd to hear you have been unwell.[2]—The Candor with wch. you write merits my best thanks, but I can't help thinking but that time, reflectn. the definitive Treaty, & the Recoms. of Congress, must give me strong hopes of your succeeding for me, as far as the appln. you intended to put in, goes. —It is drawn in a very masterly manner.[3]—Two things in it, I however request, & depend on your altering:—1st. after the words, "adequate Compensation" in parag the 4th. add,—in Sterling Value, all my letters exprest this to you, & I do not wish you to apply for a Compn. of an inadequate, uncertn. or depreciating Nature;—& 2dly.—I wod. have the Petn. to conclude with the words "public faith," leaving out all that follows, & adding only, a general, & respectful Conclusion, as it is my most earnest Wish & desire, that the Assembly in April, (who will doubtless have the Definitive Treaty, & the Recoms. of Congress, before them,) shod. finally decide upon my Case,—and I beg you to be informed, & assured, that nothing can be more distressing, & injurious to me,—than any further delay;—and as to residence, I wod. wish you to avoid saying anything like a pledge on that Subject, as that Circume. must depend on health, reception, & many—other things, utterly impossible to foresee at present—Shod. the Application have been—presented before this letter reaches you, I shall depend you will endeavour notwithstang. the concluding part, to get it finally determd. upon, & the Compn. made fixt & certain.

You have done very right in stating so fully, my circums. as a British Subject, in wch. character, under the 5th. & 6th. Artles of the Definitive Treaty, I am certainly, taught to expect the uncondl. restoratn. of all my Rights, & Property, but circumd. as things are, I shall readily receive back the lands not disposed of, (tho' I have every reason to fear they make but a very poor, & trifling part of the great landed Property I held,) & to accept an adequate Compn. in Sterling Value, made certain to me, for the Rest.—By an adequate Compn. can hardly be understood, the amot. of the Sales of my lands made flagrante Bello, when it was morally impossible to know what the ultimate decision of a Peace would be,—and when, Men bot. not the Lands, but the Expectancy of an uncertain Title only.[4]—I am however, ignorant of the amot. of such Sales, Save from your & other letters, that compared with the Real value, they were very trifling.—I must therefore leave it to you, havg. the facts—before you, to determine:—if you find the amot. of such Sales, anywise adequate, & that it will be secured to me, not subject to depreciation, you will endeavour to procure it,—but if it is not so,—& cannot be made certain, & fixt, I wod. rather you shod. decline that part of the Case, at present, & press for the Restoration of the unsold lands, only: And in case of Success, I must then depend, you will procure, & transmit me, with all Speed, an accurate accot. of the particulars, Locations, & amot. of such lands as are restored, &

wch. believe me, it will very much import me to have, without delay.[5]—BMC. can assist in this matter, & as to the lands to the Westwd. Col. T. Polk, Mr. Frohock, & Mr. Holt, & Mr. Johnston of Little river, can furnish partrs., & either Col. Felix, or Jas. Kenan, as to the lands in Duplin.[6]

I approve your omitting the two points you mention, & make no doubt All Impedts. in the way of the 4th. Artle of the Def. Treaty, will be removed.

I write my ackts. to my good friend Willis, to whom I refer to this letter, from wch. you will conclude that I cannot hope to be present at the Assy. in April, & that under God, I commit my hopes in the first place to you, & I earnestly adjure you, if possible to be present in person, offering as I ought, to make good all you may lose by it.[7]

I shall depend upon recg. from you, the earliest & fullest Accots. of the proceedgs. of the Assy. & of the State of my Affairs, & if your Accots. are happy, it wod. not be long before we meet,—as an obliged man, I wod. certainly make my grateful & personal ackts. to the State, & my friends, the Soonest, I cod. settle my affairs here.—I shall certainly attend to the Hint with wch. you conclude your friendly letter of the 28th of Novr. & with that view, I press for a final determn. in April, & a Compn. certain in it's Nature, & specific, & early Accots. of the lands restored.[8] —I am most affectly. &c.

H.E.MC.

Triple.

My dear Sir,

25th. Feb. 84.

The time of Mr. Black's departure being uncertain, I send this & the above, via, Virginia, & by wch., <via> to the care of Mr. Driver, or Jos. Scott Esq. Mercht. in Nansemond.—you may best write to me.[9]—I do not think of anything to add to the Subject on wch. I wrote you the 20th.—further, than that I dread, & depreciate nothing somuch, as delay, or Uncertainty.—The letters I expect to receive from you next July, must determine my future hopes, & plan.—Suppg. only the unsold Lands restored, & the right in my debts, I shod. in that Case, certainly come out to Carolina, as soon as I can finish, & settle my Affairs here.—

as to George, I can only desire your care of him till I know what my Carolina prospects are.[10] I shod. suppose he wod. wish his Settls. there, & I shod. wish him in the Service of the State, either on Shore, or at Sea, as his inclinations turn, preferably, the former, & that you cod. procure him an entrance into it.

At present, as to my debts, I think it only necessary to mention, that I make no doubt my Duplin Secs. are safe in the hands of Col. Felix Kenan, but of which fact, I wish you to enquire & to write me.—BMC. informs me Mr. Frohock has all those to the Westd. safe, & so I make no doubt has Mr. Johnston of Little River.—When Mr. Donaldson (of Suffolk) left Halifax in the Spring of 1776, he deposited the follg. Securities wch. I had left with him in 1773, with Mr. Tho. Gilchrist, Brother in law to our friend W. J.[11]—viz! a Bond from Mr. Agnew to Mr. Child assd. me by Mr. Montfort, for 200/£/. Virg. mon., a Bill drawn by me on BMC. favor Gibson, Granberry & Co. & accepted by him in 1772, or 1773, for 700/£/ odd proc.,—two bonds from Col. John Willis (now of Glocester Co. in Virga.—to BMC. for 700/£/ odd. Virg. mon. assigned me by BMC. & some Orders & Rects. relative to Mr. Montfort, & BMC.[12] I wish you to apply to Mr. Gilchrist for these Securities, & to take them into your care. I have w[*ink spot*]te W. J. to desire Mr. G. to deliver them to you, & wch. that Gentln. I am sure will readily do. Col. Willis, bonds were assd. to me in part at the last Settlt. Acct. BMC. & me. I shall hereafter empower you to reassign them to BMC. for him to apply for, & recover In Trust for me, & wch. I am sure he will readily do, & can do sooner, & with more effect than I cod. hope to do, & till receivd. BMC. is liable to me.

As to Mr. Montfort's protested bill for 1000/£/ Stg. that I make no doubt is safe in your possn., & as to that, & what is due me by cousin Ben, I am sure both He, & Harry Montfort will behave friendly & honorably, & I shall hereafter write you what I hope, & expect they will do.

I write you in mine of the 1st. of Nov. that I had in feb. 1776, given the late Mr. Cornell, my bond for 450/£/ Sterl. in paymt. of the 700/£/ proc. due him on my two notes, he assuring me, that he wished it only to be settled in Sterling, & that he wod. never wish to have it paid otherwise than in Carolina, & in Proc.—[13] Col. Bryan of Newbern, is Mr. C's acting Exer, as I am informed.—[14] Now, what I wish you in conjunction with BMC. to do for me, is, either from money you may receive for me from Mr. J. J. for the Ind. land, or otherwise, or by BMC's or Mr. J. J's entering into security to Col. Bryan, for the Amot. payable. by them, & for wch. I will immedy. give them credit as so much paid me if you cod. procure an order to have my sd. bond (wch. I beleive is, or was in the hands of Mr. Davison,—Grocer, in Fenchurch street,) delivered up to me.—[15] Be assured, if You BMC. & Mr. J. can anyhow, manage & settle this matter for me, (& I shod. think circd. as I am, their engagts. wod. be preferred to mine, especially as if paymt. is demanded here, I wod. dispute it in Equity.) I will acknowledg it as a very great Service, & Obligation, & I earnestly beg leave to recommend it to you, as such

I firmly trust, that long ere this, Harry Montfort has settled & got up the bond his father gave Mr. Cornell in 1773 for 1700/£/ proc. & for wch. A. Mc.C. & I, were Securities.[16] Pray enquire into this affair, & as BMC. is equally interested in having it settled,—please write him on the Subject,—& I hope to hear from you, it is settled.

Another point I wish you to enquire into, but not to let your reasons be known; is, where the Childn. & their repres. of the Secy. H. McC. live, & whether it wod. not be agreable to them, if I had it in my power to Settle & pay them in Carolina, the full Amot. of the Trust money & Int. they have a claim to, in Ireland.[17]

I hope my lot in Edenton is safe.—I beseech you to write me fully in answer to every matter contd. in my letters, & to have them by you to refer to.—In any Event, I do not believe it wod. be possible for me to settle my affairs, so as to be in Carolina, sooner than the Summer after next,—of which, please to take Notice. I am &c.

12th. March 1784.

I send this by Mr. Black who has been very polite in offerg. me his Services, for wch. pray thank him for me.—I do not think of any thing to add to the above.—Direct all letters in future to me at No. 22. Ironmonger lane, London.—I beg your care of the inclosed. <u>My affairs here must be settled</u> before I can come out to Carolina, & I am afraid, the soonest I can expect them to be so, will be the <u>Summer after next</u>. In the mean time, I wod. send you a power to <u>superintend</u> my affairs, &c. I rely on your friendly & zealous Exertions, & on hearing fully from you. My Respects to enquiring friends, & affectiond. Complts. to Mrs. Iredell, & your good self conclude me as ever, Your sincere friend &c

Henry E. Mc.Culloh

RC, Iredell Papers, Duke. Addressed "Jas. Iredell Esq. Edenton, No. Carolina."

---

[1]Henry Eustace McCulloh (ca. 1737-ca. 1810), an attorney and JI's cousin, claimed 800,000 acres in North Carolina in 1783. Because of his questionable allegiance during the Revolution, most of his land was confiscated, and he employed JI to try to recover his property. *DNCB*, s.v. "McCulloh, Henry Eustace."

[2]Letter of November 28, 1783, *PJI*, 2:467-469.

[3]The petition, which has not been found, was sent to McCulloh with JI's letter of November 28, 1783. See *PJI*, 2:469n.

[4]The phrase "flagrante Bello" means "ardently at war."

[5]See Loyalist Claim of Henry Eustace McCulloh, English Records, Audit Office Papers, State Archives.

[6]BMC is Benjamin McCulloch (d. 1792). Despite the variation in the spelling of the surname, he was Henry E. McCulloh's cousin. Henry referred to him as BMC in his correspondence. Benjamin represented Halifax County in the General Assembly (1781-1785, 1786). *PJI*, 1:20n; Cheney, *North Carolina Government*, 208-217 passim, 343n, 345n.

Thomas Polk (1732-1794) of Mecklenburg County had led his neighbors in a violent revolt against Henry E. McCulloh in 1765, when McCulloh was a land agent. Polk was a member of the Council of State (1783-1784). Thomas Frohock (d. 1794) of Rowan and Anson Counties was an agent for Henry E. McCulloh and clerk of court in Anson County. Michael Holt Jr. (1723-1799) was a blacksmith and farmer in Alamance County. William Johnston (1737-1785) was a merchant and land speculator in Orange County. Though a Patriot during the Revolution, Johnston worked after the war as an agent for Loyalist Edmund Fanning. *DNCB*, s.v. "Polk, Thomas"; *PJI*, 1:21n; *DNCB*, s.v. "Johnston, William," "Holt, Michael, Jr."

Felix Kenan (d. 1785) was sheriff of Duplin County (1760-1761, 1769-1776) and justice of the peace (1758-1770). He was also an attorney and land agent for Henry E. McCulloh. James Kenan (1740-1810) was sheriff of Duplin County (1762-1766, 1785-1786) and a state senator (1777-1783, 1787-1788, 1790-1792, 1793-1794). *DNCB*, s.v. "Kenan, Felix," "Kenan, James"; Cheney, *North Carolina Government*, 201-229 passim.

[7]John Willis (ca. 1764-after 1834) of Bladen and Robeson Counties served in the General Assembly (1782, 1787-1789, 1791-1792, 1794-1795, 1798) and appears to have moved to Tennessee before 1800. Massengill, *North Carolina Votes*, 64.

[8]The "hint" refers to JI's recommendation in his letter of November 28, 1783, that McCulloh apply for compensation in England because his prospects in America were poor. *PJI*, 2:467-469.

[9]John Driver was a merchant in Suffolk, Va. *PJI*, 1:18.

[10]George McCulloh (ca. 1767-1833) was the illegitimate son of Henry E. McCulloh and a woman named Molly. George was sent back and forth between McCulloh in England and JI in North Carolina before settling in North Carolina and becoming a lawyer. Estate of George McCulloh, 1833, Lincoln County Estates, State Archives; *PJI*, 1:29n, 2:374n.

[11]Gilchrist married Martha Jones, sister of Willie Jones. *DNCB*, s.v. "Gilchrist, Thomas."

[12]Mr. Agnew was a minister. No further information has been found. Francis Child (d. 1792) of New Bern was a clerk in the office of the state comptroller of public accounts. On November 20, 1784, he was elected comptroller and served in that position until his death. Henry "Harry" Montfort (d. 1793) of Warren County served in the General Assembly (1779-1786, 1788, 1792-1793) and was Willie Jones's brother-in-law. Henry E. McCulloh to JI, February 18, 1789, in this volume; *DNCB*, s.v. "Child, Francis"; Cheney, *North Carolina Government*, 205-228 passim, 345n; Ashe, Weeks, Van Noppen, *Biographical History*, 6:378.

Gibson, Granberry & Co. was a mercantile company owned by Joseph Gibson of Rockingham County and Josiah Granberry of Chowan County. The firm was in operation as early as 1770. Marguerite Butler McCall, ed., *Business as Usual: Edenton Merchant Ledgers, 1759-1819* (Edenton, N.C.: County of Chowan, 1988), ix.

[13]Samuel Cornell (1730-1781), a native of New York, was a wealthy merchant in New Bern and a member of the Royal Council (1770-1775). Because of his Tory sympathies, much of his property was confiscated by the state. *DNCB*, s.v. "Cornell, Samuel"; Clark, *State Records*, 19:672, 24:424.

[14]Nathan Bryan (1748-1798) of Jones County was a colonel in the county militia until 1779. He served in the General Assembly (1787, 1791-1794) and the U.S. House of Representatives (1795-1798). *DNCB*, s.v. "Bryan, Nathan."

[15]J. J. is John Johnston (1735-1791) of Bertie County, brother of Samuel Johnston and member of the General Assembly (1779-1780, 1782, 1784, 1787-1789). Johnston agreed to buy land from McCulloh in an area in central Bertie County called Indian Woods, but the property was confiscated before McCulloh received payment. Johnston attempted to buy the land from the state in December 1787. *PJI*, 1:137n; Massengill, *North Carolina Votes*, 32; A. B. Pruitt, *Abstracts of Sales of Confiscated Loyalist Land and Property in North Carolina* (n.p.: A. B. Pruitt, 1989), 163; William S. Powell, *The North Carolina Gazetteer* (Chapel Hill: University of North Carolina Press, 1968), 245.

[16]Joseph Montfort (d. 1776) of Halifax County, father of Henry Montfort, served in the colonial assembly (1762, 1764, 1766-1774) and was an active Freemason. A. Mc. is Alexander McCulloch (d. 1798) of Halifax and Warren Counties, Joseph Montfort's brother-in-law. *DNCB*, s.v. "Montfort, Joseph," "McCulloch, Alexander." See also *PJI*, 1:20n-21n.

[17]Henry McCulloch (d. 1755) was a British naval officer who served in several posts in North Carolina shortly before his death. He was a vice-admiralty court judge, member of the Provincial Council, and secretary of North Carolina. McCulloch and his wife, Mary, had four daughters. *DNCB*, s.v. "McCulloch, Henry."

Arthur Iredell to Hannah Iredell

Crewe Hall Feby. 25th. 1784.

I wrote a few Days ago to my Brother, & I shall now, my dear Sister, indulge a few moments in writing to You.[1] They will, I fear, be but few as I have an Engagement to day a few miles from this Place which I cannot neglect. It is at a very particular Friends of mine, a most amiable, accomplished, & agreable Young Woman, whose least recommendation, (which I therefore omitted) is that She is extremely pretty.—She has been married near four Years, tho' She is now but twenty two, & has no Children living. She is, you must know, my greatest Friend. no two People were ever more united in <u>mind</u>, I believe, than we are.[2] Her Sister is the one I have promised shall be your's. And, if ever I am so happy as to have it in my Power, I will keep my Word with You. I wish to God <u>that</u>

Time was near, & that We were all to live withen reach of each other. Is such Happiness think You, my dear Sister, in store for us, or are we for ever to be 'sundered by the Wide Atlantick? I have formed a thousand pleasing Schemes all of which will not, I trust, be denied us. Tell my Brother since I wrote to him I have received the Letter I was in Expectation of from my Uncle. It did not prove the decisive one I had wished. He talks of settling 100£ a Year upon me, which may possibly after two Year's be enlarged, & he recommends, tho' he does not insist upon my attaching myself to the Law.—It is a very kind Letter on the whole, & I think augurs very well for me. But after all I am the Jacob who stept rather stily or so into Your Husband Esru's Inheritance; who has not even had the paltry Compensation of a Mess of Porridge.[3] He will acquit me however of sinister measures to get what lay, as I think Falstaff says of Worcester's Treason, "in my Way, & I found it"[4]—Apropos, my dear Sister, are you a bit of a Politican? If you are, I could send you such Accounts to feast upon of Animosities & Feuds in our Island, as sounding & portentous as Your continental ones some ten Years ago. A Dwarf can sometimes roar like a Giant. At least I have seen very little Men who have made as free with their Lungs. But my Allusions & Politicks will run away with me if I don't take great Care. And perhaps you are not very inquisitive at this time to know about a distant Country called Great Brittain. Tho' a very good sort of a Gentlewoman & formerly a near relation of Your Mother's, She lives at such an inconvenient Distance that She cannot be very often in Your Mind, & is possibly never very near your Heart. I am obliged to think very much about Her, for I am not only a bit of a Politician myself by nature, but I am in the very Centre of Information. How fine that sounds! & yet after all I shall tell You nothing. I had better be quite <then> silent than leave off as I must do very unsatisfactorily. I shall therefore refer You to the Papers *&c.* I mean when I go to London, which will be very soon, to collect Pamphlets which are nevertheless in such heated times, somewhat like the Insects that are born & die in one day. Mr. Black has promised to let me be very troublesome to him. I shall /write/ you so soon by him that I have less ceremony on this Occasion So, my dear Sister, with the heartiest Prayers for Your Health & Happiness, I am as ususal & with all Truth

most affectionately your's

Arthur Iredell

RC, Iredell Papers, Duke. Addressed to "Mrs. Iredell."

---

[1]See Arthur Iredell to JI, February 18, 1784, in this volume.

[2]Arthur Iredell is referring to Mrs. Bayley of Hope, Staffordshire, who was Amanda Felton's sister. *PJI*, 1:114, 160.

[3]This is a reference to the Biblical story of Jacob, who, through trickery, gained the inheritance intended for his older brother, Esau. Gen. 27:1-40 RSV.

[4]Sir John Falstaff, a character in Shakespeare's *Henry IV*, part 1, says of Thomas Percy, Earl of Worcester, "Rebellion lay in his way, and he found it" (act 5, scene 1).

To Henry E. McCulloh

Edenton March 3d. 1784

Dear Sir,

I have but a moment to acknowledge your favour of the 1st. Nov:, which I received yesterday. I have acquainted you by several letters, that the Assembly did not meet as was expected, nor will they now until after a new election in April.[1] There is no change in any thing to make a difference in my expectations, but I think you had better not rely on any favour here so as to defeat your chance from the Parliamentary Committee[2]

I have the great pleasure to acquaint you, that your Son is now with me and in perfect health.[3] He was so unfortunate as to be taken, carried a Prisoner into England (Plymouth) where he was confined for some months, without knowing how to find out you, released after the Peace, and by way of France and a very circuitous route found his way here. I had been very uneasy about him, & was greatly relieved by his arrival. He is really as fine a boy as can be, with an excellent & lively capacity, a good heart, an obliging disposition, uncommon sobriety, and capable I am sure with a good education, of being a most respectable Man. He has a taste for reading, which discovers genius, and I think the sooner you can place him at a good school in England the better. In the meantime, I shall take care of him here, and to keep him employed think of putting him to a school of Mr. Earl's.[4]

The only two children of Mr. Henry McCulloch's now living, are <u>Dolly</u> & <u>Betsey</u>. The former is a distressed Widow, the latter is very happily married to a very respectable Man, Capt. Joseph Meredith, and who is also in very good circumstances. He having occasion lately to go to France, requested a letter from me to Mr. William McCulloch, that he might endeavour to settle with him.[5] I did not know that you had now to settle for more than the £200. Stg. I formerly wrote you, that Betsey had refused her Share, and since the confiscation her husband presented a <u>claim against your</u> Estate <u>and had it allowed for the sum she was entitled to. Execution was levied upon your lots</u>, of which I had never taken possession; having no authority to do so. It was not in my power, had I been inclined, to stop these proceedings, but I really thought it would be a means at any rate of securing you so much in England.

I have but just time to add that I am, Dear Sir, Your very affectionate humble Servant

Ja: Iredell

RC, English Records, Audit Office Papers, Loyalist Claims, NCSA. Endorsed "Letter from J Iredell dat. 3. Mar. 84 Ansd. 28. April do. as to Lotts."[6]

---

[1]JI is referring to his letters of ca. May 1, July 7, and November 28, 1783. *PJI*, 2:395-397, 419-421, 467-469.

The October 1783 session of the General Assembly did not conduct business because of the lack of a quorum. The next session took place at Hillsborough, April 19-June 3, 1784. Cheney, *North Carolina Government*, 212, 343.

[2]Parliament established a commission to examine Loyalists' claims in 1783 to continue until July 1785. This commission began hearing claims in August 1783. No new claims were to be heard by this commission after March 25, 1784. The commission was renewed twice, however, and continued functioning until 1799. Robert O. DeMond, *The Loyalists in North Carolina during the Revolution* (Baltimore: Genealogical Publishing, 1979), 203-204, 210.

[3]George McCulloh, Henry E. McCulloh's illegitimate son.

[4]Daniel Earl (d. 1790) of Chowan County was an Anglican clergyman, teacher, and missionary of the Society for the Propagation of the Gospel. He was the rector of St. Paul's in Edenton from 1759 to 1778. The school building, which was located on his plantation fifteen miles from Edenton, was taken in 1964 to the grounds of the James Iredell home in Edenton. *DNCB*, s.v. "Earl, Daniel." See also Lawrence Foushee London and Sarah McCulloh Lemmon, eds., *The Episcopal Church in North Carolina, 1701-1959* (Raleigh: Episcopal Diocese of North Carolina, 1987), 542 n.164.

[5]William McCulloch, a Dublin merchant, was a trustee for Henry McCulloch's accounts. *PJI*, 1:6n; Henry E. McCulloh to JI, April 28, 1784, in this volume.

[6]See Henry E. McCulloh to JI, April 28, 1784, in this volume.

To Pierce Butler

Edenton March 14th. 1784.

My dear Sir,

I received your most friendly and obliging letter of the 4th. February a few days ago with the greatest pleasure.[1] Your kind and generous concern for me, the recovery of Mrs. Butler, and a sympathy of Sentiment which so highly and so strongly flatters me, made me read it with extreme emotion. My ambition has ever directed me, next to the approbation of my own heart, to wish for the Esteem of Men of sense and virtue. I thank God, I have hitherto been fortunate in that respect, and I am exceedingly happy that so respected and so valued an approbation [*torn*] yours is not with-held from me. I have long <sought> /learnt/ to despise that sort of popularity which is to be gained by flattering the passions of the multitude. It is not only dishonest, but I am convinced is weak and impolitic, for one kind of submission makes way for another, and a Man must never stop, and so become despicable, or if he is disposed to recover his reputation, he has lost by unworthy sacrifices so much dignity of character that it is ten to one if he is able to effect it. <A steady undeviating course of virtue is the best basis> Mr. Johnston and myself have been almost the only Persons here who have opposed /the favourite/ violences against the Refugees The consequence of which was, that we were looked upon by the Patronizers of those with a very hated eye, and lately at an election of Assembly Men they openly opposed Mr. Johnston's reelection, altho' last year he had been courted to serve, and was then against his inclination chosen. His triumph however was complete, for tho' his name was not originally set on the list of <the> Candidates, tho' he was absent the whole time owing to sickness in his Family, and <not the least pains were taken by any of his intimate Friends> the utmost pains were taken (even by setting up 3 Candidates agns. Him, most if not all of them unwilling), & his intimate Friends suffered /all/ their <utmost> efforts to have vent, yet when the Poll was closed he had very near double the number of votes of any of the others, & in spite of them is now Senator for the County. This too, altho' the weather was so bad scarcely any could come in from the County & the whole opposition came from our Town Other Elections that I have heard of <had> /have/ proceeded in the same spirit, <so that I trust in God> which gives me hopes that we may yet be a composed & respectable & happy People Had one of the old Members declined as was expected, and I been chosen in his room, I would have served altho' it was extremely inconvenient to me, but the circumstance did not take place, and I therefore did not propose myself.

I am very much obliged to you for your information as to Dr. Bancroft & for your account of your Assembly's proceedings. They certainly do them honour, and your proposition of the Bank I hope will take effect, being obviously a most judicious & useful one. I see nothing that can be objected to in so rich a State as yours. And you are fortunate in having a great number of Gentlemen of Fortune and Education to conduct your Affairs, which we unhappily want.

Your observations on the unhealthiness of this Town are certainly Just Mr. Johnston & myself and our Families suffered so severely last year that we have expressed serious thoughts of removing to Hillsborough, a very healthy Town in this State in the back Country

FC, Johnson Collection, NCSA. Printed, McRee, 2:93-94. Endorsed "Substance of a letter to Major Butler March 14th. 1784."

---

[1]See Pierce Butler to JI, February 4, 1784, in this volume.

From William Hooper

Hillsb. 15 March 1784

My dear Sir

With our friend Capt Stokes I set off for Salisbury Court on Saturday last & proceeded on my Journey more than 20 miles.[1] When from a Sudden and prodigious fall of Water the creeks & rivers became impassable, as I was not very sanguine in my purpose of attending the court I returned, but he having a pressing call thither upon some private business, thought proper to wait the fall of the Waters, & was to proceed when that happened.

I regret this accident the less as I now can avail of an opportunity to write you which would otherwise <would> have passed in my absence.

Our Election which was the most warmly contested of any which has ever happened in this county has terminated in favour of Genl. Butler and your humble Servant for Commoners & Major Macaulay for a Senator.[2] More than 650 persons voted. I had 100 Votes more than Alex Mebane and 7 more than Butler.[3] My friends exult at the success, but I /who/ have been so long hackneyed in publick business know too well the levity of the people and the caprice of popularity to exult much in this momentary preference

I am anxious to know what has been the event of the Chowan & Edenton Election Nothing could have induced me to make the Sacrifice which I necessarily must from the Step I have taken than a confidence that I should be united with your self & Mr. Johnston in the business of legislation.[4] Should I fall Short on this expectation I shall very truly regret that I was ever a candidate for this laborious distinction. Macl. will be elected for Wilmington & if he would bring a little temper with him might be essentially Serviceable. Tib Gracchus had hopes of being elected for Duplin county.[5]

Judge of my mortification when I inform you that altho I have heard that <u>Cusatti Sully</u>, <u>the Citizen</u>, <u>the true Citizen</u> have Stepped forth as combatants in the war kindled by that redoubted Champion for the constitution, Atticus, & yet I have seen none of them except <Cusa> Sully which Capt Stokes ascribes to Davy.[6] I believe it to be the performance of Macl, but I judge only from the fire of the composition. Cusatti is Said to be Martin.[7] I suspect it from the quaintness of the Signature. Is there such a name recorded in ancient or modern history? I believe not. But observe that Cusatti is a transposition of all the letters which compose the word atticus & this may have given occasion to this ingenious fiction. The Citizen it is Said is the product of a joint committee on Nutbush.[8] All this however I have by vague report & have nothing certain to ground my conjectures upon. I anxiously wish to get a Sight of these political Squibs & if by this or any other Opportunity you could Send me the papers which contain them, /& any other papers/ you would much oblige me & your other friends at Hogg Hall.

Our Spring Scarcely begins to open upon us. the extreme Severity of the Winter, has destroyed as it is apprehended great part of the Wheat in this part of the country which has already had an effect upon the price of Indian Corn & the Wheat of the last year

My family enjoy uninterrupted health I have Scarcely administered a doze of Medicine for a twelve month past.

I hope in God that you and your's are well. I have yet hopes that we shall e'er long be nearer to each other & I shall then be very moderate in my further demands upon Providence.[9] Adieu, My dear Sir. Remember us all most affectionately & respectfully to Mrs. Iredell Mrs. Blair & the rest of the good family & believe me to be Ever Sincerely Yours,

Will Hooper

RC, Iredell Papers, Duke. Printed, McRee, 2:94-96.

---

[1]John Stokes (1756-1790) of Halifax, Rowan, and Montgomery Counties was an attorney who in 1790 became the first federal judge for the North Carolina district. He served less than three months, however, before he died. Stokes had been a captain in the Sixth Virginia Continental Regiment during the Revolutionary War. He was severely wounded at the Waxhaws in 1780, losing a hand to a British sword. *DNCB*, s.v. "Stokes, John"; Cheney, *North Carolina Government*, 753.

[2]John Butler (d. 1786) of Orange County had been elected to the General Assembly on three previous occasions (1777, 1778, 1781). During the spring 1784 term, he led two committees, served on a third, and sponsored legislation to provide relief for Quakers and Loyalists. He had been a brigadier general in the militia during the Revolution. William Macaulay (before 1755-1826) was a veteran of five terms in the General Assembly (1778-1780, 1782-1783). After the spring 1784 election, he would be elected to six more terms. *DNCB*, s.v. "Butler, John"; Massengill, *North Carolina Votes*, 38.

[3]Alexander Mebane (1744-1795) of Orange County held numerous political offices and was active in the militia. He served in the General Assembly (1783-1784) and in the U.S. Congress (1793-1795). *DNCB*, s.v. "Mebane, Alexander."

[4]Samuel Johnston was elected to the state senate for Chowan County. Because of financial concerns, Iredell refused requests to run for the General Assembly in the

1780s to focus on his law practice. He often worked on legislative issues, however. Cheney, *North Carolina Government*, 212; Whichard, *Justice James Iredell*, 23.

[5]Archibald Maclaine was elected to represent Wilmington in the house of commons. John Hay, "Tib Gracchus," was not chosen. Cheney, *North Carolina Government*, 212-213.

[6]Pseudonymous political writing was common during this period, and prevalent topics included the treatment of Loyalists and the discord between attorneys and judges. Atticus was thought to be Samuel Spencer (1734-1793) of Anson County, a justice of the superior court (1778-1793). JI held Spencer in low regard, deploring his undignified courtroom behavior and ignorance of the law. Nevertheless, Spencer sought help from JI in getting an essay signed by Atticus published in a Virginia newspaper. Sully was believed to be William R. Davie (1756-1820), a young attorney of Halifax. He would later be a delegate to the U.S. Constitutional Convention and play a key role in the founding of the University of North Carolina. *PJI*, 2:178n, 466-467; Whichard, *Justice James Iredell*, 20; *DNCB*, s.v. "Spencer, Samuel," "Davie, William Richardson"; Blackwell P. Robinson, *William R. Davie* (Chapel Hill: University of North Carolina Press, 1957), 164.

[7]Alexander Martin (1738-1807) of Guilford County served in the state senate (1778-1782, 1785, 1787-1788, 1805) and the U.S. Senate (1793-1799). When Gov. Thomas Burke was captured by Tories in 1781, Martin became acting governor. He subsequently served seven terms in that office (1781-1785, 1789-1792). *DNCB*, s.v. "Martin, Alexander"; *BDC*, 1427; Cheney, *North Carolina Government*, 160; *PJI*, 2:219n.

[8]Hooper believed "The Citizen" to be the pseudonym for a committee consisting of John Williams, Alexander Martin, and Richard Henderson. Williams (1731-1799) of Granville County was an attorney, planter, and superior court judge (1779-1799). After his death, Nutbush was renamed Williamsboro in his honor. Henderson (1735-1785) was also a Granville County attorney. He served in the house of commons (1781) and on the Council of State (1782-1783). Williams and Henderson were Hanover County, Va., natives, law partners, and members of an unsuccessful land development company in the 1770s. William Hooper to JI, March 18, 1784, in this volume; *DNCB*, s.v. "Williams, John," "Henderson, Richard."

[9]This is one of Hooper's more subtle attempts to encourage JI to move to Hillsborough. Touting the healthy climate of Orange County and using other enticements, Hooper repeatedly and unsuccessfully tried to persuade the Iredells to relocate. Hooper was not alone in this endeavor. "The removal of Mr. Johnston & Mr. Iredells families to Hillsboro would compleat my happiness," Elizabeth Hogg wrote to Nelly Blair on April 12, 1784. She repeated this sentiment in another letter to Nelly Blair on June 2, 1784, in which she declared, "I still hope your Uncles will move here yet." John Stokes, taking a stronger tack, wrote JI directly in an undated letter: "I wish you could prevail on yourself and Mrs. Iredell to remove to Hillsbo. or some other healthy situation. whenever I see any person who I think can give me any account of you I dread to enquire for fear the intelligence should not be such as I could wish. For God's sake if you have any regard for yourself or <such of> your friends who wish your life preserved remove

from that sickly hole Edenton." The letters cited above are from the Iredell Papers, Rare Book, Manuscript, and Special Collections Library, Duke University, Durham. See also Hooper's letters of March 18, July 8, September 8, 1784, and February 12, 1786, in this volume.

From William Hooper

[*Hillsb. 18. March 1784*]

My dear Sir

Your obliging favour by Cochrain came to hand yesterday.[1] Previous to the rect. of it I had wrote you and had committed the letter to the care of the bearer of this.[2] I cannot Suffer him to depart without pouring my most grateful acknowledgments forth to you for the newspapers. They are a feast of the most exquisite kind to us. What a whirlwind has the Judge raised about his ears.[3] Where the Devil is he that the publick do not hear again from him. Never was a better opening than the Citizen has given him both to support himself & bestow abuse upon his adversaries. Judge Wms. passed thro this yesterday. M Hogg charged him home with the Citizen He Sincerely disclaims, but I do not believe him. I suspect that he furnished the materials. Hendersen connected them, & that Prince of Parnassus, Gov. Martin gave them the finishing polish.

I rejoice to hear that you and Mr. Johnston talk Seriously of coming amongst us. When I see you we will cast about for houses to accommodate you.

I delivered your Miss Nellys letter to Miss yet Miss Hogg but who will not long remain So. Such is the instinctive appetite of that said Animal for Huske that she has consented to Sacrifice her very name for it. Alas! I gave you this Pun before, but am so pleased with my first essays in that way that I cannot forbear repeating it[4]

Remember me most affectionately & respectfully to your own & Mr. Johnstons. family & believe me Ever

My dear friend yrs.

Will Hooper

Neither you or Mr. Johnston have replied to a part of my former letter which requests information relative Mrs. Aitchesons negroes in possession of Dr. Burkes Widow.[5]

RC, Iredell Papers, Duke. Printed, McRee, 2:96.

---

[1]James Cochran (1761-1817) was an Orange County planter. *DNCB*, s.v. "Cochran, James."

[2]William Hooper to JI, March 15, 1784, in this volume.

[3]Hooper is presumably referring to Judge Samuel Ashe and his quarrel with attorney John Hay. Hooper described a heated encounter between the two in a letter to JI of February 7, 1784, in this volume. McRee states in a note to the March 18 letter that "I suppose the reference to be to Judge Ashe, between whom and the Bar raged, about this time, a violent feud. However deficient the Judge may have been in legal learning, the tradition of the profession is, that he got the better of his adversaries. Some very competent judges, who had seen his controversial efforts, have expressed to me great admiration of their vigor and sarcasm. The object of the Bar was to write Ashe off the Bench." McRee, *Life and Correspondence*, 2:96n.

[4]See William Hooper to JI, January 4, 1784, n. 15, in this volume.

[5]See William Hooper to JI, January 4, 1784, n. 10, in this volume.

From John Stokes

Salisbury March 26th. 1784

Dear Sir,

I must beg forgiveness for suffering so long a time to elapse after receiving your very friendly and polite letter, without sending you a letter of acknowledgments I feel much indebted to you, for making me acquainted with Mr. Du Chesnel.[1] I was highly pleased with him I am highly gratified in receiving from you, a letter so full of friendly expressions, both from yourself and Mrs. Iredell, who seem to value my small services and warm wishes, during your illness, far beyond any thing that was in my power to do for you.

I am extremely sorry that I cannot see you this circuit, having determined to reside in this town for a few years, because the practice of the law is more profitable here than at Halifax, and will the sooner enable me not only to buy books but to live also. Capricious Fortune has Frequently <dealt> /lavished/ out misfortunes to me, <with a bounteous> but the prospect begins to brighten.

Be so obliging as to make my compliments acceptable to Mrs. Iredell. I expect to see you the ensuing fall, when I shall have it in my power to assure that I am

My dear Sir your most obedient and very humble servant

Jno. Stokes

RC, Johnson Collection, NCSA. Addressed "James Iredell Esquire at Hillsborough favd. by Colo. Davie." Endorsed "Salisbury March 26th. 1784. John Stokes Ansd. 10th. April."

[1]Mr. Du Chesnel of France is briefly identified in a letter from William J. Dawson to JI dated January 16, 1784: "You will have an Old Gentleman in with Mr. T. C. by the name of DeChesnell Comissans of War of the French Troops." No further information has been found. Iredell Papers, Rare Book, Manuscript, and Special Collections Library, Duke University.

To Hannah Iredell

Elk Marsh[1] March 28th. 1784.

My dear Hannah,

We have hitherto had a very agreeable Journey, the weather being uncommonly fine, and our stages good. We found Mrs. Pearson in high spirits, and Mrs. Dawson's Family tolerably so till they received the unhappy account of G which quite confounded them, tho' Mrs. Dawson said she had long been apprehensive of it. We separated in the evening, your Brother going to Mrs. Gray's, and I to Dr. Lenox's, who seemed highly rejoiced to see me, and I was therefore, as well as on account of some business I had to do for him, very glad I went.[2] He is greatly mended, tho' he still uses crutches, and the young Ladies and John quite well. Their going down I believe is uncertain tho' talked of—. I went early the next morning to Mr. Gray's, and after break fast your Brother and I proceeded, and reached Mr. Mackensie's in very good time in the evening.[3] Mrs. Mackensie was much afflicted with the tooth ach, but otherwise pretty well; He entirely so. She expressed herself disappointed at not seeing you and Nelly. We came here to dinner yesterday, and are just going on before break fast. The Family here are all in perfect health—Stokes is in the back Country. Your Brother is perfectly well, and my own health is much mended, and I doubt not will in a few days be entirely recovered—Mr. Hooper is a Member for Orange, and Colo. Ashe from Cape Fear says there was no doubt Mr. Maclaine would be chosen for Wilmington.[4] They have begun to print a newspaper at Halifax, which is to be continued weekly[5] The only one of them I have seen contains Instructions from the County of Northampton in the highest stile of moderation, and it seems to be the general sentiment this way.

Pray remember me most affectionately to Mrs. Blair and her Family. It is not possible for me now to write to Nelly—Do not forget me either to Gaby, and Mrs. Johnston and her sweet home Children[6] My best respects also to Mr. Barker.[7] I would have sent the Halifax paper if I could have commanded it. Your Brother sends his love to you all. Adieu! my dear

Hannah. God grant you may preserve your health—. I assure you I will take the best care of mine, and am ever

Yours most affectionately

Ja. Iredell.

RC, Johnson Collection, NCSA. Printed, McRee, 2:96.

---

[1]Elk Marsh, in northern Halifax County, was the location of the home of Alexander McCulloch, father of Benjamin McCulloch. It appears on the Collet map of 1770 and is now known as Marsh Swamp. JI wrote numerous letters from this location. *PJI*, 1:20n-21n; Powell, *Gazetteer*, 160, 313.

[2]This is probably a reference to the wife of George Gray (d. 1806) of Bertie County. "Grays" appears on the 1770 Collet map west of the Cashie River. Robert Lenox (d. 1789) of Bertie County was a physician. Mitchell, *North Carolina Wills*, 196; *PJI*, 1:219n, 2:360n.

[3]William McKenzie (before 1755-1810) of Bertie and Martin Counties was a planter and member of the General Assembly (1786-1787, 1797, 1800). Massengill, *North Carolina Votes*, 40; *PJI*, 2:227n.

[4]Archibald Maclaine was elected to represent Wilmington in the house of commons. Cheney, *North Carolina Government*, 213.

[5]Thomas Davis may have transferred the *North Carolina Gazette* from New Bern to Halifax in March 1784. No issues have survived. Davis moved the newspaper to Hillsborough by July 1785. Alan D. Watson, *An Index to North Carolina Newspapers, 1784-1789* (Raleigh: North Carolina Department of Cultural Resources, Division of Archives and History, 1992), xii.

[6]Gabriel "Gaby" Johnston (1775-1800) was Samuel Johnston's son. Frances "Fanny" Cathcart Johnston (1751-1801), wife of Samuel Johnston, is mentioned frequently throughout the letters, especially regarding her health, which was apparently fragile. *PJI*, 1:460n; *DNCB*, s.v. "Johnston, James Cathcart."

[7]Thomas Barker (1713-1787) of Bertie and Chowan Counties was a planter who had held numerous positions in the colonial government, most conspicuously as a member of the assembly. By this time, he had retired from public life. *DNCB*, s.v. "Barker, Thomas"; *PJI*, 1:103n-104n.

To Hannah Iredell

Hillsborough April 8th 1784.

My dear Hannah—

Your Brother and I arrived here very well, and after a very agreeable journey, the day before Court. Mr. Hooper would not suffer either of us to lodge any where but at his house, and therefore I need not tell you our situation has been quite agreeable. We have been both a little affected by the water, but that is pretty well over, and we have no reason to complain I had got quite well until that renewed a little of my complaint. I should have had more leisure now to write to you but that we expected Mr. Strudwick's cause would come on this morning, and we were obliged to be busy in our preparations for it.[1] This must excuse the shortness of my letter to you, and my not writing to Nelly. Your Brother I believe will not leave this until after the Assembly is over. I have had a little new business here, but not much. I am very anxious to hear of you, and hope to get some intelligence by some of our Members before I leave this. I had hoped to get away on Sunday, but an unexpected delay of Mr. Strudwick's cause, by an accident one of his Witnesses met with, may perhaps detain me till Tuesday. Scarcely any Members are yet arrived—Mr. Huske is not yet married, but expected in two or three days when the wedding will certainly take place. Preparations are busily making. Your Brother seems in earnest about a settlement here, but there is a difficulty owing to the want of houses, and of convenience and workmen to build. Adieu! My dear Hannah—Remember me affectionately to all our Family, and give my best respects to Mr. Barker—I have at present no news for him.

Believe me, my dearest Hannah, Most truly and affectionately yours

Jas Iredell.

RC, Johnson Collection, NCSA. Printed, McRee, 2:97. Addressed "Mrs. Iredell Edenton."

---

[1]While living in England, Samuel Strudwick (d. 1797) purchased thirty thousand acres of land in North Carolina in 1761. He subsequently moved to the state and held positions in the colonial government. In 1780, Strudwick hired JI and Thomas Burke to try to prevent the state from confiscating his land. While some property was taken, he retained his plantation on the Upper Cape Fear River. *DNCB*, s.v. "Strudwick, Samuel."

Arthur Iredell to Hannah Iredell

London Apl. 9th. 1784—

Mr. Black has just informed me of a Ship that is to sail in a few Days for Virginia, & that he will consign any Letter I may have to send, either to You or my Brother, to a Friend of his in that State. I embrace, my dear Sister, with the utmost eagerness so happy an Opportunity of acknowledging & returning You my best Thanks for a Letter from You of no long Date, in which You are pleased to mention my Amanda, & to speak of her in terms of Cordiality & Affection. She will be equally gratefull when I shall have made her acquainted with the Interest You take in our Happiness—and I can with Confidence assure You of the warmest & fullest return on her Part to You & every Branch of my Family. You ask for her Name—Names, my dear Sister, are empty Sounds, unless one is acquainted with the Persons & Families to which they belong; it is with the less regret therefore I keep an engagement with Another at the time I refuse to gratify Your Curiosity—The truth is our Attachment is yet a Secret to all her Family except a Sister, & She would have great reason to be angry with me if I did not keep up some reserve with my own. But I am running over the whole of the Paper, as Men in such a Situation are apt to do, upon one Topic. I ought sooner to have informed You that Tom has accepted his Brother's kind Invitation, & is preparing to accompany Mr. Black to Carolina in a Ship that will soon Sail for Edenton. He will probably therefore have the Happiness of being introduced to You within a short time after You will have received this. I envy him an Interview [*which*] is to lay the Foundation of so warm & lasting a Friendship. You will find him an amiable Young Man extremely deserving of your regard, with a very good head (uncultivated it is true, indeed miserably neglected) and with an excellent Heart. He has, I am persuaded, much Happiness in Prospect, nor can he fail of thriving in America under the watchfull Eye of an able & affectionate Brother.[1] I have seen much of Mr. Black since my Arrival in London, &, as we have only had one Subject in Conversation, you may, perhaps, give me Credit for knowing a great deal about you all on the other side of the Atlantick, & for being, in short, every thing but an American myself. I am quite in Love with the Life You lead—I was before with the People—& tho the Country about you be such a dead flat, as we should call it here, & at times not quite so healthy as might be wished, for the Sake of the two first Blessings Who would not brave an Ague, & shiver away two or three Months in every Year to be happy the remainder of It? No wise Man I am sure. I wish I had any thing to communicate that could possibly entertain You; but Politicks are the only Things talked of here, & our's can be no longer interesting to an American Lady, tho your [*St*]atesmen may pry with Pleasure into what is "rotten in the State of Denmark"[2]—They would find it easily enough—the English, who were always a silly People in Politicks, are now more so than ever. They have been vilifying their best Friends in Addresses to the Crown; & they are now as fast as they can returning the avowed Advocates of Prerogative to the New Parliament. The great Contest is at Westminster where Mr. Fox is a Candidate.[3] It is now going on & the result of It no one can say, but all are anxiously waiting for It. Will you believe that I am a very active Partizan—?—I am, I can assure you, & have actually canvassed not without Success. Mr. Black will tell you that he saw me with one of

Charles Fox's Favours in my Hat—that is Proof positive, yet I will give You more. [*I d*]ined yesterday with a select Party of the leaders on that [*side*]—Charles Fox, Sheridans, Hare, Mr. North Ld. North's Son, Godfrey Webster, Fitzpatrick, Pigot one of the Commissioners [*of*] Accounts, Mr. Gunning a Son of Sir Robert's—& a Mr. Dudley, & I had the Satisfaction of seeing Charles Fox scratch off an Address to the Electors which will cutt a flaming Figure in to<morro>day's Papers[4]—It is a most excellant one—I went from [*thence*] to Mr. Crewe's, where I met with the Duchess of Portland & some other fine Ladies, who were equally ardent, but not quite so able in the Business as the Party I have named to you.[5] I ought to apologise for giving You so much dry Stuff but I am sure you will forgive me without intreaties—I had thoughts of writing to my Brother, but I really have not time. Pray remember me most affectionately to him—tell him my Mother & Tom are perfectly well & that I never am other I must request You likewise to present my best respects to all your Family with whom I am now better acquainted than I have yet told you—for I have seen Mr. Dawson of whom I could not say too many civil Things if I had time, which I have not, more than to assure You that I am ever, my dear Sister

most truly & affectionately Yr's.

A Iredell

RC, Johnson Collection, NCSA. Printed, McRee, 2:97-98.

---

[1]Thomas Iredell, brother of James and Arthur, was careless with money and caused his mother much concern. This was one reason JI invited both of them to come to North Carolina. Thomas reached Edenton about September 1, but Mrs. Iredell demurred because she wanted to pay Thomas's debts before leaving England. She eventually joined James six years later. Whichard, *Justice James Iredell*, 228.

[2]This well-known line from Shakespeare's *Hamlet* was spoken by a lesser-known character, Marcellus, in act 1, scene 4.

[3]Charles James Fox (1749-1806), Whig leader and adversary of George III, wanted to limit the royal prerogative to appoint ministers. Fox and Lord North, once a target himself of Fox's ire, formed a coalition government in April 1783. For a variety of reasons the coalition was unpopular, and in December 1783 the government was dismissed. In the subsequent election Fox was returned to Parliament, but many of his supporters were not. William Pitt the younger, who had the king's support, became the dominant force in Parliament. *DNB*, s.v. "Fox, Charles James," "Pitt, William"; A. Goodwin, ed., *The New Cambridge Modern History*, vol. 8, *The American and French Revolutions, 1763-1793* (Cambridge: University Press, 1965), 553-554.

[4]Richard Brinsley Sheridan (1751-1816), the playwright who penned *The Rivals* and *The School for Scandal*, was first elected to Parliament in 1780. He was an ally of Fox and during the Fox-North coalition government served as secretary to the treasury. James Hare (1749-1804) was a noted wit, member of Parliament, and longtime friend of Fox. George Augustus North (1757-1802), 3d Earl of Guilford, was a Whig member of Parliament and undersecretary to his father during the Fox-North coalition. Sir Godfrey Webster (ca. 1748-1800) served in Parliament (1786-1790, 1796-1800). Richard Fitzpatrick (1747-1813) had been Fox's friend since their school days. He was a member of Parliament for thirty-three years and secretary of war in the Fox-North coalition government. Sir Arthur Leary Pigott (1752-1819), a lawyer, was appointed as a commissioner of public accounts by Lord North under the act of 1780. George William Gunning was the son of Robert Gunning, a diplomat who held a variety of posts in Europe. Sir Henry Bate Dudley (1745-1824) was a clergyman, journalist, and man-about-town, who published a newspaper in London. In 1780, he was sentenced to prison for a year for libel. *DNB*, s.v. "Sheridan, Richard Brinsley," "Hare, James," "North, Frederick," "Fitzpatrick, Richard," "Pigott, Sir Arthur Leary," "Gunning, Sir Robert," "Dudley, Sir Henry Bate"; Bernard Burke and Ashworth P. Burke, *A Genealogical and Heraldic History of the Peerage and Barontage, The Privy Council, Knightage and Companiage*, 76th ed. (London: Harrison and Sons, 1914), 1999, hereafter cited as *Burke's Peerage*, 76th ed.

[5]Lady Dorothy Cavendish, Duchess of Portland, was the wife of William Henry Cavendish Bentinck, who had been prime minister from April to December 1783 in the Fox-North coalition government. Lady Cavendish was the only daughter of William, 4th Duke of Devonshire. *DNB*, s.v. "Bentinck, William Henry Cavendish."

From Samuel Johnston

Hillsborough April 14th. 1784

Dear Sir

The enclosed papers from Mr. Ruffin I received after you left this.[1] you will do what is proper with respect to them. I must request the favor of you to forward the enclosed Letters to Mr. Allen & Mr. Collins[2]

Very few of the Members are yet come to Town God knows when we shall make a House the Governor came to Town on Monday a few minutes after Atkins left it as if by concert.[3] I have seen him but he has nothing new that I can learn, he had never seen the Letter of our Ministers which accompanied the Treaty and knows nothing of the Copies That were intended for the Members. My Brother and his Collegues came in yesterday and the Members from Sullivan County.[4] Mr. Huske is likewise come but I do not yet understand when the happy moment is to be. he gives us reason to expect Mr. Mc.Laine this day or to morrow. I begin to be very impatient at being so long idle tho I could pass my time no where more agreeably under such circumstances at so great a a distance from my family. Mr. Hooper has carried me over all his plantations & improvements the Situations of which are very delightfull and the Soil good

I shall hope to hear from you by the first Opportunity I begin to repent my not having gone down as the time of the meeting is so uncertain, be so good as present my best respects to all such as you know I would wish to appear civil and believe me

Dear Sir Yours Affectionately

Sam Johnston

RC, Johnson Collection, NCSA. Printed, McRee, 2:98. Addressed "James Iredell Esquire."

---

[1]The enclosed papers have not been found.

[2]Nathaniel Allen, previously identified, and Josiah Collins Sr. (1735-1819). Collins was a successful merchant in Edenton and the senior partner in the firm of Collins, Stuart, and Muir. *DNCB*, s.v. "Collins, Josiah, Sr."

[3]Alexander Martin was governor. Mr. Atkins is possibly Ica Atkins of Cumberland County, who served in the state senate (1782-1783). Cheney, *North Carolina Government*, 160, 209, 210.

[4]John Johnston (1735-1791), a senator from Bertie County, was Samuel Johnston's brother. Andrew Oliver and Zedekiah Stone represented Bertie County in the house of commons. From Sullivan County, Joseph Martin served in the senate, and William Cage and David Looney in the house. *PJI*, 1:137n; Cheney, *North Carolina Government*, 212-213.

From Nelly Blair

Edenton April 14th. 1784

I daresay my Dear Uncle if I were to take up 3 sheets of paper in assuring you that it is not my fault I have not wrote to you before, you would not beleive me, so I may as well let it alone, & not pretend to excuse myself tho' I coud very well do it

& now as it is the thing nearest my Heart, give [*me*] leave to ask what success you have had in getting a [*House*] at Hillsborough. none at all. you dont wish for any there you have got a surfeit of the place, and are surprised how you coud ever like it, will I hope be the answer.

You cant think how merry we have been since you went away. there have been no less than 5 dances besides Capt Fuets Ball, & last Monday we went to breakfast on board the Capts. Brig & really spent a most agreable Morning.[1]

I have recevd. a Letter from Miss Hogg since you went away as allso one from Miss Henderson.[2] it seems it will not be possible for Miss Henderson to come down this Spring, which not a little mortified me Mr. Amis says she is going to be Married to one Mr. Lamb Alston.[3] Miss Hogg is <going> Married I suppose before this time—

Mamma went over the Sound with Aunt Johnston & is not yet returned. she stays on Peggys account. who has been very sick since you went away. & Dr. Lennox advised her to try a change of Air. Capt. Cross has Sold his House to Egan for 1200£, & intends to go to Charleton the first of next Month.[4]

if Uncle Sam should take the trouble to enquire [*a*]fter me, do pray remember me to him in the most respec[*tful*] & Affectionate manner you can think of. I hope your juant up the country, my Dear Uncle has been of as much service to you as you seem'd to expect it would be. & that you will return to us in perfect Health. that you may is the most ardent desire of your—

Affectionate Neice

H Blair

RC, Johnson Collection, NCSA. Addressed "James Iredell Esqr. Halifax."

---

[1]Captain Fuet's identity is uncertain. There is a record of the marriage of a Capt. Thomas Fuet, stepson of Rev. Thomas P. Irving of Newbern, in 1811. Irving, a native of Maryland and graduate of Princeton, was the principal of New Bern Academy and rector of Christ Episcopal Church. Lois Smather Neal, comp., *Abstracts of Vital Records from Raleigh, North Carolina, Newspapers*, vol. 1, *1799-1819* (Spartanburg, S.C.: Reprint Company, 1979), 172; *The Star* (Raleigh), August 16, 1811; Alan D. Watson, *A History of New Bern and Craven County* (New Bern: Tryon Palace Commission, 1987), 175; Barbara M. Howard Thorne, ed., *The Heritage of Craven County, North Carolina* (New Bern: Eastern North Carolina Genealogical Society, in cooperation with Hunter Publishing, Winston-Salem, 1984), 23, 57.

[2]Elizabeth "Betsy" Hogg wrote Nelly Blair on March 6, 1784. In that letter she remarked on William Hooper's comments concerning her upcoming marriage: "I wish you would tell Mr. Hooper or who ever it was that was so busy with their news from Wilmington, I think they might find something of more consequence to imploy their time in then writing about me. I really believe every body takes a pleasure in teasing me. as Mr. Iredle says I can easily see it is envy in you, Poor Girl! how I pity you, but dont despair if you will come up with Mr. Iredle to the court, and stay while the Assembly sits who knows what may happen their are sometimes two or three smart young men amongst the members & Gentlemen

who attend it." Iredell Papers, Rare Book, Manuscript, and Special Collections Library, Duke University.

[3]Miss Henderson is probably Fanny Henderson (b. 1764), daughter of Richard Henderson of Granville County. Fanny Henderson had visited the Blairs and Iredells in May 1783. She, however, married Spruce McKay (Macay), a judge from Salisbury, on May 27, 1785. While the name Alston was common in Granville County at this time, no one named Lamb Alston has been discovered. Since this information had been passed along by several people before reaching Miss Blair, it is possible that what she thought was Lamb Alston was actually Lemuel Alston (1760-1836). The latter lived in Granville County before moving to South Carolina soon after the Revolution. He was twice elected to Congress from that state. Nelly Blair's apparently misinformed informer, Thomas Amis (d. 1798) of Halifax County, was a Revolutionary War veteran and the brother-in-law of Richard Bennehan, a successful planter and merchant. *DNCB*, s.v. "Henderson, Richard," "Alston, Lemuel James," "Bennehan, Richard"; *PJI*, 2:400, 404, 407, 421-422; Brent H. Holcomb, comp., *Marriages of Granville County, North Carolina, 1753-1868* (Baltimore: Genealogical Publishing, 1981), 216; Worth S. Ray, ed., *Colonial Granville County and Its People* (Baltimore: Genealogical Publishing, 1973), 230; Mitchell, *North Carolina Wills*, 10.

[4]Captain Cross is frequently mentioned in the correspondence but has not been identified. Robert Egan (d. 1796) of Chowan County was a tavern keeper, watch repairer, and auctioneer. Raymond Parker Fouts, *Abstracts from the State Gazette of North-Carolina*, 3 vols. (Cocoa, Fla.: GenRec Books, 1982), 1:12, 44; 2:29, 32; 3:29; *State Gazette of North-Carolina* (Edenton), December 25, 1788; October 8, 1790; April 11, May 2, 1794; October 27, 1796.

To Hannah Iredell

Halifax April 17th. 1784.

My dear Hannah,

I was very much mortified, at my arriving here yesterday, to find that Harry Bond had left this for Edenton in the morning, which would have been an excellent opportunity of writing.[1] However, as he was so very much obliging as to take great pains to enquire about me and waited upon Judge Spencer on purpose with whom I had parted the day before going to Colo. Mc.Culloch's I hope you would receive a good deal of satisfaction from his in formation.[2] I left Hillsborough on Sunday, but came down leisurely, and staid a whole day on the road at Mr. Faulcen's because the weather was a little suspicious, a degree of caution I hope I shall have credit for.[3] The water at Hillsborough affected me a good deal. I am sure it was that, for I have been infinitely better ever since Your Brother was affected in a degree in the same manner, but was pretty well when I left him. He staid very properly to attend the whole of the

Assembly, by which he avoided a good deal of fatigue as well as enabled himself to render more service Mr. Hooper staid also. I sent letters to Mrs. Johnston and Mrs. Mackenzie yesterday. The former had gone to Dr. Peat's, and Peter did not see [*her*] here, but I understand Charles is to be here this morning, and I hope to have an opportunity of sending this to you by him.[4] I had the pleasure to receive your letter of the 7th. which Mr. Johnston brought up, & just received before I left Hillsborough the one you were so obliging as to write me by Cumming, and which made me and your Brother very happy.[5] Your Brother seems to have serious thoughts still of fixing at Hillsborough, if he can accomplish it, at which let Nelly not be frightened from any thing I have said in this letter, for use will soon harden our bodies, as well as others, to the laxative water. Very few Members had arrived, but I met several on the road, among others your Brother John who was kind enough to let me pass without a scolding. He was very well, and I saw nothing amiss about him but his long beard, which was a great contrast to mine as I had very handsomely shaved myself that morning. I unluckily met him as we were travelling along, and not at any house, so that I had but a few moments conversation with him. We tried one of Mr. Strudwick's causes, and gained it, for after all the bluster that had been made the Jury did not stay out five minutes. He gave your Brother a note for 100 Guineas, and put me off again with excuses of not having money at that time, but promised to contrive it for me between this and the next Court, and said he would make mine equal to Mr. Johnston's, so that I hope to get very near double the sum he engaged. By this disappointment I received only about £10. at Hillsborough, and but little since, so that I am afraid I shall go down very poor[6]—Pray give my best respects to Mr. Barker.[7] I would write him but there is not yet word of news. I will ask your Brother and Mr. Hooper both to write to him, which indeed they intended doing by me, but did not. Their correspondence I dare say will be equally valuable & acceptable with that of the little Wretch who withheld his Remember me most affectionately to your Sister & her Family. I must write a line now to Nelly, or I suppose she would never forgive me. I am most impatient to be with you again, and in the mean time beg you to believe me, as I truly am.

Your entirely faithful and affectionate
Jas Iredell.

P.S. I wrote to you from Hillsborough
about the 7th. Inst.[8]

Booth, Saturday night. I have just time to acquaint you of my having come here this evening. I had been alarmed with an account of Mrs. Johnston's ill health, but find her better than I expected. Just as I left town I h[*ad the*] pleasure to receive a letter from your Brother which I send you[9]—Mrs. Mackenzie still complains much of the tooth ach—He is very well I inclose you a large packet—I can't form a conjecture when I shall be at home, but God knows I heartily long for it—I should have no objection to meet you & Nelly on this side the sound, but just as you please—I found my Hillsborough letter here & send it[10]—Adieu! my dearest Hannah—Heaven bless you—

I am Yours most affectionately

Jas Iredell

RC, Johnson Collection, NCSA. Addressed "Mrs. Iredell Edenton."

---

[1]Henry "Harry" Bond (d. 1817) was a merchant in Edenton. Mitchell, *North Carolina Wills*, 49; *PJI*, 2:226n.

[2]Judge Spencer is Samuel Spencer, and Colonel McCulloch is Alexander McCulloch.

[3]Mr. Faulcen is probably John Faulcon (d. 1812) of Warren County, a member of the state senate (1779) and Council of State (1791). Mitchell, *North Carolina Wills*, 162; Cheney, *North Carolina Government*, 166, 204.

[4]Samuel Peete (d. 1794) of Halifax and Northampton Counties was a physician and state legislator (1789). Peter and Charles were slaves. Massengill, *North Carolina Votes*, 47; JI's List of Taxable Property, 1784, in this volume.

[5]William Cumming (1724-ca. 1797), an attorney of Edenton, served in the General Assembly (1783-1784, 1788) and the Continental Congress (1785-1786). *DNCB*, s.v. "Cumming, William"; Cheney, *North Carolina Government*, 212, 213, 222, 659, 739n.

[6]The £10 included £3.4 toward the £10 owed by Daniel Williams for services rendered in the Hillsborough Superior Court. JI often complained of financial problems during this period, and one reason was the unwillingness of clients to pay their bills promptly. Legal Fee Books, vol. 6, James Iredell Papers, Southern Historical Collection. For JI's declarations of penury, see his letters to Henry E. McCulloh, January 6, 1785; Margaret Iredell, January 22, 1785; and Thomas Iredell Sr., May 28, 1784, in this volume.

[7]Thomas Barker.

[8]JI to Hannah Iredell, April 8, 1784, in this volume.

[9]Samuel Johnston to JI, April 14, 1784, in this volume.

[10]JI is referring to his letter of April 8, 1784.

To Nelly Blair

Halifax April 17th. 1784.

My dear Nelly,

Tho' you have not thought fit to favour me with a letter, tho' quite at leisure, I will not give myself an air of being offended, even in the midst of business, so as to deny you one, a proof I think that my affection for you outweighs both your duty and affection together.[1] Your friend Miss Hogg was on the eve of Matrimony, and waiting only, contrary, to the usual forms, for the Bridegroom, the Bride, Cloaths &c. being all ready. But he had to chuse between a hasty marriage with a short stay, or one more dilatory with time to enjoy the full honeymoon, and he preferred the latter. Which, had you been the expecting Bride, would you have thanked him for? I suppose Miss Hogg's letter discovers the secret, tho' it is [*no*] secret up there. I had the pleasure to see Miss Henderson on Tuesday. She was at Mr. Burton's, and had been very much indisposed, but was a little better.[2] well enough indeed to be doing mischief. for she had contrived to hide a young Man's shirts, waistcoat, breeches &c, and palmed the deed upon a strolling Waggoner's Wife that had just been there, & sent the poor young Fellow in full pursuit of her—She is very anxious to come down this Spring, and it appears a little doubtful whether she will not. Her Mamma says she shall if possible. Her Father is willing, and I, as your Proxy (thank me for that) strongly solicited the Grandmother's Interest. You will I suppose hear more about it from her letter by Judge Williams, who is expected tomorrow or Monday—Sickness prevented her writing by me.

I have no other news, and as I know you care not a farthing for any thing else I shall only add the old true story of my being, my dear Nelly,

Your very affectionate

Jas Iredell

RC, Johnson Collection, NCSA. Addressed "Miss Blair Edenton."

---

[1]Apparently JI had not received her letter of April 14, 1784, in this volume.

[2]Robert Burton (1747-1825) was a Revolutionary War officer, planter, and member of the Council of State and Continental Congress. His home was Montpelier at Williamsboro. *DNCB*, s.v. "Burton, Robert"; *PJI*, 2:289n; McRee, *Life and Correspondence*, 1:540n.

From Samuel Johnston

Hillsborough April 21st. 1784

Dear Sir

I have only a moment to inform you that the Assembly met on Monday. the Commons chose Mr. Benbury the Senate Mr. Caswell, Speaker.[1] The Governor proposed making a Speech to them but they rather chose to receive his Communications in a Message alledging that it would save him trouble.[2] whenever any thing Occurs of consequence to communicate, you may depend on hearing from me if an Opportunity offers

I hope to hear from you to day. I am very anxious to know the State of your health pray take care of it. I am

Sir Yours Affectionately

Sam Johnston

P. S. Mr. Hooper and all friends here are well. he had all the Wedding people with the Govr. and other Company dancing last night.[3]

RC, Johnson Collection, NCSA. Printed, McRee, 2:98-99. Addressed " James Iredell Esquire Halifax."

---

[1]The General Assembly convened April 19, 1784, in Hillsborough. Thomas Benbury (1736-1793) of Chowan County had previously served in the General Assembly (1776-1782) and as Speaker (1778-1782). During the 1784 session, the assembly appointed Benbury as a state customs collector. Richard Caswell (1729-1789) of Dobbs County served in numerous colonial and state public offices, including state controller general (1782-1785) and governor (1776-1780, 1785-1787). *DNCB*, s.v. "Benbury, Thomas," "Caswell, Richard"; Clark, *State Records*, 24:552; Cheney, *North Carolina Government*, 160.

[2]A message sent to Gov. Alexander Martin stated: "The General Assembly have received your Excellency's message of this day [*April 20*] and think it unnecessary to trouble your Excellency with the communication of the public dispatches in person but are ready to receive them when your Excellency thinks proper." Clark, *State Records*, 19:493.

[3]This refers to the wedding of Elizabeth "Betsy" Hogg and John Huske.

From Baron de Poellnitz[1]

New York the 22 April 1784

Dear Sir,

I have received Letters from London witch enforce my Speedy Return, and blaste for the present my favourite hopes of Setteling in this happy and independent Staete—

One odious plot is laid against my property, the object is of upwards 34000 Pd.Ss.[2] if lost, it ruins me for ever; my Rhigt is Clear and undoubted, but the Law has Quibles in Europe more than elsewehre, and the poeple witch attak me are of Ranck, influence, and Wealth; besides they trust that my means must be exhausted, and that as Such I will be incapable to go and face the Sto [*torn*] now Sir Life and human attchievement being uncertain I must taeke my Childeren with me, and I Thinck to Send them to Ireland for their Education

This all maekes me very unhappy. I Thougth my Self in port, and Shielded for ever against the Huricanes of European Despotisme and malice; but Tho I have hunted it repose is not my Lot—

Never Sir Shall I forget your Generous behaviour towards me, Your politeness, and <Your> /the/ trouble witch my childeren hav' given You, if I live I Shall be Victorious over my Ennemies, and greatfull to my friends, in Case You have Somthing in Europe that I can Execute for You <in Europe> give me the charge it will do me pleasure, Ly. Anne desires her Compliments to Mrs. Iredell and I am for ever, Dear Sir,

Your most oblgd. and Obd. Servent

FCHB Poellnitz

I Wrote to Mr. Ritzen at Norfolk to find occasion of Sending the Childeren by Sea as the less Expensif way, and to Settle Acct with Rd. D. Earl in Caese talk You was in the back Country = Your bill of Exq*e* of 22th. Septbr. 1783 Dllrs. 149 1/2 I have paid to [*torn*] Gentlemen at <Shigt> Sight the 31 Jan 1784 the naeme of bearer was Captn. Tomas Sanders

RC, Iredell Papers, Duke. Addressed "To Jams. Iredell Esqr. Edenton North Carolina." Endorsed "New York 22d. April 1784. Baron de Po[*torn*] Ansd."

---

[1]Friedrick Charles Hans Bruno, Baron von Poellnitz, had been chamberlain to Frederick the Great. He and his family visited the Iredells in September 1782 while en route to New York. The baron's children from an earlier marriage stayed with the Iredells in Edenton at least until January 1783, as the baron and his current wife continued their journey. The baron eventually became the owner of an experimental farm in Manhattan. Poellnitz's sister-in-law, Jane, was the wife of George Macartney. *PJI*, 2:349n, 369-370.

[2]The "odious plot" against the baron may have been related to a scandal that was revealed later concerning his wife, Lady Anne Stuart, daughter of Lord Bute. In a 1788 letter to JI, Poellnitz reported that his wife had run away with another man and that he was besieged by her creditors. Among this group was Lady Anne's first husband, Hugh Percy, who had since become the 2d Duke of Northumberland. Their fifteen-year marriage had ended in divorce in 1779. *PJI*,

2:349n; Mrs. E. Stuart Wortley, *A Prime Minister and his Son* (London: John Murray, 1925), 40n; Baron de Poellnitz to JI, February 20, 1788, in this volume. See also JI to Hannah Iredell, November 22, 1787, in this volume.

To Hannah Iredell

Halifax April 23d. 1784

My dear Hannah,

I was in great hopes to have got away this afternoon, but some business that I expected to have finished is still unavoidably depending, and more has presented itself, so that I do not know whether I may not be confined till after Monday, the last day of the Court. I will however if possible get away sooner. Some ugly weather that we had affected my health a little. but I am now nearly as well as before and a great deal better than I was at Hillsborough. so that I hope to present myself before you in tolerable plight. I really am as cautious as possible. My last letter from your Brother was of the 17th. He was very well, but your Brother John had had a fit of the ague & fever, for which however he had taken an emetic that had a good effect. They expected to make a house on the 19th. Miss Hogg was married the 15th., and all I am told was bloom and joy. This for Nelly, and it is all the particulars I can give her—. I have a letter for her from Miss Henderson which I shall give her myself. Judge Williams only came yesterday, his Family and Friends having been very sick. It is uncertain whether Miss Henderson, /can come/ tho' I heartily wish she could, for there is a putrid fever in the neighbourhood, tho' it has yet reached none of her Friends, That may be very dangerous. I have had no opportunity of writing to you before since I left Booth on Sunday. God grant, my dear Hannah. I may find you well. My spirits have been a little revived by the sight of a little money, tho' it would do no great good to any but a very poor Man. I have received here about £70.[1] Adieu! my dearest Hannah. Give my love & respects where they are most cordially due, and be assured I am ever

Entirely & most faithfully yours

Ja. Iredell.

RC, Johnson Collection, NCSA. Addressed "Mrs. Iredell Edenton—By favor of Mr. Price—."

---

[1]The £70 JI received at Halifax included half of a £20 debt that had been owed to JI by E. Ruffin since October 1783. The remainder was paid in 1786 and 1787. Legal Fee Books, vol. 6, James Iredell Papers, Southern Historical Collection.

From Henry E. McCulloh

No. 22. Ironmonger lane London, 28th. Apr. 1784.

My dear Sir

I this day receive your favor of the 3d. Ulto.[1]—The fluctuating State of this Country, gives me but little hopes from the quarter you allude to.—What you write me as to George, both grieves, & surprises me.—The least Inquiry at the Carolina Coffee House, or Merchts. would have found me out.[2] Probably, all is for the Best, and a better fate awaits him I hope in Carolina, than might here.—Let him continue what I have great pleasure in your describing him to be, & assure him as far as my ruined fortunes will admit, I will take kind Care of him.—It is too late now, to think of putting him to School. I earnestly wish you would take him into your house, & under your Care, and Get him perfected in writing, & accompts., & use him in your business & breed him up to the law, & take him under Articles for 3, or 5 years & I will pay you whatever annual Sum you see proper for his Board & Lodging, & other expences.—My Dear James, Let me be an earnest Suitor to you to comply with this my request, & you will make me, & the young man both happy, & probably save him from being lost, for a life of Idleness is a dreadful one, especially in Youth.—Under my present Uncertainties I cannot enlarge more at present. At any event, I expect, my debts will be left open to me to receive, & I purpose to send out a power of Atty. to You & George, to collect & Manage.—You will direct & assist, & he can ride about, & act, & I trust may do both me, & himself, good Service.—I suppose, he goes by my Name, of which, as it will be necessary, please inform me. This will employ him, & you will by taking him as your articled Clerk make me the most pleasing return possible for every good Wish you ever experienced from myself, & your good Uncle, who sincerely loved you. Get him perfected in writing, Accts. & french. Books & Cloaths I will find him, & if you chuse it, as soon as my affairs settle, will pay the amot. of his Board & Lodging to your Order here. Let him know, it is my express desire that he will think himself happy in being with You, & doing every thing to merit your kindness And I [*illegible*] happy in the hopes of his being thus settled, & will write him myself soon

If you had recollected the Papers I sent you out, by Mr. Burgwin in 1778, you wd. have observed I had a power to settle the whole of the Legacy to H M's children.[3]—As I understand your last letter, Betsy recovered (thro her husbands) her Share of the 200 bill I sent out in June 1776, or her Share of the Legacy, I dont understand which,—on my Lots,[4]—To enable me to recover whatever Sum She recd. so, or in any other manner from me or my Estate, it will be absolutely necessary for you to send me under such National or other legal proof. (The Seal of the State for instance) as may be legal & satisfactory here, an Accot. of the proceedings, & the Sums actually recovered & recd. & when, in order to enable me to recover it from the Trustee Mr. Wm. Mc.Culloch, who before payment must have Such proofs.—You will please also to send me proofs as above, of all monies on acct. of sd. bill or otherwise, recd by Doley;[5]—I shall depend on your sending me these proofs, by the very first Opportunity. I shall confine this letter to these two points;—both, in your power to Serve & oblige me in & I therefore rest assured of your friendly complyance. May God in his mercy, bless & protect You, & yours, & Me & my future Life,—directing what is—Best for Me, & teaching me to know it!—Ever Yr. affect. &c.

H. E. Mc.Culloh

RC, Iredell Papers, Duke. Addressed "Jas. Iredell Esq. Edenton, State of North Carolina."

---

[1]See JI to Henry E. McCulloh, March 3, 1784, in this volume.

[2]The Carolina Coffee House in London was used as a headquarters by some merchants engaged in trade with America. *PJI*, 1:52n.

[3]John Burgwin (1731-1803), a lawyer and merchant of New Hanover County, held various colonial offices, including serving as Gov. Arthur Dobbs's secretary. In 1775, Burgwin went to England seeking medical care for a broken leg and did not return until the summer of 1778. "H M" is Henry McCulloch. *DNCB*, s.v. "Burgwin, John"; Ashe, Weeks, and Van Noppen, *Biographical History*, 8:61.

[4]See JI to Henry E. McCulloh, March 3, 1784, in this volume.

[5]Dolly McCulloch White was the daughter of Henry McCulloch. JI to Henry E. McCulloh, September 26, 1784, in this volume.

From Samuel Johnston

Hillsborough May 1st. 1784

Dear Sir

I have only a few minutes to inform you that the enclosed should have gone by Genl. Skinner but he did not call on me[1]

The fifth Article of the Treaty has been under consideration of both Houses where it has met with the /most/ illiberal reception they have paid no regard to the recommendations of Congress and there appears a settled resolution against the restoration of any part of the Confiscated property, in arguing Genl. Rutherfurd denied that Govr. Tryon, Govr. Martin,

Mr. Mc.Culloh or Sir Nathl. Duckenfield were British Subjects,[2] I despair of doing any good and heartily wish myself away from this place, Mr. Hooper supported the recommendations of Congress in the House of Commons with the most masterly Eloquence tho without support or success,[3] poor Mc.Laine is laid fast with the Gout, I said every thing that occurred to me this day in the Senate supported by Willey Jones who spoke very sensibly on the same side and tho there was not a word of common sense spoke on the other side it was carried against us by a great Majority. There is a strong party for fixing the Seat of Government at Tarborough.[4] They talk of great Alterations /in/ the Court Law, also of changing the time of holding the Annual Elections & Assembly.[5] I am called from my dinner to write this I will be more particular by Capt Boritz[6]

My Compliments to Mr. Barker & all friends, my love to my Sisters and the Children & believe me, Dear Sir

Yrs.

Sam Johnston

P. S. I have recd. all your Letters

RC, Johnson Collection, NCSA. Printed, McRee, 2:99. Addressed "To James Iredell Esquire Edenton by favr. of Mr. Henley."

---

[1]William Skinner (1728-1798) of Perquimans County was an admiralty court judge, General Assembly member, and during the Revolution, a brigadier general of militia. *DNCB*, s.v. "Skinner, William."

[2]Griffith Rutherford (ca. 1721-1805) was a brigadier general of militia during the Revolution and led campaigns against Loyalists and the Cherokee. He represented Rowan County in the state senate (1777-1781, 1783-1784, 1785-1787) and there continued to wage war against Loyalists by supporting the confiscation and sale of their property and opposing the articles of the Treaty of Peace, 1783, that benefited them. Rutherford challenged the citizenship of those listed in the letter because article five of the treaty, which called for the return of confiscated property, specified that "real British subjects" were eligible for restitution. *DNCB*, s.v. "Rutherford, Griffith"; "Treaty of Peace," *Treaties and Other International Agreements*, 12:11-12.

[3]Article five of the Treaty of Peace, 1783, required Congress to "recommend" to each state legislature to return confiscated Loyalist property. Despite efforts by Samuel Johnston, Hooper, and others, "An Act Directing the Sale of Confiscated Property" passed, which permitted the sale of the as yet unsold confiscated property. "Treaty of Peace," *Treaties and Other International Agreements*, 12:11; Clark, *State Records*, 24:661-664.

[4]Tarborough was nominated along with Smithfield, New Bern, Fayetteville, Salem, Hillsborough, the plantation of John Abernathie in Wake County, and Halifax. Clark, *State Records*, 19:578, 583-584, 587, 623.

[5]On May 28, 1784, the General Assembly established that the annual election of assembly members would begin on the third Friday in August and that legislative sessions would start on the first Monday in October. The April session, which coincided with spring planting, was discontinued. Clark, *State Records*, 24:547.

[6]William Borritz (d. 1803) of Edenton was an agent for Rey and Brandenburg, exporters in Cadiz, Spain, who sold cannons to America during the Revolution. Borritz served in the state senate (1784-1785) and on the Council of State (1789-1790). Mitchell, *North Carolina Wills*, 51; Clark, *State Records*, 19:708-710; *Heads of Families, 1790 Census*, 19; Cheney, *North Carolina Government*, 165, 214.

From William Hooper

May 1st. [1784]

My Dear Sir:

I thank you a thousand times for your attention to me and my wants since you left us. The tea came safely by Mr. Davis: and Mr. Penn has since delivered me your letter inclosing the money. I had been happy to have heard, with a full assurance of its being true, that your health was confirmed.

I have waited with impatience for some time that something might occur in our political operations decisive with respect to the temper of the Assembly, and which might be an earnest to you and every good man in the country, that they intended to avail themselves of the present great occasion to establish a national character, and to do justice to the treaty of peace. My hopes are at an end! This day has put the matter beyond a controversy: and there is not a phrenzy of misguided political zeal—avarice cloaked in the cover of patriotism—or private passion and prejudice, under the pretence of revenging the wrongs of the country—let these be carried to what excess they will—that can give me the least surprise hereafter.

The inclosed resolves, which (supposing they would afford you some satisfaction) I have had copied, are the result of the labors of a committee where Mr. Johnston, Maclaine, and myself, worked for many days.[1] Every resolve but the 5th passed, almost "nem. con." yesterday in the Commons; but that, in spite of every thing I could do[2]—and alas! I labored without support—not a speaker with me but Cummings, whose conduct does him honor, (Mr. Maclaine being ill with the gout)—was rejected, scarce 20 of 80 for it. It fared worse in the Senate. Mr. Johnston spoke longer, with less hesitation, more firmness; and as much sound solid reasoning as I ever heard him or any other man. Willie Jones stept forward in a very becoming manner—their labor was lost! Griffith Rutherford called the objects of the recommendatory clause Imps of Hell. The vote was called, and not ten in favor of the clause of the report which applies to the recommendatory article of the treaty. We are here in the dumps—doubtful of doing any good.[3]

Although the Quakers are at my elbow, urging me to finish; yet I must inform you that in a letter, which appears in the public collection, from Dr. Williamson, there is a passage to this purpose, and nearly in these words.[4] "On the last summer, Mr. Henry E. McCulloh wrote to us: he seemed to be pretty well satisfied that his property would be restored to him; we were, perhaps, pretty well satisfied before that it would not be restored to him." This, be assured, has had its effect.

Any thing in this letter that you may think proper to communicate to Mr. Barker, please inform him is at my desire. Remember me to Mr. Spencer; and do so to him also, assuring him at the same time that I will embrace the first opportunity to write. The Quakers had promised to wait until Monday: they disappoint us. I fear the session will hold till 1st of January. Expect a long letter from me by next opportunity. This family, my dear Iredell, hold you among their own first affections. Remember us to your worthy Mrs. Iredell, and the rest of the good family. I am

ever yours, affectionately,

Will. Hooper.

RC, Johnson Collection (Filed with undated correspondence), NCSA. Printed, McRee, 2:99-100.

---

[1]This copy of the resolves has not been found.

[2]The phrase *nem. con.* means "no one against."

[3]William Cumming, Archibald Maclaine, Samuel Johnston, and Willie Jones supported leniency for refugees and Loyalists.

[4]On Saturday, May 1, the date of this letter, a bill entitled "An Act to prescribe the Affirmation of Allegiance and Fidelity to this State to be taken by the People called Quakers, and for granting them certain indulgences therein mentioned" was introduced in the house of commons and passed on the first reading. The legislation, which became law, included the wording of a loyalty oath and permission for Quakers to wear hats in court. Hooper was at this time a member of the house of commons. Clark, *State Records*, 19:532, 24:593-594; Cheney, *North Carolina Government*, 213.

Hugh Williamson (1735-1819) of Chowan County, a physician and merchant, was a member of the Continental Congress (1782-1785, 1787, 1788) and a signer of the U.S. Constitution. *DNCB*, s.v. "Williamson, Hugh"; *PJI*, 2:106n.

Samuel Johnston to Hannah Iredell

Hillsborough May 15th. 1784

My dear Hannah

Tho I am very unwell I cannot let Capt. Boritz leave this without a line to you, I cant write to Mr. Iredell b[*ut*] inclose you an open Letter for Mr. Barker which, after you have read, be so good as put a Wafer in it and send to him [1]

I have been in a great deal of pain all night and to day if the Captain does not go till to morrow I hope to have it in my power to tell you I am better. My Brother was sick when he first came up but is now pretty well

I repent sincerely my having any thing to do with the Assembly I lose much more to my self than I gain to the Publick. The most illiberal dispositions prevail in most of the Members. they seem determined to hold on upon the confiscated Property I dont believe Mc.Culloh will get back a single <Acre> Acre, <u>but of this say nothing</u>

Mr. and Mrs. Hooper with their Children are well and very kind & attentive to me. I have not heard of Mr. Iredell since he left Roanoke

Give my love to my Sister and her Children, tell Gaby I expect he will be a good boy, if I get a little easier in the afternoon I will write to him. Compliments to Mrs. Dawson

Yours Affectionately

Sam Johnston

17th. I am now very well again. a Bill was brot. in on Saturday for selling all confiscated Property[2] Adieu

RC, Johnson Collection, NCSA. Printed, McRee, 2:100-101. Addressed "Mrs. Iredell at Edenton favd. by Capt. Boritz."

---

[1]A wafer is a concoction of gum and flour used to seal an envelope. *OED*, s.v. "wafer."

[2]See Samuel Johnston to JI, May 1, 1784, n. 3, in this volume.

To Hannah Iredell

Newbern May 20th. 1784.

My dear Hannah.

I have the pleasure to acquaint you with truth that I am a great deal better than when I left you, and have no doubt that Dr. Lenox's prescriptions with the care I take will soon restore my health entirely. None of the Lawyers have come from the Assembly nor have we had a line from one of them, so that I hope the Court will finish on Saturday, and I may [*be*] able to leave this on Sunday. I shall go first to Mrs. Dawson's, and if I don't find you there immediately to Dukinfield.

I flatter myself I shall see you very soon after you receive this letter, which I only write lest by any accident I should be delayed longer than I expect, and you be uneasy about me.

I have my Landlady & her Daughter all to myself, Hay having diverted for the present the Newbern resentment (tho' I don't know that he did so designedly) by a trip to the Assembly.[1]

Give my love to Nelly, & my affectionate respects to Mrs. Dawson's Family & Mrs. Pearson's. God grant, my dear Hannah, I may find you perfectly well—Then will be truly happy

Your most faithful & affectionate

Ja Iredell.

RC, Johnson Collection, NCSA. Addressed "Mrs. Iredell."

---

[1]The "Newbern resentment" refers to John Hay's continuing conflict with the bench. Hay had written an inflammatory pamphlet on the subject, which had not been well received in New Bern. See William Hooper to JI, February 7, 1784, in this volume, and *PJI*, 2:466n.

To Thomas Iredell Sr.

Edenton May 28 1784

My dear & honoured Sir,

I have wrote you several letters within these few months, but not yet been happy enough to receive any from you, which I am very anxious to do, remembering with great gratitude & pleasure the satisfaction I derived from <your> /the/ correspondence you honoured me with before the war, and earnestly wishing for a <revival> /renewal/ of it.[1] I begin to receive letters now & then from my Mother and Arthur, tho' I find several have miscarried, and I am willing to hope the same cause may have <occasioned my be> prevented my having the pleasure to hear from you—My situation in this County is /almost/ as favourable as I could wish it, my attention being entirely devoted to the profession of the Law, which is altogether suitable to my inclination, and my success in it equal to that of any Lawyer here. It is however in this Country a very laborious one, & has already so much affected my health, that I have been obliged to contract my circuit, but thank God, if I have life and health, I have a very fair prospect of gaining an independent & genteel competency by it, tho' there is no such thing <as making> /as/ a large fortune to be expected, or even for a great number of years a cessation from severe business and fatigue—During the war my situation was distressing, but the effect it had on my circumstances I hope soon to get over, & have indeed little reason to complain, when my lot was so much better than that of many thousands.

I was extremely glad to find, by a late letter from my Brother Arthur, that in consequence of your advice he was likely to change his profession, and that you appeared to prefer that of the law for him.[2] I had myself been persuaded, that that in all probability would be a better one, as in his present situation he is altogether dependent on others, and I am satisfied he possesses abilities, & application, <and> accompanied with an uncommon goodness of heart, that qualify him for any thing. Indeed I admire & love him with an extraordinary fervor of affection, and I see your kindness & attention to him, of which he speaks in high terms, with the greatest pleasure. I hope he will be enabled by it to chalk out a path of distinction & honour in which I flatter myself he will one day be distinguished, and reflect, as I am sure there is great reason to expect, lustre on a Family of which he is so great an ornament.

I informed you, that upon reflexion I had thought it best to give Tom an invitation to come & live with me, as the Army was a dangerous situation for him, & he was a burthen on my Mother. I do not find that he has any vices, but the gaiety of his disposition, indulged too much by a military life, has led him into imprudent expenses, which are </indeed/> too naturally to be expected from a young Man in his situation, & who unfortunately has had a very slender education—If I can possibly induce him to apply to my profession, he may do very well here: but if not, I shall be very much at a loss what to do with him. I have given my Mother an invitation to come & live with me also, which I hope she will do, so that I flatter myself /for/ the future the situation of our Family will not be so marked with misfortunes as it has for so many years been. My resources I trust will be sufficient if my life & health be spared to me, the latter of which has for many months, been extremely bad, but it is now beginning to revive—

I hope I have sufficiently obviated in my former letters the cause of your displeasure against me, on account of my taking part with the Americans[3]—Lest any of those letters should have miscarried, I will just again say, that I took no active part till long after the exercise of my office, & all British power, was impracticable—that however mistaken I might be, I really acted from principle, & conceived I <mad> /had/ as good a right to vindicate american privileges <to> /of/ which I was intitled to <a share> /partake/ as any Man in the Country,—that the part I took being evidently disinterested, my sincerity is not reasonably to be doubted, & as Man is only answerable for the errors of his heart, not of his understanding,—and that the mere circumstance of my being an officer of the Crown, & having taken an oath of allegiance, when the office could not be exercised, and the claims of G. B. appeared subversive of american Rights (as I really thought them), no more precluded me from taking an active part, than such considerations prevented many of the greatest & best Men of the Revolution in England taking a most active & decisive part against James the 2—You and I may differ in the application, but I am persuaded we agree in the principles, & as in making the application I could only exercise my own Judgment so I can truly say I did it deliberately, disinterestedly, & honestly—And I hope I shall be excused for <saying> /adding/, that I have frequently rejoiced since, I did not go as many others did, to be a despicable Dependent upon a Crown Pension, & to have disabled me perhaps for any respectable independent situation in life—

As Opportunities may offer very rarely here, I beg the favour of you at other times when you may have the goodness to write to me to direct your letters to the care of Mr. Alexander Diack Merchant in Norfolk, or Mr. William Lindsay Merchant in Charleston.[4]

Mrs. Iredell desires her most respectful Compts. may be presented to you and that you will be persuaded of her sincerely joining at all times in the most earnest wishes for your health & happiness, with, my dear Sir

Your most dutiful & affect. Nephew

Ja Iredell

FC, Johnson Collection, NCSA. Printed, McRee, 2:101-103. Endorsed "Copy of a Letter to my Uncle, May 28th. 1784."

---

[1]See *PJI*, 2:469-472, and JI to Thomas Iredell Sr., February 11, 1784, in this volume.

[2]See Arthur Iredell to JI, February 18, 1784, in this volume.

[3]See *PJI*, 2:469-472, and JI to Thomas Iredell Sr., February 11, 1784, in this volume.

[4]William Lindsay (d. 1786) was in business with his brother Robert at 46 The Bay in Charleston. James W. Hagy, *People and Professions of Charleston, South Carolina, 1782-1802* (Baltimore: Genealogical Publishing, 1992), 3; Caroline T. Moore, ed., *Abstracts of Wills of Charleston District, South Carolina, 1783-1800* (Columbia, S.C.: R. L. Bryan, 1974), 117.

To Catharine Macartney

<Dear Sir,>

<Edenton June 15th. 1784.>

<I received your favours>

Edenton June 15th. 1784

Madam

I had but a few days ago the great pleasure to receive the letter you did me the honour to write me of the 17 Dec. last, & by which I think myself highly obliged.[1] It is not indeed a new thing for any of my Family to be obliged by you, <Madam> /Madam/, but the generosity of the manner with which all your favours are conferred greatly enhances their value. At the time I took the liberty to write you before I knew much of your goodness, but was not acquainted with the whole extent of it.[2] I have since <been informed> /heard/, with an emotion I am utterly unable to express, of the Annuity afforded my Mother by you & Lord Macartney.[3] Heaven only can adequately reward such goodness, but if the most fervent gratitude can in any manner compensate for the weakness of any other return I trust I may assure you of that. My Lord M. & you, Madam have saved one of the best of Women & of Mothers from distress it makes my heart bleed to think of <& as such> /for that alone, if I had not been already bound by innumerable other favours/ I <shall> /must/ ever look up to you both with the most grateful respect & veneration. I am happy to hear also of my Uncle's kind attention to her, & have expressed my ack.n.t. in the best manner in my power to him, as I beg leave to do particularly to you for making my Mother's situation known to him. Mrs. Iredell thinks herself greatly honoured & obliged by your Compliments to her & desires me to assure you in return of her participating with me, as one of a Family she /has the kindness to consider/ in every respect <considers> with /nearly/ as much partiality as her own, in the warmest gratitude for your goodness to them & the most anxious wishes for all manner of happiness & prosperity to yourself, of which your noble relief of the distresses of others makes you so eminently worthy.

I am, Madam, with the greatest respect Your most obliged & most faithful humble Sert.

Jas Iredell

FC, Johnson Collection, NCSA. Endorsed "Copy of a Letter to Mrs. Catharine Macartney June 15 [*illegible*]."

[1]See letter of December 17, 1783, *PJI*, 2:472-473.

[2]See letter of ca. August 1, 1783, *PJI*, 2:432-433.

[3]See letter of May 30, 1783, *PJI*, 2:409-413.

To Archibald Neilson[1]

Edenton N. Carolina, June 15th. 1784.

Dear Sir,

I had not the pleasure to receive your letter of the 6th. Oct. last until long after the date, but should have acknowledged the kindness of it much sooner if I had not been prevented by very ill health, and frequent absences from home upon an extensive Circuit of Courts to which now I devote my whole attention.[2] It gave me great satisfaction to hear of you after so long an interval, and I shall engage with much pleasure in a renewal of our correspondence. I flattered myself indeed, after the Peace had taken place, there might have been an unreserved communication between old Friends, however separated by the war or political sentiments, but the extreme violent spirit that has been excited against the Refugees indiscriminately, on account of the particular ill conduct of some, forbids without great danger the return of any who left the Country after the War began. Some Persons, who were not remarkably obnoxious, have tried it and suffered by it, in spite of every effort of their Friends, and Mr. Johnston and myself in particular, for discountenancing such violence, have lost in this part of the Country at least much of our weight and influence. It is to be hoped this intemperate spirit will subside by degrees, but I am persuaded it will be a long time before any Persons, how respectable in private character soever, who are supposed to have taken any part in the war against America, can find that cordiality of reception among People in general in the Country without which no Gentleman who valued his peace of mind would wish to appear in it. This is very painful for me to feel or to write, but I think it my duty to be explicit on this subject lest for want of knowing the temper of the People you might be unexpectedly drawn into any disagreeable situation, as I have unavailingly had the misfortune to see others for whom I had a very sincere regard.

My own sentiments upon the subject I hope at the same time you will do me the justice to believe, remain unaltered—that no Man is either good or bad, merely for his opinions—that in political questions there is room for almost an infinite diversity of sentiment, among even the wise, as well as Men of <Integrity merely> /little understanding/—and that no Man in a civil war is justly censurable for any thing but insincerity in chusing his side, or in fidelity in adhering to it, or in the course of his political conduct deviating in any instances from principles of humanity and virtue. And I heartily wish, that the termination of the war could have been followed with an oblivion of its offences, tho' I cannot but observe that it was conducted in <many> /some/ respects in such a manner as too naturally to cause a deep and lasting resentment in many who have particularly suffered by it.

This Town flourished during the war, but has been very dull and inconsequential since. That amusing study, the Law, is my principal employment. I make a Circuit twice a year from Hillsborough by way of Halifax and this Town to Newbern—A County Court or two forms an episode, and this is my whole present history.

Are you a Foxite or a Pittite, for I suppose no Man is allowed to remain neuter, nor is the thing possible.[3] Scotland we hear too is putting in her claim for a little more liberty, so that I <suppose>/imagine/ very soon the whole three Kingdoms will be in a flame. /H/as not all this /been/ kindled by the American spark?

Mrs. Iredell, and Mrs. Blair desire their best Compliments to you, and I am,

Dear Sir, with great truth and regard, Your very faithful humble Servant

Ja. Iredell.

FC, Johnson Collection, NCSA. Printed, McRee, 2:104-105. Endorsed "Copy of a Letter to Mr. A. Neilson—June 15th. 1784."

---

[1]Archibald Neilson (ca. 1745-1805), born in Dundee, Scotland, came to North Carolina in 1771 as Gov. Josiah Martin's secretary. He became a merchant and held several positions in the colonial government. Neilson, as a Loyalist, fled to England in 1775, eventually returning to his home in Dundee. *DNCB*, s.v. "Neilson, Archibald"; *PJI*, 1:251n.

[2]See letter of October 6, 1783, *PJI*, 2:454.

[3]Foxite and Pittite refer to supporters of British political foes Charles James Fox and William Pitt the younger.

To Henry E. McCulloh

Edenton June 15th. 1784

Dear Sir,

I received your favours of the 20th. and 25th. Feby., but too late to make any alteration in the terms of your Petition.[1] The reasons of my inserting those two passages in the Petition to which you object were these. As for the words Sterling value I thought adequate compensation implied a full recompense as strongly as the other, but in less exceptionable language, for I am sure had the words Sterling value been inserted in the Petition it would have been rejected at once, as holding forth terms upon which a favour you were earnestly soliciting was to be granted, and implying a want of confidence in our recent paper Emission which would have been deemed disrespectful.[2] Could I have said to them, "Grant Mr. M. his Estate, or he will apply for redress elsewhere," then indeed I need not have been delicate about the expressions, but as I was suing for a favour supposed to be altogether in their own option either to grant or refuse, and for which I did not then know any alternative was in contemplation, & if I had could not without folly have hinted at it, I thought too much care could not be used to avoid <hazarding any offence> /saying anything offensive./

In regard to the other point of Pendence, your former letters expressed the strongest desire of it, and I thought it an ingredient in the Petition that might have some effect.—Notwithstanding these reasons, I should certainly however have accomodated it to your directions had they arrived in time—

I have now the great concern to acquaint you, that your Petition has been presented, and rejected, and in such a manner, and by so great a majority that I am persuaded all further application would be fruitless. Scarcely any Person of any consequence supported it, as I am informed, but Mr. Johnston, Mr. W. Jones, Mr. Hooper, and B. Mc.C.—The latter can give you more particular information, for /he was upon the spot &/ mine principally respects the Senate where Mr. Johnston sat. He and Mr. Jones in that house, and Mr. Hooper in the other, supported your cause and that of others in similar circumstances warmly, but without any other effect than a great diminution of their influence and popularity.[3] A Bill was brought in for the restoration of /the unsold <such> part of/ your Estate, and <that> /those/ of other/s/ <British Subjects, <that had been confiscated or (that was unsold)> according to the recommendatory Article> /that had been confiscated (except Lord Granville's)/, upon condition that within a limited time the Proprietors should become Citizens, or dispose of their Property—but <this> /it/ was rejected, & I believe at the first reading, by a great majority.[4] A Bill was afterwards brought in for the immediate sale of them, but was at length postponed to the next Session, not however from any dislike of the measure, but merely because it was introduced so late they could not settle the mode to their satisfaction[5]— <The next Assembly are to meet at Newbern the first Monday in October—You will perceive, from this detail>, /Thus you will <therefor> perceive/ you are <now> so circumstanced that you may if you think proper consider the rejection of your Petition as a final decision of your Pretensions, or make one effort more—An Effort however from which I am satisfied the smallest hopes cannot be /rationally/ entertained.

Mr. Nash was at the head of the large Majority which opposed any compliance with the Recommendatory article, and he also opposed, and with success, the removal of Obstacles to the bringing Suits according to the fourth.[6] The Preamble however stated it only as doubtful whether such an act was necessary. I should hope the next Session of Assembly would provide for this, but have already seen such a torrent of illiberality and <want> /disregard/ of public faith prevail that I think it is to be questioned.—In the act proposed for selling confiscated Estates, there was even included a provision for the recovery of the Debts that had been confiscated, for the use of the Public, tho' there can be little doubt, I think, but that these, as well as other debts, come within the provision of the 4th. article of the Treaty.[7]

My personal attendance at the Assembly was not practicable, and would have been useless. My very ill health had <obliged me to contract my> /prevented my attending some Courts on my/ former Circuit, which greatly injured my affairs, and prejudiced many of my Clients. I had however resolved, with other Lawyers, to have made a sacrifice of the last, could I have been chosen a Member of Assembly, in which character /only/ I could have appeared with any chance of effect. But tho' Mr. Johnston and myself had been courted to serve the year before, when the interference of the Courts prevented us, our known moderation upon the subject of the obnoxious Articles /(& in regard to me, my being a Relation & Connexion of yours, particularly)/ prevented any application to us this time that enabled me with any propriety to offer myself a Candidate, <(as none of the old Members declined)>, and <Mr. Johnston, who had been chosen before, was with difficulty rechosen> /Mr. Johnston's reelection /for he had been elected, tho' he did not serve /the year/ before,/ was openly opposed—/<My being a relation & connexion of yours was one reason secretly mentioned why I should not be a proper Member.> Thus circumstanced, I had no decent excuse to my clients to be absent upon the approaching Circuit, and as I could not have done it without the utmost distress to my private affairs so I knew I should have met with nothing but <the extremest> mortification from a personal application where not one out of ten would have heard me with any patience. As to my appearing professionally, tho' that might have done in England where Reason upon Subjects of Policy, in the midst of the most violent passions, can be heard, it would have been considered rather with ridicule /here/, for I conceive there was no point <of Law either municipal or national> /peculiarly belonging to my profession/ to speak to, as the subjects of the Recommendatory article appear to me to be altogether at the mercy of the different Assemblies, <in point of authority>, and any thing that could be said in favour of it /<in other respects> from principles of policy or natural or political justice/ would come with much greater propriety and effect from disinterested Members of Assembly, /acting in the express line of their duty, they were by no means inclined to favour,/ than from an avowed advocate of a particular Individual /addressing prejudiced minds in <a manner altogether unusual /as/ that of c[*torn*] upon political subjects certainly is in this Country>/ /an unusual manner/.—All I have spoke to on the subject agree with me in the same opinion, and I hope you will give me credit for being able to form /what I am entitled to think/ a proper Judgment on this occasion, not only from their united Sentiments, entirely concurring with my own, but from my former experience of such an application when I staid several weeks at the Assembly for no other purpose, and did every thing in my power for you with all the delicacy I could think of, notwithstanding which the Senate would not even <grant your case a hearing, and the Memorial I at that time presented for you was treated with some degree of ridicule & indignity out of doors> /refer my memorial to a Committee, but instantly rejected it/, and it did not even escape some degree of ridicule & indignity out of doors

One great object among my particular Friends at the Assembly was such an alteration of the time of its annual meeting as would have enabled the Lawyers who practise at the Sup. Courts to attend it—an alteration was made, but not so as to promote this purpose in any respect, for the only difference is that instead of the first Monday in April it is now to meet the first Monday in October, which interferes exactly in the same manner with the Courts as before, only at a different season.[8] There is to be a new election in August, </& the Assembly are to meet the 1st. Monday in Oct. at Newbern/> and I could easily be a Member now, but it is not <now> in my power <to be present> under any Circumstances to be present at the time it will be held (the first Monday in October) <u>at Newbern</u>, /the place where it is next to sit/ as I am under an indispensable necessity, which no consideration but <unavoidable> /absolute incapacity by/ ill health can change, of being employed the whole month of October, and <until the 12th.> /till near the middle/ of November, at Hillsborough, Halifax, & Edenton Courts, where there are such arrears of business as will not admit without the justest room for censure, & the most distressing Inconvenience /& some injustice/ to Individuals, of any further voluntary delay. Mr. Johnston & Mr. Hooper are in the same predicament, so that I greatly fear the proceedings of the next Assembly will be even more violent /& exceptionable/ than those of the last.

In consequence of the Proceedings I have informed you of I do not imagine Mr. J. J. can have the Indian Land secured to him, for he certainly had no real ground for a demand in Equity as no conclusive Agreement was ever made, and the only expectation I ever had from the suit was that it would occasion a delay in the Sale so as to afford you a chance from a more moderate temper of the People of a restitution in future[9]—That now being out of the reasonable expectation, I conceive that object both to you & him is at an end

I shall not fail to attend to every matter [*inkblot*] you have wrote me as particularly as I can, & write you as I may be [*inkblot*] enabled—

The only Children of <Mr. H. M.> Secretary M. living are Betsey & Dolly, the former married to a very worthy, clever Man, Capt. Joseph Meredith, who probably may deliver you this, the other now a Widow with several children. All the rights to the money due them in Ireland are now vested in Capt. Meredith, his Wife having purchased them before marriage, except Job Parker's share who married Penny, if that entitled him to a part—The purchases were made by Betsey, when there was a danger of other People getting them for trifles—She however gave a Declaration of Trust, which is in my hands, serving only £100, Stg., with /Int./ of Dolly's /share/ for her <own use> /self/, the remainder to be <paid > /</reserved/> /kept in trust/ for her /Sister's/ separate use, /&/ to be <laid out> /paid to her/ either Principal or Interest at Betsey's direction, or to be laid out, with Dolly's consent Signified under /her/ hand & seal in the presence of 2 Witnesses, in the purchase of any Property for her use to be held by Betsey in trust for her Sister (exclusive of any Husband), and in case any of it should remain in Betsey's hands, &c at her Sister's death, then to be divised equally among her children or lineal surviving Descendants—This precaution was taken, as Dolly was very indiscreet, & had already almost ruined herself by marriages—Henry having turned out in a most wretched manner, the purchase from her was absolute.—I believe Capt. Meredith is not going to endeavour to receive this money in Ireland himself [*inkblot*] & that he would prefer receiving it there, as he is trusting Man [*inkblot*] [*to any receipt*] of /the value of/ it in this Country.

Your lots in Town were sold at an Execution at Capt. Meredith's suit for Betsey's share of the £200. Stg. You had received, as she would not receive the money of this Country. I offered her, it being then very much depreciated—I had no means, had I been inclined, to prevent this proceeding, & rather <it> thought you might prefer this mode to a payment of it in England—I long ago acquainted you of this—

Your Son George being a Boy of an uncommon fine capacity, & of a very good disposition, and now of an age to receive an education of which he appears to me to be very worthy, I am endeavouring to obtain a passage for him to you, as he can get no education of any consequence in this Country, and there is /at present/ no Army or Navy to place him in, nor shall We I believe in time of Peace have either.—I wished rather to have received your directions first, but considering his critical time of life (now upwards of 17), and that there is <if not ent> /now/ a very favourable opportunity, which may not happen a long time again, & as he is very desirous of going himself, it appears to me upon the whole to be much better, & that you will think so when you see him, for I am sure he is capable of being qualified to make a figure in life. I shall be under a necessity of drawing upon you for his passage money, as I am absolutely unable to pay it, my disappointment in business occasioned by my ill state of health having left me very bare of money, scarcely enough to pay for common necessaries, & not indeed enough /to enable me/ to pay some money I was <obliged> sometime ago obliged to borrow even for daily expences.

I expect to have an opportunity of writing to you again in a day or two. In answer to your obliging enquiry about my Family, I have not at present any Children, but Mrs. I is now pregnant[10]—

I am, Dr. Sir, Your affect hble Sert.
J. I.

June 20. The Letter of which the above is a copy I have sent by way of Virginia, to the care of Capt. Joseph Meredith who not improbably may deliver it in person. I have since absolutely engaged a passage for George, in a Ship called the Balgra Packet, Capt. George West Commander. I could not get his passage for less than 20 Guineas, for which I must draw on you. Tho' now I suppose it is of no consequence, yet I have endeavoured to obtain the best opinion I could for you about the adventure you spoke of. I do not find there is the least probability you could get immediate payment either in Bills or Commodities, tho' you might probably in a few months. The advance would be uncertain as depending on the demand, which at present is great & the supply precarious, on account of a Paper Emission of about £100000 made since the Peace which has greatly injured our trade. As to the particular articles, the usual Fall goods (chiefly coarse) would have the best chance of a Sale; the particular assortment may easily be known from any Merchant who used to trade here before the war. But I assure you as my private opinion, I think all adventures in Trade here are greatly to be distrusted. Adieu I think of nothing further to add but my sincere and affectionate good wishes.[11]

J.I.

FC, Johnson Collection, NCSA. RC, English Records, Audit Office Papers, Loyalist Claims, NCSA. Printed, McRee, 2:103-104. FC endorsed "Copy of a Letter to Mr. Mc.Culloh June 15th. 1784." RC endorsed "Iredell—15 June 1784."

---

[1]See Henry M. McCulloh to JI, February 20, 1784, in this volume. The letter of February 25, 1784, is included with it.

[2]In 1783, the General Assembly authorized the issuance of one hundred thousand pounds in paper money. McCulloh had reason to lack confidence in this money because the currency issued by the state during the Revolutionary War had drastically depreciated. In fact, monetary depreciation was such a problem that in 1783 the legislature passed a bill that included a chart to determine the worth of the state's devalued paper money. Though the 1783 currency did depreciate somewhat, it proved to be more stable than that issued during the Revolution. It is ironic, considering that McCulloh was concerned about the confiscation of his North Carolina property, that the state backed the 1783 currency with funds obtained from the sale of land seized from Loyalists. Clark, *State Records*, 24:475- 478, 485-488; Alan D. Watson, *Money and Monetary Problems in Early North Carolina* (Raleigh: Department of Cultural Resources, Division of Archives and History, 1980), 41.

[3]McCulloh's cousin, Benjamin McCulloch, introduced a petition on his behalf. To further aid his cousin, Benjamin McCulloch also wrote to Richard Caswell on May 27, 1785, about McCulloh's request for copies of the confiscation laws. Petition of Benjamin McCulloch, November 27, 1784, in this volume; Governors Papers, Richard Caswell, 1785, State Archives. See also letters concerning the petition and the confiscation acts dated June 9, 1784, and December 1, 1784, from Benjamin McCulloch; December 30, 1784, from Willie Jones; and January 22, 1785, from Archibald Maclaine in the Loyalist Claim of Henry Eustace McCulloh, State Archives.

[4]The proposal to which JI refers, called "the Bill to amend and reduce to system the Confiscation Laws now in force in this State," was defeated at its first reading in the house of commons on May 29, 1784, by a vote of 62 to 18. Clark, *State Records*, 19:671-673.

[5]The assembly did pass a bill during the October 1784 session authorizing the sale of the remaining confiscated property. Clark, *State Records*, 24:661-664.

[6]Abner Nash (ca. 1740-1786) had been governor (1780-1781) and a member of the Continental Congress (1782-1783). At the time of this letter, he represented Jones County in the house of commons. The "Recommendatory article" refers to article five of the Treaty of Peace, 1783, which required Congress to recommend to state legislatures that confiscated property be returned to its owners. The fourth article of the treaty prohibited any interference with the collection of debts. In the April session of the General Assembly, a bill was proposed repealing any state law that contradicted the fourth and sixth articles of the treaty. The sixth banned future confiscations and prosecutions of individuals based on their role in the war. The

bill was defeated in the house of commons on its first reading, 37 to 32. *BDC*, s.v. "Nash, Abner"; Cheney, *North Carolina Government*, 213; "Treaty of Peace," *Peace Treaties and other Agreements*," 12:11-12; Clark, *State Records*, 19:674-675.

[7]The law approved in the October session did not include a provision for the collection of confiscated debts. Clark, *State Records*, 24:661-664.

[8]See Samuel Johnston to JI, May 1, 1784, n. 5, in this volume. In a letter to George Hooper dated June 14, 1784, Archibald Maclaine declared, "The annual Assemblies are altered from April to October which is much more suitable to the people in general but makes no alteration with respect to the lawyers." Clark, *State Records*, 17:146.

[9]"J. J." is John Johnston. See JI to Henry E. McCulloh, February 20, 1784, in this volume.

[10]Hannah Iredell gave birth to a son on October 1, 1784. The infant, named Thomas, died two days later. Whichard, *Justice James Iredell*, 247.

[11]The postscript portion of this letter is taken from the Loyalist Claim. Apparently McCulloh hoped to establish trade with North Carolina.

From Edward Rice[1]

Washington 27th. June 1784.

Sir,

Upon reconsidering the matter of suffering a Judgment of Doctor Dickinson to pass against /me/ as Ex<u>or</u>. to Doctor Savage, I am clearly of opinion against it, as it must still run me into a greater Expence.[2] therefore Sir you will much oblige me in not Suffering the Judgment to pass against me on Any account whatever. I am certain Captn. Collins don't mean to press me untill I receive my Tobacco from the State of Virginia, but should Doctor Dickinson urge Capt. Collins to issue his Execution I can raise a sufficient sum of Paper Money in the Course of a fortnight to pay the Debt, but I hope you'll be persuaded that nothing could prompt me to Discharge a just Debt in that manner, except my property's being laid hold of, in which case I do think myself justifiable in getting clear of it in the best manner possible. As to Doctor Dickinsons fears they are entirely groundless, the Security he has from Doctor Savage is perfectly good, and I do declare that I would sell every inch of property I have in the world sooner than the Doctor or any other Man on Earth should suffer on my Account. therefore I hope & request that a Judgment may not be suffred to pass against me. I have the Honor to be with Due respect

Sir Your most Obedt. Hble. Serv*t*.

Edward Rice

RC , Iredell Papers, Duke. Addressed "James Iredell Esqr. Edenton Hond. by Doctor Hicks." Endorsed "Washington 27 June 1784. Edwd. Rice Recd. & ansd. the 28th."

---

[1]Edward Rice was the executor of the estate of Chowan County merchant and physician William Savage (d. 1784). *PJI*, 2:29n.

[2]Rice, in a June 21 response to a letter from JI, stated, "Your Friendly & Polite note I recd. this Morng., & have to request, that you'll do whatever you Conceive to be necessary respecting Doctr. Dickinsons Security for me, & should any matter appear against the Estate of Doctor Savage or myself, you will please to appear or enter a plea against them." Iredell Papers, Rare Book, Manuscript, and Special Collections Library, Duke University.

In June 1784, Samuel Dickinson (d. ca. 1802) filed suit against the estate of William Savage to collect a £4,800 debt. Dickinson, a Chowan County physician, was represented by Samuel Johnston. In the September session of the Chowan County Court of Pleas and Quarter Sessions, a jury ruled in Dickinson's favor. Dickinson then filed a suit against Edward Rice. Dickinson's suit was one of several filed against the Savage estate in 1783 and 1784. Mitchell, *North Carolina Wills*, 135; *Dickinson v. Savage*, 1784, *Dickinson v. Rice*, 1784-1785, Trial, Appearance, and Reference Docket, Chowan County Court of Pleas and Quarter Sessions, State Archives; Estate of William Savage, 1780s, Chowan County Estates, State Archives. See also JI to Hannah Iredell, May 27, 1785, in this volume.

From William Hooper

Hillsb July 8th. 1784

My dear Sir

Should this Scrawl pursue the direction in which I let it off it may possibly Strike Edenton, but like the air Balloon its progress I fear will be excentric so that it is in the chapter of contingencies when or whether ever it will reach you. Its manner of travelling is not very honourable as it has taken its passage in a common cart to Halifax, but the scandal is much alleviated by its having the publick records for its companions.[1] I have consigned it to the care of Hanse Bond at Halifax.[2] And now having given you the history of its intended movements it is necessary that I should come at the subject matter of it.

Know then that the return of Mr. Alfred Moore has relieved us from much anxiety on the score of your health.[3] When you left this I considered it as by no means estabilished against the influence of the air of the lower country. And I was too well acquainted with your devotion [*torn*] Study and business to imagine that you would be disposed to give yourself the indulgence which your delicate habit of body So well deserves of you & so pressingly demands after the severe shock which it has So lately met with. Mr. Moore informs us that tho' you were better than when you left this yet that you were not perfectly /well./ Let me intreat of you not to Stop Short of the latter, but with unremitting care and attention follow up the prescriptions which heretofore have proved so beneficial to you. Give me leave to hope that we may have the pleasure of Seeing you and Mrs. Iredell with us in the course of the Summer. Sure I am that the jaunt and change of air would be beneficial to you both & you would make this family truly happy. You know our accommodations & have experienced our homely fair, Such as they are—they are your's with the most hearty welcome. To your horses I will promise to send them back full and fat. To yourself and Mrs. Iredell what Edenton cannot give an exemption from the fever and ague.

My family enjoy uninterrupted health. I had hopes from several conversations which I had with Mr. S Johnston upon his first arrival here & while it was yet probable that Hillsb. might be the seat of Government that he would fix at lest an occasional /residence/ [*torn*] near this town. When the Assembly had resolved upon a flight to Newbern I thought he became more indifferent about the change he had premeditated. Frequent indisposition while here arising from constant attention to business, the agitation of mind & disappointments which accompanied it & the want of the many conveniencies which he left at home, have I very much fear banished every intention he had of becoming a citizen of this western world. I do not however yet despair and have accordingly wrote to Pennsylvania concerning a tract of land which Mr. Johnston has Seen and very much approves. Should the man close with the terms which I have offered him the land is mine, that is Mr. Johnstons if he chooses it upon the Same terms. It will perfectly accommodate both you and him, and in the neighbourhood may be had two Small pieces of land with houses on them which with very little alteration may answer the purposes of both families until you think proper to build upon a larger Scale. The distance only 3 miles from the town. What say you to this, do not be peremptory in refusal. Let me at lest enjoy the delusion for a while, for it is essential to my happiness.

Mr. Johnston has given you the history of the Session which will be a catalogue of blunders and disappointments. The political frenzy ran high beyond any thing that I had foreseen. Those obnoxious [*torn*] men the lawyers prevented some mischief being done But for them we should have been Saddled with Some acts of Assembly that would have marked the annals of this country with an infamy that no time or atonement could have wiped away. A Court of Chancery with [*blank*] for a Judge.[4] Unlimited Jurisdiction to county courts.[5] A law continuing confiscations and directly violating the treaty of peace.[6] these are a Small part of the evils which died abortions & owe their extinction to the men whom scoundrels reprobate.

I have absolutely refused to Serve in the Assembly again, Butler doubts.[7] At the close of the Sessions his and my conduct were Severely animadverted upon by a few fools in the county, for having patronized the Cession bill.[8] Wretches Stimulated to it by that prince of fops & fools A M whose conduct Mr. Johnston will inform you was highly Singular and unbecoming while the bill was in agitation.[9] To Mr. Johnston he wrote an apology & he called upon /me/ before he left town expressing great contrition & making many apologies, declaring that his heat was aimed at N—h & not at any other of the company,—that N had played double promised him to oppose the bill & then duped him.[10] [*torn*] Johnston will give you the particulars of this diverting Fracas. All clamour here is at an end & Butler & I may go if we choose it. The people only want information to do right.

Mr. Hogg has been at <Hillsborough> Fayette for many weeks. I miss him much as I have not a Single male /in town/ with whom I can converse, and the ladies, God bless them, like Patridges and other very delicate food one cannot feed upon them always, a little Bacon & Greens now and then by way of Solids makes a pleasing variety. Huske left this a few days ago. He and his Betsy were destined for each other Surely. "Happy if aught's happy here on earth." He returns this month to his better half. Mrs. Hogg at the Springs trying their influence, I have very little hopes from them. Hope however is a Sovereign balsam & she has a large portion of it.

Let Mr. Johnston know that Mrs. McCarroll enjoys her usual health and Spirits & the Widow B like the Sun which for some time has been under a [*clo*]ud begins to beam forth in meridian lustre.[11] The Small specks of black which appear upon her, like spots in that luminary serve to beautify what is uncovered. She looks as if she was disposed to make a Second hazard and trust to Providence for the event. Oh the poor dear Doctor! But it is not in flesh and blood to weep for ever & every one who has tried it knows that a living husband is much warmer than a dead one and as the saying is, a live dog is better than a dead Lyon.[12] If you have any thing about your town that could minister comfort to Mrs. Mc Cal., it would be charity to help her. She is as our Hawfielders have it upon Sufferance.

We talk of a post from Halifax hither, as Soon as it takes place you cannot want opportunities to us. In the mean time write as occasion offers to the care of Hans Bond. We hear from Halifax generally once in a fortnight.

We are happily relieved from an insect which threatned destruction to all the grain in the country. The Wheat and Oats are greatly injured but the Indian Corn will escape them

My Wife & daughter & Sons join in most respectful compliments to yourself & Lady Mr. Johnston & his family I Sincerly unite with them. Remember my best regards to the worthy Mr. Barker Mr. Allen & family & my other friends.

Please to Submit this Scrawl to Mr. Johnston as I have not time to write another to him before the last moves & I hope he will consider this as addressed to himself & <consider> counts himself in my debt accordingly

Adieu My dear Iredell Ys.

Will Hooper

RC, Iredell Papers, Duke. Printed, McRee, 2:105-108. Addressed "James Iredell esqe Edenton." Endorsed "Hillsborough July 8th. 1784. W Hooper. Ansd. Aug. 30th."

---

[1]The public records were transported whenever the business of the state moved until 1794 when Raleigh was established as the capital. H. G. Jones, *For History's Sake: The Preservation and Publication of North Carolina History, 1663-1903* (Chapel Hill: University of North Carolina Press, 1966), 64-65.

[2]Hanse Bond (d. 1796) was named entry taker, that is the official who recorded land claims, in Halifax County on August 17, 1785. During the Revolution, Bond served as a marine captain aboard the ship *Caswell.* Raymond Parker Fouts, *Abstracts from the North Carolina Journal, Halifax, North Carolina*, 5 vols. (Cocoa, Fla.: GenRec Books, 1988-1994), 2:99; *North Carolina Journal* (Halifax), June 20, 1796; Appointment of Hanse Bond, August 17, 1785, Minutes of the Halifax County Court of Pleas and Quarter Sessions, State Archives; Clark, *State Records*, 15:221, 24:43.

[3]Alfred Moore (1755-1810) of New Hanover County succeeded JI as attorney general of North Carolina and served from 1782 to 1791. In 1799, he followed JI on the U.S. Supreme Court and remained on the high court until 1804. *DNCB*, s.v. "Moore, Alfred." See also *PJI*, 2:321n.

[4]The house of commons rejected a bill to establish a court of chancery on its second reading on May 24, 1784. John Sitgreaves of New Bern had introduced the bill on May 14. Clark, *State Records*, 19:598, 649.

[5]The General Assembly approved an act during the November 1785 session increasing the jurisdiction of county courts of pleas and quarter sessions. Clark, *State Records*, 24:716-718.

[6]Contrary to the impression given in this statement, the General Assembly continued to support the confiscation of Loyalist property. A bill to amend and systemize the confiscation laws, which would have returned unsold confiscated land to Loyalists, was defeated, as was a proposal to repeal state laws inconsistent with the peace treaty. Clark, *State Records*, 19:671-673, 714-716. For Hooper's arguments in support of these bills, see Clark, *State Records*, 19:714-716.

[7]John Butler, like Hooper, represented Orange County in the house of commons. His doubts were well founded, for Hooper did serve in the house during the 1786-1787 session. Cheney, *North Carolina Government*, 213, 218.

[8]The General Assembly passed a bill ceding state lands west of the Appalachian Mountains to the federal government. The U.S. Congress had requested that states do this to help pay the national debt and to encourage a sense of national unity. The North Carolina General Assembly repealed this act, however, during the next legislative session. They did so for a variety of reasons, including the failure of all states to comply with Congress's request and the unwillingness of the federal government to absolve North Carolina of debts incurred during the Revolutionary War for military campaigns conducted outside the state. Clark, *State Records*, 24:561-563, 678-679.

[9]The only assembly member during the 1784 session with the initials "A M" was Archibald Maclaine, who represented Wilmington in the house of commons. Cheney, *North Carolina Government*, 212-213.

[10]"N—h" is Abner Nash.

[11]"Widow B" refers to Mary "Polly" Freeman, the widow of Thomas Burke. *DNCB*, s.v. "Burke, Thomas."

[12]This adage is from the Bible: "But he who is joined with all the living has hope, for a living dog is better than a dead lion." Eccl. 9:4 RSV.

James Iredell's Will[1]

Edenton August 20th. 1784.

I James Iredell of Edenton in the State of North Carolina, Attorney at law, make my last Will and Testament in manner and form following, viz.

I devise my House and Lot in Edenton to my most justly beloved Wife, her Heirs and Assigns for ever, subject to the restriction herein after mentioned.

I also bequeath to my said Wife all my Negroes,[2] and other personal property of what nature or kind soever, to be hers absolutely and for ever, excepting only a Sum of Three hundred Pounds Sterling which was left me as a Legacy by my much beloved and respected Relation Miss Margaret Macartney of the Kingdom of Great Britain some years since deceased, and of whose will Henry Eustace McCulloh is Executor; which said Legacy I bequeath to the said Henry Eustace McCulloh, hoping he will accept of the same as the best consideration it is now justly in my power to make him for a Debt of Honour, which I heartily regret it has not been in my power fully to discharge, but I cannot think it right to encroach upon what I consider my Wife's peculiar property to make up the deficiency.[3]

I appoint my said Wife and my excellent Friend her Brother Samuel Johnston Esquire Executors of this my will, with full power for them or the Survivor of them to sell my said house and lot in Edenton for the payment of my Debts, if they shall think proper, and in preference if it shall appear to them to be best to the whole or any part of my personal Estate.

My Mother and Brothers will not, I hope, think their names omitted in this Will from any motive of unkindness (for God knows the tenderness of my heart towards them) but because my condition and circumstances in life only permit me to render common acts of justice, and debar me from the pleasing satisfaction of contributing to their ease and comfort, which otherwise I should be most happy in doing.

Edenton August 20th. 1784

"The above Will was signed and sealed by the said James Iredell, and by him published and declared as his last Will nd Testament, in the presence of
W. Borritz
S. Cabarrus Esq. Jurat"[4]

Ja Iredell

FC, Chowan County Wills, NCSA.

---

[1]JI amended his will on April 27, 1790, to include provision for his children. See Will of James Iredell, Chowan County Wills, State Archives.

[2]According to JI's 1784 List of Taxable Property, in this volume, he owned five slaves between the ages of twelve and fifty. It is possible that he owned others outside of this age range.

[3]Margaret Macartney, a distant relative but close friend of JI, died in August 1775. *PJI*, 1:3n; 2:69.

The "debt of honor" pertains to the assistance given the young James Iredell by Henry McCulloh and his son Henry Eustace McCulloh. In 1766, JI's father suffered a stroke and was unable to continue his only marginally successful mercantile business in Bristol, England. The McCullohs helped the financially strapped James find a position as a customs collector in North Carolina. They also loaned money to him and gave him a letter of credit as he left England. *PJI*, 1:xxxvii. See also *PJI*, 2:396-397n.

[4]Stephen Cabarrus (1754-1808), a native of France, was a member of the house of commons (1784-1794, 1800-1805) and for ten sessions was Speaker. As a result of his marriage to the widow Jeanne Henriette Damery Bodley, who was approximately seventeen years his senior, Cabarrus became one of the wealthiest men in Chowan County. *DNCB*, s.v. "Cabarrus, Stephen"; Cheney, *North Carolina Government*, 215-250 passim.

From Alexander Diack

Norfolk Septr. 3d. 1784

My Dear Sir

Since writing you about ten days ago, I have at last had the happiness of taking your Brother by the hand & most sincerely participate in the pleasure your worthy family will enjoy at meeting.[1] As Mr. Cabarrous has been kind enough to insist upon his using his Carriage, he has had very little occasion for my assistance.[2] what he put in my power I have supplied with chearfulness & for my reimbursment you will take your own time & convenience

I have nothing to add on business but that it would give me great pleasure to have the Hillsborough affair concluded & that I rely entirely on your friendship & the Candour of Dr. Burke's Exrs. for bringing it about.[3] I am with respectful Compts. to the Ladies

Dr. Sir your most obdt. hble Servt.

Alexander Diack

RC, Iredell Papers, Duke. Addressed "James Iredell Esqr. Edenton Hond. by Mr. Thos. Iredell."

---

[1]Thomas Iredell arrived from England in late August or early September. In a letter dated August 10, 1784, and written in Yorktown, Va., William Blair told his sister Nelly, "You have Mr. T. Iredell with you by this I imagine, pray let me have a description of him <by the> /in your/ next letter if he is the handsome Genteel young fellow I have heard him described Mr. Black begins to repent his having come in. if he has but half his Brothers merit & should make an attempt to Rival Mr. B., I am certain he will have very great reason." In her response, dated August 28, 1784, Nelly wrote, "Mr. Iredell is not yet come, but we are in daily expectation of his arrival, as Mrs. Iredell has wrote Uncle word that he left London the e[*n*]d. of June to go on Board the Latona bound for Virginia." Charles E. Johnson Collection, State Archives.

[2]"Mr. Cabarrous" is probably Auguste Cabarrus, brother of Stephen. He is mentioned throughout the correspondence between Nelly and William Blair as traveling to and from Virginia. *DNCB*, s.v. "Cabarrus, Stephen." See also Blair correspondence in the Charles E. Johnson Collection, State Archives, and in the Iredell Papers, Rare Book, Manuscript, and Special Collections Library, Duke University.

[3]See William Hooper to JI, January 4, 1784, n. 10, in this volume.

To Mess. Conyngham, Nesbitt, &c

Edenton Sept. 6. 1784

Gentlemen,

We were favoured with your letter of the 16th. of Aug. and take the earliest opportunity to answer it.—It would have given us great pleasure had we found it in our power, & thought it consistent with our duty, to pay the bills you drew on us, but we conceive it is indispensable that the account should be settled in the first place, <without which we should want a sufficient voucher for our justification>, and whenever that is done we do assure you you <should> /shall/ be paid with as little delay as possible. We have already acquainted [*inkblot*] with our reasons <why we think> /for thinking that/ the Account ought only to be settled here, which reasons still appear to us as powerful as ever. The principal causes of the uncertainty of the account, & which only can be satisfactorily explained upon the spot here, are the precarious & dangerous situation of the Country, for a long time in great apprehension of an invasion, <the taking every possession of it by the Enemy>, & a considerable part of it for some time actually in the Enemy's possession, which occasioned <the frequent removal of property, & sometimes an importance of it by order of government. Add to this, the [*inkblot*] loss sustained by an Enemy's galley which a considerable loss actually sustained from a Vessel of the Enemy: in our very port> /losses for which allowances must be made/, and the extreme ill health Mr. Smith had for a very long time before his death which prevented his keeping regular accounts, so that we shall be obliged in many instances to supply this defect from the information of others.[1] Under these Circumstances we think we could not be justified in sending such accounts as we might be at present enabled to do with /some/ certainty, because such would be principally to Mr. Smith's Debit, & the credit he is [*inkblot*] intitled to could not be made out, in many <respects> </instances/> </respects/> /instances/, but from such information as we have above alluded to, and the propriety of which we are sure could only be <properly> /adequately/ judged of here where the Parties concerned might receive the fullest satisfaction of what might at a distance be doubted of or deemed exaggerated—

Besides the great satisfaction we should receive in bringing to a conclusion so capital a concern, & the delay of which hitherto has been a principal means of <keeping> preventing a settlement of the Estate, we are very anxious to have a final settlement, as a Brother of Mr. Smith's with full powers from his principal Residuary Legatees is at present in this Country, & has been here ever since Nov. /last/, waiting for no other business than to settle the Concerns of the Estate with us, and Mr. Collins <in whose care> who has had the <principal> /chief/ management of the Estate since Mr. Smith's death, & is best acquainted with the circumstances of it, will be under the necessity of going to Europe next April /& in his absence <of it> a settlement of it could not be undertaken—/ <The want of this account being settled has been the pr> has <been the principal causes, greatly to his inconvenience, of preventing his going hitherto already been the chief cause of detaining him.> He has already deferred this voyage, greatly to his inconvenience, with the hope of concluding this business, but it will not be in his power at any rate to delay it longer than till next April—

In regard to the Attachment, we are still amenable to the Court, and shall be, we imagine, at least so far as Mr. Morris's interest extends until we are relieved by his putting in a special Security.

We do again assure you, Gentlemen, that it is our earnest desire to have the account settled upon & the fairest & the justest footing, & we shall do every thing in our power to expedite it, whenever you authorise any Person to <enter upon the transaction> /settle/ with us <we shall expedite the settlement by every means in our power> /interposing no difficulties but what our duty shall appear to us to render absolutely indispensable./

FC, Johnson Collection, NCSA. Endorsed "Copy of a Letter to Mess. Conyngham Nesbitt &C.—Sept. 6th. 1784."

---

[1]Robert Morris, David H. Conyngham, and John M. Nesbitt of Philadelphia had filed suit against Nathaniel Allen and others from North Carolina. The parties involved jointly owned two schooners, the *Franklin* and the *Hancock*, that traded primarily in the West Indies. Robert Smith was an agent for the owners when the ships operated from Edenton. Smith had recently died, and Josiah Collins and James Iredell were executors of his estate. During the Revolutionary War, voyages were risky. The area around Edenton was considered particularly hazardous, and the schooners' base was moved to Philadelphia. In 1782, the *Hancock*, sailing out of Philadelphia, was captured. Morris and the Philadelphians complained that Allen and his associates had been duplicitous. According to the plaintiffs, if a voyage were successful the North Carolinians shared in the profits; if the trip were unsuccessful, they claimed that they did not know or approve of the ships' journeys out of Philadelphia and therefore refused to share in the losses. The final settlement was for the plaintiffs in the amount of £4,841.16.11. *Robert Morris et al. v. Nathaniel Allen et al.*, Edenton District Superior Court, Records of Pleadings and Decrees, Equity Court, May-November 1788, 252-298, State Archives.

From Nathaniel Dukinfield

Sulham near Reading. 7th. Sepr. 1784.

Dear Sir,

A few days ago I was favored with a Letter from your brother, with an Account of your being well & that Mrs. Iredell is (in the gossiping Style) in a fair way.[1] As this is matter which will give you much happiness I do with sincere pleasure congratulate you. If I go on as I have begun & continue to do so, this Kingdom will <be> recover the Loss it has suffered by the late damned War & will be in as great a state of Population as at its commencement, for my Wife is now three month's gone with Child. my Boy is a charming Child & I have no doubt but you will soon have a like opinion of your own. 'tis not known, but to a Parent, the pleasure there is in their little Crows & attempts to talk, & scold. I shall expect an early account of your produce. Lady D. joins me in sincerest wishes for Mrs. Iredell's having a good time & getting up again as well as she did.

I wrote to you so fully by Mr. Black that I have nothing more to say on Plantation business.[2] I dined with Captain West on Saturday in London.[3] he wished to make me an Offer for part of the Plantation but I told him I had empowered Mr. Johnston & you to transact every business for me, & that <full> the entire confidence I had in you would not allow me to do any thing of myself, but should be happy to do any thing to confirm whatever you might do. He said he was enpowered by several Person to make me an Offer for the whole, & he thought it worth 6000 Guineas. I told him the Money would be very great satisfaction to me, but I must refer the Transaction to your determination.

You will not be surprized at my being desirous that the Plantation shod. be sold & the Money secured for my Use after my Mother's death, as I have entirely given up all thoughts of settling in Carolina, & if I shod. have a large family, it will be necessary, in order to keep the younger ones from being Carpenters & Mantua-makers.[4] Your Brother has promised to come & see me when it is in his power & I look forward with great hopes that I shall not be long before I enjoy the pleasure of seeing him. my best respects to Mrs. Iredell & all friends & believe me,

Yours most sincerely

N. Dukinfield—

RC, Griffith McRee Papers, SHC, UNC. Printed, McRee, 2:108-109. Addressed "James Iredell Esqr. Edenton North Carolina." Endorsed "Sulham 7 Sept. 1784. Sir N. Dukinfield. Ansd."[5]

[1]"Fair way" is a delicate reference to Hannah Iredell's pregnancy. McRee omits this portion, as he was apt to do whenever pregnancy was mentioned. In place of the euphemism used by Dukinfield, he inserted three asterisks. JI mentioned his wife's pregnancy in a letter to Henry E. McCulloh on June 15, 1784, in this volume. Elizabeth Huske, in a letter of September 14, 1784, to Nelly Blair, wrote: "Let me now congratulate you on the joyfull addition I hear you are likely to have to your family. I am sure it must make Mr. & Mrs. Iredell very happy. they seemed to want nothing else but a little pratler to divert them in their leisure hours." As previously indicated, the Iredells' son died two days after his birth. Iredell Papers, Rare Book, Manuscript, and Special Collections Library, Duke University.

[2]See Nathaniel Dukinfield to JI, January 11, 1784, in this volume.

[3]In a letter of June 10, 1785, in this volume, Dukinfield refers to West as a "friend and relation of [*William*] Brimmage's."

[4]A mantua was a woman's loose-fitting gown worn in the seventeenth and eighteenth centuries. Mantua-maker became synonymous with dressmaker. *OED*, 2d ed., s.v. "mantua," "mantua-maker."

[5]See the letter of January 9, 1785, in this volume, in which JI apologizes for his "long silence." Because of the death of his child and the demands of court, JI waited four months to reply to this letter.

From Arthur Iredell

Crewe Hall Sepr. 7th. 1784

I have lately had the Happiness of receiving two of your Letters, & whilst I thank You, my dear Brother, for your Attention & Goodness in writing them, I cannot but upbraid Myself for a very long, & yet, believe me, a very excusable remissness on my Part.[1] Tom, whom you will have seen a great while before this reaches you, is my Evidence to prove how very unable I was to write even a Letter when I left Town. Since that Time a very tedious Recovery, & which is a better reason, my Ignorance how to convey a Letter to you; (not to insist upon the Privileges of a Man in Love) furnish me with other Excuses to which you will be inclinable enough, I doubt not, to give their due Weight. Yet I plead Guilty to every charge you can bring against me, promising however in future to be every thing you could wish me. I cannot tell you, my dear James, how happy <you have> I am made <me> by the Prospect of being soon, perhaps at this Moment, an Uncle. I was scarcely myself for many Hours after I read Your Letter & now that it is a very old, it is yet a /very/ favourite Idea with me. You cannot want a Godfather or I would propose myself—May I hope for that Honour on some future Occasion?—If that will be an acceptable Bribe, I will promise you the case of my Young Julus, if I am ever to know the Anxieties of a Parent. Say every kind thing upon the Occasion to my Sister for me. I wish it was in my Power to write to her at this Time, but it really is not, & I hope therefore She will excuse me. We have lately had very fine Folks indeed here. The Duke & Dutchess of Portland, Lord & Lady Clermont left Yesterday, & Crewe is now as quiet & comfortable as ever.[2]—The Duke is a very good kind of Man, well bred & with a reserve in his Manner that, I think, becomes him, tho it borders upon Shyness. The Dutchess, who, you may know, is a Cavendish, has all the Amiable Qualities peculiar to that Family—& is upon the whole a charming Woman. But I must not expatiate upon them, or say anything of the rest; unless indeed to tell you that Lord Clermont, who is just come from Ireland, says the Disturbances there are by no means so alarming as We are taught to believe on this Side of the Channel.[3] I had a few Days ago a Letter from my Uncle, in which he acknowledges two Letters from you & says that he shall answer them.[4] So that I rejoice my dear James at the Prospect there is of an happy reconciliation between you. He still presses me very much to abandon my present Profession—but I believe I must not dream of that—By the way, I hear sad Accounts of his Affairs—My Amanda's Uncle, who is no Friend of mine, has made the most diligent Enquiry & has heard, as he says, from the Provost Marshall of the Island, that were his Debts paid, he is not worth a Sixpence. Can that be true? If it be, I shall nevertheless feel extremely gratefull for the Partiality & Attention he has of late shown to me—Oh I have received a Letter from Sr. N Dukenfield to make Enquiries about Carolina. He had not heard from thence a great while. I answered It & when I afterwards received yours of the last date acquainted him with It.[5] Adieu! My dear James, overlook the Abruptness & Incoherence of my Letter, & I shall be less scrupulous about writing them.—Assure my Sister & Tom (to both of whom I shall soon address myself) of my most ardent Affection & think me, as I am,

ever your's

A I

The D of P says there is not a shadow of doubt but that C Fox will succeed at Westr.[6]—

RC, Johnson Collection, NCSA. Printed, McRee, 2:109.

---

[1]See letters of December 31, 1783, in *PJI*, 2:476-477, and February 16, 1784, in this volume.

[2]William Henry Cavendish (1738-1809), 3d Duke of Portland, became viceroy of Ireland in 1782 and was twice prime minister. His wife, Dorothy (d. 1794), was the daughter of the 4th Duke of Devonshire. In regard to Lord Clermont, Iredell is probably referring to Dublin-born James Caulfield (1728- 1799), 4th Viscount and 1st Earl of Charlemont. He was married to Mary Hickman (d. 1807) of County Clare, Ireland. Peter Townend, ed., *Burke's Genealogical and Heraldic History of the Peerage, Barontage and Knightage*, 104th ed. (London: Burke's Peerage, 1967), 492, 2023, hereafter cited as *Burke's Peerage*, 104th ed.

[3]The British government was concerned that American independence might inspire the Irish, as suggested by the formation of armed companies in Ireland. In an attempt to pacify the Irish, Britain granted Ireland legislative autonomy in 1782. Despite the appearance of independence created by this measure, the British still controlled Irish affairs. In November 1783, a group of moderate Irish reformers met in Dublin, with Lord Charlemont presiding, and futilely proposed parliamentary reforms. At the time of this letter, more radical elements in Ireland were campaigning for change. They held a convention in Dublin in October 1784, which drew few delegates and produced insignificant results. A. B. McDowell, "The Protestant Nation, 1775-1800," in *The Course of Irish History*, ed. T. W. Moody and F. X. Martin, rev. ed. (Cork: Mercier Press, 1984), 235-236.

[4]See JI to Thomas Iredell Sr., February 11 and May 28, 1784, in this volume.

[5]See JI to Arthur Iredell, February 16, 1784, in this volume.

[6]Lord Hood and Charles James Fox were elected to Parliament for Westminster in the spring of 1784. Supporters of the unsuccessful third candidate, Cecil Wray, challenged the results. The dispute continued until March 3, 1785, when Hood and Fox were officially declared the winners. *DNB*, s.v. "Fox, Charles James."

From William Hooper

[*Hillsboro 8 Sept. 1784*]

My dear Sir,

I wrote you and Mr. Johnston Several weeks ago Since which I cannot hear of or from either of you.[1] The season of the year has now become truly critical in your part of the country, and from the accounts we have of the health of the Inhabitants of Wilmington I have many gloomy bodings about our friends in your part of the country. It is a melancholy consideration that once in every year at least you run the gauntlet for your lives notwithstanding the utmost regularity and temperance in your manner of living. In this place we know /not/ the Smallest indisposition the natural health of the country is proof against the most vigorous and uniform endeavours of the inhabitants to counteract it[2]

I rejoice with you at the prospect of the approaching increase of your family. May it fulfil the fondest wishes of its worthy parents & live to be a blessing to them.

Before this I Suppose that your brother is with you. He has fallen in at an improper Season but I hope has brought a Sufficient Stock of health to bear him thro the Sickly months & over another fall he will be prepared to encounter it.

Mr. Hoggs Son Walter a lad of 16 his daughter about 12 his cousin about 20 under the conduct of a Miss Cummings a Virgin lady about 70 arrived at Wilmington from Glasgow a few Weeks ago and on Sunday last were all lodged safe & sound in Mr. Hoggs house here.[3] Mr. Hoggs Children & kinsman are very promising their Education has been much attended to and <harps> they have profited greatly

I have now to inform you that a Circumstance has taken place which gives me most Sincere concern. In the year 1778 Peter Mallet applied to me requesting me to undertake in his behalf against a number of people who held possession against him in the Hawfields under titles denied from Mr. Pollok[4]—At that time perfectly unconnected with the latter I engaged for Mallet, drew eight writs in Ejectment & committed them to the care of Mr. Mallet. Nothing more passed upon the subject & I concluded that Mallet had dropped all thoughts of prosecuting the Suits—But to my Surprize a few days ago he informed me that for prudential reasons he had delayed carrying on the Suits, he was now resolved to begin & claims my former promises & will admit of no excuse. I cannot disengage myself and most earnestly regret that I have ever given Mr. Pollok reason to expect my Services Such as they are. Most readily would I detach myself from both parties & forego any pecuniary advantages if Mallet wou'd permit it—but alas this cannot be done. My Zeal for Mr. Polloks. interest too precipitately drew me into this difficulty & I must now pay with much distress of mind the price of my Imprudence. I have wrote Mr. Pollok upon the Subject and must intreat your friendly help to extricate me from this very disagreeable predicament.

I inclosed to you letters <lately> for Mrs. Dawson & Mr. Pollok & Mr. Johnston I hope they got safe to hand.

My Betsy is preparing her packet. My Wife unites with me in offering her kind regards to Mrs. Iredell & Mrs. Blair the young ladies and young gentlemen of your family, & begs with me to be remembered in a very particular manner to Mr. & Mrs. Johnstons family

Let me See you Some days before the court that I may have the absolute disposal of you until the court begins—& if you can, and I am sure that you can, be rustically happy I have the means of making you truley so,

I am My dear Sir Ever & Entirely Ys.

Will Hooper

RC, Iredell Papers, Duke. Addressed "To James Iredell esq Edenton."

---

[1]See William Hooper to JI, July 8, 1784, in this volume.

[2]This is a continuation of Hooper's attempts to persuade JI and Samuel Johnston to move to Hillsborough. See William Hooper to JI, March 15, 1784, n. 9, in this volume.

[3]Walter Hogg (1768-1819) served in the North Carolina General Assembly (1793-1795) and was the first treasurer of the University of North Carolina (1795-1799). In 1786, James Hogg changed Walter and his brother's surname to Alves, which was his wife's maiden name. Robina Hogg (1771-1860) was the third daughter of James and Anne McDowell Hogg. She married William Norwood, a lawyer from Granville County, in 1800. The cousin has not been identified. Miss Cumming was the aunt of artist William Cumming. *Life and Times of James Hogg*, iii, 20-22, 36.

[4]Peter Mallett (1744-1805) of Wilmington sustained heavy personal financial losses during the Revolution in provisioning state and continental troops. As a result, he resigned his position with the army. Some questioned his loyalty, and in June 1783, he was tried and acquitted on charges of treason. After the war he was a merchant and planter in Wilmington. *DNCB*, s.v. "Mallett, Peter, Jr." See also *PJI*, 2:402n-403n.

Hawfields was the name of an area between the Haw and Eno Rivers in present-day Alamance and Orange Counties. The region was once home to Saxapahaw and Sissipahaw Indians. Powell, *Gazetteer*, 217.

From Henry E. Mc.Culloh

Copy

10th. Sept. 1784.

Dear Sir

As Capt. West will hardly arrive at Edenton till Jany., I think it only necessary by this, to acknowledge the arrival of George, & the rect. of your letter by him, & to say in answer, that at the same time, I lament my misfortunes. I am fully satisfied of your friendship.—Ere this reaches you, the Oct. Assy. will probably have determined the fate of my application:—The Particulars of their Proceed[*gs.*] I hope you will be so good as to write me, & I still hope they may prove more favorable than you expected.[1]—If time is given, & my friends think, my Presence at the next Assy. wod. avail, I am rea[*dy*] to come out. At present, it is useless to add more.

I confess the sudden & unexpected arrival of George star[*tled*] me a good deal, but I hope it will prove a useful Step in the [*torn*] Life, in which in my latter letters, I wrote you, I had determined my wishes to have him placed.[2] I have agreed to send him at a very considerable expence, to the same Academy where Mr. Dawson is, and if he applies himself as he ought, in about a twelvem[*onth*] I hop[*e he*] will have obtained a sufficient Stock of Latin & french [*torn*] & have perfected himself in other things, So that he may return to study the Law under you, as I propose, with every necessary advantage.—Here, he can have no hopes of doing anything:—in Carolina, through your kind instructions, and the assistance of my friends, he may certainly do well, and that is the plan, which with his wishes, & your kind Consent, I have determined upon for him, and I pray you most earnestly, to accede to it, & I shall with pleasure, pay you the Expences he may occasion you.

I hope you have, & will be so good as to attend to what I wrote you, favor your Brother, relative to procuring and making me a Remittance. In hopes of hearing from you happily, I am &c.

No. 22. Ironmonger lane London 20th. Oct. 1784.

Dear Sir

Above is a copy of mine to you, of the 10th. Ulto. & wch. [*torn*] came to your hands, sooner than I expected. I think of nothing [*to a*]dd, save that George has been for sometime at Mr. Alexanders, is now under preparation for inoculation, & that over, hopes & means to write to You, & Mr. Earle, & which I have advised him to defer till then. I am hopeful he may turn out to your expectations, and I am sure your [*torn*] & example will be of the greatest Service to him.

As it will assuredly be of great Service to me, I [*torn*] you [*torn*]ve, if not, that you will procure & send me Copies of any [*a*]cts or [*re*]solutions of the Oct. Assy., anywise respecting <u>my Case, or absentees, generally</u>. If time & hopes are given me, I remain fixt in my determination to come out.

I have never seen Capt. Meredith, nor received the letter you sent me by him.

My Respects to all friends, & my best wishes for the Happiness of you & yours, ever attend you. In hopes of hearing from you often and happily, I am ever

Your faithful & Affecte. friend

Henry E. Mc.Culloh.

P.S. Be so good as to forward the enclosed to Cousin Ben, by the first oppy.

RC, Iredell Papers, Duke. Addressed "To Jas. Iredell Esqr."

[1]See JI to Henry E. McCulloh, June 15, 1784, in this volume.

[2]See letters of February 20, 25, March 12, and April 28, 1784, in this volume.

From James Hogg

Hillsborough 14th. Septr. 1784

Dear Sir

This evening among some letters from Fayette Ville they handed to me a letter to be forwarded to you from Mr. Strudwick which I open'd and did not find my mistake till I went to the window and saw it dated from Hawfield I read no more of it and your good nature makes me confident of a pardon.

I have been all this Summer at Fayette ville and return'd home only a few days ago. during my Stay there I never saw a news paper but what was sent to me from Hillsborough and yet notwithstanding its present dulness and all that you can say against it, I foresee it is one day to be the metropolis of this State.

I have not heard, Since I came home if you have given any orders about Sending Mrs. Atchinson's Negroes or how Mr. Johnston Settled with Col. Tuinius or Mr. Mebane the Sheriff.[1] I think he told me that you would take the price in Currency from Mebane but must have hard money or the Negro /wench/ returned from Tuinius. I understand the Latter is about removing to Kentucky and therefore I Suspect it may it may be necessary for me to make some enquiry about his determinations concerning the Negro wench, which I Shall do tomorrow.

It was perhaps my duty to have sent these negroes to you, but I expected to have heard from you about them before now. At any rate I expect to have the pleasure of Seeing you here at our Superior Court, and therefore I need not trouble you more on this Subject at present.

I hope you have kept your health <better> this Season better than usual tho' I am confident you would have a better chance for health & long life by leaving the low Country, and you have now an opportunity of buying lands in this neighbourhood that would accommodate both you & Mr. Johnston. I find the Sheriff has advertised for Sale the tract of land on which Mr. Moore lived and also the one adjoining it. None of them are very valuable, they are much broken and hilly but they are well water'd and have some tolerable meadows belonging to them. I need not Say any thing of the house where Moore lived as I believe both you and Mr. Johnston have seen it and been in it

Ladies Once in such a Town as Edenton could hardly reconcile themselves to Such lodging but it might Serve as a Shelter while you were building a better. Mr. Hooper and his family have been so well this season that I hope the Genius of Debow will inspire him with a Chapter in favour of our Climate. I have mentioned Moore's places because I think you would be no loser by buying them as I <think> Suppose they will sell probably under value. I am sorry I cannot Say more in their favour, but I believe the<y> /lands of both tracts/ are fitted to produce good small grain and <could make orchards> you could have famous orchards on the high grounds

But as I hope to have the pleasure of Seeing you before the day of Sale which is the 7th. of October I Shall be happy to take a ride with you to view them.

The interest you take in my family makes me flatter myself thatt it will not be impertinent to acquaint you that I have got my two children home from Scotland. I beg leave to offer my best respects to Mrs. Iredell and the other Ladies of your family. Be pleasd also to remember me in the most respectful manner to Mr. Johnston and believe me to be with the most sincere respect

Dear Sir Your most obedient Servant

James Hogg

RC, Iredell Papers, Duke. Addressed "Mr. Iredell." Endorsed "Hillsborough 14th. Septr. 1784. <Sam Strudwick> Jas. Hogg. Ansd. (shortly)."

---

[1]James Mebane was the sheriff of Orange County from 1782 to 1784. Hugh Lefler and Paul Wager, eds., *Orange County–1752-1952* (Chapel Hill: n.p., 1953), 355.

To Henry E. McCulloh

[*Sept. 26, 1784*]

Dear Sir,

I have to acknowledge your several letters of the 23d. March, 28th. April, and 25th. May.[1]

With regard to your request as to your Son, I hope you long before this have had the pleasure to see him in England, where he went at his own earnest desire near a month before I received your letter concerning him, by the only opportunity that <I thought might probably offer> /<it was probable would offer> appeared likely to offer/ for a long time without much greater expence, and at a time of life, perhaps the most critical of any part of it, when it was necessary to give him an education (of which he appeared to me very susceptible), or decline it altogether.[2] The latter I was satisfied you could not intend, and the former, even the most humble part of it, he could not have obtained here to any effect. I was sorry to be under the necessity of drawing on you for his passage, but it was then absolutely unavoidable, for the reasons I gave, and I could not suppose this would be an object compared to the injury the loss of such an opportunity might have been attended with. Had he remained in this Country, I certainly would have rendered him all the service in my power, but I really had not room to receive him in my house, the house being extremely small and the Family large and now since my Brother's arrival there is not a single spare room in it. Had my Brother <who is now with me> been </now/> fortunately /now/ of his age, I certainly should have far preferred placing him at some place of education in England to having him <here> /with me/, which is now his only resource, the forbearance so long of the payment of any part of Miss Macartney's legacy to him (/&/ contrary, as I am informed, to her intention expressed in her will) having made him lose, in a manner <now> never to be atoned for, the best part of his youth.—

As to the Certificates, I suppose none but the originals will do, which I will get authenticated in the best manner I can, and have them ready to transmit, but I shall be glad you would point out the conveyance for fear of any accident, which I should not chuse to be responsible for, <or be under any suspicion about> The share Betsey & her Husband recovered was of the £200. Stg., and your lots were sold to pay for it. I did not conceive she was authorized to maintain a Suit for more.—The receipts I have are, Jordan White's (Dolly's Husband) signed by himself, but without a subscribing Witness; none but me being present;—Henrietta's, with her mark, witnessed by B. Mc.Culloch. The proofs of the Recovery must be had from the Court. I suppose the proving of White's hand will be sufficient, though I am concerned now there was no Witness. I could swear to it myself, but doubt if my oath would be proper.

B. Mc.Culloch, I am satisfied, did receive the packet you mention, and it must have been owing to a mistake, I think, that he acknowledged only the letter you mention. Letters for W. Jones & W. Williams were inclosed to me at that time, the former of which I know was received, the latter I have now by me, as he was dead when it arrived. I do not remember whether B. Mc.Culloch's packet was inclosed to me, but I know the letters for Burke, Person, Johnston, Frohock, Spencer, Martin (and I believe, Polk) were forwarded, and many of them received to my knowledge before the Assembly met in October last.[3]

I formerly acquainted you, that there had been no laws passed here since the Peace in regard to British Debts, and that it was the opinion of many, and which had appeared to have the sanction of the Legislature, that such

Debts as were confiscated of Persons named, so that no future process was necessary to ascertain them as objects of Confiscation (which the Treaty would not allow) stood upon the same footing as other confiscated property; that this construction was founded upon comparing the 4th. & 5th. articles together, the latter appearing to consider all confiscated property whatsoever as objects of recommendation only, and the 4th. <(to make it consistent with that construction of the other)> providing for such Debts as either never had been confiscated at all, or belonged to British Subjects unnamed, and of course protected from any future process. Though I doubt much if this be a just, and I am sure it is a very ungenerous construction of the Treaty, yet great pains have been & will be taken to inculcate it, and I fear greatly it will have a legislative sanction.—Should this be the case, you may imagine the state of your debts, and in the mean time your chance of receiving payment of any.[4]

My Brother not being able to bring his Trunk <here> with him when he came, I have not yet received your power, and permit me to say that it is not at all suitable to me to accept it, for if your Debts are to be collected the principal scene of them will be in the back Country, far out of my way, and I have long, a great deal too long experienced the impossibility of satisfying you for any length of time. Your proneness to suspicion of me, which broke out on numberless mortifying occasions before the war, and I find could not be restrained, in the midst of all my distress, during the course of it, makes it equally unworthy of me, and unavailing to you, to continue in a course which would subject me to indignity whenever you happened to be out of humour, & /could/ be of little advantage to you when your business was conducted by a Man irritated by a sense of ill treatment and <of course> /therefore/ wanting that cordiality of attachment (I honestly confess it) which I once felt, and should have ever felt, had your conduct been as uniform as my own. What you said of me about your Son has not been told me by my Brother; I have in vain applied to him for the particulars, which convinces me it must have been unpardonably offensive, tho' I had advanced money for him when I had scarcely enough to purchase myself bread, and put him in a way of life, from necessity not choice, which was pursued by the Sons of many Gentlemen in this Country full as good as yourself.—<I knew of no title you had to be exempted from the common calamities of a Civil War, and if you had I certainly was not qualified to be the Instrument of exempting you from them. My conduct placed me greatly above an inglorious personal ease in the midst of the most imminent public distress. My fortune & that of my Family was inseparably knit to that of the public. I should have been ruined, had America failed,—the utmost economy

scarcely bore me up during the whole of the War. I had no resources to exempt those depending on me from great temporary distress—Your Son, notwithstanding my wishes to serve him, could not avoid sharing in it. Would to God you had only done half as much, in proportion to your ability, for my Mother and Brothers, as I did for him! But you know, you treated them with a neglect, & sometimes I believe an indignity, that can never be forgotten.>

<This circumstance, added to many others which your recollection can save me the trouble of recapitulating (particularly your treatment of my Mother) has <determined me> /made me resolve/ to have nothing /more/ to do with your business as your general Agent but <in> /during/ the interim 'till <the> /another/ appointment <of another> /can take place/ a Resolution <deliberately>, I do assure you, deliberately formed, of which I shall persevere in.>

<I must therefore say, that you are not to depend on me as your Agent, but expect only that I will render you what little services I can until you can appoint another. In the uncertain state of the Country I have mentioned I see no prospect of your getting any money. The Debtors will certainly hold on, until the Assembly express their sense of the Article about Debts.>

<But, for the future, I am resolved to exempt myself from continual>

You are therefore Sir not to be surprized, that this circumstance, in addition to many others which your recollection can save me the trouble of recapitulating (particularly, your treatment of my Mother, which no length of time can efface from my memory) has determined me to circumscribe my /future/ connexion with you within as short a compass as possible, & that I will not, under any circumstances, agree to be your general Agent, nor engage for any thing more but to render you what services I can (which in the present situation of things, God knows, promise to be very little) until another appointment can take place. If my opportunity of serving you has not been equal to my wishes, I can truly say my endeavours <were> /have been/ always faithful & sincere, & so far from <having> /being directed by/ any interested view that had your prosperity in this Country been equal to what it formerly was I should have spoke in this language much sooner. The present occasion rendered <sincerity> /explicitness/ unavoidable, and I heartily wish you /may find,/ in any future connexion of the same kind, more ability & success </(you can never find greater fidelity)/> than you have found in me. My heart wishes you no ill;—but I thank God, it is incapable of disguise, or pretending to an Attachment which I do not feel.[5]

You will oblige me in remembering me to <your> George, and acquainting him that I received his kind letter from the Bar which I should have acknowledged to himself, but for the increasing of postage—

I am &c

James

FC, Johnson Collection, NCSA. Printed, McRee, 2:109-111. Endorsed "Copy of a Letter to Mr. Mc.Culloh dated Sept. 26th. 1784."

---

[1]See Henry E. McCulloh to JI, April 28, 1784, in this volume.

[2]George had probably taken passage in late June or early July before JI received McCulloh's letter of April 28, 1784. He had arrived in England by the time McCulloh wrote his letter of September 10, 1784.

[3]Thomas Person (1733-1800) of Granville and Warren Counties served in the General Assembly for almost three decades. In 1788, he owned eighty thousand acres extending over ten counties in North Carolina and three in Tennessee. *DNCB*, s.v. "Person, Thomas." All others in the list have been identified previously.

[4]This is a reference to the Treaty of Paris, 1783. See Pierce Butler to JI, February 4, 1784, n. 3, in this volume.

[5]Despite JI's harsh words, he continued to assist McCulloh in his effort to retain his North Carolina property and urged him to appear personally before the General Assembly, but to no avail.

To Hannah Iredell

Edenhouse,[1] Oct. 15th. 1784.

My dearest Hannah,

We got here a little after sunset yesterday evening, and had a very pleasant passage, but I was much mortified after I left you in finding we had to cross the Creek, and that the Canoe was not immediately ready, for had I known this I could have staid with you at least a quarter of an hour longer, which short as it would have been would have been more satisfactory than being precipitated away in the abrupt and painful manner I was. Believe me, my dear Hannah, nothing can exceed the extreme anxiety I feel for you, and think of me, tho' separated, as sympathising every moment in the severity & hardship of your situation, tho' at the same time grateful, highly grateful indeed, for your own recovery. The enjoyments of life are so fleeting & transitory, so continually dashed with disappointment & distress, that perhaps upon our dear little Infant's own account we have reason to be satisfied with so sudden & so shocking a removal from us. He is gone to enjoy happiness without going through the usual gradations of misery, and I trust in the goodness of God that tho' we were denied the blessing of his society in this world we may be blest with it in another and a better—God grant, my dear Hannah, I may have the happiness to find you on my return a great deal better. I assure you I will take all possible care of myself, and endeavour by every means in my power to make the continuance of a life so valuable & so necessary to me as agreeable as possible to yourself—I shall depend upon my Brother writing me at all events by every opportunity. I will not fail on my part. Adieu! my dear Hannah. God bless you, & speedily restore your health

Give my love to the Family, & believe me, with inexpressible anxiety & affection,

Ever yours

Jas. Iredell.

RC, Johnson Collection, NCSA. Printed, McRee, 2:111-112. Addressed "Mrs. Iredell Edenton."

---

[1]Eden House was owned by Penelope Johnston Dawson, cousin of Hannah Iredell. It was located in Bertie County across the Chowan River from Edenton and was formerly the home of Gov. Charles Eden. The house was a local social center and a stopover for JI on his travels. *PJI*, 1:88n; 2:227n.

Penelope Dawson to Hannah Iredell

[*E H October 17th.*][1]

Willing to convince you my ever dear cousin that I do not always act from selfish motives or the hopes of reward I take this oppertunity by your brother of sending a few lines without hopes of a return. it gave more pleasure than I can express to all here to find by the return of the people yesterday, you continued to mend & I sincerely pray you may speedily be restor'd to perfect health be assur'd nothing could or should have prevented my seeing you but the severe indisposition I have labour'd under & from which I am not yet recover'd tho I make the best of it. I am really sorry we cannot prevail upon Mr. Iredell to spend a longer time with us which he says he would have done but for his anxiety concerning you & thinking he might be of some little service. his motive was sufficient & I was pleas'd with it indeed I think him a very amiable & agreable young gentleman & congratulate you upon so agreable an acquisition. I hope &

am assur'd that he will be a great comfort to you & his good brother. I hope we shall hear particularly from some of the family how you are & the rest of the invalids I will not fatigue you with a long letter but with my affe. compts. to Mrs. Pearson & the rest & my warmest & sincerest wishes for your perfect recovery conclude myself ever most affy.

Yours

P Dawson

RC, Iredell Papers, Duke. Addressed "Mrs. Iredell" Endorsed "Mrs. Dawson."

---

[1]This letter is presumed to have been written in 1784 because of the reference to Hannah's indisposition and JI's concern for her. Another clue is the mention of Mrs. Pearson, who died later that year.

To Hannah Iredell

Halifax, Oct. 19th. 1784.

My dearest Hannah,

I wrote you a line last night in a manner I am afraid you would scarcely thank me for by Medici who was setting off the instant we came to town, & it was all I could possibly write.[1] Your Brother and I both lodge very comfortably at Mr. Bond's. Mr. Hooper came 2 days before us, & is quite well, & left his Family so, but Mrs. Huske, who is big with child, has been in imminent danger, from which however She is happily recovered. There has been the most shocking mortality among the Children here ever known. Willie Jones, has lost two, Dr. Pasteur one, and Mr. Gilmore, H Montfort, & Colo. Davie their only ones.[2] Most of them died suddenly with Fits. Geddy in the course of a fortnight lost his Wife, two of his Children, & a grandchild, <u>and the day his Wife was buried</u> (whose funeral he attended) dined abroad, & invited company to sup with him.[3] Did you ever hear of such a Brute? Willie Jones is very sick himself & almost distracted with the loss of his Children—Good God! my dear Hannah! how melancholy are these things, & how dreadful (for it is ever present to my memory) is our share in them? To lose too our dear little Creature in the manner we did. Do what I can I cannot be sufficiently composed—A momentary gleam of cheerfulness is succeeded by the most bitter recollection. O! how I shall ever cherish the two days when the dear little Creature was spared to us, but which I too little regarded at the time, being the most distant that any Man could possibly be from the apprehension of what followed. But God grant, my dear Hannah, tho' you cannot forget it, and I cannot wish you to forget it, /you may/ think of me, & how necessary your health & tolerable peace of mind is to me, who live now only on the hopes of enjoying all possible satisfaction in your society—Excuse me to my Brother—I cannot write to him, tho' I am forced to be so unreasonable as to desire him to write to me—. Let him know, & your Sister & Family, how affectionately I think of them. God bless you!—. Let me find you almost quite well, & I will still look forward with hope & cheerfulness. Remember me too to Mrs. Pearson.

I am ever Your most affect.

Jas. Iredell

RC, Johnson Collection, NCSA. Printed, McRee, 2:112-113. Addressed "Mrs. Iredell Edenton."

---

[1]Cosimo de Medici's (fl. 1767-1789) history is obscure. During the Revolution, he served as an army officer in the Patriot cause. De Medici, however, apparently had a taste for gambling and a disdain for performing his duties, which resulted in the convening of a court-martial, the results of which have not been found. *DNCB*, s.v. "Medici, Cosimo de"; Babits and Howard, *Fortitude and Forbearance.*

[2]Of the thirteen children born to Willie and Mary Montfort Jones, eight died before reaching maturity. One of their daughters, Mary, died on June 29, 1781. Dr. Pasteur is Charles Pasteur (d. 1794), who represented Halifax in the house of commons (1785) and served as county sheriff. Mr. Gilmore has not been identified. Gilmore or Gilmour was a common name in Halifax County at this time. H. Montford is Henry Montford of Warren County, who was married to Sarah Edwards. William R. Davie married Sarah Jones, niece of Willie Jones, in the spring of 1782. *DNCB*, s.v. "Jones, Willie"; Blackwell Pierce Robinson, "Willie Jones of Halifax," pt. 2, *North Carolina Historical Review* 18 (April 1941): 169; *PJI*, 2:82n; Mitchell, *North Carolina Wills*, 396; Cheney, *North Carolina Government*, 217; Ashe, Weeks, and Van Noppen, *Biographical History*, 6:378; Robinson, *William R. Davie*, 137.

[3]While Geddy has not been identified, it is clear that this is not a reference to John Geddy (1748-1799) of Halifax, a prominent silversmith, Patriot, and legislator. John Geddy's wife, Patience McKinnie, whom he married in 1768, lived until 1814. *DNCB*, s.v. "Geddy, John."

From Michael Payne[1]

Newbern Octo. 22d. 1784

Dear Sir

this day I expect we shall be able to make a House of Commons.[2] theres three members wanting for the Senate, which I hope will arrive in the

Course of this day. I had summoned to attend the next Court the following Gentlemen as Witnesses in my Suit vs. Mary Lee,[3] Robt. Davidson, who proves the demand I made for the property, William Harrisson Senr. Jno. Stubbs Senr. Sarah Stubbs and John Jordan who will prove the Negroes and other property to belong to Richd. Fagan and given to Enoch Fagan, also Francis Ward of Martin County who proves the Will of the Old Man and the Will of his son Enoch.[4] if my presence should be necessary at the Trial please to inform me as per the next post tho I do not know what service I can be on the Trial as you have all the papers and all the Witnesses Summond that I know will be of Service and I am afraid there will be so few Members over a Majority that I should be very hard push'd to get leave to return. the Inhabitants of this Town are very sickly scarce a Day passes but one or more leaves this World this has been the Case ever since I arrived here. Genl. Green has been here Confoundedly frightned on Account of Bank's Death. the Genl. has been Security for that Man to the Amt. of £60,000 Sterlg. it was always suspected that the Genl. was in partnership with that Gentn. and that the money that was sent on to pay the Contl. Officers & Soldiers was given to Banks to pay for part of the purchase made at Chas. town. should this appear to be true as many think it will the Genl. will loose <much> a great Share of the good Character he has maintained to the Eyes of the World.[5] I hope Mrs. Iredell and self enjoy a better share of health and then when I left Edenton. excuse this scrawl as the post is just setting off. I should be exceeding happy to hear from you as per the next post

I am Dear Sir Your Obedt. Huml. Serv

Mich. Payne

RC, Iredell Papers, Duke. Addressed "James Iredell Esquire Edenton." Endorsed "Oct. 22d. 1784. M. Payne. Ansd. Nov. 1."

---

[1]Michael Payne (1740-1803) of Chowan County served in the house of commons (1781-1782, 1784-1785) and the state senate (1785). Massengill, *North Carolina Votes*, 46.

[2]The General Assembly did not officially convene until the following Monday, October 25, 1784. Cheney, *North Carolina Government*, 214.

[3]Payne was the administrator of Mary Fagan's estate in the case of *Michael Payne, ad. of Mary Fagan, v. Mary Lee*. Mary Fagan was the daughter of Enoch Fagan (d. ca. 1777), and Mary Lee Fagan was his sister. Why Mary Lee's surname was omitted from the case name is unclear. Enoch's father, Richard Fagan (d. ca. 1773), left his house and land to his wife, Sarah, and upon her death to Enoch. Enoch, who predeceased his mother, stated in his will that the property left to his mother, that was intended for him upon her death, should go to his daughter Mary. Sarah died

in 1783, and Mary Lee Fagan was the administrator of her estate. The case appears to have centered on the disposition of this property. On May 13, 1785, a jury found in favor of the plaintiff and awarded £430 in damages. The suit was continued in 1787 and appears in 1788 records as a "non suit." Edenton District Superior Court Records, State Archives; Estate of Sarah Fagan, 1784, Tyrrell County Estates, State Archives; Stephen E. Bradley Jr., *The Wills of Tyrrell County, North Carolina, 1729-1811* (Keysville, Va.: Stephen E. Bradley Jr., 1990), 24-25.

[4]Robert Davidson [Davison] was a justice of the peace in Tyrrell County in 1796. John Stubbs (d. 1790) owned plantations in Martin and Tyrrell Counties. Sarah Stubbs was Sarah Fagan's niece. When Sarah Stubbs's parents died, Sarah and Richard Fagan raised her. John Jordan of Tyrrell County was the son of Sarah Fagan from a previous marriage and the stepbrother of Mary Lee Fagan. Francis Ward witnessed the wills of Richard and Enoch Fagan. A. B. Pruitt, *Abstracts of Land Entries, Tyrrell County, North Carolina, 1778-1794* (n.p.: A. B. Pruitt, 1991), 109; Bradley, *Wills of Tyrrell County,* 24-25, 40, 66; Francis L. Stubbs, ed., *Thomas and Mary (Everett) Stubbs of North Carolina and Some of Their Descendants*, vol. 1 (Columbia, Mo.: Francis L. Stubbs, 1997), 3, 7.

[5]In 1782, American general Nathaniel Greene accepted personal financial responsibility for a contractor named John Banks in order to obtain food and clothing for his troops. When Banks died in bankruptcy, Greene was saddled with insurmountable debts and had to sell almost everything he owned. Greene spent the remainder of his life on an estate confiscated from a Loyalist and given to him by the people of Georgia. *DAB*, s.v. "Greene, Nathaniel"; *National Cyclopædia of American Biography*, s.v. "Greene, Nathaniel."

To Hannah Iredell

Halifax Oct. 24th. 1784.

My dearest Hannah,

I had once the fairest prospect of being now on my way to you, instead of writing you a letter, but the scandalous dilatoriness of the Judges, & their indifference about the trial of causes, has occasioned the necessity of our meeting again tomorrow, & possibly also on Tuesday. My mind was greatly relieved, & indeed made very happy by the receipt of your charming & unexpected letter by Medici. Thank God for his Goodness in restoring you so fast, and which is a blessing I must continually think of when the memory of our dear little Boy affects me, as it often does, very severely. The loss was dreadful in itself, but the manner & circumstances of it such as I cannot bear to recollect. Good God! What happiness this shocking Incident has deprived us of! I can too well sympathise with other melancholy Sufferers in the same way, & feel greatly for poor S. Cooke & his Wife.[1] The Daughter they lost was a remarkably fine & healthy one. I am glad Mrs. Cabarrus bears her loss so well.[2] Tho' now undoubtedly it must be very painful, her good Sense must certainly every day more & more reconcile her to it. I heartily rejoice in Mr. & Mrs. Pollok's good fortune.[3] My health is really better, and your Brother has preserved his full as well as usual—

Adieu! my dear Hannah. Remember me to your Sister & the Girls, & Mrs. Pearson, & think of me, as I truly am,

Ever most affectionately yours

Ja. Iredell.

RC, Johnson Collection, NCSA. Printed, McRee, 2:113. Addressed "Mrs. Iredell Edenton."

---

[1]Silas Cook Jr. (1753-1798), a native of Rhode Island, moved to New Bern ca. 1783 and became clerk of court, a position he held until his death. He was married to Ann Lechmere (d. 1807). Their daughter, Elizabeth (b. 1780), died on October 10, 1784. Thorne, *Heritage of Craven County*, 112-113; Mary Louise Stapleford, *Cedar Grove Cemetery* (New Bern: Historical Records Survey of North Carolina, 1939), 12.

[2]Henriette (b. 1777), daughter of Stephen and Jeanne Henriette Damery Cabarrus, died October 16, 1784. *DNCB*, s.v. "Cabarrus, Stephen."

[3]This a reference to Mr. and Mrs. Cullen Pollock. Their son died within a month of the date of this letter. Thomas Iredell Jr. to JI, November 19, 1784, in this volume.

To Hannah Iredell

Newbern Nov. 18th. 1784

My dear Hannah,

We arrived here only yesterday morning; having proceeded along with great moderation, going no further than Dr. Lenox's on Sunday for fear of the low grounds of Skewawky, and making very easy journies afterwards.[1] Your Brother is surprizingly mended, and if he has now at any time any fever he is scarcely sensible of it. For a day or two he was very unwell, but thank God he is now in as good health as he has long been. My cold was troublesome to me on the road, but is now a great deal better. I had an excellent sleep last night which has been of great service to me. We have very good accomodations, all three being in one large room at Mrs. Carruthers's, and a bed for each of us.[2] I thank you for your kind letter by Andrew.[3] I have not been unmindful of your injunction to take good care of your Brother & myself, as our moderate Journies testify which he was willing to conform entirely to our direction, & it was owing to us /(Mr. H &

myself)/ that we did not leave Dr. Lenox's on Sunday. We are in the midst of Politicians, but find nothing is yet certainly concluded. The repeal of the Cession Bill to Congress is likely to pass,—I mean the Bill for the cession of the Western Lands—But there will be, I believe, no alteration about the Courts. Mr. Nash had a majority of 30 against him in the vote for Governor.[4]

I have scarcely had a minute to spare since I came here. As usual, a great deal of business. I truly assure you, my bowels are in much better order than when I left home, & my cold is a great deal better. I am very careful of it. You may rely too on the good account I have now the pleasure to give you of your Brother. Your Brother saw Mr. & Mrs. Mackenzie at Skewawky. I did not. She had had a sore throat, but was <well> a good deal better & about again. Miss M. tolerably well. But your Brother I imagine will write himself. Excuse me to my Brother & Nelly for not writing. I have not half time for what I have to do if I could enlarge it. Give my love to them & your Sister, & believe me, my dearest Hannah, with inexpressible tenderness & truth,

Your most faithful & affectionate

Ja. Iredell

RC, Johnson Collection, NCSA. Printed, McRee, 2:113. Addressed "Mrs. Iredell Edenton."

---

[1]Skewawky and its various spellings refer to Thomas Hunter's plantation at Williamston in Martin County. *PJI*, 2:147; Powell, *Gazetteer*, 456, 536.

[2]A John Carruthers operated a tavern in Craven County as early as the mid-eighteenth century. Watson, *History of New Bern and Craven County*, 35.

[3]Andrew was a slave who often traveled with JI and served as a courier. James Iredell's List of Taxable Property, 1784, in this volume. See also letters from Jean Blair to Nelly Blair, Iredell Papers, Rare Book, Manuscript, and Special Collections Library, Duke University.

[4]The General Assembly repealed the Cession Bill, as JI predicted, and passed two acts changing the dates of court sessions. One statute established that as of January 1, 1785, sessions of the superior courts of law and equity would begin in Halifax on April 17 and October 17; in Edenton, on May 3 and November 3; in New Bern, on May 20 and November 20; and in Wilmington, on June 6 and December 6. A second law altered dates for sessions of the county courts of pleas and quarter sessions in six counties. Abner Nash and Richard Caswell were the nominees for governor. Clark, *State Records*, 24:664-668, 678-679, 688-689; 19:436.

From Thomas Iredell Jr.

Edenton 19th. Novr. 1784

Dear Brother,

I embrace the opportunity of writing to you a few lines by the French Consul who setts out for New bern tomorrow.[1] I was very happy in having it in my power to forward the copy of the Will time enough for you to take it with you, I am afraid you would find it ill wrote, I however was desirous as you seemed so anxious to have it to finish it as soon as possible which made me hurry it over.—I am sorry to hear of the Reflection cast on our Assembly by the detection of Theft by in one of the Members and so paltry a theft too as he had a particular letch for that amusement it is a pity he did not thieve more like a Gentleman.[2] The Assembly they say have dismissed Mr. Cock from the Office of Clerk[3] pray is not that an Infringment on the Judges right. If so I should suppose it will cause great contention between those two Powers.—Mr. Pollock has lost his little Boy they have really been very unfortunate in not having been able to rear any of their Children.—I have wrote three long Letters to go by Captain Cross to Charlestown one to my Mother one to Arthur and one to my Uncle, I have taken care to let each of them know your <before> being at New bern prevented your writing I am afraid you was not able to get that <c> Affidavidit finished time enough to forward by the Packet—. I was very sorry to hear Mr. Johnston was so unwell when he set out I however hope as the weather was favorable after your crossing The Sound he has not felt much inconvenience from his Journey I beg my most respectful Complits. to him.—And believe me to be with the greatest truth and sincerity Dear Brother,

your most affectionate Bror.

Thos. Iredell

RC, Johnson Collection, NCSA. Addressed "James Iredell Esqr. Newbern."

---

[1]This is probably a reference to Du Chesnel. See John Stokes to JI, March 26, 1784, n. 1, in this volume.

[2]Edward Clay, who represented Caswell County in the house of commons, was accused of stealing money from a store in New Bern. The shop's operator, a Mr. Haryon, reported that Clay stepped behind the store's counter and slipped money into a glove that he was wearing. The house conducted an investigation on November 10-11, which resulted in Clay's expulsion. Cheney, *North Carolina Government*, 214, 344; Committee of the Whole House, November 10-11, 1784, General Assembly Session Records, October-November 1874, State Archives.

[3]William Cocke became clerk of court in Washington County in August 1777, the same year that the western North Carolina county was created. The following year Cocke was elected to the house of commons but was prohibited from serving because he was also clerk of court. In 1782 and 1784, Cocke was elected to the state senate from Washington County and seated. The assembly passed legislation in November 1784, however, prohibiting any person from serving in the legislature who held another public office from which he received income. The county Cocke represented was ceded to the federal government in 1790 and became part of Tennessee. Clark, *State Records*, 15:221, 24:685-686; Cheney, *North Carolina Government*, 203, 209, 212, 341, 1302; "A Bill to Prevent Persons Holding Offices of Profit from Enjoying Seats in the General Assembly," Senate Bills, October-November 1784, General Assembly Session Records, State Archives; David Leroy Corbitt, *The Formation of the North Carolina Counties, 1663-1943* (Raleigh: State Department of Archives and History, 1950), 216-218.

To Hannah Iredell

Newbern Nov. 20th. 1784.

My dear Hannah,

I had great pleasure in receiving your kind letter by the Post, and having such favourable accounts of your and the Family's health and the chearfulness of the two eternal Opponents, who seem always quarreling but when in a private tête a tête.[1] Thank God your Brother's Family are getting better. His Hiccough left him at Dr. Lenox's, and he has been long entirely clear of it, and is in as good health & spirits as he has had for a long time. My cold, which was really a bad one, is wearing away fast, owing to my prudence in abstaining one whole day from the Court, in spite of a thousand teezing solicitations. But the consequence is, I am now in a condition to bear & comply with them.

—This evening came on the election of public officers. They are as follows, the number not being yet quite complete, one delegate & 3 Counsellors being still to be chosen—

Delegates—William Blount, John Sitgreaves, Timothy Bloodworth, Adlai Osborne, and Charles Johnson.[2] (Their time to begin next November. Speight left out, because after that time there was but a little while he could serve.)[3]

Counsellors—Colo. Leach, John Hawks, Armstrong, and James Kenan[4]—

Treasurer—Memucan Hunt (for the whole State.)[5]

Comptroller—Francis Child—

Mr. Nash put in nomination for Delegate, & not chosen. The Repeal of the Law ceding Western Lands has past. I think of no other of importance yet passed. The Assembly will certainly I believe break up next week, & to dispatch business disgracefully are to meet tomorrow—It is very uncertain when you may receive this, but I risque it. Your Brother thinks it may be necessary for him to return by Bath to see Palmer.[6] Make an Apology as before to my Brother & Nelly, Give my love to them, &c. and believe me ever

Most affectionately yours

Ja. Iredell.

RC, Johnson Collection, NCSA. Printed, McRee, 2:114. Addressed "Mrs. Iredell Edenton—."[7]

---

[1]The "two eternal Opponents" may refer to Nelly and Peggy Blair, who lived with Hannah and JI for a while.

[2]The following delegates were selected on November 20, 1784, to attend the Continental Congress. William Blount (1749-1800) of Bertie and Craven Counties was a member of the house of commons (1780-1784) and state senate (1788-1790), and a delegate to the U.S. Constitutional Convention. He had been selected as a delegate to the Continental Congress in 1782 and would be chosen again in 1785. Timothy Bloodworth (1736-1814) of New Hanover County resigned from the Continental Congress in 1787 to fight against the ratification of the U.S. Constitution. He later served in the U.S. House of Representatives (1790-1791) and the U.S. Senate (1795-1801). Adlai Osborne (1744-1814), a lawyer and land speculator of Rowan and Iredell Counties, resigned from the Continental Congress in 1785. John Sitgreaves of Craven County and Charles Johnston of Chowan County were also elected but there is no record of their attendance. The reason, in part, for the absences and resignations was the prohibitive expense incurred by delegates attending the Congress in New York. *BDC*, s.v. "Blount, William," "Bloodworth, Timothy"; *DNCB*, s.v. "Bloodworth, Timothy," "Osborne, Adlai"; Cheney, *North Carolina Government*, 658-659, 741n; Samuel A'Court Ashe, *History of North Carolina*, 2 vols. (1925; reprint, Spartanburg, S.C.: Reprint Company, 1971), 2:55.

[3]Richard Dobbs Spaight (1758-1802) of Craven County, who had been selected as a delegate to the Continental Congress on three previous occasions, was chosen on November 22 as the final delegate, but he too resigned in 1785. He would later serve three terms as governor (1792-1795) and as a member of the U.S. House of Representatives (1798-1801). *DNCB*, s.v. "Spaight, Richard Dobbs"; Cheney, *North Carolina Government*, 658-659, 742n.

[4]The following were chosen as members of the Council of State on November 20, 1784. Joseph Leech (1720-1803) of New Bern was an Admiralty Court judge (1783-1787) and colonel in the militia. He would be chosen again for the council in 1785. John Hawks (1731-1790), a native of England and resident of New Bern, was the architect who designed Tryon Palace. He would be reelected in 1785 and

1786. James Armstrong (d. 1794) of Pitt County was a Revolutionary War officer and member of the General Assembly (1788-1790). He was elected to the Council of State again in 1788. On November 22, 1784, Robert Burton, Thomas Eaton, and Abraham Sheppard were selected to complete the council. *DNCB*, s.v. "Leech, Joseph," "Hawks, John," "Armstrong, James"; Cheney, *North Carolina Government*, 164-165.

[5]Prior to becoming state treasurer, Memucan Hunt (1729-1808) of Granville County had been treasurer of the Hillsborough District. His tenure as state treasurer was marred by a controversy involving the payment of fraudulent claims for military service. He was never charged with wrongdoing, however. *DNCB*, s.v. "Hunt, Memucan."

[6]William Palmer of Beaufort County was the son of Robert Palmer (1724-ca. 1790). The elder Palmer, a member of the Royal Council and an aide to Governor Tryon, returned to England in 1771, leaving his North Carolina holdings in William's hands. William, who supported the Revolution, died ca. 1785, and the Palmer property was confiscated. *DNCB*, s.v. "Palmer, Robert."

[7]On the back of this letter is a poem written in Hannah's handwriting with the preface: "The following lines were written by the late Duke of Dorsen to a friend who pressed his Grace to marry for the sake of a large fortune." Hannah Iredell may be referring to Thomas Sackville (1536-1608), 1st Earl of Dorset, rather than Dorsen. He was a poet, playwright, and holder of various positions in the English government, including lord treasurer for life. This wealthy favorite of Queen Elizabeth I would have had no need to marry for money.

The Petition of Benjamin McCulloch

[*November 24, 1784*]

To the Honorable The General Assembly of the State of North Carolina,

The Petition of Benjamin Mc.Culloch Esquire, on behalf of Henry Eustace Mc.Culloh Esquire, one of the Persons named in the Act of Confiscation,

Humbly sheweth,

That the said Henry Eustace Mc.Culloh, being conscious that he has never taken any active part in the War against America in any manner whatsoever, and that he is only chargeable with an inoffensive residence in Great Britain, where he had for the greatest part resided many years before, and in which he was induced to continue to reside by the distressed and melancholy situation of his only surviving Parent, who had unfortunately lost all his Family but himself, is earnesstly desirous to have an opportunity in person of laying his case before the Legislature, and imploring a restoration of such part of his property as remains yet unsold.

Your Petitioner therefore, on behalf of the said Henry Eustace Mc.Culloh, most humbly prays that your honorable Body will be pleased to suspend the sale of such part of the property formerly belonging to the said Henry Eustace Mc.Culloh as remains yet unsold until the next annual meeting of the Honorable The General Assembly.[1]

BMCulloch

FC, General Assembly Session Records, NCSA. Endorsed "The Petition of Benjamin Mc.Culloch In the House of Commons 24 Novr. 1784 read & ordered to be sent to the Senate with the Confiscation Bill. By Order J. Hunt. C H."[2]

---

[1]This petition is in JI's handwriting.

[2]John Hunt (d. 1807) of Franklin County was house clerk from 1778 to 1806. Mitchell, *North Carolina Wills*, 256; Cheney, *North Carolina Government*, 203-251 passim.

From Arthur Iredell

Novr. 27th. 1784—

You have indeed, my dear Brother, the greatest Reason to be offended at my long, & as you may think, inexcusable Silence, for even you, I fear, will not be inclined to make all those Allowances for me which my Situation intitles me to. You are now an old Married Man, & have probably forgotten what it is to be in Love, to be held in Durance honourable, & to be every thing but what we ought to be, capricious, negligent, & above all forgetfull. "Brush up Your Memory," as we familiarly say in England, fight all Your Battles over again, be the "fallen, fallen, fallen, fallen" Darius (that is, poetically myself) & you will then have more [*Compassion*] for the vanquished Hero of the Day.[1] Apropos—call Tom into Your Counci[*l*.] He is by this Time, I have no doubt, the very humble & sighing Admirer of some beautifull Carolinian, & the persuasive Eloquen[*ce*] of his Plaints will speak powerfully for me.

To be more serious, I have neither Time nor Matter to amuse you with political Information. A Rupture between the Dutch & the Emperor is the grand, if not the only Topic of the Day, & of that You will hear fully from other & better Authority.[2] Our domestick Situation is just as it was—Pitt continues first Minister, with the same Cabinet that he sett out with; tho Arrangements are every day talked of & must sooner or later take Place, if he retains his Post, as there is indubitably a Want of Harmony in the Cabinet. Lord Camden, your favourite (tho by the way a shabby Politician) & the D of Grafton are Persons talked of for Office.[3]

To be still more at home,—Your Mother continues, I thank Go[*d, as*] well as usual.—Yet I am by no means satisfied with the Life She le[*ads*] Would to God She were with You! I see no near Prospect of Happiness for her on this Side the Atlantick. For myself, I am precisely as I was, a Candidate for better Fortunes, but hitherto unsuccessfull.—When, my dear Brother, will our Sky clear itself? When shall I have The Happiness to embrace you & my dear Sister, & be more known to You than I am?. The Time will come, I trust, when I shall have a roof to cover You in your native Country, & I cannot tell you the Joy with which I often anticipate this, & form Schemes of Happiness in which you are all of you included. But I will not dream of fancied <Happiness,> especially as I may by this Time riot in the Enjoyment of real Happiness—for Mrs. Iredell has before this made me of greater Consequence than I ever was. I am quite weighed down with the Load of Dignity which is necessarily attached to the Character of Uncle, & I fear (to borrow a word or two from Johnson) the Levity [*of*] my Joy will not so far counterbalance the Ponderosity of my Pride, as to make my Company even tolerable to Persons of diurnal Acquaintance.[4] In plain English, I am above measure elated at an Event which portends so much good to me. Let me know every thing about it as soon as possible. And let me put in my Claim as early as possible for the Care of the younker, whether male or female, when He, She, or They (You are a Lawyer) shall stand in need of an English Education—I can only cease to trifle by closing my Letter, which I shall therefore do instantly—I am going to write a few Lines to my Sister. My dear Fanny, & her Sister Mrs. Bayley, to whom I am very particularly attached, desire to be affectionately remembered to you & Tom—& I am ever my dear James,

Your's most Affecttely.

A Iredell

My best Wishes to Tom

RC, Johnson Collection, NCSA. Printed, McRee, 2:114. Addressed "James Iredell E[*sq*]r. Edenton North Carolina America." Endorsed "Nov. 27. 1784 Arthur Iredell. Ansd."[5]

---

[1]Darius III (380-330 B.C.), king of Persia, was defeated by Alexander in 334 B.C. and again in 333 B.C. The quotation "fallen, fallen, fallen, fallen" is from John Dryden's "Alexander's Feast, or the Power of Music" (1697). *The Poetical Works of John Dryden*, ed. George E. Noyes, Cambridge Edition (Boston: Houghton Mifflin, 1909), 731-733.

[2]The Treaty of Münster of 1648 closed the Scheldt River to non-Dutch traffic. Emperor Joseph II objected to this stricture on the trade of Austrian territories in the

Netherlands and, beginning in 1781, took steps to reopen the river. A series of clashes occurred between Austrian and Dutch forces, culminating in the Dutch seizure of an Austrian ship on October 3, 1784. War appeared to be inevitable. The matter was peacefully resolved, however, by the Treaty of Fontainebleau in November 1785, under which the Scheldt River remained shut to Austrian shipping. Goodwin, *New Cambridge Modern History*, 8:272-274.

[3]Charles Pratt (1714-1794), 1st Earl Camden, was lord chancellor (1766-1770) and president of the council from 1782 to 1783. He returned to that post on December 1, 1784, and served until his death. Augustus Henry Fitzroy (1735-1811), 3d Duke of Grafton, was prime minister (1768-1770) and lord privy seal (1771-1775, 1782-1783). *Burke's Peerage*, 104th ed., 426; *DNB*, s.v. "Pratt, Charles"; Jeremy Gregory and John Stevenson, *The Longman Companion to Britain in the Eighteenth Century, 1688-1820* (London: Longman, 2000), 56, 58, 59, 401.

[4]Arthur Iredell is paraphrasing Samuel Johnson (1709-1784), an often-quoted author, lexicographer, and literary scholar, and the subject of James Boswell's famous biography. *DNB*, s.v. "Johnson, Samuel."

[5]See JI to Arthur Iredell, March 6, 1785, in this volume.

To Nelly Blair

Edenton Dec. 13th. 1784.

My dear Nelly,

Your request for a letter came very unseasonably, just as I was sittng down to dinner & your aunt & Sister were going to occupy my ink & table, so that I have to scratch this scrawl at a distance getting a drop of ink at a time. I hope as your purpose for crossing the sound was not answered you don't mean to stay much longer, unless you can prevail on Mrs. Dawson & her Family to come & spend their Christmas with us, in which case I give you full permission to stay to accompany them, and under that word may be sent for myself as my Deputy, my Brother, to attend you all over, to commend I must wish for, & hope to receive—My Brother's constly omission of it I cannot now to become fashionable; & therefore wish for you to ascertain its right which I assure you is at present almost continually violated—This is all I can possibley write now, except to desire my respectful & affectionate Compl. to Mrs. Dawson & Miss Penny, and my best respects to Miss Young & Miss Jenny Lenox,[1] and to assure you, my dear Nelly

I am ever Most affectionately yours

Ja. Iredell.

RC, Johnson Collection, NCSA. Addressed "Miss Blair Eden House."

[1]Jenny Lenox was the daughter of Dr. Robert Lenox.

From Nelly Blair

Eden House 15th. December[1]

I am very much obliged to you my Dear Uncle for your short letter the other day[2]—you need not have been in such a hurry tho', for the Negroes did not leave Town till 4 o clock next day—I press'd Mrs. Dawson very much to give me leave to desire you or your Brother to attend in Uncle Sams barge about next Sunday week, but I could not prevail. she says if it is only on Miss J. Lennoxs account she must stay at Home—for she poor Girl dare not go to Town, or any where else, from this House where her Father has fix'd her, without his leave, which he takes care to put it out of Her power to get by not coming near her. Mrs Dawson thinks his only reason, the last time he came over, for staying a Night & part of a Day at Balgra—was <that> /because/ he was offended with her for writing him word that she should be very glad to see him, but beg'd he would not bring over a Dr. as he had intended because it was very uncertain after the Dr. was here whether or no Cousin penny would be bled.[3] besides that my Cousin had petion/ed/ to have it put off till she went to town—which she purposed to do in a short time—Mrs. Dawson seems to think he is offended that she should have the most distant idea of <staying> leaving home while it was convenient for him or his, for her to stay at it, & upon my word I beleive so too. it was by the Canoe Peggy went over in Mrs. Dawson wrote & by the return of it he sent Miss J word (without so much as his Compt. to the rest) to pack up her clothes & be ready for he should call for her next Day before breakfast. she poor thing was up at Day light & after plaguing herself to Death. he staid at Balgra /all that time/ without ever calling for her or sending her a single message—

You must excuse me for not writing to my Aunt & peggy this time—tell them it has absolutely /been/ as much as I could do to write the inclosed (which I must get the favor of you to direct to Sam—& send by the next post) & this scrawl to you—remember me Affectionately to them—& tell them as Mrs. Dawson & Cousin P—has wrote—my writing is of the less consequence however I shall not omit thanking them for their letters to me next chance—tell your Brother I am very sorry-he should be the only one in the family that won't get a letter. tell him I have been trying to prevail on—Miss J—or Miss Gracy to write to him—but they will not tho' they very readily join the other Ladies in desiring their Compts. to him & yourself

You often have <often> said my Dear Uncle that long letters are very ridiculous—am sensi/ble/ this is so—I ask ten thousand pardons for it & hope in a fit of passion you will burn it—

Your Affectionate Neice

H Blair—

Please to send us a few pens—

RC, Johnson Collection, NCSA. Addressed "Mr. Iredell, Senior Edenton."

---

[1]While the date on this letter does not include the year, 1784 is written on the envelope.

[2]See JI to Nelly Blair, December 13, 1784, in this volume.

[3]Balgray, located west of Edenton on the Chowan River, was the home of Cullen Pollock. Cousin Penny is Penny Dawson, daughter of John and Penelope Dawson. *PJI*, 1:xliii.

The ancient practice of extracting blood to cure illness was used frequently and with much enthusiasm in the eighteenth century. A barber-surgeon, using either a lancet to open a vein on the arm or hand, or leeches, usually performed the procedure. Guy Williams, *The Age of Agony: The Art of Healing, c. 1700-1800* (Chicago: Academy Publisher, 1986), 13-14.

Jean Blair to Hannah Iredell

Dukinfield[1] 24th. Decr. 1784

My Dear Sister

I got here Wedensday eveng. & was much disapointed at not meeting you as I had heard you were over. I never heard a word from this since I went up till I got to Docr. Lenox's & then I hurryed down as fast as I could. I send my Brors. Boys to your care John has long had a bad Cough Docr. Lenox says it must be taken care of he is to be in town on monday & I promised my Bror. to speak to him about him & if he did not come to speak to Docr. Ramke about him I intended over with the Corps but Miss Vail & Mrs. Pembrun say if I go they will & it is perhaps necessary that somebody should stay here till my Bror. comes.[2] be so obliging as desire Peggy to take care of her Cousins Cloaths & see that they have clean ones sometimes & she must mend their Stockings till I come my Bror. John will be down about the middle of next week with your Pork. it was my fault that the Corps did did not go over last night. Patty was very anxious to go & talked as if she was of much consequence, that Mrs. Johnston was very unwell that James was sick & she should be wanted but I knew the funeral could not be over last night & I thought they were better here than at Hayes & indeed I was afraid Mr. Iredell would get sick if he went out again last night for when they got in here yesterday he was almost black with the cold.[3] the corps has been quite long enough out of the ground. the sooner she is burried now the better if it is not done to day & I am wanted you must send for me. I have got you a little Tallow but nothing else. desire Peggy if you please to send me over a few clean cloaths in the Trunk that she had at Edenhouse by the first opportunity I want a little linen my Flanel Coat & worsted Stockings & a pr. of Pockets my love to all friends I am my dear Sister

Affectionatly Yrs.

J. Blair

RC, Johnson Collection, NCSA. Addressed "To Mrs. Iredell Edenton."

---

[1]Dukinfield, the plantation formerly owned by Nathaniel Dukinfield, was located west of Edenton on the Chowan River. Dukinfield, a Loyalist living in England, had given the property to his mother and her second husband, John Pearson (d. 1777). *PJI*, 1:xliii, 52n; Nathaniel Dukinfield to JI, September 7, 1784, in this volume.

[2]The "Corps" refers to the body of Margaret Pearson, mother of Nathaniel Dukinfield. She died on December 21, 1784. Miss Vail is probably Mary Vail (d. 1816), daughter of John Vail (d. 1765) of Chowan County. Elizabeth Vail Pembrune was the wife of Dominick Pembrune (d. before 1790), a Chowan County physician. The name Pembrune is spelled in various ways throughout the correspondence. JI to Nathaniel Dukinfield, January 9, 1785, in this volume; Mitchell, *North Carolina Wills*, 526; *PJI*, 2:339-340.

[3]Patty was probably one of Samuel Johnston's slaves.

Tax List

James Iredell's List of Taxable Property, 1784.

Lands. - A Moiety[1] of 1180 acres of Land (by estimation), at Tuckahoe on Trent River in the County of Jones.

Do. of 320 acres (by do.) on Reedy Branch in the same County; near the above.

Do. of 200 acres (by do.) on Beaver Creek in the same County.

Do. of 2130 acres (by do.) in the County of Onslow, on the North East and North West Branches of New River.—

Town Lots - One House and Lot in Edenton.

Free Males. - One only of 21 years of age or upwards.
a moiety of an Island in chowan river Cond. 400 acres.

Slaves (between 12 & 50)} Sarah, Peter, Andrew, Edy, and Sukey.

Ja. Iredell.

FC, Chowan County Tax Records, NCSA.

---

[1]Moiety means half. *OED*, s.v. "moiety."

1785

To Henry E. McCulloh

Edenton January 6. 1785

Dear Sir

I have now the misfortune to acquaint you, that <your last> /another/ Petition /for you/ <was> /has been/ presented & rejected, & that a Law has passed for the immediate sale of all the remaining confiscated property.[1] <Your Petition in the name of B. Mc.Culloch> The Petition was in the name of B. Mc.Culloch, & strongly supported by Mr. Nash, notwithstanding which, after some promising appearances of success, it was rejected by a considerable majority.[2] Had it passed that house, it most probably would have been rejected in the Senate, where a clause that had been inserted /& sent from the Commons/ in favour of Bridgen & Waller at the express recommendation of Dr. Franklin, was <rejected> /thrown out/, and I believe without a dissenting voice.[3] Clauses concerning the collection of confiscated debts were proposed by Persons not friendly to the Bill in general, with an equivocal exception "of those Debts protected by the Treaty." The Members could not agree upon the mode, & <the clauses were at length thrown out as they were introduced at the very last of> & it being at the /very/ conclusion of a very long session the clauses were at length rejected not however from any dislike of the principle, for it is a prevailing <People> /opinion/ among many who are at present the most leading People in this Country, that the Debts of Persons whose Estates were confiscated <u>by name</u> are not protected by the Treaty, upon the principle I formerly wrote you.[4] The petition presented for you was only for a suspension of the sale of your estate until next Session, that you might have an opportunity of appearing in person, as this method was thought the most eligible.

I had not an opportunity of seeing Mr. Montfort either at Halifax or Newbern, he not being in either place when I was there, but B. Mc.Culloch told me he expressed himself strongly disposed to avail of your generous offer, and that he would endeavour to remit you 40 hogsheads /of Tobacco/ this Winter.[5] He has advertised for sale the greatest part of his property, <so that he may perhaps be able to remit you remittance twice over> which <will> /I should suppose would/ enable him to pay with much greater ease. <I doubt not at all the integrity of his intentions, but he is unfortunately too fond of play, so that he cannot be so absolutely depended upon as <his> if his life was more regular, and his expences more defined.> B. Mc.Culloch expressed a desire to make you a remittance on his own account, but not knowing but he may be called upon for it by the Public, & under the necessity of paying twice, thought it would be too hazardous. You may readily suppose most of your other <Creditors> /Debtors/ would be still less willing to incur such a risque, & therefore I do not think you have a chance at present of receiving any remittance but of the Tobacco which I mention above, and which I heartily hope you may receive, it being so evidently the interest of that person to pay it. As to myself, what I owe you [on account of the office][6] I consider a debt of honour, & payable to you only /at all events/.[7] As such I stated it when formerly called upon & shall again if again called upon, but I trust you must be sufficiently sensible of the distress & embarrassment of my circumstances, occasioned by a war which annihilated all my resources, not to be surprised that it is not in my power at present to pay any part of it. I have the utmost difficulty, notwithstanding a very extensive practice, in procuring money enough for my Family's common support, & occasionally paying little debts in the country that I contracted during the war.

I beg the favour of you to send me a Copy of my Account, as I was surprised to see so large a sum <of> as £376.17.10. Proc. Money charged against me as the Ballance I owe you [in the Proc. account], & think I must be entitled to some Credits not given me. You remember your allowing me the difference between one third of the profits of your office, which Mr. H[*ardy*] used to receive, & one fourth he agreed to receive in consideration of my doing the business.[8] This sum I did not charge when you were here, as it would have left no ballance in your favour, and I wished you then to receive all the money /you/ could. But I presume you can have no objection to its being charged now. And I never charged you for postage of letters, tho' I paid a great deal, but how much it is impossible for me now to ascertain, as I confess I was a great deal too careless in keeping accounts, which I have frequently had reason to regret, and am now endeavouring to rectify.[9]

I thought till lately that Mr. Mc.Guire had gone, as <I unders> he intended it, to England last Summer but I find he has deferred it till the Spring.[10] He has sold off every thing here, & vested his property in England. <I shall write to him> /If he does not pay you sooner he undoubtedly will on his arrival in England/, but <think all application to Kenan with> /In/ regard to <others of> your <Creditors> /other Debtors/ I think great caution is to be used in the present uncertainty about the property of your debts. I shall do however in respect to them every thing I think best, but they appear to me very unfit objects for you to rely at all upon while the present uncertainty continues.

I received a few days ago your letter of the 8 Sept. by Capt. West. I was perfectly satisfied, that you would upon reflexion approve of my consenting to George's going <home> /to you/, tho' for want of your previous approbation I did it with reluctance.[11] But he could have obtained no education that would have been of any service to him here. In regard to your proposal for me to take him, I do sincerely assure you that I would render him any service in my power with the greatest pleasure, but my Family is at present so very large, & my house so small, that <it cannot> we are as it is put to the greatest inconvenience, and I have earnestly pressed my Mother to come & live with me, which I hope she will do, as she has too long suffered misery & distress in England it makes my heart bleed to think of. We shall then be eight in <Family> the house altogether, <and I cannot ask Mrs. Iredell to be put to the an additional inconvenience> a Family that will not admit of any increase.[12] If I was to continue to live in Edenton, he could easily be boarded at some other house in town, and I would instruct him in the study with all my heart, but our healths have been so much injured here, that Mr. Johnston & myself think of removing to a healthy situation in the Piney woods on the southside of Roanoke River, and there <perhaps> the difficulties could not be removed[13]—Thus am I circumstanced. I have candidly told you my situation, and I do assure you with the greatest truth that in any particular whatsoever, where I can serve George, I chearfully will. But I see no prospect of my being able to do it in this <particular> manner, for the reasons I have given you.

<Agency> &c I have already wrote you, that I could not undertake to be your general Agent. My present course of business puts <me> /it/ entirely out of <the way of> /my power to/ render <ing> you essential service, which cannot I am sure be done by any than without devoting more time to it than I can possibly spare, and journeying about in a manner I cannot do without abandoning my practice Your back Country debts would be [, at least the greatest part,] almost entirely out of my reach, and others I am sure I could not pay the attention to they require. <You must therefore, Sir, if you please as well for your own sake as mine, appoint> /It would be deceiving you were I to say or pretend otherwise. It is therefore necessary you should appoint/ some other person, & consider my declining this task as peremptory & irrevocable.

You will oblige me in remembering me kindly to George, and I trust will believe that I feel the greatest regret in being obliged to send you such melancholy, tho' faithful accounts of your affairs here. I am heartily sorry my forebodings have been so exactly verified. I flatter myself, however painful the communication was, it may however have enabled you to lay the ground-work of a handsome compensation in England. It will give me the greatest pleasure to be informed of such.

I am, Dear Sir, Your very affectionate humble Servant

Jas. Iredell

FC, Iredell Papers, Duke. RC, English Records, Audit Office Papers, Loyalist Claims, NCSA. Printed, McRee, 2:116-117. Addressed "Henry Eustace Mc.Culloh Esqr. No. 22 Ironmonger Lane, London. By favour of Capt. Hooker." FC endorsed "Copy of a Letter to Mr. McCulloh January 6. 1785." RC endorsed "Letter from Jas. Iredell Esq. dated Edenton No. Carolina, 6. Jany. 1785 recd. 21st. April. 85—."[14]

---

[1]See the petition of November 24, 1784, in this volume. During the November session of 1784, the General Assembly passed "An Act Directing the Sale of Confiscated Property." Clark, *State Records*, 24:661-664.

[2]While Abner Nash supported McCulloch's petition, he had led opposition in the previous session to the implementation of articles four and five of the peace treaty, which would have helped Loyalists collect debts and recover property. See JI to Henry E. McCulloh, June 15, 1784, in this volume.

[3]John Adams and Benjamin Franklin had expressed support for Edward Bridgen's attempts to recover his confiscated North Carolina property. Bridgen was a London merchant who Franklin called "a Zealous friend to the cause of liberty and America." In June 1785, a house and lot on Dock Street in Wilmington that had belonged to Bridgen were sold for £2100. In December of that year, the General Assembly passed legislation restoring Bridgen's property and paying him for what had been sold. Mr. Waller was also a London merchant, but no additional information about him has been found. Clark, *State Records*, 18:536, 603-604; 19:435; 24:762; Pruitt, *Abstracts of Sales of Confiscated Land*, 81; DeMond, *Loyalists in North Carolina*, 168.

[4]For a list of the rejected clauses, see Clark, *State Records*, 19:832-835. Confiscation "by name" refers to a list of individuals in a 1779 state law whose property was to be seized. Nathaniel Dukinfield and Henry Eustace McCulloh were near the top of the list, and JI represented both of them. Clark, *State Records*, 24:263-264.

[5]Benjamin McCulloch, in a letter of December 1, 1784, to Henry E. McCulloh, wrote, "I applied to Mr. Montfort respecting the protested Bill of exchange, he said the offer was so generous that he would endeavor to comply with it & would contrive to remit Mr. Boyd 30 or 40 hogsheads of Tobacco this winter or next spring & the ballance would pay as quick as he possibly could." Loyalist Claim of Henry Eustace McCulloh, State Archives.

[6]Phrases in brackets in this letter were added by JI to an earlier draft, as shown in the copy of this letter in Henry E. McCulloh's Loyalist claim. Loyalist Claim of Henry Eustace McCulloh, State Archives.

[7]For more on the "debt of honor," see James Iredell's Will, August 20, 1784, n. 3, in this volume.

[8]Robert Hardy (d. 1781), often referred to as Captain Hardy, was a merchant in Edenton. Following Henry E. McCulloh's departure from North Carolina and before JI's arrival, Hardy apparently had served as the interim customs official. Before JI's marriage, he had lived with the Hardy family. *PJI*, 1:20n, 218n; 2:259.

[9]The copy of this letter in McCulloh's Loyalist claim reads "and of late have endeavoured to rectify." Loyalist Claim of Henry Eustace McCulloh, State Archives.

[10]Thomas McGuire (fl. 1754-1802) of Bladen County was a member of the Royal Council, a vice-admiralty court judge, and North Carolina's last colonial attorney general. Despite being a Loyalist, he remained in North Carolina until July 1785, when he returned to England. *DNCB*, s.v. "McGuire (or McGwire), Thomas"; Cheney, *North Carolina Government*, 22; *PJI*, 1:248n; Gregory Palmer, *Biographical Sketches of Loyalists in the American Revolution* (Westport, Conn.: Meckler Press, 1984), 549.

[11]See Henry E. McCulloh to JI, September 10, 1784, in this volume.

[12]The Iredell household comprised JI and his wife, Hannah; his brother Tom; and five slaves. James Iredell's List of Taxable Property, 1784, in this volume.

[13]The copy of this letter in McCulloh's Loyalist claim reads "Mr. Johnston & myself have resolved to remove to a healthy situation. . . ." Loyalist Claim of Henry Eustace McCulloh, State Archives.

[14]The closing, address line, and endorsement are taken from the copy of this letter in Henry E. McCulloh's Loyalist claim. Loyalist Claim of Henry Eustace McCulloh, State Archives.

To Nathaniel Dukinfield

Edenton Jan. 9. 1785[1]

Dear Sir

<I flatter myself <the causes which have occasioned my long silence> you will have the goodness to excuse my long silence, when I acquaint you of the principal & reel cause of it.>

I wish, after so long a silence occasioned principally by a very unhappy event, & the engagements of an extensive Circuit, it was in my power in some measure to atone for it by agreeable information, but it unfortunately is not. My Feelings have been severely tried in this unhappy climate both for myself & Friends. Mrs. Iredell, on the 1st. of October, was safely delivered of a very fine Son, with every appearance of their both doing extremely well, but in a manner too sudden & <recoll> unexpected to be recollected without the utmost distress he was snatched from us in 2 days. Judge, my dear Sir Nathl. what situation mine then was. To lose with scarcely a moment's preparation an only child, so long & so anxiously wished for, & to have at the same time to dread its putting an end to his

Mother's life. God in his mercy saved me from this calamity, but the escape was a very critical one, for her state of health & mind for many days after was enough to drive one to despair, & her recovery, tho' at last effected, slow & melancholy in its progress. I thank God she is at present in perfect health, as I am at length myself, after being far otherwise for upwards of a twelvemonth with a disorder in my bowels I found the utmost difficulty in getting rid of.

I wish to God it was in my power to soften the melancholy account I am now going to give <to> you /of your own loss/, & which it is unfortunate that you are obliged to receive without any preparation in a letter. I know, tho' it is not <to> premature, it will affect you deeply and I sincerely sympathise with you on so distressing an occasion. Your Mother, after being a considerable time in a very ill state of health, died at Dukinfield on the 21st. of Dec. last.[2] She had for a good while had a severe disorder in her bowels, & it at length terminated, I believe, in a consumption of them. She was at our house great part of Sept. & Oct. & had been very sick then, but got much better, & then felt so great in anxiety to go home & attend to her affairs that our most urgent solicitations could not prevail on her to stay, a circumstance we regretted very much at the time, & still more when we had the misfortune to hear <sometime afterwards> of her illness at home, tho' this did not appear so dangerous till a very few days before her death. <Two days before, on the 19th., I attended her at her desire> She had made a will during the war, at which time your name could not /be/ safely mentioned, & therefore the whole estate was apparently given to <Mr. Pollok &> Mr. Johnston, relying upon <their> /his/ honour to secure it for you. Sometime ago Mr. J. expressed a desire she should alter it, & she had intended doing so, but deferred it till a very short time before she died. <She sent for me, and> /She sent for me, and/ I attended her <at her desire> on the 19th. A most melancholy situation it was. The faculties of her mind were as strong & vigorous as ever, her affection & regard for her Friends as lively, & her memory as perfect I believe as at any moment of her life, but her disorder had very much wasted her, & her looks too <plainly bespoke> /probably indicated/ the approaches of death, tho' I then was far from supposing her fate was so near at hand, nor indeed that it was altogether impossible to save her. She dictated her will to me with great composure. Mr. Johnston will inclose you a copy of it, but the substance was, a devise & bequest of her whole property real & personal to Mr. Pollok & Mr. Johnston in trust to sell it, & pay the proceeds to you, after deducting a legacy of £300 Stg. to Mr. Johnston (£150 of which she most kindly intended for me, & which I could not divert her from, tho' as I was to draw the will she directed me to express it in that manner)—Your

Brother's legacy to her she gave to your Son, & her Watch to Mrs. Iredell, and left Mr. Pollok & Mr. Johnston her Exers.[3] She particularly desired, that /in case of her death/ I would inform you of this melancholy event, & assure you & Lady D. of her extreme affection & /her/ anxiety for your happiness, and let you know that her deferring to answer your & Lady D. letters, & acknowledging the tenderness of the attention of both, was not owing to any want of regard or respect, but /that/ she was in hopes of being able to give you more agreeable accounts. After this she conversed with me on a great many indifferent topics, with as much ease & quickness of understanding as I ever knew her possess, & with no apparent difference but the want of that agreeable humour which in general mixed with all her conversation. <I withdrew, but purposely avoided doing it abruptly, lest she should imagine I thought her in great danger> After I had prepared her will, I read it to her, & asked her if that was conformable to her desire. She said perfectly. <The> & conversed with me freely, as before, tho' not quite so fully. I was most unfortunately at that time obliged to go instantly to Pasquotank, so that I could not stay longer. I expected she would have executed her will that day, but after waiting a considerable time for her to propose it I at length asked her if she chose to execute it then, or at another time. She said, another time if it could do as well, & put to me the affecting question whether if she was unable to sign if any body might do it for her. In this situation, with the utmost distress, I left her. The will was executed, & with sufficient form, the morning of the day she died. Her death was quite easy, & what I hope will greatly soften your grief on this occasion. Tho' Mrs. P. always before had expressed & discovered the greatest fear of death, she discovered nothing of it in this last unfortunate illness but bore & spoke of the approaches of it with extraordinary equanimity and composure. She was interred at her own desire at Hayes.[4]

I have now gone thro' an undertaking which I dreaded, the recital of particulars that must ever pain & affect me in the recollection. My own regard for her was very great, & if it had proceeded from gratitude alone, & not from a respect for a most excellent mind that I sincerely entertained, it was justly merited, for almost ever since I have been in the Country she has uniformly shewn me nearly as much attention & affection as if I had been her Son. Mrs. Iredell, who equally loved & respected her, has been most deeply affected also, & had greatly to regret that her own state of health prevented her being with her till the very morning before she died, & when she was shocked beyond expression in finding her in a situation she at that time little expected. The supreme Being certainly can never suffer such distresses to be without some compensation hereafter. Of all human evils, in my opinion the loss of Friends is the greatest, & would to me be insupportable if I thought this life terminated our existence.

All the remaining confiscated property is doomed to be sold, & yours must share the same fate unless we can succeed in setting up your Mother's <Est> title. As this has long been our only ground of hope, I think it is very unfortunate you should have /had/ any conversation with Capt. West from which he might infer you claimed it as yours,—for nothing is more clear than /that/ if it were yours & it is now the Public's & this I thought I had sufficiently explained to you.[5] The Treaty by no means protected your Estate, for it was confiscated, tho' not sold before, & the Treaty only guarded against future Confiscations, not future Sales, & left all the rest at mercy. And it has always appeared to me that you Gentl in England trill too much on the recommend Article.[6] How unwisely the event has shewn! Mr. J. will write you fully of his intentions, but as the Law will decide between your present title under your Mother, & the Public's under your former one, I think it is well worth your while to lay <the> a Copy of your Father's will (the whole of it, no extract) with all the circumstances of the case, before one or two of the first Counsel in the Kingdom, & those in preference by far whose general practice is in the Court of Chancery.[7] And let a question something /like/ this be proffered to them. "Whether, for want of such an Instrument of writing, as your Father referred to, /the Trust of/ the real Estate in this Country resolved to his Heir at law, or by the express direction for it to be sold it was to be deemed in Equity as personal Estate, & go under the strong general residency clause to your Mother. And whether, under that clause she was not entitled to all the produce of the personal Estate here"—Neither Mr. J. nor myself are satisfied with the opinions you sent. The opinion as to the personal Estate appears to be clearly wrong. The other is more doubtful, but remember your whole chance depends now on supporting your Mother's title, and could we be fortunate enough to get one or two respectable opinions in support of it from England it might have great weight here. The whole Will ought to be before Counsel, on account of the very remarkable expressions in it in your Mother's favour. Your Mother on Mr. Collet's renunciation administered in this Country.[8]

Your letters that you favoured me with, & for which I owe you acknowledgments, are dated Jan. 11., March 30, and the 7 Sept., & communicate agreeable accounts which I heartily rejoice at.[9]

You must be sensible your Power of Attorney can now be of no use. If you apply for opinions, let us have them as soon as possible.[10]

Mrs. Iredell joins in <very> respectful Compliments to you & Lady D. & in wishing you both & your rising Family all manner of prosperity.

Adieu! my dear Sir & believe me ever Faithfully & affectionately yours

Jas. Iredell

FC, Iredell Papers, Duke. Printed, McRee, 2:117-119. Endorsed "Copy of a Letter to Sir Nathl. Dukinfield Jan. 9. 1785."

---

[1]McRee dates this letter January 7, 1785.

[2]Margaret Pearson was the mother of Nathaniel Dukinfield. She had remarried following the death of Dukinfield's father.

[3]The will, written in JI's handwriting, is dated December 19, 1784. In it she declared, "I bequeath to my Grandson Samuel George Dukinfield the Legacy left me by me dear Son Robert Dukinfield deceased. I request my Friend, Mrs. Iredell, Wife of Mr. James Iredell Attorney at law, to accept of my Watch which I have usually worn as a token of my regard for her. Lastly, I constitute and appoint the said Cullen Pollok and Samuel Johnston Executors of this my Will." Will of Margaret Pearson, Chowan County Wills, State Archives.

[4]Located near Edenton, Hayes was the home of JI's brother-in-law Samuel Johnston. Although JI states that Mrs. Pearson was interred at Hayes, no record of her burial there has been found.

[5]In earlier correspondence, Dukinfield had discussed selling part of his property to Captain West through Samuel Johnston and JI. See Nathaniel Dukinfield to JI, September 7, 1784, in this volume.

[6]Article five of the Treaty of Peace required Congress to recommend that confiscated property be returned to Loyalists, while article six prohibited future confiscation. "Treaty of Peace," *Treaties and Other International Agreements*, 12:11-12.

[7]Nathaniel Dukinfield, father of the recipient of this letter, died in 1749. His will can be found in J. Bryan Grimes, *North Carolina Wills and Inventories* (Baltimore: Genealogical Publishing, 1967), 155-160. *DNCB*, s.v. "Duckenfield, Nathaniel."

[8]In his will of 1746, the elder Nathaniel Dukinfield named Joseph Collett, a London merchant, as executor of his affairs in North Carolina. Collett renounced his executorship, however, in 1755, and Margaret Dukinfield assumed that responsibility. Grimes, *North Carolina Wills*, 157, 159-160.

[9]See letters of January 11, 1784, and September 7, 1784, in this volume. Letter of March 30, 1784, not found.

[10]The younger Dukinfield had given Samuel Johnston and JI power of attorney over his property in North Carolina. The Confiscation Acts, however, had rendered that power of attorney invalid. Opinions from the Court of Chancery could have been used to support Dukinfield's claim, but no such opinions have been found. For an excerpt of Dukinfield's letter of attorney, see Nathaniel Dukinfield to JI, January 11, 1784, n. 8, in this volume.

To Arthur Iredell

Edenton Jan. 22d. 1785.

My dear Brother,

I have to acknowledge, after a very long silence on your part, a very hasty letter from you of the 7 Sepr., which gave me pleasure as all yours do, but I could not help regretting it had not been longer & more particular.[1] I fear from your letter that your health has been greatly affected but Tom will not allow it was so much so before he left you as to justify your relying on him for an excuse. However, my dear Brother, I heartily rejoice that you are at last recovered, & beg that we may not have, except from indispensable necessity, so long a chasm in your correspondence /for the future/—It is cruel in you to deprive us of agreeable letters you can write with so much ease, and of intelligence in which we are so strongly interested—<I doubt not the story of the Provost Marshall is exaggerated greatly. For your sake particularly I wish it may be so, in forwarding,> You cannot imagine the anxiety & mortification I have felt—Every week enquiring with hope & expectation at the Post Office, until at last I began to fear you had forgot every thing but your Amanda.[2] God forbid you should fail in proper devoirs to her, but for heavens sake don't let her engross you entirely[3]—I have not had a line from my Uncle, but am glad to hear he thought of writing to me—I should be extremely glad if I could recover his favour, even if the Provost Marshall's account was true, which I don't believe.[4]

Tom behaves exceedingly well, & pleases me as well as my whole Family highly. He applies with an assiduity I could not expect to the study of the Law, and I have great hopes he will conceive a relish for it[5]—He discovers not the least propensity to any vice, & is always good humoured & obliging. <Was I industrious to ferrit out a fault in me, it would be only> I only regret his still being on half pay, & owing the debt for which it was mortgaged. Was it not for that, I would get him to resign immediately, but that can't be without the debt being in some measure secured, & unfortunately it is not in my power at present to discharge any part of it.[6] I owe considerable sums, & collect with great difficulty & slowness what is due to me—I wish, by means of remittance from my Uncle or otherwise, it was possible at least to lessen that debt. I <will> readily undertake the care of Tom for the future, & anxiously expect my Mother, both of whom I fear not to provide for here, but I see no prospect of my being able to pay that heavy debt for Tom in England, and at the same time I can't bear his being here on the incumbrance of half pay. I should hope, if the Circumstance was made known to my Uncle, he might relieve us from this embarrassment—I do assure you it is not a pleasing one. Nothing but this in the least <damp> /abates/ the great happiness my Brother's arrival has afforded me.[7]

Mrs. Iredell, I thank God, after suffering a great deal in consequence of her delivery, is perfectly recovered, & enjoys her usual share of good health. Mine is as good as at any period of my life, after /being/ upwards of a twelve month <being> in a very critical & dangerous state—. We doubt not of continuing so if you will now & then enliven us with some of your letters, <but> for we have no Ranelagh's or Pantheon's to soften the mortification of being neglected by our Friends.[8] Mrs. Iredell fears she has received your last letter, and I do assure you it will require a good deal entirely to reconcile me.[9] Remember, the Post is open, & the most secure way of writing—The Packets come regularly, & the communication is certain, —only you must pay the /English part of the/ postage <to your sea side> </in England/> and I <pay to mine> /the American/. God knows how chearfully I shall pay <the entire American postage> /my share of it, & yours can't amount to a great deal/, & therefore for the future you are /not/ to excuse long silences by want of opportunities—If I am to have any of the Poetry &c you promised me, commit it to Mr. Black's care. It can be sent either directly here, or to Norfolk in Virginia—If to the latter to the care of Mr. Alex. Diack Merchant. Remember too, I watch the fortunes of Mr. Fox, & Mr. Burke, & heartily despise the present senseless clamour against them.[10]

I can never assure you too strongly of the affection of my own heart, & my anxiety for you. Mrs. Iredell's too is very strongly attached, & particularly sympathises in your & your Amanda's fate. Endeavour to prepare her to think properly of her future Brother, & Sister, & pray be a little more communicate as to the prospects or obstacles in the way of a conclusion—It is something more than a Romance to us, as the event is real, & the personages so dear, & yet you know that Readers of Romance are not satisfied without a great many particulars—

Adieu! Tom answers for himself—Mrs. Iredell makes use of me on this occasion to assure you of her <very> affectionate regard, and I promise you that I shall ever be, whether you will or will not write, but much more so if you will,

Your very affectionate Brother

J. I.

RC, Johnson Collection, NCSA.

[1]See Arthur Iredell to JI, September 7, 1784, in this volume.

[2]Amanda Felton, Arthur's fiancée.

[3]Devoirs means duty. *OED*, s.v. "devoirs."

[4]The uncle is Thomas Iredell Sr.

[5]Tom, brother of JI and Arthur, studied law as JI's apprentice. Whichard, *Justice James Iredell*, 235-236.

[6]Tom was on half pay as a lieutenant in the marines. *PJI*, 2:338.

[7]Tom had amassed a large debt in England, though how he did so was not reported in the correspondence. Iredell's mother, still living in England, refused to come and live with JI until Tom's obligations were met. Nettie Southworth Herndon, "James Iredell" (Ph.D. diss., Duke University, 1944), 190.

[8]Ranelagh was a pleasure garden in Chelsea, which featured an assembly room, almost two hundred feet in diameter, called the Rotunda. The Pantheon was built in 1772 on Oxford Street in London and was used for musical performances and theater. Frederick A. Pottle, ed., *Boswell's London Journal, 1762-1763* (New York: McGraw-Hill, 1950), 26, 256; *Brewer's Dictionary of Phrase and Fable*, 15th ed. (New York: HarperCollins, 1995), 798. See also *PJI*, 1:35.

[9]This refers to a letter to Hannah Iredell from Arthur Iredell dated April 9, 1784, in this volume.

[10]Edmund Burke (1729-1797), attorney, author, and member of Parliament, supported the coalition government of Charles Fox and Lord North. One of several controversies afflicting this unpopular government involved a proposal by Burke and Fox to diminish the power of the East India Company and place control of Indian affairs in the hands of a commission. The commissioners were to be appointed for the first four years by Parliament rather than the king. Fox presented the East India Bill in Parliament on November 17, 1784, and Burke spoke in support of it. With the king's influence, the bill was defeated, and soon after, the coalition ministers were dismissed. *DNB*, s.v. "Fox, Charles James," "Burke, Edmund"; Goodwin, *New Cambridge Modern History*, 8:553-554.

JI held Edmund Burke in high regard and called him "one of the greatest and best Men in the world." For more information on JI's opinion of Burke, see JI to William R. Davie, July 19, 1787, in this volume.

To Margaret Iredell

Jan. 22d. 1785.

My dear Mother,

Having been for a good while past very much from home I have not had it in my power to write to you at times when my Brother did. I know it will make you very happy when I assure you, as I can with great truth, that his behaviour pleases me & my Family extremely,—that he applies with an understanding & ability I could not possibly have expected to the study of the law,—& that he discovers not the least propensity to any vice,

& is uniformly good humoured & obliging. His health, thank God, is also perfectly good. Were you now to see him you would think he had come here for the benefit of his health. My principal wish now, my dear Mother, is to have you with me. This I heartily & earnestly wish for, flattering myself you would not find it disagreeable, and I am continually disappointed in my prospects of remitting money to England, which I had hoped to have done this winter, but find it impossible. My heart bleeds to think of your distresses there without my having it in my power to relieve you, but here I am persuaded I could enable you to live with comfort, and I hope with happiness, for many would be earnest to promote it. I wish to God it was possible, by means of my Uncle or otherwise, to pay Tom's debt to Mr. Woodgate, that he might get rid of his commission & half pay, the thoughts of which frequently give me pain, and it is the only thing in regard to him that does. It is really not in my power, & God knows when it may be to pay it, as I owe considerable debts contracted during the war, & collect those due to me very slowly, & my difficulties since the peace have been much enhanced by a Paper Curency in this Country that has raised the price of every thing, & almost totally prevented, except for Merchants, the means of remitting money abroad

How cruel & mortifying was the treatment of poor Charles! It has distressed & disappointed me beyond measure, after having reason to hope you would have received so liberally, to find it such a pittance![1] —O! do, my dear Mother, if possible, come to me. Rely on a Son as dutiful & affectionate as ever Son was, & a Daughter deserving of your highest confidence, & utmost affection. Let it be our pleasing <emolument> employment to soften all the cares, & increase as much as possible the satisfactions of your life. Nothing in our power that can be done for that purpose shall be omitted. Alas! my hope of presenting you with a Grandson has been dreadfully dashed. I told you the cruel fate before, and I cannot bear to repeat it,—but providence thought proper to deprive us of him! I thank God, however, he has preserved & restored my dear Wife's health, which was in the most imminent danger, and my own after being a long time in a very precarious state is thoroughly reestablished—I thank you cordially for your letter by Capt. West. We have been hoping for some since, tho' in regard to you that was rather unreasonable, but we have some cause to complain if Arthur, who did not write a line from April till September, and tho' I fear he has had ill health yet <I can't think> a good deal must <be> certainly be imputed to love or idleness, as he indeed seems candidly to acknowledge, & therefore I hope he will be less negligent for the future. I heartily rejoice in his recovering his health again, and hope it will long continue—If you can prevail on yourself to come here, and can meet with a good opportunity, the most agreeable way would be by a Ship bound to James River in Virginia, & landing at Norfolk, in which case please to apply to Mr. Alexander Diack a Merchant there, who upon knowing your name & relation to me will shew you every civility. I shall write to him on the subject, in hopes that you may leave England in the spring, which will give you the chance of a fine passage. God knows how my heart will rejoice to see you, my dear Mother, & have you at last fixt, I trust, beyond the caprices of life, and in the natural protection of your own children. Heaven grant I may not be disappointed in this delightful hope!

I am very glad you so often see Mr. Dawson, who is a most excellent young Man, and I rejoice exceedingly in the universal pleasing accounts which are given of him. His Mother and Sister are now here, and in very good health, which has been I believe not a little benefited by the removal of her anxiety about him, which, thank God, I find is at length happily restored[2]

Mrs. Iredell intends writing to you, being much obliged by the uniform kindness of your affection to her, & interesting herself always very deeply in your happiness & prosperity. God grant you may suffer as to contribute to it, as we should endeavour by all possible means, by our personal attentions. Believe me, it is now by far the fondest & most anxious wish of my heart—

Adieu! my dear Mother, and believe me ever Your most dutiful & affectionate Son

J. I.

FC, Johnson Collection, NCSA.

---

[1]Charles Iredell, brother of JI, was killed in action in 1782 while serving in the British navy. This may refer to compensation given to Mrs. Iredell by the British government. *PJI*, 2:439n.

[2]William Johnston Dawson (1765-1796) had been sent to England for his education. His mother was Penelope Johnston Dawson and his sister, Penny Dawson. *DNCB*, s.v. "Dawson, William Johnston."

To Thomas Iredell Sr.

Feb. 19, 1785

My dear & honoured Sir,

I was from home when my Brother last wrote to you, or I should have accompanied his with a letter from me expressing the very great satisfaction

I have felt on his arrival, & from his conduct since, which has far exceeded my expectation or what I thought possible, as he not only applies closely, but appears to apply with real pleasure to the dry study of my <Poss> Profession, & to comprehend what he reads with a quickness and intelligence fully equal to my wishes, & which promises the fairest fruits from his application. He has retained the principles of his education too much better than could have been imagined, & the morality & gentility of his conduct is without exception. The only pain I feel on his account is for some debts that he left undischarged in England, & which it is utterly out of my power to pay, or I readily would—. I receive no more in ready money than is barely sufficient to defray my necessary expences in a /very/ frugal /manner/, & have some old debts yet to pay, tho' I have taken care to contract no new ones. But these do not make me very uneasy, as I doubt not with the blessing of God, if I live, to get through my own difficulties, but they unfortunately put it out of my power to relieve my Brothers.

I received the greatest satisfaction from a <lett> late letter of my Brother Arthur's, wherein he told me you had acknowledged two of my letters and said you <had> intended writing to me.[1] I have been most impatiently hoping for this great favour, but tho' I have not yet been so happy as to receive any letter <permit me, my dear Sir> /I beg leave/ to express my <best thanks> /sincere gratitude/ for the kindness of your intention. It is now the first wish of my heart to be restored to your former kind opinion & regard, which whatever may be the event I thank God, so far as innocence of intentions is concerned, I have never deserved to forfeit.

I have earnestly solicited my Mother to come & live with me, & urged her if possible <to sa> & she is not averse to my proposal, to sail in the month of April, which would give her a chance of a very fine passage. I have not heard from her in answer, since I wrote so particularly, but have great hopes she will come, in which case I will readily undertake the care of her & Tom for the future.[2]

My Brother, I dare say, acquainted you in his letter of Mrs. Iredell's & my melancholy misfortune <She was safely delivered of a very fine Boy on the 1st. of Oct. & he died on the 3d.> /in losing a very fine Boy of which she was safely delivered on the 1st. Oct, on the 3d./ As this was our only Child after a marriage of so many years, it was certainly a most unhappy event, & I had the utmost reason to dread it would put an end to his Mother's life, but thank God after being in <the most> /very/ imminent danger she recovered, & has since been nearly as well as ever.

My own health is at length, after much difficulty, thoroughly reestablished. My Brother's has improved extremely since his arrival, & he has been altogether clear of sickness. Would to God I could hear as favourable accounts of yours—Mrs. Iredell desires her respectful & affectionate Compliments may be presented to you, & earnestly joins in every wish of my heart for your health & happiness.

Adieu! my dear Sir, & believe me, as I truly am, Your most dutiful & affectionate Nephew

Ja. Iredell

FC, Johnson Collection, NCSA. Endorsed "Copy of a letter to my Uncle Iredell Feb. 19th. 1785."

---

[1]See JI to Thomas Iredell Sr., February 11 and May 28, 1784, and Arthur Iredell to JI, September 7, 1784, in this volume.

[2]See JI to Margaret Iredell, January 22, 1785, in this volume.

From Arthur Iredell

Crewe Hall Feby. 28th. 17[*85*][1]

My dear Bror.

You shall have no further Cause to complain of my Silence & as a Specimen of my Sincerity, behold another Letter! for I wrote one by the last Packet, tho You have not received it yet &, perhaps, may never receive it[2]—in truth these are such strange Jumblements about your American Mails that I ne[*ver*] know how to choose New York on this Side, or Charles Town [*on*] that—Quebec, I presume, is rather out of the Way—A [*torn*] tell me what I am to depend upon in future, for I [*torn*] wonderfull Oconomist of my time, or in other words, as a [*torn*] who hardly ever devote my means, such as they are, to [*the*] Service of my Friends, or even my own Emolument. The [*torn*] Hunks keeps his Money in Bags not daring to part [*with*] It, & here am I crawling from Day to Day, & counting [*torn*] Moments which I can never bring myself to apply, & which are therefore to me as profitless,—but I am not afraid, now & then, to part with them, as you shall see—for I will now run you a Race through Politicks, & all the icks, bu[*t*] [*Ma*]thematicks & Metaphysicks which I know no more of than You—[*Fidd*]lestick—As to Politicks, thou American, thanks to the [*indust*]rious Spirit that your Country has so successfully breathed over us we have no sooner begun to bask /a little/ in the Sunshine of Peace, & to get, as it were, into half Mourning for thirteen Daugh[*ters*] [*o*]f whom alass! we have been bereaved, Than our youngest has Thought proper to call in her Fortune, & because forsooth [*torn*] little bit of a termagant, & must not be contradicted for [*torn*]as of her pulling Caps, Our Father has been promising her much [*mo*]re than a younger Child's Portion,—the Consequence of which is that [*torn*] are in high Dudgeon, & are striving by all means to get a [*torn*] fancy Prig of a Steward, who has been the Contriver of [*torn*], & had, I fancy, a sneaking kindness for Hibernia, [*torn*] out of his Place[3]—You must know there is an old Steward [*who*] was formerly in the family, ready to pop into his Place, [*torn*] he is not a whit better—& so what we shall do God knows—[*Torn*] amazing fine Estate it is true, but it is sadly [*Encumbered*], & we are besides so abominably cheated by our n[*ea*]rest Relations that we may after all find ourselves very soon in a Gaol—Do you understand all this? The plain English of it is, that Mr. Pitt is now in the Act of arranging the [*D*]istrict Claims of Ireland & Great Brittain—but he has bungled terribly in the outsett of the Business, for he opened the Propositions from this Country to that in <u>their</u> Ho[*use*] he proposed Terms for Acceptance which at last may ma[*torn*] them, & it appears indeed as if that would be the Case [*torn*] writes word that in all probability the Minister will [*torn*] on that Business—[*If he*] should, he will go out, & if he goes out, some one else will come in—All this, I hope, is orthodox, if it be not ([*torn*] hazard another if) I can send you no better, n[*torn*] Affairs are not more promising than the Irish [*torn*] is at length recalled, & our Cousin Lord Macar[tney] [*torn*] his Successor—You will be happy to hear this—I w[*torn*] for it is the first Appointment for a Subject in V[*torn*] & he may, without Injury to his reputation, "fea[*torn*]" they say[4]—I will positively tell you no more [*torn*] much richer sources of Intelligence & cannot need me [*torn*]—Tell Tom I have received his kind Letter, & will answer it, but when, this Deponent saith not—I am too poor at present to pay the Postage of another Letter. Six months have elapsed since I have expected a Remittance from Jamaica, & it is not yet come.[5] You are making Bishops in America—will you accept of me in No. Carolina?-How does my Sister?-Miss F. wrote to her by the last Packet, & is dying for an Answer—so am I for a Letter from her too tho I have not <u>one</u> Pretension—Assure her however of my best Love, Tom of D<u>o</u>. & believe me most truly & affectionately

Your's

A I.

Amanda desires her Love to you all—I have not said a Word of my Mother, because I know She will speak for herself—but least She should not, She is as well as She can be in <u>England</u>—Adieu! God bless thee—Mrs. Bayley desires her best Comps. to all

Sirs[6]
One Month after Date pay to Mr. Thomas Iredell one Sheet of [*torn*] written upon three Sides upon my Account & for Value received

To Messrs. Pen, Ink, & Paper,
Writing Sheet, Correspondence—Gentlemen, Yo[*ur*] very

A. Ire[*dell*]

RC, Johnson Collection, NCSA. Addressed "James Iredell Esqr. Edenton North Carolina America."

---

[1]This letter is filed in the undated correspondence of the Johnson Collection, State Archives. From the context it is dated 1785.

[2]See Arthur Iredell to JI, November 27, 1784, in this volume.

[3]Arthur Iredell employs terms and usages that are uncommon today. A termagant is a quarrelsome bully; dudgeon is a synonym for anger; a prig, in this case, refers to a dandy; and Hibernia is Ireland. *OED*, s.v. "termagant," "dudgeon," "prig," "Hibernian."

[4]England had imposed harsh trade regulations on Ireland, and some in England feared that the Irish, like the Americans, would revolt. Prime Minister William Pitt the younger proposed free trade with Ireland, a plan embraced by the Irish Parliament. English business interests, however, fearful of Irish competition, opposed such an arrangement. Members of Parliament representing those interests drastically modified Pitt's plan so that it was no longer acceptable to the Irish. Derek Jarrett, *Pitt the Younger* (New York: Charles Scribner's Sons, 1974), 94-95.

[5]Arthur Iredell was expecting to receive money from his uncle Thomas Iredell Sr. See Arthur Iredell to Hannah Iredell, February 25, 1784, in this volume.

[6]This section appears at the top of the first page in the original.

To Arthur Iredell

[*March 6, 1785*]

My dear Brother,

I received with inexpressible pleasure your letter of the 27 Nov., which came to my hands a few days ago[1]—The <plcharming> charming information it gives me concerning yourself has put me in so good a humour, that I am willing to pardon all your former neglects, upon condition of an entire amendment for the future & that as a great deal of your anxiety must now be removed there may be no more references to my former, or Tom's present sympathizing situation. I can allow a great deal on that score, but am much deceived if a Man may not be very violently in love, & in great uncertainty too, & yet be able in the course of many months, to write a line to a Brother, who was waiting with the utmost anxiety to hear from him, & would warmly have participated either in his pains or pleasures—You know not how much you would oblige me by communications that shewed you considered me, as I really am, interested in every movement of your life as deeply affecting myself—<that> the <most minute particulars will be highly interesting to me>, more minute the Information the more pleasing it will be to me, and the delightful happiness you enjoy of being so much beloved by one admirable Lady, & so highly esteemed by another, gives a </peculiar/> tinge to your situation capable of affecting a much less interested heart than mine. What would I give, my dear Arthur, to see you & these charming Women?[2] God knows if such happiness is in store for me. I seem chained to America & doubt not it will be for life, but I should be unhappy if I thought I never was to meet with you in person. I rest now only on uncertain hope that perpetual, but that useful Deceiver of Mankind—But in the mean time let me earnestly intreat you to write me often—You can at any rate once a month by the Packet, & I hope you will not neglect it. I shall be sure of not losing a letter, if no accident happens at Sea.

Mrs. Iredell is <perpetu> particularly obliged by your last letter to her.[3] I doubt not she will answer it by a convenient opportunity, but she thinks so highly of you, & with such extreme humility (in my opinion without <justice> /foundation/) of her capacity for writing, that her correspondence with you, tho' what she so <much highly prizes> </values/> /highly prizes/, is with difficulty preserved on her part. She thinks herself much flattered by your proposal of her corresponding with your Amanda & her Sister, but declares it is impossible that she can ever bring herself to write to them, tho' nothing could more delight her than such a correspondence could she keep it up. You can easily account for this diffidence in American Ladies, who lead such Retired lives, & want many advantages which are enjoyed by the Ladies in England—I have tried, but to no purpose, to give <Mrs. Iredell> /your Sister/ a little more courage. Her diffidence, I fear, in this respect, is unconquerable.

I can still continue to assure you, with great truth, and the utmost satisfaction, that my Brother if possible gains upon my esteem & affection & the good opinion of the whole Family every day.[4] He studies with <unceasing> /extraordinary/ assiduity, and an ability that more & more surprizes /me/,—lives with the strictest regularity <in every respect>, & maintains a constant cheerfulness & good humour that adds very much to the happiness of us all. My uneasiness in respect to him, thank God, is now at an end, and the happiest prospects await him. I wish now only for my Mother, & anxiously hope I shall not be disappointed—I have wrote her

& you so repeatedly, & hope my sincerity will not be questioned—My greatest distress is about her present difficulties, & the Debts of Tom that are unpaid—Were these satisfied, & his Commission relinquished, it would relieve me from much anxiety—My Brother and I wrote particularly to you & my Mother by a Vessel that sailed from here in January, but we unluckily hear of her putting into Virginia in great distress[5]—Tom sent by her a Certificate for his half pay, <but unluckily it> /which unfortunately however/ would entitle her to receive entry till the July Quarter—We will send another as soon as it can be done, but it is not easy to get business of this kind done here, from the remote situation of the Governor & other obstacles.

Tom desires me to tell you, that so far from feeling any sensations which prompt an excuse for you, he would readily have wrote to you now but for the increasing of postage. His heart I believe is yet very whole, & he has no notion of such fascinating powers of love as you ascribe to it. His time <may> possibly however may come, & if you should not then hear from him for a twelve month you will know how to excuse him.

<We are all at present in good health—My Brother has not been at all sick. He desires his best affection to you, as does Mrs. Iredell, & we all join>

He desires to be most affectly. remembered to you, as does Mrs. Iredell who loves you I believe nearly as well as well as we do. Present /us/ also <our> most dutifully & affecty. to my Mother, if in England when this letter arrives, which I hope she will not be, and assure <you> the two lovely Sisters in your handsomest manner of our thinking of them with every sentiment of respect, and anticipate with the liveliest joy the prospect of the more intimate connection which we, as well as you, so ardently wish for.

FC, Johnson Collection, NCSA. Endorsed "Copy of a Letter to my Brother Arthur March 6. 1785—."

---

[1]See Arthur Iredell to JI, November 27, 1784, in this volume.

[2]The two women are Amanda Felton, Arthur's fiancée, and her sister, a Mrs. Bayley of Staffordshire. See Arthur Iredell to Hannah Iredell, February 25, 1784, in this volume.

[3]See Arthur Iredell to Hannah Iredell, April 9, 1784, in this volume.

[4]JI is referring to Thomas Iredell.

[5]See JI to Margaret Iredell, January 22, 1785, in this volume.

From Archibald Maclaine

Wilmington 7 March 1785

Dear Sir

I have just now received yours of the 7th. of last month—Where it has lain so long I cannot conceive, except for the last week, when there was no rider from New Bern.

I have not yet fixed on persons for adjusting the audts. between Messrs. Spaight & Campbell—indeed it had escaped my memory.[1] I was taken dangerously ill immediately after our Superior court, & confined for five weeks, & since I have recovered, I could not find lei[*sure*] to think of any thing but what was before my eyes.

Mr. Burgwin is the surviving executor of Mr. Waddell & was joined with the late Mrs. Waddell.[2]

We have been paid off here as in other places by the sickly season—The sore throat proved fatal to several. Dr. Claypoole says it is properly a scarlet fever, attended with a sore throat, & we ought to conclude that he is no incompetent judge, as he has not lost a patient where he was called in the beginning of the disorder.[3]

Mrs. Huske has got a chopping girl, & is perfectly well some time ago[4]—Col. Clark is also well, & his wife much better[5]—she has been lately thought passed recovery in a consumptive complaint, but Fergus says she is <much better> /recovering/[6]—I have no faith in his judgement, though I hope the best—Mrs. Hooper & her daughter are now at Mr. Clark's, & we shall have them soon in town. Mr. H. is well. I heard from him a few days ago.—Mr. Hay is now in Virginia, but expected home this month—Mr. G. Hooper & his family were perfectly well a short time ago.[7]

It gives me pleasure to hear that Mr. Johnston is so much better & that Mrs. Dawson & all your friends are well. I am particularly pleased to hear that Billy Dawson promises so well

The last night of our court, Mr. B. Hoskins gave me some very extraordinary information.[8] He had <some> /a/ conversation with Mr. Singleton about the suits commenced by the Cornell family[9]—Singleton appeared perfectly easy, said he depended upon Nash as /a/ Sheet-anchor, & had nothing to fear, as he and his associates had silenced you, Mr. H. & myself. He went indeed much further. He said that all the Judges had been sounded, and were favorable to them. I wrote to Ogden, who appeared to be the agent of the gang, informing him that I would return the retainer, & looked upon myself as disengaged.[10] I also wrote to Singleton <informing> telling him that I had heard what he said, (without naming my author) and assuring him that though he had deprived me of a fee, he should not seal up my lips. I acquainted Mr. H. of all this, but he seems to think we cannot appear against these scoundrels without injuring ourselves—I think the best way will be, to consult together when we meet.—at present my own opinion is, that delicacy should prevent us from taking fees on the other side, but I do not see any reason why we should be altogether silent. if we, at the trial, should declare we are volunteers, & give the reasons for our conduct, I think I may venture to rely upon the facts for my justification, & this will probably receive some additional force from my usual disinterestedness. I suppose Johnston will laugh that we have been so damnably taken in.

Yours with great sincerity

A Maclaine

as I must write you so soon about Spaight & Campbell's affair I should not have troubled you now, had not your letter been of so old a date—Among several others, Mrs. DeRossets & Mr. J. Lillington are dead. Col. Sampson & lately old Mr. Hasell[11]

RC, Iredell Papers, Duke. Printed, McRee, 2:119-120. Addressed "James Iredell esquire Edenton." Endorsed "Wilmington 7 March 1785 A. Maclaine. Ansd. 29 March."

---

[1]In *Richard Dobbs Spaight v. William Campbell*, JI represented the plaintiff and Maclaine, the defendant. The case, heard in New Bern District Superior Court, was eventually concluded in 1787. Campbell was ordered to pay £489.1.11 in damages and court costs. Minutes of the New Bern District Superior Court, November 1787, and New Bern District Superior Court Execution Docket, November 1787, State Archives. See Richard D. Spaight to JI, March 10, 1785, in this volume.

[2]John Burgwin was Hugh Waddell's (ca. 1734-1773) brother-in-law and the executor of his estate. Waddell, a prominent merchant of Bladen County, was married to Mary Haynes Waddell (d. 1776) of Castle Haynes. Richard Dobbs Spaight filed a suit against the executors of the Waddell estate in New Bern District Superior Court. Auditors John Wright Stanly, Wilson Blount, and Thomas W. Pearson were appointed during the November 1787 term to prepare a report on the estate. A final settlement was not reached until 1792. *DNCB*, s.v. "Waddell, Hugh"; Estate of Hugh Waddell, 1788, New Hanover County Estates, State Archives; Minutes of the New Bern Superior Court, November 1787, State Archives.

[3]William Claypoole (d. 1797) was a physician in New Hanover County. Mitchell, *North Carolina Wills*, 97.

[4]Elizabeth "Betsy" Hogg Huske gave birth to a daughter, Ann Alves, on January 31, 1785. *Life and Times of James Hogg*, 21.

[5]Thomas Clark (1741-1792), a planter and native of New Hanover County, attained the rank of colonel and commanded North Carolina troops during the Revolutionary War. He married Sarah Moore Nash in 1782. She was the widow of

Gen. Francis Nash, whom Clark had served under during the war. Clark's sister, Ann, was the wife of William Hooper. *DNCB*, s.v. "Clark, Thomas"; *PJI*, 2:160n-161n.

[6]John Fergus (1741-1802) of New Hanover County was a surgeon and justice of the peace. *DNCB*, s.v. "Fergus, John."

[7]George Hooper (ca. 1744-1821) was a merchant in Wilmington and Charleston, S.C., and the first president of the Bank of the Cape Fear (1804). He was accused by some of being a Loyalist. Archibald Maclaine was his father-in-law and William Hooper his brother. *DNCB*, s.v. "Hooper, George"; DeMond, *Loyalists*, 54.

[8]Baker Hoskins (d. 1835) of Chowan County was a member of the house of commons (1806-1808). Estate of Baker Hoskins, 1835, Chowan County Estates, State Archives; Cheney, *North Carolina Government*, 251, 253, 255.

[9]Spyers Singleton (d. 1814) of Craven County served in the Third Provisional Congress (1775), the General Assembly (1784-1785), and on the Council of State (1793). The litigation in question involved Singleton's ownership of property confiscated from Loyalist Samuel Cornell. This dispute evolved into *Bayard v. Singleton* (1787), an early case involving judicial review of legislation. *DNCB*, s.v. "Singleton, Spyers"; Cheney, *North Carolina Government*, 155, 166, 215.

[10]Titus Ogden.

[11]Margaret Walker De Rosset of Wilmington was the wife of Lewis Henry De Rosset (ca. 1724-1786). He held numerous public offices, including royal councilor. De Rosset, a close associate of Gov. Arthur Dobbs, was expelled from North Carolina in 1779 and his property confiscated. John Lillington (d. 1785) of New Hanover County was a Revolutionary War officer and justice of the peace. John Sampson (d. 1784) of New Hanover and Duplin Counties was a planter, legislator, justice of the peace, and the first mayor of Wilmington. Sampson County is named in his honor. James Hasell (d. 1785) of New Hanover County was a judge, planter, and royal councilor. As president of the Royal Council, he served as acting governor after the departure of Governor Dobbs and before the arrival of Governor Martin. *DNCB*, s.v. "De Rosset, Lewis Henry," "Lillington, John Alexander," "Sampson, John," "Hasell, James"; *PJI*, 2:42n; Donald R. Lennon and Ida Brooks Kellam, eds., *The Wilmington Town Book, 1743-1778* (Raleigh: Division of Archives and History, North Carolina Department of Cultural Resources, 1973), 24n-25n; Andrew J. Howell, *The Book of Wilmington* (n.p., n.d.), 43.

From Richard D. Spaight

New York 10th. March 1785

Dear Sir,

I did not receive your favor of the 7 Feby. untill a few days ago and have taken the first leizure moment to answer it. upon reflection I do not think it would be so proper to have applied to the court to re-instate the report they had set aside. it would at least have the appearance of their having acted inconsiderately, which the characters of Judges in Equity ought not to admit of and therefore it is better that the individual should suffer pro tempore, then the least flaw be discovered in the supreme court. As it is my disposition rather to make the best of the present, then to fret at what is past, I submit with patience to the delay and must rest satisfied with the new Order of Reference. It is very immaterial to me who the referees are, provided they are disinterested men & capable of settling Accounts. Mr. James Reed, Mr. Thos. Mc.Claine and Mr. John Hurst the persons appointed by the Second order of reference, would be perfectly agreeable to me, but I believe Mr. Hurst resides at Hillsborough.[1] in that case suppose the two former should agree upon a third person and proceed to the Settlement it would be perfectly agriable to me, if it would be so to Mr. Campbell. All I want is a final settlement so that I may receive whatever may be the balance, which I have been too long kept out of, and the want of which has rendered my situation not only irksome but very disagreeable.[2]

Mr. Craike has already a power of Attorney from me to Act for me in the district of Wilmington, and whatever he may do on my account, I shall be fully satisfied with[3]—The claim against Wadell's Estate I am very Anxious to have settled, but fear nothing can be done with it till my return to No. Carolina; It is my intention, at present to be at New Bern by the 20th or 25th. of may, unless some thing happens to prevent me which I do not foresee.

The only european news we have here is the war between the Emperor & the Dutch. the season admits of nothing else but the various Opinions of the politicians, whether the Controversy will be put an end to, by the negociations of the winter or decided by arms. For my part from every Acct. I have heard, am induced to be of the last opinion. Its pretty certain that the only way of putting an end to it by negociation is, either, that the dutch must give up the free navigation of the Schildt, or the Emperor desist from his demands. The former are divided in not granting the free navigation of that river first because it is contained in that treaty which confirmed their freedom and Independence, and if they admit <of> any of the Articles of that treaty not to be valid the others are equaly so. Secondly they have kept the Schildt shut up for more than 130 years, without their right for so doing, having ever been disputed. On the contrary it cannot be supposed that the Emperor will recede from his demands, the ridicule it would throw on his Character, to have made such, as he should be obliged to recede from for want of a sufficient force (the only right he had to plead) to oblige them to comply with would be too great, for a prince of such abilities and ambition as he is supposed to possess, to submit to.[4]

Congress have lately appointed Mr. John Adams, Minister to the Court of London.[5] it was a step absolutely necessary to be taken, & I think has been delayed too long and its well for america if her saving policy don't cost her millions

The holding of our Western posts contrary to the Treaty, her different arrangements in Canada & the lakes, added to the murmurs of the nation against america, and the restraints laid upon our commerce with them, Shew so hostile a disposition in the court of Great Britain <against> /towards/ us, that I think we should at least be prepared for any think that might happen.[6] Yet the States seemed to be lulled into perfect security, few of them have Organized & armed their militia, still fewer have taken any steps to procure a sufficient supply of military Stores, without which no nation ought to be, and I think our situation at the begining of the late war for want of those articles, ought to be a warning to America, never to be unprovided.[7] The want of money and the Unsettled State of Ireland, rather than the want of Inclination, will prevent them from renewing the controversy.

Mrs. Montgomery the widdow of /the late/ General of that name requested me to write to some of my Acquaintance in Edenton to know what had become of the Statue (I believe it is) that was ordered by Congress to be erected to the memory of Genl. Montgomery. it was sent from France to Edenton and lodged in the hands of Messrs. Hues, Smith & Allen, on order of [*Congress*] passed at Annapolis for its being sent from thence to this city.[8] Shall I take the liberty of requesting you to make this enquiry and to inform me of the result?

I have the honor to be with great Regard & Esteem

Dear Sir, Your most obedient & most humble Servant

Richd. Dobbs Spaight.

RC, Iredell Papers, Duke. Printed, McRee, 2:120-122. Addressed "James Iredell Esqr."

---

[1]James Read (1750-1804) of New Hanover and Brunswick Counties was a Revolutionary War officer, justice of the peace, and port collector. He was an aide-de-camp to Gov. Thomas Burke and was captured along with the governor in 1781 by Tory David Fanning. Clark, *State Records*, 20:160; Howell, *Book of Wilmington*, 66-67; Neal, *Abstracts of Vital Records*, 1:418; *Raleigh Register and North-Carolina State Gazette*, October 29, 1804.

Thomas Maclain of New Hanover County and John Hurst of Orange County. No further information found. *Heads of Families, 1790 Census*, 96, 193.

[2]For information on *Spaight v. Campbell*, see letter of March 7, 1785, n. 1, in this volume.

[3]Thomas Craike (d. 1792) of New Hanover County. Estate of Thomas Craike, 1792, New Hanover County Estates, State Archives.

[4]Austria and the Netherlands came close to war over the closing of the Schildt River. See Arthur Iredell to JI, November 27, 1784, n. 2, in this volume.

[5]John Adams (1735-1826) served for three years as U.S. minister to England. *DAB*, 72-82; Bailey, *Diplomatic History*, 53-54.

[6]British and Canadian officials conspired to delay withdrawal from the northern United States. In addition, the British imposed numerous barriers to U.S. trade, including a prohibition against American trading ships in the British West Indies and a ban on the exporting of certain materials to the U.S. that could be used to expand American manufacturing. Richard B. Morris, *The Forging of the Union, 1781-1789* (New York: Harper and Row, 1987), 203, 139, 205.

[7]At the end of the Revolution, many Americans feared that a standing U.S. army might pose the same threat to personal liberties that British forces had earlier. The Continental army was demobilized, and only a token force was maintained. Morris, *Forging of the Union*, 52-53.

[8]Richard Montgomery (1736-1775), a native of Ireland and resident of New York, was a brigadier general in the Continental army. He led forces in the capture of Montreal on November 12, 1775, and was killed in an attack on Quebec on December 31, 1775. His widow was Janet Livingston Montgomery, daughter of Robert R. Livingston of New York. They were married on July 24, 1773. *DAB*, s.v. "Montgomery, Richard."

Hewes, Smith, and Allen was a mercantile firm in Edenton. The partners were Joseph Hewes, Robert Smith, and Nathaniel Allen. Ferguson et al., *Papers of Robert Morris*, 9:621n.

In January 1776, the Continental Congress appointed a committee composed of William Livingston, Benjamin Franklin, and William Hooper to determine a way to honor General Montgomery. The committee decided upon a monument "from Paris, or any other part of France." The Board of Treasury notified Congress of the arrival of the memorial in November 1785. *Journals of the Continental Congress, 1774-1789*, ed. Worthington C. Ford et al., 34 vols. (Washington, D.C.: Government Printing Office, 1904-1937), 4:78, 89-90; 29:895.

To Hannah Iredell

[*Halifax April 22. 1785.*]

My dear Hannah,

I had great pleasure in receiving your letter yesterday by Mr. Black, and was happy in hearing such agreeable accounts. This is the first opportunity of writing since our arrival here, which was on Sunday afternoon. I have scarcely any recollection of my cold now, and my other complaint is better than it was. Your Brother I think is also much better. Mr. Hooper is not yet arrived. I had a letter from him since Hillsborough Court, mentioning that Mrs. Hooper had just arrived, that Mrs. Clarke was dead (an event to be most deeply regretted) and that he did not expect to be here till the middle of the Court.[1] He had been very unwell, and tho' better he must naturally wish to stay a day or two with Mrs. Hooper who had been so long absent and from whom he was to be again separated for so long a time. His absence delays our business very much, tho' we do all we can, but I am very sure the Court will hold the whole time. Judge Williams was able to attend part of Hillsborough Court, and will be here. Spencer has the very countenance of Hygeia, and Ashe is not far behind him, considering the natural difference between the two Men.[2] Penn is here with his usual froth.[3] Alfred Moore came the evening before last, and looks much better than I have seen him for a long time, and is more chearful than might have been expected after the recent loss of a Sister I believe he most fervently loved.[4] Her husband, in addition to his extreme affliction, Mr. Hooper writes me, is sick also. He does not mention whether his Sister left him behind, or where. I have heard a most affecting relation of Mr. Henderson's death. He was perfectly sensible almost to the last moment, was certain of his death for a fortnight before it happened, and tho' forbidden to speak but as little as possible was urgent to do so, and frequently expressed the most poignant regret for the imprudence of his conduct.[5] The day of his death all his Family took formal leave of him. Mrs. Henderson fainted twice, and the whole was a Scene too dreadful almost for Imagination—Mrs. Henderson has been in a very low /way/ ever since, but is beginning to recover a little now.[6] Miss Henderson & the rest of the Family are quite well—Alfred Moore saw her at Judge Williams's on his way here a day or two ago—

I bought a Cask of Red Port of Mr. Clark at Windsor, and requested him to send it down. The Cask contains 7 dozen, and I am to pay him 40/ a dozen for it (which I intend to do as I go back). The Wine appears to be very good, tho' not quite fine. Mr. Marshall, whom I saw at Windsor, and who is really a very agreeable Man, told me it would grow quite fine by putting the bottles on their bottoms in the Sun or Air in which case the dregs would go entirely down. Loaf Sugar was the same price there as in Edenton, so I got none.[7]

I am sure we shall not be able to leave this place till the 29th. Be kind enough to remember me affectionately to Nelly. Your Sister told me she was desirous of going over, but Mrs. Johnston pressed her so earnestly to stay that she did not like to leave her. I said every thing you could have wished me to do on the occasion.

Capt. Collins has the ague & Fever here most severely. He was very desirous of setting out to day, but as it is his sick day he will scarcely be able. Nat Allen talks of going to morrow, but I believe it is uncertain. Capt. Collins came here I believe to settle with a number of People before he left the Country, & the absence of Muir, with whom he had large connexions has occasioned an unexpected disappointment & delay.[8] I am heartily sorry for this on Mr. Wiseham's account.[9]

Adieu! my dear Hannah. Give Compts. for me to whom you please, but don't forget your Brother's Family & Gaby.

I am ever Your most affectionate

Jas Iredell

P.S. Mrs. Mc.Culloch has a fine Son.

RC, Johnson Collection, NCSA. Addressed "Mrs. Iredell Edenton."

---

[1]Sarah Moore Nash Clark, wife of Thomas Clark.

[2]Hygeia was the Greek goddess of health. Samuel Spencer and Samuel Ashe were superior court judges. JI had a low opinion of Spencer but a higher regard for Ashe. Walter Addison Jayne, *The Healing Gods of Ancient Civilizations* (New Hyde Park, N.Y.: University Books, 1962), 248; Whichard, *Justice James Iredell*, 20.

[3]This is probably a reference to John Penn.

[4]Sarah Moore Nash Clark was Alfred Moore's sister.

[5]Richard Henderson may have been referring to his land speculation. He and five other investors organized the Louisa Company in 1774, which later became the Transylvania Company. The firm signed agreements with the Cherokee to gain control of western lands, but the governors of North Carolina and Virginia invalidated the treaties, which caused the company's decline. *DNCB*, s.v. "Henderson, Richard."

[6]Mrs. Henderson was Elizabeth Keeling Henderson, daughter of Lord Keeling and stepdaughter of Henderson's law partner, Judge John Williams. *DNCB*, s.v. "Henderson, Richard."

[7]Windsor, established in 1768, was a shipping center at the head of navigation on the Cashie River in Bertie County. The Halifax and "Cashy" Roads provided overland connections to Windsor. JI stopped there to make purchases while riding the court circuit. Harry L. Thompson, "A History of Windsor, 1768-1968," in *The Windsor Story* (Windsor, N.C.: Windsor Bicentennial Commission, 1968), 78, 81-83. See also JI to Hannah Iredell, October 1, 1785, in this volume.

[8]This is probably a reference to William Muir of Halifax County, a partner in the trading firm of Collins, Stewart, and Muir. Josiah Collins Sr. was the senior partner in the company from 1777 to 1785. *DNCB*, s.v. "Collins, Josiah, Sr."

[9]William Wiseham (d. 1805) was a merchant of Richmond, Va., and an acquaintance of Josiah Collins. Netti Schreiner-Yantis and Florence Speakman

Love, comps., *The 1787 Census of Virginia*, 3 vols. (Springfield, Va.: Genealogical Books in Print, 1987), 2:1097; Benjamin B. Weisinger III, comp., *City of Richmond, Virginia, Wills, 1782-1810* (Richmond: Benjamin B. Weisinger III, 1983), 31, 33; *Robert Morris et al. v. Nathaniel Allen et al.*, Edenton District Superior Court, Record of Pleadings and Decrees, Equity Court, May-November 1788, State Archives.

From Arthur Iredell

Cheshire April 30th. 1785

If all that you urge to induce me to write oftner than I have done was not of the most flattering Nature, I might possibly, my dear Brother, be Contrition itself, but you have taken the sure means of recconciling me to myself—I cannot repent the having extorted from you Assurances of the most cordial regard—Try, on a future occasion, (tho you will never have <another> /a second/) another mode of Reformation, an infallible one, be as negligent as I should be, if I could now be negligent. I am too interested in the hearing from You, not to rouse You by wakening myself first—Your Letter & Tom's of January reached me three Days ago—& have made me extremely happy, because you both of You appear to have been so[1]—How much I wish that my poor Mother was of your Party, & enjoyed the same Ease! I have used every Argument in my Power; but Arguments are less wanted than Money, I believe, & I have little of that God knows, to use at any time—As to Tom's Debts of every [*kind*] [*torn*] [*I*] f[*er*]vently wish it was in my Power to discharge them, & if it ever should be, I most certainly will—but I see no Prospect of this, no near one I mean—My Uncle's remittances are not only very tardy in coming, but are likewise such small ones, that I am generally more in Arrear than they can discharge—& whilst he lives, which I sincerely hope may be long, (do not think this cant) it is next to impossible that I can have any thing to spare, unless to my Mother, whose Wants should certainly have a Preference to my own—I have lately been a most delightfull Tour of four or five Days with Mr. Felton (Amanda's Father)[2] He is very intimately concerned with the great Iron Manufacturers in Shropshire, & I had anxiously wished for a Sight of their Works—He took me with him, & I saw them to the greatest Advantage—They are situated in Coalbrook Dale & the adjacent Country—& you may have an imperfect Idea of their Magnitude, when You hear that, in one Work only, they consume 500 Tons of Coal every day![3] But I will give you in my next Letter a more particular Account of my Tour—Coalbrook Dale is the most delightfull Situation I ever saw—it is just what a Place, a fine Place, should be, both beautifull & sublime—At Mr. Wilkinson's, one of the first Manufacturers we met Silas Deane, your late Plenipot[4] [*torn*] Genius? He may be so, but he cannot talk English—tho perhaps that is not necessary to an American Statesman—or your resentment against Engld. may induce you to disgrace us by deforming our Language. Give my best Love to my Sister & tell her (which will be very satisfactory Information at that time) that She must before this have received a long Letter from Miss Felton, which, I dare swear, She would prefer to one from me—but that I mean to make t[*he*] Tryal by very soon sending one from Myself—Oh! my dear James, a thousand thanks for your Solicitude on her & my Account! Every t[*hing*] I thank God! goes on thrivingly for my Happiness, but Mo[*ney*,] without which, like the rest of the World, I can do nothing—When It will enable me to rival you in all the real Comforts of Life I don't yet know—Remember me most affecttely to Tom, & thank him for his Letter—In a few Weeks I will do so myself—& now I must make my Bow—not without desiring you to present my most Affectte. Compls. to all your near Connections, whom I consider as my own—& also to Mr. Black, who is my acquaintance—Also! I had almost forgotten Amanda's strict Injunctions that I should assure you, my Sister, & Tom, of her warmest Love—Accept it, for it is worth your Acceptance, & believe me ever most truly and affectedly Yours

Arthur Iredell

I shall let you have some news Papers & [*torn*] I mean to send you soon, if I can scrape them together, some things I have scribbled—I shall do so, because it will put a stop to your Importunities. you will not ask for more.[5]

RC, Johnson Collection, NCSA. Printed, McRee, 2:122. Addressed "James Iredell Esqre. Edenton North Carolina America." Endorsed "Cheshire April 30. 1785 Arthur Iredell Ansd."

---

[1]See JI to Arthur Iredell, January 22, 1785, in this volume. Tom's letter not found.

[2]John George Felton.

[3]Coalbrookdale is located approximately twenty miles NW of Birmingham. *Reader's Digest Complete Atlas*, 32.

[4]John Wilkinson (1728-1808) was an innovator in the use of iron. He developed a method of producing cannons and was instrumental in the building of the world's first iron bridge. Newman, *Britain in the Hanoverian Age*, 773-774.

Silas Deane (1737-1789) of Connecticut was sent to France during the early stages of the American Revolution to secure supplies and support. He was recalled in 1778 to face erroneous charges that he had personally profited from the shipment of matériels from France to America. His reputation was further damaged in 1781 when letters he had written to friends calling for an end to the war and reconciliation with England became public. After the war he lived in exile in Belgium and England. *DAB*, s.v. "Deane, Silas."

[5]This note was placed at the top of the first page of the original document.

From Henry E. McCulloh

No. 22. Ironmonger lane London, 15th. may 85.

Dear Sir

I mean little more than to acknowledg the receit of your letter of the 6t. of Jany. & to thank you for the Concern you express for my hardship, & your wishes that I may meet with some Compensation here.[1] I have as you may suppose, laid the best foundn. in my power for that purpose, & with great & reasonable hopes of ultimate Success. to prove the ultimat loss of the Property, the law of Nov. 1784 for its final Sale, you as a Lawyer might have recollected, was essentially necessary for me to produce, God grant you had attended to this Idea, in that case I shd. have had litl. to apprehend & I am sure, if the matter had struck you in this important light, you wod. rather have spared expence or trouble to have procured, & sent me a written <u>Copy of it formally authenticated under the</u> <u>Seal of your State</u>. Circumstanced as I am at present, I have been able <u>only to pledge</u> myself to <u>produce</u> such a <u>Copy of the Act</u>, so authenticated. I trust to you to do me this last, this <u>most essential</u> Service, & to be at the expence of sending an Express to Newbern & procuring the Act with? as apres? & transmitting it to me by the first safe oppurtunity, either from your post or Norfolk. I will chearfully pay the expences you may be at in procuring and forwarding this <u>most important voucher</u>, here to Mrs. Iredell.—As a man of business, I am who may guess at the importance of the object, I need not to you say more: The future colour of my life & fortunes may depend on my having this voucher, & I shall depend on you for it. If you can procur the printed copy of the Confiscation Acts wherein I am named, & send them at the same time, you will render me very essential Service.[2]

I observe what you write as to my debts: My right to them by Treaty I <u>insist upon</u>. I am a born resident <u>Real British Subject</u>, who never owed any alegiance to your State, & what are the legal Impedts. directed to be removed by the Treaty but the Acts of Confiscation? but this is a matter, shod. it be insisted on,—which must be settled elsewhere.—As to your proc. debt, all the credits you propose giving yourself I acknowledg just & proper, I desire you to make them, & I dare say they will settle the Accot. in your favor.—I left it open & beleive I write you for that purpose.

Your debt of honour I shall depend on receiving as soon as it suits. your Circt. & Convenience. sooner I neither wish, expect, or desire it.

Mr. Alexander says your friend George, both for Genius & applicatn., exceeds every thing he ever met with in his whole life. & that by next Spring at farthest he will be [*seal*] to pass his examination for any University in Europe.[3] Towards the fall, he will have learnt enough here, & I propose his return to Carolina, he is happy in your kind & affectionate assurances of friendship & support,—his heart is set upon being with you. but that is a matter I shall defer entering into till I have had some conversation with Mrs. Iredell, & know whether She means to go out to Carolina. In case, She shod not, I think I have a proposal to make respecting George to You, that may <app> probably meet your approbation.—In any Event, I thank you heartily for your assurances of friendship to him, of which I dare say, you will find him very worthy. In Carolina, I dare say he will do well. here without fortune & friends to raise him, he might Starve:—Ruined myself I can do little for him. At present, I am distressing myself to do every thing that reason & affection can dictate.—

If you will please to look back, I beleive you will see, your Superintendance of my affairs was all I required, but I shall in future, observe your explicit declarations, & not trouble you on my Subject;—the procuring & sending me the voucher I have such interesting call for <you> & your kindness to George, I trust I may nevertheless still depend on. I hope to hear from you, & am

affy. & truly. Yrs.

H. E. Mc.Culloh.

P.S. In Case of the Idea of an Act of Banishment being carried into Execution I beg my friends wd. not make any effort to take my name out of it, but e contra I shod. <we> wish it in:[4]—as things are, I <can> consider myself, as it relates to North Carolina, as a person, naturally, as well as politically dead;—& after all, my heart feels an additional pang, when it reflects that to the rest of my most unmerited, & severe Usage, I am obliged to add the painful Idea, that I shall now probably never see persons both most near, & dear to me.—H. E. M.

write me I pray you & send me the law, as soon as possible.

RC, Iredell Papers, Duke. Printed, McRee, 2:122-123. Addressed "James Iredell Esq. Edenton, No. Carolina. Care of B. Mc.C. Esqr. to forward." Endorsed "London 15 May 1785. Henry E. Mc.Culloh."

---

[1]See JI to Henry E. McCulloh, January 6, 1785, in this volume.

[2]The act to which McCulloh refers was passed during the second session of the 1779 General Assembly. McCulloh wanted an official copy of the law to bolster his

case for compensation from the Loyalist Claims Commission in England. Clark, *State Records*, 24:263-264. See also Henry E. McCulloh to JI, February 20, 1784, n. 1, and JI to Henry E. McCulloh, March 3, 1784, n. 2, in this volume.

[3]"Your friend George" is McCulloh's illegitimate son.

[4]No act of banishment was passed. The phrase "e contra" means on the contrary.

To Nelly Blair

Cuffnels May 17th. 1785.[1]

My dear Nelly,

Mr. Hooper and myself came here between nine and ten this morning, and we have prevailed on ourselves without much difficulty to stay till after dinner,—the house being very cool and pleasant, the Mistress of it extremely kind, and a good dinner certain. Mrs. Iredell & my Brother came over with us. Your Aunt I think is better already, and I am persuaded will be much more so. Mrs. Dawson & your Cousin Penny and Miss Gracey tolerably well. We left your Mamma quite so, & Mrs. Johnston getting better, tho' still I believe requiring great attention. You and Peggy are much missed, and must not be too long absent. I hope your Jaunt will be of much service to the health of both. Your Mamma has had a very late letter from Billy. He was quite well. Tell your Uncle the Decree for Spaight against Jordan was upon this principle:—That as Spaight about the time of the conveyance to Jordan had agreed to take £130 Virga. money for the land he could not be injured if he was allowed that sum with Interest, and as the Judges held the conveyance to be in the nature of a Mortgage and obtained fraudulently <from> /by/ old Jordan they therefore decreed for Spaight that Sum with Interest till Jordan's death (about 20 years), which amounted to upwards of £670. They did not decree the land to be reconveyed, thinking it would be hard on the present Possessor, who did not appear to be privy to the Fraud, & had made valuable Improvements on it and as no account of Jordan's appeared, they supposed Spaight's own labour, & that of his Negroe wench, & the Interest since old Jordan's death might probably ballance what Spaight owed[2]—Do you understand any of all this?—Do you know what a mortgage is? As you are only a Lawyer's niece, & not the Wife of one, probably you do not, & must apply for information to your Uncle.—

Remember, your Uncle & Aunt are not to engross you the whole Summer. I shall be impatient to see you on my return. Give my best love to Peggy, and remember me properly to your Uncle and Aunt and Cousins, and believe me, my dear Nelly, ever

Most truly & most affectionately yours

Jas Iredell

RC, Johnson Collection, NCSA.

---

[1]Cuffnels had been the Bertie County home of planter and lawyer Jasper Charlton (d. 1782). *PJI*, 1:341n, 420n; Mitchell, *North Carolina Wills*, 92.

[2]*Thomas Jordan Spaight v. William Jordan et al., executors of the last will and testament of Joseph Jordan.* See Estate of Joseph Jordan, no date, Chowan County Estates, State Archives.

To Hannah Iredell

Newbern May 20. 1785.

My dear Hannah,

We have had upon the whole a very good Journey here, where we arrived this morning. At Windsor we found we could not pass Skewawky, & proceeded that night to your Brother's, where we found all very well except Nelly who had been complaining a little that day, but soon grew very chearful, and I am in hopes would have no return of her complaint, which appeared to be a slight one. We left your Brother's very early in the morning, crossed at Mr. Hill's ferry, & reached at least 54 miles that night, within 4 miles of the 2 Judges & Mr. Moore, whom we overtook at Mrs. Seller's before breakfast the next morning.[1] I by no means regret our roundabout Journey, since it gave me an opportunity of seeing the most delightful meadows on the road to Mr. Hill's I ever saw in my life, and which I believe can scarcely be exceeded, and they are of several miles extent. We had to traverse this town for 3 or 4 hours before we could get lodgings to our mind, but are at length very comfortably fixed at one Hunley's, & hope to get your Brother in with us when he arrives.[2] I was very unwell the day I left you, but have been ever since a great deal better, & am very attentive to my bitters & diet. Mr. Hooper is tolerably well, but a little fatigued & out of humour by our tiresome Jaunting about the Town. Remember me affectionately to Mrs. Dawson & her Family & my Brother to whom I have not time to write—I bought 10 yards of Huckaback for you in Windsor, but found the <loaf sugar> /Coffee/ no cheaper than with us, & therefore bought none.[3] Adieu! my dear Hannah. This opportunity has offered suddenly, & only permits me to add that I am

Most affectionately yours

Ja. Iredell

RC, Johnson Collection, NCSA. Addressed "Mrs. Iredell."

---

[1]Hill's Ferry was located on the Roanoke River in Martin County near Palmyra, the plantation home of Whitmel Hill (1743-1797). Hill was a member of the Continental Congress (1778-1781), state senate (1778-1780, 1784, 1785), and Council of State (1781-1782). *BDC*, s.v. "Hill, Whitmel"; Cheney, *North Carolina Government*, 163.

[2]Hunley may be Richard Hunley (d. 1800) of Craven County. Will of Richard Hunley, 1800, Craven County Wills, State Archives.

[3]Huckaback was a coarse linen used for making towels. *OED*, s.v. "huckaback."

To Richard Caswell

Newbern May 26. 1785

Sir,

I had the honour of receiving your Excellency's letter, & will with great pleasure render any assistance to your business in my power compatible with prior engagements.

I inclose your Excellency a letter from Mr. Cumming, who will be very glad to receive as early an answer as possible. Some expectation of your Excellency being in Town prevented my sending it sooner.

I also take the liberty to inclose an affidavit of my Brother, certified by Judge Williams, requesting the favour of your Excellency to affix the Colony Seal to it—He had a small office in the British Marines, but never served out of England, and his circumstances did not admit of his immediately /giving it up/ when I sent for him here for the purpose of studying the law under me, which he is now doing, with an intention of his becoming a Resident in the Country, and whenever he can divest himself of his half pay I intend he shall do it altogether.

Your Excellency will excuse the unavoidable hurry with which I assure you of my being, most respectfully,

Your faithful & obed. Serv,

Ja. Iredell.

RC, Governors Papers, NCSA. Addressed "His Excellency Richard Caswell Esq. Governor &c. &c." Endorsed "James Iredell Esqr. Newbern 26th May 1785 recd. 27 & answd. 30. May."

To Hannah Iredell

Newbern May 27. 1785

My dear Hannah,

I had great pleasure in receiving your letter by this Post, and was really very much diverted at the laughable account you gave me of one of the most ridiculous scenes that can be imagined. Mr. Hooper and myself enjoyed it highly. Your Brother lodges at Silas Cooke's, so that Mr. H. and myself have not near so much of his company as we had. He is in a great deal better health than when I came. Mine has been a little affected by the severe duty of the Court, but I take all possible precaution, and a few days rest in the happy society at Eden house will soon restore me. Mr. Hooper has taken a memorandam about Mrs. Dawson's letter, & will with pleasure attend to it. I am very sorry it miscarried. Mr. Nash has so far succeeded in Rice's business, as to obtain a declaration from the Court that tho' they could do nothing in this Court, they saw no reason at present why they should not grant a Rehearing at Edenton. But his success so far was principally owing I believe to a piece of evidence in Rice's favour known early that very morning, and given by a Man of extreme good character, of Savage's strong declarations in Rice's favour a short time before his death.[1]

I wish my time would permit me to say more to you, or to write to my Brother. Thank him for his letter, & excuse my not writing for the true reason, <u>of not having time</u>. Give my love to him & the charming Family you are with. I flatter myself I shall find you much better, & am my dear Hannah,

Yours with the tenderest affection

Ja. Iredell

RC, Johnson Collection, NCSA. Addressed "Mrs. Iredell Eden House."

---

[1]In court documents dated May 31, 1785, Samuel Dickinson was accused of taking by force "the goods & chattels of the said Edward [*Rice*] of the value &c damages [*of*] three thousand pounds." Archibald Maclaine represented Rice, and Samuel Johnston was Dickinson's attorney. In November the court summoned Dickinson to appear and answer the charge of trespass. A jurisdiction dispute subsequently arose. By 1794, the suit was still outstanding, although by that time Rice had moved to Virginia. Chowan County Civil Action Papers, State Archives. See also letters of June 27, 1784, n. 2, October 24 and 31, 1785, in this volume.

From Nathaniel Dukinfield

Sulham, near Reading, 10th June, 1785.

Dear Iredell:

At the same time that I received your letter of the 9th of January, I was favored with one from Mr. Johnston, enclosing a copy of my mother's will.[1] I am sorry to hear of the loss you have sustained, but I flatter myself that may be retrieved. There are many persons who have been married as long as you have been without having a child, and afterwards have had several. Lady D. brought me another son on the 3d February last, and his older brother was not a year old. They are both very well at present. The young one I once expected would have died; he was very bad, and even without hopes, which affected his mother to so great a degree, that we both wished for his death and release from pain—this has kept him rather backward. The oldest is the finest boy I ever saw, and is every thing a fond parent can wish. Our fear is that we shall have more than we can well provide for and as Lady D *** with great pain and distress, I hope we shall have no more: though I believe, if she could be sure of one girl and no more children, she would rather prefer that than stop here.[2]

I am much pleased with my mother's will, (for I call her intention to you a part of it,) though I was a good deal affected by the account of her death: yet I received much comfort in reflecting that though she had hitherto lived in peace and quiet, she would probably have soon felt a different situation, by the Commissioners for the sales of confiscated property entering upon the execution of their trusts, and if she had not succeeded in making good her claims, it would have been distressing to her for her to have been obliged to leave a place, which she had lived upon as her own near 30 years. With this packet I send a letter to Mr. Johnston, and a case on my father's and mother's wills, with Mr. Madock's opinion, by which it clearly appears that my mother has ever been entitled to the plantation and personal property.[3] I don't recollect any particular conversation with Captain West that can be drawn to my hurt; and if any word fell when we were talking in private and friendship, and he has used it to diserve me, he is a man to be scouted—as a friend and relation of Brimmage's I met him. I wished to have got the Attorney General's opinion. The case is before him, but my attorney says I shall not get it till the Parliament breaks up; he is so very busy in mending old acts and framing new ones—and I don't know if it will be of any use.

I am very glad that you and Mrs. Iredell were perfectly well: I hope you continue so. I am just recovering from a bilious fever which attacked me smartly for three or four days, and it was thought I would have the jaundice. I was most confoundedly low-spirited, with an universal languor, though I did not think I was immediately going "au monde des taupes."[4] It is the first of the sort I have felt since the year 1771: you will therefore think I have no great reason to complain. The beginning of this week I could not have touched a pen, but had as great an aversion to it as a mad dog has to water. But I can now say "a fig for the doctor."[5] I have never had the pleasure of seeing your brother. He has promised me, by letter, that he will embrace the first opportunity; but I suppose his engagements confine him very much. If he should attend young Crewe to Oxford, my house is not above 22 miles distant.

My best compliments to Mrs. Iredell, Mrs. Blair, and my few (alas) remaining friends, and believe me ever

Yours, most sincerely,

N. Dukinfield.

Printed, McRee, 2:123-124.

---

[1]See JI to Nathaniel Dukinfield, January 9, 1785, in this volume. Samuel Johnston's letter to Dukinfield, dated January 8, 1784, has not been found.

[2]McRee used asterisks to denote text of a delicate nature, usually relating to pregnancy.

[3]Henry Maddock was a barrister of Lincoln's Inn, London, who Dukinfield once described as "an old Practiser in Chancery." Maddock was the father of a better-known legal writer, also called Henry Maddock. *DNB*, s.v. "Maddock, Henry"; Nathaniel Dukinfield to Samuel Johnston, June 10, 1785, Hayes Collection, Southern Historical Collection.

[4]This French phrase translates as "the world of moles," or underground, implying being buried.

[5]A "fig" is a gesture of disdain. The literal gesture, which dates at least to the sixteenth century, is made by inserting the thumb either in one's mouth or between two fingers. *OED*, s.v. "fig."

Smith's Academy Minutes[1]

At a Meeting of the Trustees of Smith's Academy, at the house of Samuel Johnston Esquire at Hayes in Chowan County, on Saturday the second day of July in the year one thousand seven hundred and eighty five.

Present, the following Members—

Samuel Johnston }
Hugh Williamson } Esquires.
Charles Johnson }
Mr. Iredell.

The Board proceeded to the choice of a President, Secretary, and Treasurer for the ensuing year, when Samuel Johnston Esquire was again chosen President, Mr. Iredell Secretary, and Laurence Baker Esquire Treasurer.[2]

Resolved, That the academy be erected in the Town of Edenton, and that Dr. Williamson, Mr. Charles Johnson, and Mr. Iredell be a Committee to examine and report to the Trustees their opinion what part of the Town it would be most eligible to erect the buildings upon, and whether any lot or lots that would be suitable for that purpose remain to be taken up, or could probably be purchased at a moderate price.

Resolved, That the following be the Form for a Subscription to be presented to the Public, and that each Member be furnished with a Copy of it, viz.

"We the Subscribers do severally promise to pay to the Treasurer of Smith's academy (which [*torn*] Town of Edenton) the several Sums annexed to our respective Names, to be applied by the Trustees of the said Academy for the use of the same; one half of the Subscription to be paid on the tenth day of January in the year one thousand seven hundred and eighty six, and the other half on the tenth day of January in the year one thousand seven hundred and eighty seven."

Resolved, That the Treasurer make a demand of the Executors of the last Will of Robert Smith Esquire deceased of the Legacy he so generously left for the use of this Academy.[3]

Ja. Iredell, Secretary.

FC, Johnson Collection, NCSA.

---

[1]JI, as secretary of the board of trustees, recorded these minutes, and they were filed among his papers. Note that while he applies the courtesy title "esquire" to others, he does not use it himself.

In 1782, the General Assembly passed "An Act for the promotion of learning in the District of Edenton," which established the board of trustees of Smith's Academy as a corporate body and listed their powers and obligations. Clark, *State Records*, 24:454-455.

[2]Laurence Baker (1745-1805) of Chowan and Gates Counties was a major in the Continental army during the Revolutionary War and clerk of court in Gates County. *DNCB*, s.v. "Baker, Laurence."

[3]Robert Smith died without children in 1782 and bequeathed "£500 toward support of a public academy that may be erected in Edenton." Will of Robert Smith, 1782, Chowan County Wills, State Archives. See also JI to Mess. Conyngham, Nesbitt & Co., January 3, 1784, n. 3, in this volume.

From Tristrim Lowther[1]

Eden House 4th. July 1785

My dear Sir

I have the pleasure to inform you that I returned here yesterday in good health from Halifax & that I have met with nothing to make me regret my journey on /the/ contrary I have received the most flattering marks of attention & hospitality from all the inhabitants of that polite & agreeable place of which I had formed a pleasing idea but I must confess I found my expectations greatly exceeded. I consider myself under particular obligations to you for the letters of introduction you were so obliging as to favor me with to Col. Mc.Cullochs family & I have only to lament that I had it not in my power longer to cultivate the acquaintance of a family whose manners hospitality & politeness cannot fail of strongly attaching every person who has the happiness to know them. I have had the good fortune during my journey considerably to extend my acquaintance among the inhabitants of this Martin & Halifax Counties & the pleasure to find that the prejudices which unfortunately have been imbibed against me in this Country are confined to a very narrow circle.[2]

Remember me in the most affectionate & respectful manner to Mrs. Iredell Miss Blair & the rest of your amiable family also to Mrs. Iredell & give me leave dear Sir to assure you that I shall ever consider your late goodness & reflect upon it with a heart replete with the most grateful sensations & that I shall remain while I live with the greatest sincerity & regard your truly affectionate

& much obliged

T. Lowther

RC, Iredell Papers, Duke. Printed, McRee, 2:124-125. Addressed "James Iredell Esqr. Edenton." Endorsed "Eden house 4 July 1785. T. Lowther. Ansd."

---

[1]Tristrim Lowther of Bertie and Chowan Counties was the son of William Lowther (d. 1794), a merchant of Edenton and New York. The elder Lowther had provided the British with intelligence about privateers during the Revolutionary War, and as a result, his property in Edenton was confiscated. Tristrim represented Bertie County in the house of commons (1792-1793). He married Penny Dawson, niece of Hannah Iredell, on January 14, 1786. *PJI*, 1:20n; Palmer, *Biographical Sketches*, 508; Loyalist Claim of William Lowther, English Records, Audit Office Papers, State Archives; Cheney, *North Carolina Government*, 228; William Hooper to JI, February 12, 1786, in this volume; D. L. Corbitt, ed., "Historical Notes," *North Carolina Historical Review* 9 (January 1932): 91.

[2]The taint of Toryism followed Lowther for years after the war as revealed in letters of the Iredell family. For example, JI wrote to Hannah on October 22, 1785, "Your information about T. L. gives me concern, as I see no prospect of his situation mending, & the People of G. B. appear to me to take pains to keep up the spirit of Enmity that unfortunately too much prevails against particular Persons." In a letter of February 3, 1787, Nelly Blair told JI, "T. Lowther blusters about very much. he is determined to attend next Subscription Ball. is sorry he did not go to The last. in short he talks quite ridiculously & will I fear revive all The Old prejudices." The 1785 letter is from the Johnson Collection, State Archives; the 1787 letter is from the Iredell Papers, Rare Book, Manuscript, and Special Collections Library, Duke University.

From William Hooper

Hillsboro 6th. July 1785

Dear Sir,

This will be handed to you by a messenger whom we Send to Mr. Pinto to assist him with horses in his progress hither.[1] I have not heard of you or any of my friends at Edenton Since I parted with you at Newbern, and as your health at that time was by no means confirmed, & the accounts from Mrs. Johnston by no means the most favourable I have been truly anxious to learn how heaven has conducted itself to you & your friends Since your return to them.

We here enjoy our usual good health, not an individual of my family had been indisposed during my absence. I found them all in high health and spirits, enjoying in common with the rest of the town an event which had taken place just before my return, of which I have given Mr. Johnston an account & it will therefore be unnecessary to repeat it to you—Glorious example to all husbands in the like case offending![2]

Our Court at Wilmington went on in the old dilatory mode of doing business. Great threats of dispatch accomplished in the usual way. Much conversation from Germanicus on the bench, his vanity has become insufferable & is accompanied with the most overbearing insolence.[3] Maclaine & he had a terrible fracas Germanicus with those Strong intuitive powers with which he is inspired took up Maclaines defence in an Ejectment & ran away with it before it was opened. Maclaine expostulated Scolded Stormed called names, abandoned the cause. All was confusion. The Jury took the cause. I prevailed—Spencer made condescensions. Hostilities ceased & peace was restored.[4]

It is a doubtful circumstance whether I shall be in the next assembly. I have no desire to make any condescensions to men whom I heartily despise to Secure their votes or interest. The Courts must be altered &

most earnestly do I hope that you and Mr. Johnston will have a principal share in planning a new establishment[5] Against the present system the cries of the people are loud. they must be heard—they ought to be heard. But what affects me most is that the censure is pointed at the bar when the occasion is Seated much higher. It is a melancholy consideration that we have not proper materials in this country to form the officers which our constitution makes necessary. We must do the best we can with such stuff as we have until our Academies & colleges supply us with something that may be more equal to the purpose.

Our little town of Hillsb. begins to thrive Some new buildings are begun & many more in contemplation. The Academy will give it a very considerable spring & should the Assembly return hither our importance is Sealed[6]—and then Squhawkay. what will become of thy healthy barrens—they will be as they were intended by Providence a desolate uninhabited waste to make poverty & wretchedness comforted in their condition by shewing them that bad as the soil may be to which Providence /has determined them/ that Still there is a worse. The alteration of courts I flatter myself will again draw your attention this way and give me what alone I want to make my situation here compleatly happy—your & Mr. Johnstons family.

I visited your old friend Genl. Clark when I was at Cape Fear. A deep melancholy has fixed itself upon him & he denies all comfort. His complexion is that of a deep Jaundice—has lost all his flesh—his conversation turns upon nothing but the occasion of his distress, & when he is told that he can not live long in that unhealthy place, he says with utmost earnestness that he fears he shall. I think a very few months will end him & alas! I tremble for the effects such an event would have on my wife. I earnestly wish that I could draw him hither; but of that I despair.

At Wilmington I saw Mrs. Tho Hooper who was there to attend the nuptials of her sister Betsy, who gave her hand to a Mr. Mackenzie (Billy Campbells nephew) while I was at Wilmington.[7] Mrs. Hooper is a very fine woman much polished with her tour thro Britain but alas! yet but a little while & how useless all her accomplishments—She is in a consumption—my brother Tom in the same condition—both going to Rhode Island flying from death—which I fear is at no great distance from them [*illegible*] Geo Hooper & his wife were also at Wilmington he is much improved in his health and appearance. She has not her health in So. Carolina but is grown much more easy & affable than she was. Our Meeting was awkward—distant, distressing to me.

Your dunnery letters were delivered & the most Solemn promises made to deposit the money immediately with Mr. Th. Maclaine. I had not entire faith in them.

I flatter myself that I shall by Mr. Pinto get a long letter from you. Be not discouraged from any apprehension that I may in return distress you with another Scrawl of equal length with this—There is no probability that I shall find another opportunity before I see you, as there is as little intercourse betwixt this & Edenton as between this & another world. And now My dear Sir, Let me entreat you to offer Mrs. Hooper Betsys & my kind regards to Mrs. Iredell, Mrs. Blair Miss Blair & Miss Peggy & your brother Accept our best wishes for their & your health & happiness & believe me Ever with unalterable esteem & affection

Your friend & Obedt. Set

Will Hooper

P.S. Let me ask the favour of you to assist Pinto to come forward Should he meet any Obstructions Be pleased to assist to obviate them

RC, Emmet Collection, NYPL. TSS, Thomas Addison Emmet, NCSA. Printed, McRee, 2:125-127.

---

[1]Solomon Pinto (1758-1824), a graduate of the College of New Haven, was a schoolmaster at Hillsborough Academy. Receipt, June 3, 1788, Hillsborough Academy Papers, State Archives; *Vital Records of New Haven, 1649-1850,* 2 pts. (Hartford: Connecticut Society of the Order of the Founders and Patriots of America, 1917), 1:357, 2:610; Ruth Blackwelder, *The Age of Orange: Political and Intellectual Leadership in North Carolina, 1752-1861* (Charlotte, N.C.: William Loftin, 1961), 121.

[2]The "event" has not been identified but was probably a wedding.

[3]Germanicus is Samuel Ashe.

[4]This incident was but one battle in a war between lawyers and judges. For information on the conflict, see Waldrup's "James Iredell and the Practice of Law in Revolutionary Era North Carolina," 300-323.

[5]Many North Carolina lawyers favored such reform, including JI, who had drafted and introduced legislation in 1777 to create the state's first system of courts. The distance between the towns where court was held and an insufficient number of judges caused the wheels of justice to turn slowly. In addition, personality clashes between lawyers and judges, and the accompanying accusations of incompetence, undermined the system. When cases involved controversial issues, such as Loyalist claims, proceedings were often marred by displays of bitter partisanship. In 1782, William R. Davie introduced reform measures in the General Assembly. In subsequent sessions, including that of November 1785, other proposals were made. Despite the general recognition of the need for

change, reform was gradual and piecemeal. The changes proposed by Davie were for the most part implemented by 1805. Whichard, *Justice James Iredell*, 19-20; Robinson, *William R. Davie*, 159-160; Waldrup, "James Iredell," 300-323.

[6]In 1778, the General Assembly passed legislation to found a school in Hillsborough to be called Science Hall. In 1784, the assembly amended this act and incorporated the board of trustees of Hillsborough Academy. The school, which was funded through private subscriptions, had two faculty members when it opened, and classes were held in the renovated St. Matthew's Church. The school operated for approximately sixty years. Clark, *State Records*, 24:250-251, 605-607; Miscellaneous Papers, Hillsborough Academy Papers, State Archives; Francis Nash, "The History of Orange County-Part 1," *North Carolina Booklet*, 10 (October 1910): 107-109.

[7]Mary Heron Hooper was the wife of Thomas Hooper (ca. 1746-ca. 1821) of Wilmington and Charleston, South Carolina. He was a merchant and William's brother. Elizabeth "Betsy" Heron married John McKenzie. *DNCB*, s.v. "Hooper, Thomas," "Heron, Benjamin."

From Henry E. McCulloh

No. 22. Ironmonger lane London, 25th. July 1785.

Dear Sir

I did myself the favor to write you the 15th. of may in answer to your letter of the 6th. of January.[1]—I am convinced it will give you sensible Concern to hear that for want of my being able to produce an authentic & <u>certified</u> Copy of the Act passed at your Assembly in Nov. last, (directing the Sale of the Confd. Property,) to the Commissn of American Claims, I am excluded from all participation of a paymt. of /£/ 150,000. Stg. made by Govt., this Sessions, on that accot.—Since the passing of the said Act I relinquish all thoughts of ever being restored to an acre of my lost landed Property in No. Carolina.—A Copy of the said Act, duly extracted from your Records, & Certified under the Seal of your State is required of me to be produced here.—I wrote to B Mc.Culloch to procure & send it me, and if you can be assistant in so doing, you will essentially serve me.

No cognizance is taken here, of the debts due me in your State, as it is insisted on that they are preserved to me by the Treaty, & that the legal Impediments referred to in the 4th. article, are clearly the Confiscation acts,—if your State says otherwise,—the matter must be settled between the higher Powers.—It will be very essential to me to know what proceedings take place in your State on this matter, and I shall be much obliged to you to inform me thereof, for my government, <u>here</u>.[2]

I inclose you a letter from Mrs. Iredell, & another from George—who is by Mr. Alexander's accot., making a very rapid & surprising progress. He has the greatest respect for you, & Reliance on your kindness, & when you recollect my Father's & my wishes to serve you in days past, I hope you will return them, by being a friend to this young man.—If you can take him under your direction, I shod. greatly prefer it:—his being in your home, is of no great consequence; if he is near, & under your eye. He possesses immense application. You are pleased to write me that you hold yourself my Dr.—for the 300/£/ & odd Sterl. remaining of your Engagemt. to me for the 600/l/. Sterling, after deducting the Legacy left you by Miss Macartney, & that you would pay me that Sum at your first conveniency:[3]—Take care of George, & his Board for two years,—and take whatever part of this Sum you please for your remuneration, and if you agree to take him, I have mentd. to Mrs. Iredell, that I will exert myself to assist her getting out to you, as far as 20 or 25 Gs.—which in my present great distress, is the utmost in my power.[4]

I beg your answer on this matter by the very first opporty. and if you will inclose & transmit your letters for me as above, to the care of Mr. Watson Stott, Merchant, at Suffolk in Virginia (who is a Nephew of my friend Mr. Jas. Gibson,) he will forward them Safely.

I hope you have recd. the letters I wrote you in Octr., Novr., Feby. & may last, to which I hope to be favoured with answers.[5]

I am Dear Sir Your assd. friend & Obedt. Servt

Henry E. Mc.Culloh.

P.S. I beg your care of the inclosed for Mr. Maclane, to be forwd. by <u>a safe hand only</u>.

RC, Iredell Papers, Duke. Addressed "Jas. Iredell Esqr. Edenton, No. Carolina."

---

[1]See JI to Henry E. McCulloh, January 6, 1785, and Henry E. McCulloh to JI, May 15, 1785, in this volume.

[2]See JI to Henry E. McCulloh, June 15, 1784, in this volume.

[3]Margaret Macartney (d. 1775) left £300 to JI. *PJI*, 1:69, 397n.

[4]Mrs. Iredell is JI's mother, Margaret McCulloh. JI had been trying to persuade her to move from England to North Carolina. "Gs" are guineas, which are coins worth twenty-one shillings.

[5]See Henry E. McCulloh to JI, February 20, 1784, and May 15, 1785, in this volume.

From Arthur Iredell

Cheshire July 31st. 1785—

"The Tables are turned," my dear James—you are become negligent, & I am the most punctual Correspt. in the World! I cannot give a more convincing Proof of it than by writing at this time, when I really have not ten minutes at my Disposal.—"Haven't you heard from America?" is now Miss F's constant Question, for; if you have not received, I mean Mrs. Iredell, a Packet She sent her, such an one went, & was expected before this to have produced a very valuable Return, hence Fears, Anxieties, & every thing that Modesty & Nerves can produce—I certainly told you in my last Letter of my intended Voyage to the West Indies, & my Motives for undertaking it[1]—If I did not know briefly that it is a Scheme my Friends have all united in reccommending, as the most likely means of facilitating an establishment for me. He has approved of a Marriage with Miss F, but he has not yet enabled me to compleat it; & added to interested Motives, I have really a very great desire to be known by & to know one to whom I am (at your Expence) so considerably indebted—When I shall sett out or from Whence I cannot tell you, for at present I am not rich enough to arrange Matters—some Sugars my Uncle promised to send me long before this not having yet arrived but you shall know almost as soon as myself, for I have News Papers, Pamphlets &c. for you, & they must be sent off before I leave England. You will doubtless hear from my Mother by this Packet, but least you should not, She is as well as She can be here, & as obstinate as ever in keeping the resolution of paying off Tom's Debts before She enjoys the Quiet & Happiness of Carolina—Apropos—how happy should I be in seeking for them myself! The Idea alone electrifies me with Joy, but, I fear, after all I must be content with a future Prospect, till more of our Clouds disperse—

Tom has written, I find, to my Mother who will grow fat upon the Strength of his having done so, & furnish Work for her Mantua Maker, because the Taylor has been letting out his Cloaths—Am I an Uncle yet? Pray take great care, & let me be, & <u>continue</u> so—My best Love to my Sister & Tom—Why not to many other People, who, I am sure, deserve it? So let dispense it liberally amongst the Blood of the Johnston's (for I would not confine it to the Name as there are <u>Blairs</u> & Dawsons I <u>know</u>) & in return accept M[*iss F*]eltons—<u>who dies</u> to know [*torn*] may She do so, after Mr. Phoebus, who [*faded*] me, & in a few Hours will be equally busy with your Worship, shall have viewed a few more of our revolutions!—

May he then be able to scorch us with the same Rays![2]—God bless you all I am ever, most truly & affectionately your's

A Iredell—

I cry Mrs. Bayley's Mercy!—She desired her best Comps.—She has just got a Son who may be seen thro' a Microscope but not by the naked Eye. it is littleness itself—

RC, Johnson Collection, NCSA. Addressed "James Iredell Esqr. Edenton North Carolina America."

---

[1]See Arthur Iredell to JI, April 30, 1785, in this volume.

[2]Phoebus is the Greco-Roman god of the sun.

From Samuel Cutler[1]

Hartford Augt. 7th. 1785

Dear Sir

Your very obliging Letter of the 20th. of March, I recd. by Mr. Lowther. Since which I have had no Opportunity of writing you, As I am now going to N York I hope to find Some Conveyance from there

Mr. Webster last Spring Set of for the southern States and did me the Honor to take Charge of a Letter for you, But as it is very uncertain wheather he took Edenton in his Way, or wheather you have recd. it, I will now tell you that I have formed a Connection with an english Gentleman in a little Business in Connecticut, by which I hope to live comfortably the Remainder of my days; I have here recd. every Civility I could wish, yet the forming new Connections, at my Time of Life, amoung a People in their Genius & manners totally different from those that I have lived amoung for near twenty years past, to me is truly disagreable. But the most unpleasing Circumstance of all, is my Seperation from my Friends in every Quarter for whom I have the most tender Regard: This State is remarkable for having the first Bishop settled in it. Dr. Seabury has arrivd. within this few Weeks with Powers of Ordination & from whom four Gentlemen have already receivd. holy Orders;[2] his coming meets the Approbation of the Legislature & I belive of the Generality of the People. One unfavorable Circumstance however attends it. this is the Society withdrawing the Salaries from the Clergy they have keept upon their Books till very lately. they having discovered that it is inconsistant with their Charter to continue their Missionaries in the United States, but have given Assurances that they will provide for those that will remove to any of the British Settlements[3]

Notwithstanding our distance from each Other, the many pleasing Hours I have spent in your Family and the most agreable Conversation I have enjoyed, often occur to my Mind, and make the Subject of my most pleasing Reflection in my solitary Hours; and when I consider the great Improbability of ever participating again of those Enjoyments, (melancholly Reflection) I feel the Obligations that I am under to your Goodness, with double Force; Be assured my Dear Sir, my best Wishes are and ever will be for your & your Families Welfare; You well know who my Friends are. will you in your manner, make my Compliments to them, particularly to Mrs. Iredell & Family

& Belive me Dear Sir yours most

Saml. Cutler

RC, Iredell Papers, Duke. Printed, McRee, 2:127-128. Addressed "James Iredell Esq Edenton North Carolina."

---

[1]Samuel Cutler, formerly of North Carolina, moved to Connecticut and later to Vermont. He was a physician, merchant, farmer, miller, distiller, and legislator. He was probably a Loyalist during the Revolution and may have received legal counsel from JI. In a letter to Hannah, JI mentions Cutler and refers to "the little cloud on his political character during the war." Cutler held JI in such high regard that he named his son after him. McRee, *Life and Correspondence*, 2:444-445; Whichard, *Justice James Iredell*, 222-223.

[2]Samuel Seabury (1729-1796) became Episcopal bishop of Connecticut in 1784. During the Revolution he had been chaplain in Edward Fanning's Loyalist regiment. George L. Clark, *A History of Connecticut: Its People and Institutions*, 2d ed. (New York: G. P. Putnam's Sons, 1914), 141-142; Richard J. Purcell, *Connecticut in Transition, 1775-1818* (Washington, D.C.: American Historical Association, 1918), 53.

[3]After the Revolution, the Society for the Propagation of the Gospel in Foreign Parts no longer paid the salaries of clergymen in the former colonies. In addition, the Church of England could not consecrate American bishops because they were no longer subjects of the Crown. Samuel Seabury of Connecticut had to go to Scotland for consecration. Parliament passed a law in 1786, however, allowing English bishops to consecrate Americans without requiring that they declare loyalty to the king. London and Lemmon, *Episcopal Church in North Carolina*, 66, 77.

To Nelly Blair

Dukinfield 15th. Sept. 1785.

My dear Nelly

I thank you for the favour of your letter, and for remembering at last to send my Razors, after my patience was almost exhausted, making a most scandalous appearance, and being prevented half a day going to Mrs. Dawson's. However your apology is so ingenuous that I can no longer be angry, especially when I was so negligent myself as to omit sending letters from your Uncle John which I had in my pocket. They were brought by an old Wench of Mrs. Dawson's. You will find he has had the ague and fever, but is better. Neither your Aunt or I had any letter. Mrs. Pearson and Miss Vail are much better, and your Aunt I think improved by her expedition. We are just going to Mrs. Dawsons. I know not whether she will write to your Mamma. You will therefore give her love as well as mine to her and the rest of her Children, and accept of it yourself. We are very unhappy about Gaby. Pray write to us, for we expect to be here again tomorrow night.

I am ever, my dear Nelly, Your very affectionate

Ja Iredell.

RC, Johnson Collection, NCSA. Addressed "Miss Blair Edenton."

To Hannah Iredell

Hornes, Sept 29. 1785[1]

My dear Hannah,

We arrived at Mrs. Charlton's before sunset last night, and did not leave it till past sun rise this morning, and having taken a fine quantity of Snake root last night, and being in an excellent Bed, I am much better of my cold to day.[2] I recollect another thing I had forgot, of which I entreat you for Pity's sakes to say nothing to a single Mortal. It is <u>my Notes of hand</u>. They are in one of my Drawers in the inside of the desk. (the lowest I believe to the left hand) and I beg the favour of you to send them to me (at least those for Halifax) by your Brother—Mr. & Mrs. Pollok dined here last Monday. My Fellow Companion is very well. Adieu! my dear Hannah. Give my love & respects to your Sister and her Daughters, and Mrs. Dawson and hers &c. and believe me ever

Most affectionately yours

Ja. Iredell.

P.S. Remember me to Tom.

RC, Johnson Collection, NCSA. Addressed "Mrs. Iredell Edenton."

[1]Hornes was located near Norfleet's ferry, which was situated near the point where Halifax, Northampton, and Bertie Counties meet. *PJI*, 2:147; Powell, *Gazetteer*, 353, 439; "A Compleat Map of North Carolina from an actual Survey by Capt. Collett, 1770," in W. P. Cumming, *North Carolina in Maps* (Raleigh: State Department of Archives and History, 1966), plate 6.

[2]Abigail Charlton of Bertie County was the wife of Jasper Charlton, who is often mentioned in JI's correspondence. She was one of the signers of what has become known as the Edenton Tea Party resolution. *PJI*, 1:286n.

Snakeroot was made into a tea to treat rheumatism and fevers. Danielle Lopes, Joan Moser, and Annie Louise Perkinson, *Appalachian Folk Medicine: Native Plants and Healing Traditions* (Asheville, N.C.: Warren Wilson College Press, 1996), 6, 20.

To Hannah Iredell

Elk Marsh Oct. 1 1785.

My dear Hannah,

The evening of the day I left Mrs. Charlton's, finding we could not reach Gen. Jones's in time, we put /up/ at Bryan's, where I expected we should meet very bad fare, but was agreeably disappointed, so much so that I declined a very kind invitation from the old Man in the new house to stay with him. I breakfasted yesterday at Gen. Jones's, whose heart I made easy by the Papers I gave him, and Mrs. Jones was particularly obliging indeed, and very earnestly & repeatedly expressed a great desire to see you at her house.[1] I dined at Mr. Bond's, & came on here in the afternoon, where we found Mr. & Mrs. Pollok arrived but about an hour before us.[2] Mrs. Pollok has been a good deal unwell. He is extremely well & Th. Buncombe.[3] They don't go from here till to morrow, we to day, and I hope to be in Hillsborough with great ease on monday. Mrs. Pollok seemed disappointed at not having /a letter/ from Mrs. Dawson, but I blundered the best apology in my power. The Family here are all very well, except Mrs. Mc.Culloch who looks far from being so, but that may be occasioned by grief for her Sister, Mrs. Long, who died about 3 weeks ago.[4] The old Man is in Warren. I went to every store in Windsor to enquire for Flat Irons, but could get none. Bryer promised to engage Tallow, if he could, but he said it was very scarce.[5] I ought to have mentioned this in my letter from Horne's.[6] The Papers I wrote about to my Brother from Dukinfield I afterwards found. Ah! my dear Hannah! what does this day suggest to me.[7] Heaven bless you! and grant you a more confirmed state of health than that I left you in. Billy is quite well and desires me to be joined in love & respects to, thank God, too numerous a set of Friends to be readily named.

I am ever Most affectionately yours

Ja. Iredell.

RC, Johnson Collection, NCSA. Addressed "Mrs. Iredell Edenton."

---

[1]Allen Jones (1739-1798), brother of Willie Jones, was a brigadier general in the Revolutionary War. He served in the Continental Congress and the 1788 state ratification convention. *BDC*, s.v. "Jones, Allen."

[2]Mr. Bond is probably Hanse Bond, and Mr. and Mrs. Pollock are Cullen Pollock and his wife.

[3]Thomas Buncombe (b. 1769) was the son of Col. Edward Buncombe (1742-1778) of Tyrrell County, who died after being wounded during the Battle of Germantown. Thomas's mother had died earlier. The Pollocks raised the Buncombes' two daughters and possibly Thomas after the colonel's death. Buncombe County was named in honor of Thomas's father. *PJI*, 2:393n; *DNCB*, s.v. "Buncombe, Edward."

[4]Rebecca Hill Long was the wife of Nicholas Long Jr. (d. 1819) and sister of Mrs. Benjamin McCulloch. *DNCB*, s.v. "Long, Nicholas."

[5]Benjamin Bryer (d. 1789) of Bertie County was licensed to operate an ordinary in his home in August 1786. Mitchell, *North Carolina Wills*, 70; *Bertie County, North Carolina, County Court Minutes, 1781-1787*, vol. 5 (Durham: Weynette Parks Haun, 1982), 140.

[6]See JI to Hannah Iredell, September 29, 1785, in this volume.

[7]October 1 was the first anniversary of the birth of JI and Hannah's son. The baby died after only two days.

To Hannah Iredell

Hillsborough Oct. 5. 1785.

My dear Hannah,

I have the pleasure to acquaint you that Billy and I arrived here last night, both perfectly well, and both lodged at Mr. Hooper's, sharing one bed.[1] I endeavoured to be off, but to no purpose, as he had reserved a room expressly for me. Mrs. and Miss Horne are still here, as well as Mrs. Huske, who expects her Husband for her in a few days. Every one here, except one or two in Mr. Hog's Family (his Son from Scotland, and Nelly, who have had a little of the Ague and Fever—what think you of that?) extremely well.[2] Mr. Hooper's house is much enlargd, and really very commodious and elegant. He was much pleased with his Chair. We were fortunate enough to escape all the heavy rain on the road, & made very moderate Journies.—I hoped to have had more time; as Mr. Blount did not intend to go till morrow morning; but he has just informed he shall go immediately after dinner; and it is now past 3 o'clock. Give my love to your Sister and Nelly and Peggy, Mrs. Dawson and Miss Penny (you see I am in Sam's manner) and your Brother and his Family. God grant you may be now perfectly well. Upon my honour I am so. As a proof of it, my complexion is greatly admired & complimented. Snake root has entirely conquered my cold.

—Adieu! Heaven bless you, and believe me; my dearest Hannah, Most affectionately yours,

Ja. Iredell.

RC, Johnson Collection, NCSA. Addressed "Mrs. Iredell Edenton."

---

[1]Billy Blair was the son of George and Jean Johnston Blair and the brother of Nelly Blair. *PJI,* 1:100n, 158n.

[2]Mr. Hogg's son from Scotland is Walter Hogg (Alves), previously identified. Nelly is Helen Hogg (1769-1846). She married William Hooper, son of JI's friend of the same name, and after his death, Joseph Caldwell, first president of the University of North Carolina. William Hooper to JI, September 8, 1784, n. 3, in this volume; *Life and Times of James Hogg*, 21.

JI's remark "what think you of that" is in reference to the efforts of William Hooper and others to persuade the Iredells to move to Hillsborough because of its healthy climate as opposed to that of Chowan County. See William Hooper to JI, March 15, 1784, n. 9, in this volume.

From Nelly Blair

Edenton October 14th.

You see my Dear Uncle I am determined notwith/standing/ all your endeavours to The contrary to continue a correspond/ence/ which has constantly been The source of so much pleasure to me. it is I own very selfish in me to insist upon it, but I will be doubly disinterested on some other occasion to make amends.

Mrs. Dawson has been over The Creek now a fortnight. it is impossible for me to express how dull The House seems since Yourself & They have left it—I assure you we pray for your safe & speedy return—we have lost all our visitors too—Mr. Black is in Virginia. Dr. Ramkee has so much business he scarcely ever has time to call & Poor Mr. Bornicke, he has been at the point of Death & is hardly able now to go about, & all These things were not mortifying enough, but you must go <about> & write to Aunt Iredell & your Brother, without even making an apology for neglecting me—

Dr. Williamson & I are become great Friends. he has sent me The Translation of Sophocles, & Euripedes Plays to read, & spoke as if he had some other Books to lend me, when I was done with them, which I fear will not be shortly, for Tho' I read the Plays with eagerness, yet there are long comparisons between the Plays between The Ancient & modern Theatre's & an account of the rise & origin of the greek Theatre which I suppose The Dr. thought would be the most useful part, & which some how or other I never can find time to read[1]—

Mamma & Peggy join in love to you with

Your ever Affectionate

H Blair

RC, Johnson Collection, NCSA. Printed, McRee, 2:128-129. Addressed "James Iredell Esqr. Halifax favor'd by Mr. Johnston." Endorsed "Edenton 14 October 1785 Helen Blair."

---

[1]The anthology that Dr. Hugh Williamson gave to Nelly Blair may have been all or some of the seven volumes of English translations of Greek plays entitled *The Greek Tragic Theatre: containing Aeschylus by Dr. Potter, Sophocles by Dr. Franklin, and Euripides by Mich. Wodhull, with a dissertation on ancient tragedy by Thomas Franklin* (London, 1777).

To Nelly Blair

Halifax October 18. 1785

My dear Nelly

You did great wrong to my gratitude & taste in supposing I meant to discourage so valuable a correspondence as yours, for such it has ever been to me, and I hope will long continue so. Far from slighting it, I received your agreeable favour by your Uncle with very great satisfaction.[1] I relied on your Candour to excuse me without a formal apology, not suspecting the inference you have drawn from the want of one, for my affection would of itself have prompted a letter had I had time to write it, and I am sure for the future my vanity will be an additional incentive, since I am flattered with finding it of consequence. It gives me concern to hear you have been a little indisposed, tho' upon the whole I have great reason, as I truly am, to be thankful for the accounts I have received. I am sure you must miss Mrs. Dawson & her charming Daughter very much. Happy shall I again be in mixing with our agreeable circle.—I am glad to hear of Dr. Williamson's attention, & that it displays itself in a manner which may be useful to you. My Books have come by mistake here, but no letters for me, at which I am very much surprised, but I really am more grieved at Mrs. Dawson's disappointment than my own, thinking it peculiarly severe & provoking. I hope however she is thoroughly satisfied of his health, since it is so well vouched by that severe Man Mr. Elmsley.[2] I am quite vexed (between ourselves) at the levity & indifference of Sir N. D.'s letter wrote in answer to mine giving a very particular & to me a very affecting account of his Mother's death.[3] He bears it with all the cursed stoicism of a Philosopher, and is still afraid that his Wife will ruin him with a great number of Children. He would well deserve a Xantippe for his next Wife, and a double set of Children into the bargain.[4] It is insufferable to see a young Man so insensible & so avaricious.

I have a letter for you from Mrs. Huske, but I don't know whether I shall enclose it now.[5] Your Friend Mrs. Mc.Coy and her Gentlemen are well. I enclosed your letter under a cover to him, and put it in the care of Governor Martin.

Contrary to a Custom you have complained of, I have wrote this letter first, determined you should not go without one. You will be so good as to remember me affectionately to your Mamma & Sister. Your Brother left Hillsborough very well on the 7th. Instant. Adieu! my dear Nelly, and believe me ever, whether I do or do not write,

Most sincerely & affectionately yours

Ja. Iredell.

RC, Iredell Papers, Duke. Printed, McRee, 2:129-130. Addressed "Miss Blair Edenton."

---

[1]See Nelly Blair to JI, October 14, 1785, in this volume.

[2]The nature of Mrs. Dawson's disappointment has not been determined. Mr. Elmsley may be Alexander Elmsley, previously identified.

[3]See JI to Nathaniel Dukinfield, January 9, 1785, and Nathaniel Dukinfield to JI, June 10, 1785, in this volume.

[4]The name Xantippe, the wife of Socrates, has become a synonym for an ill-tempered woman. *OED*, s.v. "Xantippe."

[5]In her letter of October 14, 1785, to Nelly Blair, Elizabeth Huske wrote, "This place [*Hillsborough*] will soon be very dull. Mr. Iredell, and Mr. Hooper, are to set out tomorrow on the circuit. . . . Mr. Malletts family are gone and I suppose not to return for he is in a manner bannished from this. the circumstances are too tedious for me to relate but your Uncle will tell much better then I am capible of doing." Iredell Papers, Rare Book, Manuscript, and Special Collections Library, Duke University. For information on Peter Mallett, see William Hooper to JI, September 8, 1784, n. 4, in this volume.

To Hannah Iredell

Halifax October 19th. 1785.

My dear Hannah,

In consequence of my waiting for Mr. Hooper till Saturday we did not arrive here till yesterday morning. I am really a great deal better than when

I left home, and every body tells me I look so. I had not the slightest complaint when I left Hillsborough, but have caught a very trifling cold (scarcely perceivable) on the road, & which I should not think worth mentioning if your kindness did not induce you to doubt my word when I am not very particular. I have not the least symptom, nor had since I parted from you, of my former Complaint. Mr. Hooper caught a slight cold also, tho' we were not much exposed, but obliged to ride a little later than we wished one evening, tho' it was a very fine one. Thank God, I have such pleasing accounts of you & my other Friends, so much better than might be expected at this season—Mr. Black arrived here yesterday, & poor Fellow! looks very ill. It greatly affected me to see him, and I fear he will have to go immediately to Petersburg, which I shall be much concerned for, as his health is far from being good enough for such a Journey. My Books are arrived by mistake here, but no letters, which I am much surprised at, but I am much more at Mrs. Dawson's getting no Letter, which is certainly extremely provoking. I am very glad to hear however Billy is well. I can easily make allowance for my Mother's not writing in the midst of Hookey's confusion after so long a delay—.[1] I have a letter from Sir N D. which I am almost tempted to burn, it discovers such scandalous insensibility on his Mother's death, and the usual cant of his being likely to be ruined with children, as he had another Son born last February.[2] He says tho' he believes he & his Wife would put up with one more, if they could be sure it would be a Girl.—I left all our Friends well at Hillsborough. Miss Johnston still for Market, & preparing to go to Cape Fear with Mrs. Huske, who was very well, & has the biggest child I believe in the whole Country. We left Mr. & Mrs. Pollok, & Nelly, at Mr. Bennehan's on their way down.[3] I am to have a quarter Cask of very fine Port from him in part of a Fee, & got at Hillsborough 16 1/4 yards very fine linen for another. The debt was critical, and I was advised to take it tho at 12/ a yard. Mrs. Heron told me such cost at Wilmington 10/6, for I consulted her & Mr. Hooper about the quality of it, and they pronounced it extremely good.[4] I believe Judge Williams's Wife will come to Edenton with him. Nothing I believe will prevent it, except the illness of Mrs. Henderson's eldest Son who was supposed to be a good deal in danger as we came along.[5] A great number of Criminals are to be tried here. One was condemned for horse stealing at Hillsborough, and a very affecting circumstance so far as affects his Family, took place in regard to Ja. Williams, his conviction on an Indictment for very scandalous practices as an Attorney, for which he was dismissed from the Bar.[6] His poor Wife was almost distracted, got no sleep for five nights, & at length scarcely obtained any by means of laudanum which was in a manner forced upon her How melancholy! when her own character is so worthy! and what a Lesson against precipitate & incautious marriages! They have too 5 remarkably fine children.

I shall be very glad, if Woods cannot be got, to have some other Person employed to repair our house. Your Brother is very well. Pray remember me with particular affection to Mrs. Dawson & Penny, & your Brother's Family, & in a proper manner to the rest of my Friends, and be assured I am, my dear Hannah,

Most faithfully & Most affectionately yours

Ja. Iredell

RC, Johnson Collection, NCSA. Addressed "Mrs. Iredell Edenton."

---

[1]"Hookey's confusion" has not been identified.

[2]See Nathaniel Dukinfield to JI, June 10, 1785, in this volume.

[3]Richard Bennehan (1743-1825) was a successful merchant and planter. In 1768, he became William Johnston's business partner and settled on Johnston's plantation called Snow Hill, located fifteen miles northeast of Hillsborough. This partnership lasted until Johnston died in 1785. Bennehan later established Stagville plantation. *DNCB*, s.v. "Bennehan, Richard."

[4]Alice Marsden Heron (d. 1813) was the second wife of Benjamin Heron (1722-1770), who held several public offices during the colonial era, including membership on the governor's council. He is credited with building one of the first drawbridges in the colonies. Will of Alice Heron, 1813, New Hanover County Wills, State Archives; Estate of Alice Heron, New Hanover County Estates, State Archives; *DNCB*, s.v. "Heron, Benjamin"; Mitchell, *North Carolina Wills*, 232.

[5]Agnes Bullock Keeling Williams was the wife of Judge John Williams. Her daughter from a previous marriage was Elizabeth Keeling Henderson, wife of Richard Henderson. John Henderson (b. 1766) was their oldest son. *DNCB*, s.v. "Williams, John," "Henderson, John."

[6]On October 7, 1785, William Roach was found guilty of horse stealing and sentenced to be hanged. His execution was set for October 28, 1785, between noon and 4 P.M. *State v. William Roach*, 1785, Hillsborough District Superior Court, Minute Docket, 1768-1788, pt. 2, State Archives.

William Stewart testified that attorney James Williams, who had prosecuted Stewart in Chatham County for theft, had agreed to help Stewart gain an acquittal in return for twenty to twenty-five barrels of corn. The first bill of indictment against Stewart was dismissed because of errors that Williams had intentionally made in order to help Stewart. When a second bill of indictment was issued, Williams advised Stewart to abscond, which he did. A jury found Williams guilty of a misdemeanor on October 10, 1785. He was fined £5 and forbidden to practice law in any North Carolina court. Deposition of William Stewart, June 13,

1785, Hillsborough District Superior Court, Criminal Action Papers, 1784-1786, State Archives; *State v. James Williams*, 1785, Hillsborough District Superior Court, Minute Docket, 1768-1788, pt. 2, State Archives.

Elizabeth Huske in an October 14, 1875, letter to Nelly Blair wrote, "Mr. Williams and family are going to live at Newbern & as matters have turned out, this court I am not sorry for it, for he has com/m/itted crimes which made the Judges suspend him. I am very sorry for Mrs. Williams they say she is much distressed about it, and she is really a very agreeable woman and a good neighbour, but it would rather be dissagreeable to visit there now." Iredell Papers, Rare Book, Manuscript, and Special Collections Library, Duke University.

From Archibald Maclaine

Wilmington 24 Oct 1785

Dear Sir

I once intended to have been with you at Edenton court, but the assembly intervening, and there being little probability that the Judges (ever tenacious of an opinion once given) will give Mr. Rice a hearing without formal notice from Edenton court, I have been obliged to postpone a journey over the sound for the present. In truth I have such various business upon my hands, that I see no probability of going through it. The testimony of Captain Willis must be sufficient to induce the Judges to give Mr. Rice a re-hearing, for from what I can recollect of the whole affair, they <Judges> set aside the will proved by Rice, upon a presumption that Savage had a will by him, but had lost all memory of it. I wish it was possible to get the matter argued at New Bern, as I my attendance at Edenton must be very uncertain, and I do not think Mr. Nash will go there. If reasons are shewn for a rehearing, Rice is intituled to every indulgence, especially where there is no impropriety in it.[1]

During the last of New Hanover county court in the beginning of this month, I was served with a subpona in equity, & a copy of a bill, in a suit brought by Mr. Johnston to Edenton next term. The complainants are, a Jacob Monk and his wife, who is a niece of the late Mr. Wilkinson of this town.[2] Mr. W. left the children of his brother Robert (except one who has 2000 dollars) £500 each. This woman is one of them, & her husband claims that sum in specie, or in the present currency. I agreed that the value of the legacies should be settled by the Judges at this place next December term, & Monk & his father-in-law even consulted me what counsel they should employ. I mentioned all those who practised here, but declined advising, & thought we should adjust it amicably, when I was surprised with a suit to Edenton. I have sent you a plea which <per> though perhaps not very formal in some parts of it, appears to me sufficient, & I have given you a copy of the clause where the testator gives 2000 dollars to his nephew & £500 to each of Nephews & nieces, with a list of Other legacies of the same nature as the last. Should I be ruled to answer, which I am strongly inclined to believe will not be the case, you must endeavor to get four months time to answer, as the Assembly and courts will give me full employment for some time. Let me add that Mr. W. at the time of his death was possessed of above £12000 in dollar bills of the state & about the same sum in continental money, & I believe he intended the legacies to be paid out of this money, even if it should appreciate, but I am persuaded he never meant to give so much away otherwise. I have scarcely time to finish my letter, as the post will be going out. Complimts. to Mr. Hooper & tell him I request his assistance if he is not engaged. remember me to Mr. Johnston

Dr. Sir Yours sincerely

A Maclaine

To W. Wilkinson son of Robert 2000 Spanish dollars		
To each of the other children of Robert, I believe four	£500	2000
To W. Maclaine son of A Maclaine[3]		500
To E Maclaine wife of the same[4]		250
To the revd. Mr. Tate as per year for five years £5[5]		25
To C. H. J. Holt[6]		250
To W. Hen. Hill[7]		250
For a presbyterian church[8]		500
		£3775

I give devise and bequeath to my nephew W. Wilkinson son of my brother Robert my house & lot in Wilmington near the church and three acres of land on the island and further I give and bequeath to my said nephew the sum of two thousand spanish milled dollars, which if paid to him in depreciated currency my will is that he shall receive as much of such currency as shall be equal in value to so much specie to be pd. him &c.[9] To each of the other children of my <sd.> bror. Robt. I give the sum of five hundred pounds, payable when each shall respectively arrive at the age of 21 years, or day of marriage

The above will shew what the testator intended, & how much I am interested in a decision in favor of Mr. Monk. It is therefore necessary that I should have the opinion of the Judges upon a full and fair hearing

A Maclaine

RC, Iredell Papers, Duke.

---

[1]For more information on this case, see Edward Rice to JI, June 27, 1784, n. 2; JI to Hannah Iredell, May 27, 1785, n. 1; and Archibald Maclaine to JI, October 31, 1785, in this volume.

[2]Jacob (d. 1831) and Sarah Monk of Duplin County. Will of Jacob Monk, 1831, Duplin County Wills, State Archives.

William Wilkinson (d. 1780) of Wilmington, brother of Robert Wilkinson, was a merchant, town commissioner, constable, and justice of the peace. He also owned, along with Cornelius Harnett, a rum distillery. Lennon and Kellam, *Wilmington Town Book,* 160n-161n, 193, 194.

[3]William Maclaine did not live beyond infancy. *DNCB*, s.v. "Maclaine, Archibald."

[4]Elizabeth "Polly" Rowan Maclaine (1731-1806). *DNCB*, s.v. "Maclaine, Archibald"; Neal, *Abstracts of Vital Records*, 1:330; *Minerva* (Raleigh), January 13, 1806.

[5]James Tate (d. 1795) of Wilmington and Orange County was a schoolmaster and Presbyterian clergyman. During the Revolution he was a chaplain of North Carolina troops. *DNCB*, s.v. "Tate, James"; McRee, *Life and Correspondence*, 2:217n.

[6]Cornelius Harnett Jacob Holt of Wilmington was the orphan son of Obediah Holt. Cornelius Harnett (1723-1781) was named as Holt's guardian in 1775. Harnett was a prominent Wilmington merchant who served in the colonial assembly and the Continental Congress. Granting of Guardianship, October 1775, Minutes of the New Hanover County Court, 1771-1779, State Archives; *DNCB*, s.v. "Harnett, Cornelius, Jr."

[7]William Henry Hill (1767-1809), a Wilmington attorney and planter, was U.S. district attorney for North Carolina (1790-1797) and a member of the U.S. House of Representatives (1799-1803). *DNCB*, s.v. "Hill, William Henry"; *BDC*, s.v. "Hill, William Henry."

[8]On December 29, 1785, the General Assembly passed "An Act to Impower Certain Persons Therein Named to Receive, Sue for and Recover all Such Bequests, Donations, Benefactions and Other Things as Have Heretofore Been Bequeathed, Given or Made by Any Person or Persons Whatsoever, for the Use of the Congregation or Society of the Presbyterian Communion at Wilmington." This law established a board of Presbyterian trustees in Wilmington to receive money for the church and, if need be, to file suit to collect diverted bequests. Clark, *State Records*, 24:757-758.

[9]The Spanish milled dollar was a coin minted in Spain's American colonies during the reign of Philip V (1700-1746). "Milled" refers to grooves on the edge of the coin put there to discourage shaving the metal. The Spanish milled dollar was the most common coin in the British colonies in America and was the standard form of payment for business transactions into the Confederation period. Burton Hobson and Robert Obojski, *Illustrated Encyclopedia of World Coins* (Garden City, N.Y.: Doubleday and Company, 1970), 402, 433; Morris, *Forging the Union*, 154.

From Archibald Maclaine

Wilmington 31st. Octr. 1785

Dear Sir

I wrote you last post, inclosing a plea to a suit in equity brought against me by one Monk & his wife.[1] It was so late before I could prepare all my letters & business for New Bern &c that I omitted to make oath to the plea before Dr. Geekie, the commissioner for this county.[2] But though it is usual to swear to pleas in chancery, I do not see the propriety of it, unless where matters of fact are set forth. It is too late to draw another, so that if it is not admitted (which however I cannot believe will be the case) you will be kind enough to procure time for me. I have since seen young Wilkinson, the brother of Monk's wife, & I find there are only four children of Robert Wilkinson in all, consequently the list I gave of the legacies, is £500 too much, as I supposed there were five.

I cannot help being anxious about Rice's affairs, & yet I do not know that I could have been of any service, could I have gone to Edenton, for from what the Judges threw out, I believe they will not determine it now, if Dr. Dickinson urges a delay. Considering, however, how Rice was precipitated into a defence of his property, upon the oath of a woman of no credit, they certainly ought to give him a re-hearing without delay, unless his opponent alleges upon good grounds the want of testimony

I very earnestly wish for a decision of this business at New Bern, that I may discharge my engagement. If nothing is determined upon at Edenton, I propose drawing a bill to regulate proceedings of this kind, & perhaps it is necessary at all events. I wish therefore you Mr. Johnston & Mr. Hooper may think of it, & communicate your opinions when I see you. Though Mr. Johnston is against us, I am sure he will promote any necessary regulation.[3]

My compliments to Mr. Hooper—Tell him Billy has had the ague since his return from Hillsborough, but is now recovered, and takes special care to keep himself warm.

I am very sincerely Dear Sir yours

A Maclaine

RC, Iredell Papers, Duke.

---

[1]See Archibald Maclaine to JI, October 24, 1785, in this volume.

[2]James Geekie (d. 1793) of Wilmington was a physician, justice of the peace, and county commissioner. During the Revolutionary War, he was surgeon in the

First Regiment North Carolina Continental Troops. Lennon and Kellam, *Wilmington Town Book*, 225n.

[3]Maclaine is referring to regulation of the proceedings to settle the estates of those who died without wills. In 1787, the General Assembly passed "An Act Authorizing and Empowering the County Courts of Pleas and Quarter-sessions to Divide and Appropriate the Real Estate of Intestates." Clark, *State Records*, 24:903-904.

Smith's Academy Minutes

At a Meeting of the Trustees of Smith's Academy, in the Town of Edenton, on Friday the fourth day of November in the year one thousand seven hundred and eighty five

Present

Samuel Johnston Esquire, President

Hugh Williamson }
Isaac Gregory[1] } Esquires
Laurence Baker }

Mr. Iredell, Secretary.

Dr. Williamson from the Committee appointed "to examine & report to the Trustees their Opinion what part of the Town it would be most eligible to erect the Buildings upon, and whether any lot or lots that would be suitable for that purpose remain to be taken up, or could probably be purchased at a moderate price:"
Reported, That in their opinion it would be most eligible to erect the Academy on a part of the Town Common in the Town of Edenton, provided a Law could be obtained authorising the Commissioners to convey a sufficient part of the same for the purpose of erecting the public Buildings of the Academy thereon.
The Board therefore resolve, That the Inhabitants of the Town of Edenton be requested to give their Assent to a Law to be passed for the said purpose, and that Dr. Williamson, General Gregory, and Charles Johnson Esqs. be a Committee to apply to the Inhabitants, and collect their Sentiments thereupon.[2]

Colonel Baker, the Treasurer, reported, that agreeable to the order of the Board he had applied to Josiah [*Collins*] the [*torn*]erfial acting Executor of the Will of Robert Smith Esquire deceased and demanded payment of the Legacy left to the Academy by the said Robert Smith, but that Mr. Collins had not paid it.

Colonel Baker, on account of his distant situation from the Town of Edenton where the Academy is intended to be erected, desired leave to resign his office of Treasurer.

His resignation was accordingly accepted, and Charles Johnson Esq. appointed Treasurer in his room.

Ja. Iredell, Secretary.

FC, Johnson Collection, NCSA.

---

[1]Isaac Gregory (ca. 1737-1800) of Camden County was a Revolutionary War officer, member of the house of commons (1780-1781) and the state senate (1782-1795), and a delegate to the 1788 and 1789 state ratification conventions. Gregory was also a trustee of the Currituck Seminary of Learning. *DNCB*, s.v. "Gregory, Isaac."

[2]The General Assembly approved a bill on December 29, 1785, allowing the Edenton board of commissioners to convey part of the town common, not to exceed six acres, to the board of trustees of Smith's Academy. Clark, *State Records*, 24:754.

To Hannah Iredell

Newbern Nov. 24th. 1785.

My dear Hannah,

After one of the most difficult & disagreeable Journies we ever had (owing to the great floods of water) your Brother and I arrived here on Tuesday morning, his cold a great deal better than it was, and myself quite well. We are both now in very good health. By Mr. Hooper's extreme kindness I have together with him the best lodgings in the whole Town, tho' they were procured with great difficulty. Each of us has a good room in Mr. Cogdell's house, where we breakfast, and we have in another house a tab[*le*] every day for your Brother, Mr. Moore, & ourselves.[1] Your Brother sleeps in a different house, the same where Dr. Williamson is. The Assembly met last Saturday. Hitherto no business has been done decisively, and it is not easy to conjecture what will be. To day we expected some sport at a horse race, between Mr. Nash's horse & a Mr. Dekeyser's, but the latter flying the way was distanced the first heat.[2] There is to be a Ball to night, to which I shall unwillingly go out of compliment to the Invitation, it ill suiting my Court business, otherwise I should like it very well. People in general are very well here. God grant you may continue so, and my other Friends. I can't wait to thank you for your letter by the Post, for fear of losing it. I hope to have the pleasure of receiving a letter from you, & another from Nelly to night. Give my love particularly to her. I know she will have the goodness to excuse my [*not wri*]ting this time. Adieu! Remember me to all my Friends, [&] believe me

Most faithfully & Most affectionately yours

Ja. Iredell

RC, Johnson Collection, NCSA. Addressed "Mrs. Iredell Edenton."

---

[1]Richard Cogdell (1724-1787), a native of Beaufort and resident of New Bern, served in a variety of posts, including justice of the peace, sheriff, postmaster, and member of the house of commons. He retired from public office in 1783. *DNCB*, s.v. "Cogdell, Richard."

[2]In 1790, L. Dekeyer operated a boardinghouse in Fayetteville to accommodate members of the assembly. John A. Oates, *The Story of Fayetteville and the Upper Cape Fear* (n.p., n.d.), 322.

From Samuel Cutler

New London Decr. 13th. 1785

Dear Sir

Altho Business at the Approach of Winter is pressing, I cannot neglect so good an Opportunity as presents by the Sloop Friendship, now going to Carolina to write you

It is now a long Time Since I have had the Pleasure to hear from you, not Since you wrote by Mr. Lowther, when I find you did not enjoy so good Health as for some Time before; I have, my Dear Sir, often remonstrated against your too close Application to Study, and want of Exercise. I now tell you that I fear your Perseverance will deprive you of your Health & me & Thousands of your Friendship. the very Means you take to render yourself usefull to your Friends will disapoint them. You know very well when I was at Edenton, I was at best but a Convalescent, which I have not the Vanity to charge to Attention to Books, but rather a Shamefull Inactivity. I am now engaged in Business that calls me up before the Sun I am on Foot the whole Day and often Times by night very much fatigued, yet I never enjoyed half so good Health, which I attribute as much to change of my Manner of Life, as of Place, and was it not for my Seperation from a few for whom I retain a most tender Regard I Should bless God for the Cause that removed me. Medicines may <for> my dear Sir, for a while relieve you but it must be change in your Manner of Life that will keep you in Health. you will excuse my Freedom in writing, when I assure you that it is your Life & Health and the Happiness of your Friends that dictates it —

When you have one half Hour of Leasure lend it me in telling me how you are and of the Welfare of my Friends. where is Lenox? has he left you for Charleston the Westindies or the other World? for I hear nothing of him

Remember me with tender Regards to Mrs. Iredell and Family and believe me

Dear Sir Yours most Sincerely

Saml. Cutler

RC, Iredell Papers, Duke. Printed, McRee, 2:130-131. Addressed "James Iredell Esq Edenton North Carolina Favd. by Capt Brown."

To James Gordon[1]

Edenton Decr. 16th. 1785

Sir

I duly received, though not till long after the date (owing to my absence from home upon a Circuit) your favour of the 25th. August, with the Power of Attorney and Accounts inclosed, and yesterday a duplicate of that letter, with a few additional lines of the 8th. November.—I had hitherto delayed answering your former letter in hopes of being able to obtain some information of Hutching, whom I know nothing of, and flattered myself <and flattered myself> I should have heard something of him before this time but my inquiries, such as I have been able to make in the midst of a great deal of business abroad, have hitherto been unsuccessful. Tulloch is dead, and has made a Will, but died I am afraid in very bad circumstances.[2]

Our Assembly is now sitting, and about making very material alterations in our Courts, so that I think it <is proper> /adviseable/ to wait to see what those alterations may be, before I bring suit against Tulloch's Executors as I could only sue them myself to Halifax Superior Court, and it is in contemplation to deprive the Superior Courts of all original jurisdiction in which case your Suit must be brought to the County Court where the Executors reside and there I do not attend.[3] Hutching in that case must also be sued to the County Court of the County wherein he is to be found, and as it is highly probable that may not be in the very few I go to in this part of the Country it may possibly not be in my power to serve you in either respect. Further, Sir, I think it is proper I should inform you that it may happen in consequence of some alterations projected, if they should take place, tho' <all original jurisdiction should not be taken away from the Superior Courts> /they should not proceed so far as to take away all original jurisdiction from the Superior Courts/, that it may be for your advantage to bring suit in a County Court in preference to give you a chance of an earlier decision.

You will therefore be pleased to be prepared for such circumstances, and advise me of your determination, observing that I cannot engage to act under your power of Attorney but merely as a Lawyer

I am Sir Your very obedient humble Servant[4]

FC, Johnson Collection, NCSA. Endorsed "Copy of a Letter to Mr. James Gordon Merchant in Charleston, dated Dec. 16. 1785. One Copy sent by the Post. Another by Dr. Lenox."

---

[1]James Gordon was a merchant in Charleston, S.C. Hagy, *People and Professions of Charleston*, 2, 14, 40, 53.

[2]This is probably a reference to Thomas Tulloch, whose will was filed in Halifax County, though he was a resident of Beaufort County. A Thomas Tulloch represented Hillsborough in the house of commons from 1779 to 1781. Margaret M. Hofmann, comp., *Genealogical Abstracts of Wills, 1758-1824, Halifax County, North Carolina* (Weldon, N.C.: *Roanoke News*, 1970), 67; Cheney, *North Carolina Government*, 205, 207, 208.

[3]The General Assembly passed "An Act for Encreasing the Jurisdiction of the County Courts of Pleas and Quarter Sessions, and of the Justices of the Peace out of Court, and Directing the Time of Holding the Several Courts of this State" on December 26, 1785. The law contained a list of disputes that were to fall within the jurisdiction of the county courts of pleas and quarter sessions. The legislation also included provisions intended to discourage appeals to the overburdened superior courts. Clark, *State Records*, 24:716-718.

[4]The letter was written by Thomas Iredell; insertions and endorsement are in JI's handwriting.

Archibald Maclaine to Samuel Johnston

New Bern 24th. Decr. 1785

Dear Sir

From your letter and /that/ of Mr. Iredell I have drawn a short bill, now on its progress, to amend the act of last Session relative to the real estates of deceased debtors[1] —It was impossible to find sufficient time to give it that attention which the subject deserves; but I hope it will be found to remove the difficulties which the act laid us under, & I have no reason to believe that it will be opposed.

The money-bill for £100,000 finds a great majority in both houses in its favor—Persons are to be appointed to purchase tobacco at Halifax Tarborough & Fayetteville; the price not to exceed 50/s.[2] As that article is fallen and falling in all parts of the world, so high a price is damning the money in embrio. I am told that a member has already offered it at five for one. The only thing we can do to save the country from ruin is to sink its credit as quick as possible.[3]

The bill for regulating the superior court system, & making three additional Judges, is damned[4]—What makes it worse the bill for giving the county courts jurisdiction of land causes will pass; so that we are in a heavenly situation[5]

A bill for confirming all titles <to property> under sales of Commissioners of confiscated property, was read yesterday for the second time—It was long debated, & Nash with all his address endeavored to support it; but it was attacked from all quarters, and an amendment proposed to the senate, saving rights reserved by any law, and bona fide sales made by persons before any confiscation could have taken place—Whether this will be adopted as part of the bill, I do not yet know, but I believe it will be rejected by the commons. The most curious part of it is, that it confirms sales hereafter to be made.[6]

A bill was introduced directing the manner of trying judges upon impeachments—As the court <consisted> was to consist of the Governor and his honorable council, and as it was pointed at the Judges alone, a committee was appointed to prepare a general bill [*torn*] Hay & myself prepared one, but as it was found that members of Assembly & Justices of the peace might be impeached & tried, the bill was rejected last night upon the second reading, or which amounted to the same thing, was laid over.[7]

The Judges are in a fair way of becoming favorites with the Assembly; for they have had Frank Brice and a doctor MacNeill (Mrs. DuBois's nephew) indicted for <a> misdemeanors, in returning to the State without permission[8]—The indictment recited treasons committed by these persons; but the treasons were not proved, & indeed no proof could be received—When the Jury asked if there was any law which made their return a misdemeanor, they were told that they had to find the facts only; that the treaty was the law of the land, & that the misdemeanor was implied in the treaty. Both the prisoners were found guilty, find, & ordered to give security to leave the State in sixty days—Brice is preparing to go—MacNeill who has a family has sent in a petition to the Assembly, as there is a condition; that is, unless the Assembly permits their stay. I do not think of presenting it, as I know it will be to no purpose.[9]

When I sat down I thought of writing to Mr. Iredell, but as I have not time, this must serve you both for the present

Yours very sincerely

A Maclaine

RC, Hayes Collection, SHC. Addressed "Samuel Johnston or James Iredell esquires Edenton Favored by M. Cabarrus."

---

[1]The General Assembly passed "An Act Directing the Mode of Proceeding Against the Real Estates of Deceased Debtors, Where the personal Estate is Insufficient for the Payment of the Debts" during the 1784 session. Clark, *State Records*, 24:671-672.

[2]"An Act for Emitting One Hundred Thousand Pounds Paper Currency, for the Purposes Therein Expressed" was passed on December 29, 1785. A provision in this act allocated not more than £36,000 to purchase tobacco at a set price that exceeded the current market rate. The state would then sell the tobacco abroad and use the money to pay North Carolina's debt to the U.S. government. The General Assembly's decision to pay more for the tobacco than the going rate made the public, who already doubted the worth of state-issued paper money, believe that the assembly had little faith in the sustained value of the new currency. Clark, *State Records*, 24:722-725; Watson, *Money and Monetary Problems*, 45.

[3]The United States experienced an economic depression in the mid-1780s caused by, among other things, excessive use of credit, a dependency upon imports, and a scarcity of specie. For a discussion of the country's financial problems during this period, see Morris, *Forging of the Union*, 130-161.

[4]"A Bill for increasing the number of Judges, for dividing the Superior Courts into different Circuit and for establishing a Court for the decision of Appeals . . ." was passed by the house but defeated on second reading in the senate on December 20, 1785. House Bills, December 10-26, Session of November-December 1785, General Assembly Session Records, State Archives.

[5]See JI to James Gordon, December 16, 1785, n. 3, in this volume.

[6]The General Assembly passed "An Act to Secure and Quiet in Their Possessions all Such Persons, Their Heirs and Assigns who Have Purchased, or May Hereafter Purchase Lands and Tenements, Goods and Chattels, Which have Been Sold, or May Hereafter Be Sold by Commissioners of Forfeited Estates, Legally Appointed for That Purpose" on December 29, 1785. This legislation protected purchasers of confiscated property from "expensive and vexatious lawsuits" by former owners attempting to reclaim their property. This law was amended the following year to allow legal recourse to those who believed that their property had been wrongly confiscated. Clark, *State Records*, 24:730-731, 794-795.

[7]In 1785 "A Bill for directing the mode of proceeding on impeachments," written in Maclaine's handwriting, was introduced in the General Assembly. The constitution of 1776 allowed the impeachment of the "governor and other officers" but did not establish a method by which this could be done. The bill, which passed on its initial readings in the house and senate, was laid over until the next Assembly, but during that session the measure again failed to become law. House Bills, December 10-26, November-December 1785, and House Bills, December 1-January 4, November 1786-January 1787, General Assembly Session Records, State Archives; Cheney, *North Carolina Government*, 814.

[8]Francis Brice of New Hanover County was a tax collector, commissioner of the port of Wilmington, and a member of the Wilmington-New Hanover Safety Committee. In 1781, he left Wilmington with the British army. He eventually made his way to Jamaica and became an exporter of rum, sugar, coffee, and slaves. Daniel McNeill, a North Carolina native and Cumberland County resident, joined British forces in 1779. He became a captain of North Carolina Loyalists in 1781 and raised a company of more than one hundred men. Leora H. McEachern and Isabel M. Williams, eds., *Wilmington-New Hanover Safety Committee Minutes, 1774-1776* (Wilmington, N.C.: Wilmington-New Hanover County American Bi-centennial Association, 1974), 122; Palmer, *Biographical Sketches*, 575; Raymond Parker Fouts, *Abstracts from Newspapers of Wilmington, North Carolina*, vol. 1, *1765-1775, 1788-1797* (Cocoa, Fla.: GenRec Books, 1984), 48, 50.

[9]Bladen County citizens presented a petition dated December 13, 1785, to the General Assembly asking that McNeill be permitted to stay because of his "skill as a Phisician and the Readiness with which he has Exercised it." Nine residents had signed the appeal. Petition of Doctor Daniel McNeill, 1785, Miscellaneous Petitions, Session of November-December 1785, General Assembly Session Records, State Archives.

To Henry E. McCulloh

[*December 26, 1785*]

Dear Sir,

I have received your favours of the 15th. of May, and 25th. of July, and a <short line> /few lines/ together with the last by Colo. Palmer, as also a day or two ago a duplicate of that /letter/ of the 25th. of July from Virginia.[1] All these letters came to my hands long after the date, <& the letter> /that/ of the 15th. of May /in particular/ I received /but/ very lately at Newbern.—The other letters you mention dated in Oct, Nov, & Feby. I never received

I am extremely concerned that for want of a Certificate from this Country you lost your share of the full Dividend, and it would give me great pain if I could in any manner blame myself on that account, but I don't recollect that you ever desired me to send you s[*uc*]h a Certificate, and my knowledge as a Lawyer could not suggest to me any information in regard to an entirely new proceeding of which I <heard> /knew/ nothing but from loose suggestions in Newspapers—Ben Mc.Culloch has been for a long time attending the Assembly at Newbern. I saw him there at the Court. He <intended> /had already taken steps/ to procure two authenticated Copies of the last Act, & <a Copy> of the former [*torn*] you at [*torn*] transmit you, one Copy of which, at my desire, he promised to send me, that I might forward it by a safe opportunity.[2] You may depend on my attention to this matter, and if by any accident I should not receive the Cop<y>/ies/ he promised me I will exert myself to procure <an> other—I shall not fail also to acquaint you of any thing done here in regard to the disputable objects of the 4th. Article of the Treaty

I hear with great pleasure such agreeable accounts of George, who I always thought had a very fine Genius. Without exactly <measuring> /weighing/ the scales of reciprocal obligation (tho' I trust I have never been deficient in gratitude) I shall be very ready to render George any services that are really in my power, & which I can faithfully undertake to perform. At present it is with great difficulty that I can barely support my Family with the little ready money I collect, and <it> /my Family/ being so large is already a great inconvenience to me, from the smallness of my house, so that it will not be <possible> /practicable/ for George either to lodge or board with me. Neither could I be answerable to pay for his lodging or boarding, uncertain whether I should be able. But if you are willing that he should be lodged and boarded in a different Family, dependent on you only with certainty for his support, I would render him any assistance in my power in regard to the study of the law. At the same time, it is proper I should inform you that Mr. Johnston & myself have had views of removing /from/ here, which may be realized in a <much> less time than you allott for his study, and I could engage only to assist him during my residence <here> in this Town.

I was very sincere in my declaration, that I held myself indispensably bound to discharge my debt of honour, whenever I was enabled to do so, notwithstanding it was a tie which <unfortunate> subsequent /unfortunate/ events rendered peculiarly heavy—but when you consider, that I had beneficially the enjoyment of the office but little more than 12 months, that the War not only deprived me of that but also of the profits of my professions so that I could not possibly avoid running pretty deeply in debt even for my necessary support, and that I have had but a very short time to begin to recruit from [those] embarrrassments, the increasing of which I have carefully avoided by observing as strictly as possible a rule I have laid down as a very essential one, to pay for every thing [I] purchase in ready money[3]—I trust, when you consider these things you will believe my ability to discharge this debt is far inferior to my wishes, especially as when it was contracted it was agreed <it> /the <pay time of its> payment of it/ should depend upon my convenience, & therefore I cannot think it reasonable to take any part of my Wife's capital for such an application, or provide any other fund for it but my own industry & the little property I <have been> </may be/> /have been/ able to acquire as the fruits of it[4]—The part I held myself bound to take during the war left my whole hopes at stake upon the event of it—I provided no resource in case the event should be unfortunate. Misery in its most dreadful degree must then have been my part in, and its Success has left me a great deal to struggle with in order to make myself clear & independent. But by the blessing of God I will exert every nerve to be so—

I have the pleasure to acquaint you that Mrs. Iredell on the 22 last was safely delivered of a Daughter, & that they are both in very good health.[5] I beg to be remembered to George, & wish you & him many happy returns of this season. I will send a duplicate of this letter by way of Virginia, & take that occasion to write to him—

I am & c Dr. Sir Your very affect hon Ser.

FC, Johnson Collection, NCSA. Endorsed "Copy of a Letter to Mr. Mc.Culloh, Dec. 26. 1785. (Sent by the Post, (Dec. 26) and a Duplicate by Virginia, 2d. Jan—)."

---

[1]See Henry E. McCulloh to JI, May 15 and July 25, 1785, in this volume.

[2]Henry E. McCulloh had received a copy of the act by July 19, 1786, but who sent it to him is unclear. Loyalist Claim of Henry Eustace McCulloh, State Archives. See also JI to Henry E. McCulloh, June 15, 1784, n. 3, in this volume.

[3]For information on the "debt of honour," see James Iredell's Will, August 20, 1784, n. 3, in this volume.

[4]For information on Hannah Iredell's inheritance, see *PJI*, 1:124n.

[5]Annie Isabella Iredell (1785-1816) was born December 22, 1785.

1786

From John Burgwin

Hermitage near Wilmington 14th. Jany. 1786

Dear Sir

when I last had the pleasure of seeing you at New Bern I was flattered with the Strongest hope that the Assembly would relieve me from the dilema I was under respecting my Property which the Comr. of forfeited Estates had Advertized for Sale—

The fact is this—in 1781 I left this State on more private Business by the leave of a Genl. Officer under his hand & Seal and as soon as my Business was compleated & I could find an Opperty. to return I embraced it—I did not leave the State in an Hostile or private manner. on retaking my Business to the Colo. of the County he he advised my going—<But> And on my return all would have been well, but unfortunately I had an Ejectmt. Cause on the Supr. Cot. Docket hanging some years—The Deft. last June Court plead my Disability & the issue made up & tried instantez—in short I was surprized into it—for it was a mere chance that I was that day in Town & in half an hour after my Arrival I was Sent for into Cot. was informed of the issue, but my proof<s> I had not with me & the matter was determined before I could recollect myself, & having no Evidence it went against me—This Induced the Comr. to Advertize my property for Sale—I obtained a prohibition from One of the Judges—This was dismissed at the last Superr. Cot. without a hearing & now the Sale is it seems to take place, but I think I can by consent bring on a discussion of the matter before the next Superior Cot. at Wilmington—The Object to me is great, no less than the preservation of an Innocent family from ruin[1]—

I am extreamly Anxious to get your Assistance as one of my Council—altho I have both Law & Justice on my Side I am not insensible of the popular prejudices against those under my Situation & requires the weight &—assistance of Gentn. of the greatest eminence in the Law to eradicate—to you Sir who formerly knew the Character I supported, I must then Crave <for> Assistance & did you know how Cruelly & unjustly I have been persecuted I am convinced you'd feel for me—Your fee shall be equal to your Own wishes & the Magnitude of the Cause—I think I shall have Interest enough to have it brot. on any day in the Cot. so that you will not meet with much detention from your family—and at the same time please to consider you may preserve a worthy family from utter destruction—

believe me to be my Dear sir Your Mt. Obed. Servt.

J Burgwin

RC, Iredell Papers, Duke. Endorsed "January 14th. 1786. John Burgwin. Ansd. But an Opinion to be formed &c."[2]

---

[1]Burgwin had traveled to England in 1775 for medical reasons. In 1777, while he was still abroad, the North Carolina assembly authorized the confiscation of property belonging to those who were absent from the country on July 4, 1776, and had not returned. Burgwin's situation was complicated by his failure at an earlier date to provide gunpowder requested by the Wilmington Committee of Safety. After the passage of the 1777 confiscation law, Burgwin returned to Wilmington only to leave again in 1781 when the British occupied the town. He traveled in Europe, including England, and while there married an English woman. After the war's end, he returned to Wilmington and eventually regained his property. *DNCB*, s.v. "Burgwin, John"; Clark, *State Records*, 24:123-124. For Burgwin's account of events, see the enclosure with John Burgwin to JI, March 30, 1786, in this volume.

Archibald Maclaine suggested that those who opposed Burgwin were motivated by the fact that they owed him money and that he was a business competitor. A. Maclaine to George Hooper, June 14, 1784, in Clark, *State Records*, 17:144-147.

[2]See JI to John Burgwin, February 6, 1786, in this volume.

From James Hogg

Hillsborough 19th. Jan. 1786

Dear Sir

The Law passd at last Assembly for quieting in their possession the Purchasers of Confiscated property makes it again necessary for Mr. Johnstons Exrs. to apply for advice.[1]

You have received no fee from us but you have been so good as to allow us to consider you as retaind for the business regarding Fannings Lots and Lands and we Shall pay your fee with pleasure[2]

I have written a long letter to Mr. Johnston on this Subject and have sent him a Copy of this wonderful Law by which the Assembly have arrogated to themselves the judicial power in all Suits regarding Confiscated property[3] How the people at large will like this innovation, I know not, but when you have read it I Suppose you will see reason to give us an opinion different from your former one for if we do not make use of Wylies judgement I see no ground of hope that we Shall be able to retain any part of Fannings property[4]

I need not trouble you with a repetition of what I have written to Mr. Johnston: He will be so good as to Shew it to you as it may perhaps contain some particulars that were not taken notice of in my former letters

I do not recollect any news worth your notice if there are any you will have them from Mr. Hooper who tells me he is to write to you—

At length the Southern & Western people have prevailed & fix'd next meeting of Assembly at Fayette[5]—Mr. Hooper says it will never sit there again but I must differ with him. to me it appears that the interest of that place will yearly increase, tho' I Suspect the Duty laid on British goods will give a great check to their trade for a time and I am afraid the new emission of paper Currency will be of no service[6] The Laws of this State seem very favourable to the knavish Debtor

Mrs. Hogg & Nelly join me in offering their best respects and I am with the most sincere regard

Dear Sir Your most obedt. humble Servant

James Hogg

RC, Johnson Collection, NCSA. Printed, McRee, 2:132. Addressed "James Iredell Esquire Edenton." Endorsed "Hillsborough 19 Jan. 1786. Ja. Hogg. Ansd."[7]

---

[1]In 1782, William Johnston (d. 1785) purchased land on the Little River, in what is now Durham County, that had belonged to Henry E. McCulloh. Before the Revolution, Johnston had worked as an agent for McCulloh and after the war, for Loyalist Edmund Fanning. Pruitt, *Abstracts of Sales of Confiscated Land*, 88; A. B. Pruitt, *Abstracts of Henry E. McCulloh's Survey Book and Petition to the Crown and Warrants (Money) Issued in 1787 by Gov. Richard Caswell* (n.p.: A. B. Pruitt, 1992), 33; Will of William Johnston, 1785, Orange County Wills, State Archives. For information on the law to which Hogg refers, see Archibald Maclaine to Samuel Johnston, December 24, 1785, n. 6, in this volume.

[2]Edmund Fanning, a New York native, moved to North Carolina prior to the Revolution to practice law. He served as recorder of deeds in Orange County, and his conduct in that office was said to have inspired the Regulator movement. Early in the Revolutionary War, Fanning moved to New York and became a colonel in the British army. After the war he moved to Canada and by 1808 had been promoted to general. Fanning's North Carolina property included nine lots and part of two others in Hillsborough. These were confiscated and sold. Pruitt, *Abstracts of Sales of Confiscated Land*, 85-86, 92, 97-98; Lorenzo Sabine, *Biographical Sketches of Loyalists of the American Revolution with an Historical Essay*, 2 vols. (Boston: Little, Brown and Company, 1864), 1:416-417.

[3]"Mr. Johnston" in this case is Samuel Johnston.

[4]William Wyley had purchased land from William Johnston in 1782. The land apparently had been Loyalist property that Wyley was not permitted to keep. Minutes of the Orange County Court of Pleas and Quarter Sessions, May 1784, State Archives; William Hooper to JI, February 12, 1786, in this volume. See also JI to James Hogg, January 29, 1786, in this volume.

[5]On December 12, 1785, the General Assembly voted to hold its next session at Fayetteville. Hillsborough, New Bern, Tarborough, and Halifax had also been nominated. Clark, *State Records*, 17:311, 338; 20:28-29, 50.

[6]On December 29, 1785, the General Assembly passed "An Act for the Regulation of Commerce," which prescribed duties on imports, and "An Act for Emitting One Hundred Thousand Pounds Paper Currency, for the Purposes Therein Expressed," which included authorization to pay a portion of the foreign debt and part of the operating expenses of the national government. Clark, *State Records*, 24:716-718, 718-720. For more information on this emission of paper money, see Watson, *Money and Monetary Problems*, 43-46.

[7]See JI to James Hogg, January 29, 1786, in this volume.

To James Hogg

[January 29, 1786]

Dear Sir,

I had the favour of your letter of the 19 Inst. by the Express.[1] Mr. Johnston & myself both concur in thinking, that it may be now proper to avail yourself of Wyllie's Judgment. The claim as to the lands I always thought very doubtful, <& rather thought a> /considered <that> a/ pursuit of the title /was rather/ adviseable as a meer discharge of your trust than because there was a probability of supporting it—But this late omnipotent Law will serve to satisfy all scruples of that kind, and I do not think Mr. Johnston's Executors could be justified in giving up the benefit of the Assignment tho' I have great doubts whether, tho' <there be a> /the/ Warranty /be special/ as the consideration has failed (supposing the title not to have been originally good) a Court of Equity would not entitle Wylie to the benefit of that Judgment.[2] of this however I am by no means clear; & <it> /the subject/ would require much more consideration then it is possible for me now to give it, nor is any opinion upon that point at present absolutely necessary.—

For the Ballance due to Mr. Johnston's Estate we conceive all Attachments will be proper, & that in consequence of that a Jury may estimate the value of Mr. Johnston's services upon a quantum measure, a law phrase the meaning of which you may easily collect from the words. If

<such> /however you should be at a loss for its full meaning/, Mr. Hooper can explain it—

<By an attachment we conceive the lands levied on will be absolutely bound, until <it is satisfied>—the Judgment is satisfied—For which reason, I think, it would be proper not to levy on more than what may be considered the value of <what> /the sum/ you are likely to recover.>

It is a melancholy thing, that in support of a favourite system every principle of decency & justice <has been> /should be/ so wantonly sacrificed as /it has been/ in this last act concerning Confiscation, and barefaced as it is, the conduct of the Cour[*t of Wil*]mington gives [*torn*] very little prospect of relief from them[3]—

You will be so good as to present my best respects to Mrs. Hogg and your <Miss H> young Ladies & Gentlemen. I know it will give you pleasure to hear, that I have been blessed with a very fine Daughter, that is now about 5 weeks old, and /that/ both her & her Mother have been remarkably well ever since her birth.

—Mrs. Iredell considers herself as having a great interest in the welfare of your Family, tho' <not having> /she has not/ the pleasure to be /personally/ known to them, and I am sure no one can be with /a/ greater sincerity & respect than I am,

Dear Sir Your very faithful and obed. Ser,

J.I.

FC, Johnson Collection, NCSA. Endorsed "Copy of a Letter to Mr. Hogg Jan. 29th. 1786—."

---

[1] See James Hogg to JI, January 19, 1786, in this volume.

[2] This is a reference to the act protecting purchasers of confiscated property. See Archibald Maclaine to Samuel Johnston, December 24, 1785, n. 6, in this volume.

For information regarding the Johnston-Wyley land sale, see James Hogg to JI, January 19, 1786, n. 4, and William Hooper to JI, February 12, 1786, in this volume.

[3] JI is referring to a case involving two Loyalists who had been arrested for returning to North Carolina without permission. The Loyalists were fined and ordered to leave the state. Waldrup, "James Iredell," 307-308; Archibald Maclaine to Samuel Johnston, December 24, 1785, in this volume.

From Arthur Iredell

Doddlespool Jany. 29th. 17[*torn*][1]

You know nothing of this Place, & I must tell you that it belongs to the Brother in Law of my Amanda; [*He*] is the Husband of Mrs. Bayley, whom I have before mentioned to you, & who is my most intimate Friend. I came here [*torn*] the breaking up of the Family at Crewe Hall, Mr. & Mrs. [*torn*] having left it, the one to attend his Duty in Parliame[*nt*] the other to pay a visit to her Mother in Ireland.[2] Y[*ou*] will think me a very happy Fellow, for I found Amand[*a*] here, & She is now at my Elbow whilst I tell you so. I have just extorted a Promise from her that She will write a few Lines to my Sister, with whom I am very desireous She should keep up a regular Correspondence. I have endeavoured to prevail upon Mrs. B to do the sa[*m*]e. so that Mrs. Iredell would have had no small Labour upon her hands, if extreme Delicacy had not prevented her from listening to My request. I had a Letter a f[*ew*] Days ago from our Tom of a remote Date—I find he expects, & has probably taught You to believe, that I shall soon be married. I wish this were to be; but at present I see no immediate Prospect of It—for I am resolved not to incur the Expences of a Family till I shall have the Means of defraying them, & when that will be God only [*kn*]ows. Mr. Crewe the other Day told me he should make [*a p*]oint of getting some Preferment for me from the Bp. of [*torn*]borough, but that his Patronage at present was by no means extensive—it was probable, however, that he would be soon translated into a better See[3]—This looks well—but I have other Strings to my Bow. Miss Felton is not without her Connections, & they are very good ones. My Uncle besides has just wrote to tell me, in answer to some injurious Reports that had been circulated about him, that three fifths of his Property are perfectly clear, & that he will, tho he is active in removing the Incumbrances that are yet upon it, allow me in the mean [*wh*]ile, nay make his Estate chargeable with an Annuity of 100£ for Miss F's & my Lives, & double that Sum as his Debts are wiped away. So that you see by degrees I may be able to become Benedick the Married Man.[4] one bad Consequence, perhaps, from my living so long in <u>a great</u> Stile is that I shall require so much the more to live [*torn*] to the Ideas I have imbibed in it. This I should despair of doing if my Views from my Uncle were removed—& [*torn*] I feel conscious that they ought to be, & that you sh[*ould*] be in appearance, as you are in fact, the head of your [*torn*]

[*torn*] James! I rob you of your Birth rig[*ht*] even without the Mess of Porridge—It is true, but there shall always be one at your Service, & I cannot tell you how unhappy I should be if I did not frequently anticipate

the Time when we should be mutually benefitted by my Plantation either on this or the other Side of the Atlantick. Amanda is equally fond of encouraging the same pleasing Ideas, & is equally sanguine in her Expectations. May they in time, & in good time, be happ[*ily*] realized! I can tell you no News. Our Parliam[*ent*] is assembled, but I have as yet only read the King's Speech, which breathes Peace all over the World.[5] This Sessions will be a very busy one, & as you are in America not wholly insensible, perhaps, to the Affairs of a Country [*torn*] so intricately connected with your own, they will probably interest you. I may from time to time send you [*ac*]counts of what I hear—indeed I will do so—at present [*torn*] I have said I know nothing—My Mother I thank God [*has*] been tolerably well. She has not yet determined on [*a v*]isit to you, but I am yet full of the Thoughts of [*torn*] rejoice very much that you & Tom entertain strong Opinions of each other, & I am confident you will every day find better reasons for having formed them. Oh! my dear Brother how enviable you, how enviable we all are! In this old rotten Country—Fathers are against Sons, Sons against Brothers, in short every Man against every Man—Well Heaven bless thee & my dear Sister. Assure her of my best Love. Mrs. Bayley desires to be affecttely. remembered to you both & Amanda will answer for herself—I am ever your's most truly

A I__

RC, Johnson Collection, NCSA.

---

[1]Doddlespool Hall is in northwest Staffordshire, six and a half miles northwest of Newcastle-under-Lyme. Bartholomew, *Survey Gazetteer*, 212.

[2]John Crewe, previously identified, and his wife, Frances Anne Crewe (d. 1818), daughter of Fulke Greville. *DNB*, s.v. "Crewe, Frances Anne."

[3]John Hinchliffe (1731-1794) was the bishop of Peterborough from 1769 to 1794. He also became the dean of Durham on September 24, 1788. This latter office was a rich and influential position and is probably the "better See" to which Iredell refers. W. D. Sweeting, *The Cathedral Church of Peterborough: A Description of its Fabric and a Brief History of the Episcopal See* (London : G. Bell, 1898), 132-133; *DNB*, s.v. "Hinchliffe, John."

[4]"Benedick the Married Man" is one of the central characters in Shakespeare's *Much Ado About Nothing.* A confirmed bachelor, Benedick devotes himself to Beatrice after being led to believe that she is in love with him.

[5]The speech of January 24 included a call for reducing the national debt, praise for the increase in revenues, and an emphasis on the amiable relations between England and other European nations. Donald Groves Barnes, *George III and William Pitt, 1783-1806* (New York: Octagon Books, 1965), 139.

To John Burgwin

Edenton Feb. 6th. 1786.

Dear Sir

I received your favour of the 14th. January by Mr. Wooldridge, and sincerely feel for the truly distressed /& critical/ situation you and your Family are in.[1] I should be extremely glad if it was in my power to render you any service, but I fear the nature of my Engagements will not permit me to attend at Wilmington Superior Court, could I even entertain a hope that by so doing you could be at all benefited. Had it not been for that unfortunate conviction, upon an Issue voluntarily consented to, I should have supposed, consistently with the Treaty of Peace, no Confiscation Act could be carried into Effect against you[2]—An opinion, <however>, that I know is not very popular, and I believe has not the countenance of the Judges, but one which at all times I should deem it my duty to support. There is however some doubt & difficulty attending even this, as the Legislature has not thought proper to <remove by an express law the impediments the Treaty declares against>—/alter their laws conformably to the provisions in the Treaty/—But when <the Fact has been found by a Jury against you> /a Jury, circumstanced as your case was, have found the <fact> against you /the fact/ upon which the Confiscation arises, I despair of your being able to obtain any relief.

At the same time, Sir, I do assure you, abstracted from any pecuniary consideration, I feel so much for your present unfortunate situation, that I will at least promise you to think with all possible care of your case, and give You the best advice which may be the result of my enquiries in my power. <In the mean time which> It will be necessary for that purpose that I should have a Copy of the <for> pleadings in your Ejectment Suit, /so far as they concern this point/ and I should wish also to see a Copy of the Permission you obtained for leaving the Country.

Mr. Wooldridge & Mr. Waddell left this Town quite well on the 2d. Inst.

I am &c

FC, Johnson Collection, NCSA. Endorsed "Copy of a Letter to Mr. Burgwin Feb. 6. 1786."

---

[1]See John Burgwin to JI, January 14, 1786, in this volume.

[2]In *John Burgwin v. David Russ*, June 1785, the Wilmington District Superior Court ruled that Burgwin had departed North Carolina "to avoid giving assistance agt the Enemies of the State." Wilmington District Superior Court, Trial Docket, State Archives. See also John Burgwin to JI, March 30 and May 23, 1786, in this volume.

From Samuel Johnston

Hayes February 7th. 1786

Dear Sir

The inclosed is the rough of the Opinion I have formed in Capt. Merediths Case. as it is a case you have had reason to consider and it is of some importance to him I would take it kind if you will take the trouble to look over it and correct it where you think it is wrong that I may be the more certain of <being> giving <a pro> proper advice

Yrs.

Sam Johnston

[*Enclosure*]

I am of Opinion that as William Topping never reduced his Wife's Interest in the trust money to possession, it remained a Chose in Action and survived to his Widow.[1] That Jordan while on his intermarriage with her might well dispose of it, and that the Interest of himself and his Wife vested in Miss Elizabeth McCulloch under the Conveyance referred to in the Case. That the Interest which Henrietta Mary McCulloch had in the said Trust Money is well conveyed to Miss Elizabeth McCulloch by the Deed from Mark Browning referred to in the Case[2] I am further of Opinion that Captain Joseph Meredith in consequence of his intermarriage with Miss Elizabeth McCulloch is entitled to reserve three fourths of the said Trust-Money, to wit, the share due to his Wife and the shares which were assigned to her by her two Sisters. And that Job Parker on obtaining Letters of Administration on his /Wife's/ Estate is entitled to reserve her part.[3]

To exonerate the Representative of the Surviving Trustte There should be the most full and ample Certificates of all the Marriages properly Authenticated by the Governor under the Great Seal of the State. The Deeds proved before the proper Court or Officer Authorized to take the probate of Deeds, with the Governor's Certificate under the Great Seal that the Deeds were proved agreeable to the Laws of this State and that the Certificate of the probate was Authentick. Job Parker's Letters of Administration with the Governor's Certificate as aforesaid that the Letters were properly obtained and that they are signed by the Officer who had a right to issue them.

This I should presume would be sufficient to satisfie the Court of Chancery in a Case where there was no adverse Suit, otherwise that Court would insist that these facts should be made manifest by Depositions certified by Commissioners specially appointed by the Court for that purpose Should the Trustee, however, be satisfied, as I think he well may, that these transactions are bona fide. I should suppose he would find no difficulty in paying the Money as there is not the most distant probability that any person will ever molest him or give /him/ any further trouble in this business

RC, Hayes Collection, SHC. Addressed "Mr. Iredell."

---

[1]William Topping (d. ca. 1773) of Chowan County had been the husband of Dorothy "Dolly" Berisford McCulloch. Will of William Topping, 1773, Chowan County Wills, State Archives.

A "chose in action" is a claim to property, money, or a debt recoverable through a lawsuit. *Black's Law Dictionary*, 7th ed., 234.

[2]A Mark Browning appears as a resident of the St. Mark's District, Orange County, in 1790. *Heads of Families, 1790 Census*, 96.

[3]Job Parker (d. 1812) of Chowan County. Estate of Job Parker, 1812, Chowan County Estates, State Archives.

To Samuel Johnston[1]

Dear Sir,

I am perfectly of your opinion in every particular & am extremely glad we happen so entirely to agree in it.

Ja. Iredell.

As Job Parker's child survived the Mother, would not it be more secure for him to take our Administration on the Estates of both? Tho' I think he would be entitled to his Wife's choses in action without it. Squib v Wyn, 1 P. Wms. 378.

RC, Hayes Collection, SHC.

---

[1]JI's note to Samuel Johnston is written on Johnston's letter of February 7, 1786.

1786 Tax List

Edenton Feb. 8th. 1786.

List of the Number of Persons in the Family of James Iredell in the Town of Edenton.—

White Males from 21 to 60	2
Do.——under 21 & above 60	1
White Females	5
Blacks from 12 to 50	8
Blacks upwards of 50, and under 12} (Doubtful as to one, whether under or above 50)}	6

Edenton Feb 8th. 1786.
Ja. Iredell.

FC, Johnson Collection, NCSA.

From William Hooper

[February 12, 1786][1]

My dear Sir.

By accident I have heard that Skinner is in this Town, at the same time I learn that he leaves it immediately. I cannot however suffer him to escape without making him the bearer of my most Sincere & ardent congratulations to you and Mrs. Iredell upon the happy addition to your family. Mrs. Hooper & my daughter most cordially sympathize with you <o>in the joyful event & desire me to assure you of it. May it live to be a lasting blessing to its worthy parents & be the forerunner & harbinger of many such causes of rejoicing. Come hither with the dear babe to us. Snatch it from the air of your Unhealthy climate, and give it in early life a vigour of constitution that may bear it up against accidents hereafter & so

Penny Dawson has changed her name for one she likes better. Mr. Johnston in his letter to me says that Lowther would be unconscienable to refuse to be hanged after enjoying so fine a girl. Might he not add<ed> damned too. I mean a temporary damnation. If I had time I would rant a little upon the luscious subject. It sets my old blood afloat with youthful heat & I find a glow about my heart that such a theme only could excite. But I was early taught "Thou Shalt not covet thy neighbour's" you know the rest. I rejoice that the wedding has been conducted with So much address. It may perhaps pave the way for peace & Security to Lowther. Pray present my congratulations to the happy pair & family

Mr. Hoggs family dined with me yesterday being the anniversary of Genl. Washingtons. <family> /birth./ You occupied much of Mrs. Hoggs. thoughts, and as it is customary among great people on great occasions to register their toasts Mrs. Iredell & the little one followed close at the heels of our Hero by order of Mrs. Hogg. Mr. Hogg is not here. He has been at Fayette for some time past.

I perfectly agree with you as to the right which Wiley has to relief in equity against Johnstons. estate in case of eviction under the confiscation law. Mr. Hogg's Ideas are as Johnstons were that the Warranty <wa>is Special & that Wyley bought at his own peril. But the Assignment of a Judt. for 1200£ is a solid consideration & surely a court of equity will not substantiate it without some consideration to support it.[2] Mr. Hogg's hopes have been sanguine until lately. I have given him very little encouragement. Lytle has advertised the tract called Nugents for sale.[3] It holds about Seventy families Seated upon it. They menace loudly, & the event may possibly be another <u>regulation</u>. In this case I may escape a whipping as I am very earnestly on the Side of the tenants, which fortunately is the Strongest.[4] Should Strudwick's men take the Infection, you perhaps may get a Scouring.

Skinner will not give me time but to add my most respectful compliments to Mrs. Iredell & yourself & the rest of your good family. <The &> My Wife & Betsy unite with me & I am

My dear Sir Truly & affectionately Yours

Will Hooper

RC, Iredell Papers, Duke. Printed, McRee, 2:90-91. Addressed "James Iredell esquire Edenton By favour of Mr. Skinner." Endorsed "Hillsborough Feb. 12. 1786. Wm. Hooper."[5]

---

[1]While McRee dates this letter 1784, it is filed with the 1786 documents in the Charles E. Johnson Collection in the State Archives. References to the birth of Annie Iredell and the wedding of Penny Dawson indicate that 1786 is the correct year.

[2]For more information on the Wiley-Johnston land transaction, see James Hogg to JI, January 19, 1786, n. 4, and JI to James Hogg, January 29, 1786, in this volume.

[3]Archibald Lytle (1730-1790) was the commissioner of confiscated property in the Hillsborough District. He was a military officer during the Revolutionary War and later served as a Hillsborough town commissioner (1784) and as a member of the house of commons (1784-1785). *DNCB*, s.v. "Lytle, Archibald."

[4]Hooper, as deputy attorney general of the Salisbury District, was often in conflict with the participants in the Regulator uprising of the late 1760s and early

1770s. A mob of Regulators was said to have attacked him in Hillsborough in September 1770. *DNCB*, s.v. "Hooper, William."

[5]The endorsement is taken from a loose page filed with miscellaneous papers in the Johnson Collection, State Archives.

From Arthur Iredell

London Feby. 21st. 1786.

My dear Brother

I had yesterday the Favor of a Visit from Mr. Dawson who informed me that the Ship in which he has taken his Passage will sail to morrow, & that the Parcel I design for you must be sent this Morning to Mr. Blacks. Unfortunately I had not prepared the few Articles I intended to collect, such as a Calendar, the late Reviews &c., & you must therefore for the present take up with a few old Papers I scraped together in Cheshire. I am indeed going to Woodfall's to purchase, if I can, the Morning Chronicles since the Meeting of Parlt., but whether I shall succeed or not is a matter of great Uncertainty[1]—I am extremely sorry my Finances will not suffer me to extend my Plan to all the new Publications, & Books of intrinsic Value, but the plain truth is that I am as poor as a Rat. My Uncle is a year behind hand in remittance, & that is now the only Fund I subsist upon. Apropos of his Fortune—I hear sad Acccounts of it from all Quarters to damp my Expectations, wch. are by no means so sanguine as they were. So much the better, for should I be disappointed, it will be on the right Side, & no harm can arise from an Activity I have long wanted. I mean therefore to stir my Stumps, "as the saying is," & who knows but I may be Persona Ecclesia in due time[2]—My Mother's Situation is much more distressing to me than my own. I had hopes of her getting out to Carolina with Mr. D—but they are blasted—Mc.Culloh, with his usual Shabbiness, has promised her a small Sum of Money <u>if</u> you take his Son—I incline to think his Application wd. have had more weight with you had he advanced it unconditionally—For my own part I had rather run all hazards & procure the Money Myself than be indebted to him for a Stiver[3]—And I think it will end in <u>my</u> furnishing her with the means I every day expect a remittce. from Jamaica of 50£—This & much more I stand in need of to pay off Debts of my own & enable me to jog on thro' the Summer—Yet I will forego such Considerations & bestow it upon her Equipment & Passage if no unforeseen Accident should intervene & put it out of my Power. My Friend Mr. Kempe has lost, or rather buried his Wife. A most fortunate Event, for he may now live comfortably if he will—he had no Option before. I have already passed some time with him in Sussex, & he has desired me to consider Malling as my Home, when I have no better Place to go to. So you see my Stars do now & then twinkle kindly upon me.

There is nothing momentous upon the political Carpet at present, but an Impeachment against Mr. Hastings instituted by your Friend Mr. Burke, & now in It's Infancy[4]—I hardly think it will attain to Manhood, notwithsg. the apparent Impartiality & Candour of the Minister. Burke will certainly not relax, or flinch from the Business but there are few in either House, or out of them, so zealous or hearty in the Cause as himself. I was yesty. Morng. with Mr. Crewe & he fairly confessed that he thought the only Point that wd. be gained by the Attack wd. be that of exposing Dundas, whose Character was never Specious enough in my Opinion to be mistaken.[5] Adieu my dear Brother! I am in a great hurry, & want to beset Mr. Woodfall. My best Love to my Sister & Tom, of whom I augur great Things. My Mother has written her own History & all I need now assure you of is that I am ever Most truly Your's

A I

It will give you great Pleasure I am sure to learn that Miss F. is perfectly well, & entirely devoted to You & your's. I have just heard from her—<Don't you pity me?> I must not see her—don't you pity me? Well—I must get a Living & be more eligible than they chuse to think me at present.

I have been fortunate enough to procure the Papers from Woodfall, & I have ordered the Morning Chronicle to be sent in to me regularly in future, so that you may depend upon having the following ones up to the time that my Mother shall sail, or, if that Event shd. not take Place, by the first favorable Opportunity. once more Adieu! God bless you all! I am in a prodigious hurry & want to dispatch the Box.

A I___

Direct your Letters for me to the Care of Francis Vincent Esqr Threadneedle Street—Tell Tom that Wilson has got the Command of an Indiaman. He bought the whole Ship indeed, & gave it to himself, but he has since disposed of 2 thirds of the Concern.

RC, Johnson Collection, NCSA. Printed, McRee, 2:134. Addressed "James Iredell Esqr."

---

[1]William Woodfall (1746-1803) was the editor of the *Morning Chronicle*, a leading Whig organ. Newman, *Britain in the Hanoverian Age*, 504.

[2]"To stir stumps," a phrase dating from the sixteenth century, means to move one's legs, either literally, by walking or dancing, or figuratively, by taking action. Bartlett Here Whiting, *Early American Proverbs and Proverbial Phrases* (Cambridge,

Mass.: Belknap Press of Harvard University Press, 1977), 422; *Oxford Dictionary of English Proverbs*, 3d ed. (Oxford: Clarendon Press, 1970), 775.

Persona Ecclesia refers to someone associated with the church.

[3]A stiver is a coin of small denomination or a small sum of money. *OED*, s.v. "stiver."

[4]Warren Hastings (1732-1818), a high-ranking official of the East India Company, was charged with corruption and cruelty by the House of Commons in April 1787. His trial in the House of Lords, which dragged on for more than seven years, ended in his acquittal. Edmund Burke, who in 1783 had served on a select committee to investigate the activities of the East India Company, led the prosecution. *DNB*, s.v. "Hastings, Warren," "Burke, Edmund."

[5]Henry Dundas (1742-1811), 1st Viscount Melville, was a member of Parliament, lord advocate, and treasurer of the navy. Beginning in 1784, he was a dominant member of the Board of Control, a body established to oversee Indian affairs in the wake of Pitt's India bill. *DNB*, s.v. "Dundas, Henry"; Goodwin, *New Cambridge Modern History*, 8:555.

To Thomas Iredell Sr.

Edenton N. Carolina Feb. 23d. 1786.

Hond. Sir,

I confess a letter which my Brother yesterday received from you has given me very great pain, not from a consciousness that I deserve in any degree the reflections you think proper to bestow upon me, but <because> /that/ the manner in which those reflections are made implies an inveterate prejudice against me I can entertain little hope of removing. It is not my intention, Sir, to force upon you a correspondence which has become disgusting: This letter is the last probably you will ever receive from me, unless you shall condescend to desire otherwise, and being so I trust you will forgive an attempt, which if troublesome will not be renewed, to convince you I have neither been that bad Man you have figured to your imagination, nor do my letters <duly considered>, if expressive of my present sentiments, as I believe they are, <carry those marks> /merit the <epithets> reproach/ of disingenuity and prostitution of good sense which are the severe characteristics you fix <upon> /on/ them. As I may perhaps have suffered before from too little distinctness of expression, I beg leave now, though at the risque of being thought pedantic, to take slight notice of your objections to my particular conduct in order, carefully avoiding however any thing on the great subjects of controversy, which it would be equally improper, as it is unnecessary to discuss.

The objections, as I understand them, are, 1. My having taken an Oath of Allegiance. 2. My holding an official Character. 3. My being an Englishman by birth—

To the first I say, that admitting the resistance of the Subject is [*allowable in*] any case, the circumstance of an Oath of Allegiance is of no weight, since Allegiance is as much due without an Oath as with it, and if all who had taken such an Oath were debarred from resistance no effectual one ever could be formed. This every Whig must agree in as a principle. The Revolution in 1688 clearly proves so much, tho' it does not indeed ascertain, nor is it possible for any single case ever to do so, the particular instances in which this principle may be applied. This must be left to every Man's conscience and judgment, taking due care to be well informed of all circumstances, & being as much aware on the one hand of the great duty & indispensible obligation of Allegiance until forfeited, as of the clear right to resistance when it is.

In regard to my official Character, I was scrupulously careful so long as the least vestige of a British Government remained to do nothing in consistent with it. But afterwards, I thought myself as much at liberty to chuse my side as any Man. I should have disdained any office which was to be purchased by a sacrifice of public duty, nor could I conceive any such abject condition annexed to it when the King himself is merely a Trustee for his People, and certainly, in the distribution of public offices, to be considered rather in that light than as a Distributor of private Favours. This I do not say with any view to detract from the obligations conferred upon me. I admit them fully, but they were in my opinion always subordinate to public motives, and if Instances were wanting in so plain a point I recur to the many great examples at the time of the Revolution you so justly call a glorious one. Permit me also to say, that I was not altogether fed by the Bounty of England. The offices I held had severe duties annexed to them, which I performed faithfully. The first was a mere Pittance, and the latter which I held for little more than 12 months I purchased of Mr. Mc.Culloh for £600 Stg. with Interest, great part of which is still due.[1]

The remaining objection against me, is that I am an Englishman by birth. I glory in being so; I glory that I was in truth brought up in that Country in the Bosom of Liberty, and in principles which I have never departed from. I left England, as I had a right to do, to become an Inhabitant of an American Province. I then belonged to a new Society, whose welfare by all possible means it became my indispensable duty to promote. Nothing could be more painful to me than a Conflict between the Country of my Birth, and the Society of which I was an actual Member long before the War broke out. It imposed a distressing alternative upon me. But I never doubted, whether or not it was not my duty to defend my own rights as well as those of the Society I belonged to. I never considered myself as a Spy placed in America to prosecute the views of England upon it. Thus circumstanced therefore, I had only to fix my principles, & doing so to chuse my side. I did so, to the best of my judgment, and have acted accordingly, but with so little bigotry of mind that I do assure you, in the very heat of the war, I held in equal respect, so far as personal character was concerned, Men of principle on both sides, for such there are & will be in every civil war—The very nature of one supposes something difficult in the question. And I cannot but think myself peculiarly unfortunate, that entertaining such sentiments even in regard to Strangers, some of my own nearest Relations should be unwilling to exercise the same candour towards me.

I never meant, in respect to the two Revolutions (as you will find if you will condescend to look at my letters, in case you have preserved them) to compare the personal or political character of the 2 Kings. God knows nothing was further from my heart, and in respect to the American Revolution I look upon it to have been much more brought about by the intemperate violence of the People of England themselves than from any other cause. The Effect however as to us was the same, and it would have been a poor consolation in viewing the miseries of our Country to have said "The People of England are much more to blame for this than the King."

You will observe, I wave altogether particular Questions of the Controversy, as those perhaps we should never agree in. I contend only, and have a right to contend with warmth against any construction of Immorality in my Conduct, since I was obliged to act according to my own Judgment, and I call God to witness I did so, honestly, sincerely, & voluntarily. If it shall nevertheless in spite of any thing I can say, continue to preserve your /strong/ prejudices against me, though I shall lament this as one of my greatest misfortunes, I shall never repent of obeying the dictates of an honest Mind—

I have troubled you with this long letter, for no other purpose but to clear myself of misrepresentations which I think nothing but the strongest prejudices against me, and the want of a little attention to my letters, has occasioned. Your favours are at your own disposal, and God knows I had never any selfish presumptuous views upon them. But my Character I hold sacred, and as your estimation of it is a matter of great moment I hope you will condescend to consider again whether you are warranted in renouncing me as unworthy of your name & blood, a sentence of too awful a nature to be pronounced by a Man of principle without very good reason.

I should sometime ago have had hope, that it would have given you pleasure to hear I had a fine Daughter born on the 22d. of December, and that both Mother & child have been since in remarkable good health.

I have now only to add (which I cannot but do with particular earnestness, as this may possibly be my last letter), that whatever may be your sentiments towards me I shall never cease to pray for your prosperity & welfare, and that I ever am,

with the greatest respect, Most dear & honoured Sir [*Your sincerely*] affe[*ction*]ate Nephew

J. I.

FC, Johnson Collection, NCSA. Printed, McRee, 2:134-137. Endorsed "Copy of a Letter to my Uncle Iredell, Feb. 23d. 1786."

---

[1]JI arrived in Edenton in 1768 to fill the post of comptroller of customs, while Henry Eustace McCulloh held the superior position of collector of customs. McCulloh, however, had returned to England in 1767 leaving JI to perform the duties of both positions as well as taking care of McCulloh's personal business. JI acquiesced to this arrangement, no doubt, because McCulloh and his family had secured the job for him. They had also helped him financially in other ways at a time when JI's immediate family faced economic difficulties. In addition, JI was only seventeen when he came to America and probably lacked the confidence to challenge this arrangement. McCulloh finally relinquished the collectorship to JI in 1774. *PJI*, 1:xxxvii, xlviii, lv.

From Archibald Maclaine

Wilmington 6th. March 1786

Dear Sir

Blyth being some time absent, and never having given me proper instructions, & having no copies of the proceedings at New Bern court, I am not able to make out a bill in equity as I would wish it should be done[1]—I have however sent you a sketch which I believe <will> contains the substance; and I must rely upon you to let me amend it in any <form> /matter/ that may be deficient, filling up blanks &c

I do not at present see Mr. Burgwin's case in a very desperate point of view, considered in itself; but I think he has every thing to fear from the Judges. On a plea of his disability to sue under the last clause of the court law, for that he had withdrawn to avoid giving his assistance to the State, and had resided in the british dominions, both these facts were found against him, though there was not the least proof of the first; and it now lies over to be determined, whether this conviction is sufficient at this day, to preclude him from maintaining a suit. The Judges seem to extend the clause referred to, to every british subject, so far as to prevent the recovery of any old Debt; but I do not know that Mr. B— can come under any of the confiscation acts, but that passed in 1782 (about a year after he left the State). The 20th. Section is a sweeping clause, and was apparently intended to take all the property that could be reached; but notwithstanding the words, "heretofore attached themselves selves in any manner whatsoever to the enemies of this, or the United States," I take it for granted that before any confiscation can possibly take place upon such an act, a legal inquiry must be had, and a criminal attachment must be proved.[2] As this was not done during the war, and of course the property not confiscated when the State had a power to do it, can it /now/ be done, consistent with the treaty of peace?[3] The Assembly and the Judges have indeed found an easy way to evade the treaty—The former refuse to point out any method to ascertain what is confiscated (for they know they cannot) and the Judges refuse to let any person [*torn*] whose property may be taken by a rapacious commissioner, maintain a suit; so that we seem to be at the mercy of a set of needy adventurers, whose interest it is to pillage us; and that no loop- hole may be left unguarded, an act was passed last Session, intended to give a sanction to every thing that has been done, & may be done for the future.[4]

The commissioner in this district has I believe so far relaxed as to consent that only part of B's property shall be sold in such manner as that he may have the legality of the sale tried.[5] I wish you could do something more than give advice, as I am persuaded that if the Judges are beset by the principal gentlemen of the bar in a proper manner, they will not venture to go any great length—I believe indeed that Williams was long since determined; and I know that Spencer is a man of firmness; but I know also that he is an apostate from his principles. The conduct of all these worthies at last Wilmington court, shews what we have to expect from them. You know the sneaking part they acted, in order to avoid determining against popular prejudices—They found that the Assembly would not interfere, and they learned that there was a clamor against them for the little good which they attempted—They therefore determined to plunge through thick and thin, and now they rise like the diver in the Dunciad,

Shaking the horrors of their sable brows,
And each ferocious feature grim with ooze.[6]

They believe that the Assembly will not censure them for misbehavior in office, when Their vengeance is aimed at a defenceless tory, and as they are not under the impulse of fear, they luckily /for themselves/ have no principle to restrain them

How it happened I know it, but notwithstanding the intention of so many of the gentlemen to get into the assembly last year, they almost all failed—To this we owe the want of a reform in our court system; and possibly to this we owe a fresh influx of paper money—To this it is owing that we have so many wicked and scandalous acts of last Session, and it is certainly owing to this, that the bills which I introduced, and which were recommended by you and Mr. Johnston, fell to the ground in the Senate[7]—Want of principle and want of knowledge have occasioned these evils—I am sick of Legislating—There is no dealing with fools and knaves, unless they are powerfully opposed—There will be no living in the country without a reform, and in truth it will be a disgrace to live in it. If there are no hopes of having a better legislature, I shall bid adieu to public business forever.

What effect has the approaching paper money upon you at Edenton? No body gets tobacco in this quarter but the commissioner, though many thousands /of pounds/ were to be discharged in that article; but the merchants will not take it at the public price[8]—This is a new way of monopoliz[*ing*] the staple commodities of the country, but the monopoly will not last long. I believe those who have sold their property for paper, will be good boys, and never do so again.

Mr. Hay is lately married to Col. Rowan's daughter, who is I am told a very fine girl, for I have not seen /her/ for upwards of three years[9]—I expect to see him in about a month, & will then deliver your compliments Mr. Huske and a number of commissoners of pilotage are now at Baldhead, with Genl. Howe, Mr. B Smith &c fixing the place for a lighthouse, and expect to begin it very shortly[10]—All your friends that are here, desire their compliments—Present mine to Mrs. Iredell, your family & Mr. Johnston's

I am with very sincere respect and esteem Dear Sir yours

A Maclaine

The Assembly of S. Carolina have continued their valuation law for a year; so that there will be no collection of debts[11]—Mr. G. Hooper is now there, and will /come/ back with his finger in his mouth.

I have no copy of the bill I send you, & therefore you will take care of it for me

RC, Johnson Collection, NCSA. Printed, McRee, 2:137-139. Addressed "Mr. Iredell."

---

[1]See *John Doe on demise of James Lassers guardian v. Samuel Blyth*, November 1785, New Bern District Superior Court, Trial, Appearance, Argument and Reference Docket, State Archives, and *Samuel Blyth v. William Blackman Excor.*, June 1786, Wilmington District Superior Court, Equity Docket, State Archives.

Samuel Blyth was a resident of the Salisbury District, Mecklenburg County. *Heads of Families, 1790 Census*, 160.

[2]Section 20 of "An Act directing the sale of Confiscated Property" states "that every person who has been a resident in this State, and have heretofore attached themselves in any manner whatsoever to the enemies of this, or the United States, it is hereby fully and entirely expressed, that all the property of such person or persons, shall be considered as having been forfeited to and for the use of this State, from the time that such person so joined the enemy as aforesaid; and that all bargains and sales, wills and devises, made so as to interfere with this Act, is, and are hereby declared to be null and void, to all intents and purposes." For the text of the entire act, see Clark, *State Records*, 24:424-429.

[3]For more information on the Burgwin case, see John Burgwin to JI, January 14, 1786, in this volume.

[4]See Archibald Maclaine to Samuel Johnston, December 24, 1785, n. 6, in this volume.

[5]Griffith John McRee, a Revolutionary War veteran from Brunswick County, was the commissioner for the Wilmington District. He was the grandfather of Griffith John McRee (1819-1872) of New Hanover County, author of *Life and Correspondence of James Iredell*. Clark, *State Records*, 24:662; *DNCB*, s.v. "McRee, Griffith John."

[6]"The Dunciad" is a satirical poem by Alexander Pope. The complete work was published in 1743. Margaret Drabble, ed., *The Oxford Companion to English Literature*, rev. ed. (Oxford: Oxford University Press, 1998), 295-296.

[7]The senate rejected "A Bill for increasing the number of judges, for dividing the Superior Court into different circuits, and for establishing a Court for the decision of appeals, writs of errors and matters of Laws and courses in Equity" on its second reading on December 20, 1785. General Assembly Session Records, House Bills, December 10-26, 1785, State Archives.

[8]See Archibald Maclaine to Samuel Johnston, December 24, 1785, n. 2, in this volume.

[9]John Hay married Susannah Rowan in February 1786. She was the daughter of Col. Robert Rowan (ca. 1738- 1798) of Cumberland County, a Revolutionary War officer, sheriff, and legislator. *DNCB*, s.v. "Hay, John"; Roy Parker Jr., *Cumberland County: A Brief History* (Raleigh: Division of Archives and History, North Carolina Department of Cultural Resources, 1990), 15.

[10]The General Assembly passed "An Act for regulating the Pilotage and facilitating the navigation of Cape Fear River" in 1784. Section 17 called for the erection of a lighthouse on Bald Head to "greatly facilitate the navigation of vessels trading to Cape Fear river." The beacon was to be built at "the extreme point of Bald-head or some other convenient place near the bar of said river, in order that

vessels may be enabled thereby to avoid the great shoal called the Frying-Pan." Clark, *State Records*, 24:586-592.

Robert Howe (1732-1786) of New Hanover and Brunswick Counties fought in the French and Indian War and in the war against the Regulators. During the Revolution, he attained the rank of major general in the Continental army. Howe retired to his plantation after the war and in 1786 was elected to the house of commons. *DNCB*, s.v. "Howe, Robert."

Benjamin Smith (1756-1826), a lawyer and planter, was a member of the house of commons for three terms and the senate for eighteen terms. He was also governor (1810-1811). Smith, owner of Bald Head, donated ten acres of land as a site for the lighthouse in 1789. *DNCB*, s.v. "Smith, Benjamin"; David Stick, *Bald Head: A History of Smith Island and Cape Fear* (Wendell, N.C.: Broadfoot Publishing, 1985), 30-31.

[11]In 1784, the South Carolina legislature prohibited lawsuits to collect debts until 1786. In the postwar economic chaos, debtors dominated the state assembly and acted in their own interests. David Duncan Wallace, *South Carolina: A Short History, 1520-1948* (Chapel Hill: University of North Carolina Press, 1951), 332.

From John Burgwin

Hermitage near Wilmington 30th. March 1786—

My Dear Sir

You will no doubt be greatly Surprized at a delay in the Acknowledgemt. of of yo[*ur*] Kind favour of the 6th. Feby. but the fact has been that soon after the Rect. of [*it*] I w[*ent*] [*torn*] into the back Country & am but just Returned, and I now take the first Post to thank you for your Polite & friendly Letter & promise of your best Advice in my truly unfortunate Situation[1]—Inclosed I have taken the liberty to send you a S[*torn*] of my case from the begining & the Several papers Relative—My Case is [*pec*]uliar & if I may be Allowed to Judge from an Appeal to my Own heart, I may Justly say that I am persecuted—how many Men do I see around me in full possession of their property & priviledges who I am told had Actually Joined the Enemys of this Country: Overt Acts had been proved & other Circumstances evincing their Attachment Contrary to the Laws of this State—Yet by the glorious uncertainty of the Law have been honorably Acquitted—whilst I who have not by any One Act of my life been guilty of the smallest Crime to the prejudice of this my Country—Yet am pitched upon as the Scape Goat, and thereby by the prejudices of peoples minds, heightened for the purpose, am made the Sufferer—

Who have I to look up to, but to Gentn. who have hearts Capable, Spirit & abilities & Humanity too, to Assist me in Steming the torrant of Popular

Injustice. To you then My Frd. I apply not from any right of early or long Acquaintance or Act of former Friendship which I daily experience have no Avail in this Country and if they had on these Considerations I have no real right to your Services because I lived at a distance from you & was but little [*known*] to you—But I claim a Right to your friendship & Services on [*faded*] & more Substantial Motive, the Principles of Natural Justice & Humanity to a Family who has been born down by Oppression in a most unparralle<l>led manner—upon the whole I claim it as a Persecuted Man, to save a worthy Woman & two lovely Children from inevitable want & destruction—I am convinced these incentives will have their weight provided your Affairs will Admit me to have your Assistance at the next Superior Court—If your Affairs will not Admit it then I hope for Your friendly Advice &c

as what I write as what I now Write to you I hold most Sacred between us and under that confidence I will venture to say to you that I have been most Cruelly treated which by your leave I will One day make you Acquainted with. The point is <at present> delicate & I had Rather bury the Injury in my own [*hear*]t for the present. Only I will Just say that our Mutual Frd. G M[*torn*]n has been the innocent Cause of all my Sufferings

You will please to excuse the inaccuracys of this Scrawl which I hurry over to Save the post & not time to Correct—I am with Real & true Regard for your person & Character

Dear Sir Your Obliged & Obedt. Hbl Servt.

Jno. Burgwin

P.S. it may be necessary to say that the Plea of Disability was filed in a Suit in Ejectmt. brought by me against one David Russ abt. the year 1779 & so long continued over that I had nearly forgot there was Such a Suit of myne in Court[2]—The Plea was founded on a Clause at the end of the Superior Court Law—I am extreamly tender in giving Sanction to blame in these delicate Cases—but it strikes me that in a matter of so much Consequence I ought to have been made acquainted with the Plea & issue previous to the trial—but /unfortunately/ the Plea was filed, issue made up & Jury drawn, before I was Acquainted with either of the Circumstances & had I not by Chance that day gone to Town, it would have been Tried too, before I knew any thing of the matter—and all this I believe was Owing to my Council being perhaps Over Sanguine on my behalf—I had not even My Pasport or any of my papers in Town so that the Deft. in Ejectmt. had only to prove my going to Charleston which indeed was Admitted. yrs.

J. B

[*Enclosure*]

Case

In 1775 I had the misfortune to fracture my leg, in July the same year by the Advice of my Phisicians I went to England—immediately on hearing of an Act of Assembly having Passed Subjecting the property of Absentees to Confiscation I returned [*to*] No. Carolina and at the next Assembly held at Halifax in Jany. 1779 I was admitted a Citizen & soon afterwards was appointed a Justice of the Peace for the County of Bladen which Office I discharged with fidelity firmness & integrity[3]—That I had been appointed Exor to my Brother-in-law Genl. Waddell & Sole Guardian to his three Sons in case of their Mothers Death or intermarriage—the two eldest I carried to England with me and I placed them at a Public School on my Own Credit—on my Departure from England in 1778 My worthy Frd. Edmund Radcliff Esqe. promised me to Supply their Expences & Support till Remittances could be made—That in 1776. Mrs. Waddell died leaving M. Faithful Graham one of her Exors who in consequence possessed him self of the whole Estate of Genl. Wadd[*ell*][4] the begining of 1780 I had information of the Death of my Frd. Mr. Radcliff and no provision made for my Nephews Support—which created me great uneasiness on their Acct. as well as <for> /on Acct. of/ the Youngest Son who was growing up without any Education whatever & whom his Mother had Committed to the Care of Mr. & Mrs. Graham, it was [*torn*] delicate point in me to Notice his Situation &c.—I however frequently Advised with Mr. Harnett & Genl. Lillington intimate frds. of the late Genl. Waddell whose Advice was to Send the Youngest to England & depend on their Fathers Relations for their Support till Remittances could be made—

In December 1780 I Obtained a passport from Genl. Lillington to carry the youngest Son to Charleston being the nearest Port from whence I could Convey him to England—but as I was not Able to get more from Mr. Graham than £10.18.4 Stg. towards his Support I was under a Necessity of going to Wilmington previous to my Departure for Charleston—Whilst I was at Wilmington the British Arrived in the River and as soon as the intelligence came I left the Town & went back to my Plantation the day before the Enemy entered the Town—

The deplorable Situation of my Nephews was ever upp[*ermo*]st in my Mind I began to think it would be easier & less expensive to convey my Youngest Nephew from Wilmington than to Run the Risque of going to Charleston & for that purpose I Obtained a passport from the Justices of Bladen but on Reconsidering the matter & advising with [*torn*] on whoes friendship Integrity & Honr. I had the most unlimitted Confidence I thought it most prudent to proceed to Charleston with my Nephew; where soon after my Arrival I met with Letters under the care of Mr. John Edwards which determined me immediately to embark for England[5] On my Passage I was taken very ill & it was near 8 Months after my Arrival before my health was tollerably Re established—after this I married my present wife and soon after I embarked for Flanders & Germany &c to Settle Correspondencys in the Merchantile line previous to my return to America[6]—during this period the provisional Articles of Peace were Settled and on my Return to England I purchased a Ship & prepared a Cargo to Carry out with my self & family.[7]

That on my Return to No. Carolina I was Surprized to find my property had been hired out by the Sheriff of New Hanover County and afterwards advertized for Sale by the Comr. of forfeited Property without any trial whatever consistant with the Bill of Rights & Constitutions of this State—Except—That in 1782 the County Court of Bladen in the Month of December illegally confiscated some small property I had in that County, the proceedings thereon were brought up to the Superior Court by Certiorari & Remains undetermined; And—Except at last June Court for the District of Wilmington a Verdict was given against me on a plea of Disability hastily filed & issue as hastily taken, on an Old Cause in Ejectmt.—without my privity & which now lies before the Cor. on a Motion in Arrest of Judgmt.[8]

On the Comrs. Advertizing my property for Sale I was advised to Obtain a Prohibition from One of the Judges to Stop the Sale till [*torn*] matter was finally determined in the Superior Court and I was [*torn*] Advised to lay a Memorial before the last Assembly—which I did Stating the Several facts mentioned praying Relief

The Assembly Referred the Memorial to the Gd. Committee [*torn*] on which they Reported "That Mr. Burgwin be Referred to the Decision of the Laws of the Land to which they are informed he has had Recourse"

In the Commons this Report was Concurr'd but Rejected in the Senate[9]—

I am now Advised to bring the matter again before a Jury in an Action of Trespass against the Comr.—My Relyance is on the Justice of my Case—On the Bill of Rights & Constitutions of this State, On the Treaty of Peace & on the urgent Necessity I was under of leaving America, when I did

I conceive the most powerful Act against me is that of April 1782—but then surely what is done by Bladen [*torn*] Court for that County cannot or ought not to influence the Comr. to Sell property in another County without a legal Conviction—

RC, Johnson Collection, NCSA. Addressed "James Iredell Esqe. Edenton."

---

[1]See JI to John Burgwin, February 6, 1786, in this volume.

[2]In 1786, David Russ of Brunswick County was appointed to a commission to draw the boundary between Bladen County and the newly created Robeson County. Clark, *State Records*, 24:839.

[3]For the joint legislative committee's recommendation to receive Burgwin as a North Carolina citizen, see Clark, *State Records*, 13:650-651.

[4]Hugh Waddell employed Faithful Graham as an overseer. *DNCB*, s.v. "Waddell, Hugh."

[5]A John Edwards is listed in the Charleston city directories of 1794 and 1796 as an auctioneer and the manager of an unidentified business at 7 Meeting Street. Hagy, *People and Professions of Charleston*, 39, 52.

[6]Burgwin and Elizabeth Bush (1753-1787) of Bristol, England, were married on April 27, 1782. Burgwin's "Correspondencys in the Merchantile line" stemmed from his businesses in North and South Carolina. Walter Burgwyn Jones, *John Burgwin, Carolinian; John Jones, Virginian: Their Ancestors and Descendants* (n.p.: privately published, 1913), 17, 20; *DNCB*, s.v. "Burgwin, John."

[7]American negotiators signed a preliminary peace treaty with Great Britain on November 30, 1782. The final document was signed September 3, 1783. Bailey, *Diplomatic History*, 45, 47.

[8]See JI to John Burgwin, February 6, 1786, and John Burgwin to JI, May 23, 1786, in this volume.

[9]See Clark, *State Records*, 17:312-313, 373; 20:30, 79.

To Hannah Iredell

Halifax April 18th. 1786.

My dear Hannah,

I cannot express the great delight I had in hearing on my arrival in Town this morning that you and my lovely Annie are so well. God be praised for his great goodness. Your charming letter filled with such pleasing particulars has made me very happy. My anxiety, at all times great during my absence from home, has now been extreme, but thank God, it has been this day amply rewarded. Your Brother & mine are full of the dear little creature's praises. I thank you for talking to her of me. God knows she is almost every moment in my thoughts, and I eagerly anticipate the time I hope I shall be happy enought to see when she can both know & love me. Heaven grant, my present very great happiness may be continued to me. I will every day more & more study to deserve it.

Mr. Hooper & myself did not leave Hillsborough till Saturday afternoon. I was there in my usual happy situation which indeed is as great as I can possibly enjoy any where in the absence of you & our charming Girl. My anxiety about you both sometimes clouded the pleasing hours I enjoyed in one of the most excellent Families in the whole creation. Mrs. Hooper is uniformly herself; the finest understanding, with the greatest goodness of heart, constantly exerted to make all about her happy. Her Daughter, notwithstanding the utmost liveliness of <her> disposition, saving her Mother all the trouble possible in her Family affairs. The Sons (for they are both now at home) both amiable, and obedient and affectionate to their Parents. No scolding, no irregularity, nor disorder or disagreement of any kind ever to be heard in the Family or near it. You would be delighted to be among them, and I wish you could comply with their very kind & I am persuaded genuine invitation to spend the Summer—the approach of which I dread on our lovely Girl's account, among them at Hillsborough. But I fear this is too great a thing to be hoped for. Mrs. Hogg is much better & can walk a little without any assistance. But one of her Sons has still the Fever & Ague. The rest are quite well, & all made the kindest inquiries about you and your Daughter.

I wrote the inclosed from Hillsborough, & it was given to me here, which I send to shew you I was not negligent, and I am sorry there was no opportunity to send it.[1] For want of Survey, nothing was done in the great land causes. I received no money from Strudwick who made many excuses. I have however been very explicit with him, both in person, and in a letter I wrote when it was doubtful if I should see him.[2] I was employed in [*one*] or two cases tried during the Court, but received only £5. in ready money.[3]

April 20. Eccleston going sooner than he told me I must finish abruptly. I wish you to purchase what linen you chuse, but that yours shall be as fine as mine. I hope to get some money /of consequence/ here, having begun tolerably already. Mr. Lowther arrived last night, quite well—So is your Brother—I had fully intended writing to Nelly, but Eccleston's going much sooner than he proposed alone has prevented me. Adieu! Heaven bless you & my dear Girl—Love to all,

Your very affectionate

Ja Iredell

RC, Johnson Collection, NCSA. Addressed "Mrs. Iredell Edenton By favour of Mr. Eccleston."

---

[1]In his letter of April 6, 1786, JI wrote of his daughter Annie: "How much that lovely Angel has added to our anxiety, tho' it has increased our happiness! I think

constantly of her with a kind of trepidation that almost makes me miserable. But I will trust in the good providence of God, hoping she may be spared to us, and devoutly grateful for so great a blessing." Charles E. Johnson Collection, State Archives.

[2]Samuel Strudwick had hired JI in 1780 to save his property from confiscation but had been lax in paying his bill. In April 1784, JI told Hannah that Strudwick had paid Samuel Johnston one hundred guineas but had "put me off again with excuses of not having money at that time." JI to Hannah Iredell, April 17, 1784, in this volume. See also JI to Hannah Iredell, April 8, 1784, n. 1, in this volume.

[3]JI received £5 from James Stuart, who had been charged with high treason, and a promissory note for £10 from a Mr. Potter. Legal Fee Books, vol. 7, James Iredell Papers, Southern Historical Collection.

To Hannah Iredell

Halifax April 21. 1786

My dear Hannah,

I wrote you a few lines yesterday, which somehow or other are mislaid. There was a grand ball last night, to which I did not go, having a cold which I was afraid of increasing, & to night I was invited to a dance at Bond's, but tho' my cold, owing to care last night, is almost gone, I prudently have abstained on account of business. My Brother is a partaker of this, as well as the last. The grand Cock fight is at last ended, N. Carolina victorious by two battles. Such a scene of gaming & confusion as there is here now can hardly be imagined.[1] I shall be heartily glad when the Court is over, not only from my extreme impatience to get home, but to be clear of so disagreeable a place. Mr. Lowther was very uncomfortably accomodated the first night, but sleeps now at Bond's. I am afraid we shall have but an indifferent Court in point of money. My expectations are much disappointed. [*Please to*] send this by Jonathan Skinner, who I believe will have occasion to send [*torn*] Town for Dr. Williamson[2]—I think every moment of you & my dear Annie. God grant I may find you both well. I have no expectations of [*leaving this till*] Friday, after which I shall make all possible haste, tho' with due discretion, home. O! How I long to see you & that lovely Infant! God bless you both, & long spare you to me—Give my kindest love & respects to Mrs. Dawson & Mrs. Lowther—[*torn*] Compliments I have entrusted to Nelly, and I can assure you with the [*utmost*] sincerity that I am

my dear Hannah, Most faithfully & affectionately yours

Ja. Iredell.

RC, Johnson Collection, NCSA. Addressed "[*Mrs. Iredell*] Edenton."

[1]For information on cockfighting in North Carolina, see B. W. C. Roberts, "Cockfighting: An Early Entertainment in North Carolina," *North Carolina Historical Review* 42 (summer 1965): 306-314.

[2]Jonathan Skinner of Perquimans County served in the house of commons (1779, 1781-1784). Cheney, *North Carolina Government*, 205, 208, 210-212.

From Nelly Blair

Eden House April 1786

Your Brother I hope my Dear Uncle excused me sufficiently to you for not writing by him, & has told you as he truly might That it was entirely his fault I did not. I asked him to send me a Sheet or two of Paper from Town when he went over & one or two good Pens, but he was so taken up with his own Dear Sweet Self & Thinking of The figure he should make among The Halifax Beaux, That he could not recollect even That one poor trifling request & so I had like to have been entirely deprived of The plea/sure/ of writing to you, which without joking would have been a very great mortification, as I cannot now hope for a letter from you, without I write first & petition for it, & Then it is only a short answer. I know my Dear Uncle you have a great deal of Business, but you always used to find time to write, & I fancy still could if it was equally as agreable, indeed your indulgence has spoilt me, for The least mark of indifference or disregard from you gives me more pain Than it is possible for me to express.

We have been over here eight Days to Day, & I can scarcely believe you are more impatient to be at home Than I am. to Morrow Morning we are to go, & Mrs. Dawson & my Cousin are to accompany us over to stay a few Days. They both express The greatest desire to see my Aunt & our Dearest little Annie. The sweet little Angel. I dont know scarcely how to live without her. Mrs. Dawson, my Cousin, & Peggie join in Love to you, & my Uncle Sam & in Compts. to your Brother, with Your Affectionate Neice

H Blair

RC, Johnson Collection, NCSA. Addressed "James Iredell Esqr."

From Arthur Iredell

South Malling May 1st. 1786

My dear James,

Yours of the 2d of January arrived here Yesterday & very satisfactorily confirmed what I had been told two Months ago—But pray remember I have an unconquerable Aversion to old Dates, & that the speediest Conveyance (cite as many Proverbs in point agst me /as you may/) is with me the best. If a Balloon therefore shall leave Edenton for Europe, write by that, & direct to the Care of Francis Vincent Esq. Threadneedle Street London Per Favour Monr. Blanchard or Doctr. Franklin, who, I suppose, reviews your Continent in an Aiery Car, & seldom creeps (for an ordinary Man may do that even better than the Doctor) upon the Surface of this vile Globe.[1] He has already mastered one Element you know, & since he has lost his Fire, it is natural enough that he shd. have to contend with Wind. You will pity me for writing such trash, to a Man of Business too, whose Circuit Continued from Sepr. to Jany. (I want Faith, James)—but what can I do who am neither a Man of Sense, nor a Man of Business?—Why I must write Stuff, aye & nonsensical Stuff, for there are good Stuffs as well as bad ones. By the way Tom must be made of the latter for robbing me of the honor of being God father to Annie Isabella—But I'll be even with him when I have an Annie Isabella of my own. As to your Honorary Sponsorships, I beg leave most willingly to decline them. No, a young James will want a God father, & I will be his, upon condition that you will send the young Dog over to me for Instructions spiritual & moral, that is, look you, if I shall be able to keep him sleek & in as good Case as my good Sister wd. wish him to be in. "In Witness whereof the aforementioned" &c—To be serious, you are all very good in thinking so much & so affectionately of Miss Felton. She is as sensible to your Kindness as I am, & we both of us endeavour to deserve it by cherishing, on our parts (does not that rather smell of Parchment?) an equal tenderness & Regard for our dear Carolinians. But we are not so inclinable to croak as you are; for it is part of our Creed that in some future happy Day we shall meet either in Europe or America, in your House or mine, & examine the Lines of each other's Countenances, which shall be frequently discomposed by loud laughs (yes, my Lord Chesterfield, loud laughs) & every Species of hilarity.[2]—I must say something too for Mrs. Bayley, who believe me, is well deserving of your best Regard, & who will felicitate herself very much upon the Professions you make of it. She has her Sister at this time in her House, at a cruel Distance from hence, but I am not without hope that some <fortunate> /auspicious/ Event will soon bring us nearer to each other, tho I have none immediately in view, & have only that hope to feed upon which, perhaps, every other Man has in as large Quantities as myself. I left London a fortnight ago & till something shall fortunately happen, these will be my Head Quarters. My old friend the Serjeant is vastly good to me, & you may be sure I do not like him the less for being very partial to you.[3] My Mother was tolerably well when I took my leave of her, but She will doubtless write more fully than I can upon her Subject. I saw Ld. Macartney who was very civil to me & indeed during my Stay in London I was so much in the great World that I could not miss of [*torn*] (as they say) Just before I quitted it Mrs. Crewe invited me to [*torn*] Party at her House consistg. of the Duchess of Portland, & your favourite Mr. Burke & his Wife—He is really a wonderfull Man—I will get you in time the printed Accts of his Impeachmt. of Hastings & send them to you.[4] Adieu, my dear Brother! Assure my Sister & Tom, with your charming Annie Isabella (tho She be not my God daughter) of my supremest Regard & give my Love, for they are my relations, to all your own, particularly to that young Lady who was to have been my Wife—I long to know her—She has already made a very deep Impression upon me, & is one of my most esteemed Friends. Will She be my Second? God bless you all! now this strange Letter ends

Yours ever

A I—

RC, Johnson Collection, NCSA. Printed, McRee, 2:139-140. Addressed "James Iredell Esqr. Edenton North Carolina." Endorsed "May 1. 1786. A. Iredell Ansd. July 16th. 1786."

---

[1]Jean Pierre Francois Blanchard (1753-1809) was a French balloonist. By traveling from Dover to Calais in 1785, Blanchard became the first person to cross the English Channel by balloon. Benjamin Franklin, too, was interested in balloon flight but only as an observer. While a diplomat in Paris, Franklin rose from his sick bed to witness the ascent of a piloted balloon from the spot that is now the site of the Eiffel Tower. *Chambers Biographical Dictionary*, s.v. "Blanchard, Jean Pierre Francois"; David Schoenbrun, *Triumph in Paris: The Exploits of Benjamin Franklin* (New York: Harper and Row, 1976), 391-392.

[2]Philip Dormer Stanhope (1694-1773), 4th Earl of Chesterfield, wrote letters of advice to his son for more than three decades. After the earl's death, his widow published a collection of these, which became a popular guide to etiquette. Chesterfield suggested, among other things, to avoid laughing because laughter distorts the face. Drabble, *Oxford Companion to English Literature*, 188.

[3]The searjeant is a Mr. Kemp, who was Arthur Iredell's law instructor. *PJI*, 1:78n.

[4]See Arthur Iredell to JI, February 21, 1786, n. 4, in this volume.

To Hannah Iredell

Friday, May 19th. [*1786*]

Within 25 miles of Newbern.

My dear Hannah,

This is about one o'clock, and the other Gentlemen and myself are just arrived here, very well, and hitherto quite satisfied with our Journey. We were doubtful about being able to cross at Skewawky, and went to Taylor's Ferry, and have found the roads extremely good.[1] I am told the Stage will soon pass by this place, and I write to be ready for it. I forgot to tell Andrew he must work out, and to look out for a place for him. I would rather he should hire out by the month if you approve of it than otherwise. I omitted also to apologise to Edmd. Blount for not paying my taxes. Pray ask my Brother to do it, and to acquaint him I had intended doing it before I left home, but will certainly /pay him/ immediately on my return—I shall hope to hear from you by every Post, and I will not wilfully miss any. Remember of how much importance every motion & look of my dear Annie is to me, and give me a faithful report. I had meant to give a caution about the Candle burning in your room of a night. I think sometimes it is placed too carelessly. Pray do you, or your Aid de camp carefully watch it. Nelly & my Brother must both be convinced I cannot write to them now, expecting the Post every minute. Adieu! God bless you & my lovely Girl. Give her a thousand kisses, remember my love to all the Family, and believe me, my dear Hannah,

Most faithfully & affectionately yours

Ja. Iredell.

RC, Johnson Collection, NCSA. Addressed "Mrs. Iredell Edenton." Endorsed "May 19—1786 or 1787. Ja. Iredell."

---

[1]Taylor's Ferry crossed the Roanoke River between Bertie and Martin Counties. Powell, *Gazetteer*, 488.

From John Burgwin

[*May 23, 1786*]

Dear Sir

I had this day the Honr. of receiving your favour of the 15 Inst. I need not express to you my feelings on perusing its Contents—I have for some time had it hinted that the J—dges were determined to Offer Sacrifices to the Goddess of Popularity and that I was /to be/ devoted as one—I confess I was weak enough not to believe it—because I could not bring myself to believe that the Tribunal of Justice in this State (over famed for its Judicious & Upright decisions) was at so low an Ebb as to require Support from such a baggatelle—and more especially as my Conscience tells me I am not deserving of the treatment. But what cuts me to the Soul is the ruin brot. upon a Worthy Woman & two fine babes[1]—

When I last Wrote, I was not possessed of the Inclosed Papers[2] I now send them for your perusal & consideration And Admitting that the Judgment of the Inferior Court of Bladen is legal & Just, yet I conceive it can only affect my Property in the hands of John Young in that County, because the <County> Court of New Hanover County had they proceeded to Judgment, /the Judgmt./ might have been reverse /to that of Bladen,/ but that Court has not Confiscated any property of Mine or even mentd. my name in any of its Confiscations And yet the Property—Advertized of myne by the Commissioner for Sale all lies in New Hanover County—I have no doubt but all the County Courts in the State have an equal power in their respective County either to Confiscate or not, as to their Wisdom & shall save much—If therefore Our County Confiscates & another does not, is it legal is it agreable to the Laws & Constitutions—that That my Property shall be sold by the Comr. where it has not been Condemned——wod. it not be contrary to the Spirit & meaning of Law—and yet this stands the case—

I have a reverential respect for my Old frd. Mr. M. and yet I have too much reason to say all my Political Misfortunes has Arose from his Managemt.—but this my Dear Frd. is a matter Sacredly between ourselves till I can give you my reasons &c from this hint you may be Assured I shall be happy in receiving your Advice &c under Cover to Doctr. Fergus in Wilmington or inclosed to Colo. Reid[3]—

I have retained Mr. Jones, & he has brot. a Specl. Action on the Case agst. the Comr. for Dams. Sustained by his Advertizing <these> /my Property/ for Sale as Confiscated property &c but whither it will be safe to risque a trial or not is the question or whither it wd. not be best to delay it for a hearing before another Assembly[4]—Your <advice> Opinion & advice will be the greatest favr. <[*illegible*]> to

Dear Sir Yr. Much Obliged

Hermitage

Tuesday afternoon — Jo. Burgwin

23rd May- — please to excuse the hurry in wch.

I write to save post

RC, Iredell Papers, Duke. Addressed "James Iredell Esquire Atty. at Law New Bern."

---

[1]Burgwin is referring to the decision of the Wilmington District Superior Court that Burgwin had left North Carolina to avoid supporting the war against the British. In this letter he is suggesting that the judges were appealing to the prevalent anti-Loyalist sentiment in the state at a time when some lawyers were highly critical of the bench. See JI to John Burgwin, February 6, 1786, and John Burgwin to JI, March 30, 1786, in this volume.

[2]Enclosed papers not found.

[3]Col. James Read (Reid) was appointed collector for the port of Brunswick in 1784 and appears later to have become collector in Wilmington. Clark, *State Records*, 24:552; *DNCB*, s.v. "Smith, Benjamin."

[4]Marmaduke Jones was Burgwin's lawyer.

To Hannah Iredell

Newbern May 24. 1786.

My dear Hannah,

I steal a few minutes from Sleep to thank you most cordially for your letter by the Post this evening, which has given me the finest spirits in the world. I certainly was very uneasy, but not vexed at my disappointment by the former, being assured the neglect would not be a wilful one, and afraid only, tho' I struggled all I could against such thoughts of some misfortune that might have occasioned it. But the Post really comes surprisingly quick upon us. I sent Peter this afternoon to enquire when the next Post was expected, having no idea of its coming in to day, and behold he returned with the happy tidings I had so much wished for. It is to return at 11 to morrow, and I steer to wind ward of my Clients by writing to night. Mr. Hooper is on his legs again, & with his usual spirits. Your Brother arrived Yesterday evening, & is well, but seems very low spirited, having left poor Jemmy sick, he fears with a nervous fever.[1] My God! what he is doomed to undergo—God grant his fears may be groundless. I hope his alarms are greater than there is occasion for. He has a very good room, much better than we have, tho' 3 of us are in one house—He is of our Party at dinner, so that we do very well. I am not quite determined about Wilmington, but rather think I shall go. It would grieve me if Mr. Burgwin, in case of ill success, should suppose my non-attendance was in any respect the cause of it. I should hope too to get a handsome fee by going, and my being at Mr. Huske's, tho' I should be a little concerned for the trouble I gave them, would be a great alleviation, for there is no getting tolerable public accomodations in the Town. The manner of his invitation too, in his letter to Mr. Hooper on a report of my being to be there, is extremely genteel and encouraging.[2] I am very much concerned for Mrs. Whedbee.[3] Tell Nelly I intend occasionally to write to her, but not to trouble her every time I write to you. I am much obliged to her for her intentions towards me. God bless our lovely little Angel. How I delight in the sweet praises you give her! Heaven preserve her to us, & make her a most valuable Member of Society. Apropos! I have been complimented on my command of temper this Court, on an occasion or two where sometime ago I should have stormed with fury. I hope to mend a little every day, and in that particular I assure you I am ambitious of doing so, not only for my own peace, but in regard to your kind & friendly admonitions. [*Torn*] Adieu! God bless you, my dear Hannah! I must go to [*sleep to*] prepare for the fatigues of tomorrow. My Cold is quite gone, and I am perfectly well. My love & remembrance to Annie! I hope, by being often repeated, my name will be one of the first her dear lips will lisp.

Your ever affectionate

Ja. Iredell

P. S. My love very sincerely to your Sister & the Girls—

RC, Johnson Collection, NCSA. Addressed "Mrs. Iredell Edenton." Endorsed "Newbern. 24 May 1786 Ja. Iredell."

---

[1]"Jemmy" is James Cathcart Johnston (1782-1865), son of Samuel Johnston. *PJI*, 2:359n.

[2]The letter from Burgwin to Hooper has not been not found. JI remained uncertain about going to Wilmington for several days. "I am not yet fully determined about Wilmington," he wrote Hannah on May 27, " but rather think I shall go." Charles E. Johnson Collection, State Archives.

[3]A number of people named Whedbee lived in Chowan County at this time. JI may be referring to Elizabeth Whedbee, who, when she died in 1811, was said to have been "an old inhabitant of the town." Raymond Parker Fouts, *Abstracts from the Edenton Gazette and North Carolina General Advertiser*, 4 vols. (Cocoa, Fla.: GenRec Books, 1990-1996), 2:86; *Edenton Gazette*, August 6, 1811.

From William Hooper

1 Augt. 1786

My dear Sir

Your very kind favour by Mr. Johnson has relieved me from much concern upon account of yourself and family. I have with much anxiety Since my return home Sought an opportunity to get a letter to your hands and I flattered myself that I had Succeeded. I inclosed one to Davy by a very special messenger & urged his utmost care and assiduity to forward it to you—What has become of it he best knows.

We are all mortified that you are determined to balk the flattering expectations we had of having Mrs. Iredell and others of your family under our roof this fall. I was the more encouraged to hope this as Miss Nelly in a letter to Mrs. Huske at wilmington mentions that after your return home from New bern you talked as if your purpose was Serious. My letter to you via Halifax, was to press the propriety of this Journey upon you, not only as your own & the health of Mrs. Iredell might profit by it but to awaken your apprehensions on the Score of that dear lovely infant with whose health your own happiness (I might say perhaps your life) is inseparably united—I wish that you may yet have occasion to alter your resolution provided the want of health has no share in producing it. I confess I should be gratified at your feeling a few fears and apprehensions if they should induce you to fly to us for allaying them. My Wife, My Betsy had anticipated some pleasing rural scenes, to the pleasure of which Miss Nellys human vivacity & good Sense would have greatly contributed—

All of Mr. Hoggs family are here except himself, he is busied in preparing the Capitol for the reception of the Assembly at Fayette. A thousand Obstacles are cast in his way and I am Somewhat doubtful if he will Surmount them all.[1]

Our Election will present a very busy Scene of tumult and altercation. A vast variety of candidates amongst whom I am not. I have received three deputations from the Hawfields, all they have drawn from me is that I shall think it my duty to Serve if I am elected, but that I am not a candidate & shall bestow no pains to procure a seat in the Assembly. what will be the event is in the book of contingencies. The present competitors for the county are Butler. Two Mebanes Carrington, Mc.Cauley, Cain some others of more ignoble note.[2] For the town Lytle Taylor Watters. the latter has Some chance of success tho I think it rather doubtful.[3]

I shall be happy to hear that the people of your county <were> are restored to a lucid interval and that they have given an earnest of their future Sanity by electing Mr. Johnston & yourself.[4] Much good you may do them. You may temper the ardour of Maclaine & keep under /you/ the combustible Stuff which is ready to burst & blaze forth in our friend Hay (tho' perhaps the latter may fall short in his Election of which he is indecently Sanguine in his expectations. He boils with as much fury against the Judges as Saul did against the Christians—

Perhaps you have not heard of the adventure in court at Wilmington the last hour of the last term. Williams pressing his opinion upon the Treaty of peace to Hay and craving his attention to him "So this is your Opinion Judge Williams. Your Servant Sir I wish you a good night," & waving his hand & hat & dodging his elegant bow he marched out of the court house. Williams highly incensed in Strong terms proclaimed the insult to the bench and himself personally. He proposed that Hay Should be struck off the roll of Attornies—Ashe acquiesced—Spencer sat Silent—Huske was ordered to make the entry—It was partly finished—Ashe desired time to cool Stopped Huskes hand—the court adjourned without any thing more decisive[5]—This was part only of the disgraceful business of the day. From the beginning to the close of it Spencer & Williams were engaged in the most bitter altercation, nothing was wanting but blows to complete the farce—Thrice Williams furiously descended from the bench & fifty times Spencer interrupted him attempting to speak "Suffer me to do Justice if you will not I wash my hands clean I wish others could" This becoming altercation took place upon the question of Mallet's suits being suspended. Mallet prevailed.[6]

Burgwins business is as it Should be. Upon my arrival at Wilmington I discouraged Marmadukes action for Slandering title and proposed that the whole merits of the question should be discussed in a Suit in Ejectment to be brought by Burgwin vs. the Commissioner. It was agreed & it Stands for hearing.

I moved for a new trial in the pitiful suit that has given occasion to so much uneasiness. Suggesting that Burgwin was surprized into it unprepared, I prevailed with the opinion of three Judges—I think him now in a favourabl way if he does /not/ mar every thing by his mean low Servile condescensions. I would not for the best estate in the country condescend to such indignities as I witnessed in his behaviour at Wilmington—He talks of seeing you here at our Sup Ct. I have taken the liberty to hint to him that if he expects your Services he must talk of Sterling money & something considerable. He professes great promptitude. "Caveto, Hic niger est"[7]

I regret that our press here has Stopped Davis has failed to supply it with paper.[8] I am Some what at a loss how to act. I would certainly forward the inclosure with which I am highly pleased to Newbern, but my power is circumscribed by your letter & perhaps you can find a more direct and immediate convenience from Edenton—

I will no longer trespass upon you. I am highly favoured with a letter from Mr. S. Johnston I will answer it as Soon as I have a belief that he is returend from Roanoake. Make the cordial regards of Mrs. Hooper, Betsy

& myself to your Lady Mrs. Blair & the others of your amiable family—Accept them yourself & believe me ever

My dear Iredell, Your Affectionate friend and humble Sert.

Will Hooper

Verte

P.S. We have had our annual Commencement or examination. The Boys exceeded our most earnest expectations. They were examined in Latin—English—Natural Philosophy—Geography—Geometry—Euclid. Spoke a little in Latin & English & diversified the scene by some ludicrous well chosen dialogues—to the high Satisfaction of a vast concourse of people. Believe me, my dear Sir, my heart expanded with Joy at this promising appearance of a School which is a Child of my own & which I shall continue to rear with unremitting care. Pardon this effusion of vanity in an overweaning parent.[9]

Tell Miss Nelly she looses a play by not Spending the Summer with us—

Compts. to my worthy friend Mrs. Dawson Mr. Dawson Mr. Lowther & Lady—To Mr. & Mrs. Pollok & all our other friends

I had almost for got to tell you that a letter from Hay to a friend of his has this passage "I had wrote you before but have been busily employed in collecting materials for a history of the last Wilmington Sup Ct., which I shall short[*l*]y entertain the publick with"[10]

What a feast have Johnston you & I preparing for us?

RC, Iredell Papers, Duke. Printed, McRee, 2:140-142. Addressed "James Iredell Esq To the care of the Honourable Charles Johnston Esq who will be pleased to deliver it himself." Endorsed "Hillsborough 1st. August. 1786. W. Hooper."

---

[1]James Hogg was part of a mercantile firm with business interests in Fayetteville. In addition, Hogg owned large tracts of land there, including much of what has become downtown Fayetteville. The General Assembly met at Fayetteville from November 20, 1786, to January 6, 1787. *Life and Times of James Hogg*, 55; Cheney, *North Carolina Government*, 217.

[2]John Butler was elected to the house of commons but died before the session began. Jonathan Lindley, a prominent Quaker and delegate to the 1788 ratification convention, was chosen to take his place. Hooper was also elected to represent Orange County in the house, and William McCauley (McCawley) was selected for the senate. Cheney, *North Carolina Government*, 217-218, 345n; Lefler and Wager, *Orange County*, 16, 65.

The Mebanes were Alexander, previously identified, and probably William (before 1755-1803), who served in the state senate (1782) and was a delegate to the 1788 ratification convention. John Carrington was elected to the house of commons from Orange County in 1790. William Cain (d. ca. 1827) served in the house of commons (1785) and the senate (1794-1796, 1802). In 1800, he was the largest landowner in Orange County. Massengill, *North Carolina Votes*, 42; Cheney, *North Carolina Government*, 216, 225, 231, 232, 234, 244; Lefler and Wager, *Orange County*, 16; Estate of William Cain, 1834, Orange County Estates, State Archives.

[3]Archibald Lytle, previously identified. John Taylor, the incumbent, was returned to the house to represent Hillsborough. He would be elected for a third term in the following election. Watters is possibly William Watters, an Orange County justice of the peace. Cheney, *North Carolina Government*, 217, 218, 220; Minutes of the Orange County Court of Pleas and Quarter Sessions, February 1787, State Archives.

[4]In Chowan County, Jacob Jordan was elected to the senate, and Josiah Copeland and Lemuel Creecy to the house of commons. Stephen Cabarrus was elected to represent Edenton in the house. Cheney, *North Carolina Government*, 217-218. In *North Carolina Government*, Josiah Copeland is erroneously listed as Joshua.

[5]For another account of this fracas, see Archibald Maclaine to JI, August 3, 1786, in this volume.

[6]Though Peter Mallet was acquitted on charges of treason in 1783, his right to file lawsuits was denied by the General Assembly in 1785. At that time, Mallet was involved in one suit and had yet to collect on a favorable decision in another case. The judges in the Wilmington Superior Court debated whether the acquittal or the legislation should take precedence in determining Mallet's right to continue his suits. A key point of contention was the authenticity of the 1783 acquittal, even though the documentation supporting its legitimacy was in the handwriting of one of the judges then presiding in Wilmington. After three days the court ruled in Mallet's favor. The court's decision to override a legislative act would become a key issue in the General Assembly hearings on the conduct of the judiciary later in the year. Waldrup, "James Iredell," 310-311.

[7]From Latin, meaning "Beware, This is dark."

[8]Thomas Davis had moved publication of the *North Carolina Gazette* to Hillsborough in July 1785. He ceased operations there in July 1786. Watson, *Index to North Carolina Newspapers*, xii.

[9]Hooper was a trustee of the Hillsborough Academy. See letter of July 6, 1785, n. 6, in this volume.

[10]Letter and Hay's "history" not found.

From Archibald Maclaine

Wilmington 3d. August 1786

My dear Sir,

Since our Superior court, I have frequently determined to write to you, but at the close of the term, and several days before, I was greatly indisposed,

& continued /so/ almost the whole month, so that I was utterly unable to attend to any thing—At the county court in the beginning of last month, I was seized with a slight fit of the gout, which confined me in no small pain for about ten days—Since that I have /been/ constantly engaged

I am sorry the paper which you inclosed me, and which I received this day, did not come to my hands sooner. It is forwarded with this, but I am afraid will not get abroad as soon as might be wished.[1]

At the Superior court, we did business as usual—Tried about half a dozen jury causes, wrangled with the Judges, & they with each other—at least Spencer and Williams—The latter has sworn solemnly and openly, never to sit with the former again. The most shameful partiality disgraced the bench, but the most curious case was that of Mallet—It cost the court nearly three days, tho' the judgement of May 1783 on his acquittal, restored him to all the rights and privileges of a citizen, and ordered his causes which had been suspended, to be put in their their proper places on the docket—When their own judgement was produced against them, Williams boldly questioned the authenticity of it, tho' in the hand writing of Lillington, and prior to the answer of Nat. Allen & Collins on Brailsford's attachment. Ashe disavowed all knowledge of it. We suspected this, and were prepared for it—Luckily for the memory of poor Lillington, and as lucky for the reputation of Mallet's council, the entry was drawn up by Spencer, under one that Hay had offered, and which was thought not full enough. This paper had been with other loose ones, <been> carefully preserved in the office—Spencer, when called upon, acknowledged that the entry was word for word with his paper, which however I believe was pocketed by him or Williams, for it is not now to be found. The court took till next day to deliver their opinion, and then very wisely determined that the question had been decided before. When Mr. Ashe declared that he did not recollect any thing of it, Mr. Moore pertinently remarked that he was not surprised at it, for he remembered that his Honor had carried a recognizance to the Necessary.[2]

Our friend Hay is in disgrace with Ashe and Williams. The latter at the last hour of the court (8 or 9 o'clock) began to preach with his usual effrontery, in order to convince Mr. Hay, that the treaty of peace the constitution & articles of confederation, had nothing to do in a question /in/ which Mr. Hay had made a motion, and which was decided against him. Mr. Hay made a low bow & wished his Honor a good night, leaving, <u>their</u> Honors, their /Honors'/ clerk, Spiller and a constable. Williams still proceeded, till Ashe asked him, to whom he was speaking? for that Mr. Hay was gone. Williams replied that Mr. Spiller was present, and willing that somebody should have the benefit of his sermon, continued, as follows;—

"I say, I will convince you Mr. Spiller &c"—Ashe not willing to lose an opportunity of striking at Hay, observed, that he thought the latter did not use them well—Williams assented, & replied, that he /should be/ struck off the list of attornies—To this Ashe said that he had no objections—Spencer was silent. The clerk was directed to make the entry, but before it was finished, Mr. Ashe observed, that they might be too fast, and that it would be better to cool upon it. It seems however that the virtuous duumvirate have determined that Hay shall apologize before he will be admitted to practice before their Honors[3]

I believe Mr. Burgwin is now perfectly safe, as the commissioner has been prevailed upon to institute two suits against him

I am happy to hear that Mr. Johnston may be one of the Legislature; I shall be doubly so, if you will consent to be chosen—I have no idea of attending New Bern, though I have some business there which should not be neglected—I have reason to believe I shall be chosen in preference to any who may offer, but though my o[*ld*] friend Walker has been long doing his best for others as well as himself, not a man in the place thinks he can succeed[4]—Genl. Howe will I believe be returned for Brunswick, though opposed with great assiduity—He openly avows the most liberal principles, and execrates the Judges and other officers, particularly the district commissioners. If Mr. Hooper should be returned, as I expect will be the case, I believe he does not intend to be at New Bern, nor do I imagine that Col. Davie will be there[5]—Every thing depends upon mustering all our forces, attending early, maturing our plans, and engaging auxiliaries. It will be easy for the lawyers to inform their Honors the Judges, that the importance of the approaching session prevents their attendance at court; and with respect to our clients, they had better wait a term (and as business has been conducted, few of them will be obliged to wait) than have their causes continued for ever—Consider how much depends upon a reform, & how few men of business we have among us

Present my respectful compliments to Mrs. Iredell and your family, and to Mr. Johnston & his family

Yours with great sincerity

A Maclaine

RC, Iredell Papers, Duke. Printed, McRee, 2:143-145. Addressed "James Iredell esquire Counsellor at Law Edenton." Endorsed "Wilmington Aug. 2d. 1786. A. Maclaine."

---

[1]Enclosure not found.

[2]For more information on the Mallet case, see William Hooper to JI, August 1, 1786, n. 6, in this volume.

[3]For another report of this altercation, see William Hooper to JI, August 1, 1786, in this volume.

[4]Maclaine was re-elected to represent Wilmington in the house. Cheney, *North Carolina Government*, 218.

[5]Robert Howe was chosen to represent Brunswick County in the house of commons but died en route to a meeting of the assembly. Hooper was returned for Orange County, and William R. Davie was elected to represent the town of Halifax. Cheney, *North Carolina Government*, 218; *DNCB*, s.v. "Howe, Robert."

To the Public[1]

As the Question concerning the Power of the Assembly deeply concerns every Man in the State, I shall make no apology for delivering my Sentiments upon it. They are indeed only the sentiments of an obscure Elector, [*but*] one who he trust has rights that he as much values, though with less ability to defend them, as the proudest Member of Assembly whatever.

I have not lived so short a time in the State, nor with so little interest in its concerns, as to forget the extreme anxiety with which all of us were agitated in forming the Constitution, a Constitution which we considered as the fundamental basis of our Government, unalterable but by the same high power which established it, and therefore to be deliberated on with the greatest caution because if it contained any evil principle the Government formed under it must be annihilated before the evil could be corrected. It was of course to be considered, how to impose restrictions on the Legislature that might still leave it free to all useful purposes, but at the same time guard against the abuses of unlimited power, which was not to be trusted without the most imminent danger to any Man or Body of Men on Earth. We had not only been sickened and disgusted for years with the high and almost impious language from Great Britain, of the omnipotent power of the British Parliament, but had severely smarted under its Effects. We felt in all its rigour the mischiefs of an absolute and unbounded authority claimed by so weak a Creature as Man, and should have been guilty of the basest breach of Trust, as well as the grossest Folly, if in the same moment when we spurned at the insolent despotism of Great Britain, we had established a despotic power among ourselves. Theories were nothing to us, opposed to our own severe experience. We were not ignorant of the theory, of the necessity of the Legislature being absolute in all cases, because it was the great ground of the British Pretensions. But this was a mere speculative principle, which Men at ease and leisure thought proper to assume. When we were at liberty to form a Government as we thought best, without regard to that or any theoretical principle we did not approve of, we decisively gave our sentiments against it, being willing to run all the risques of a Government to be conducted on the principles then laid as the basis of it. The instance was new in the Annals of Mankind. No People had ever before deliberately met for so great a purpose. Other Governments have been established by chance, caprice, or mere <brut> brutal force. Ours, thank God, sprang from the deliberate voice of the People. We provided, or meant to provide (God grant our purpose may not be defeated) for the security of every Individual, as well as a fluctuating majority of the People. We knew the value of liberty too well to suffer it to depend on the capricious voice of popular favour, easily led astray by designing Men, and courted for insidious purposes. Nor could we regard without contempt a Theory, which required a greater authority in Men than (with reverence be it spoken) exists even in the supreme Being. For his power is not altogether absolute. His infinite power is limited by his infinite wisdom.

I have therefore no doubt, but that the power of the Assembly is limited and defined by the Constitution. It is a Creature of the Constitution. (I hope this is an expression not presentable.) The People have chosen to be governed under such and such principles. They have not chosen to be governed, or promised to submit upon any other. And the Assembly have no more right to obedience on other terms, than any different power on Earth has a right to govern us. For we have as much agreed to be governed by the Turkish Divan, as by our own General Assembly, otherwise than on the express terms prescribed.[2]

These are Consequences that seem so natural, and indeed so irresistible, that I do not observe they have been much contested. The great argument is, that though the Assembly have not a right to violate the Constitution, yet if they in fact do so the only remedy is, either by an humble Petition that the Law may be repealed, or an universal resistance of the People. But that in the meantime, their Act, whatever it is, is to be obeyed as a Law, for the judicial power <are> /is/ not to presume to question the power of an Act of Assembly.

To these Positions, not unconfidently <supported> /urged/, I answer,

1. That the Remedy by Petition implies a supposition, that the Electors hold their rights by the favour of their Representatives. The mere stating of this is surely sufficient to excite any Man's indignation. What! if the Assembly say, we shall elect only once in two years, instead of electing annually, are we to petition them to repeal this Law? to request, that they will be graciously pleased not to be our Tyrants, but to allow us the benefit of the Government we ourselves have chosen, and under which they alone derive all their Authority?

But 2. The whole People may resist a dreadful Expedient indeed. We well know how difficult it is to excite the resistance of a whole People, and what a calamitous contingency at best that is to be reduced to. But it is a sufficient answer, that nothing can <have strength> /be powerful/ enough to effect such a purpose in a Government like ours, but universal oppression. A thousand injuries may be suffered, and many hundreds ruined, before this can be brought about. A Majority may see A. B., C. D., and E. F., and hundreds of others quietly injured one after another, and not stir a step towards a civil War. Let any Man then ask himself. Suppose a law is passed by which I am ruined! Have I interest enough to overturn the Government of my Country? If I have, we still may be a ruined People, and myself ruined among the rest. If I have not, upon what footing do my liberties depend? The pleasure of a Majority of the Assembly! God forbid! How many things have been done by Majorities of a large Body in heat and passion, that they themselves afterwards have <repented> of! Besides, would the Minority chuse to put themselves in the power of a Majority? Few Men I presume are always in a Majority. None therefore could <be absolutely secure> /have even <have> a chance of being secure/ but Sycophants that will forever sacrifice reason, conscience, and duty, to the preservation of a temporary popular favour. Will this not put an end to all freedom of deliberation, to all manly spirit, and prove the utter extinction of all real Liberty?

But this resource is evidently derived from the principle of unbounded Legislative Power that I have noticed before, and that our Constitution reprobates. In England they are in this condition. In England therefore they are less free than we are. A very Parliament in that country chosen for *3* years continued itself for 7.[3] This is an absolute fact that happened long within the present Century. Would this be a fit Precedent for us? May our Assembly do so, because their Parliament did! May our Governor have a negative on the Laws, because he has a faint image of monarchical Power!—As little I trust is the Government of Great Britain to influence in other things, equally inconsistent with our Condition, and equally preposterous as these.

These two Remedies then being rejected, it remains to be enquired whether the Judicial Power hath any Authority to interfere in such a case. The duty of that Power, I conceive, in all cases, is to decide according to the Laws of the State. It will not be denied, I suppose, that the Constitution is a Law of the State, as well as an Act of Assembly, with this difference only, that it is the fundamental Law, and unalterable by the Legislature which derives all its power from it. <An> /One/ Act of Assembly may repeal another Act of Assembly. For that reason the latter

Act is to be obeyed, and not the former. An Act of Assembly cannot repeal the Constitution or any part of it. For that reason an Act of Assembly inconsistent with the Constitution is void, and cannot be obeyed without disobeying the Superior Law <of the Constitution> to which we were previously and irrevocably bound. The Judges therefore must /take care/ at their peril <so> /<take care>/ /since/ that every Act of Assembly they presume to enforce <be> /is/ warranted by the Constitution, <otherwise> / <for> if it is not/ they act without lawful authority. This is not an usurped or a discretionary Power, but one inevitably resulting from the constitution of their Office, they being Judges for the benefit of the whole People, not mere Servants of the Assembly. And the danger, about which there is so much alarm, attending the exercise of this power, is, in my opinion, the least that can be imagined to attend the exercise of any important power whatever. For the Judges, besides the natural desire which must be entertained by every Man living in a popular Government of securing the favour of the People, are in fact dependent on the Assembly, <even> /for/ though their duration in office is permanent, at least as long as the Act is in being which establishes their Court, their Salaries are precarious, and in vain are they nominally independent in point of station, when the Assembly may every session determine how much they shall have to subsist upon. Did any Man in England previous to the Revolution apprehend any injury to the Prerogative from the Judges /of those days/? They depended indeed both for Salary and Place on the breath of the Crown. But the dependence here, I am persuaded, will <be> in general /be/ found equally effectual, at least to prevent a wanton abuse of power, and it <must> is much to be feared may in some instances produce an actual bias the other way, which in my humble opinion is the great danger to be apprehended. It may also be observed, that if the Judges should be disposed to abuse their power, merely for the sake of the abuse, they have means enough of doing so, for every Act of Assembly may occasionally come under their Judgment in one shape or other, and those Acts may be wilfully misconstrued as well as the Constitution.

But it is said, if the Judges have this power, so have the County Courts. I admit it. The County Courts, in the exercise of equal judicial power, must have equal Authority. But every Argument, in respect to the Judges (except their dependance for Salary), and other obvious ones, occur in great force against this danger, besides the liberty of appeal, which <ultim> ultimately rests every thing almost with the Superior Courts. The objection however urged by some Person, that Sheriffs and other ministerial officers must exercise their Judgment too does not apply. For if the power of judging rests with the Courts, their decision is final as to the subject matter. Did ever a Sheriff refuse to hang a Man, because he thought he was unjustly convicted of Murder?

These are a few Observations that have occurred to me on this subject. They are given by a plain Man, unambitious of power, but sincerely and warmly interested in the prosperity of his Country, feeling every respect for the constitutional authority of the Legislature, which in his opinion is great enough to satisfy an ambitious, as well as to support the Efforts of a public-spirited Mind, but a determined Enemy on all occasions to arbitrary Power in every shape whatsoever, and reverencing beyond expression that Constitution by which he holds all that is dear to him in life.

An Elector.

FC, Iredell Papers, Duke. Printed, McRee, 2:145-149. Endorsed "The Elector."

---

[1]This essay appeared in a New Bern newspaper on August 17, 1786. McRee attributes the article to JI and declares it to be the first discussion of judicial review in the United States. McRee, *Life and Correspondence*, 2:145.

[2]The "Turkish Divan" is the Turkish privy council. *OED*, s.v. "divan."

[3]The Parliament elected in 1715 passed the Septennial Act in 1716, establishing parliamentary elections every seven years instead of every three. Gregory and Stevenson, *Longman Companion to Britain in the Eighteenth Century*, 104.

From Archibald Maclaine

Wilmington, N. C., August 24th, 1786.

Dear Sir

We have had the heaviest and most constant rains in this part of the country which I have known for years. They began the 17th, and continued, almost without ceasing, for two days and nights. I am afraid we shall have no corn on the low lands; and if the waters have been as high in Roanoke, I do not know what will become of us.

I should have wrote you sooner, but I wished to inform you of the elections in this neighborhood; and though I have waited so long, I have heard very little; for this country is yet afloat. Gen. Howe is returned for Brunswick. For New Hanover and Wilmington the old members. Duplin nearly the same.[1] From the other counties in this district, I have not had any certain news. I am particularly anxious to hear from Bladen and Cumberland; from the former, in hopes that they have exchanged a very bad man for a very good one; and from the latter, in hopes that Mr. Hay and Mr. Winslow are chosen.[2] When I learn I shall acquaint you in hopes that you will communicate the names of those elected in your district, especially those for Chowan and Edenton.[3] About these two places and Orange I am more solicitous than any others; if I do not think of them in my prayers, which are generally very short, I make it up in dreaming of them. Next to the places I have mentioned, I wish to know the fate of Craven and Newbern, as that arch-scoundrel, Coor, has been doing every thing that cunning and malice could suggest, to keep Spaight and Sitgreaves out.[4] Yesterday came to my hands the New Bern paper of the 17th, in which I observe a piece signed "An Elector," which I wish had been sooner published, as in the light reading which my time permitted me to give it, it appears to me to contain true constitutional principles. It is however to be lamented that those who may be esteemed tolerably qualified for giving information on subjects of so much importance to the people, are so widely scattered over an extensive country, and the greatest part of them so distant from the press, that it is extremely difficult to discuss such subjects to so as to have the intended effect. Very extraordinary exertions are necessary to arouse the people to a sense of their danger; for notwithstanding the plain principles of the constitution, they seem to think themselves safe from every species of internal tyranny, having succeeded so well in freeing themselves from a foreign yoke—a palpable proof of their ignorance, or want of virtue. Pray let me hear from you, &c., &c.,

A. Maclaine.

Printed, McRee, 2:149-150.

---

[1]Robert Howe was elected to the house from Brunswick County. In New Hanover County, John A. Campbell was elected to the senate, and James Bloodworth and John Pugh Williams to the house of commons. Archibald Maclaine was elected to represent Wilmington in the house. In Duplin County, James Gillespie was elected to the senate, and Joseph Dickson and Joseph T. Rhodes to the house. Cheney, *North Carolina Government*, 217-218.

[2]To represent Bladen County, Thomas Brown was chosen for the senate, and James Richardson and Peter Roberson for the house. In Cumberland County, Thomas Armstrong was elected to the senate, and John Hay and Edward Winslow were elected to the house of commons. Cheney, *North Carolina Government*, 217-218.

[3]For the names of those elected from Chowan County, see William Hooper to JI, August 1, 1786, n. 4, in this volume.

[4]James Coor was elected to the senate from Craven County and was chosen as Speaker for the 1786-1787 session. Abner Neale and Richard Dobbs Spaight were elected to represent Craven County and John Sitgreaves the town of New Bern in the house of commons. Cheney, *North Carolina Government*, 217-218.

From Arthur Iredell

My dear Brother

Trin: Coll: Camb
Sept. 5th. 1786—

What in the Name of Wonder is become of you, of my Sister, & of Tom? I shudder when I think upon the Time that has elapsed since your last Letter. Do write more punctually in future, for you cannot conceive how much so long a Silence affects both my Mother & myself. The inclosed Letter is for my Sister—It was sent to me by Miss F to be forwarded by the last Packet, but it came unfortunately a Day too late. I send it now because It's Contents are as applicable at this time as they were a Month ago. I wish they were not! but alass, I wish in vain for that Change in my Situation which alone can make me happy! To add to my Difficulties, the last Crops in the West Indies were terribly bad, & I have no Remittance from Jamaica. My Uncle however continues to write as cordially as ever, & in time all will be well. I have been here two months. I came to take a Master of Arts Degree, & have been somehow or other very unexpectedly induced to stay thus long—My Degree was perfected in the Course of a very few Days. We are going to have a Visit from their Majesties—Lord Howard (whose Seat is to be their head Quarters) has received an Intimation of the Honour intended him, & we are brushing ourselves up to receive him with all due Respect.[1] As you do not deal in Kings upon Your Continent I ought perhaps to define what I mean by the word—tho You have Books to consult, & they will inform you that he is our great excentrics Power &c &c Apropos to Kings, Frederick the great is at last dead![2] That Scourge of the North! & yet the Stocks fell but little after his Death, & are now as high as ever. Have you any Relish, [*for*] English Politicks? I will prove your Palate—tho, to say true, ours are at present at a low Ebb—yet we have a Commercial Treaty with France in great forwardness, our Ministry is lessening the National Debt, there is no German War going forward[3]—fine Topics these to expatiate upon, & infinite are the Speculations to which they might give rise—I hope they will all conduce to Peace, & Above all to a lasting Amity with America—I know not whether the latter wd. have even entered my Thoughts, if you & my valuable Connections in Carolina were not always present to my Mind, & sure to interest me in her Cause. Hence She has undoubtedly my best wishes, & I must always be more than a common Friend to her Cause.

My Mother is, I thank God, very well—She has lately written either to you or Tom, I know not which—and will probably write by this Mail.

How does my lovely Niece go on? I am very Anxious to hear of her, and be sure the Moment She can be made to comprehend that there is such a Person as myself to let her know that no one is so highly in favour with me as herself—In a few years I shall begin to think of borrowing her of Mrs. Iredell—Will She trust her with me, & in England too! a licentious & profligate Island where the Women can only emulate the Americans in [*external*] Charms—I shall make the Experiment when [*stain*] Miss F my Amanda to take Care of her.

Adieu! my dear Brother! You have all my Warmest Wishes—May they be gratified! Present to my Sister & Tom my most affectionate Remembrances—Smother your little Cherub with Kisses—& believe me ever with all Truth & Regard

Your's ever

Arthur Iredell

Direct to me as usual at Francis Vincent Esqre's. Threadneedle St London—

RC, Johnson Collection, NCSA. Addressed "James Iredell Esqre. Edenton North Carolina."

---

[1]Lord Fredrick Howard (1748-1825), 5th Earl of Carlisle, was a close friend of Charles James Fox and served as president of the Board of Trade (1779-1780), lord lieutenant of Ireland (1780-1782), and lord privy seal (1783). Gregory and Stevenson, *Longman Companion to Britain in the Eighteenth Century*, 57, 59, 77; *DNB*, s.v. "Howard, Frederick."

[2]Frederick II, king of Prussia, died August 17, 1786.

[3]England and France negotiated a treaty to lower tariffs to encourage trade. English manufacturers and French wine producers were the chief beneficiaries. A parliamentary committee predicted that Prime Minister Pitt's tax and trade policies would produce an annual surplus of one million pounds. Based on this, Pitt proposed a sinking fund to reduce the national debt. J. Steven Watson, *The Reign of George III, 1760-1815*, The Oxford History of England, ed. George Clark (Oxford: Clarendon Press, 1960), 288-289, 290-293.

To Hannah Iredell

Halifax 29 Sept. 1786.

My dear Hannah,

I left Mrs. Charlton's yesterday morning, & not knowing any decent house beyond Peale's to stop at put up for the heat of the day only 9 miles from Windsor at one Rhoads's, & just as I drove up met Mr. Allen's

Family who had that moment alighted. We dined very sociably together, and then I proceeded to Peale's from whence I came here to Dinner, and tell my Brother I had the luxury to dine with Miss Lucas. She & Miss Cook were both at Bond's, where I was pressed to dine. Very luckily Bond has proposed giving me a room, on proper terms, at the Court, [*torn*] to provide on the same for Mr. Johnston also, if he chuses it, and perhaps other Lawyers. He tells me he is laying himself out for it. They are now at A. Miller's old house well repaired, & he has offered me a room either there or at Thompson's old house, which is now vacant. I shall prefer the latter as much more convenient, & hope to have some of my other Friends with me—Colo. Mc.Culloch's Family are in great affliction. They have had the misfortune to lose one of their lovely Children Nancy. I go there with infinite pain—Mrs. Charlton wishes to sell her house, & will let Mrs. D. have the preference if she chuses it—I am perfectly well, upon my honour. God Almighty grant you & my dear Annie may be so. Don't lose a single opportunity to write to me. Love to all. Kiss my lovely girl for me, & talk to her often of me. Adieu! Heaven bless you!

Yours most affectionately

Ja. Iredell.

Turn over[1]

Elk Marsh. Sept. 30. Not hearing of any opportunity to Edenton, I put this letter in my pocket to write you a few more lines this morning, as I was obliged to conclude abruptly. Be so good as to mention Bond's plan to your Brother. If there be an opportunity I wish he would write him a line about it. Mr. Pollok's Family had arrived here about half an hour before me. Both he & his Wife complained very much last night, but he says they are very well this morning. He is going however to be let blood notwithstanding. I have not seen her yet this morning. The fine little lovely girl died out of this Family last Sunday week. Ben & his [*torn*] in great affliction indeed, and both sick. I have not seen [*torn*] them, but have the satisfaction to hear they are better this morning. They have had another Child, Sam, very near the grave, but he is recovering. To the former they had no other Doctor, I am told, but old Eelbeck. Possibly, with better assistance she might have recovered. I never saw a finer child in my life than she was. I greatly flatter myself, this fine weather, & the care I doubt not you have taken, have entirely relieved you from your complaint. I shall be most anxious & impatient to hear. Every moment I think of you & my most lovely Annie, as comprising my dearest Interests in this world. May Heaven preserve you both to me! I shall be devoutly thankful for its goodness. I am surprisingly well, & my tetter worm I think is entirely healed.[2] Remember me with great affection to all our Family. If I had had a little more leisure I would have done myself the pleasure to write to Nelly, but writing to her or not she <w> has always my tenderest attachment. Kiss Annie as long as you can for me, and when you are tired get Nelly & Peggy to relieve you. I will faithfully repay you all on sight. Adieu! once more. & always think of me, as I truly am,

Most faithfully & affectionate[*ly*] yours

Ja. Iredell.

P.S. Don't forget me to your Brother & Family.

P.S. It is reported, that Capt. Fenner is to be married to Miss Houson, and tell my Brother that that Porpoise, Capt. Pasteur, is so much in love with Miss Lucas, that he would fan her the other evening, tho' the weather was extremely cold to every body but himself.[3]

RC, Iredell Papers, Duke. Printed, McRee, 2:151. Addressed "Mrs. Iredell Edenton." Endorsed "State Tax 29 Sept 1786 Ja. Iredell."

---

[1]This is written at the bottom of the first page of the original document.

[2]Tetter is a term used for a variety of skin diseases, including herpes, ringworm, and eczema. *OED*, s.v. "tetter."

[3]Robert Fenner (ca. 1755-1816), a Revolutionary War officer and prominent Halifax planter, married Mary Howson (1765-1831). *DNCB*, s.v. "Fenner, Robert."

To Hannah Iredell

Hillsborough Oct. 10th. 1786.

My dear Hannah,

God knows when, or whether ever this letter will reach you, but if it does it can honestly give you the satisfaction of knowing I am perfectly well. I was a little unwell for 3 or 4 days after my arrival, having been obliged in spite of my utmost precaution to expose myself a good deal to the very warm Sun we had for a few days. But I am now as well as ever I was in my life. Mr. Pollok has a sore leg, otherwise all here are as well as I am Nelly was left at Nutbush with Mrs. Burton. We tried one of Strudwick's Causes yesterday, & succeeded for him.[1] I am extremely anxious to hear of you & my dearest little Annie. God Almighty grant I may hear of your being perfectly well. With what Joy shall I embrace you both again! I count every day almost that brings me nearer to so great a blessing. Give the lovely creature ten thousand kisses for me, & say every thing tender to her on my behalf. I anticipate the charming appearance I hope she will make when I see her. Present my best affection to your Sister & Nelly & Peggy, and believe me, my dear Hannah, with inexpressible affection,

Faithfully & sincerely yours

Ja. Iredell.

RC, Johnson Collection, NCSA. Addressed "Mrs. Iredell Edenton."

---

[1]See JI to Hannah Iredell, April 8, 1784, n. 1, in this volume.

To Hannah Iredell

Halifax Oct. 17th. 1786.

My dear Hannah,

Mr. Hooper & myself arrived here in very good time this evening, having left Hillsborough on Sunday, and I have had the great happiness, for which I am devoutly thankful, to hear by your & my Brother's Letters which Mr. Amis left here, that you & my dearest Annie were well at least on the 7th. Inst. I met Mr. Amis on the road, & he assured me so, but evidence under your own hand is much better. It mortifies me however not to meet your Brother here, but I impute it to the very rainy day which I am told it has been here. We had some, but not so much, and contrived to escape the greatest part. I am glad you met with a little recruit of money. I received altogether at Hillsborough £55, but the expences every where /are/ enormous.[1] Here a Dollar is rated at the least at 12/, owing principally I believe to the very ill behaviour of Kinchen in bidding up at the most extravagant rates for hard money.[2] Tell Annie I will excuse her not sending any message by you if she will tell me her sweet little wishes in person. I hear with great concern of your Brother's sickness and the other Indispositions in his & our Family. But I hope all are by this time much better. Adieu! Kiss my lovely Annie, & tell her all expression of my love for her is unutterable. My affectionate remembrance to the rest—

Ever, my dearest Hannah, Most affectionately yours

Ja. Iredell.

RC, Johnson Collection, NCSA. Addressed "Mrs. Iredell Edenton." Endorsed "Halifax October 17th 1786. Ja. Iredell."

---

[1]JI's records indicate that as of the date of this letter he had been paid £85 for the year for cases in Hillsborough. He had received £5 from James Stuart on April 8; £60 from Cullen Pollock on July 10 for twelve ejectment suits at £5 apiece; and £20 from William Johnston's executors on October 3 in a case involving confiscated land. Legal Fee Books, vol. 7, James Iredell Papers, Southern Historical Collection.

[2]John Kinchen (ca. 1745-1794), an attorney and merchant of Halifax and Orange Counties, had a long-standing interest in monetary policy. As a member of the Fourth Provincial Congress in 1776, Kinchen served on the committee to issue currency. In 1779, he was appointed to the state board of auditors, which was to address the state's economic woes. *DNCB*, s.v. "Kinchen, John."

Inflation occurred throughout the Confederation period, and the paper money issued by the state in 1785 had depreciated faster than the emission of 1783. Within a week of this letter, JI told Hannah, "The Paper is very little credit here indeed." Watson, *Money and Monetary Problems*, 45; JI to Hannah Iredell, October 22, 1786, Charles E. Johnson Collection, State Archives.

To Mr. Hamilton[1]

[*Tuesday (Nov. 7.)*]

Dear Sir

I recd. the favour of your letter last night, but too late to answer it then. Upon the Judges requiring such /a/ certificate as you recd. from Mr. J. & myself at the last Court, though I was then sensible it might be the means of leading us into difficulties hereafter if such a practice should become common, yet I gave with pleasure, considering it as perhaps a necessary means of serving you at a <particular> /critical/ time. I have since however very seriously thought of the subject, & can by no means agree to take upon myself voluntarily the odium of such a situation as the Judges seem willing to place us in, since your own good sense must easily point out to you what a source of passionate ill will we should create to ourselves in those who were unsuccessful in their application. These reasons have for some time in a manner determined me never to renew such a Certificate as I gave to you. But I am much surprized at another Certificate being required from us by the Judges, and that extending, not to character (with respect to which our Certificate was very full before) but to ability, and the Bar's inclination for your admittance—

In regard to the first, the Judges by the express words of the Act are to form an opinion from their own examination, and surely that is a much properer method than making one Lawyer a Judge of another's qualifications, the most insidious situation any Man can be placed in, since whenever <in> /a/ Person is refused it will be imputed to the <most> meanest & /most/ dishonourable of all motives (such as I should ever hold in the <most> utmost disdain) a desire to exclude Competitors in the profession. I could easily say your <of> obtaining a license would be by no means disagreeable to me, but I do not <understand> know that the Bar have a right to be consulted as to their personal inclinations. It is a matter, I conceive, entirely of duty & conscience with the Judges.[2]

I am persuaded you will believe, Sir, <that it is with great pain I find myself <thus> /thus/ under a necessity of declining to comply with </your/> any request of yours, but> /it would give me pleasure to serve you in any instance within my power, and that /I can rely upon your liberality of mind in estimating the reasons I have given, <and though the reference of the Judges and which I trust will have their full weight in convincing you of the propriety of my unwillingness to take upon /me/> /for declining to assume/ a most odious & insidious department without the least necessity, & intreat you must be sensible & must exercise in all instances, or refuse to exercise in any, however far my Inclinations may extend—

I am, Sir with great regard, Your faithful & obed. Serv.

FC, Johnson Collection, NCSA. Endorsed "Copy of a Letter to Mr. Hamilton Nov. 7th. 1786."

---

[1]This is possibly John Hamilton of Chowan County. *Heads of Families, 1790 Census*, 19.

[2]Section 6 of "An Act for Establishing Courts of Law, and for Regulating the Proceedings therein" (1777) required those wishing to practice law in state courts to pass an examination administered by two or more superior court judges. If the applicant possessed sufficient knowledge of the law and was of good character, the judges would certify the candidate and indicate in what courts he was qualified to practice. Clark, *State Records*, 24:50-51.

In the 1786-1787 assembly session, a bill was proposed to alter that system. The proposal called for the examination of prospective lawyers by a panel of three attorneys, who, if satisfied, would issue a certificate attesting to the candidate's legal knowledge and character. This document would be presented to at least two judges who would then conduct their own investigation. With their approval, the governor would permit the candidate to practice law. This measure, however, was rejected. "A Bill prescribing the method of admitting attorneys to practice in the several Courts of Law and Equity of this State and ascertaining how they shall be tried for misbehavior," December 18, 1786, House Bills, General Assembly Session Records, State Archives.

From Richard Caswell

Kinston 10th. Novr. 1786.

Dear Sir

Your favor of the 26th. September last has come to hand, it should have been answered before this, but I was in daily expectations of going to Newbern where I might have been able to give you full information in the Suit Lindsay vs. Herring, but as I have not been able to effect my design that way & being now about to set /out/ for the Assembly, I will give you the best information my Memory will enable me to do, the papers being Lodged in the Clerks office[1]—

The Suit was instituted to recover the possession of three or four Tracts of Land which at the Time of bringing the Suit I did beleive Joined each other, but since I have learned that, I think, 400 Acres are at some distance from the others & are totally disclaimed by the defendant, who sets up a Title under a Supposed Grant from the Crown for 300 Acres to Robert Riely who left a son & two daughters—the Son is dead & one of the daughters is married to the defendant in whose right he Claims, these three hundred acres, if he can establish his Boundaries, which I suppose he cannot, will include (one) one hundred Acres which the plaintiff Claims under a Grant to Joshua Sarsnett which is of an elder date than the Supposed Grant which the Defendant Claims under.[2] This latter Claim is of prior date to the other Grants of the plaintiff but I presume neither the Grant or Boundaries can be established—Mr. William Dickson was appointed to Survey the Lands, by a rule of court,[3] And he has returned very Accurate plans, one of which you will find among my papers, filed with all the Titles in this Cause with the Clerk, except John Dicksons will which I know was proved in the Superior Court at Newbern, but Mr. Cooke cannot he says find the record the papers being distroyed by Storm, however I have no doubt it may be found on a proper Search or that a Copy can be Obtained from Mr. Lindsay.

This Suit I understood was Compromised, but Mr. Hall did not give me any directions to dismiss it, I do not think it can well be tried without Mr. Dickson, who was Summoned, is present.

The fees of Office on the Testimonials you have been furnished with are so trifling that I am sorry you should be (at) at any trouble about them, my Secretary is entitled to 2/ for the Testimonial & 2/8. the Seal for each, Mr. Glasgow to whom I spoke on the Subject intimated that the fees to him were trifling also.[4] I think he usually charges for each Copy of the Laws 20/. But as these Accounts cannot now be furnished I beg you will not be at any trouble about them, they shall be forwarded you when the

Secretary & my Secretary [*torn*] together and I can prevail o[*torn*] to make them out

I am Dr. Sir with the greatest esteem, Your Most obedt. Servt.

R Caswell

RC, Hayes Collection, SHC. Addressed "James Iredell esquire Edenton."

---

[1]*Robert Lindsay v. Solomon Herring and wife*, November 1786, New Bern District Superior Court, Argument, Reference, and Appearance Docket, State Archives.

[2]Robert Rielly (d. before 1767) owned an area known as "Johnston's old fields" in Dobbs County, south of the Neuse River. Joshua Sarsnett acquired property in Craven and Johnston Counties, including land south of the Neuse, in the 1740s. Margaret M. Hofmann, *Colony of North Carolina, 1735-1764: Abstracts of Land Patents*, 2 vols. (Weldon, N.C.: Roanoke News, 1982-1984), 1:232; A. B. Pruitt, *Colonial Land Entries in North Carolina*, 4 vols. (n.p.: A. B. Pruitt, 1994-1995), 1:48, 118, 145; 3, pt. 2: 38.

[3]William Dickson (1739-1820) of Duplin County was clerk of the Court of Pleas and Quarter Sessions from 1777 to 1819. He served in the militia, the colonial assembly (1769, 1770-1771), and the General Assembly (1795). He was the author of the "Dickson Letters," which contained his observations on political affairs. His father, John Dickson (1704-1774), was a native of Ireland who, after living in Pennsylvania and Maryland, moved to North Carolina in the 1740s. *DNCB*, s.v. "Dickson, William."

[4]James Glasgow (ca. 1735-1819) of Dobbs County was North Carolina secretary of state (1777-1799). *DNCB*, s.v. "Glasgow, James."

From Arthur Iredell

Reigate Surry Decr. 5th. 1786[1]

My dear Brother

I should certainly have written to You by the last Packet, had I not prolonged my Stay in Cheshire a few Days beyond the Time to which I had at first limited myself. Can you blame me, tho you are an old married man, & may partially conceive Yourself a Sufferer by my Silence?—No! you have too much Sensibility, perhaps too much Sympathy, in your Nature, not to rejoice with me upon being once more, even for a short time, restored to my Amanda; & upon every Event that kept us longer together—I passed indeed a most delicious Month at her Sister's, & at the same time contrived to pay a Visit at Crewe Hall, where I stumbled upon Lord Macartney—They were all vastly civil to me, but in my then temper of mind, the very Sight of a great House, a large Establishment, fine Folks, &, above all, the glittering of a Star was hatefull to me! I pined (as you did some ten years ago) for shady Walks & purling Streams, the breathing Zephyrs & the cooling Grove—Without burlesque, I was miserable till I returned to my small, but infinitely rich Circle at Doddlespool—where <u>you</u>, I do assure you, & your Circle were a very frequent Topic—The little Annie was often dandled on the Knee; & sometimes her awkward Uncle, in the riot of his Imagination, would caricature the Attitudes of a Nurse—And, (by the way, Sir) when I get a House of my own, & you get a few more Children, I shall lay in a very serious Claim to the Possession of the <u>aforesd</u> Annie, that I may realize the <u>abovementioned</u> ideal Happiness <u>to wit</u>, the dandling on the Knee; for I shall then be potent enough, be She fifty times as broad as She is long. But, to return to Cheshire—I was at last constrained to leave it, & all my Consolation was that both Amanda & her Sister were vastly well—the former better than ever I saw her—They have charged me with all manner of fine Speeches for you all, & <u>your</u> Imaginations must run riot in conceiving them, for really they have escaped my resolution. You will ask, when we are to meet not to part?—Alas, my dear Brother, I know not—some fortunate Event must happen before I dare Marry, & when it will, God only knows! My Uncle continues to write, & indeed much oftener & in a more affectionate Stile, I think, than usual—Tho he treats <u>you</u> in so cool a Way, I am persuaded he will do every thing he can for <u>me</u>; &, to say true, he is my Sheet Anchor—I observe what you say about him; & I think you do right in not continuing a Correspondence that would probably answer no good Purpose—Of this you may be assured, should his Property ever descend to me, one of my first & most gratefull Objects will be to add to your Ease & Independence. These are troublesome Times, I fear, in America, & from what I could learn from Mr. Traill, the Situation of N Carolina is not so enviable an one as I could wish it to be. However that Gentleman, (whom I had the Pleasure to see on my return from Cheshire, & who is a very agreable Man) gave me the best Accounts of your Family, & with them I will be for the present contented. I mean to call upon him whenever I go to Town, where he resides, I find, during the Winter; but that will be very seldom, as entre nous, my Finances are at this time, like the National ones, not in the most flourishing Condition. I have therefore a Curacy near this Place, to which I stick remarkably close. One of the worst Effects of my Poverty is the not being able to send you any News Papers, Pamphlets &c. as I most ardently long to do, because I know of what extraordinary Value they must be in America, & especially to <u>You</u>, however I hope to have that in my Power in the Spring when my Uncle promises me a remittance. He has been sadly behind hand in that respect, & has run me into debt in consequence of his Arrearages—but I will stretch a Point, if possible, to allay your political Thirst—A Commercial Treaty with France has been concluded, & will be ratified by Parlt. the Moment it meets after Xmas.[2] You will have seen the Articles long before this reaches You one of them greatly affects the West Indies, that of Brandy, wch. is to be imported at the reduced Duty of 7s/ pr Galln.—What will become of the Rum Trade I know not; but a Meeting of the West Indian Proprietors, Merchts. &ca has been held, & a Committee has waited upon Mr. Pitt who has refused, I hear, to lower the Duties on Rum in a proportionate Degree, wch. was the Proposition they submitted to him. Mr. Eden is about to return to Paris to conclude another Commercial Arrangement by which the English & french Islands are to be sufferred to trade with each other[3]—How will that affect the united States? All the Papers & Conversation here are engrossed by Mr. Bowes, who has forcibly taken away Ly Strathmore, his Wife, & confined her in the Country—A habeas Corpus [*was*] issued—he paid no Obedience to it, & an Attachment followed, under wch. he is now [*torn*] in the King's Bench. The Fact is Ly. S: is & ever was, a strange Woman. She was an immense Heiress—a poor Scotch Lord married her—She broke his Heart—Bate, (the famous fighting Parson & Editor of the Morng. Post at that time) put some Paragraphs agst her into his Paper—Captn. Stony who wanted <u>her Fortune</u>, fought him & was wounded—She marrd. him, havg. the night before lain with <u>another</u> Man—Since that time it has been a constant Struggle wch. shd. behave the worst & no one can say which has succeeded.[4] By this time Ld. Mansfield, that venerable Sage of the Law; has quitted it.[5] Buller succeeds him, <u>without a Title</u>[6]—Pepper Arden fills the vacant Seat on the Bench, with the Chief Justiceship of Chester (1500 £ per year) in commandum[7]—Ld. C. B. Skinner (who is almost blind) retires on a Pension, & is succeeded by Eyre.[8] Macdonald succeeds <u>him</u>.[9] Bancroft is to be Atty. Genl. & Scotts Solicitor.[10] Such, I understand, are the legal arrangements. But it is high Time that I should bid you Adieu! you will not be able to read what I have already written—My Mother will I dare say speak for herself. She is however (least She shd. not) very well. I beg my most affectte. remembrances to my Sister, Tom, & little Annie , all of whom I trust are well—

& I am ever most truly & faithfully Your's

A. Iredell

Tom must excuse my not writing to him at present.

RC, Johnson Collection, NCSA. Printed, McRee, 2:151-152. Addressed "James Iredell Esqr. Edenton North Carolina America By the American Packet." Endorsed "Surrey Dec 5 1786 A. Iredell."

---

[1]Reigate, Surrey, is located twenty-one miles south of London and nineteen miles east of Guilford. *A Topographical Dictionary of England*, 3d ed., 5 vols. (London: S. Lewis, 1835), s.v. "Reigate, Surrey."

[2]Parliament ratified a commercial treaty with France in September 1786. This was followed by a commercial convention in January 1787. See Arthur Iredell to JI, September 5, 1786, n. 3, in this volume.

[3]William Eden (1744-1814), 1st Lord Auckland, was a member of Parliament and a diplomat. In 1778, he had been part of a mission to America to quell the revolution. In 1785, he negotiated a commercial treaty with France at Versailles, which was a key element in Pitt's plan for economic reform. *DNB*, s.v. "Eden, William."

[4]Andrew Robinson Stoney (1745-1810), who had squandered a fortune obtained from a previous wife, persuaded the wealthy Mary Eleanor Bowes (1749-1800), Countess of Strathmore, to marry him. For the countess, this was also a second marriage. Soon after the wedding, which occurred on January 17, 1777, Stoney assumed his wife's surname.

The countess's life was marked by scandal. Between marriages, she had been involved in several indiscreet relationships. Henry Bate Dudley published unflattering stories about her in a London newspaper, and this led to a duel between Stoney and Dudley. In addition, shortly after the wedding, rumors spread that her former fiancé, George Grey, had dined with her the night before the ceremony.

The marriage was not a happy one. Stoney was cruel and unfaithful, and in 1785, she left him and began divorce proceedings. On November 10, 1786, thugs employed by Stoney kidnapped the countess on a London street. She was eventually rescued, and her husband and his henchmen were fined and sentenced to prison. The divorce was finalized on March 2, 1789. *DNB*, "Bowes, Mary Eleanor," "Dudley, Sir Henry Bate."

[5]William Murray (1705-1793), 1st Earl of Mansfield, was a privy councilor, Speaker of the House of Lords, and lord chief justice. He resigned the latter position on June 4, 1788. *DNB*, s.v. "Murray, William."

[6]Francis Buller (1746-1800) was Lord Mansfield's choice as his successor as chief justice. The position went, however, to Lloyd Kenyon on June 9, 1788. *DNB*, s.v. "Buller, Sir Francis," "Kenyon, Lloyd."

[7]Richard Pepper Arden (1745-1804), a Cheshire attorney, was first elected to Parliament in 1782. He served as solicitor general from 1782 to 1783, and became attorney general and chief justice of Chester in 1784. *DNB*, s.v. "Arden, Richard Pepper."

[8]John Skynner (1724-1805), after serving for ten years, retired as chief baron of the Exchequer in 1787. James Eyre succeeded him on January 26, 1787. Alan Valentine, *The British Establishment, 1760-1784: An Eighteenth-Century Biographical Dictionary*, 2 vols. (Norman: University of Oklahoma Press, 1970), 2:794; *DNB*, s.v. "Eyre, Sir James."

[9]Archibald MacDonald (1747-1826) replaced Richard Pepper Arden as solicitor general on April 7, 1784, then became attorney general on June 28, 1788. He succeeded James Eyre as chief baron of the Exchequer on February 12, 1793. *DNB*, s.v. "MacDonald, Sir Archibald."

[10]John Scott (1751-1838), 1st Earl of Eldon, replaced Archibald MacDonald as solicitor general in 1788. He again followed MacDonald in office in 1793, this time as attorney general. *DNB*, s.v. "Scott, John."

From Alfred Moore

Wilmington 14th. of Decr. 1786.

Dear Sir

The court has risen, and the Judges have notice of charges against them before the Assembly; that they may attend if they please[1]—We have very little news of importance from the Assembly except the above; I beleive indeed, that little has been done, if we except the zealous measures that are persued against the forgers of military claims; many of these are in close confinement & their money seized as we hear; this iniquity does not seem to be confined to Dobbs county, which can only claim the greatest rogues[2]—Judge Spencer shewed me to day an abstract from a letter of Mr. Hay containing the charges against the Judges, some of them are quite new to me

High fines & a shameful appropriation of them
Admitting new & illegal prosecutions (depreciation &c.)
The banishment of Brice & Mc.Neil
Dispenseing with laws (the Newbern case)
Negligence of their duty & delay of business
Ill behaviour to Mr. Hay at Wilmington[3]

These & a few other charges which I did not understand when I read them, nor can remember now; are urged against their Honors with great violence—Mr. Ashe says he has clean hands & a pure heart & disregards the clamour, he stays at home;[4] but Mr. Spencer & Mr. Williams will sett off with me tomorrow for Fayette—The Assembly have resolved that I shall attend them, but do not say for what purpose; a day or two ago this resolve was handed to me, by the express who brought the notice to the Judges—

It is supposed that our present courts will be continued; because they cannot agree on a plan to succeed this, of which however they have a multitude.

The line between this State & So. Carolina is to be run, to the great delight of Dr. Williamson who I learn, is to be the Palinurus to guide them thro' darkness & difficulties[5]—

There have been three grand balls & two horse races at this place within a week, and at this moment five fiddles are playing a lively tune, and the whole town are dancing to it <&> I am struck with a vain conceit of my superiority over you, being able to write, when you could do nothing but dance—I hope however if you are not dancing that you are well enough to do so & that your whole family are in perfect health. be pleased <d>to give them my best respects & beleive me Dr. Sir

very sincerely yours,

A. Moore.

My Compliments to Mr. Johnston & Mr. & Mrs. Pollok.

Nothing has been done in Mr. Burgwin's business. Genl. Howe is at the verge of the grave it supposed he will die in a few days.[6] he has only got as far as Genl. Clark's

RC, Johnson Collection, NCSA. Printed, McRee, 2:153-154. Addressed "James Iredell Esquire Edenton." Endorsed "Wilmington 14 Dec. 1786. A. Moore."

---

[1]At the instigation of John Hay and Archibald Maclaine, the General Assembly agreed to investigate the conduct of superior court judges Samuel Spencer, John Williams, and Samuel Ashe. A seven-member legislative committee, headed by Maclaine, conducted the initial investigation and reported the charges to the full legislature but without offering a verdict of its own. The assembly met in joint session to hear the defense offered by Williams and Spencer. Ashe did not attend. After hearing their testimony, the assembly exonerated the judges and passed a resolution expressing gratitude for their service on the bench. Waldrup, "James Iredell," 311-319; Robinson, *William R. Davie*, 176. See "Committee of the Whole of two Houses in Conferences, Jan. 1 & 2, re administration of justice," Joint Resolutions, 1786-1787, General Assembly Session Records, State Archives.

[2]In 1784, a state commission was established to make final payments to North Carolina soldiers of the Continental army. The process was rife with corruption. Claims were forged and submitted by individuals who had never served, yet the commissioners approved them. In November 1786, the legislature granted Governor Caswell's request for an inquiry. In January 1787, a special court was convened in Warrenton, and among the indicted were commissioners Henry Montford and Benjamin McCulloch. Alfred Moore, as state attorney general, prosecuted the case, while JI and William R. Davie defended Montford and McCulloch. Montford, who before the trial had been expelled from the house of commons, was acquitted. McCulloch, however, was found guilty, fined £4,000, and sentenced to a year in the Halifax jail. Like Montford, McCulloch had earlier

been expelled from the General Assembly. Robinson, *William R. Davie*, 173-175; Cheney, *North Carolina Government*, 345 n. 191.

[3]For an elaboration of the charges against the judges, see "Report of the committee to whom was referred the examination into the present mode of the administration of justice in the Superior Courts of Law and Equity," January 1, 1787, in "Committee of the Whole of two Houses in Conferences, Jan. 1 & 2, re administration of justice," Joint Resolutions, 1786-1787, General Assembly Session Records, State Archives. For more information on the case involving Brice and McNeill, see Archibald Maclaine to Samuel Johnston, December 24, 1785, in this volume. For more information on the Hay incident, see William Hooper to JI, August 1, 1786, and Archibald Maclaine to JI, August 3, 1786, in this volume.

[4]Ashe offered his defense in a letter to the Speaker dated December 14, 1786. The letter appears in Clark, *State Records*, 18:137-142.

In explaining his unwillingness to attend the session, Ashe wrote, "Indeed I am at a loss to know what purpose my being present would answer. . . . Can I go from member to member out of doors assuring each of them in turn of my innocence, and thus endeavor to exculpate myself and do away offences that never existed, this would be lessening myself. . . . I cannot stoop to it, the measure itself would indicate guilt." Clark, *State Records*, 18:137.

[5]In 1784 and 1785, Gov. Alexander Martin had urged the General Assembly without success to form a committee to define the state's border with South Carolina. In March 1786, however, the South Carolina assembly did establish a boundary commission. The following November Martin's successor, Richard Caswell, pressed the North Carolina legislature to take action. In response, the General Assembly considered a joint resolution to create a commission to settle and extend the boundary line in coordination with South Carolina. Little came of this, however, and the state line remained ambiguous for years. Marvin Lucian Skaggs, *North Carolina Boundary Disputes Involving Her Southern Line*, James Sprunt Studies in History and Political Science, vol. 25 (Chapel Hill: University of North Carolina Press, 1941), 98-99; House Joint Resolution, December 26, 1786, General Assembly Session Records, State Archives.

Palinurus piloted Aeneas's ship in Virgil's *Aeneid*. M. C. Howatson, ed., *The Oxford Companion to Classical Literature*, 2d. ed. (Oxford: Oxford University Press, 1989), 405.

[6]Robert Howe died in Bladen County on December 14, 1786, while traveling to a meeting of the General Assembly. *DNCB*, s.v. "Howe, Robert."

To Hannah Iredell

Nixonton Dec. 21. 1786.

My dear Hannah,

Your Brother and I are very well, but I cannot express my mortification in finding it utterly impossible that I should be at home to morrow to enjoy among you the delightful Anniversary of our dear Annie's birth. God Almighty be praised for his great goodness in sparing her to us hitherto! May she still live; to be a comfort & happiness to us, and a useful & respectable Member of Society! Say every thing dear & tender for me to her. Kiss her most fervently, & congratulate her on the most happy occasion. My thoughts will be every moment fixed upon it. My heart indeed will be with you tho' I shall be necessarily & cruelly absent. Remember my love to all the Family. Pray do you or my Brother kiss Nelly & Peggy on my behalf to morrow, tho' I mean that only by way of memento, & not to preclude my own privilege after my return. Adieu! God bless you. Tell Annie to think of her and

Your ever affectionate

Ja. Iredell.

RC, Johnson Collection, NCSA. Addressed "Mrs. Iredell Edenton By favor of Mr. Eccleston."

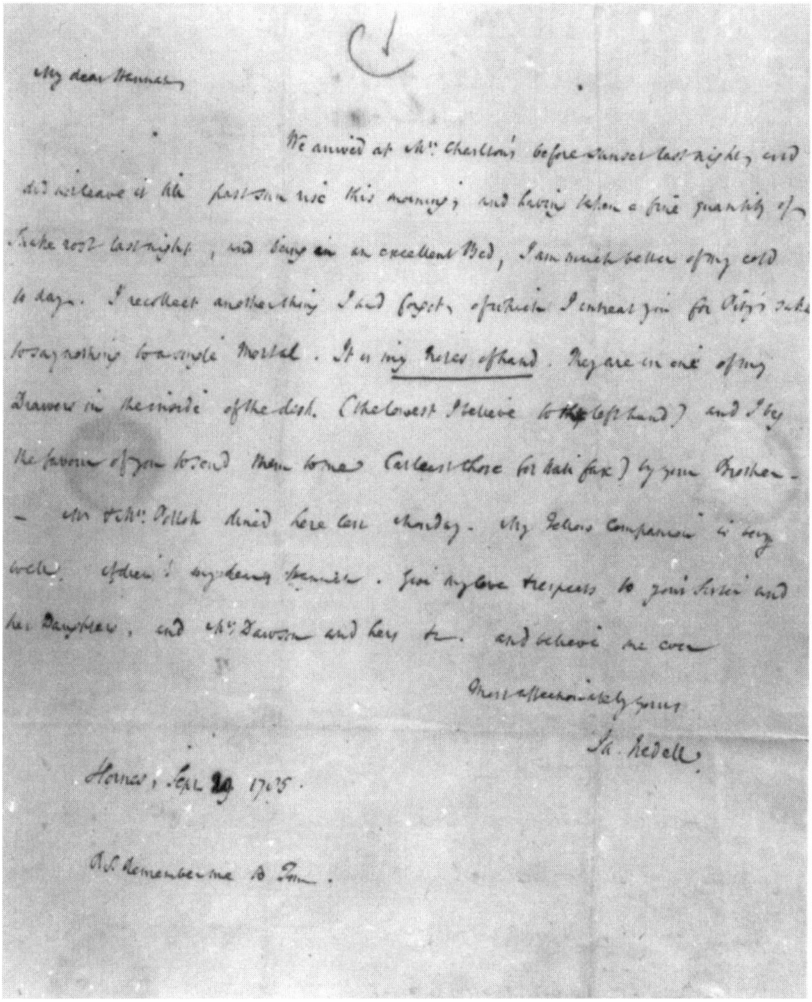

My dear Hannah,

We arrived at Mr. Charlton's before sunset last night, and did not leave it till past ten this morning; and having taken a fine quantity of [illegible] last night, and lying in an excellent Bed, I am much better of my cold to day. I recollect another thing I had forgot, of which I entreat you for Pity's sake to say nothing to a single Mortal. It is my Notes of hand. They are in one of my Drawers in the inside of the desk. (The lowest I believe to the left hand) and I beg the favour of you to send them to me (at least those for Halifax) by your Brother. — Mr & Mrs. Pollok dined here last Monday. My fellow Companion is very well. Adieu! my dearest Hannah. Give my love & respects to your Sister and her Daughter, and Mrs. Dawson and her [illegible]. and believe me ever

Most affectionately yours

Ja. Iredell.

[illegible], Sept. 29 1785.

P.S. Remember me to Tom.

This is one of many letters that James Iredell wrote to his wife, Hannah, while riding the court circuit. As a practicing attorney, Iredell spent much of his time away from home. In this correspondence, dated September 29, 1785, he is mortified at having forgotten some of his notes for a case at Halifax. "They are in one of my Drawers in the inside of the desk." He asks her to "send them . . . by your Brother." *Charles E. Johnson Collection, State Archives, Office of Archives and History, Raleigh.*

Samuel Johnston was James Iredell's brother-in-law, mentor, and friend. As attorneys they sought fair treatment for Loyalists, and both supported ratification of the U.S. Constitution. Johnston was unanimously elected as president of both state ratification conventions. He also served as governor and as a U.S. senator. *State Archives.*

William Hooper, a Hillsborough attorney and signer of the Declaration of Independence, was one of Iredell's closest friends. Hooper often encouraged Iredell to leave Edenton's unhealthy climate and move to Hillsborough. "It is a melancholy consideration," he wrote, "that once in every year at least you run the gauntlet for your lives notwithstanding the utmost regularity and temperance in your manner of living." *State Archives.*

Richard Dobbs Spaight (1758-1802) of Craven County served nine terms in the General Assembly and from 1783 to 1785 was a member of the Continental Congress. As a signer of the U.S. Constitution, Spaight joined Iredell in supporting ratification at the 1788 convention in Hillsborough. Spaight was subsequently elected to three terms as governor (1792-1795) and as a member of the U.S. House of Representatives (1798-1801). *State Archives.*

William Richardson Davie, an attorney from Halifax, was a delegate to the U.S. constitutional convention. Soon after arriving in Philadelphia, he wrote and asked Iredell for advice, adding, "I [*shall tr*]ouble you frequently and I [*shall*] expect your opinion without reserve." Davie, an ardent Federalist, was a delegate to both state ratification conventions. He later led a successful movement to found a state university and in 1798 was elected governor. *State Archives.*

Hugh Williamson was a merchant and physician in Chowan County. As a delegate to the constitutional convention and a member of the Continental Congress, he kept Iredell abreast of national events. Williamson, an advocate for education, helped to establish academies and was one of the first trustees of the University of North Carolina. *State Archives.*

John Burgwin, a Cape Fear merchant, was wrongly suspected of being a Loyalist during the Revolutionary War, and the state confiscated his property. After the war he sought help from Iredell in recovering his holdings. Iredell's schedule prevented him from representing Burgwin, but the two men often corresponded. *State Archives.*

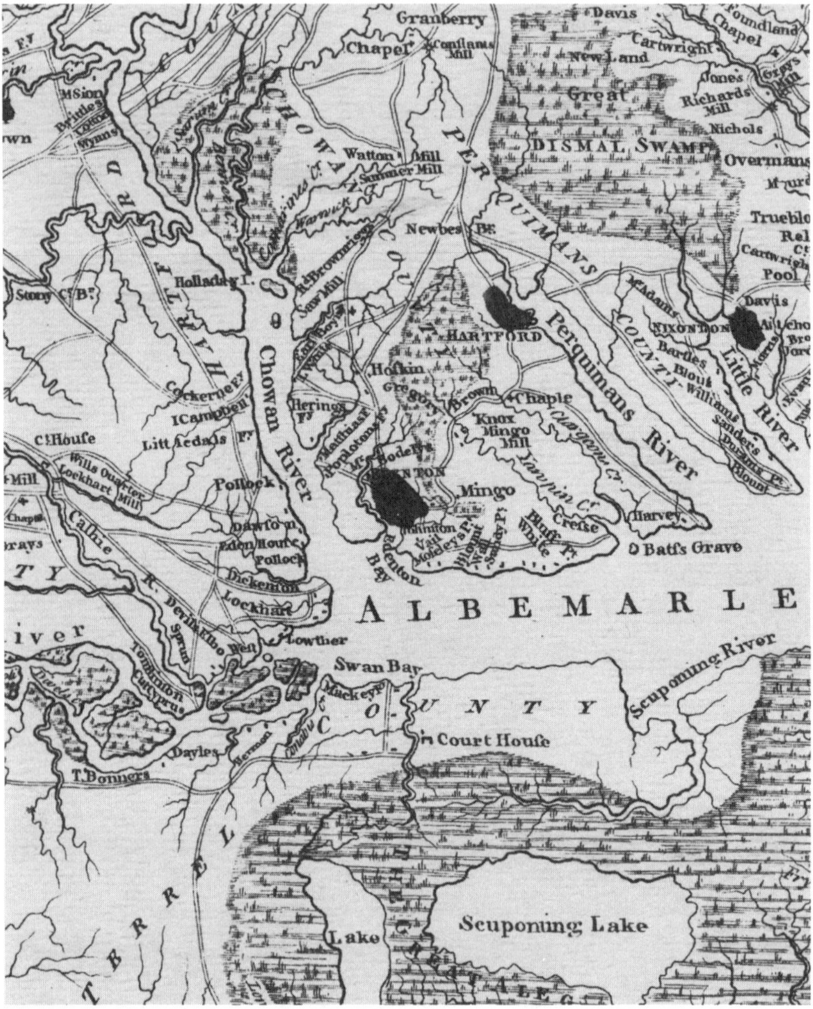

After moving to Edenton in 1768, James Iredell established friendships with the prominent families in the area. Names that appear in his correspondence, such as Blount, Pollock, and Lowther, can be seen on this 1770 map of Edenton and vicinity. Detail from "A Compleat Map of North Carolina from an actual Survey" by John Collet. This map is reproduced in facsimile within *North Carolina in Maps* by William P. Cumming (Raleigh, N.C.: N.C. Division of Archives and History, 2001). The original map is housed at Davidson College.

1787

From John Witherspoon[1]

Princeton Jany. 8. 1787

Sir

On the 25 of November I received a Letter from Mr. Hooper desiring me to send a Tutor for the Hillsborough Academy of which by his Letter you are one of the Trustees[2]—On the 28th. of that Month I wrote him an answer under Cover to my Son at Newbern informing him that I would endeavour to supply the Academy with one agreeable to his Request.[3] The Person whom I first applied to who is one of our last years graduates and now employed in the Academy at Trenton seemed disposed to go but lately has declared being as I suppose tempted by superior offers to continue where he is—Immediately on receiving this Intelligence I wrote to another who is at present at the Academy at Newark but have not yet received his Answer As soon as I do if he agrees I will send him on if he refuses to shew my earnest Desire to gratify those who have put this Confidence in me I will send one of those who are employed by my self in the Grammar School here though it will be somewhat inconvenient for me—

I write this because I have just received a second Copy of Mr. Hoopers Letter & have addressed it to you according to Mr. Hoopers Direction if Letters are sent to Edenton Please to advise me of the Receipt of this Letter. I shall however write again oftener as I receive further Intelligence

I am Sir your most obedient humble Servant

Jno. Witherspoon

RC, Iredell Papers, Duke. Addressed "James Iredell Esqr Edenton N. Carolina." Endorsed "Princeton Jan. 8. 1787. John Witherspoon Recd. Feb. 24. Ansd. Feb. 25."

---

[1]John Witherspoon (1723-1794) was president of the College of New Jersey, now Princeton University. He was a clergyman, signer of the Declaration of Independence, and member of the Continental Congress. *BDC*, s.v. "Witherspoon, John."

[2]JI served on the board of trustees of Smith's Academy in Edenton and was a close friend of William Hooper of the Hillsborough Academy board of trustees, but no record has been found placing JI on the board of the Hillsborough school.

[3]David Witherspoon (d. 1801) was a New Bern attorney and the husband of Gov. Abner Nash's widow, Mary Whiting Jones Nash. *DNCB*, s.v. "Witherspoon, John Knox."

From William Hooper

22 Jany 178[7][1] Hillsboro

My dear Sir,

Mr. Moore forwarded me from Wilmington your very affectionate letter dated at Newbern. I also received a few lines from you acknowledging that my scrawl by the quakers had reached you.

I had availed of some one of the many opportunities which offered to Edenton at the close of the session to have informed you of what had been done in the Assembly, but I found myself so crowded with business in the moment of departure, my passions so agitated with the unbecoming means which had been used to cast a stigma upon the bar, and upon the whole that so large a portion of our time had been occupied to accomplish purposes either nugatory or disgraceful that I forbore to give you a detail of our proceedings. It now becomes unnecessary, you have had frequent opportunities I doubt not to mix with your legislators and were it only to give you proper ideas of their own parliamentary consequence they would not fail to inform you of all that had passed in the Assembly and the distinguished share which they had taken in it. In the New Court law, if it merits the name, for it had been much better christened as I proposed a bill inflicting pains and penalties on Attornies, Edenton District conducted themselves, with a very few exceptions, very differently from what I expected.[2] Cabarrus Sawyer Everagen acquitted themselves honourably.[3] Cabarrus' conduct thro the whole Session was upright, sensible and independent and in the investigation of the publick frauds he proved himself a very useful and industrious committee man[4]

I inclose you without a comment certain papers which made their appearance in the course of the investigation of the conduct of the Judges. This ridiculous pursuit of Hay's ended as we expected. It was conceived in Spleen and conducted with such headstrong passion that after the charges were made evidence was wanting to support them.[5]

You have inclosed a letter (a copy) of Mr. Ash's it carries its own commentary with it I leave you to judge how far we have merited the charges it alledges against us.[6]

I will not spin this scrawl to a greater length and will only add that there is no time of my life has been so decidedly mispent as that which I passed in the last session of the Assembly. God forgive me this publick political sin and I will do so no more[7]

Make Mrs. Hooper's Betsy's and my kind regards to your own and Mr. Johnston's family. Comp to Mr. and Mrs. Pollok

Hand this and the inclosed to Mr. Johnston and beleve me ever

Most Affectionately Your's

Will Hooper

The inclosed are hurredly copied, perhaps you can make them out.

RC, Emmet Collection, NYPL. TSS, Thomas Addison Emmet Collection, NCSA. Printed, McRee, 2:132-133.

---

[1]Though the original of this letter is dated 1786, the contents indicate that it was actually written in 1787.

[2]On January 7, 1787, the General Assembly passed "An Act to Amend an Act Passed at New Bern, In December, One Thousand Seven Hundred and Eighty-Five, Entitled, 'An Act for Encreasing the Jurisdiction of the County Courts of Pleas and Quarter Sessions, and of the Justices of the Peace Out of Court, and Directing The Time of Holding Courts In This State.' " The act includes the assertion that "the frequent abuses of attornies have occasioned distress to many of the good people of this State." To remedy this, the legislation contains provisions regulating the conduct of lawyers and establishing legal fees. Clark, *State Records*, 24:804-807.

[3]Stephen Cabarrus, previously identified. Enoch Sawyer (1758-1827) of Camden County was a member of the house of commons (1784, 1785-1790) and a delegate to the 1788 and 1789 state constitutional ratification conventions. Edward Everagin (d. 1793) of Pasquotank County served three terms in the Colonial Assembly and eleven terms in the General Assembly. He was also a delegate to the 1788 and 1789 state constitutional ratification conventions. Massengill, *North Carolina Votes*, 19, 52.

[4]Cabarrus was appointed to the Committee of Finance in 1786. This legislative committee had the responsibility of producing "a full statement of the debts, funds and revenues of the State." Clark, *State Records*, 18:7-8, 13.

[5]Enclosures not found. For more information on "this ridiculous pursuit of Hay," see Alfred Moore to JI, December 14, 1786, n. 1, in this volume.

[6]In Samuel Ashe's letter to the General Assembly, answering charges made against the bench, he leveled accusations of his own against attorneys. The judges had been accused of failing to conduct court expeditiously, but Ashe claimed that the attorneys were to blame for the delays. The lawyers, according to Ashe, delayed court while "scouring and hunting after fees" and with "unnecessary long and rambling harangues, calculated only to amuse the client, and pay him in empty words for the extravagance of the fee." He went on to complain of the lawyers' "insufferable rudeness." Clark, *State Records*, 18:137-142.

[7]Hooper had expressed similar sentiments earlier. In 1784, he told JI, "I have absolutely refused to serve in the assembly again." This time, however, he meant it. William Hooper to JI, July 8, 1784, in this volume.

To Hannah Iredell

Edenhouse, Thursday Morning.[1]

My dear Hannah,

I have been particularly fortunate in the time I had to cross the Sound, since it scarcely rained at all the whole way, and I kept myself perfectly dry, and the weather now has a very unpromising appearance. I abandon all thoughts of being either at Halifax or Colo. Mc.Culloch's any time tomorrow; my principal object shall be to get to the Marsh some time on Saturday, and therefore you may be assured of my taking all possible care of myself. I shall not attempt getting further than Mrs. Charlton's tonight at any rate. if the weather continues very bad I shall probably stay here all night. Pray thank your Brother, when you see him, for his Canoe, and Mrs. Dawson for my comfortable Quarters here. I should grow raving tired almost at Ryan's. All the Family here are quite well. Tell my lovely Annie how much I was disappointed at not getting another kiss from her. I can scarcely bear the thoughts of so long an absence in what I had some right to think my own time. But I console myself with the hopes it may ultimately serve you both, & particularly enable me (upon which my heart is set) to carry you both to Hillsborough the ensuing Summer. What in this world is equal to Annie's health! But I grow too much affected. Smother her as Arthur says, with kisses for me, and tell her I will see her again as soon as I can. Give my love to all the Family. I am sure you will have the goodness to think of my Brother's health. God preserve your own & my lovely Girl's. Adieu!

Yours most affectionately

Ja. Iredell.

I wish you would write a line to my Mother. Surely you need not be so ceremonious with her. I have not said half enough to her of Annie.

RC, Johnson Collection, NCSA. Addressed "Mrs. Iredell Edenton." Endorsed "Edenhouse. Jan. 1787."

---

[1]This letter was probably written on January 25, 1787, since it was written on a Thursday while JI was traveling from Edenton to Warrenton.

To Hannah Iredell

Warrenton Jan. 31st. 1787.

My dear Hannah,

I arrived here perfectly well on Monday, and though I was obliged to ride a little in the rain I have not suffered the least inconvenience from it. Judge Williams & Mr. Moore arrived the same day I did. Ashe & Williams are this moment come. None of the charges are yet brought forward. I am convinced the matter against B. Mc.Culloch has been greatly exaggerated. What I [*torn*] can only be justly proved against him is, his undertaking to negociate certificates for a certain proportion, but not with any view to pass any but such as were entitled to it.[1] Colo. Davie and myself are very comfortably lodged in a room together. I shall be extremely impatient to hear from you, and hope you will neglect no opportunity to write. Express my love in the tenderest manner to my lovely Annie. God knows how impatient I shall be to see & converse with her. Remember me affectionately to your Sister & the Girls. It is impossible for me now to write to Nelly. I will if I can write a line to my Brother, though I know not if I shall have time—

I am, my dearest Hannah, ever Most affectionately yours

Ja. Iredell.

RC, Johnson Collection, NCSA. Addressed "Mrs. Iredell."

---

[1]In the legislative committee hearings, which were a prelude to the Warrenton trial, McCulloch was accused of having arranged with various individuals to accept their claims in return for a quarter or more of the amount they received. He was also said to have conspired with John McNees to accept "sixteen or seventeen" claims from him. Clark, *State Records*, 18:72. See also Alfred Moore to JI, December 14, 1786, n. 2, in this volume.

To Hannah Iredell

Warrenton Feb. 13th. 1787.

My dear Hannah,

I am still perfectly well, but our situation with such bad weather is extremely disagreeable. Three Men of the name of Price, Butcher, and Reid of Halifax have been convicted, the two former of presenting fictitious Accounts, and the latter of signing blank Accounts for pay.[1] H. Montfort has been acquitted, but poor B. Mc.Culloch convicted.[2] He was tried on much the same charge as against Montfort, and their case was nearly equal, but he had strong prejudices both of the People and Court to encounter, and I really believe was convicted of more than he had done, or been capable of doing, which was, taking Accounts to pass right or wrong. Had his Conviction been for making himself voluntarily interested in Accounts he was to pass, and by that means disabling himself from performing his Trust impartially, I should have thought it right. No Judgments have yet been pronounced. In respect to him, I fear it will not only be a large Fine, but Imprisonment also. I did not forget your birth day, any more than G. Washington's. God grant you, my dear Hannah, many happy returns of it. I think myself very unfortunate in not having heard a single word from you since I left home—I have heard but this minute of the present opportunity, so that I can write to nobody else, for which you will properly & truly apologise. O! my little lovely Annie! how I long to see her. Tell her so, with many warm kisses. Give my love to all our Family, & respects to your Brothers,

and believe me, my dear Hannah, Sincerely & most affectionately yours

Ja. Iredell.

RC, Johnson Collection, NCSA. Addressed "Mrs. Iredell Edenton."

[1]John Price of Dobbs County was convicted and fined £1,000. Thomas Butcher of Dobbs County was also convicted. He and a confederate had collected £186 by presenting a claim in the name of Hardy Robertson, even though Robertson had never been in the army. Robertson subsequently demanded a share of the money. Capt. Jesse Read of Halifax was accused of signing twenty blank account forms for a Capt. Sherrod Barrow, who in return gave Read more than 1,200 acres in military land claims. Clark, *State Records*, 18:73, 108; 20:630.

[2]See Alfred Moore to JI, December 14, 1786, n. 2, in this volume.

To Hannah Iredell

Warren February 19th. 1787.

My dear Hannah,

The letters I received from you and my other Friends by Mr. Dawson gave me the greatest pleasure. It was the first account I had had of any of you. The delightful little Circumstances you mentioned, & my Brother mentioned, of my lovely Annie, affected me beyond measure. How I long for an opportunity to thank the sweet little Creature for her tenderness and affection for me, manifested in so extraordinary a manner—I am now at

Mr. Montfort's, of whom I could get no more than this scrap of Paper, of which be good enough to inform Nelly, and your & my Brother, with my best acknowledgments for their obliging letters.[1] Never did I receive such a shock as in the barborous & inhuman sentence passed on B. Mc.Culloch—£4000 Fine, & 12 months Imprisonment in Halifax Gaol. Though his whole Trial he met with the greatest tyranny & injustice from 2 of the Court. I need not say which. He was charged I am sure beyond his real offence—All the People here speak with the utmost horror & resentment of his Sentence—How can I bear to see his poor miserable Family! I have had 2 letters from his Father, dreadful beyond what I have ever read.[2] I may be obliged to stay at Warrenton till tomorrow night, when the Court must end, in order to see some little business done for the People who have employed me. I shall have occasion to call on Faulcon, on some business, but hope that will not detain me long—after which I shall push down with the utmost expedition. Billy Dawson is very well. He dined here yesterday. Give my love to all—Tell my Annie how I have been delighted with her kissing my letters and give her many tender kisses for me. I am very well.

Adieu! my dear Hannah—Yours most affectionately

Ja. Iredell

RC, Johnson Collection, NCSA. Addressed "Mrs. Ired[*ell Edenton*] By favor of Mr. Craven."

---

[1]The letters from Samuel Johnston and Tom Iredell have not been found. In a letter of February 3, 1787, Nelly Blair told JI, "We are all of us extremely impatient to hear from you, & know how you come on in defending your Clients after The proofs of Innocence They gave you. I shall never have an opinion of your eloquence again, if you do not succeed in clearing Them /from/ The aspersions cast on them." Iredell Papers, Rare Book, Manuscript, and Special Collections Library, Duke University.

[2]In a letter dated February 15, 1787, of which only a small portion has survived, Alexander McCulloch, father of Benjamin McCulloch, wrote "upon any but you two, give my Service to the Collo. and /tell/ him I bege he will exerte himself to get the fine as low as posseble, and for God Sake let there be no imprisonment. if there is I am Sertain it will end my days for what has hapned—I can Scarcely go about. I think if the Judges Ash and William knew in what broke and grief I suffer they wou'd not ofer to imprison him. it can't be of any Service. if you think it proper you may let those two Gentlemen know it's in there power to end, or prolonge my days, for if he is put in prison I am Shure I shall not Survive many days. I am Shure Since I heard of it which was Sunday I have not Sleept four house nor Eat a pound of any thing, and I realy would be Glad I was Clear of the world, if it was Gods will—I should be glad how Soon, if /I/ could but see my Son I wou'd not care." Charles E. Johnson Collection, State Archives.

From John Witherspoon

Princeton Feb. 19. 1787

Sir

I wrote you some time ago of my receiving Mr. Hoopers Letter desiring me to send a Tuter to the Academy at Hillsborough & of my Attention to that Commission though for some Time without Success.[1] I now embrace the first Opportunity of informing you that I have engaged a young Gentleman for that Purpose. He will set out without Delay but is in some Difficulty as to Money for his outfit & the Expences of the Journey & Voyage.[2] I have therefore written to Mr. Blount & Mr. Hawkins with both of whom I am acquainted requesting them to see whether som Crdor from our acctt N. Carolina could be negotiated on N. York for 30 or 40 Dollars.[3] This Import may be done & that he will be on his Way soon. Their is no Mention made in the Letter to me of bearing his Expences but if the Trustees do not allow of it he agrees that it may be deducted from his Salary. In Case this Schem takes place I will draw the Crdor on the Gentleman to whom he is addressed accordg as he finds a Passage to Edenton Wilmington or Newbern

The first Letter not coming till after our Commencement in September made it much more difficult for me to provide for you as at that Time all the Graduates for that year go home & get themselves fixed in different Ways

I am Sir your most obedt. humble Servant

Jno Witherspoon

RC, Princeton. Addressed "James Iredell Esqr."

---

[1]See John Witherspoon to JI, January 8, 1787, in this volume.

[2]Ladoc Squire began teaching at Hillsborough Academy in April 1787. School records indicate that JI lent Squire £6 and was reimbursed from Squire's first month's salary. Copy of the Account of Mr. Squire, Hillsborough Academy Papers, State Archives.

[3]Witherspoon knew William Blount, previously identified, and Benjamin Hawkins (1754-1818) from when they served together in the Continental Congress. Witherspoon's tenure in Congress overlapped with that of Hawkins in 1781-1782 and with Blount in 1782. Hawkins, a native of what was then Granville County, also attended the College of New Jersey while Witherspoon was president. Hawkins was, in addition, a delegate to the North Carolina ratification convention (1789) and a U.S. senator (1789-1795). *BDC*, s.v. "Blount, William," "Hawkins, Benjamin," "Witherspoon, John."

To Richard Caswell

[*Feb. 1787*][1]

Sir,

At the desire of a most respectable and afflicted Father, I take the liberty to write to your Excellency on the unfortunate subject of a late most heavy Judgment pronounced by the Judges at Warrenton upon Mr. B. Mc.Culloch. I have not a copy of the Indictment, which was for <a> Misdemeanors in his office of Commissioner of Army Accounts and one Charge in it was, his corruptly bargaining <for a share> to pass accounts, without regarding whether they were right or wrong. The other, I believe, was, for his passing such accounts /under the influence of a Corrupt Interest/ without duly exercising his Judgment upon them. These, to the best of my recollecting were the substantial Charges. However, it is probable a Copy of the Indictment itself will be laid before you.

In regard to the first Charge, the two /principal/ Witnesses (Faircloth & Moring, the first of whom was a Party to the Agreement, whatever it was, the other introduced to shew a Conversation in the subject in <regard> /respect/ to other accounts)[2] both disclaimed in the most solemn manner any knowledge or belief that Mr. Mc.Culloch meant, in consequence of what passed, to pass Accounts right or wrong, but /declared/ that they understood, the share he was to receive was <for> of such money as the Persons should be entitled to draw out of the Treasury upon such accounts as should pass the office, the exercise of his Judgment upon them not being in any manner precluded by the agreement made, but the Agreement extending simply to the trouble of taking the accounts, & upon such as should appear to be good afterwards drawing the Money out of the Treasury for a certain proportion. It appeared further that all the accounts he received were regularly certified by Continental officers, agreeable to the act of Assembly, (at least nothing was suggested to the contrary), and that he had no Evidence to counteract the officers Certificates, unless (as it was strongly contended) the mere face of the accounts, from the suspicious manner in which they were drawn the great number of them, & the obscurity of the Characters who preserved them to so great an amount, could constitute sufficient Evidence to that purpose.[3] In regard to this, the Testimony of Mr. John Macon, one of the Commissioners, was very important, & therefore I shall presume to mention it to your Excy. at time Compt. His Evidence, as near as I can recollect it, was to this effect.[4] He said, upon the first opening of the Board, Mr. Mc.Culloch presented a great number of acccounts, he thinks to the amount of 4 or 500, upon which he immediately <proposed shutting up the office, & supposed>

said, he was convinced many of these accounts must be bad, and proposed shutting up the office, & suspending all proceedings till the next meeting of the Assembly. <That Mr. Mc.Culloch answered, /he supposed some of the Accounts might be bad, but <he> did not think they were at liberty to <do so> /shut up the office/, and that he <supposed> /considered/ they were bound by the Certificates of the officers unless upon examination there should be express evidence of fraud or mistake. /That at this time Mr. Macon had not seen the Act of Assembly, but having seen it he concurred in opinion, that the Certificate of the officers did bind them to pass the accounts, unless they had clear evidence to the contrary/ It was <upon this> /therefore/ mutually agreed, as these two were only present, that it should be referred to Mr. Montfort, and if he was of opinion that </that they had no way to prevent [*illegible*] accounts passing but by shutting upon the office altogether/> the office should be kept open, that they should proceed in the exercise of it, and the accounts should be received /and therefore he thought it unnecessary to consult Mr. Montfort <and> the office was <kept> accordingly kept open. <Mr. Montfort having been consulted, & being of opinion they were under a necessity of proceeding, the office was kept open. Mr. Macon /who/ acted as well as the others>> / That Mr. McC. answered, he supposed some of the accounts might be bad, but he did not think they were at liberty to shut up the office, and that he considered they were bound by the certificates of the officers, unless upon examination there should be express evidence of fraud or mistake. It was upon this mutually agreed, that as those two were only present, it should be referred to Mr. Montfort the other Commissioner, and if he was of opinion that the office should be kept open, that they should proceed in the exercise of it, and the accounts should be received. At this time Mr. Macon had not seen the Act of Assembly, but having seen it he concurred in opinion, that the certificates of the officers did bind them to pass the accounts, unless they had clear evidence to the contrary, and accordingly afterwards acting as well as the others,/ did conceive himself bound, notwithstanding all the suspicious Circumstance /relied upon as a clear proof/ of Mr. Mc.Culloch's guilt, by the Certificates of the officers, and concurred, in passing the greater part of the accounts, there being no Evidence before them which he thought would justify them in rejecting them. Mr. Macon further declared, that Mr. Mc.Culloch discovered no particular anxiety to pass any of the accounts, as if he had been indifferent whether they were good or bad, and that on the contrary Mr. Mc.Culloch detected several as bad which he himself had overlooked. <He further said, that he thought> Your Excellency will please to observe that Mr. Macon is neither charged nor suspected, but universally believed to have been altogether disinterested. If he therefore thus circumstanced was not sensible of the force of these Presumptions now ingeniously, and easily suggested after the frauds are fully made known <under all the Circumstances there be> /with all that particulars <plainly> /clearly before us/ there Presumptions alone are now a <utter> /decisive/ proof of any such criminal Intention as is suspected to Mr. Mc.Culloch, from <them alone of knowingly> /that ground only/ of his intending to pass accounts right or wrong. Especially, when it was plainly proved, that he himself pointed out many as bad which Mr. Macon had overlooked, a thing utterly improbable under the former supposition, and when a Character as good as any Man's in the State belonged to him until the unfortunate Transactions took place which have caused his present /unhappy/ situation. I humbly presume, even where the ballance of his ability hangs <ever> /equal/, Character <is> must weigh it down one way or the other, of much more moment is it when thrown into the heavier scale already greatly in a Man's favour from the Circumstances attending his Conduct.

As to the second Charge, It must be admitted, that previous to the passing of the accounts (upon which a Judgment of some kind, however fitting, was necessary to be exercised) Mr. Mc.Culloch ought well to have made himself in any manner however remotely, interested in them, because tho' he might sufficiently confidence the Integrity of his Intentions, he could not be sure but that there might be some bias upon his mind, & this might disable him from the dire execution of his Trust. In this particular, in my opinion his Criminality consisted, not in any deliberate Treachery to the Public, of which I presume to say I believe him at this moment as <incapabel> incapable as any Man in the State. Your Excellency must perceive that I write with all the warmth, possibly with the partiality of a Friend. I can only say, I mean not to mistake a single Circumstance. My passions indeed are strongly interested in his favour. Never have I felt in such a manner /before/ and the sight of his numerous & afflicted Family among whom I now write (his Father, a most lovely Wife, and six small children, /the eldest/ almost too young to <have> comprehend the nature of their Father's distress) would be enough to melt the most [*illegible*] heart. What Effect then must it have on me, who am related to them, have lived on the happiest & most intimate terms with them all for a great number of years, and am indebted to the goodness of this very Family in this very house for the preservation of that life which enables me with so much zeal, tho' hitherto with so little need to endeavour to rescue theirs from misery & ruin. The Sentence passed upon Mr. Mc.Culloh is a Fine of £4000. Imprisonment till he pays it, & after he pays it a further Imprisonment of 12 months in Halifax Gaol, a place which from its unwholesomeness, its being filled with a number of <other> /low/ unhappy Watchers &c <thousand> /other Circumstances too <miserable> /painful/ for me to think of as [*illegible*], must certainly [*illegible*] to his life, unless your Excellecy with the goodness natural to you, & which I am sure if you deem it consistent with your public duty you will with pleasure exercise on the present occasion <exercise> /should exert/ that blessed attribute of Mercy which the Constitution has intrusted to you. I shall only add, that I desire only to be credited for my account in his letters as you will find it confirmed by the declaraton of a great number of respectable Persons who interest themselves in this late nearly with as much warmth as I do, though <could>/they have/ infinitely less reason to be partial to the Man, and that whatever your Excellency may determine on I am sure you will find in my troubling you with this letter, at the instance of a most unhappy Father you have [*illegible*] a more respectable point of view, & whose days will probably be <thou> shattered by this <most calamitous> /truly melancholy/ event [*illegible*].[5]

FC, Johnson Collection, NCSA. Endorsed "Copy of my Letter to the Governor in favour of B. Mc.Culloch."

---

[1] This letter was probably written soon after the conclusion of the trials in Warrenton in late February.

[2] For information on William Faircloth's dealings with the commission for liquidating army accounts, see Clark, *State Records*, 18:73-74.

Burwell Mooring (ca. 1745-ca. 1809) of Wayne County, though questioned, was not accused of wrongdoing. He was a major in the Wayne County militia during the Revolution and served eleven terms in the General Assembly. Mooring was also a delegate to the 1788 and 1789 state ratification conventions. Massengill, *North Carolina Votes*, 44; Clark, *State Records*, 19:17.

[3] See "An Act to amend an Act, intituled, 'An Act for the relief of the Officers and Soldiers of the Continental line, and for other purposes.' " Clark, *State Records*, 24:566-568.

[4] John Macon (ca. 1754-1828) of Warren County was one of the three commissioners for liquidating the army accounts. He replaced Willie Jones after Jones resigned. Macon was questioned about the commission's activities, but no evidence suggested that he had acted illegally. He had been a cavalry major in the Revolution and served sixteen terms in the General Assembly. Macon was also a delegate to the 1788 state ratification convention. He was the brother of Nathaniel Macon. Clark, *State Records*, 18:73; 24:567; Massengill, *North Carolina Votes*, 40.

[5] Scattered notes from these trials can be found among the miscellaneous papers in the Charles E. Johnson Collection in the State Archives. In addition, a petition, in JI's handwriting, from Tarborough citizens expressing support for Benjamin McCulloch is filed among Governor Caswell's papers. Richard Caswell, 1785-1787, Governors Papers, State Archives.

From William Hooper

Hillsborough, March 1st, 1787.

Dear Sir

Your kind favor by Mr. Moore, together with a letter of a later date, came safe to hand. Accept my grateful acknowledgments for your kind remembrance of me.

I have just now returned from the most painful visit that I ever paid in my life. Your old friend, Gen. Clarke, is struck with blindness. He went to bed in perfect good health; rose at the accustomed hour; opened his window shutters; the yard of the house appeared to be in an undulating motion; black and yellow spots floating upon the surface of the earth; the floor of his chamber covered with dry brush, which he attempted to kick away; complained to his servants that the day was dark and cloudy, who informed him that the sun shone with remarkable brightness; bound up his eyes, and the next morning awakened stone blind. My hand was in his without his knowing me; my voice helped him to the discovery. His firmness is beyond all description. Thus, he tells me, he reasoned when he was first attacked: "Shall I blow my brains out? It will be pusillanimity. I can do it. But to dare to be blind for life, will be an effort that will discover real resolution." Not a single complaint, no repining. He is now on his plantation, without a single white person. It is a school to which I would recommend youth, to learn philosophy, and to bear misfortune. I always loved the man; I reverence him blind; he is something more than man. I shall carry a statement of his case to Dr. Lennox, when I visit Edenton, that we may avail ourselves of his advice.

I rejoice that your dear little girl is well—that you are all well. God bless you all! May you never feel the affliction with which Providence has wounded us! Love to Mr. Johnston and family.

Bring your gown with you. The judges have issued their edict, that we shall wear gowns, or not have the supreme honor to appear in their presence, &c., &c.[1]

Will. Hooper.

RC, Printed, McRee, 2:158.

---

[1]In May 1785, the judges of the superior court advised lawyers to wear black robes in court, a practice dating from the colonial era. Most of the attorneys disregarded this request, however. In 1787, the judges, emboldened by their triumph in the legislature, directed the lawyers appearing before them to wear the gowns. Waldrup, "James Iredell," 304-305, 321.

From John Stokes

Salisbury March 27th. 1787

My dear Sir,

I have received your very obliging favour by the hands of Colo. Davie—I am singularly happy to learn that you are (after so many severe attacks of illness) now in good health

It was not necessary for you to have mentioned to me the extreme pain which the situation of BMC. gave you. my knowledge of your goodness had informed /me/ as much long before I received your letter—It is needless to add more on that subject. You can readily imagine how I feel on the occasion without my informing you—The subject is too disagreable to dwell on—I wish I was ignorant of it—I think of it by day—It is represented to me in my dreams, which are wont to make it nothing but a fantom—The blushing morn <destroys> establishes the reallity & renews my grief.

I forgot to send you the money by Mr. Mc.Kenzie but I will do it by Colo. Davie—

Believe me my Dear Sir that there is not a man in the world more happy to hear from you or more solicitous for you happiness than

Jno. Stokes

RC, Iredell Papers, Duke. Printed, McRee, 2:157. Addressed "James Iredell Esquire at Hillsborough Hond. by Colo. Davie."

To Hannah Iredell

Wheelers March 31. 1787.

My dear Hannah,

After eating half a shad, and two or three eggs for breakfast, I do myself the pleasure to acquaint you of my arrival here in perfect health, supposing I am now at a sufficient distance from home to write to you without ridicule. As the weather was so excessively bad on Thursday, I staid at Copeland's till the afternoon, & only got to Bennet's Creek Bridge that night.[1] I should have gone to Lawrence Baker's, but that I was afraid on account of the recent death of Mrs. Granbery it might be inconvenient.[2] I reached one Horn's on the Winton Road last night, & find it a pretty good house which is a valuable discovery. His Wife's fame as a scold used to deter People formerly, but she is fortunately now dead. I was in my chair by sunrise this morning; found an excellent Breakfast here which is now a public house, & intend to be 15 miles beyond Halifax to night, so that I hope to be at Hillsborough early in Tuesday Morning. I shall be very anxious to hear of you & my dear little girl, who I hope will cut her remaining teeth easily. Tell her I think of her every minute, & wish the utmost possible anxiety & affection. Remember me kindly to all the rest of the Family, your Brothers, Mrs. Dawson's &c. and believe me, my dear Hannah, ever

Most affectionately yours

Ja. Iredell.

P.S. Accept this as a letter from Halifax, where I shall be in 2 hours, & I write here to save time there.

RC, Johnson Collection, NCSA. Addressed "Mrs. Iredell Edenton."

---

[1]This is probably Josiah Copeland, a member of the house of commons from Chowan County. Cheney, *North Carolina Government*, 218, 219.

Bennett's Creek originates in central Gates County, near Merchants Millpond, and flows southward into the Chowan River.

[2]Mrs. Josiah Granberry of Chowan County. See *PJI*, 1:111n.

To Hannah Iredell

Hillsborough April 6th. 1787.

My dear Hannah,

I arrived here quite well on Tuesday morning, but had the misfortune to leave poor Fox lame about 42 miles behind. He will be however I believe taken great care of. That very rainy day obliged me to push along afterwards faster than I would have chose. Mr. Pollok's Causes are appointed for Trial next Tuesday. God knows when we shall get rid of Moore's.[1] But the Court have done an amazing quantity of business both here and at Salisbury. They begin punctually at ten, and continue sitting till near Sun set every day. I am heartily glad of it. The People about Salisbury say—they are convinced the fault before was in the Judges, not in the Lawyers, the latter discovering no kind of reluctance at the present amendment.[2]

The Families here are quite well. Gen. Clark, we hear, has begun to see a little with one eye.[3] It is expected Miss Johnston will be married soon.[4] There is much reason for regret at some things. Different Accounts are given of the Insult offered to young Hogg, and a Justice of the Peace prevented their going further.

I think day and night of you & my lovely Annie. Say ten thousand tender things for me to her. I hope to see a few more teeth, & hear a few more words from her on my return. You will be good enough not to lose any oppportunity of writing to me at Halifax. I beg to be most affectionately remembered to your Sister & her Family, your Brother's, Mrs. Dawson's &c—God grant I may find you all well—Kiss Annie once, twice—a hundred times for me. And believe me, my dear Hannah ever

Most Affectionately yours

Ja. Iredell.

P. S. I can't possibly write to Nelly now.

RC, Johnson Collection, NCSA. Printed, McRee, 2:158-159. Addressed "Mrs. Iredell Edenton."

---

[1]John Moore of Orange County. *Heads of Families, 1790 Census*, 96. For more information on Moore's case, see JI to John Moore, August 30, 1787, in this volume.

[2]See William Hooper to JI, January 22, 1787, n. 2, in this volume.

[3]See William Hooper to JI, March 1, 1787, in this volume.

[4]Walter Alves married Amelia Johnston (d. 1827), daughter of William and Ann Johnston, on May 11, 1787. Alves was the son of James Hogg. His surname had been changed in 1786. *Life and Times of James Hogg*, 20, 21, 37. See also William Hooper to JI, September 8, 1784, n. 3, in this volume.

From Henry E. McCulloh

No. 71 Newman street, London, 10th. April 1787.

Dear Sir,

I am favd. with your letter of the 24th. of Jany., & am much obliged to you, for your anxious Concern as to the important Certificates I request. It is true, I have wrote Mr. Frohock full 100 letters; it is equally so, I have never recd. a single line from him since July <u>1774</u>,—so, that you see,—my expectations from him, are <u>hopeless</u>—My great dependance is on Ben. Mc.Culloch, (for whose Situation, I feel the most anxious Concern.) He has been so kind as to send me Dupls. of all the Confiscation—acts, under Seal; these establish the general point of the Confiscation;—but the information & Certificates—<u>requisite</u> for <u>my particular case</u>—are, Certifs.—proofs, & information of <u>the Sales</u> of my late lands in your

State,—as far as they can be possibly got,—and the best information, how the remainder is situated, and become lost—The Certificate BMC. sent me, was an Extract from the Secys. Office, (very properly certified, & under Seal,)—of the Sales of some of my lands in Rowan, Guilford, Randolph, & Orange Counties, returned to that office, to the 20th. of Nov. 1786, to the amot. of 47,000 acres, which is not much more than the half of the lands I held in those 4 Counties:—the remainder must be, either not sold, and left out on the new Surveys, (a fact of great importance to me, to have ascertained, in the best manner possible)—or the Sales not returned.—I held near 140,000 acres in your State, when my Property was confd.—full 60,000 acres in Wake, Chatham, Johnston, Granville, Anson, Meclenburgh, Duplin, & Bertie Counties, of wch. no returns of Sales are contained in the Certificate sent me by BMC.—& no proper information of what has been done with these lands since the Confiscation, has yet reached me; so that without I receive further Certifs. & information on this subject, it might probably do me harm to lay the certificate I have recd. from BMC. before the Board here, as the proof wod. appear so inadequate to the Loss claimed;—and I therefore lay it by, & reserve it in hopes of recg. further proofs & information to accompany it.—I wrote BMC. the 28th. Ulto. so fully, & plainly of all the further particulars wanted from the Westward, that thro' his kindness, I trust, I shall certainly, obtain them.[1]—The particulars, which with your leave, I beg you will kindly take the trouble to procure & send me, are,—1st.—Certificate under Seal,—(a Notorial one I shod. think wod. do, for so small a quantity) of the Sale of the Indian land:—2dly—a Certife. or Certs. from Mr. Glasgow, under the State-Seal, of all Sales of any of my lands, returned to the Office since the 20th. of Nov. 1786, brought down to as low a period as possible, so as to reach me here, by this time twelve months,—certainly, not later, as the Commission here, will certainly close in May 1788 for ever,—and their final reports—probably made up, a month before—Be pleased to obtain & forward this Cert. to me,—the same as if I had not writ BMC.—as I wish Dupls. at least, to be forwarded—If you are at the Assembly, you will be kind enough to procure them, yourself, —if not, instruct some friend to do so, & forward it with other papers to the Care of Mr. Stott at Suffolk, & on whose further care of it, I can depend.[2]—The Importance of these Vouchers to me, (every acre wherein, may tell in my Compensation)—will readily strike a Man of your Judgment, and knowledge in business:—& I beg leave firmly to rely on receiving the abovementd. Certifs. from your hands, & <shall> Mr. Stott, shall pay you the Expences.

I am also to beg the favor of you to send me as abovementd.—the receits, proofs & proceedings you mention, relative to all the monies recd. or recovered by the Children of the late Secy. Henry Mc.Culloch of or from me, my Agents, or Property,—certified & proven in the best manner before a Notary, or as you judg best:—Also an Accot. stated by yourself of the Proc monies you recd. from Mr. Mc.Gwire &, Mr. Frohock in consequence of my bills on them in your favor, drawn in 1776,—and how the same was applied by you,—and if you please, be so good as to attest the Same, as without the best proofs, I shall lose all this money advanced by me,—and if I receive proofs, I shall be able to compell payment, and therefore I beg leave to depend on your forwarding every proof, and paper you can to me, in the fullest manner, & please inclose a few lines with your letters to Mr. Stott, begging him to forward them by some Captain or other person who will deliver them into my hands,—as the charge of Postage, is excessive high.

I am glad to hear from you, such good accots. of George's behaviour & Application. I beg leave to refer you to a letter I write him of this date, & that you will do me the justice to beleive, I do not wish or mean you shod. be at any expence on his accot.—Your friendship, Protection, & superintendance, is all I request of you for him, and I urge him to do every thing in his power to merit your favor—In limiting his board & Lodging not to exceed 25 a year Sterl. & 5 for his pocket Expences, I was advised by Hamilton, Martin & others here, I had done it on very liberal, & sufficient Terms;[3]—however if his Necessary & unavoidable Expences /must/ exceed that Sum, I must pay it,—and all I will now add is, that I intreat you to keep them within the closest bounds possible, & to write me fully and particularly on this subject,—and you will please from time to time, to draw upon Mr. Stott to furnish you Currency to pay the Year's expences incurred,—and I shod. suppose I cannot desire you to apply for this purpose to any Gentleman more convenient, & agreable to You;—and I pray you to controul this matter as close as you can;—as my Circumstances still continue very narrow, tho' I trust I have considerable hopes at no great distance, if I receive in time, the Certs. papers & informs. I request from you, & BMC.

I pray you to write Harry Montfort concerning his father's protested bill taken up by Allen, Marlow & Co. paid in 1773, & sent out to you & Mr. Johnston,—if only to make a demand:—I have letters from him writ in 1783 & 4 promising paymt. which he never performed.[4]—Pray write me whether you wod. have any objections to bring an Action on the protested bill—and to furnish me the Proceedings under Seal.—I was authd. to offer Harry Montfort, very good Terms,—and if he wod. even pay the Principal by Installments,—the Interest & Protest wod. be given up. I pray you write him at least, & forwd. me his answer.

I am, and have been for a long time, in a very indifferent State of Health. let me depend on your kindness, and on hearing often from You; and give me leave to present You, & Yours, with my best wishes & to write myself Your old, sincere, & affectionate friend, Henry E. Mc.Culloh.

RC, Johnson Collection, NCSA. Addressed "James Iredell Esqr. Edenton, North Carolina."

---

[1]McCulloh wanted these certificates as evidence to support his petition to the British Loyalist commission. After filing claims for £54,265, he received £11,747, the greatest amount given to any individual from North Carolina. DeMond, *Loyalists*, 207. For details on the certificates of the sale of McCulloh's land, see Loyalist Claim of Henry E. McCulloh, State Archives.

[2]This is probably a reference to Watson Stott of the Upper Parish of Nansemond County, Virginia. Netti Schreiner-Yantis and Florence Speakman Love, *The State Census of 1784/5, The 1788 Land Tax Lists, Insolvent Lists & Legislative Petitions for Nansemond County, Virginia* (Springfield, Va.: Genealogical Books in Print, 1987), 1329.

[3]John Hamilton was a wealthy merchant and land speculator in Virginia and North Carolina. A Loyalist, he organized and commanded the Royal North Carolina Regiment during the Revolution. After the war he moved to London and successfully sought payment from the British government for his losses in America. Martin was probably either Angus Martin, who served in the British army and fled to England in 1783, or John Martin of Cumberland County, who served with Loyalist forces and went to England in 1784. *DNCB*, s.v. "Hamilton, John"; Palmer, *Biographical Sketches*, 588-589.

[4]Henry Montford's father, Joseph, was selected in 1771 to serve on a committee to oversee North Carolina's British interests. Henry E. McCulloh was the committee's agent in England. Ashe, Weeks, and Van Noppen, *Biographical History*, 6:377-378.

To Hannah Iredell

Halifax April 14th. 1787.

My dear Hannah,

I wrote you twice yesterday, and Nelly once, and have nothing to add but that I continue quite well, and your Brother is tolerable, tho' much plagued with the pain in his arm. Tom is very well. We tried Blake Baker's Cause yesterday, but the Judges being divided in opinion we agreed to withdraw a Juror.[1] It seemed generally agreed, that he would be entitled to the Land, but there were doubts about the mode.

Give my tenderest love to Annie. And remember me to your Sister & her Family. I really have not time to write to Nelly now. Remember me also to your Brother's & Mrs. Dawson's Families &c.

Adieu! and believe me ever Most affectionately yours

Ja. Iredell.

RC, Johnson Collection, NCSA. Addressed "Mrs. Iredell Edenton By favor of Mr. Bond."

---

[1]JI represented Blake Baker Jr. (ca. 1755-1818) in two ejectment suits in the Halifax District Superior Court. Baker, of Chowan and Warren Counties, was clerk of the Edenton District Superior Court from 1784 to 1787. Later he was state attorney general (1794-1803), a member of the house of commons (1807), and a superior court judge (1808, 1818). Legal Fee Books, vol. 7, James Iredell Papers, Southern Historical Collection; *DNCB*, s.v. "Baker, Blake, Jr."; Minutes of the Edenton District Superior Court, 1782-1790, State Archives. See also JI to Hannah Iredell, October 25, 1789, in this volume.

To Hannah Iredell

Halifax April 21st. 1787.

My dear Hannah,

I wrote to you and Nelly already this morning by Capt. Fuet, who was so obliging to acquaint me of his intention to leave Town this morning. I understood he was going to Edenton very soon after his arrival at Windsor; and as Mr. Pegrinnant may be taken out of the direct road by business I considered that that would probably be the most early opportunity. I am quite well. Your Brother, I think, is as much so as usual, but still continues troubled with the pain in his arm. My Brother, and the rest of our Friends are very well. I bought a handsome Sorrel horse, and I believe a very good one at Hillsborough, for £57. He goes very well either with a Saddle or Chair, and is only about 7 or 8 years old. I wish much to match him, by way of Swap for the Grey, but know not if my Funds will enable me. Fox soon got quite well, and I have him with me. Miss Johnston I believe will be very soon married to young Alver. She seems full as impatient himself. You may imagine how happy I was in hearing on my arrival here you were all so well. God grant I may find you so. Talk to my dear little Annie a great deal about me that [*torn*] she may be properly prepared to meet me. Give my love to your Sister & the Girls &c. &c. and believe me

Most truly & affectionately yours

Ja. Iredell.

RC, Johnson Collection, NCSA. Addressed "Mrs. Iredell Edenton. By favor of Mr. Pegrinnant."

To Hannah Iredell

Halifax April 22d. 1787.

My dear Hannah,

This is the third day running that I have done myself the pleasure of writing to you.[1] I went yesterday with Mr. Hooper to Colo. Mc.Culloch's, and was in town from there this morning at a quarter past 6. I got up with great reluctance, but was so charmed with the morning afterwards I could not help reading a lecture to myself, who could relish it better than you, on the pleasures & advantages of early rising. We must somehow or other contrive to teach it to Annie, but how to accomplish it at our lazy house I am entirely at a loss. I left Mr. Hooper in bed, but by an unusual effort he was in town very soon after me. The Family at the Marsh are greatly to be compassionated. Poor Ben is still in Gaol. I have gone to see him frequently, and at times have found the stench insufferably offensive. I am sure it will be utterlly impossible he should survive 12 months in it. His prospect of relief is very precarious. His poor Father & Wife look miserably.—On Saturday night the Spanish Fryar was to be acted here, but there were not 5 Tickets sold at Sunset, so that there was none acted.[2] I am told the indelicacy of it was the cause, and if so I suppose it is very indelicate indeed. Your Brother is pretty well, the pain in his arm excepted. The rest perfectly so. We have fine Rock & Sturgeon to make up for your Asparagus. I count the days now very minutely which are to intervene before I am to have the happiness of seeing you, I intend to return the same way, it being infinitely most convenient. I find you have not weaned Annie. I thought it would be a painful task, & so delayed as long as possible. Teach the dear little Creature to look out for me, that I may not appear a Stranger to her when I come. Kiss her most tenderly for me. I had intended writing a line to Nelly again, but find my paper exhausted. Remember me affectionately to her, your Sister, Peggy &c. &c. and be assured, my dear Hannah, I am ever

Most affectionately yours

Ja. Iredell.

RC, Johnson Collection, NCSA. Addressed "Mrs. Iredell Edenton By favor of Mr. Baker."

[1]See letter of April 21, 1787, in this volume.

[2]*The Spanish Fryar* (1681) by John Dryden challenged some of the commonly held political and religious views of its day. Drabble, *Oxford Companion to English Literature*, 918.

From Nelly Blair

Edenton April 25th.

My Aunt Iredell was unlucky enough Yesterday my Dear Uncle, to get a severe fall, as she was running in to The Room to her little Annie (who had just waked & was crying) & hurt The same Hip which she did when she fell out of the The Chair it will prevent her writing. she says she is afraid as she cannot sit in any position long enough without great pain to write. She has desired me do it. That if Mr. Craven should <leave> /reach/ Halifax before you leave it, or if you should meet with him, that you may not be alarmed by hearing of The accident without any particulars. She has not been able to set her foot to The Ground since it happened, but has had no fever. The Dr. was immediately sent for. he bled her, sent her something to rub her hip with, & has ever since attended with his usual kindness. Your little Annie is in perfect Health, as are the rest of the family (not even your humble Servant excepted) They All join in love to you—it is not in the power of language to express our impatience to see you.

Your Affectionate Niece

H Blair—

PS. Captn. Fuet's letters are not yet come tho' them by Mr. Bond & Mr. Pegrinnant are.[1] Penny Johnston begs I will not forget to mention her Affectionately to you she has been here These two Days. it was after eleven o'clock when I began to write, my Dear Uncle, & I have yet a thousand Things to do before I go to Bed so I hope you will excuse The many faults my letter abounds with—

RC, Johnson Collection, NCSA. Addressed "James Iredell Esqr. Halifax favour'd by Mr. Craven." Endorsed "Edenton April 25. 1787. Helen Blair."

[1]See letters of April 14 and 21, 1787, in this volume.

From Alexander McCulloch

Elk Marsh April 29th. 1787

Dear Sir

I hope you got Safe home and found Mrs. Iredell and the litle Gerl in good health. I inclose you two letters bege you'll be so good to Deliver them as Soon as posseble, and Should be glad you wou'd Speake to the Govr. about Beney's releasement. for it is Certain if he is keep'd much longer it will be his Death, and you Can informe him the propriaty of it, <th> and that maney people Calls out against the Judgment, and the Judges. pray see him as Soon as posseble, at least before he has an oppertunity of seeing any of the Judges. Shall depend wholely upon your Care in this afair. the fine will be paid tomorrow. my best respects to my Cosen and beleve me to be

Dear Sir Yours Most affectionedly

Alexr. Mc.Culloch

RC, Iredell Papers, Duke. Addressed "To Mr. Iredell." Endorsed "April 29th. 1787. Alex. Mc.Culloch Ansd."

From John Burgwin

Wilmington 1st. May 1787.

Dear Sir

If I had looked on you as a Gentn. surely as a Man of Punctillo, I shod. have replyed to your last kind favr. from New Bern Novr. Court—but I know you to be a Gentn. of too much Sterling Understanding to take amiss that, which a Moments reflection will tell you, cod. not be intended to give you Offence, but which you may be Assured proceeded from other Causes[1]—what those were, is not at present Material. When I have the pleasure to see you here, I will explain all those matters—But the Seeing <of> you at the next Sup. Court, is the Material Matter to me—On this Subject I have already said as much as is necessary between Men of real Honr. & a Sense of feeling, to Induce you to come forward, in the Defence of Innocence & a distressed, yet, worthy family—In short, Notwithstanding your New Punctillo, with respect to your Brother Lawyers, I must be allowed to say that I now & then peep thror. as Impartial a Glass as any of you, And that I perceive things in a different light than you appear to conceive them to be;—I do boldly Affirm that I am not that Obnoxious Character you have been persuaded to believe me—I Assert that the Voice of the People at large, are with me, I have lived among them 36 years, they are Acquainted with my Good, & bad qualities;—they have Observed & are Sensible how Cruelly & how treacherously I have been treated, by those I have deserved better usage from; And except Interested and designing Men, None will Injure me: but alass—I want a Man of uninterested Views & of Integrity to speak out for me & to represent me as I realy am—not what Speculators & Confiscated property Purchasers, would represent me—you will find you will be Attended to, with ecclat, And I can venture to say you will receive more public as well as self applause than you have yet experienced—But I may yet be deceived, tho' my own Mind clears me of Deception I trust to that good Providence which brings about all things right, in his own good time, and on him I rest

with Affte. regard D. Sir Your Mo. Obed Servt.

Jo. Burgwin

this Letter is a Letter Of Privacy Between Men of Honr & is wrote in Confidence Mr Iredell you have no conception of the base manner I have been treated.

RC, Iredell Papers, Duke.

[1]Punctillo, in this case, means a fussy formality. *OED*, s.v. "punctillo."

Whitmel Hill[1] to Messrs. Johnston & Iredale

11 May 1787.

Gentn.

The uncommon fate of my Suit vs. Seawell gives me real Concern, and expect, there may possibly be a new Tryal obtained or perhaps the matter be carried to a Court of Chancery, but if the present Judgment be given up, & his Estate be then at his Disposal I may probably lose the whole, but perhaps as there is a Judgment obtained it will fix his Land, altho the Enquiry be continued /on/ to Chancery;[2] I wish to know, as my Judgment took place before Stanleys, whether his Land is already fixed so that Stanleys Execution cant be levied on it in preference to mine, provided the Sherriff is disposed to do it, and whether it be necessary that my Execution be actually levied to stop any other Demand that may come against his Land, & whether the Sherriff is obliged to levy and sell as soon as I deliver him the Execution, or whether he may at his Option withhold the levying, with an Assurance from Seawell that the Money shall be ready by October Court,[3] if I could compel the Sherriff to levy & sell after ten Days Notice for ready Money, I expect it might be in my power to purchase his property to great Advantage, so as in some degree to make up my Loss at least partially. I am told the Sherriff is in Friendship with him, and a Scoundrell of course—

I have wrote a Letter to the Judges on the Subject open for yr. perusal before delivery, I have summoned all my Hypocrisy on the occasion, for I most cordially despise the Puppies, and have likewise wrote a species of Address to them which when put in proper order & corrected, I wish to put into the Press, provided you are of Opinion that they cannot punish me for it, as probably they will deem it a Libel, and harrass me severely for delivering those Sentiments of them, which I believe all the good men in the State heartily concur with me in Opinion respecting those Monsters in Power—

If they are disposed to afford me another Hearing I shall suppress the ps. for the Press of [*c*]ourse, but if not, I shall feel a great propensity to expose them to the World, and am in earnest to endeavor their Removal at the ensuing Assembly: I wish you could be elected, surely your Enemies are a blind stupid set, that wish Damnation to their Country; I wish I knew who was most pointedly against you, I would take some pains to set them right, I expect it is within your own Town—

from Gentn. yr. most Obdt. hml. Sert.

Whitmell Hill

RC, Johnson Collection, NCSA. Printed, McRee, 2:159. Addressed "Messrs. Johnston & Iredale Edenton." Endorsed "May 11th. 1787. Whitmell Hill. Ansd."[4]

---

[1]Whitmel Hill (1743-1797) of Martin County was a wealthy planter and shipowner. He was a militia officer and held numerous political posts, which included serving in the Continental Congress, state senate, and on the Council of State. After the war, he actively supported internal improvements in Martin County. *PJI*, 2:82n; *DNCB*, s.v. "Hill, Whitmel."

[2]JI represented Whitmel Hill in his lawsuit against Benjamin Seawell in the Halifax District Superior Court. Hill's suit was terminated, but the reason has not been determined. Iredell Fee Books, vol. 6, James Iredell Papers, Southern Historical Collection. For more information on this suit, see JI to Whitmel Hill, May 1787, in this volume.

Benjamin Seawell (1741-1821) of Bute and Franklin Counties served in the Provincial Congress (1776) and the state senate (1777, 1779). During the Revolution, he was an officer in the militia. *DNCB*, s.v. "Seawell, Benjamin."

[3]John Wright Stanly (1742-1789) of New Bern was a merchant who, during the Revolution, supplied the Continental army and sent privateers against the British. After the war he continued his shipping business and became a distiller. *DNCB*, s.v. "Stanly, John Wright."

On October 22, 1787, Stanly received a promissory note from Benjamin Seawell for £63 14s. 4½d., perhaps to satisfy the judgment mentioned in this letter. Stanly sued to collect on the note, and asked for £140 to cover the debt and damages. In November 1788, he was awarded £67 4s. 5½d., which was the original amount plus interest. Seawell was also assessed £7 14s. in court costs. New Bern District Superior Court, Civil Action Papers, 1785-1788, State Archives.

[4]See JI to Whitmel Hill, May 1787, in this volume.

To Hannah Iredell

Newbern May 23. 1787.

My dear Hannah,

It is with extreme pleasure I acknowledge your letter of the 20th. God be praised my Annie is so well. I wish you had been more particular about yourself. I was led into a strange embarrassment, for I received two other letters from you that I could make nothing of, until I recollected those that had miscarried last November, for these were of that date. I really was frightened at first. Your Brother and I, and the rest of us went to the Play (the Miser) last night, and I never was so disgusted in my life.[1] They are a most execrable set, infinitely worse than ours, and the great Mr. Smith appeared to me the greatest Blockhead I ever saw. This opinion was pretty general and the place was a most abominable one. One half the audience could neither hear nor see.[2] Your Brother, I think, is much better than he was, and I suffer only from fatigue. From 9 to 6 are our usual hours. My cold is much better.

I am sorry I must write so abruptly, as I only received the letter past 8, and the Mail is to be made up tonight. Continue your goodness in writing to me. I thank my dearest Annie for her kind Enquiries. Impress my gratitude with most tender kisses. Remember me with great affection to our Family, and believe me, my dear Hannah, ever

Most affectionately yours

Ja. Iredell.

RC, Johnson Collection, NCSA.

---

[1]*The Miser* is a comedy by Henry Fielding based on Molière's *L'Avare*. The play premiered at the Drury Lane Theater in London on February 17, 1733, and

was produced repeatedly throughout the eighteenth century. Martin C. Battestin, *A Henry Fielding Companion* (Westport, Conn.: Greenwood Press, 2000), 182-183.

[2]A few traveling troupes of actors performed in New Bern before the Revolution, but their numbers increased after the war, with most coming from Charleston. The professional performances inspired local amateurs, and the founding of hometown thespian societies often followed in a touring company's wake. For more information on the theater in early New Bern, see Alonzo Thomas Dill Jr., "Eighteenth Century New Bern: A History of the Town and Craven County, 1700-1800," part 8, "New Bern at Century's End," *North Carolina Historical Review* 23 (October 1946): 524-529.

To Hannah Iredell

Newbern May 27th. 1787.

My dear Hannah,

I had the pleasure of hearing by my Brother's letter the last Post, that you were all well—I am much obliged by Nelly's wishing me not to go to Wilmington, and am pretty well persuaded that will be the case. For a day or two I was a little troubled with a feverish Complaint, but a little Rhubarb & Magnesia set me to rights again. I cough a little yet, but not so much as I did. On Saturday Evening the Spanish Fryar was acted here, and two of the actors (Kidd & Mc.Grath) fought behind the Scenes, which were soon filled by a vast number of People. The Curtain was down when the Fight began. I forgot to tell you that young Alver [*and*] his Girl ran off & were married at a Mr. Hall's near Hillsborough. Their own doors were shut upon them on their return, and they are now at Mr. Hooper's. Previous to their going off however he had applied in person <however>, pursuant to our recommendation, to Mr. Williams of Chatham to draw a Marriage Settlement, but he refused to do it as he thought it could not be valid when both Parties were under age.[1]

Apologise to my Brother for my not writing to him. I have just slipped out of Court for a few minutes, but must return again. I am very impatient for this night's post. God grant I may hear well by it. I dread almost, & yet wish to hear about Annie's weaning. Tell her I will kiss her in a few days myself, and in the mean time she must accept of some from you. Give my love & respects to all the rest—Your Brother is very well. I assure you much better, I think, than when he came here.

Adieu! my dear Hannah & be assured I am Most affectionately yours

Ja. Iredell.

RC, Johnson Collection, NCSA.

[1]John Williams (d. 1816), a native of London and resident of Pittsboro, began practicing law in North Carolina in 1785. Wade Hampton Hadley, Doris Goerch Horton, and Nell Craig Strowd, *Chatham County, 1771-1971*, 2d ed. (Durham, N.C.: Moore Publishing, 1976), 421; Neal, *Abstracts of Vital Records*, 1:539; *Raleigh Minerva*, November 22, 1816.

From William R. Davie

Philadelphia, May 30th. 1787

D Sir

After a very fatiguing but rapid journey I arrived here on the 22d, the Gentlemen of the Convention had been meeting from day to day waiting for the presence of seven States. on the 25th. the members from Jersey attended, and General Washington was chosen president[1]

Yesterday nine States were so represented, and the great business of the meeting was brought forward by Virginia, with whom the proposition for a Convention had originated.[2]

As no progress can yet be expected in a business so weighty and at the same time so complicated, you will not look for any thing new from this quarter—

Be so good as to favour me, by the next post, with your opinion how far the introduction of Judicial and executive powers derived from Congress would be politic or practicable in the States? And whether absolute or limited powers for the regulation of trade both as to exports and imports &c.[3] I [*shall tr*]ouble you frequently and I [*shall*] expect your opinion without reserve Make my Compts. to Mr. Johnston and believe me with

great respect your mo obd.

W. R. Davie.

RC, Iredell Papers, Duke. Printed, McRee, 2:161. Addressed "James Iredell Esquire Edenton No. Carolina."

[1]On January 6, 1787, the General Assembly selected William R. Davie, Richard Dobbs Spaight, Willie Jones, Alexander Martin, and Richard Caswell as delegates to the constitutional convention in Philadelphia. Jones and Caswell resigned prior to the meeting and were replaced by Hugh Williamson and William Blount. Robinson, *William R. Davie*, 178-179.

George Washington, who had retired to Mount Vernon, faced financial and health problems. As a result, he hesitated going to Philadelphia but was persuaded to do so by James Madison and others. As the convention's president, Washington was prohibited from participating in the debates. He worked behind the scenes, however, helping to formulate the Virginia Plan and taking part in discussions outside the convention hall. Alfred H. Kelly and Winfred A. Harbison, *The American Constitution: Its Origins and Development* (New York: W. W. Norton, 1976), 108; James Thomas Flexner, *Washington: The Indispensable Man* (Boston: Little, Brown and Company, 1974), 204-207.

[2]The notion of holding a constitutional convention grew out of a commercial meeting that had been held in Annapolis in September 1786. The Continental Congress did not endorse the idea, but the Virginia assembly passed a resolution supporting it, and other states followed Virginia's lead. In Philadelphia on May 27, 1787, delegate Edmund Randolph introduced the Virginia Plan, which became the basis for the initial debates of the convention. Kelly and Harbison, *American Constitution*, 106-107, 113-114.

[3]The Articles of Confederation did not include a method to determine the separate areas of national and state authority. The Virginia Plan authorized Congress to define these roles, and to nullify state laws and use force against recalcitrant states to enforce its conclusions. JI's response to Davie's inquiry has not been found. Kelly and Harbison, *American Constitution*, 114-115.

To Whitmel Hill

[*May 1787*]

Dear Sir,

We received the favour of your letter of the 11th. Inst. and do assure you few things have given us greater concern than the unfortunate termination of your Suit with Seawell.[1] We thought as the value of the Article in question was unascertained by any act of Assembly, & therefore was a mere subject of evidence that the Verdict finding the value ought to have been correspondent to the evidence, & that this was an occasion which might have been laid hold <off> of with pleasure to avoid the inequity of a Defendant under colour of law. Every argument that occured was pressed with great force & the Court were particularly informed that according to their own standard (the proportion of 8 Shillings to a dollar) an ounce of Silver was equal to at least 9/. <[*illegible*]> But <[*illegible*]>, much to our surprize, we were unsuccessful in both points, in the manner you have heard. We think that by the Judgment as it now stands, Seawell's Lands are bound, whether an Execution be taken out or no; so that any subsequent Judgment of Stanley, or any other Person, even if he should take out one before you, will not avail as to them to your prejudice. If an Exec is taken out we believe the Sheriff is not compellable to levy immediately, but may do it at any time so as to make his return to the next Term, but if by his delay in levying an opportunity should be lost of getting any of the property we think he would be liable to answer you in damages at least to the full value of that property. According to the common Ideas that we believe have been entertained in this Country, it appears to us that personal property would be probably considered as bound only from the delivery of the Writ to the Sheriff, though we are inclined to think that upon a right construction of the law as it stands here it should be considered as bound from the <set> time of taking out the Execn., if that appears, otherwise from the title of the Writ. But of this matter we are doubtful, so that it would be safer in all cases to act upon a supposition that the former is the law, where <a distinction> the necessity of a distinction to the contrary can be avoided.

Your letter to the Judges, in regard to the expressions, appears to us perfectly unexceptionable, but we apprehend they cannot with propriety <receive> /regard/ an application on the subject but in Court. In respect to your /proposed/ Publication, the reasoning & <your particular case> the principles of your case is exactly agreeable to our own Sentiments <[may have]> we think such a publication in its present form might <perhaps> /probably/ be deemed a Libel, and if judged of by the objects of it certainly would be so, and it is unfortunately one of those subjects which with regard to the Charge itself, & the mode of punishing, leaves a most dangerous, discretionary, & to a certain degree arbitrary power in the Court.

We are much obliged by your wishes of our being Members in the next Assembly. No Persons are more sensible of the critical situation our Government is in, or better disposed to lend our assistance for its relief, but besides that the business of our profession. Interests of some of our clients might suffer by our attendance as Members, if chosen, we have somehow or other become so unpopular among People here that we have no reason to think we shall become the voluntary objects of <their> choice, & we are resolved not to <[*risque to*] attempt to observe one [*illegible*] off[*er ourselves to a*] People [*who*] we think [*certain any number of whom*] have taken pains to represent us as unfriendly to the public Interests> solicit Votes, or use any electionary arts, <among People who evidently either entertain a distrust of our public principles, or have [*views*] for some rejection> for the purposes of carrying a bare election by a People who evidently have not a proper confidence in us, or <have> /entertain/ views altogether different from our own.

We are, Dear Sir, &c.

If a new Trial should be granted, from that moment we conceive the lien by the Judgment ceases, and an Excen. at the suit of any other Person might be instantly levied—

FC, Johnson Collection, NCSA. Endorsed "Copy of a Letter to Colo. Whitmell Hill, May 1787."

[1]See Whitmel Hill to Messrs. Johnston & Iredale, May 11, 1787, in this volume.

From William R. Davie

Philadelphia June 19h. 1787.

My Dear Sir

I am under great obligations to you for your letter of the 4h. instant I was agreeably surprised at the unexpected firmness and independence of Judge Williams. he has deceived the whole party they counted upon him as "dead sure." how misterious are the ways of providence. this is the effect of the Fayetteville business[1]—Mr. Blounts case is a remarkable instance of the deep political sagacity of our Judges, and the high and delicate sense they have of their duty.[2] what a blessed trio for the reformation of morals, and to preserve and promote the happiness of a community—so all actions are to be deemed laudable or criminal by their consequences to the society without any respect to the cause or motive—

Among the late publications of particular merit a performance of Mr. J. Adams the American Minister at the B. Court now generally engages the attention of the public; this book which he calls a defence of the Constitution of the U. States against the opinion of Mr. Turgot is one continued encomium on the British constitution, and that unequalled balance and security produced by the admirable mixture of Democracy, aristocracy and monarchy in that Government.[3]

I have nothing worth inclosing to you but a paper containing a list of the members—be so kind as to forward the inclosed letter to Mrs. Davie and believe me

with Sincere esteem your mo obd.

William R. Davie

Pray let me know by the next post how you are and make my Compts. to Mr. Johnston and your brother.

RC, Iredell Papers, Duke. Printed, McRee, 2:161. Addressed "James Ired[*ell Esq.*] Edenton No. Carolina." Endorsed "Philadelphia June 19. 1787. W. R. Davie. Ansd."

[1]Davie may be referring to Judge John Williams's willingness to support judicial review in *Bayard v. Singleton*. Davie was a lawyer for the plaintiffs in that case. "The Fayetteville business" refers to the General Assembly's exoneration of the superior court judges during the previous legislative session, which was held in Fayetteville. Robinson, *William R. Davie*, 166. For more information on *Bayard v. Singleton*, see Richard D. Spaight to JI, August 12, 1787, n. 2, and JI to Hannah

Iredell, November 27, 1787, n. 2, in this volume. For more information on the legislative hearings on the judges, see Alfred Moore to JI, December 14, 1786, n. 1, in this volume.

[2]"Mr. Blount's case" is difficult to identify because of the number of Blounts and their prominent role in legal affairs.

[3]In *A Defence of the Constitutions of Government of the United States of America, Against the Attack of M. Turgot, in His Letter to Dr. Price, Dated the Twenty-Second Day of March, 1778,* John Adams advocates a government with separate branches and a bicameral legislature, like that found in his own Massachusetts constitution. This three-volume work was a response to the arguments of Anne Robert Jacques Turgot, former controller general of France, and Benjamin Franklin, who supported unicameralism. Peter Shaw, *The Character of John Adams* (Chapel Hill: University of North Carolina Press for the Institute of Early American History and Culture, Williamsburg, Va., 1976), 206-207; James J. Cooke, *France, 1789-1962* (Hamden, Conn.: Archon Books, 1975), 261-262.

To Mess. William Mc.Cleod & Co.[1]

[*June 26, 1787*]

Gentlemen,

I received a few days ago your favour of the 2nd. May, but have not received the Proceedings on the Attachment, without which I cannot venture a trial of your Suit against Mulrain & Keegan. The Court is just over, & Mr. Black & myself had a Conversation with Mr. Mulrain, who appears anxious to pay you the ballance he acknowledges to be due, as soon as he can have it in his power.[2] I made a merit with him, as I did before, of continuing the Suits and he delivered Mr. Black a Bill of lading of a Vessell which I dare say has sailed before this time. The Cargo is consigned to you, and Mr. Black has forwarded the Bill of Lading by Post. I found greatly to my surprise that the Writ upon the Bond which I had made out at the Court before the last had not been executed. The Sheriff returned "not to be found." Upon enquiry I found Mr. Mulrain had been really absent the whole time between the two Courts. I immediately ordered another. I cannot tell what proof will be necessary, or be authorised to send a Commission, till his plea is put in.

Mr. Mulrain objects to the Demurrage, alledging that their Letter authorised no more than one Vessell to be sent, that in regard to the first he had made a particular agreement with Mr. Price, to pay for any loss sustained (which he says was not the case), and further, that the promise to provide a Cargo being upon a supposition of a friendly settlement he considers the seizure of their property upon the attachment at Charleston sufficiently absolved them from any promise of that kind.[3] And as to this last suggestion, in my opinion he is right.

As to the charge of 25 Per Cent, I think you never can recover it in a Court. This promise evidently respected a friendly settlement here also. <And> /had/ no consideration to validate it unless such a settlement was made, and therefore all you will be entitled to, in my opinion, will be the difference of exchange between your money & ours. This in a mercantile concern ought certainly to be upon a very liberal footing, but you are to understand that though the current value of a Dollar be 12/-, yet in all legal proceedings it is reckoned at 8/- (a valuation by Act of Assembly making it a Tender), and our Judges will not allow this value to be altered even by the consent of Parties, of which we have had one or two very recent determinations.[4] You see therefore the critical situation in which your Debt stands, considering your chance of recovery in Court, to which permit me to add that your Cause will not be tried by a Jury of Merchants, nor in all probability by a Jury in which their is one Merchant, but by a common Jury probably composed <by> of very ignorant Men, and who knowing nothing of trade will pay little regard to any thing that can be urged to them in respect to a Merchant's diasappointment &c. Such indeed is the State of our Country, that I am really in almost all instances afraid to bring on a Suit for a considerable Creditor, knowing that the chances of his obtaining full justice are in general infinitely against him. In this situation therefore, I should think it most adviseable in case your Debt can be secured, to rely on some accomodation that may perhaps be made more to your advantage than urging an immediate trial of the Suit, for you certainly gain by every Shilling remitted to Charleston, at least 50 Per Cent, besides in all human probability the difference of Exchange in other respects.

I ought also to mention to you, that I am under a considerable embarrassment in regard to your blending the charge upon the Bond with the other Account, because you have credited on the Bond Payments made by Mulrain & Keegan, & they will have a right to insist that those payments shall be credited to the Company Account, which will put me to great difficulties on the trial of the Bond itself, upon which these Payments are indorsed.

You will be so obliging as to acquaint me as early as possible with your determination on this subject.

I am, Gentlemen, very respectfully, Your obedient Servant

Ja. Iredell

FC, Johnson Collection, NCSA. Endorsed "Copy of a Letter to Mess. Wm. Mc.Cleod & Co. (Charleston). June 26. 1787."[5]

---

[1]In 1785, William McCleod & Co. operated at 6 Elliot Street in Charleston, S.C. Hagy, *People and Professions of Charleston*, 6.

[2]JI represented William McCleod in his suit against James Mulrain in the Pasquotank County Court of Pleas and Quarter Sessions. Mulrain was a merchant, and Keegan appears to have been his business partner. McCleod was attempting to collect a debt from Mulrain of £1,870 80s. 4d. dating from May 2, 1785. Because of the depreciation of the state's paper money, the 1787 value of the debt was determined to be £3,210. Mr. Black is Alexander Black, previously identified. Legal Fee Books, vol. 6, James Iredell Papers, Southern Historical Collection; Civil Action Papers, 1786-1788, Pasquotank County Court of Pleas and Quarter Sessions, State Archives.

[3]Demurrage is the additional money someone chartering a ship must pay to use the vessel beyond the time period specified in the contract. Robert E. Rothenberg, ed., *The Plain-Language Law Dictionary* (Harmondsworth, England: Penguin Books, 1981), 93.

[4]"An Act for the establishing [*of*] a Scale of Depreciation, with a provision for Suits commenced for Paper Currency, . . .", enacted in 1783, deemed that "one Spanish milled dollar, weighing seventeen penny-weight six grains, to be of the value of eight shillings specie." Clark, *State Records*, 24:485-488.

[5]JI wrote only the endorsement on this document. The letter itself is in the handwriting of Thomas Iredell, JI's brother and clerk.

From Arthur Iredell

Reigate July 2nd. 1787

We are both of us, my dear Brother, wretched Correspondents, and if you had not the Plea of Business to advance, which alass! I have not, it would be difficult to determine upon whom the Blame might more properly be laid. As it is, I fear, I am the great Offender, & must sue for Mercy on the Score of my present embarassed Situation which, I do assure You, has demolished the little Stock of Philosophy I had before scraped together, & renders even the writing of a Letter to my dearest Friend almost an impracticable Task—Having said thus much, I must give you a short History of It, to convince you of It's Truth—At the Age of Thirty, I am barely existing in a strange Place, sans Preferment, sans Curacy, sans every thing, for I am nearly two hundred Miles from my dear Fanny, & without the Privilege of visiting her; at least such a Step would be attended with such disagreable Circumstances to her that I dare not undertake It. My Uncle writes cordially to me, but he seldom remits—and, tho he assures me he would willingly part with his Property, could he get any thing like It's Value for It,—it is very possible I may continue a great while longer in the same anxious State of Suspense—His Estate however is a large one, & could I overlook the intervening Prospect, I might feast largely on the distant View of possessing what may render not only myself, but you & all my Family comfortable at the least.—Preferment, whilst the present Men continue in Office, is not what I must look for—& they have taken such deep root that God only knows when they will be removed. Such, my dear Brother, is the present Posture of my Affairs. Yours, I hope, are in a much more flourishing State, in spight of all the dismal Paragraphs that are crammed into our public Prints respecting the Politicks of America. Apropos to News Papers, I have made a tolerable Collection for you, & the Moment a remittance from Jamaica enables me to purchase the few Books you desired in a late Letter, I will dispatch a small Box, by the first Virginia Ship. Would to God It's Contents could be more valuable than it is in my Power to make them!—But I must have done with Croaking. Yet I could say much on the not hearing of so long a time from any of You. What is my Friend Tom about? and my Sister too? I am half angry with both of them, ill as I have used them both—However I see a little Mediatrix, who is sure to reconcile all Parties—One Smile, and I am pacified—By the way, that same Niece of mine must be sent over to me, the Moment I have a House [*torn*] [*to recei*]ve her. By that Time Mrs. I, I hope, will [*seal*] other Objects to engage her Attention, and I am de[*termined*] Annie shall be an English Girl. Adieu, my dear Brother. Your Mother is tolerably well, indeed as much so as I can expect her to be in her present Circumstances. She unites with Miss F. & me in every affectionate Wish for you all, and with my particular regards to Tom, who I trust is not only better in Health, but more Sage also than when he left England, I remain, my dear James

Most truly yours

A. I.

Direct to me as usual My best Comps. to Mr. Dawson, not forgetting my older Friend Mr. Black.

RC, Johnson Collection, NCSA. Addressed "James Iredell Esqre. Edenton North Carolina America." Endorsed "July 2d. 1787. Arthur Iredell Ansd. Sept. 30th."

From Richard D. Spaight

Philadelphia 3d. July 1787.

Dear Sir,

Your favor of the 17th. June I had the pleasure of receiving a few days ago. Colonel Davie, agreeable to your request, informed me of the termination, in my favor, of my suit against Campbell.[1] I have as yet recd.

no copy of the Decree of the Court, but cannot conceive why I Should be obliged either in person or by my attorney to demand the money from Campbell on the very day. surely in Justice the Decree ought to have compelled him to have paid the money by a certain day, and in case of failure an execution issue against him returnable to Novr. term. Suppose Mr. Campbell should absent himself to avoid a demand being made for the money on the day appointed? where is the remedy? or has the Court put it in the power of the Defendant, by their desire, to evade the payment? surely not. If they have I am sure Campbell is rascal enough to avail himself of their indulgence. I shall be glad to hear from you on this subject, & shall in the mean time write to Mr. Hawks to forward me a copy of the Decree.

The convention has made as yet but little progress in the business they have met on, and it is a matter of of uncertainty when they will finish. Secrecy being enjoined I can make no communications on that head.

By advices from France we are informed that great confusion prevails there on Acct. of the total derangement of their finances. M. De Calonne is removed from Office and is impeached by the Marquis De la Fayette for malpractice & imbezzlement &c.[2] its consequences has had a disagreeable effect upon the merchantile transactions here. it is said to have occationed a number of Mr. Morris bills to have been protested, to a very considerable amt.[3] the particular sum I don't know report sais from 50 to 150,000 Sterg. what effect it will have I know not a number of persons are interested in the event.

The Genl. Court of Massachusetts have lately passed an Act for raising a body of regular troops for the support of government not to exceed 800 men, nor less than 500. this is strictly within the Articles of Confederation[4]— The genl. Assembly of Connecticut have reprobated in very severe terms, in the course of their debates & proceedings, the conduct of the State of Rhode Island, and have ultimately come to a determination to remonstrate to Congress, and Rhode Island agt. the injustice of their proceedings. I should not be surprised if they were to compell them by force to do Justice to their Citizens (Citizens of Cont.) it seems their laws enables them to pay the citizens of any other State off with their paper money which is depreciated to 8 or 9 for one, but does not allow the citizens of any other State to pay them off with it. their mode of process, is that any citizen of R. I. who is indebted to the citizen of any other State, or a foreigner, may go and lodge the debt in paper money, in the hands of any majistrate who gives him a discharge for the same, and advertises the payment that the Creditor may come & take his money, <while> which if he does not do in a certain limitted time, the law requires that it shall be paid into the public treasury for the benefit of the State.[5]

I am sorry to find by letters from the Governor that the Conduct of the Franklinites is likely to involve that western Country in a civil war.[6]

I am with esteem & regard Dear Sir, Your most Obt. Servt.

Richd. Dobbs Spaight.

RC, Iredell Papers, Duke. Printed, McRee, 2:162. Addressed "James Iredell esquire Edenton No. Carolina."

---

[1]See Archibald Maclaine to JI, March 7, 1785, n. 1, in this volume.

[2]Charles Alexandre de Calonne (1734-1802) was controller general of finance with the responsibility of resuscitating the dying French economy. Calonne proposed, among other things, a centralized national bank, taxation of the nobility, and an end to the corvée, which required peasants to labor for a certain number of days in the service of the king. Queen Marie Antoinette opposed Calonne, and in 1787 he was driven from office by members of the court. Cooke, *France, 1789-1962*, 55, 82.

[3]Robert Morris and his partners, under a contract with the Farmers-General of France, were to supply sixty thousand hogsheads of tobacco to France in 1785, 1786, and 1788. The decline of tobacco prices, the shortage of currency, and the unstable French economy made this arrangement more complex and less lucrative than planned. The affair ended with Morris and his partners suing one another. Morris suffered additional financial losses during the 1780s through unsuccessful land speculation in Virginia and Georgia. William Graham Sumner, *Robert Morris* (New York: Dodd, Mead and Company, 1903), 137-138; Eleanor Young, *Forgotten Patriot: Robert Morris* (New York: Macmillan, 1950), 172.

[4]The decision to raise troops in Massachusetts followed the suppression of Shays' Rebellion earlier in the year. Farmers in central and western Massachusetts, angered over the state's monetary policies, had taken up arms under the leadership of Daniel Shays, a former military officer. The rebels prevented courts from meeting, attacked militia guarding the federal arsenal in Springfield, and horrified the well-to-do. Norman A. Graebner, "New England and the World, 1783- 1791," in *Massachusetts and the New Nation*, ed. Conrad Edick Wright (Boston: Massachusetts Historical Society, 1992), 23.

Article 6 of the Articles of Confederation, while permitting a "a well regulated and disciplined militia," prohibited any state from maintaining "any body of forces" during peace time except those that Congress deemed necessary "to garrison the forts necessary for the Defence of such state."

[5]After the Revolution, Rhode Island faced enormous public and private debt. In response, the Rhode Island legislature in 1786 authorized the issuing of £100,000 in paper money, the largest per capita emission of currency in the country. Creditors who refused to accept the money at face value were subject to a £100 fine. The debtor could then place the payment with a court, and if the creditor did not claim the money within three months, the money went to the state and the debt was erased. This law became known as the "Know-Ye Law"

because the placement of the money with the court was announced for three consecutive weeks in newspapers. Irwin H. Polishook, *Rhode Island and the Union, 1774-1795* (Evanston, Ill.: Northwestern University Press, 1969), 126; Morris, *Forging of the Union*, 157. See also Hugh Williamson to JI, July 7, 1788, in this volume.

[6]After the General Assembly ceded the western part of the state to the U.S. government in 1784, inhabitants of the area began creating a new state to be called Franklin. Despite the repeal of the act later in the year, the Franklinites continued their move toward statehood. By 1787, the situation had reached a crisis. In some cases two people—one representing the state of Franklin and the other North Carolina—held the same public office. The situation worsened when Governor Caswell ordered residents to vacate Cherokee hunting lands. Many of those affected supported the formation of the state of Franklin and did not want to leave. In March, the Franklin assembly made serving in an official capacity for the state of North Carolina illegal. First offenders were fined £5. Those found guilty a second time had to pay £10 and were jailed for a year. As the August election approached, armed bands from both sides tried to intimidate their adversaries. By autumn, the state of Franklin's fortunes began to wane under pressure from North Carolina. In 1789, the General Assembly again ceded the land to Congress, and in 1790, the area was officially transferred to the U.S. government. Louise Irby Trenholme, *The Ratification of the Federal Constitution in North Carolina* (New York: AMS Press, 1967), 56-57; Samuel Cole Williams, *History of the Lost State of Franklin*, rev. ed. (New York: Press of the Pioneers, 1933), 135-136, 161-164; McRee, *Life and Correspondence*, 2:162n-163n.

From Hugh Williamson

Philadelphia, July 8th, 1787.

Dear Sir:

I received your favor by which you were so good as to inform me of the issue of my suits. I was by no means surprised that all your endeavors proved fruitless to obtain the proper value of tobacco.[1] When it becomes a man's interest to do wrong, Judges themselves may try to pervert justice. I hope the necessary steps have been taken to recover the adjudicated balance from Montford, for it would be grievous "post omnia perdere naulum."[2] In this State, the season, which has been rather wet, is becoming dry. I have wished very much to hear what prospects there are for crops of corn in North Carolina, but nobody thinks it worth while to mention such a subject. Our accounts from Virginia are that great complaints of drouth prevail. I think it more than likely that we shall not leave this place before the middle of August. The diverse and almost opposite interests that are to be reconciled, occasion us to progress very slowly. I fear that Davie will be obliged to leave us before our business is finished, which will be a heavy stroke to the delegation. We have occasion for his judgment, for I am inclined to think that the great exertions of political wisdom in our late Governor, while he sat at the helm of our State, have so exhausted his fund, that time must be required to enable him again to exert his abilities to the advantage of the nation.[3]

If the good citizens of Chowan should think fit on the present year to dispense with the abilities and labor of Squire Jordin, and should submit to such services as Mr. Samuel Johnston can render, I hope that he will not refuse to serve.[4] My reason, as you may readily believe, is that some men of understanding may be in the House who are capable of explaining and promoting such measures as may be recommended by the Convention. &c.

Hu. Wiliamson.

Printed, McRee, 2:163.

---

[1]Williamson was the plaintiff in three cases heard during the May 1787 session of the Edenton District Superior Court. The defendants were William Jordan, Henry Machen, George Ogg, and Henry Montford. All of the cases involved the collection of debts, and the Montford suit included a dispute about the value of tobacco. Edenton District Superior Court, Trial Reference, and New Action Docket, 1783-1793, State Archives; Minutes of the Edenton District Superior Court, 1782-1790, State Archives.

[2]This Latin phrase means "to waste the whole fare."

[3]Alexander Martin was the only member of the state's delegation to the constitutional convention to oppose strengthening the national government. He left the convention during the latter part of August. Martin had been governor from 1782 to 1785 and would serve in that capacity again from 1789 to 1792. Robinson, *William R. Davie*, 177, 179; *DNCB*, s.v. "Martin, Alexander"; Cheney, *North Carolina Government*, 791, n. 4; Beth G. Crabtree, *North Carolina Governors, 1585-1974: Brief Sketches*, rev. ed. (Raleigh: Division of Archives and History, Department of Cultural Resources, 1974), 49-50.

[4]Jacob Jordan represented Chowan County in the state senate (1786-1787). Charles Johnson was elected to replace him for the 1788 session. Johnson, like Samuel Johnston, favored ratification of the Constitution. Cheney, *North Carolina Government*, 217, 219; *DNCB*, s.v. "Johnson, Charles."

From Archibald Maclaine

11th. July 1787

Dear Sir

Mr. Rutherfurd sending to Edenton upon business, affords me an opportunity of writing to you; and sincerely /expressing my/ hopes that you have recovered from your late indisposition.

Constantly as my time was employed in New Bern, it was nothing to what I have had to do here. Numbers of plaintiffs were nonsuited, some of them whose witnesses were not above 30 or 40 steps from the court; but if my clients were not known /by the Judges/ (for some of them were favored) they had no quarter. My whole time has been employed both in and out of court in drawing declarations, whenever there was a leisure moment. The equity business, except a very few causes (one of which was determined most inequitously) all lie over, and in such confusion, that it is impossible <that> they should ever be decided properly, but by chance. The criminal business has been trifling, & no otherwise remarkable than for trifling fines for atrocious trespasses, where the favorites of the court were defendants; and heavy fines where the<ir> malice of the Judges was to be gratified. In one of these against the gentlemen who are commissioners of the town, /for pulling down the old courthouse/ Ashe reflected upon me with his usual rancour, & I returned it with my usual warmth; to the great satisfaction of the by-standers.[1]

Upon the new trial upon Burgwin's disability to sue, he was triumphant, the Judges in particular being strongly in his favor. The confiscation suits lie over, and we may be assured will end in smoke[2] I have in addition to other torments, been tormented with the rheumatism. Complimts and so forth

A Maclaine

This letter though of so late a date, was written long since; Mr. Rutherfurd having put off his journey. Out of 240 causes on our county court docket, we did not get over 30. The Rocky point Justices and their adherents are numerous, and they kept possession of the bench the whole term.[3] I am told they alleged that the judgements given in the Superior courts last circuit amounted to more than all the money in the country would pay, & that the people ought to have a respite—The truth is, they and their friends were all sued.

Mr. Jones continues still in a very debilitated state, & has not been able to attend the courts; but he eats like a dragon

The lawyers' letter to Judge Ashe is now ready, & will be delivered immediately—Spiller put his hand to it last Saturday. I Shall give his Honor a week or two to answer, and then send it to the press, that it may be printed with his curious address to the Assembly, & such justification or apology (if any) <which> /as/ he may think proper to make[4]

A M

12 July.

Yesterday afternoon Mr. S Swann was killed in a duel by Mr. John Bradley.[5] Mr. Rutherfurd will give you the particulars—on monday was lost in the river a Mr. Murley and a captain Love, with a negroe[6]—The boat filled and sunk in a thunder storm—a sailor made the shore with difficulty

RC, Johnson Collection, NCSA. Printed, McRee, 2:163-165. Addressed "James Iredell esquire Edenton." Endorsed "July 11th. 1787—A. Maclaine__ Ansd."

---

[1]The criminal docket of the June 1787 session of the Wilmington District Superior Court includes the names John Allen, John Huske, James Walker, Joshua Potts, Alexander Hostler, and Robert Wells—all prominent citizens of New Hanover County and all charged with trespassing. The case against Hostler was dropped for an undetermined reason. Allen was fined £5, and the others £25 each. On November 26, 1787, Joshua Potts presented a memorial in the house of commons asking for the recision of the fines. The matter was referred to a committee and subsequently rejected in the senate. *State v. John Allen et al.*, Criminal Docket, June 1787, Wilmington District Superior Court, State Archives; Clark, *State Records*, 146, 333.

[2]John Burgwin, once suspected of being a Loyalist, had filed lawsuits to recover property that had been confiscated and sold. A 1785 state law prohibited such suits, however. The superior court ruled, as in *Bayard v. Singleton*, that Burgwin could continue his lawsuits despite this statute. Burgwin was eventually successful in reclaiming most of his property. For more information on Burgwin's plight, see John Burgwin to JI, January 14 and March 30, 1786, in this volume. For more information on *Bayard v. Singleton*, see Richard D. Spaight to JI, August 12, 1787, n. 2, and JI to Hannah Iredell, November 27, 1787, n. 2, in this volume.

[3]Rocky Point is an area on the northeast fork of the Cape Fear River in what is now Pender County. Alfred Moore Waddell, *A History of New Hanover County and the Lower Cape Fear*, vol. 1, *1723-1800* (n.p., 1909), 38; Powell, *Gazetteer*, 424.

[4]During the 1786-1787 legislative session, the General Assembly, at the urging of some lawyers, conducted an inquiry into the performance of the judges of the state superior court. One of the justices, Samuel Ashe, rather than attending the hearings wrote a letter to the assembly excoriating the attorneys. Members of the bar felt compelled to respond. JI wrote a rejoinder to Ashe's attack, and eight other lawyers joined him in signing it. JI's prominent role in this is curious. He had not been one of the vocal critics of Ashe, nor had there been any conspicuous animosity between the two men. Subsequently, Ashe personally told JI that his condemnation of attorneys was not meant to include him, and Ashe reiterated this in his written response to the lawyers' letter dated August 30, 1787. Nevertheless, JI believed that Ashe had unfairly denigrated the legal profession even if he personally was not intended as a target. Consequently, JI wrote a second letter challenging Ashe's charges. This letter was signed by JI alone and appeared in a New Bern newspaper on November 26, 1787. Waldrup, "James Iredell," 300-323. For more information on the legislative hearings, see Alfred Moore to JI, December 14, 1786, n. 1, in this volume. The text of Ashe's letter to the General

Assembly can be found in Clark, *State Records*, 18:137-142. The lawyers' letter to Judge Ashe has not been found. An excerpt of Ashe's response to that letter appears in McRee, *Life and Correspondence*, 2:601, n. 1. JI's letter of November 26, 1787, is included in this volume.

[5]John Bradley, a Wilmington merchant, accused an English officer named Tabb of stealing rings from his store. The officer, who had been shipwrecked and lost everything, had been given shelter by Samuel Swann (1747-1787), a former military officer himself and the son of a wealthy attorney. Hugh Waddell, an early historian of New Hanover County, described Swann as "a highstrung gentleman of fortune." Accordingly, Swann took offense at the accusation against his guest and demanded an apology from Bradley or satisfaction in a duel. No apology was given. In the ensuing confrontation, Swann wounded Bradley in the hip. As Bradley fell, he fired a bullet into Swann's brain, which killed him instantly. Bradley was charged with manslaughter but pardoned by the governor. The Wilmington District Superior Court disallowed the pardon. Bradley petitioned the General Assembly during the 1789 session and was granted a full pardon by the legislature. *DNCB*, s.v. "Swann, Samuel"; Archibald Maclaine to JI, January 20, 1789, in this volume; McRee, *Life and Correspondence*, 2:165n-166n; Waddell, *New Hanover County*, 54, 225-226; *Connecticut Courant* (Hartford), August 13, 1787, typescript, State Archives; Clark, *State Records*, 25:39.

[6]The following appeared as an "Extract of a letter from Wilmington, dated July 12" in the *Connecticut Courant* (Hartford): "On Monday the 9th a Captain Love of this place, left town by water in the afternoon, accompanied by Mr. Thomas Murley, merchant, a sailor and a negro: They went in a sailing boat, Captain Love being ready to put out to sea on an out-bound voyage. At the time he left town the weather appeared very unfavorable and a violent thunder storm immediately succeeded. The boat being ballasted with stone suddenly filled and sunk. Mr. Murley, Captain Love and the negro were drowned; the two former being encumbered with clothing against the impending storm, and the latter having one of his feet entangled by a rope. The sailor made the shore with great difficulty. The bodies have since been found and interred." *Connecticut Courant* (Hartford), August 13, 1787, typescript, State Archives.

From William R. Davie

Philadelphia, July 17h. 1787

My dear Sir,

I have the pleasure of acknowledging your letter of the 3d.—I am obliged to you for the information relative to our "vindicatory letter" a circumstance my feelings are much interested in, and which I really was afraid would be neglected untill the length of time would have formed an objection against the measure. The two Great characters you enquire after, move with inconceivable circumspection—This hint will satisfy you,—their situations though dissimilar, are both peculiar and delicate. —

I shall not stay untill the business may be finished. I am sorry it will be out of my power, as soon as the general principles are established, I shall set out—My Compts. to Mr. Johnston and Mrs. Iredell and believe me with great regard

your mo obd.

William R Davie

Mr. Martin begs me to present his Compliments to you.

RC, Iredell Papers, Duke. Printed, McRee, 2:165. Addressed "To James Iredell, Esqr. Edenton, No. Carolina."

To William R. Davie

Edenton July 19th. 1787.

Dear Sir,

I have had the pleasure of receiving your favour of the 27 June, for which I thank you, and /also for/ the Pamphlet inclosed. What Blockhead is it that supposed it was wrote by Junius, for I have some where or other seen it ascribed to him.[1] Though it is certainly well wrote, yet in my opinion <He /the Writer/> /the author whoever he be/ has evidently affected Junius's stile (at a becoming distance however), and by his 3 or 4 times nauseously mentioning him wanted to make the resemblance catch. I take it the Pamphlet was wrote on purpose to serve Rodney, and Hastings, both of whom seem in a fair way of meeting with their deserts, for whatever may have been their successes they certainly have been guilty of the basest barbarities, and England would be as infamous as Algiers if it was to suffer the excess of Plunder to be a cover for its villainy.[2] I am glad to see that Country has still so much virtue left as to hold forth such Examples of Punishment. It may be a means of redeeming its character, and preserving much longer its Constitution and Government. A few more Hastings's to pass with impunity would transmit the name of Englishmen with destation to all future ages, and make the Government the most odious and corrupt that ever yet existed. You may suppose this Writer's supercilious treatment of Mr. Burke has kindled my indignation a little, and I assure you it has. <A Man must be a compleat Scoundrel, to be capable of using such language of one of the greatest and best Men in the world, for none can question his ability, and most I believe admire his virtue.> /The manner in which he speaks of him <serves only to show his

contempt of all decency outrage a littleness, or a baseness of mind; which cannot be viewed without emotion> is so <evidently> detractive from his acknowledged character, that <nothing but the [venom] of Stanly [*illegible*] spits so forth the mere rage of Party cannot alone account for it> /nothing but the utmost rancor of Party could spit it forth/ But the cause is evident—The prosecution of his great Favourite (perhaps Paymaster) Hastings. This is the flight of Imagination, unregulated by temper or judgment, which has drawn down the Reviewer's resentment upon him. This is not a means of giving that kind of strength most pleasing to the Reviewer, a Strength derived from enormity of Villainy, and Satiety of Cruelty and Plunder. It is indeed astonishing, and a thing greatly to be lamented, to see Men of Parts prostituting themselves to purposes so notoriously base. But it is perhaps equally so, to find a Pamphlet, consisting indeed for the most /part/ of very good words (tho' in many places in my opinion they are by far too gaudy and affected), but containing matter <calculated so justly to excite every humane Person's indignation> </so justly offensive to every humane <mind> & reflecting mind/> /so destructive of every principle of public justice & humanity/ greedily caught up as a thing <so> /highly/ deserving of admiration. I am persuaded you think of it just as I do; a temporary Catch-penny to serve a vile purpose, and as little fit to go down to Posterity, which the Writer has the <vanity> /effrontery/ to speak of, as the late Proceedings of Rhode Island, if it was possible to bury them in oblivion.[3]

I am indeed extremely obliged to you for the kindness of your attention to me, and wish I could repay it with any thing interesting from here. But ours is a dead, dull calm, unanimated with any thing but now and then a few Fevers and Agues &c. from which I hope you are exempt. Your Family was very well, when I heard last (which was very lately) from Halifax. Colo. Ashe intends going to New York by water from here, I hear not a word <by> about our Election <here>, so that I imagine there is some such maneuvring going on as formerly. I flatter myself there will be no doubt of your<s> /being elected/.[4] I heartily wish success to the great business you are engaged in, and should not doubt it if less than an entire unanimity would do. But where that is the case it is difficult to carry any thing.

My Brother is much obliged by your remembrance of him, and desires his respectful Compliments. My best wishes are ever with you, and I sincerely assure you that I am,

Dear Sir, with the greatest respect,
Your much obliged and obedient Servant

Ja. Iredell

P.S. I beg pardon for sending you torn paper, which I did not observe till my letter was nearly finished.

FC, William Richardson Davie Papers, SHC. Printed, McRee, 2:165-167. Johnson Collection, NCSA. Endorsed "Copy of a Letter to Colo. Davie July 19th. 1787."

---

[1]Junius was the pseudonym of a Whig polemist who wrote letters attacking George III and members of the Grafton government. These appeared in the *Public Advertiser* (London) from 1769 to 1772. The true identity of Junius has never been established, though theories abound. As evidenced by JI's letter, the name continued to be used in later years, perhaps by a number of authors. Newman, *Britain in the Hanoverian Age*, 383. For more information on Junius, see John Cannon, ed., *The Letters of Junius* (Oxford: Oxford at the Clarendon Press, 1978).

[2]George Brydges Rodney (1719-1792) in 1781 captured the island of St. Eustatius, a Dutch possession in the West Indies. Without legal process, he confiscated merchandise on the island belonging to English merchants, who, Rodney believed, were traitors for dealing with the enemy. He sold some of the goods and sent the rest to England. En route much of the cargo was captured by a French fleet. At the time of this letter, the elderly, sickly, and financially hard-pressed admiral was beset with lawsuits from angry merchants trying to recoup their losses. *DNB*, s.v. "Rodney, George Brydges."

[3]For information on the "late Proceedings of Rhode Island," see Richard D. Spaight to JI, July 3, 1787, in this volume.

[4]Davie was elected in August to represent the town of Halifax in the house of commons. Robinson, *William R. Davie*, 190.

From Hugh Williamson

Philadelphia, July 22d. 1787.

Dear Sir:

After much labor the Convention have nearly agreed on the principles and outlines of a system, which we hope may fairly be called an <u>amendment</u> of the Federal Government. This system we expect will, in three or four days, be referred to a small committee, to be properly dressed; and if we like it when clothed and equipped, we shall submit it to Congress; and advise them to recommend it to the hospitable reception of the States. I expect that some time in September we may put the last hand to this work.[1] And as Congress can have nothing to do with it but put the question—pass or not pass,—I am in hopes that the subject may be matured in such time as to be laid before our Assembly at its next session.[2] This being my expectation, I hope that our friend, S. Johnston, if asked, may not refuse to succeed Mr. Jordin, for surely there will be much need of abilities in the Senate as well as in the Commons. I also think that if he shall be in the Assembly he will, in all probability, be our next Governor, which certainly is a particular object to the town of Edenton, as well as a general one to the State.[3] Two delegates from New Hampshire arrived yesterday, so that we have every State except Rhode Island, &c., &c.[4]

Hu. Williamson.

Printed, McRee, 2:167.

---

[1]The Constitution was signed on September 17, 1787. The following day William Blount, Richard D. Spaight, and Hugh Williamson sent a copy to Governor Caswell. Clark, *State Records,* 20:775-779.

[2]The delegates in Philadelphia decided that with the approval of at least nine state conventions the Constitution would be ratified and in effect in those states. A proposal to seek congressional approval, consistent with Article 13 of the Articles of Confederation, was defeated. Delegates were apprehensive about Congress's willingness to sanction the document. Kelly and Harbison, *American Constitution,* 137.

[3]Jacob Jordan continued to represent Chowan County in the senate. Samuel Johnston was elected governor on December 12, 1787. Cheney, *North Carolina Government*, 160, 219.

[4]The New Hampshire legislature did not meet until June 1787. After debating the method of choosing delegates, the assembly selected four people, with the understanding that the state could not advance travel expenses and that if any two of the four could get to Philadelphia they would be the state's official delegation. The two who made it to the convention were John Langdon and Nicholas Gilman. Lynn Warren Turner, *The Ninth State: New Hampshire's Formative Years* (Chapel Hill: University of North Carolina Press, 1983), 68.

Rhode Island did not send a delegation to the constitutional convention. Advocates of the state's monetary policy feared that a stronger central government would end their fiscal plan. Polishook, *Rhode Island and the Union*, 187; Kelly and Harbison, *American Constitution*, 139. For information on Rhode Island's emission of paper money, see Richard D. Spaight to JI, July 3, 1787, in this volume.

From Fred Ramcke

[*July 1787*][1]

Mr. James Iredell,
Dear Sir,

What distress the unfortunate birth of a Child in my Family by P. H. must have given me is, I supose unnessary to describe, but the augmentation of it by a report that I am the father of it is more than I shall be able to suport. every Gentlemen in town which I have seen lately shuns me, &

their behaviour towards me convinces me, that a general dissolution of Friendship has taken place, & a horible Opinion of my Carracter <is> must be the cause. it is impossible to Express what I suffer on this occation, number of stories are Spread about town of which is no truth, & which renderes my case still more desperate. Mrs. Ramckes distress is very great on account of her sisters Reputation being lost to all intense & purposes, & her distress is allso greatly augmented by the general report in town tho she does not believe nor has the least Suspicion that I should be the father to that unfortunate baby in the contrary she is as carefull to the Child & as attentive to her sister & comforts her as much as possible.[2] is it then possible that a Lady could be so carefull to a bastard of her husband or could continue that same tenderness for him which she formerly had if he had been so base as to be connected with her Sister & she be sensible of his baseness & now nurse the fruit <of> the Consequence of such a Connection. Miss Hardy also her distress must be great undoubtedly, being sensible of a total ruination of her Carracter for ever, but I assure you Dear Sir, since she has been informed of the dreadfull report that I should be the father of her Child her distress is greatly increased & seemes quit uncomfortable, Shedding tears continually & not the least Nourishment can we prevail on her to take. Yet she is not inclined to Expose the father of her Child & I suppose as long she conceales the father I shall not be able to clear up my Carracter & before this is done I shall with the greatest Reluctance make my appearance in any Company Except whose Opinion I know vary from others, I can not stoop so low as to go to every man in town & tell <t>him the Circumstance of my family & were I to do it very little Effect it would have on the mind of som of them, I see no other prospect then a true confession of P H. & I hope we may prevail on her after her mind is a little Settled.

I have furnished Mr. Johnston with an acct. againt Capt Dunscomb favor F. Hardys Estate, who has brought a Suit against that Estate last Court,[3] should Doctor Laines Suit come on I beg the favor to defend them, unless it is absolutely necessary for my attention in this Court I shall with the greatest reluctance appear, & do heartily wish I might be excused this time, I hope your Family are all well Mrs. Ramcke Joins me in Respectfull Compliment to you & Family I beg you will excuse my taking the liberty of writing so long letter to you on a Subject which probably is highly disagreeable to you

I am with the highest Esteem Dr. Sir, Your most Obedient & very devoted humble Servant

Fredr. Ramcke

Monday Morning 8 oClock

RC, Iredell Papers, Duke. Addressed "James Iredell Esqr. Present." Endorsed "July 1787 Fred. Ramcke."

---

[1]The year is difficult to determine on the original and could be either 1787 or 1789.

[2]Mrs. Ramcke was Elizabeth Hardy of Edenton. She was the widow of Edenton merchant Joseph Smith. *DNCB*, s.v. "Ramcke, Frederick."

[3]Francis Hardy was Ramcke's brother-in-law, and Robert and Agnes Hardy were his father- and mother-in-law. By 1787, these three had died, and Ramcke was the administrator of their estates. Five suits against the Hardy estates are listed in the records of the March 1787 session of the Chowan County Court of Pleas and Quarter Sessions, one of which was filed against Francis Hardy's estate by Edward Dunscomb. Estates of Robert, Agnes, and Francis Hardy (filed together), 1781-1798, Chowan County Estates, State Archives; Will of Robert Hardy, 1781, Chowan County Wills, State Archives; Minutes of the Chowan County Court, March and June 1787, State Archives; Trial, Appearance and Reference Docket, March and June 1787, Chowan County Court of Pleas and Quarter Sessions, State Archives.

From William R. Davie

Philadelphia, Aug. 6th. 1787.

My dear Sir

I have the pleasure of acknowledging your letter of the 19h. last.[1] The <u>author</u> of the political review has, <u>poor dog</u>, suffered what I expected, a most merciless criticism—His partiality, servility and prostitution indeed merited no quarter—The temper, dignity and judgment with which Mr. Burk has conducted the prosecution against Hastings, even to the last parliamentary stage of the business, notwithstanding the influence of wealth, and the favor of the Court doe not seem to be the effect of an "eccentrick ill-regulated imagination" but the result of experience and abilities, which reflect a dignity even on national measures.

This writer is often happy in his expression, but so frequent an affectation of elegant ornament, has rendered his stile extrem[*ly u*]nequal, and far inferior to the [*graceful*] and venerable solemnity [*of Junius*]

[*I*] wish it was in my power to forward to you Mr. Adams celebrated defence of the American constitution. I think you would be pleased with it, altho' it is rather an encomium on the British constitution than a defence of American systems.

I shall leave this place on monday next and probably be in Halifax by the time you receive this, as the great outlines of the business are now marked

<out>, and have been detailed by a Committee, the residue of the work will rather be tedious than difficult.

Inclosed are the current news. Major Butler requests me to make his respects to you, and is constantly inquiring after you[2]—My Compliments to your brother and believe me with great regard

your very huml. Servt.

William R Davie

RC, Iredell Papers, Duke. Printed, McRee, 2:167-168. Addressed "To Mr. Iredell, Edenton." Endorsed "Philadelphia Aug. 6th. 1787. W. R. Davie. Ansd."

---

[1]See JI to William R. Davie, July 19, 1787, in this volume.

[2]Pierce Butler.

From Richard D. Spaight

Philadelphia 12th. August 1787

Dear Sir,

Last week I had the pleasure of receiving your favor of the 19th. July. I did not expect or suppose that the Court would or could ordered an execution against the property of Mr. Campbell in the first instance, but I expected their decree would have been in some measure similar, to the one they passed last November term, that is, if the money was not paid on the day appointed, the Clerk should issue execution in the usual manner. The former decree was, "that if exceptions were not filed in three months, then execution to issue &c. there may be some difference between exceptions & payment that I am not aware of, but I supposed that if they had power to do it in one case, they had it equally in the other. I shall agreeable to your advice, have notice given to Mr. Campbell, that I shall either in person or by my attorney be there on the day to demand the money, and shall in the mean time, direct the Clerk to send him an official copy of the decree, least he might neglect it.[1]

The Convention having agreed upon the out lines of a plan of government, for the United States, refered it to a small committee to detail. that committee have reported, and the plan is now under consideration. I am in hopes we shall be able to get through it by the 1st. or 15th. of September.

It is not probable that the United States will in future be so ideal, as to risque their happiness upon the unanimity of the whole, and thereby put it in the power of one or two States, to defeat the most salutary propositions, and prevent the Union from rising out of that contemptable situation to which it is at present reduced. There is no man of reflection, who has maturely considered, that must and will result, from the weakness of our present federal government, and the tyranical and unjust proceedings of most of the State governments, if longer persevered in, but must sincerely wish for a strong and efficient National government. We may naturaly suppose that all those persons who are possed of popularity in the different States, and which they make use of, not for the public benefit, but for their private emolument, will oppose any system of this kind.

The late determination of our Judges at New Bern, must in my opinion, produce the most serious reflections, in the breast of every thinking man, and of every well wisher to his Country. It can not be denied, but that the Assembly have passed laws unjust in themselves, and militating in their principles against the constitution, in more instances then one, and in my opinion of a more alarming & destructive nature than the one which the Judges have, by their own authority, thought proper to set aside and declare void.[2] The laws I alude to are the tender laws, and the laws for increasing the Jurisdiction of the Justices of the peace out of Court,[3] the latter they have allowed to opperate without censure or opposition, the former they have openly and avowedly supported, to the great disgrace of their Characters. I do not pretend to vindicate the law which has been the subject of controversy. it is imaterial what law they have declared void. it is their usurpation of the Authority to do it that I complain, as I do most positively deny that have any such power; nor can they find any thing in the constitution either directly or impliedly, that will support them, or give them any colour of right to exercise that authority. Besides it would been absurd, and contrary to the practice of all the world, had the constitution vested such powers in them, as it would have operated as an absolute negative on the proceedings of the legislature which no Judicial ought ever to possess. And the State, instead of being governed by the representatives in general Assembly would be subject to the will of three individuals, who united in their own persons, the legislative & Judiciary powers, which no monark in Europe enjoys, and which would be more despotic than the roman decemvirate was, and equally as insufferable.[4] If they possessed the power, what check or controul would there be to their proceedings? or who is there to take the same liberty with them, that they have taken with the legislature, and declare there opinions to be erroneous? none that I know of. In consequence of which, whenever the Judges should become corrupt, they might at pleasure set aside any law, however just or consistant with the constitution, to answer their designs and the persons and property of every individual would be compleatly at their disposal. many instances might be brought to shew the absurdity and impropriety of such a power being lodged with the Judges.

It must be acknowledged that our constitution, unfortunately has not provided a sufficient check, to prevent the intemperate and unjust proceedings of our legislature, tho' such a check would be very beneficial, & I think absolutely necessary to our well being. The only one I know of, is the annual election, which by leaving out such members as have supported improper measures, will in some degree remedy, tho' it can not prevent such evils as may arise. I should not have intruded this subject upon you, but as it must certainly under go a public discussion, I wish to know what is the general opinion on that transaction.

Since I wrote you, Mr. Morris has had the satisfaction of receiving accounts that his bills, that <has been> /had/ protested for non acceptance, have been paid.[5]

I am with respect and Esteem Dear Sir, Your most obt. Servt.

Richd. Dobbs Spaight.

RC, Iredell Papers, Duke. Printed, McRee, 2:168-170. Addressed "James Iredell Esq."

---

[1]For more information on *Spaight v. Campbell*, see Archibald Maclaine to JI, March 7, 1785, n. 1, and Richard D. Spaight to JI, July 3, 1787, in this volume.

[2]This refers to the superior court's decision to allow lawsuits to reclaim property that had been confiscated and sold, despite a state law prohibiting such suits. Samuel Cornell was a wealthy colonial merchant in New Bern and a Loyalist. In 1777, after returning to North Carolina from England, he refused to swear allegiance to the new nation and, as a result, was forced into exile. In an attempt to thwart confiscation of his property, Cornell gave his holdings to his wife and daughters. Still, the state appropriated and sold the property. After the war, members of the family, including daughter Elizabeth Cornell Bayard, attempted to reclaim through the courts what had been lost, but in 1785 the General Assembly forbade such lawsuits against the purchasers of confiscated property. The court's decision to allow the Cornells to pursue their claims, despite the state law, is an early example of judicial review, a principle championed by JI. The case is known as *Bayard v. Singleton*, though numerous suits involving a variety of plaintiffs and defendants were involved. Whichard, *Justice James Iredell*, 9-16; Waldrup, "James Iredell," 254-284; New Bern District Superior Court, Argument, Appearance and Reference Docket, May and November 1787, State Archives. For more information, see JI to Hannah Iredell, November 27, 1787, n. 2, in this volume.

[3]Spaight is referring to "An Act for Emtting One Hundred Thousand Pounds Paper Currency, for the Purposes Therein Expressed" and "An Act for Encreasing the Jurisdiction of the County Courts of Pleas and Quarter Sessions, and of the Justices of the Peace out of Court, and Directing the Time of Holding the Several

Courts of this State." Both laws were passed in 1785; the latter was amended in 1786. Clark, *State Records*, 24:716-718, 722-725, 804-807.

[4]The Roman Decemviri was a ten-member commission established in 461 B.C. to write laws. Eventually the commission itself became the absolute authority in Rome. Harry Thurston Peck, ed., *Harper's Dictionary of Classical Literature and Antiquities* (New York: Harper and Brothers, 1898), 474.

[5]See Richard D. Spaight to JI, July 3, 1787, in this volume.

To Mr. Littlejohn[1]

[*August 18, 1787*]

Dear Sir,

As I am told you are one of the gentlemen appointed to take the Poll, & have always been my particular Friend, in order to prevent any misunderstanding in regard to my being put in nomination as a Candidate, I do assure you I neither knew of such a thing being done, or even intended, until later than 5 o'clock yesterday afternoon. Had I meant to offer myself, I certainly should not have conceiled it from you who had been so obliging as to speak to me on the subject, & knew my reasons for wishing that my Friends might decline proposing me again. Circumstanced as I now am, I can only declare that I am undoubtedly highly sensible of the honour at present done /me/, & if chosen (which as things now are I have no expectation of) I shall consider it my particular duty to attend the Assembly so far as it is possibly in my power, which cannot in all events be until after my attendance at Newbern where many causes of great importance indispensably oblige me to go. Being situated in so delicate a manner I beg the favour of you to communicate as generally as you can the purpose of this letter, that none may be deceived in their expectations of me, or from an improper Judgment of my Conduct—I am &c.

FC, Johnson Collection, NCSA. Endorsed "Copy of a Letter to Mr. Littlejohn. August 18th. 1787."

---

[1]William Littlejohn (1740-1817), a native of Scotland, was a merchant in Edenton. He owned property on Broad Street in Edenton and a plantation at Durant's Neck in Perquimans County. JI was his attorney. William Harris Littlejohn and F. S. Littlejohn, *William Littlejohn Descendants* (n.p., n.d.), 1; Fouts, *Abstracts from the Edenton Gazette*, 1:12, 52; Legal Fee Books, vol. 6, James Iredell Papers, Southern Historical Collection.

To Stephen Cabarrus

[*Edenton Aug. 18. 1787*]

Dear Sir,

Though Mr. Littlejohn informed me he had shewn you my Letter to him this morning, mentioning to him my entire ignorance of my being proposed as a Candidate, or that it was intended I should be, till late yesterday afternoon, yet I feel so much concern in standing <in a manner> /again/ in competition with you, that I cannot avoid assuring you personally I had no share directly or indirectly in my nomination, and if it had been proposed to me with any prospect of success I should have been the more unwilling to consent, as my particular Friends who were Members of the last Assembly spoke of your conduct there with the highest respect, a thing I have had the greatest pleasure in taking every opportunity to mention. At the same time, Sir, I <cannot think it consistent with> /am persuaded you must think it would be highly inconsistent with /my duty to refuse Serving in a public capacity, so far as is in my power when really called upon, and I trust you will do me the justice to believe that /I act/ upon no other principles <do I act> upon the present occasion. I am &c.

FC, Johnson Collection, NCSA. Printed, McRee, 2:171. Endorsed "Copy of a Letter to Mr. Cabarrus, August 18th. 1787."

From Stephen Cabarrus

[*Edenton August 18th. 1787*]

Dear Sir,

I received your Kind favour Before dinner, and most Sincerely thank you for the very obliging manner in Which you are pleased to Express yourself about the present Election—Give me leave to inform you, of my Conduct in the business, I owe it to your Character I owe it to myself. Before I left this place Some Weeks ago, I declared in a large Company of our mutual friends, that if you proposed yourself as a Candidate for the Town of Edenton at the Ensuing Election, I would decline that honour; but that on the Contrary and my friends were desirous I Should represent them once more, I would accept of it. I returned to this place the day before the poll was opened and not hearing that you had any intention to Stand as a Candidate for the Town, I most Chearfully offered myself. But Judge of my Surprise, when yesterday in the afternoon, I was informed of the greatest Exertions been made to overset my Election. The manner in

Which it was Carried was more than a Sufficient proof that you was Entirely unacquainted with it and when Some of my friends informd me of a Tavern been open for all friends that Would vote for you, I declared publickly that I was Certain of your not having being Consulted or Even asked wether you would offer as a Candidate. This Sir gave me much uneasiness I thought I discovered A disposition in Some of your friends rather to turn me out than to accept of my resignation.

I thought it ungenerous, it Would be a Triumph over me, I did not merit after the Concesions I had made you, at the Same time I declare to you once more my Dear Sir, that I was Sensible of your total ignorance of this Matter and felt in my own heart that I had never merited the ungenerous treatment of Some of your friends—

I am as ever Dear Sir With very great respect your mo. faithfull and Obedient Servant

S. Cabarrus

RC, Johnson Collection, NCSA. Printed, McRee, 2:171. Addressed "James Iredell Esquire."

To James Cotton[1]

[*Edenton August 20, 1787*]

Sir,

As /I am told it was/ you /who/ did me the honour to put me in nomination at the <last> /late/ Election, without <even> /either/ my previous application or knowledge, I <do> /think it proper to/ assure you /that/ I am not the less gratefully sensible of the zeal of my Friends because they were unsuccessful in their wishes.[2] I should undoubtedly have been proud of so great a distinction, as being chosen without the least solicitation on my part to represent the Town of Edenton, and in that case should have discharged the duties incumbent upon me in that high character to the best of my abilities </so far as my election would admit of a/>. But this was much more than in such circumstances I could expect. I shall however always reflect with gratitude on the <warm> /disinterested/ voluntary support I met with, nor </do/> I think <can> /can/ any reasonable Man </can/> disapprove of a resolution I have long formed & inflexibly adhered to, to be always ready to obey the wishes of the Town, so far as it was in my power, if they thought proper to chuse me their Member, but never to use the least solicitation for that purpose. I think every Man's mind ought to be left perfectly free & unbiased upon so momentous an occasion, nor would I wish to owe to private favour & influence what ought to be the result of a proper confidence, <in me> in expectation of public service.

As I am in a great measure ignorant who my Supporters were, I beg the favour of you to communicate to such of them as you are acquainted with my best thanks for the good opinion which dictated their earnest wishes on my behalf.

I am, Sir Your very obedient Servant

J. I.

FC, Johnson Collection, NCSA. Addressed "Mr. Cotton."

---

[1]James Cotton (d. ca. 1791) owned three lots in Edenton valued at £500 in 1788. Estate of James Cotton, 1791, Chowan County Estates, State Archives; *Chowan County Taxables, 1788* (Edenton, N.C.: Robert Bland Smith Sr. and Grayson Hamilton Harding, 1964), 2.

[2]In an election held August 18, 1787, Stephen Cabarrus defeated JI to be re-elected as Edenton's representative in the house of commons. Cheney, *North Carolina Government*, 220.

From James Cotton

[*Edenton August 20th, 1787*]

Sir

In Answer to your very Polite Letter, permit me to Address you, in the following Lines. The Day previous to the Election, I candidly made every Effort in my power to the Intere/s/t of Mr. Iredale. not that I wish't to cancel the Opinion of any Voter, interested for Mr. Caburrus to the Interest of Mr. Iredale

Or, Meanly tell them their Interest should suffer if they did not Vote for Mr. Iredale. far from it. Mr. Iredale would have Scorn'd such a Vote. I wish't every Man to Vote, Disinterestedly, as I did myself, those that were neither bias'd by private Influence, party Prejudice, Or any thing contrary to the Dictates of an Honest Heart

The Gentlemen who where so Obliging to give their Disintested Votes, I shall Return them Your Sincere thanks

I am Sir, Your Most Obt. Humble Servant

Ja. Cotton

RC, Johnson Collection, NCSA. Addressed "Ja. Iredale Esqr."

To Stephen Cabarrus

[*Edenton August 21st. 1787.*]

Dear Sir,

I had the pleasure of receiving your obliging answer to my letter on Saturday, which I should immediately have acknowledged, in order to have expressed my thanks for the liberality of your conduct in respect to me, but that I thought you would probably /be/ at that time <be> a good deal engaged.[1] The very polite Declaration you mention I casually heard of, but it was not mentioned to me with the particular circumstances you relate, and which certainly made it of much more importance than it otherwise would have been. I have long resolved, and hitherto uniformly adhered to the resolution, never to offer myself, but never to refuse serving, so far as I could, if I had the honour of being applied to. A Friend of mine spoke to me a considerable time ago to know if I would suffer my name to be /put/ again <put> in nomination /this year/, and I expressly declined it, assigning my reasons particularly. It was introduced, as I informed you before, without my knowledge, and I have had no other concern in the election than in saying (which I thought my duty indispensably required) that I would serve, if chosen, to the utmost of my power, and I took care to explain how /far/ that might be. I have the pleasure of thinking the report of an open house being kept <open> on my account was founded on a mistake. Common as that practice is, I should have been sorry if the zeal of any of my Friends had induced such a step as that.

Feeling the greatest satisfaction in thinking that the accidental conflict of our names will cause no change in our sentiments of each other, I subscribe myself,

with great truth and respect, Dear Sir Your most faithful humble Servant

Ja. Iredell

FC, Johnson Collection, NCSA. Printed, McRee, 2:171-172. Endorsed "Copy of a Letter to Mr. Cabarrus, August 21. 1787."

---

[1]See Stephen Cabarrus to JI, August 18, 1787, in this volume.

From Samuel Johnston

Windsor August 23d. 1787

Dear Sir,

I received your two Letters and the News papers for which I thank you, I heard yesterday from Skewackey our friends there were all very well. Business here goes on very heavily, my Brother and myself are both well. I have heard of the following Elections, Martin, Mayo, Bryan & Smithwick.[1] Halifax, Long, Branch and Dawson.[2] Northampton, Jones, Vaughan & Peebles.[3] Craven, Coor, Spaight & Nixon.[4] Pitt. Redd J. Blount and two Williams's.[5] Beaufort, two of the name of Smaw & Bonner, John Blount declined.[6] Bertie, Johnston, Oliver & Horn.[7] these are all I have yet heard of. A short time before the Election at Hilsbro' our friend Hooper had an engagement with McCauley in which he came off second best with his eyes blacked.[8] I have not heard who is elected for the Town of Halifax.[9] I have enclosed an open Memo. to W Blair if he should not be at Home please to make it out. Be pleased to make my best and most Affectionate Respects to all your family and believe me

Your Affectionate & Obedt. Servant

Sam Johnston

RC, Johnson Collection, NCSA. Addressed "James Iredell Esquire Edenton by favr. of Mr. James Hayes."

---

[1]In Martin County, Nathan Mayo was elected to the senate, and Joseph Bryan and Edward Smithwick to the house of commons. Cheney, *North Carolina Government*, 219.

[2]Nicholas Long won the senate race in Halifax County, while John Branch and John Dawson were chosen for the house. Cheney, *North Carolina Government*, 219.

[3]In Northampton County, Allen Jones was elected to the senate, and Robert Peebles and James Vaughan were elected to the house of commons. Cheney, *North Carolina Government*, 219, 220.

[4]James Coor was chosen to represent Craven County in the senate. Richard Nixon and Richard Dobbs Spaight were elected to the house. Cheney, *North Carolina Government*, 219.

[5]In Pitt County, John Williams was elected to the senate, and Reading Blount and Robert Williams were elected to the house. Cheney, *North Carolina Government*, 219, 220.

[6]John Smaw was elected senator from Beaufort County. Henry Smaw and John Bonner were chosen for the house. Bonner died soon after the election, and the General Assembly on December 19, 1787, authorized an election to be held in

March 1788 to select his replacement. Cheney, *North Carolina Government*, 219, 345 n. 205, 206; Clark, *State Records*, 20:264.

[7]In Bertie County, John Johnston was elected to the senate, and Andrew Oliver and William Horn to the house. Cheney, *North Carolina Government*, 219.

[8]The McCauley in this incident may have been either William or his brother Matthew, both of Orange County. William (before 1755-1826) served in the house of commons (1778-1780, 1782, 1824-1826), the senate (1783-1788), and as county sheriff (1789-1790). He was also a delegate to the 1788 constitutional convention. Matthew, a miller and blacksmith, was a Revolutionary War veteran. Lefler and Wager, *Orange County*, 76, 348, 355; Massengill, *North Carolina Votes*, 38.

[9]William R. Davie was elected to represent the town of Halifax in the house of commons. Cheney, *North Carolina Government*, 220.

From Nathaniel Dukinfield

Sulham, 24h. Augt. 1787.

Dear Iredell,

I am very sorry to hear a bad account of your Health from Mr. Johnston,—the month of June is not used to be so unhealthy, & I shall begin to fear your Indisposition may increase with the Fall of the Leaf. I shall be very happy to hear the contrary. Mr. J. says that Mrs. Iredell & your little Girl are very well. this is some counterballance but it would give me pleasure to hear that you are all well—my Wife is but recovering her Lying-In. she was delivered of a third S[*on*] the 11h. of last month & for the first week, we had every reason to hope she would have been stout & well /in a/ short time, but she has been unlucky & is not yet well. <but> We are going into Kent tomorrow to visit her Brother—I hope she will recover by change of Air, which is recommended—& I expect to be amused with killing Partridges—From Mr. Johnstons letter it appears that the people of North Carolina are not so unwilling to pay their Debts as is represented of some of the Provinces. I wish him to collect all my Mother's & then I shall be sure they are in honest Hands, & that some time or other & by some means I shall be benefitted, but take Care that you receive your Legacys before I get any thing, as it might not be convenient to me after some time of possession to make a Refund, not being one of the most thoughtful & attentive to these matters.

I have never [*yet*] been able to see your Brother. I have not any acquaintance with Mr. Crewe, nor am I much in London. I hope to hear better Accounts of your Health. Lady D. joins me in best respects to you & Mrs. Iredell

believe me Yours very sincerely

N. Dukinfield

P.S. Will you be so good as to tell me how you make Yeast in Carolina.

RC, Iredell Papers, Duke. Addressed "James Iredell Esqr. Edenton North Carolina." Endorsed "Aug. 24. 1787 Sir N. Dukinfield. Ansd."

To Richard D. Spaight

August 26th. 1787

In regard to the late decision at Newbern, I confess it has ever been my opinion, that any Act inconsistent with the Constitution was void; And that the Judges, consistently with their dut<y>ies, could not carry it into effect.[1]

The Constitution appears to me to be a fundamental law, limiting the powers of the Legislature, & with which every exercise of th<eir>/ose/ powers must, necessarily be compared. Without an express <of> Constitution, the Powers of the Legislature would undoubtedly, have been absolute (as the Parliament in Great Britain is held to be); & any Act passed, not inconsistent with natural justice (for that curb is avowed /by the Judges/ even in England) would have been binding on the People. The experience of the Evils, which the American War fully disclosed, attending an absolute Power in a Legislative body, suggested the propriety of a real, original, ·Contract between the People & their future Government, such perhaps as there has been no instance of /in the world/ but in America. Had not this been the case, Bills of Attainder, & other Acts of party violence, might have ruined many worthy Individuals here, as they have frequently done in England, where such things are much oftener the Acts of <the> /a/ Party than the result of a fair judicial enquiry. In /a/ Republican Government<s> (as I conceive) Individual Liberty is a matter of the utmost moment, as if there be no check upon the public passions, it is in the greatest danger. The majority having the rule in their own hands may take care of themselves; but in what condition are the Minority, if the power of the other is without limits? These Considerations, I suppose, or similar ones, occasioned such express provisions for the personal Liberty of each Citizen, which the Citizens, when they formed the Constitution, chose to reserve as an unalienated right, & not to leave at the mercy of any Assembly whatever. The restriction might be attended with inconvenience; but they chose to risque the inconvenience for the sake of the advantage; & in every transaction we must act in the same manner: we must cho/o/se between evils of some sort or other: the imperfection of Man can never keep entirely clear of all. The Constitution therefore, being a fundamental Law, & a law in writing of the solemn nature I have mentioned (which is the light in which it strikes me) the Judicial power, in the exercise of their

Authority, must take notice of it as the Ground work of that as well as of all other Authority; & as no Article of the Constitution can be repealed by a Legislature, which derives its whole Power from it, it follows either that the fundamental unrepealable Law must be obeyed, by the rejection of an Act unwarrented <or> /by and/ inconsistent with it, or you must obey an Act founded on an authority not given by the People, & to which therefore the People owe no obedience. It is not that the Judges are appointed Arbiters, & to determine as it were upon any application whether the Assembly have or have not violated the Constitution; but when an Act is necessarily brought in Judgment before them, they must unavoidably, determine one way or another. If it is doubted whether a subsequent Law repeals a former one, in a case judicially in question, the Judges must decide this; & yet it might be said, if the Legislature meant it a repeal & the Judges determined it otherwise, they <conceived> /exercised/ a negative on the Legislature in resolving to keep a Law in force which the Assembly had annihilated. This kind of objection, if applicable at all, will re[*ach*] <check> all judicial Power whatever, since upon every abuse of it (& there is no power but what is liable to abuse) a similar inference may be drawn; but when once you establish the necessary existence of any power, the argument as to abuse ceases <so as> to destroy its validity, though in a doubtful <manner> matter it may be of great weight. Suppose therefore the Assembly should pass an Act, declaring that in future in all criminal Trials the Trial by Jury should be abolished, & the Court alone should determine. The Attorney General indicts; the Indictment is found; the Criminal is arraigned, & the Attorney General requires his trial to come on. The Criminal objects, alle<d>ging that by the Constitution all the Citizens in such Cases are entitled to a Trial by Jury; & that the Assembly have no right to alter any part of the Constitution; /& that/ therefore the Act appointing the Trial by the Court is void. Must not the Court determine some way or other, whether the man shall be tried or not? Must not they say whether they will obey the Constitution or an Act inconsistent with it? So, suppose <in> a still stronger case, that the Assembly should repeal the Law naming the day of election (for that is not named in the Constitution), & adjourn to a day beyond it, & pass Acts, & these Acts be attempted to be enforced in the Courts. Must not the Court decide whether they will obey such Acts or no? And would it be approved of (except by a Majority of the de facto Assembly) if they should say, "We cannot presume to declare that the Assembly who were chosen for one year have exceeded their authority by acting after the year expired." It really appears to me, the exercise of the power is unavoidable, the Constitution not being a mere imaginary thing, about which ten thousand different opinions may be formed, but a written document to which all may have recourse, & to which therefore the Judges cannot wilfully blind themselves. This seems also to have been the idea of some of the early Assemblies under the Constitution since in the Oath of allegiance are these expressions I, A. B. do sincerely promise & swear, that I will be faithful & bear true allegiance to the State of N. C. & to the Powers, & Authorities /G or C/ which are or may be established /G or C/ for the government thereof, not inconsistent with the Constitution (Act of Nov. 1777). In any other light than as I have stated it, the greater part of the provisions of the Constitution would appear to me to be ridiculous, since in my opinion nothing could be more so than for the Representatives of a People solemnly Assembled to form a Constitution, to set down a number of political dogmas, which might or might not be regarded, whereas it must have been intended as I conceive, that it should be a system of Authority, not depending on the casual whim or accidental ideas of /a/ Majority either in or out of doors for the time being; but to remain in force until by a similar appointment of Deputies specially appointed for the Same important purpose, an alteration should be with equal solemnity & deliberation made. And this, I apprehend, must be the necessary consequence since surely equal authority is required to repeal as to enact—That such a Power in the Judges may be abused is very certain, That it will be, is not very probable—In the first place, in a Democratical Government like ours, it is the interest of every Man ambitious of public distinction to make himself pleasing to the People. This is so much the case, that there is great danger of Men sacrificing their honour to their popularity, if their principles & firmness of mind are not of a texture to keep them steady in an honorable <cause> /course/. It can be no Man's Interest, certainly to make himself odious to the People, by giving unnecessary & wanton offence. It is also to be considered, that though the Judges are permanant in station (at least as long as the Act of their appointment is in force*), yet as their Salaries are during pleasure, they are in fact dependent on the Assembly, few Men likely to be Judges being rich enough to consider them as a trifle. Besides if they are disposed, by a gross abuse of power, (for the mere pleasure of abusing it) to put their negatives on our laws by giving them a false construction, cannot they do this every day with other Acts of Assembly, (few of which I believe are more exempt from cavil than any article of the Constitution)? So that it really seems to me, the danger is the most chimerical that can be supposed of this Power being abused; & if you had seen as I did, with what infinite reluctance the Judges came to this decision, what pains they took by proposing expedients to obviate its necessity, you would have seen in a strong light how little <possible> /probable/ it is a Judge would ever give <a> such a Judgment where he thought he could possibly avoid it. But whatever may be the consequences, formed as our Constitution is, I cannot help thinking they are not at liberty to choose, but must in all questionable instances decide upon it. It is a subject indeed of great magnitude, & I heartily lament the occasion for its discussion. In all doubtful cases, to be sure, the Act ought to be supported. it should be unconstitutional beyond dispute before it is pronounced such. I conceive the Remedy by a new election to be of very little consequence, because this would only secure the views of a Majority, whereas every Citizen in my opinion should have a surer pledge for his constitutional Rights than the Wisdom & /activity/ of any occasional Majority of his Fellow Citizens, who if their own rights are in fact unmolested may care very little for his—I believe many think as you do upon this subject, though I have not heard much said about it, & I only speak on the general question, independant of an application to any case whatever.[2] Most of the Lawyers, I believe are of my opinion, in regard to that. The Power of the Judges, take it alltogether is indeed alarming, as there is no Appeal from their jurisdiction, & I don't think any Country can be safe without some Court of Appeal /that has no original Jurisdiction at all, since Men are commonly careful enough to correct the Errors of others, though seldom sufficiently watchful of their own, especially if they have no check upon them/[3]

Jas Iredell

*I mean the act constituting their Courts

FC, Johnson Collection, NCSA. Printed, McRee, 2:172-176. Endorsed "Extract of a Letter to Mr. Spaight, August 26th. 1787."

---

[1]The "late decision at Newbern" refers to *Bayard v. Singleton*.

[2]For Spaight's views, see Richard D. Spaight to JI, August 12, 1787, in this volume.

[3]This last section, within solidi, was inserted by JI. The rest is in Thomas Iredell's handwriting.

To the Editor of the State Gazette[1]

"Hic murus aeneus esto:
Nil conscire sibi; nulla pallescere culpa."—Horat.[2]

Sir:

You have shown an impartiality becoming the editor of a paper, in the publication of the two pieces under the signatures of B. and C., which appeared in your last Gazette. It is to be lamented that the prevalence of party spirit is so great as to render such impartiality a subject of praise. To a benevolent mind there cannot be a more distressing prospect than that which our country presents, distracted as it is, and threatened with ruin, by the violence of this fatal spirit of party. Addison observes that, "There cannot a greater judgment befall a country than such a dreadful spirit of division as rends a government into two distinct people; and makes them greater strangers, and more averse to one another, than if they were actually two different nations."[3] This picture is, unfortunately, too applicable to the present state of our own country. In such a condition of things, the only check which is left to this spirit, and the only remaining support of the peace of society, is to be found in that system of politeness and urbanity, which characterizes modern manners. This system forbids all exterior signs of angry and turbulent emotions; and prevents the expression of any sentiments which may disturb the peace and security of society. And surely some degree of the same temper should preside over the productions of the press. No gentleman, in a publication designed for general circulation, should allow himself to be so far hurried away by the violence of passion, as to use expressions which would not be allowed in general society; or to indulge in personal reflections, which would be equally inadmissible.

I have been led to these remarks by the perusal of the piece under the signature of C., the latter of the two to which I alluded in the beginning of this address. This production appears to me to be written with a violent rancor, and a grossness of personal invective altogether unbecoming any man pretending to the character of a gentleman. In addition to these capital faults, it is not only a most wretched composition; but, notwithstanding the rudeness of the author, written in a most dastardly and pusillanimous spirit. As to the facts alleged by the two writers, I shall enter into no examination of them: they were public transactions, and are only to be proved by public testimony. I can only express my own belief that the former writer was perfectly correct in his statement; and that the latter has been guilty of a most monstrous perversion of truth. Indeed the author's own violence is a strong argument against him: rage and passion seldom produce conviction; and we are strongly tempted to suspect the merits of a cause are insufficient to support it, when we see such auxiliaries called in to its aid. As to the composition of this essay, it is by no means worthy of a minute criticism; and would have passed altogether unnoticed, had not the author provided some attention to it by his attempted witticisms on the expressions used by the former writer; though, so wretched as these efforts that they recall to mind the satiric poet's charge to dulness—

"If e'er to wit a coxcomb makes pretence—
Mark the sure barrier between that and sense."[4]

Diffuseness and obscurity are the prevailing characteristics of his style. The writer, either from inability to express himself in clearer terms, or purposely with a view to afford himself subterfuges beneath which he might escape responsibility for any of his assertions, has written in so confused and perplexed a manner, that it is extremely difficult to sift a meaning from many of his phrases. But as this writer professes to have taken his pen in defence of truth and virtue, in so noble a cause we might overlook the comparatively trivial faults of composition. Let us see then how he supports his boast. He begins with asserting that the publication under the signature of B., "is the undoubted offspring of mortified pride and disappointed ambition: the sullen bantling of a vindictive, unforgiving temper." What does he mean by this sentence? What can he mean, but that he is certain, the piece in question was written by the Federal candidate, on whom he is pleased to confer these amiable qualities. An assertion so positive he ought to be prepared to support by proof: yet, a few sentences after, shrinking even in his anonymous character from any responsibility, he explicitly declares that he is "unable to point a suspicion." And thus sheltered himself, he ventures to assert, that "a more gross and detestable misrepresentation never saw the light." So much for the consistency of this pretended champion of virtue and truth. I do not mean to undertake the defence of the gentleman against whom his attacks are aimed. His character cannot be injured, though it should be assailed by an abler pen, guided by a cooler mind. For its worth and excellence, private friendship might appeal to public opinion, and to the suffrage of all who are acquainted with it. But it is unncecessary. To malevolence and aspersions such as these

"Let his only answer be his life."[5]

Printed, McRee, 2:176-178.

---

[1]This document is printed in McRee's *Life and Correspondence* between the letters of August 26 and August 29, 1787. McRee indicates that the document was in the handwriting of JI's niece (probably Nelly Blair), thus it was either copied by her or dictated to her. McRee also states that this may be a response to a denunciation of either JI or Charles Johnson, who had recently lost an election in Chowan County. McRee, *Life and Correspondence*, 2:176, 178.

[2]"Be this your wall of brass, your coat of mail; a guileless heart, a cheek no crime turns pale." From the *Epistles* of Horace (Quintus Horatius Flaccus). Thomas Benfield Harbottle, *Dictionary of Quotations (Classical)* (New York: Frederick Ungar Publishing, n.d.), 84.

[3]Joseph Addison (1672-1719) filled several political posts, but he is best known as a poet, playwright, and essayist. His writings appeared in periodicals such as the *Tatler, Spectator*, and *Guardian*. The particular source of this quotation has not been identified. Drabble, *Oxford Companion to English Literature*, 7.

[4]Quotation not identified.

[5]Quotation not identified.

From Archibald Maclaine

Wilmington 29h. Augt. 1787

Dear Sir

I am much obliged to you for your election-intelligence, and am not surprised at any part of it, but that which relates to C. Johnson, who I thought was so popular that he would have been chosen at an hour's notice. But the truth is, that we have a set of fools and knaves in every part of the State, who seem to act as by concert, and are uniformly against every man of abilities & virtue. The lawyers of character are particularly obnoxious to them, but if they can find a profligate character at the bar, they caress him as one of themselves.

I am clearly of opinion that it is for the interest of the State, that certain lawyers should (for some time at least) decline all public business. Possibly they might indeed be of some service at the next Assembly, when the convention-business will probably be considered; but I hope we shall have some men of understanding, who will endeavour to do what is necessary. Happily our Assembly, except where particular interests interfere, have generally appeared well disposed to coincide with the proposals of Congress. Possibly, indeed, apprehensions may arise from the expectations of heavy taxes when the federal government have sufficient power to compel the payment. In that case, we shall be opposed by a nest of hornets, with Tom Person at their head.[1]

I had long been thinking of withdrawing myself from public business, and the conduct of last Assembly determined me. I am now no longer a legislator, and feel myself happy in having thrown off the load, which so long oppressed me. Before I declared my intentions, I had with the concurrence of a few friends, and the principal mechanics, fixed upon a successor—Joshua Potts, the partner of Boritz.[2] Several undertook to secure his election, which would have been easily effected, but secure in their own opinion, they neglected using any exertions, and Jack Walker, who had been aiming at the county, the moment he was acquainted with my intentions, went secretly to work among the lowest of the people, and what with misrepresentations on one hand, and a number of illegal voters, who were admitted when the poll first opened, he had almost succeeded—Potts carried it by a single vote.[3]

J. A. Campbell is the Senator, & Tim. Bloodworth & T Devane in the commons.[4] In Brunswick, where Ben Smith was an unsuccessful candidate, one Forster is senator, & Col. Leonard & Lewis Du Pre in the commons[5]—Col. Owen is Senator for Bladen, a brother of Brown's and Saml. Cain in the commons.[6] Cumberland has sent to the senate old Mc.Alester, & Col. Thackston & Mr. Grove (Mr. Rowan's son-in-law) to the other house[7]—These are all I have heard of.

This day-week we buried Mr. M. Jones, & yesterday, Mrs. Schaw.[8] She had been long declining, & I am afraid did not confine herself to a proper regimen.

I do not recollect any other news, except that we have recommended your old acquaintance, the revd. doctor Boyd, to the American bishops for ordination. He has been some time in Georgia, from whence I suppose he will go to Philadelphia for holy orders.[9]

Mr. & Mrs. Hooper & my brother with your friend Mr. Huske have requested that I would present you their compliments

I am very sincerely Dear Sir yours

A Maclaine

RC, Iredell Papers, Duke. Printed, McRee, 2:178-179. Addressed "James Iredell esquire Edenton." Endorsed "Wilmington 29th. Aug. 1787. A. Maclaine. Ansd."

---

[1]Thomas Person, as a member of the senate in 1787 and house of commons in 1788, stridently opposed both ratification conventions. He continued his fight against the Constitution as a delegate to the conventions. William C. Pool, "An Economic Interpretation of the Ratification of the Federal Constitution in North Carolina," parts 1-3, *North Carolina Historical Review* 27 (April-October 1950): 2:296.

[2]Joshua Potts represented Wilmington in the house of commons for one term. McRee described Potts as "a very shrewd but illiterate Yankee," who after living in Wilmington for several years returned to New England. Cheney, *North Carolina Government*, 220; McRee, *Life and Correspondence*, 2:179n.

[3]John "Jack" Walker (1741-1813) was a planter and merchant in New Hanover County. During the Revolution he participated in the battles of Moore's Creek Bridge and Sullivan's Island, and was an aide-de-camp to General Washington. The General Assembly of 1790-1791 gave him five thousand acres in what is now Tennessee in gratitude for his service during the war. *DNCB*, s.v. "Walker, John (Jack)."

[4]John Ablen Campbell (d. 1794) of New Hanover County served eleven terms in the General Assembly. He was an admiralty court judge (1782-1783) and a

delegate to the 1788 and 1789 state ratification conventions. Thomas Devane (before 1755-1805) of New Hanover County was also a delegate to the 1788 state ratification convention. Timothy Bloodworth, previously identified. Massengill, *North Carolina Votes*, 11, 15.

[5]Benjamin Smith, previously identified. Alexious Medor Forster (d. 1794), Jacob Leonard (1747-1790), and Lewis Dupre (1744-1791) were delegates to the 1788 state ratification convention. Massengill, *North Carolina Votes*, 20, 36, 18.

[6]Thomas Owen (1735-1806) served six terms in the General Assembly. During the Revolution he was an officer of state troops and saw action in the battles of Camden and Elizabethtown. He was also a delegate to the 1788 and 1789 state ratification conventions. John Brown was elected to the house. He was probably the brother of Thomas Brown (1744-1814), a distinguished Revolutionary War veteran and legislator. Samuel Cain (d. before 1797) served nine terms in the house of commons and was a delegate to the 1788 state ratification convention. *DNCB*, s.v. "Owen, Thomas," "Brown, Thomas"; Massengill, *North Carolina Votes*, 46, 11; Cheney, *North Carolina Government*, 219.

[7]Alexander McAlester (d. 1796) served four terms in the senate and was a delegate to the 1788 state ratification convention. James Thackston (d. 1792) of Orange and Cumberland Counties was a merchant and Revolutionary War officer. William Barry Grove (1764-1818) served four terms in the house of commons. He was a delegate to the 1788 and 1789 state ratification conventions and a U.S. congressman (1791-1803). Massengill, *North Carolina Votes*, 38, 24; *DNCB*, s.v. "Thackston, James."

[8]This refers to Marmaduke Jones and probably Anne Schaw, wife of Robert Schaw, a Wilmington merchant and planter. *DNCB*, s.v. "Jones, Marmaduke"; *PJI*, 1:19n; Alexander McDonald Walker, comp., *New Hanover County Court Minutes*, part 3, *1786-1793* (Bethesda, Md.: Alexander M. Walker, 1960), 11, 26; Lennon and Kellam, *Wilmington Town Book*, 104 n.104.

[9]Adam Boyd (1738-1803) was a newspaper publisher and clergyman. In 1769, he established the *Cape Fear Mercury* in Wilmington and during the war was a chaplain of North Carolina troops. At the time of this letter, he was serving a parish in Augusta, Ga.; the following year he moved to New London, Conn. In Connecticut, Boyd was accepted into the Holy Order of Deacons of the Protestant Episcopal Church in the United States by Bishop Samuel Seabury and ordained. Durward T. Stokes, "Adam Boyd, Publisher, Preacher, and Patriot," *North Carolina Historical Review* 49 (January 1972): 1-12.

To John Moore

Edenton August 30th. 1787.

Sir,

As the Judges upon the last Circuit determined, that the prohibition of more than one Lawyer speaking on a side should extend to Suits already in being, as well as to such as should be commenced after the Act passed, I must conclude <any> /my/ further attendance on your Suits at Hillsborough will be useless, not only because Mr. Hooper's superior abilities would justly give him the preference in the conduct of them, but because his being originally employed, and living upon the Spot, naturally point him out as the person to be principally relied on.[1] But as by this means my hopes of recompensing you fully for my fee by attending your Causes to their final Issue are frustrated without any fault of yours, I think it reasonable to give up what now remains due upon your note, and shall be ready to surrender it to your order cancelled at any time. I flatter myself you will be sensible of the propriety of this arrangement, and shall be glad to receive your approbation of it. If in any particular, without personal attendance (which now appears quite unnecessary) I can be at all serviceable to you hereafter in any matter concerning these Suits, it will give me great pleasure to testify my sincere attachment to you in them

I am Sir with great regard Your faithful and Obedient Servant

FC, Iredell Papers, Duke. Addressed "John Moore Esq." Endorsed "Copy of a Letter to Mr. John Moore Aug. 30th. 1787."

---

[1]This provision is found in Section 2 of "An Act to Amend an Act Passed at New Bern, in December One Thousand Seven Hundred and Eighty-Five, Entitled, 'An Act for Encreasing the Jurisdiciton of the County Courts of Pleas and Quarter Sessions, and of the Justices of the Peace Out of Court, and Directing the Time of Holding Courts in This State,' " which was passed on January 7, 1787. Clark, *State Records*, 804-807.

To Henry E. McCulloh

Edenton N. Carolina Sept. 7th. 1787.

Dear Sir,

I received your favour of the 10th. April, and should have acknowledged it <much> sooner but that my health <this summer> /for some time past/ has been <often> very bad, and my business in consequence a good deal in arrear.[1] I am very sorry the Certificates transmitted to you were so defective. I think <it is probable> /perhaps/ it may have arisen from some of the Commissioners not knowing of all your lands, and I recommended it to B. Mc.Culloch not only to apply to Mr. Frohock, that he may give full information if that be the case, or if the Commissioners have been negligent in transmitting their accounts, to urge the doing of this without delay, but also to interest in this business his Brother in law, Capt. Stokes, a very worthy Man who is a Lawyer resident at Salisbury, and attends either all or the greatest part of their County Courts, and I am sure from his obliging disposition he would render all the service he could. B. Mc.Culloch has promised me to do this, and /that/ if necessary he will send a Man to some places for that particular purpose, and tho', poor Fellow, he is still under confinement in Halifax Gaol, he meets with so much indulgence as to enable him to do any business of this kind nearly as well as if he was quite at liberty. You may be assured of my doing every thing I can to fulfill your wishes perfectly as to all the Papers you write for, and that I will by no means rely on any but myself for the Certificates as to the Indian land, and all additional accounts of Sales transmitted to Mr. Glasgow's office, as I well know, & feel with great anxiety, the extreme importance of your receiving them before the allotted time, & not risquing the chance of any further indulgence in a matter so merely discretionary. I will take care also to send you the other papers in the best manner in my power, though I should have been glad <for> /to have received/ some particular directions in regard to the original receipts, as I know no means of authenticating them, or supplying their loss, in case they should not arrive safely.

Upon receiving your directions for not drawing on account of George </for not drawing on account of/> /tho' they arrived after the year expired/, I waited till you signified the mode of payment by Mr. Stott. He in consequence supplied me with £77"0"0. <Proc.> /Curr./ Money <(Current Money I should have said)> to pay for George's board &c, & desired me to draw for the amount, which I did <in the manner> /at 60 days sight as he/ he directed. I have also been obliged to advance <him> /George/ some small sums, which I have charged in my general Account with you, but I do assure you it appears to me he has lived with very great frugality indeed, and it is in vain for any Persons who formerly lived in this Country to form an imaginary estimate of the prices of things here now, since the disadvantageous condition of our trade, and bad effects of paper money, have occasioned so great a change that no former knowledge of <this> the Country can enable any Man to make a tolerable conjecture of its present condition. I intend to <make out> /send you/ a full share of my account <with you> altogether, <so far as I am able to do it> /made out in the best manner I can/ considering my former negligence of accounts, <and send you a Copy of it>, and by comparing it with yours we may perhaps be able to strike a ballance with some degree of justice—George still continues to apply & behave himself with great propriety, & I hope by next May he may be able to procure a licence. In the mean time therefore it might be proper for you to supply him with some of the most necessary Books. I doubt not he will make a very respectable Man. His conduct hitherto has gained him universal esteem, <and his application, I believe, would receive an additional pleasure,

Without giving him too great expectations, /and permit me to add,/ /that/ I think, your frequent notice of him /(without giving him too great expectations)/ would have a happy affect on his Spirits, & induce him to apply with greater pleasure.>

Mr. Montfort, tho' acquitted at Warrenton, is still not clear of prosecution, & by an act of the last Assembly is disabled from disposing of any part of his property until the end of the next Session[2]—I imagine his Father's Estate has long been divided, so that tho' he is in Law liable for his Father's <Estate> /Debts/ to the value of the assets yet I don't believe there is any of the Estate remaining (or if any very little) so specifically the Estate of his Father that he as Execr. could dispose of it without a breach of that law. In this situation therefore no hopes can be entertained of any speedy payment by him. I however will make a demand, as you desire it. I should have no objection at your request to commence an action against him. In this case, you will judge whether the former Power is sufficient <I am told, but can not be certain, that Allen Merchat &Co. have since become Bankrupts.> I am in great hopes, as Congress have so earnestly recommended it, that this State will at length /at least/ leeve the construction of the Treaty to the Courts <at last>.

It gives me great concern to hear of your ill health. But I hope it has long before this been re-established—

I am ever Dr. Sir, with great sincerity, Your very faithful and affectionate

J. I.

FC, Johnson Collection, NCSA. Endorsed "Copy of a Letter to Mr. Mc.Culloh Sept. 7th. 1787."

---

[1]See Henry E. McCulloh to JI, April 10, 1787, in this volume. In a letter of September 1, 1787, to John Cameron of Petersburg, JI apologized for his delinquent response, stating, "I was taken very ill at Newbern, and continued so a considerable time after my return." JI had been in New Bern in May. Charles E. Johnson Collection, State Archives.

[2]This refers to the trial of the commissioners for liquidating the state's army fund. Charges of fraud were made, but Henry Montford, a member of the commission, was found innocent. Nevertheless, the accused were prohibited by state law from selling their property until the end of the 1787 legislative session. Clark, *State Records*, 24:1788. For more information on the trial, see Alfred Moore to JI, December 14, 1786, n. 2, in this volume.

From Arthur Iredell

London Sept. 20th.: 1787

Would to God, my dear Brother, my Finances were but equal to my Esteem & regard for you! The Proofs I give of my Attention would not be so few, & so inconsiderable as they are now of Necessity, for what can a Pauper do?—I assure you I am very little better; for my Uncle has sent me no Remittance, & I have been several Months without a Curacy—When the Tide will turn God only knows—but till it does, you must exercise your Faith, & believe me to be what I certainly cannot prove myself.

I have sent you besides the Trifles you desired Hawkins's Pleas of the Crown & a Court Calendar, the former I imagine you will find a most usefull Book, as it is carried down to the present Day, & enriched with all the Modern Cases & Practice.[1] The latter will tend to divert a leisure Hour (if you have such) & indeed, for my own Part, I consider it as an inexhaustible fund of Amusement. I had hopes of being able to send my Niece some little Presents; but by <Finances> Purse revolted at the Idea, & I was obliged, like the Emperor, to listen to the Remonstrances of my Subjects which, after all, I must <comply> conform /to/. I will positively send her some the Moment I have a Prize in the Lottery. Your News Papers are compleat to a very late Date. I need not therefore upon the Subject of Politicks say one word more than that the Idea of all People here is that we must be shortly involved in a War. Time will determine the Point, & I hope in a contrary Way, for we cannot afford, I fear, to attack another Continent[2]—

I shall write a few Lines to my Sister & Tom, so adieu, my dear Brother! I am always, be assured, most truly & most affectionately Your's

A Iredell

21st.

I have this Moment been made infinitely happy by your's of the 3d. July—I thank God you are so well recovered & pray keep Yourself in better plight for the future—What Business had you in Court with a Fever, Sir?—You should have thrown their Briefs at your Clients Heads, & at all Events have spared yourself a little—Woe is me! Fearne's Book is not to be had![3] I have been with his Bookseller, & he tells me so. The strangest Part of the St[ory is] that half of it has been reprinted these six Years, & no more—However the Moment it comes out, I will secure <you> One for you, &, for Your Comfort, there are to be many Additions—The Dean of St. Asaphs Trials are likewise not to be had—at least I have not been able to rummage them out[4]—I will try further & send them at a future time—In their Room I have purchased two late Publications wch. may be usefull—I cannot, my dear James, answer Your Letter so fully as I wish—but I must tell you that your Account of Annie makes me inexpressibly happy—Positively, when I get settled, you must send her over to me—<At> If the Mountain cannot go to Mahomet, Mahomet must come to the Mountain—I pray Heaven She may continue to thrive & to bless you with her thousand Charms—&—I beg, as She understands English, that You will say every thing upon that, & every other Subject for me—Once more Adieu! I have scribbled a few unintelligible Lines to my Sister & Tom wch. I hope they will excuse— Sett them the Example by pardoning this—& believe me ever

most affecttely. your's

AI

My Uncle complains of Crops &ca., & has not sent me any thing to live upon—Judge how I shall be able to pay off Tom's half pay Debt—I wd. not hesitate a moment if I could—

My Mother's going to America depends alone upon that supply of money wch. God knows may not soon arrive. You are not more anxious to receive her than I that she shd. go, for She leads a terrible Life here, & it is not in My Power to alleviate her Sufferings—but Times may change[5]

RC, Johnson Collection, NCSA. Addressed "James Iredell Esqr."

---

[1]Five editions of William Hawkins's *Treatise of the Pleas of the Crown* were published between 1716 and 1771. *DNB*, s.v. "Hawkins, William."

[2]The United Provinces (forerunner of the Netherlands) was divided politically between a pro-French faction called the "Patriots" and supporters of the Prince of Orange. The English tried unsuccessfully in 1786 to create a pact with Prussia in opposition to the growing French influence in the United Provinces. The Prussians, however, were more concerned about threats from Austria and Russia than from France. In July 1787, the Patriots seized the Princess of Orange, who was also the sister of Frederick William II, ruler of Prussia, and held her for several days before releasing her. The Prussians, in response, and with the assurance of English assistance, invaded the United Provinces in September. The Patriots were soon toppled, and Orangist supremacy reestablished. In addition, the success of the Prussian intervention led to treaties uniting the interests of Prussia, England, and the United Provinces. Ian R. Christie, *Wars and Revolutions: Britain, 1760-1815*, The New History of England, ed. A. G. Dickens and Norman Gash (Cambridge, Mass.: Harvard University Press, 1982), 194-195.

[3]"Fearne's book" could refer to any of several publications by Charles Fearne (1742-1794) of London. *DNB*, s.v. "Fearne, Charles."

[4]Part of the proceedings of the trial of William Davies Shipley, dean of St. Asaph, was published by the Society for Constitutional Information of London in 1783. The full transcript appeared in 1784 under the imprint of H. Goldney of London. Shipley had been accused of seditious libel because of a pamphlet he published urging political reform. The arguments of his barrister, Thomas Erskine, which called for the broadening of the jury's role in libel cases, led to the reform of libel laws in 1792. Ralph E. McCoy, *Freedom of the Press: An Annotated Bibliography* (Carbondale: Southern Illinois University Press, 1968), S341-S342.

[5]In the original document, this final paragraph was written at the top of the first page, above the date. Iredell had run out of space on the last page of his letter and had to return to the top of page one to finish his postscript.

From John Burgwin

Wilmington 6t. October 1787.

Dear Sir

You are entitled to my best Acknowledgemts. for your very friendly & wholesome Advice given me in my public embarrassments for altho' you was not made Acquainted with many Circumstances which led to my unhappy dilema, & indeed was the cause of it, and which perhaps too nice a delicacy has prevented my disclosing yet from your Statemts. of the Laws I recd more real Information than I ever obtained from all the rest of my frds. from your Observations, & a consciousness of my own innocence as to the charge against me, raised surely to serve particular purposes & persons, I was led to pursue the Step I took in bringing the matter forward last Superior Court, contrary to the Opinion of my Lawyers, and it was happily decided in my favour.[1]

Thanks Sir, are but a poor reward to a Lawyer—I have nothing else at present to Send you. My losses by that Cruel issue & Verdict at June Cot. 1785 has been beyond conception great <by> that matter has been the cause one way or other of Sinking, & being plundered I may say, of upwards of Seven thousand Guinays.[2]—it is a true saying "that no One knows where the shoe pinch but he that wears it."[3] It is with difficulty I can at present support my family.

I remain with sentiments of the greatest respect & true regard

Dr. Sir Yr. Obliged Frd. Evr.

J Burgwin

RC, Iredell Papers, Duke. Addressed "James Iredell Esqe. Atty. at Law Edenton." Endorsed "Wilmington 6 October 1787. John Burgwin. Ansd."

[1]See Archibald Maclaine to JI, July 11, 1787, n. 2, in this volume.

[2]See JI to John Burgwin, February 6, 1786, n. 2, in this volume.

[3]"Where the shoe pinch" refers to the source of a problem. A variation of this aphorism dates to ancient Rome. *Brewer's Dictionary of Phrase and Fable*, 1149-1150.

From Archibald Maclaine

Wilmington 10h. Octr. 1787

Dear Sir

I now send you my answer to Monk's bill in the best manner I could draw it, without recollecting what is particularly set forth, except the claim of the legacy in specie; for I have mislaid the copy, and do not even remember Mrs. Monk's name. I think it will be very singular if the court should determine this legacy to be paid in the value of the money at the time when the will was made, as the other legatees will be concluded by it without a hearing; and it will be no less extraordinary if all the legacies should be deemed equal to the like sums in the present currency, without hearing the residuary legatee, or making him a party to the bill. The court having determined that I should answer, I could not attempt another plea, and I believe what I formerly pleaded, did not comprehend what I now mention. I am not a little desirous to defeat Monk, as he has acted insidiously; for having informed him that unless he agreed to bring his suit in Wilmington, I would file a bill against all the legatees, he agreed & expressly promised in presence of his wife's father to do so; and now he has evaded the act of Assembly; for though at the time of commencing his suit, he had not actually removed his property from Edenton district, he was married and determined to live here, from whence I think his wife had not removed; and he has ever since been a settled inhabitant of Sampson county, so that it appears he formed a design to deceive me, in order the more effectually, as he thought, to effect his purposes at a court where I told him I could not attend.[1]

You will have seen at Hillsborough Judge Ashe's letter to the Bar.[2] In this quarter, where we are not famed for any intimacy with scripture, we were for some time at a loss to know who Gallio was; but a New-England man, one George Hooper, found in the 18h. chapter of the acts of the apostles, that Gallio, before whom the Jews brought Paul, was deputy of Achaia.[3] The application would have better suited his purpose, had the

Judges substituted the Assembly in place of Judge Gallio, himself for the apostle, and the lawyers for the Jews; but the fool had not understanding sufficient to apply the text, so as to prove from scripture his own righteousness. Having taken the name of Judge Gallio upon himself, it may very properly be applied to him for the future. It is scripture would have been very expressive of his own feelings, had he <plead> compared the lawyers to Sosthenes, whom all the Greeks (the Assembly) beat before the judgement seat; for undoubtedly, he cared not for any of those things.[4]

Present my compliments to Mr. Johnston, & let him know that there is no copy of Governor Dobbs's will to be had here. The copy which Mr. Gregg had, was destroyed with Mr. Campbell's house by the fire.[5]

If I should without much trouble find the copy of Monk's bill, and I should have omitted any thing material I will send a further answer.

I am very sincerely Dear Sir yours

A Maclaine

RC, Iredell Papers, Duke. Printed, McRee, 2:179-180. Addressed "James Iredell esquire Edenton."

---

[1]This refers to the case of Jacob and Sarah Monk. See Archibald Maclaine to JI, October 24, 1785, in this volume.

[2]See Archibald Maclaine to JI, July 11, 1787, n. 4, in this volume.

[3]George Hooper, a Boston native, was the brother of William Hooper. *DNCB*, s.v. "Hooper, George."

Lucius Junius Gallio Anneaus was governor of Achaia, a Roman province in southern Greece. Paul appeared before Gallio to answer charges that his teachings were contrary to Jewish law. Gallio refused to hear the case because, he said, the question was of a religious nature and not the court's responsibility. Paul J. Achtemeier, ed., *Harper's Bible Dictionary* (San Francisco: Harper and Row, 1985), 9, 331; Acts 18:12-17 Revised Standard Version (RSV).

[4]After Gallio's ruling in Paul's case, a mob attacked Sosthenes, who was a leader in a Corinth synagogue. Though Gallio was present, he did not intercede, again claiming that it was a religious matter. Achtemeier, *Harper's Bible Dictionary*, 982; Acts 18:12-17 RSV.

[5]Arthur Dobbs (1689-1765) of New Hanover County was the colonial governor of North Carolina from 1754 to 1765. Crabtree, *North Carolina Governors*, 38-39. His will is filed among the Secretary of State's Office Wills, State Archives, and is abstracted in Grimes, *North Carolina Wills*, 145-148.

To Hannah Iredell

Halifax Oct. 21st. 1787.

My dear Hannah,

I wrote to you a few lines the other day by Mr. Dawson, who has ever since been detained by the rain. I continue quite well, and your Brother is as well as usual. Mr. Hooper's not being here makes this Court much duller than usual. Gen. Pinckney & his Lady arrived yesterday on their way to So. Carolina, & stay at Bonds.[1] I think they are both very agreeable. I have nothing new to acquaint you of except that Gen. Pinckney thinks the Constitution will be pretty generally adopted to the Northward of us, & he speaks with a good deal of confidence of his own state. Gen. Washington had lately a very narrow escape from a most imminent danger. He had to pass a bridge upon the Elk or <rather> near it, but fortunately got out of his carriage[2]—The horses fell in. Thank God, he was perfectly safe himself & arrived well at home. What a dreadful misfortune it would have been had he remained in the Carriage. I am very impatient to hear from you. Speak of me with the utmost possible affection to my dear Little Girl. I hope she won't object to receive kisses from me through you. Let them be most tender ones. God grant she may have preserved her health, & that I may find you & my other Friends perfectly well. Remember me affectionately to your Sister & Nelly & my Brother, & over the Creek. Adieu! I can write to nobody else. I am ever

my dear Hannah, Yours most affectionately

Ja. Iredell

RC, Johnson Collection, NCSA. Addressed "Mrs. Iredell Edenton By favor of Mr. Dawson."

---

[1]Charles Cotesworth Pinckney (1746-1825) of South Carolina fought in numerous campaigns during the Revolutionary War, including the defense of Charleston where he was captured. By war's end he had attained the rank of brigadier general. An active delegate at the constitutional convention, Pinckney was returning to South Carolina from Philadelphia when he stopped at Halifax. Earlier in his journey, he had visited George Washington at Mount Vernon. Pinckney and his second wife, Mary Stead, wealthy daughter of a Charleston merchant, had been married only a little more than a year when this trip took place. *National Cyclopædia of American Biography*, s.v. "Pinckney, Charles Cotesworth"; Marvin R. Zahniser, *Charles Cotesworth Pinckney: Founding Father* (Chapel Hill: University of North Carolina Press for the Institute of Early American History and Culture, Williamsburg, Va., 1967), 80, 96.

[2]George Washington's carriage almost plummeted into Maryland's Elk River on September 19 while the general was returning to Mount Vernon from Philadelphia. Unable to ford the river because of high water, Washington chose to cross on an old disused bridge. Washington got out of his carriage before attempting the crossing. Soon thereafter one of the horses harnessed to the carriage slipped and fell about fifteen feet. The other horse and the carriage were in danger of being pulled after the fallen animal. People from a nearby mill came to the rescue and removed the harness from the fallen horse, thereby saving Washington's carriage. *The Diaries of George Washington, 1748-1799*, ed. John C. Fitzpatrick, vol. 3 (Boston: Houghton Mifflin for the Mount Vernon Ladies Association, 1925), 237-238.

To Hannah Iredell

Halifax Oct. 23d. 1787.

My dear Hannah,

This is my fourth or fifth letter since I came here, without my having the pleasure to hear from you, which I am very impatient to do. I hope in God my dear little Annie has continued to recover, & that I may have the delightful happiness to find her looks and spirits better. I hope you take care to keep me in her remembrance. Your Brother is pretty well. I don't expect to get away till Sunday, & hope to be at home on Tuesday. We have no news. Mr. Baker's cause is to be tried today, for which I am busily preparing.[1] Tell Nelly & my Brother they must excuse my not writing to them. I have really not had time. Remember me affectionately to them and your Sister & to your Brother's Family. Give at least half a dozen sweet kisses to Annie, & believe me, my dear Hannah, Your very affectionate

Ja. Iredell

RC, Johnson Collection, NCSA. Addressed "Mrs. Iredell Edenton By favor of."

---

[1]For more on the Baker case, see JI to Hannah Iredell, April 14, 1787, in this volume.

Grand Jury to the Edenton District Court[1]

Edenton, November 12th, 1787.

We, the Grand Jury for the district of Edenton, considering the present as a very important crisis in the affairs of America, and being deeply sensible of the necessity of a firm and lasting union among the American States, to ensure the common safety and liberty of all, hope it will not be deemed presuming in us, that we take this occasion to express our sentiments on the subject of the new Constitution, proposed by the late respectable Convention. We believe none can be so ignorant as not to know, and we hope few are so unfeeling as not to regret, the disordered and distracted state in which the affairs of the Union have been for a long time past. No sooner was the danger of a common enemy removed, than the States immediately detached themselves from the general concerns of the whole, as if our future fate was out of the power of fortune. The consequence has been, our public debts unpaid, the treaty of peace unfulfilled on both sides, our commerce at the very verge of ruin, and all private industry at a stand, for want of a united, vigorous government. Quotas demanded which we can never pay, and Congress preserving merely the shadow of authority, without possessing one substantial property of power. These evils dictated the necessity of a change, and the same happy expedient of an union of counsels which formed the confederation, was adopted to remedy its defects. Experience had pointed these out, and we believe it would be difficult to draw together in any country, a body of abler men than the persons appointed on this important occasion. They were not only able men, but entitled to the highest confidence which can be bestowed by any people upon illustrious and successful leaders; and the same patriotism of character which formerly distinguished so many of them in the most trying scenes, was visible in the anxious and deep attention they employed on this momentous subject. A work coming from such men, after such long deliberation, is entitled to the utmost respect, especially as all the States assembled were unanimous, a circumstance that strongly shows the purity of their intentions, their sense of the absolute necessity that a new constitution should be immediately formed, and that little subordinate attentions to local interests ought to give way to the great object of the general good.[2] There is nothing we hold in greater disdain, nor is there any thing more inconsistent with common prudence, as well as the most ordinary share of public spirit, than that we should cavil about trifles when our all is at stake; that we should slight the present favorable opportunity, which may be the only one we may ever enjoy, to establish a free and energetic government, when we now lie at the mercy of the most inconsiderable enemy, and have an union in nothing but in name. We admire in the new Constitution a proper jealousy of liberty mixed with a due regard to the necessity of a strong authoritative government. Such a one is as requisite for a confederated, as for a single government, since it would not be more ridiculous or futile for our own Assembly to depend for a sanction to its laws on a unanimous concurrence of all the counties in the State, than for Congress to depend for any necessary exertion of power on the unanimous concurrence of all the States in the Union. One weak, corrupted, or unprincipled State might in such a case destroy the whole. This evil, the effect of which we have already felt, is, in our opinion, happily remedied by the constitution proposed, with an advantageous addition of a popular representative of the people at large, accompanied with useful checks to guard against possible abuses. It is also a part of the constitution, that we observe with particular pleasure, that nine States may at any time make alterations, so that any changes which experience may point out can be made without the danger of such calamities as are incident upon changes of government in all other countries, where they can be only brought about by a civil war.[3] Nor can we avoid dwelling with delight upon those many provisions, calculated to make us as much one people as possible, and to impress upon the minds of all that useful and important truth, that our strength consists in union, and nothing can hurt us but division. May this great truth, so important for us, so formidable to our enemies, rest upon the minds of all well-wishers to their country, as the watch-word of American liberty and safety! The various attempts that were made to divide us during the war, and the danger of similar efforts being used on the present occasion to make us distrust our best and ablest characters, ought to put us upon our guard, that we may not suffer ourselves to be the dupes of an insidious policy, working for our destruction. But we trust in God, that the same all-powerful Providence, which has hitherto so wonderfully preserved us, will still continue to protect us from the machinations of all our enemies, internal and external, and that by a wise use of the vast advantages in our possession, this country may become, as it seems destined to be, an asylum for all the oppressed upon the globe.

Entertaining these sentiments, which the warmth of our feelings hath carried to a greater length than we intended, we most earnestly wish that the General Assembly may appoint the meeting of a Convention on as early a day as possible, that no reproach of unnecessary delay may lie on us, when, in all human probability, upon our speedy adoption or rejection of this constitution it may depend, whether we shall be truly a nation, happy in ourselves, and respected by the rest of mankind; or an inconsiderable scattered people, perpetually driving to and fro, in search of a perfection which never can be found, amusing ourselves with visionary ideas, when we might be enjoying real blessings, and at length doomed to feel the curse of all human discontent, the consciousness that, by rejecting the means Providence had put into our power, we had become both wretched and contemptible.

Printed, McRee, 2:181-183.

---

[1]A group of Chowan County citizens met on November 8, 1787, and passed a resolution, written by JI, calling for a state convention to ratify the proposed national constitution. Four days later the grand jury of the Edenton District presented the document above, also penned by JI, to the district court. McRee, *Life and Correspondence*, 2:180-181.

[2]The phrase "all the States assembled were unanimous" is somewhat misleading. There were individual delegates who dissented, including some who bolted the convention. Three who remained declined to sign, each for a different reason. Seventy-four delegates were named to the convention, fifty-five attended, and only thirty-nine actually signed the document. At Benjamin Franklin's recommendation, however, the Constitution's final paragraph states that the work was completed with "the Unanimous Consent of the States present." Kelly and Harbison, *American Constitution*, 108, 137-138.

Two of North Carolina's delegates, William R. Davie and Alexander Martin, did not sign. Davie left Philadelphia on August 13, though he supported the Constitution. He told JI that at the time of his departure the major issues had been settled and what remained would "be tedious [*rather*] than difficult." Martin left the convention in late August; his reasons are unclear. William Blount signed for the sake of the appearance of unity, though he had reservations about the document. Cheney, *North Carolina Government*, 765, 791 nn. 3, 4; Robinson, *William R. Davie*, 189; Trenholme, *Ratification*, 98.

[3]Under Article 5 of the Constitution, approval by three-fourths of the states is necessary to ratify an amendment, while Article 13 of the Articles of Confederation required consent from all states.

To Hannah Iredell

Newbern Nov. 22d. 1787.

My dear Hannah,

We arrived here without much inconvenience on Tuesday to dinner, and are both in a great deal better health than when we left home—I feel perfectly well, but my bowels are not entirely in so good a state as I could wish them. Mr. Hooper was taken very sick at Kinston on the road, but came yesterday evening, & is in extreme good spirits today. He seriously declares, that he will endeavour to bring his Family to Edenton in the spring. Mr. Le Roi, who married one of the Miss Cornells, is here, & is really a very genteel agreeable Man.[1] He speaks of it as a matter of certainty, that Lady Ann Stuart either went with Mr. Sayre from N York soon after the Baron left it, or associated with him afterwards, & that he being confined to the Fleet Prison she has chosen to stay with him, & that the Baron has returned with another Woman, of a vile temper & apparently low character who used his charming Daughter (of whom Mr. Le Roi speaks highly) very ill indeed.[2] I had great pain in hearing this.

He says if the Baron & Lady Ann had continued together a year longer they would have been visited by all the first Families in New York. How much he is to be pitied if the account is true! I am likely to have a tolerable Court. Brown has not yet come, but I am told is preparing to visit me properly, tho' I have had no particulars. I am very impatiant for the post, & am afraid I must send this letter before I acknowledge yours. I hope my sweet little Annie begins to recover finely, & that I am often in her thoughts. Her frequent remembrance of me is one of my fondest wishes. Kiss her most tenderly for me—I beg to be affectionately remembered to all our Family & your Brother, and sincerely assure you I am ever, my dear Hannah,

Your most affectionate

Ja. Iredell.

P.S. Let my Brother have money, if you please, to pay the Printer for his blanks.

RC, Johnson Collection, NCSA. Addressed "Mrs. Iredell Edenton."

---

[1]Herman LeRoy founded the international mercantile firm of LeRoy, Bayard, and Company in New York. He and Hannah Cornell were married on October 19, 1786. Walter Barrett, *The Old Merchants of New York City*, 5 vols. (1870; reprint, New York: Greenwood Press, 1968), 1:160; Lynne Belluscio, "It is a Great Portrait," *LeRoy (N.Y.) Pennysaver and News*, September 25, 2000, *www.leroyny.com/common/news/2000/sep00/20000925183230001.html*, March 18, 2002.

[2]For more information on Lady Anne Stuart, see Baron de Poellnitz to JI, April 22, 1784, n. 2, and February 20, 1788, in this volume.

From a Newbern Newspaper

[*Newbern, Nov. 26, 1787.*]

Judge Ashe, in his reply to the letter addressed to him by some other gentlemen of the Bar and myself on account of his letter to the Assembly, wherein the whole profession of the law were, as I thought, very unjustly aspersed, having been pleased to impute to my signature a motive I hold in the utmost disdain (that of making a sacrifice of his reputation) I beg leave shortly to state my motive for joining in the letter to him, notwithstanding the conversation he speaks of at Warrenton.[1] It is true Judge Ashe did speak to me much to the effect as stated in his let[*t*]er (though I do not recollect he mentioned Mr. Johnston) and I received his explanation with as much politeness as it was offered, but I never could suppose Judge Ashe would think such a private explanation to me was sufficient to do away in the opinion of the whole public a stigma, which, as it was universal in its expression, might have been made so, by many at least, in its application, especially as it is known how many mean minds there are always ready to catch at any piece of malignity, and who would receive with great eagerness a slander from such high authority. It would be natural to conclude, that if any distinctions ought to have been made, a Judge of great experience in life, and who had been so long either in the practice of the law, or in the habit of administering justice, would not have failed to make them. I was therefore from the first of opinion, that a public explanation was necessary, though as I wished in so new a case to consult with my friends who were equally concerned with me to resent such calumnious imputations on the Bar in general, I did not intimate any such opinion to the Judge, not being at that time prepared to point out a mode I could recommend, and I was not selfish enough to think merely of my own case when a number of respectable characters, with whom I am willing at all times either to stand or fall, stood exactly in the same situation with me.

I for my part cannot see, when Judge Ashe himself admits his expressions comprehended more than he meant, what harm there is in requiring him to say how much he did really mean, and to support so much at least. His sounding such heavy charges on bare suspicion, unaccompanied with any proof, is not reconcileable to my notions of justice, or of that propriety of conduct which is due even from men in the most retired situations, to say nothing of that of a Judge. Nor do I by any means admit, that a lawyer may continually harrass the court with trifling debates, absent himself from business, when his presence is necessary, for scandalous purposes of his own, and purchase an extravagant fee by a base sale of his honor and conscience in using deceitful language to delude his client, without being guilty of more than an indecorum not judicially inquirable into, and punishable by the court. In proportion to the importance of any trust is the danger of its abuse, and ought to be the security of the public against it. The lawyers enjoy their privilege upon the tenure of their good behaviour. Many acts of negligence, or one act of moral turpitude in their profession, would in my opinion amount to a misdemeanor in office, upon which a forfeiture of their privilege is incurred of course. It is necessary at all times to adapt the proof to the nature of the crimes it is to detect. Where positive proof can be had, that may be required. Where it cannot, circumstantial must be admitted. Nor do I believe there is a lawyer of any eminence in the state, who either thinks he can practise with impunity the acts of baseness stated by Judge Ashe, or deems his situation unsafe or dishonorable because he must ultimately rely for his protection on the tenure by which every thing is happily held in th[*i*]s country, the verdict of an impartial jury.

Judge Ashe represents the charge as to extravagant fees unquestionably sounded, because laws have been recently made to remedy the abuse.[2] If he will condescend to consult his memory, or refer to the proceedings of the Assembly, he will find that laws have been long made to remedy that abuse, that it is a complaint of ancient standing, and submitted as well when the Bar received a lustre from his presence, as since he has been exalted from it. The truth is, I suppose there always have been, and probably there always will be, some lawyers deserving of censure on this account, but that the charge is true of the profession in general I do not believe. Judge Ashe however is very generous in providing means for our exculpation, no less than by the ingenious method of publishing a list of our suits and fees since the revolution. This is a very excellent specimen of justice in a free country, to prefer a complaint, and then tell the person accused, Sir, I cannot prove you guilty, but you shall be deemed so unless you shew yourself to be innocent. However, I am willing to close with the Judge in the method of administring justice in his new tribunal, and I do hereby solemnly assure him, that if he will employ an amanuensis, and be at the expence of the publication, he shall have the liberty of transcribing all my account-books in my possession, and depositing a copy if he pleases in every Clerk's-office in the state, or making what other use of it he thinks proper.[3]

Notwithstanding the provocation we received, I should have been very sorry if we had been capable of writing any illiberal language. There is only one part of our letter which the Judge particularly points out as exceptionable in this respect. If he had had a copy of his letter, he might have found what we alluded to, was that part wherein he takes pains to shew that a Judge is not accountable for an error in judgment, and that there is no reproach in a man's acknowledging any mistake he had committed. It would have been no discredit to Judge Ashe, had he pursued upon the present occasion the many excellent examples which would have justified him in such a step, if in so plain a matter authority was of any consequence in support of justice. By such a conduct he would have saved the necessity of an altercation that can be pleasing to no man of feeling, and I can truly say has been very painful to myself; but I trust it will appear, that as we were driven into a defence by an unprovoked attack, so our method of conducting it has been consistent with the character every man of honor would wish to maintain.

JA. IREDELL.

Printed, *North-Carolina Gazette; or the Edenton Intelligencer.*

---

[1]See Archibald Maclaine to JI, July 11, 1787, n. 4, in this volume.

[2]The statute establishing legal fees was passed on January 7, 1787. Clark, *State Records*, 24:804-807.

[3]An amanuensis is someone who takes dictation or copies from what someone else has written. *OED*, s.v. "amanuensis."

To Hannah Iredell

Newbern Nov. 27th. 1787.

My dear Hannah,

I had great pleasure in hearing of your being all well by my Brother's letter, tho' I should have /had/ greater satisfaction in receiving one from yourself. However, I impute it to Mrs. John Johnston being there.[1] I shall be sorry if I lose that opportunity of seeing them, but I hope you will in all events keep Annie. I wonder how our dear little Annie is reconciled to her name. I am extremely impatient to see you all again. One of the Cornell Causes was decided yesterday, against the Family, in consequence of which I imagine the rest will be discontinued.[2] Your Brother talks of leaving this today, but he will scarcely be able to do it. He is very anxious indeed to return. George Pollok (who is much cleverer than the other) is to come in either with him or me.[3] We pass our time here very dully, having almost as few dinners given to us as the Judges had at Edenton.

I have had no application from Bradley. I am told he has employed Mr. Williams from the back Country. If I don't go to Tuckahoe (which I think not improbable, tho' I don't expect to conclude on any thing decisively) I shall leave this on Saturday.[4] Give my tenderest love to Annie. God Almighty grant I may find you both & my other Friends well. Remember me to them, & believe me ever

Most affectionately yours,

Ja. Iredell.

P. S. The little complaint I had is entirely removed—

RC, Johnson Collection, NCSA. Addressed "Mrs. Iredell Edenton."

---

[1]Elizabeth Williams Johnston (d. 1789) was the wife of John Johnston and sister-in-law of Hannah Iredell. *PJI*, 1:137n.

[2]This a reference to the anticlimactic end to the noted case of *Bayard v. Singleton.* The superior court confirmed the right of the Cornell family to a jury

trial in their suits to reclaim family property that had been confiscated and sold. One of the daughters, Elizabeth Cornell Bayard, lost her case against Spyers Singleton. The jury ruled that her father was an alien when he deeded his property to her and other family members. Because aliens were prohibited from owning property, the confiscation and subsequent purchase of the property by Singleton were allowed to stand. The family dropped the remaining suits. Whichard, *Justice James Iredell*, 9-16; Waldrup, "James Iredell," 278; New Bern District Superior Court, Argument, Appearance and Reference Docket, May and November 1787, State Archives. For more information on *Bayard v. Singleton*, see Richard D. Spaight to JI, August 12, 1787, n. 2, in this volume.

[3]George Pollok (Pollock) was probably related to Cullen Pollock, who may be "the other" referred to in the letter. George was a common name in the Pollock family, which makes further identification difficult. *PJI*, 1:219n.

[4]Hannah Iredell had inherited land along the Trent River called Tuckahoe Meadows in what is now Jones County. *PJI*, 2:27n.

To Hannah Iredell

Newbern Nov. 28 1787.

My dear Hannah,

I was made extremely happy by your letter yesterday, for which I am very much obliged to you. God be praised for his goodness in preserving you & my dear Annie so well. Tell her she is in truth my sweet Pet and I am most impatient to see her. I wish she had finished her letter. Pray kiss her most tenderly for me. I am much obliged to Nelly for her intention of writing, & wish I could spare time to have the pleasure of writing a line to her. Had I known a day or two ago Mr. Johnston could have gone so soon I would have endeavoured to do it. I don't believe now I shall go to Tuckahoe, but I must at all events see Brown. If he comes in the meantime I intend to leave this on Saturday. Mrs. Williams & G. Pollok I expect will come in /with me/. By all means engage our Corn of Mr. Tredwell.[1] I hope I may be able to pay him all the money very shortly. God knows how we are to get Pork. Adieu! my dear Hannah. Remember me particularly, & most kindly to all, <for the> especially my little Angel, [*a*]nd be assured I am ever

Most affectionately yours

Ja. Iredell.

I leave to you the quantity of Corn [*torn*]ng care it be rather too much [*torn*] too little.

RC, Johnson Collection, NCSA. Addressed "Mrs. Iredell Edenton By favor of Mr. Johnston."

---

[1]Mr. Tredwell is probably Samuel Tredwell, husband of Nelly Blair.

From Arthur Iredell

Decr. 4th. 1787

My dear Brother,

I did not write by the last Packet depending upon my Mother who engaged to communicate my heartiest Wishes for you all, with which alone I must have filled my Letter if I had written. It seems a prodigiously long time since I heard from either you or Tom—and it really is so—How comes it about (for I feel as if it were my own Case too) that we are so much affraid of one another's Correspondence? You have, to be sure, a Multiplicity of Objects to attend to—I have none, and yet I am not certain that my Negligence is not of a more venial kind than Your's, for I have, I hope, infinitely more anxiety to derange my Mind & reduce it to that State, in which the writing even a Letter, & to a Brother too whom I dearly love, is an Herculean Labor! It is even so with me I do assure You—I can think of you all forever—I can cherish my Affection as much as possible, but it is irksome in the extreme to me to tell you this, & I could wish it were possible for you to be satisfied without receiving a Line from me till I am in a better Mood for writing—Isn't it tiresome to you to hear over & over again that my Affairs, & that my Mother's, are in some dull Train they have been God knows how long? I am sure it must be, I am sure I feel it so to harp always on the same disagreeable Topic—Were my Instrument in Tune I would "discourse most excellent Music."

The Peace will be old News to You and so will every publick Information I can give you?[1] And me thinks I hear you say, so much the better! "You are writing a Letter, not a News paper." But suppose your Worship, I have nothing for your private Ear? Which is the Case, unless, in his Mother's Name, I rail at Tom for not sending Certificates, without which She will go on very poorly indeed, I fear, for the next few Months. My Uncle puts it out of my Power to assist her, & God only knows when it will be otherwise. In time You shall all be the better, if I live, for his Partiality to me, but at present I am a Pauper myself, but enough of our private Histories, which, I trust you will now agree with me, are not half so entertaining as that of the Times. The Box I had the Pleasure of making up for You, was delivered on board the Friendship Captn. Saml. Milford bound for Virginia the 8th. of October, & it was directed to the Care of

Mr. Diack. I please myself with the Hopes of your receiving it very soon, and I am the less affraid of your opening it because I know you are prepared to receive the Crumbs from a poor Man's Table. In return however, I shall expect a very rich Packet. Gratitude is a great Virtue, convince me that you possess [*it by*] sending me a long Account of the Life & Adventures [*of*] dear little Anie together with Anecdotes of Her Parents & Uncle interspersed, with as much other Matter as you please. As for Tom the very rust upon his Pen will speak more forcibly to him than I can.

I can tell you little of my Mother. It is an Age since I heard from her. She was then as well as usual. My dear Fanny is entirely so, & forever enquires after You all—Assure my Sister, Tom, & my littlr prattling Niece of my utmost regard, & yourself, my dear James, of the Entire Affection with which

I am always Your's

A Iredell

RC, Johnson Collection, NCSA. Addressed "James Iredell Esqre. Edenton North Carolina America."

---

[1]For information on the "Peace," see Arthur Iredell to JI, September 20, 1787, n. 2, in this volume.

From William R. Davie

[*Decr. 13h. 1787.*]

My dear friend,

I have the pleasure of informing you, that we have accomplished our wishes in the appointment of Mr. Johnston, whose election was entered by a very respectable poll.[1]

Judge Spencers bill has in his language been damd in spite of every thing I could do for it in the Senate, and their Memorial has been treated with the most contemptuous neglect.[2]

My Compts. to your brother & believe me with great friendship and respect

your mo. obd.

William R. Davie

RC, Iredell Papers, Duke. Printed, McRee, 2:183. Addressed "James Iredell Esquire Edenton." Endorsed "Dec. 13th. 1787. W. R. Davie. Ansd."

[1]The General Assembly elected Samuel Johnston governor on December 12, 1787. He received eighty-three votes, while his nearest competitor, John Williams, garnered only thirty-two. Cheney, *North Carolina Government*, 160; Balloting for Governor, December 1787, General Assembly Session Records, State Archives.

[2]During the 1787 legislative session, the judges of the superior court—Samuel Ashe, Samuel Spencer, and John Williams—asked the General Assembly for an increase in pay. The last raise the judges had received was in 1782, when their wages were increased from £40 to £50 for every court they attended. Davie's remarks regarding this issue are facetious. Clark, *State Records*, 20:150; 24:406, 444, 796.

From Archibald Maclaine

Wilmington 25 Decr. 1787

Dear Sir

You will probably have heard before this time that we are to have a convention at Hillsborough in July[1]—As any freeholder can be chosen to represent any county, Mr. Moore, some time ago, upon that supposition, proposed to set you up for Brunswick county; doubting, I conceive whether you would be chosen in your own town or county.[2] If you are of the same opinion I will certainly give in aid what little influence I have, not only from my own knowledge of your general principles, but as I wish to have as many of the friends of the new constitution as possible in the convention—There are a set of interested people, and petty tyrants (among whom are the Judges) that are and will be exerting all their influence, and straining every nerve, to prevent the new government taking place.

From the presentment of the Edenton Grand Jury, and the instructions of the town, I should conclude that you would be one of the members chosen, and in that case, if you should at the same time be elected here, we might lose a good vote[3]—This is a matter of some consequence, and I wish to hear from you on the subject. I hope Mr. Johnston will be chosen, which is no way incompatible with his new dignity[4]—I am indeed concerned that his promotion has been attended with a diminution of salary, which if we did not know our Assembly-men so well, might be interpreted into an insult.[5] No people ever more fully made good the old saying of "penny wise, and pound foolish." I hope however this will not occasion him to decline the government, to which, in my opinion, he will give a dignity which it has <long> /generally/ wanted.

It is some comfort to me under the abuse of "A Farmer," that the the profession of the law, as well as myself, lie under his tremendous lash, and that your observations on Judge Ashe's letter, have the honor to be placed beside that elegant <writer> /performance/ in the same paper[6]—I have been too much engaged to give it more than a slight reading—I would readily submit my conduct to men of sense and candor, without taking notice of the numerous falsities which that paltry scribbler has asserted; but unfortunately many of those who read have neither understanding nor honesty, or at best <want> /have but/ one of them. The difficulty with me is, how to disprove the assertions, without discovering a resentment, of which the writer is unworthy—I must endeavor to lo[*wer*] myself to a proper temper to turn him into ridicule. You will hear more of him soon relative to an affair that will place him in a still more contemptible and detestable point of view.

Oblige me with an answer as soon as your convenience will permit, to the first part of my letter.

I had almost omitted to write you that I had a notice from Monk that by virtue of a commission from your court, he was /to/ take the examination of Robt. Wilkinson and his wife—Can you tell me to what purpose? For neither of them were present at making of the will[7]—At least I believe so.

I am with sincere respect and esteem Dear Sir yours

A Maclaine

make my respectful congratulations acceptable to our Governor—Compliments of the season &c

RC, Iredell Papers, Duke. Printed, McRee, 2:183-184. Addressed "James Iredell esquire Edenton." Endorsed "Dec. 25. 1787. A. Maclaine. Ansd."

---

[1]On December 5, 1787, the General Assembly agreed to meet in a joint session to consider the proposed constitution. The following day the assembly scheduled elections for the last Friday and Saturday in March to select delegates to a ratification convention, which would begin the third Monday in July. Hillsborough was chosen as the site of the convention, though Halifax, Tarborough, New Bern, and Fayetteville were also considered. Clark, *State Records*, 20:369-374, 378-379.

[2]Mr. Moore is probably Alfred Moore of New Hanover County. Maclaine may have felt some trepidation about JI's chances in Chowan County because of JI's recent loss to Stephen Cabarrus in an election for the General Assembly. Maclaine's fears were unfounded, however, for JI was elected to represent the town of Edenton at the ratification convention. Massengill, *North Carolina Votes*, 30.

[3]See Grand Jury to the Edenton District Court, November 12, 1787, in this volume.

[4]Samuel Johnston, though a resident of Chowan County, owned land in Perquimans County and was elected to represent that county at the 1788 and 1789

constitutional ratification conventions. He was chosen as president of both conventions. Massengill, *North Carolina Votes*, 32.

[5]Johnston had recently been elected governor, an office that paid an annual salary of £750. At the time of his election, Johnston's income had come from his law practice and plantation. Clark, *State Records*, 24:796; *DNCB*, s.v. "Johnston, Samuel."

[6]See "From a Newbern Paper," November 26, 1787, in this volume, for JI's response to Ashe's letter.

[7]See Archibald Maclaine to JI, October 24, 1785, in this volume.

From William Hooper

Point Repose, 31st Dec.'87.

My Dear Iredell:

Immediately upon my arrival at Wilmington, it was announced to me that my son William, at midnight, had left his uncle George Hooper's house, to vist Gen. Clarke, who had been attacked with a violent disorder in his head, which had utterly deprived him of his senses, and left him (stone-blind) to the care or inattention of nearly 40 slaves, without a white person on his plantation to attend to his distresses.

Judge of my feelings from your own, such as they would have been on such an occasion. I sought an early opportunity to come hither; it happened in the most busy and interesting part of the court; I lost two days of it, but to the friendly offices of Mr. Moore and Mr. Maclaine I am indebted that my clients did not suffer. I found the general ill indeed; he consented that I should send for his sister, proof positive that he thought himself near his dissolution. With poor Drinker, and another horse which bore Spencer to Portsmouth, Jem left this; and, with an aid of two plow-horses, delivered Mrs. Hooper and Tom here the fifth day, before noon, after they left this—going and returning 348 miles, with scarce as much flesh on my horses as would protect them from the depredation of the buzzards before they died.

Mr. Clarke is in a recovering state of health; his sight is, however, very bad, and I suppose will never be better. Mrs. Hooper and I are here; she waiting his consent to return, I preparing to leave this to-morrow or next day.

Thus have I troubled you with a detail of my private family affairs. I shall not attempt an apology. I know too well the share you take in my family feelings to conceive it necessary.

I am happy to hear that the Convention is so appointed that you can take your seat in it without interfering with your law engagements. Mr. Moore has thought of proposing you for Brunswick, lest by any possibility you should not be elected for Chowan or Edenton. Your election for Chowan, I think (if the Devil has not made himself an uniform inmate of the souls of the voters for your county), must be certain. Make it so there, or somewhere, for in the Convention you must be. I shall exert my powers to be there, but I conceive the chances very much against me. Watters proposes for the town; if I divide against him Taylor goes in, and Watters surely is to be preferred to him.[1] The county members are opposed to me—some from interest—and from ignorance oppose the new constitution—and I have been explicit and decided in my approbation of it.

During the court nothing happened to the disadvantage of Maclaine. The Judges and he kept up a kind of apparent respect for each other. If there was any deficiency, Maclaine was the aggressor. He talked loud, laughed in court, carried on business in a kind of conversation, attended with much delinquency, yet never met with a reproof.

Geo. Hooper, after court, called Spencer, with due spirit and decency, to account for expressions which he had made use of respecting himself and Maclaine in Burgynn's business. Spencer degraded himself. Of this when I see you, &c. &c.

Will. Hooper.

Printed, McRee, 2:184-185.

---

[1]Neither Watters nor Taylor won. Absalom Tatum (1742-1802) represented Hillsborough in the 1788 state ratification convention. Tatum served nine terms in the house of commons between 1779 and 1802, representing Randolph County and the town of Hillsborough. He was also a member of the U.S. House of Representatives (1795-1796). Massengill, *North Carolina Votes*, 59.

1787 Tax List[1]

List of the Taxable Property of James Iredell 1787.

Lands. A Moiety of a Tract of Land estimated at 1500 Acres at Tuckahoe on Trent River in the County of Jones (being the remaining quantity of a Tract of 2000 Acres by Patent, the other 500 having been some time since alienated. —)

A Moiety of 320 Acres (by estimation), on Reedy Branch near the above.

Sold {A Moiety of 200 Acres (by estimation), on Beaver Creek in the same County.

A Moiety of 2130 Acres (by estimation) in the County of Onslow, on the North East & North West Branches of New River.

A Moiety of an Island (estimated at 400 Acres, by Patent dated 21 March 1742) lying in Chowan River; —This Patent but lately discovered.

A House & Lot in the Town of Edenton.

<Free Males. Two.

Slaves from 12 to 60} Dundee, Sall, Peter, Andrew, Edy, Sukey, Sarah, Pink or Sappho (These two last in my Employ, tho' not my property).

Carriage Wheels, Two. —(I <suppose Cart Wheels are not & therefore have not mentioned them> /have a Cart, but suppose Cart Wheels are not intended/>

FC, Johnson Collection, NCSA.

---

[1]Most of the text of this document is in the handwriting of someone other than JI. Information about Sarah, Pink, and Sappho and the carriage wheels was inserted by JI, as well as the word "Sold" by the two hundred acres on Beaver Creek.

1788

To Mr. Mason[1]

[January 8th, 1788][2]

Answers to Mr. Mason's Objections to the New Constitution recommended by the late Convention at Philadelphia. By Marcus.[3]

I. OBJECTION.

"There is no declaration of rights, and the laws of the general government being paramount to the laws and constitutions of the several States, the declarations of rights in the separate States are no security. Nor are the people secured even in the enjoyment of the benefit of the common law, which stands here upon no other foundation than its having been adopted by the respective acts forming the Constitutions of the several States."

ANSWER.

1. As to the want of a declaration of rights. The introduction of these in England, from which the idea was originally taken, was in consequence of usurpations of the Crown, contrary, as was conceived, to the principles of their government. But there no original constitution is to be found, and the only meaning of a declaration of rights in that country is, that in certain particulars specified, the Crown had no authority to act. Could this have been necessary had there been a constitution in being by which it could have been clearly discerned whether the Crown had such authority or not? Had the people, by a solemn instrument, delegated particular powers to the Crown at the formation of their government, surely the Crown, which in that case could claim under that instrument only, could not have contended for more power than was conveyed by it. So it is in regard to the new Constitution here: the future government which may be formed under that authority certainly cannot act beyond the warrant of that authority. As well might they attempt to impose a King upon America, as go one step in any other respect beyond the terms of their institution. The question then only is, whether more power will be vested in the future government than is necessary for the general purposes of the union. This may occasion a ground of dispute—but after expressly defining the powers that are to be exercised, to say that they shall exercise no other powers (either by a general or particular enumeration) would seem to me both nugatory and ridiculous. As well might a Judge when he condemns a man

to be hanged give strong injunctions to the Sheriff that he should not be beheaded.*[4]

2. As to the common law, it is difficult to know what is meant by that part of the objection. So far as the people are now entitled to the benefit of the common law, they certainly will have a right to enjoy it under the new Constitution until altered by the general legislature, which even in this point has some cardinal limits assigned to it. What are most acts of Assembly but a deviation in some degree from the principles of the common law? The people are expressly secured (contrary to Mr. Mason's wishes) against ex post facto laws; so that the tenure of any property at any time held under the principles of the common law, cannot be altered by any future act of the general legislature. The principles of the common law, as they now apply, must surely always hereafter apply, except in those particulars in which express authority is given by this constitution; in no other particulars can the Congress have authority to change it, and I believe it cannot be shown that any one power of this kind given is unnecessarily given, or that the power would answer its proper purpose if the legislature was restricted from any innovations on the principles of the common law, which would not in all cases suit the vast variety of incidents that might arise out of it.

II. OBJECTION.

"In the House of Representatives there is not the substance, but the shadow only of representation; which can never produce proper information in the legislature, or inspire confidence in the people; the laws will therefore generally be made by men little concerned in, and unacquainted with their effects and consequences."

ANSWER.

This is a mere matter of calculation. It is said the weight of this objection was in a great measure removed by altering the number of 40,000 to 30,000 constituents. To show the discontented nature of man, some have objected to the number of representatives as being too large. I leave to every man's judgment, whether the number is not sufficiently respectable, and whether, if that number be sufficient, it would have been right, in the very infancy of this government, to burthen the people with a great additional expense to answer no good purpose.*[5]

III. OBJECTION.

"The Senate have the power of altering all money bills, and of originating appropriations of money, and the salaries of the officers of their own appointment, in conjunction with the President of the United States;

although they are not the representatives of the people or amendable to them.—These, with their other great powers (viz. their powers in the appointment of Ambassadors, and all public officers, in making treaties and trying all impeachments) their influence upon and connection with the supreme Executive, from these causes, their duration of office, and their being a constant existing body almost continually sitting, joined with their being one complete branch of the legislature, will destroy any balance in the government, and enable them to accomplish what usurpations they please upon the rights and liberties of the people."

ANSWER.

This objection, respecting the dangerous power of the Senate, is one of that kind which may give rise to a great deal of gloomy prediction, without any solid foundation: An imagination indulging itself in chimerical fears, upon the disappointment of a favorite plan, may point out danger arising from any system of government whatever, even if angels were to have the administration of it; since I presume none but the Supreme Being himself is altogether perfect, and of course every other species of beings may abuse any delegated portion of power. This sort of visionary scepticism therefore will lead us to this alternative, either to have no government at all, or to form the best system we can, making allowance for human imperfection. In my opinion the fears as to the power of the Senate are altogether groundless, as to any probability of their being either able or willing to do any important mischief. My reasons are,

1. Because, though they are not immediately to represent the people, yet they are to represent the representatives of the people who are annually chosen, and it is therefore probable the most popular, or confidential, persons in each State, will be elected members of the Senate.

2. Because one-third of the Senate are to be chosen as often as the immediate representatives of the people, and as the President can act in no case from which any great danger can be apprehended without the concurrence of two-thirds, let us think ever so ill of the designs of the President, and the danger of a combination of power among a standing body generally associated with him, unless we suppose every one of them to be base and infamous (a supposition, thank God, bad as human nature is, not within the verge of the slightest probability), we have reason to believe that the one-third newly introduced every second year, will bring with them from the immediate body of the people, a sufficient portion of patriotism and independence to check any exorbitant designs of the rest.

3. Because in their legislative capacity they can do nothing without the concurrence of the House of Representatives, and we need look no farther than England for a clear proof of the amazing consequence which

representatives of the people bear in a free government. There the King (who is hereditary, and therefore not so immediately interested, according to narrow views of interest which commonly govern Kings, to consult the welfare of his people) has the appointment to almost every office in the government, many of which are of high dignity and great pecuniary value, has the creation of as many Peers as he pleases, is not restricted from bestowing places on the members of both Houses of Parliament, and has a direct negative on all bills, besides the power of dissolving the Parliament at his pleasure. In theory would not any one say this power was enormous enough to destroy any balance in the constitution? Yet what does the history of that country tell us?—That so great is the natural power of the House of Commons (though a very imperfect representation of the people, and a large proportion of them actually purchasing their seats) that ever since the revolution the Crown has continually aimed to corrupt them by the disposal of places and pensions; that without their hearty concurrence it found all the wheels of government perpetually clogged; and that notwithstanding this, in great critical emergencies, the members have broke through the trammels of power and interest, and by speaking the sense of the people (though so imperfectly representing them) either forced an alteration of measures, or made it necessary for the Crown to dissolve them. If their power, under these circumstances, is so great, what would it be if their representation was perfect, and their members could hold no appointments, and at the same time had a security for their seats? The danger of a destruction of the balance would be perhaps on the popular side, notwithstanding the hereditary tenure and weighty prerogatives of the Crown, and the permanent station and great wealth and consequence of the Lords. Our representatives therefore being an adequate and fair representation of the people, and they being expressly excluded from the possession of any places, and not holding their existence upon any precarious tenure, must have vast influence, and considering that in every popular government the danger of faction is often very serious and alarming, if such a danger could not be checked in its instant operation by some other power more independent of the immediate passions of the people, and capable therefore of thinking with more coolness, the government might be destroyed by a momentary impulse of passion, which the very members who indulged it might for ever afterwards in vain deplore. The institution of the Senate seems well calculated to answer this salutary purpose. Excluded as they are from places themselves, they appear to be as much above the danger of personal temptation as men can be. They have no permanent interest as a body to detach them from the general welfare, since six years is the utmost period of their existence, unless their respective legislatures are sufficiently pleased with their conduct to re-elect them. This power of re-election is itself a great check upon abuse, because if they have ambition to continue members of the Senate they can only gratify this ambition by acting agreeably to the opinion of their constitutents. The House of Representatives, as immediately representing the people, are to originate all money bills. This I think extremely right, and it is certainly a very capital acquisition to the popular representative. But what harm can arise from the Senate, who are nearly a popular representative also, proposing amendments, when those amendments must be concurred with by the original proposers? The wisdom of the Senate may sometimes point out amendments, the propriety of which the other House may be very sensible of, though they had not occurred to themselves. There is no great danger of any body of men suffering by too eager an adoption of any amendment proposed to any system of their own. The probability is stronger of their being too tenacious of their original opinion, however erroneous, than of their profiting by the wise information of any other persons whatever. Human nature is so constituted, and therefore I think we may safely confide in the free admission of an intercourse of opinion on the detail of business, as well as to taxation as to other points. Our House of Representatives surely could not have such reason to dread the power of a Senate circumstanced as ours must be, as the House of Commons in England the permanent authority of the Peers, and therefore a jealousy, which may be well grounded in the one case would be entirely ill directed in the other. For similar reasons I dread not any power of originating appropriations of money as mentioned in the objection. While the concurrence of the other House must be had, and as that must necessarily be the most weighty in the government, I think no danger is to be apprehended. The Senate has no such authority as to awe or influence the House of Representatives, and it will be as necessary for the one as for the other that proper active measures should be pursued: And in regard to appropriations of money, occasions for such appropriations may, on account of their concurrence with the executive power, occur to the Senate, which would not to the House of Representatives, and therefore if the Senate were precluded from laying any such proposals before the House of Representatives, the government might be embarrassed; and it ought ever to be remembered, that in our views of distant and chimerical dangers we ought not to hazard our very existence as a people, by proposing such restrictions as may prevent the exertion of any necessary power. The power of the Senate in the appointment of Ambassadors, &c., is designed as a check upon the President. They must be appointed in some manner. If the appointment was by the President alone, or by the President and a Privy Council (Mr. Mason's favorite plan), an objection to such a system would have appeared much more plausible. It would have been said that this was approaching too much towards monarchical power, and if this new Privy Council had been like all I have ever heard of, it would have afforded little security against an abuse of power in the President. It ought to be shown by reason and probability (not bold assertion) how this concurrence of power with the President can make the Senate so dangerous. It is as good an argument to say that it will not as that it will.*[6] The power of making treaties is so important, that it would have been highly dangerous to vest it in the Executive alone, and would have been the subject of much greater clamor. From the nature of the thing, it could not be vested in the popular respresentative. It must therefore have been provided for with the Senate's concurrence, or the concurrence of a Privy Council (a thing which I believe nobody has been mad enough to propose), or the power, the greatest monarchical power that can be exercised, must have vested in a manner that would have excited universal indignation in the President alone.—As to the power of trying impeachments:—Let Mr. Mason show where this power could more properly have been placed. It is a necessary power in every free government, since even the Judges of the Supreme Court of Judicature themselves may require a trial, and other public officers might have too much influence before an ordinary and common court. And what probability is there that such a court, acting in so solemn a manner, should abuse its power (especially as it is wisely provided that the sentences shall extend only to removal from office and incapacitation) more than any other court? The argument as to the possible abuse of power, as I have before suggested, will reach all delegation of power, since all power may be abused when fallible beings are to execute it; but we must take as much caution as we can, being careful at the same time not to be too wise to do any thing at all.—The bold assertions at the end of this objection are mere declamation, and till some reason is assigned for them, I shall take the liberty to rely upon the reasons I have stated above, as affording a belief that the popular representative must for ever be the most weighty in this government, and of course that apprehensions of danger from such a Senate are altogether ill-founded.

IV. OBJECTION.

"The judiciary of the United States is so constructed and extended, as to absorb and destroy the judiciaries of the several States; thereby rendering law as tedious, intricate and expensive and justice as unattainable by a great part of the community, as in England; and enabling the rich to oppress and ruin the poor."

ANSWER.

Mr. Mason has here asserted, "That the judiciary of the United States is so constructed and extended, as to absorb and destroy the judiciaries of the several States." How is this the case? Are not the State judiciaries left uncontrolled as to the affairs of that State only? In this, as in all other cases, where there is a wise distribution, power is commensurate to its object. With the mere internal concerns of a State Congress are to have nothing to do: In no case but where the union is in some measure concerned, are the federal courts to have any jurisdiction. The State judiciary will be a satellite waiting upon its proper planet: That of the Union, like the sun, cherishing and preserving a whole planetary system.

In regard to a possible ill construction of this authority, we must depend upon our future legislature in this case as well as others, in respect to which it is impracticable to define every thing, that it will be provided for so as to occasion as little expense and distress to individuals as can be. In parting with the coercive authority over the States as States, there must be a coercion allowed as to individuals. The former power no man of common sense can any longer seriously contend for; the latter is the only alternative. Suppose an objection should be made that the future legislature should not ascertain salaries, because they might divide among themselves and their officers all the revenue of the Union.*[7] Will not every man see how irrational it is to expect that any government can exist which is to be fettered in its most necessary operations for fear of abuse?

V. OBJECTION.

"The President of the United States has no constitutional Council (a thing unknown in any safe and regular government), he will therefore be unsupported by proper information and advice, and will generally be directed by minions and favorites—or he will become a tool to the Senate—or a Council of State will grow out of the principal officers of the great departments; the worst and most dangerous of all ingredients for such a Council in a free country, for they may be induced to join in any dangerous or oppressive measures, to shelter themselves, and prevent an inquiry into their own misconduct in office: Whereas, had a constitutional Council been formed (as was proposed) of six members, viz., two from the eastern, two from the middle, and two from the southern States, to be appointed by vote of the States in the House of Representatives, with the same duration and rotation of office as the Senate, the Executive would always have had safe and proper information and advice: The President of such a Council might have acted as Vice-President of the United States, pro tempore, upon any vacancy or disability of the Chief Magistrate, and long-continued sessions of the Senate would in a great measure have been prevented. From this fatal defect of a constitutional Council has arisen the improper power of the Senate, in the appointment of public officers, and the alarming dependence and connection between that branch of the legislature and the Supreme Executive. Hence also sprung that unnecessary and dangerous officer, the Vice-President, who for want of other employment, is made President of the Senate; thereby dangerously blending the Executive and Legislative power; besides always giving to some one of the States an unnecessary and unjust pre-eminence over the others."

ANSWER.

Mr. Mason here reprobates the omission of a particular Council for the President, as a thing contrary to the example of all safe and regular governments. Perhaps there are very few governments now in being deserving of that character, if under the idea of safety he means to include safety for a proper share of personal freedom, without which their safety and regularity in other respects would be of little consequence to a people so justly jealous of liberty as I hope the people in America ever will be. Since however Mr. Mason refers us to such authority, I think I cannot do better than to select for the subject of our inquiry in this particular, a government which must be universally acknowledged to be the most safe and regular of any considerable government now in being (though I hope America will soon be able to dispute that pre-eminence). Every body must know I speak of Great Britain, and in this I think I give Mr. Mason all possible advantage, since in my opinion it is most probable he had Great Britain principally in his eye when he made this remark, and in the very height of our quarrel with that country, so wedded were our ideas to the institution of a Council, that the practice was generally if not universally followed at the formation of our governments, though we instituted Councils of a quite different nature, and so far as the little experience of the writer goes, have very little benefited by it. My inquiry into this subject shall not be confined to the actual present practice of Great Britain; I shall take the liberty to state the constitutional ideas of Councils in England, as derived from their ancient law subsisting long before the Union, not omitting however to show what the present practice really is. By the laws of England*[8] the King is said to have four Councils,—1. The High Court of Parliament; 2. The Peers of the realm; 3. His Judges; 4. His Privy Council. By the first, I presume is meant, in regard to the making of laws; because the usual introductory expressions in most acts of Parliament, viz., "By the King's most excellent Majesty, by and with the advice and consent of the Lords spiritual and temporal, and Commons," &c., show that in a constitutional sense, they are deemed the King's laws, after a ratification in

Parliament. The Peers of the realm are by their birth hereditary Counsellors of the Crown, and may be called upon for their advice, either in time of Parliament, or when no Parliament is in being: They are called in some law books Magnum Concilium Regis (the King's Great Council). It is also considered the privilege of every particular Peer to demand an audience of the King, and to lay before him any thing he may deem of public importance. The Judges, I presume, are called "a Council of the King," upon the same principle that the Parliament is, because the administration of justice is in his name, and the Judges are considered as his instruments in the distribution of it. We come now to the Privy Council, which I imagine, if Mr. Mason had any particular view towards England when he made this objection, was the one he intended as an example of a Constitutional Council in that kingdom. The Privy Council in that country is undoubtedly of very ancient institution, but it has one fixed property invariably annexed to it, that it is a mere creature of the Crown, dependent on its will both for number and duration, since the King may, whenever he thinks proper, discharge any particular member, or the whole of it, and appoint another.*[9] If this precedent is of moment to us, merely as a precedent, it should be followed in all its parts, and then what would there be in the regulation to prevent the President being governed by "minions and favorites?" It would only be the means of riveting them on constitutional ground. So far as precedents in England apply, the Peers being constitutionally the Great Council of the King, though also a part of the legislature, we have reason to hope that there is by no means such a gross impropriety as has been suggested in giving the Senate, though a branch of the legislature, a strong control over the Executive. The only difference in the two cases is, that the Crown in England may or may not give this consequence to the Peers at its own pleasure, and accordingly we find that for a long time past this great Council has been very seldom consulted; under our constitution the President is allowed no option in respect to certain points wherein he cannot act without the Senate's concurrence. But we cannot infer from any example in England, that a concurrence between the Executive and a part of the legislative is contrary to the maxims of their government, since their government allows of such a concurrence whenever the Executive pleases. The rule, therefore, from the example of the freest government in Europe, that the Legislative and Executive powers must be altogether distinct, is liable to exceptions; it does not mean that the Executive shall not form a part of the Legislative (for the King, who has the whole Executive authority, is one entire branch of the legislature, and this Montesquieu, who recognizes the general principle, declares is necessary); neither can it mean (as the example above evinces) that the Crown must consult neither House as to any exercise of the Executive power.[10] But its meaning must be, that one power shall not include both authorities. The King, for instance, shall not have the sole Executive and sole Legislative authority also. He may have the former, but must participate the latter with the two Houses of Parliament. The rule also would be infringed were the three branches of the legislature to share jointly the Executive power. But so long as the people's representatives are altogether distinct from the Executive authority, the liberties of the people may be deemed secure. And in this point surely there can be no manner of comparison between the provisions by which the independence of our House of Representatives is guarded, and the condition in which the British House of Commons is left exposed to every species of corruption. But Mr. Mason says, for want of a Council, the President may become "a tool of the Senate." Why? Because he cannot act without their concurrence. Would not the same reason hold for his being "a tool to the Council," if he could not act without their concurrence, supposing a Council was to be imposed upon him without his own nomination (according to Mr. Mason's plan)? As great care is taken to make him independent of the Senate as I believe human precaution can provide. Whether the President will be a tool to any persons will depend upon the man, and the same weakness of mind which would make him pliable to one body of control, would certainly attend him with another. But Mr. Mason objects, if he is not directed by minions and favorites, nor becomes a tool of the Senate, "a Council of State will grow out of the principal officers of the great departments; the worst and most dangerous of all ingredients for such a Council in a free country; for they may be induced to join in any dangerous or oppressive measures, to shelter themselves, and prevent an inquiry into their own misconduct in office." I beg leave to carry him again to my old authority, England; and ask him, what efficient Council they have there but one formed of their great officers. Notwithstanding their important Constitutional Council, every body knows that the whole movements of their government, where a Council is consulted at all, are directed by their Cabinet Council, composed entirely of the principal officers of the great departments; that when a Privy Council is called, it is scarcely ever for any other purpose than to give a formal sanction to the previous determinations of the other, so much so that it is notorious that not one time in a thousand one member of the Privy Council, except a known adherent of administration, is summoned to it. But though the President under our constitution may have the aid of the "principal officers of the great departments," he is to have this aid, I think, in the most unexceptionable manner possible. He is not to be assisted by a Council summoned to a jovial dinner perhaps, and giving their opinions according to the nod of the President; but the opinion is to be given with the utmost solemnity, in writing. No after-equivocation can explain it away. It must for ever afterwards speak for itself, and commit the character of the writer, in lasting colors, either of fame or infamy, or neutral insignificance, to future ages, as well as the present. From those written reasons, weighed with care, surely the President can form as good a judgment, as if they had been given by a dozen formal characters, carelessly met together on a slight appointment; and this further advantage would be derived from the proposed system (which would be wanting if he had constitutional advice to screen him), that the President must be personally responsible for every thing—for though an ingenious gentleman has proposed, that a Council should be formed who should be responsible for their opinions, and the same sentiment of justice might be applied to these opinions of the great officers, I am persuaded it will in general be thought infinitely more safe, as well as more just, that the President who acts should be responsible for his conduct, following advice at his peril, than that there should be a danger of punishing any man for an erroneous opinion which might possibly be sincere. Besides the morality of this scheme, which may well be questioned, its inexpediency is glaring, since it would be so plausible an excuse, and the insincerity of it so difficult to detect, the hopes of impunity this avenue to escape would afford would nearly take away all dread of punishment. As to the temptation mentioned to the officers joining in dangerous or oppressive measures to shelter themselves, and prevent an inquiry into their own misconduct in office, this proceeds upon a supposition that the President and the great officers may form a very wicked combination to injure their country, a combination that in the first place it is utterly improbable, in a strong respectable government should be formed for that purpose, and in the next, with such a government as this constitution would give us, could have little chance of being successful, on account of the great superior strength and natural and jealous vigilance of one at least, if not both the two weighty branches of legislation. This evil, however, of the possible depravity of all public officers, is one that can admit of no cure, since in every institution of government the same danger in some degree or other must be risked; it can only be guarded against by strong checks, and I believe it would be difficult for the objectors to our new Constitution, to provide stronger ones against any abuse of the Executive authority than will exist in that. As to the Vice President, it appears to me very proper he should be chosen much in the same manner as the President, in order that the States may be secure, upon any accidental loss by death or otherwise of the President's service, of the services in the same important station of the man in whom they repose their second confidence. The complicated manner of election wisely prescribed would necessarily occasion a considerable delay in the choice of another, and in the mean time the President of the Council, though very fit for the purpose of advising, might be very ill qualified, especially in a critical period, for an active Executive department. I am concerned to see, among Mr. Mason's other reasons, so trivial a one as the little advantage one State might accidentally gain by a Vice President of their country having a seat, with merely a casting vote, in the Senate. Such a reason is utterly unworthy of that spirit of amity, and rejection of local views, which can alone save us from destruction. It was the glory of the late Convention, that by discarding such they formed a general government upon principles that did as much honor to their hearts as to their understandings. God grant, that in all our deliberations, we may consider America as one body, and not divert our attention from so noble a prospect to small considerations of partial jealousy and distrust. It is in vain to expect upon any system to secure an exact equilibrium of power for all the States. Some will occasionally have an advantage from the superior abilities of its members; the field of emulation is however open to all. Suppose any one should now object to the superior influence of Virginia (and the writer of this is not a citizen of that State), on account of the high character of General Washington, confessedly the greatest man of the present age, and perhaps equal to any that has existed in any period of time; would this be a reason for refusing a union with her, though the other States can scarcely hope for the consolation of ever producing his equal?

VI. OBJECTION.

"The President of the United States has the unrestrained power of granting pardons for treason; which may be sometimes exercised to screen from punishment those whom he had secretly instigated to commit the crime, and thereby prevent a discovery of his own guilt."

ANSWER.

Nobody can contend upon any rational principles, that a power of pardoning should not exist somewhere in every government, because it will often happen in every country that men are obnoxious to a lawful conviction, who yet are entitled, from some favorable circumstances in their case, to a merciful interposition in their favor. The advocates of monarchy have accordingly boasted of this, as one of the advantages of that form of government, in preference to a republican; nevertheless this authority is vested in the Stadtholder in Holland, and I believe is vested in every Executive power in America. It seems to have been wisely the aim of the late Convention, in forming a general government for America, to combine the acknowledged advantages of the British constitution with proper republican checks to guard as much as possible against abuses, and it would have been very strange if they had omitted this, which has the sanction of such great antiquity in that country, and if I am not mistaken, a universal adoption in America.*[11] Those gentlemen who object to other parts of the constitution as introducing innovations, contrary to long experience, with a very ill grace attempt to reject an experience so unexceptionable as this, to introduce an innovation (perhaps the first ever suggested) of their own. When a power is acknowledged to be necessary, it is a very dangerous thing to prescribe limits to it, for men must have a greater confidence in their own wisdom than I think any men are entitled to, who imagine they can form such exact ideas of all possible contingencies as to be sure that the restriction they propose will not do more harm than good. The probability of the President of the United States committing an act of treason against his country is very slight; he is so well guarded by the other powers of government, and the natural strength of the people at large must be so weighty, that in my opinion it is the most chimerical apprehension that can be entertained. Such a thing is however possible, and accordingly he is not exempt from a trial, if he should be guilty or supposed guilty, of that or any other offence. I entirely lay out of the consideration the probability of a man honored in such a manner by his country, risking, like General Arnold, the damnaton of his fame to all future ages, though it is a circumstance of some weight in considering whether for the sake of such a remote and improbable danger as this, it would be prudent to abridge this power of pardoning in a manner altogether unexampled, and which might produce mischiefs the full extent of which is is not perhaps easy at present to foresee. In estimating the value of any power it is possible to bestow, we have to choose between inconveniences of some sort or other, since no institution of man can be entirely free from all. Let us now therefore consider some of the actual inconveniences which would attend an abridgment of the power of the President in this respect. One of the great advantages attending a single Executive power is the degree of secrecy and dispatch with which on critical occasions such a power can act. In war this advantage will often counterbalance the want of many others. Now suppose, in the very midst of a war of extreme consequence to our safety or prosperity, the President could prevail on a gentleman of abilities to go into the enemy's country, to serve in the useful, but dishonorable character of a spy. Such are certainly maintained by all vigilant governments, and in proportion to the ignominy of the character, and the danger sustained in the enemy's country, ought to be his protection and security in his own. This man renders very useful services; perhaps by timely information, prevents the destruction of his country. Nobody knows of these secret services but the President himself; his adherence however to the enemy is notorious: he is afterwards intercepted in endeavoring to return to his own country, and having been perhaps a man of distinction before, he is proportionately obnoxious to his country at large for his supposed treason. Would it not be monstrous that the President should not have it in his power to pardon this man? or that it should depend upon mere solicitation and favor, and perhaps, though the President should state the fact as it really was, some zealous partisan, with his jealousy constantly fixed upon the President, might insinuate that in fact the President and he were secret traitors together, and thus obtain a rejection of the President's application. It is a consideration also of some moment, that there is scarcely any accusation more apt to excite popular prejudice than the charge of treason. There is perhaps no country in the world where justice is in general more impartially administered than in England, yet let any man read some of the trials for treason in that country even since the revolution: he will see sometimes a fury influencing the judges, as well as the jury, that is extremely disgraceful. There may happen a case in our country where a man in reality innocent, but with strong plausible circumstances against him, would be so obnoxious to popular resentment, that he might be convicted upon very slight and insufficient proof. In such a case it would certainly be very proper for a cool temperate man of high authority, and who might be supposed uninfluenced by private motives, to interfere and prevent the popular current proving an innocent man's ruin. I know men who write with a view to flatter the people, and not to give them honest information, may misrepresent this account as an invidious imputation on the usual impartiality of juries. God knows no man more highly reverences that blessed institution than I do; I consider them the natural safeguard of the personal liberties of a free people, and I believe they would much seldomer err in the administration of justice than any other tribunal whatever. But no man of experience and candor will deny the probability of such a case as I have supposed sometimes, though rarely, happening; and whenever it did happen surely so safe a remedy as a prerogative of mercy in the Chief Magistrate of a great country ought to be at hand. There is little danger of an abuse of such a power, when we know how apt most men are in a republican government to court popularity at too great an expense, rather than do a just and beneficent action in opposition to strong prevailing prejudices among the people. But says Mr. Mason, "The President may sometimes exercise this power to screen from punishment those whom he had secretly instigated to commit the crime, and thereby prevent a discovery of his own guilt."

This is possible, but the probability of it is surely too slight to endanger the consequences of abridging a power which seems so generally to have been deemed necessary in every well regulated government. It may also be questioned, whether supposing such a participation of guilt, the President would not expose himself to greater danger by pardoning, than by suffering the law to have its course. Was it not supposed, by a great number of intelligent men, that Admiral Byng's execution was urged on to satisfy a discontented populace, when the administration, by the weakness of the force he was intrusted with, were perhaps the real cause of the miscarriage before Minorca?[12] Had he been acquitted, or pardoned, he could perhaps have exposed the real fault: as a prisoner under so heavy a charge his recrimination would have been discredited, as merely the effort of a man in despair to save himself from an ignominious punishment. If a President should pardon an accomplice, that accomplice then would be an unexceptionable witness. Before, he would be a witness with a rope about his own neck, struggling, to get clear of it at all events. Would any men of understanding, or at least ought they to credit an accusation from a person under such circumstances?*[13]

VII. OBJECTION.

"By declaring all treaties the supreme law of the land, the Executive and the Senate have, in many cases, an exclusive power of legislation; which might have been avoided by proper distinctions with respect to treaties, and requiring the assent of the House of Representatives, where it could be done with safety."

ANSWER.

Did not Congress very lately unanimously resolve, in adopting the very sensible letter of Mr. Jay, that a treaty when once made pursuant to the sovereign authority, <u>ex vi termini</u> became immediately the law of the land? It seems to result unavoidably from the nature of the thing, that when the constitutional right to make treaties is exercised, the treaty so made should be binding upon those who delegated authority for that purpose. If it was not, what foreign power would trust us? And if this right was restricted by any such fine checks as Mr. Mason has in his imagination, but has not thought proper to disclose, a critical occasion might arise, when for want of a little rational confidence in our own government we might be obliged to submit to a master in an enemy. Mr. Mason wishes the House of Representatives to have some share in this business, but he is immediately sensible of the impropriety of it, and adds "where it can be done with safety." And how is it to be known whether it can be done with safety or not, but during the pendency of a negotiation? Must not the

President and Senate judge whether it can be done with safety or not? If they are of opinion it is unsafe, and the House of Representatives of course not consulted, what becomes of this boasted check, since, if it amounts to no more than that the President and Senate may consult the House of Representatives if they please, they may do this as well without such a provision as with it. Nothing would be more easy than to assign plausible reasons, after the negotiation was over, to show that a communication was unsafe, and therefore surely a precaution that could be so easily eluded, if it was not impolitic to the greatest degree, must be thought trifling indeed. It is also to be observed, that this authority, so obnoxious in the new Constitution (which is unfortunate in having little power to please some persons, either as containing new things or old), is vested indefinitely and without restriction in our present Congress, who are a body constituted in the same manner as the Senate is to be, but there is this material difference in the two cases, that we shall have an additional check, under the new system of a President of high personal character chosen by the immediate body of the people.

VIII. OBJECTION.

"Under their own construction of the general clause at the end of the enumerated powers, the Congress may grant monopolies in trade and commerce, constitute new crimes, inflict unusual and severe punishment, and extend their power as far as they shall think proper; so that the State Legislatures have no security for the powers now presumed to remain to them: or the people for their rights. There is no declaration of any kind for preserving the liberty of the press, the trial by jury in civil causes, nor against the danger of standing armies in time of peace."

ANSWER.

The general clause at the end of the enumerated powers is as follows:—

"To make all laws which shall be necessary and proper for carrying into execution the foregoing powers, and all other powers vested by this constitution in the United States, or in any department or office thereof."

Those powers would be useless, except acts of legislation could be exercised upon them. It was not possible for the Convention, nor is it for any human body, to foresee and provide for all contingent cases that may arise. Such cases must therefore be left to be provided for by the general Legislature as they shall happen to come into existence. If Congress, under pretence of exercising the power delegated to them, should in fact, by the exercise of any other power, usurp upon the rights of the different Legislatures, or of any private citizens, the people will be exactly in the same situation as if there had been an express provision against such power in particular, and yet they had presumed to exercise it. It would be an act of tyranny, against which no parchment stipulations can guard; and the Convention surely can be only answerable for the propriety of the powers given, not for the future virtues of all with thom those powers may be intrusted. It does not therefore appear to me that there is any weight in this objection more than in others. But that I may give it every fair advantage, I will take notice of every particular injurious act of power which Mr. Mason points out as exercisable by the authority of Congress under this general clause.

The first mentioned is, "That the Congress may grant monopolies in trade and commerce." Upon examining the constitution I find it expressly provided, "That no preference shall be given to the ports of one State over those of another;" and that "citizens of each State shall be entitled to all privileges and immunities of citizens in the several States." These provisions appear to me to be calculated for the very purpose Mr. Mason wishes to secure. Can they be consistent with any monopoly in trade and commerce?*[14] I apprehend therefore, under this expression must be intended more than is expressed, and if I may conjecture from another publication of a gentleman of the same State and in the same party of opposition, I should suppose it arose from a jealousy of the eastern States very well known to be often expressed by some gentleman of Virginia. They fear, that a majority of the States may establish regulations of commerce which will give great advantage to the carrying trade of America, and be a means of encouraging New England vessels rather than Old England. Be it so. No regulations can give such advantage to New England vessels, which will not be enjoyed by all other American vessels, and many States can build as well as New England, though not at present perhaps in equal proportion.†[15] And what could conduce more to the preservation of the Union than allowing to every kind of industry in America a peculiar preference! Each State exerting itself in its own way, but the exertions of all contributing to the common security, and increasing the rising greatness of our country! Is it not the aim of every wise country to be as much the carriers of their own produce as they can be? And would not this be the means in our own of producing a new source of activity among the people, giving to our own fellow-citizens what otherwise must be given to strangers, and laying the foundation of an independent trade among ourselves, and of gradually raising a navy in America which, however distant the prospect, ought certainly not to be out of our sight. There is no great probability however that our country is likely soon to enjoy so glorious an advantage. We must have treaties of commerce, because without them we cannot trade to other countries. We already have such with some nations; we have none with Great Britain, which can be imputed to no other cause but our not having a strong respectable government to bring that haughty nation to terms. And surely no man, who feels for the honor of his country, but must view our present degrading commerce with that country with the highest indignation, and the most ardent wish to extricate ourselves from so disgraceful a situation. This only can be done by a powerful government which can dictate conditions of advantage to ourselves, as an equivalent for advantages to them; and this could undoubtedly be easily done by such a government, without diminishing the value of any articles of our own produce; or if there was any diminution it would be too slight to be felt by any patriot in competition with the honor and interest of his country.

As to the constituting of new crimes, and inflicting unusual and severe punishment, certainly the cases enumerated wherein the Congress are empowered either to define offences, or prescribe punishments, are such as are proper for the exercise of such authority in the general Legislature of the Union. They only relate to "counterfeiting the securities and current coin of the United States," to "piracies and felonies committed on the high seas, and offences against the law of nations," and to "treason against the United States." These are offences immediately affecting the security, the honor or the interest of the United States at large, and of course must come within the sphere of the Legislative authority which is intrusted with their protection. Beyond these authorities, Congress can exercise no other power of this kind, except in the enacting of penalties to enforce their acts of legislation in the cases where express authority is delegated to them, and if they could not enforce such acts by the enacting of penalties those powers would be altogether useless, since a legislative regulation without some sanction would be an absurd thing indeed. The Congress having, for these reasons, a just right to authority in the above particulars, the question is, whether it is practicable and proper to prescribe limits to its exercise, for fear that they should inflict punishments unusual and severe. It may be observed, in the first place, that a declaration against "cruel and unusual punishment" formed part of an article in the Bill of Rights at the revolution in England in 1688. The prerogative of the Crown having been grossly abused in some preceding reigns, it was thought proper to notice every grievance they had endured, and those declarations went to an abuse of power in the Crown only, but were never intended to limit the authority of Parliament. Many of these articles of the Bill of Rights in England, without a due attention to the difference of the cases, were eagerly adopted when our constitutions were formed, the minds of men then being so warmed with their exertions in the cause of liberty as to lean too much perhaps towards a jealousy of power to repose a proper confidence in their own government. From these articles in the State constitutions many things were attempted to be transplanted into our new Constitution, which would either have been nugatory or improper. This is one of them. The expressions "unusual and severe" or "cruel and unusual" surely would have been too vague to have been of any consequence, since they admit of no clear and precise signification. If to guard against punishments being too severe, the Convention had enumerated a vast variety of cruel punishments, and prohibited the use of any of them, let the number have been ever so great, an inexhaustible fund must have been unmentioned, and if our government had been disposed to be cruel their invention would only have been put to a little more trouble. If to avoid this difficulty, they had determined, not negatively what punishments should not be exercised, but positively what punishments should, this must have led them into a labyrinth of detail which in the original constitution of a government would have appeared perfectly ridiculous, and not left a room for such changes, according to circumstances, as must be in the power of every Legislature that is rationally formed. Thus when we enter into particulars, we must be convinced that the proposition of such a restriction would have led to nothing useful, or to something dangerous, and therefore that its omission is not chargeable as a fault in the new Constitution. Let us also remember, that as those who are to make those laws must themselves be subject to them, their own interest and feelings will dictate to them not to make them unnecessarily severe; and that in the case of treason, which usually in every country exposes men most to the avarice and rapacity of government, care is taken that the innocent family of the offender shall not suffer for the treason of their relation. This is the crime with respect to which a jealousy is of the most importance, and accordingly it is defined with great plainness and accuracy, and the temptations to abusive prosecutions guarded against as much as possible. I now proceed to the three great cases: The liberty of the press, the trial by jury in civil cases, and a standing army in time of peace.

The liberty of the press is always a grand topic for declamation, but the future Congress will have no other authority over this than to secure to authors for a limited time an exclusive privilege of publishing their works.—This authority has been long exercised in England, where the press is as free as among ourselves or in any country in the world: and surely such an encouragement to genius is no restraint on the liberty of the press, since men are allowed to publish what they please of their own, and so far as this may be deemed a restraint upon others it is certainly a reasonable one, and can be attended with no danger of copies not being sufficiently multiplied, because the interest of the proprietor will always induce him to publish a quantity fully equal to the demand. Besides, that such encouragement may give birth to many excellent writings which would otherwise have never appeared.*[16] If the Congress should exercise any other power over the press than this, they will do it without any warrant from this constitution, and must answer for it as for any other act of tyranny.

In respect to the trial by jury in civil cases, it must be observed it is a mistake to suppose that such a trial takes place in all civil cases now. Even in the common law courts, such a trial is only had where facts are disputed between the parties, and there are even some facts triable by other methods. In the Chancery and Admiralty Courts, in many of the States, I am told they have no juries at all. The States in these particulars differ very much in their practice from each other. A general declaration therefore to preserve the trial by jury in all civil cases would only have produced confusion, so that the courts afterwards in a thousand instances would not have known how to have proceeded.—If they had added, "as heretofore accustomed," that would not have answered the purpose, because there has been no uniform custom about it.—If therefore the Convention had interfered, it must have been by entering into a detail highly unsuitable to a fundamental constitution of government; if they had pleased some States they must have displeased others by innovating upon the modes of administering justice perhaps endeared to them by habit, and agreeable to their settled conviction of propriety. As this was the case it appears to me it was infinitely better, rather than endanger every thing by attempting too much, to leave this complicated business of detail to the regulation of the future Legislature, where it can be adjusted coolly and at ease, and upon full and exact information. There is no danger of the trial by jury being rejected, when so justly a favorite of the whole people. The representatives of the people surely can have no interest in making themselves odious, for the mere pleasure of being hated, and when a member of the House of Representatives is only sure of being so for two years, but must continue a citizen all his life his interest as a citizen, if he is a man of common sense, to say nothing of his being a man of common honesty, must ever be uppermost in his mind. We know the great influence of the monarchy in the British government, and upon what a different tenure the Commons there have their seats in Parliament from that prescribed to our representatives. We know also they have a large standing army. It is in the power of the Parliament, if they dare to exercise it, to abolish the trial by jury altogether. But woe be to the man who should dare to attempt it. It would undoubtedly produce an insurrection, that would hurl every tyrant to the ground who attempted to destroy that great and just favorite of the English nation. We certainly shall be always sure of this guard at least upon any such act of folly or insanity in our representatives. They soon would be taught the consequence of sporting with the feelings of a free people. But when it is evident that such an attempt cannot be rationally apprehended, we have no reason to anticipate unpleasing emotions of that nature. There is indeed little probability that any degree of tyranny which can be figured to the most discolored imagination as likely to arise out of our government, could find an interest in attacking the trial by jury in civil cases;—and in criminal ones, where no such difficulties intervene as in the other, and where there might be supposed temptations to violate the personal security of a citizen, it is sacredly preserved.

The subject of a standing army has been exhausted in so masterly a manner in two or three numbers of the Federalist (a work which I hope will soon be in every body's hands), that but for the sake of regularity in answering Mr. Mason's objections, I should not venture upon the same topic, and shall only presume to do so, with a reference for fuller satisfaction to that able performance.[17] It is certainly one of the most delicate and proper cases for the consideration of a free people, and so far as a jealousy of this kind leads to any degree of caution not incompatible with the public safety, it is undoubtedly to be commended. Our jealousy of this danger has descended to us from our British ancestors; in that country they have a Monarch, whose power being limited, and at the same time his prerogatives very considerable, a constant jealousy of him is both natural and proper. The two last of the Stuarts having kept up a considerable body of standing forces in time of peace for the clear and almost avowed purpose of subduing the liberties of the people, it was made an article of the bill of rights at the revolution, "That the raising or keeping a standing army within the kingdom in time of peace, unless it be with consent of Parliament, is against law;" but no attempt was made, or I dare say ever thought of, to restrain the Parliament from the exercise of that right. An army has been kept on foot annually by authority of Parliament, and I believe ever since the revolution they have had some standing troops; disputes have frequently happened about the number, but I don't recollect any objection by the most zealous patriot, to the keeping up of any at all. At the same time, notwithstanding the above practice of an annual vote (arising from a very judicious caution), it is still in the power of Parliament to authorize the keeping up of any number of troops for any indefinite time, and to provide for their subsistence for any number of years. Considerations of prudence, not constitutional limits to their authority, alone restrain such an exercise of it—our Legislature however will be strongly guarded, though that of Great Britain is without any check at all. No appropriations of money for military services can continue longer than two years. Considering the extensive services the general government may have to provide for upon this vast continent, no forces with any serious prospect of success could be attempted to be raised for a shorter time. Its being done for so short a period, if there were any appearances of ill designs in the government, would afford time enough for the real friends of their country to sound an alarm, and when we know how easy it is to excite jealousy of any government, how difficult for the people to distinguish from their real friends, those factious men who in every country are ready to disturb its peace for personal gratifications of their own, and those desperate ones to whom every change is welcome, we shall have much more reason to fear that the government may be overawed by groundless discontents, than that it should be able, if contrary to every probability such a government could be supposed willing, to effect any designs for the destruction of their own liberties as well as those of their constituents; for surely we ought ever to remember, that there will not be a man in the government but who has been either mediately or immediately recently chosen by the people, and that for too limited a time to make any arbitrary designs consistent with common sense, when every two years a new body of representatives with all the energy of popular feelings will come, to carry the strong force of a severe national control into every department of government. To say nothing of the one-third to compose the Senate coming at the same time, warm with popular sentiments, from their respective assemblies. Men may to be sure suggest dangers from any thing, but it may truly be said that those who can seriously suggest the danger of a premeditated attack on the liberties of the people from such a government as this, could with ease assign reasons equally plausible for distrusting the integrity of any government formed in any manner whatever; and really it does seem to me, that all their reasons may be fairly carried to this position, that inasmuch as any confidence in any men would be unwise, as we can give no power but what may be grossly abused, we had better give none at all, but continue as we are, or resolve into total anarchy at once, of which indeed our present condition falls very little short. What sort of a government would that be, which, upon the most certain intelligence that hostilities were meditated against it, could take no method for its defence till after a formal declaration of war, or the enemy's standard was actually fixed upon the shore? The first has for some time been out of fashion, but if it had not, the restraint these gentlemen recommend, would certainly have brought it into disuse with every power who meant to make war upon America. They would not be such fools as to give us the only warning we had informed them we would accept of, before we would take any step to counteract their designs. The absurdity of our being prohibited from preparing to resist an invasion till after it had actually taken place*[18] is so glaring, that no man can consider it for a moment without being struck with astonishment to see how rashly, and with how little consideration gentlemen, whose characters are certainly respectable, have suffered themselves to be led away by so delusive an idea. The example of other countries, so far from warranting any such limitation of power, is directly against it. That of England has already been particularly noticed. In our present articles of confederation there is no such restriction. It has been observed by the Federalist, that Pennsylvania and North Carolina appear to be the only States in the Union which have attempted any restraint of the Legislative authority in this particular, and that their restraint appears rather in the light of a caution than a prohibition; but that notwithstanding that, Pennsylvania had been obliged to raise forces in the very face of that article of her bill of rights. That great writer, from the remoteness of his situation, did not know that North Carolina had equally violated her bill of rights in a similar manner. The Legislature of that State in November, 1785, passed an act for raising 200 men for the protection of a county called Davidson county against hostilities from the Indians; they were to continue for two years from the time of their first rendezvous, unless sooner disbanded by the Assembly, and were to be subject to the same "rules with respect to their government as were established in the time of the late war by the Congress of the United States, for the government of the continental army." These are the very words of the act.[19] Thus, from the example of the only two countries in the world that I believe ever attempted such a restriction, it appears to be a thing incompatible with the safety of government. Whether their restriction is to be considered as a caution or a prohibition, in less than five years after peace the caution has been disregarded, or the prohibition disobeyed.*[20] Can the most credulous or suspicious men require stronger proof of the weakness and impolicy of such restraints?

IX. OBJECTION.

"The State Legislatures are restrained from laying export duties on their own produce."

ANSWER.

Duties upon exports, though they may answer in some particulars a convenience to the country which imposes them, are certainly not things to be contended for, as if the very being of a State was interested in preserving them. Where there is a kind of monopoly they may sometimes be ventured upon, but even there perhaps more is lost by imposing such duties, than is compensated for by any advantage. Where there is not a species of monopoly, no policy can be more absurd. The American States are so circumstanced that some of the States necessarily export part of the produce of neighboring ones. Every duty laid upon such exported produce operates in fact as a tax by the exporting State upon the non-exporting State. In a system expressly formed to produce concord among all, it would have been very unwise to have left such a source of discord open; and upon the same principle, and to remove as much as possible every ground of discontent, Congress itself are prohibited from laying duties on exports, because by that means those States which have a great deal of produce to export would be taxed much more heavily than those which had little or none for exportation.

X. OBJECTION.

"The general Legislature is restrained from prohibiting the further importation of slaves for twenty odd years, though such importations render the United States weaker, more vulnerable, and less capable of defence."

ANSWER.

If all the States had been willing to adopt this regulation, I should as an individual most heartily have approved of it, because even if the importation of slaves in fact rendered us stronger, less vulnerable and more capable of defence, I should rejoice in the prohibition of it, as putting an end to a trade which has already continued too long for the honor and humanity of those concerned in it. But as it was well known that South Carolina and Georgia thought a further continuance of such importations useful to them, and would not perhaps otherwise have agreed to the new constitution, those States which had been importing till they were satisfied, could not with decency have insisted upon their relinquishing advantages themselves had already enjoyed. Our situation makes it necessary to bear the evil as it is. It will be left to the future legislatures to allow such importations or not. If any, in violation of their clear conviction of the injustice of this trade, persist in pursuing it, this is a matter between God and their own consciences. The interests of humanity will, however, have gained something by the prohibition of this inhuman trade, though at the distance of twenty odd years.

XI. OBJECTION.

"Both the general Legislature and the State Legislatures, are expressly prohibited making ex post facto laws, though there never was, nor can be, a legislature but must and will make such laws, when necessity and the public safety require them; which will hereafter be a breach of all the constitutions in the Union, and afford precedents for other innovations."

ANSWER.

My ideas of liberty are so different from those of Mr. Mason, that in my opinion this very prohibition is one of the most valuable parts of the new constitution. Ex post facto laws may sometimes be convenient, but that they are ever absolutely necessary I shall take the liberty to doubt, till that necessity can be made apparent. Sure I am, they have been the instrument of some of the grossest acts of tyranny that were ever exercised, and have this never failing consequence, to put the minority in the power of a passionate and unprincipled majority, as to the most sacred things, and the plea of necessity is never wanting where it can be of any avail. This very clause, I think, is worth ten thousand declarations of rights, if this, the most essential right of all, was omitted in them. A man may feel some pride in his security, when he knows that what he does innocently and safely to-day, according to the laws of his country, cannot be tortured into guilt and danger to-morrow. But if it should happen, that a great and overruling necessity, acknowledged and felt by all, should make a deviation from this prohibition excusable, shall we not be more safe in leaving the excuse for an extraordinary exercise of power to rest upon the apparent equity of it alone, than to leave the door open to a tyranny it would be intolerable to bear? In the one case, every one must be sensible of its justice, and therefore excuse it; in the other, whether its exercise was just or unjust, its being lawful would be sufficient to command obedience. Nor would a case like that, resting entirely on its own bottom, from a conviction of invincible necessity, warrant an avowed abuse of another authority, where no such necessity existed or could be pretended.

I have now gone through Mr. Mason's objections; one thing still remains to be taken notice of; his prediction, which he is pleased to express in these words: "This government will commence in a moderate aristocracy; it is at present impossible to foresee, whether it will in its operation produce a monarchy, or a corrupt, oppressive aristocracy; it will most probably vibrate some years between the two, and then terminate in the one or the other." From the uncertainty of this prediction, we may hope that Mr. Mason was not divinely inspired when he made it, and of course that it may as fairly be questioned as any of his particular objections. If my answers to his objections are, in general, solid, a very different government will arise from the new constitution, if the several States should adopt it, as I hope they will. It will not probably be too much to flatter ourselves with, that it may present a spectacle of combined strength in government, and genuine liberty in the people, the world has never yet beheld. In the mean time, our situation is critical to the greatest degree. Those gentlemen who think we may at our ease go on from one convention to another, to try if all objections cannot be conquered by perseverance, have much more sanguine expectations than I can presume to form. There are critical periods in the fate of nations, as well as in the life of man, which are not to be neglected with impunity. I am much mistaken if this is not such a one with us. When we were at the very brink of despair, the late excellent Convention, with a unanimity that none could have hoped for, generously discarding all little considerations, formed a system of government which I am convinced can stand the nicest examination, if reason and not prejudice is employed in viewing it. With a happiness of thought, which in our present awful situation ought to silence much more powerful objections than any I have heard, they have provided in the very frame of government a safe, easy and unexceptionable method of correcting any errors it may be thought to contain. Those errors may be corrected at leisure; in the mean time the acknowledged advantages likely to flow from this constitution may be enjoyed. We may venture to hold up our head among the other powers of the world. We may talk to them with the confidence of an independent people, having strength to resent insults; and avail ourselves of all our natural advantages. We may be assured of once more beholding justice, order and dignity taking place of the present anarchical confusion prevailing almost every where, and drawing upon us universal disgrace. We may hope, by proper exertions of industry, to recover thoroughly from the shock of the late war, and truly to become an independent, great and prosperous people But if we continue as we now are, wrangling about every trifle, listening to the opinion of a small minorty, in preference to a large and most respectable majority of the first men in our country, and among them some of the first in the world, if our minds in short are bent rather on indulging a captious discontent, than bestowing a generous and well-placed confidence in those who we have every reason to believe are entirely worthy of it, we shall too probably present a spectacle for malicious exultation to our enemies, and melancholy dejection to our friends; and the honor, glory and prosperity which were just within our reach, will perhaps be snatched from us for ever.

Marcus.

Printed, McRee, 2:186-215.

---

[1]George Mason (1725-1792), a planter of northern Virginia and a delegate to the constitutional convention, refused to sign the Constitution and gave his reasons in his "Objections to the Federal Constitution." Mason first sent his "Objections" to Richard Henry Lee, a Virginia member of the Continental Congress. Within a few weeks, Mason's essay was published, but it contained

errors and was done without Mason's knowledge. Approved versions subsequently appeared, and Mason's work became part of the Antifederalist canon. *DAB*, s.v. "Mason, George"; Helen Hill Miller, *George Mason: Gentleman Revolutionary* (Chapel Hill: University of North Carolina Press, 1975), 267.

[2]McRee dates this document January 8, 1788. Portions of it appeared in the *State Gazette* of New Bern. The entire essay, along with an "Address" to the people by Publicola (Archibald Maclaine), was published in pamphlet form. McRee declared it to be "greatly superior to any defence of the Constitution published in North Carolina anterior to its adoption." McRee, *Life and Correspondence*, 2:186.

[3]Marcus was JI's pseudonym. His reason for choosing this name is unknown, though perhaps he likened himself to Marcus Aurelius. Despite the pseudonym, his style was easily identifiable "by his vigor, as a giant by the imprint of his foot." McRee, *Life and Correspondence*, 2:186.

[4]JI's notes to this essay are indicated primarily by asterisks in the text in McRee's publication. Each note appears here in its entirety. "It appears to me a very just remark of Mr. Wilson's, in his celebrated speech, that a bill of rights would have been dangerous, as implying that without such a reservation the Congress would have had authority in the cases enumerated, so that if any had been omitted (and who would undertake to recite all the State and individual rights not relinquished by the new Constitution?) they might have been considered at the mercy of the general legislature." McRee, *Life and Correspondence*, 2:187.

James Wilson (1742-1798), a Pennsylvania lawyer and signer of the Declaration of Independence, was a delegate to the constitutional convention and the Pennsylvania ratification convention. Wilson was also a law professor at the University of Pennsylvania, a congressman, and, along with JI, an associate justice of the U.S. Supreme Court. *BDC*, s.v. "Wilson, James."

[5]"I have understood it was considered at the Convention, that the proportion of one Representative to 30,000 constituents, would produce at the very first nearly the number that would be satisfactory to Mr. Mason. So that I presume this reason was wrote before the material alteration was made from 40,000 to 30,000, which is said to have taken place the very last day just before the signature." McRee, *Life and Correspondence*, 2:188.

[6]"It seems by the letter which has been published of Mr. Elsworth and Mr. Sherman, as if one reason of giving a share in these appointments to the Senate was, that persons in what are called the lesser States might have an equal chance for such appointments, in proportion to their merit, with those in the larger, an advantage that could only be expected from a body in which the States were equally represented." McRee, *Life and Correspondence*, 2:192.

Oliver Ellsworth (1745-1807), a prominent lawyer from Connecticut, was a delegate to the constitutional convention and the 1788 state ratification convention. He later served as a U.S. senator (1789-1796), chief justice of the U.S. Supreme Court (1796-1800), and commissioner to France (1799-1800). *BDC*, s.v. "Ellsworth, Oliver"; *DAB*, s.v. "Ellsworth, Oliver."

Roger Sherman (1721-1793) of Connecticut was a merchant and lawyer. He represented the state in the Continental Congress (1774-1781, 1783-1784) and was a member of the committee to draft the Declaration of Independence. Sherman was a delegate to the constitutional convention and introduced what became known as the "Connecticut Compromise." The compromise broke an impasse between large and small states by prescribing, among other things, equal representation among the states in the Senate and one representative in the House for each forty thousand state residents. *DAB* , s.v. "Sherman, Roger"; Kelly and Harbison, *American Constitution*, 120-121.

[7]"When I wrote the above, I had not seen Governor Randolph's letter. Otherwise, I have so great a respect for that gentleman's character I should have treated with more deference an idea in some measure countenanced by him. One of his objections relates to the Congress fixing their own salaries. I am persuaded, upon a little reflection, that gentleman must think this is one of those cases where a trust must unavoidably be reposed. No salaries could certainly be fixed now so as to answer the various changes in the value of money that in the course of time must take place. And in what condition would the supreme authority be if their very subsistence depended on an inferior power! An abuse in this case too would be so gross that it is very unlikely to happen, but if it should it would probably prove much more fatal to the authors than injurious to the people." McRee, *Life and Correspondence*, 2:193.

Edmund Randolph (1753-1813), governor of Virginia and delegate to the constitutional convention, would not sign the final version of the Constitution and on October 10, 1787, wrote a letter listing his reasons. While Randolph wanted to change the proposed Constitution, he did not want it—even in its flawed state—defeated. Thus, he withheld his letter to avoid aiding the Antifederalists. Growing public curiosity and increasing hope among partisans that his words would help their cause created pressure on Randolph to release the letter to the public, which he finally did in late December 1787. Despite the ten objections listed in his letter, Randolph eventually supported ratification. John J. Reardon, *Edmund Randolph: A Biography* (New York: Macmillan, 1974), 125-127, 130; *DAB*, s.v. "Randolph, Edmund"; *BDC*, s.v. "Randolph, Edmund."

[8]"See Coke's Commentary upon Littleton, 110. 1. Blackstone's Commentaries, 227 and seq." McRee, *Life and Correspondence*, 2:195.

[9]"1. Blackstone's Commentaries, 232." McRee, *Life and Correspondence*, 2:196.

[10]Baron de Montesquieu (1689-1755) was a French political philosopher who believed that the best way to protect individual freedom was to divide government into three parts so that each branch could check the excesses of the others. *The Encyclopedia of Philosophy*, s.v. "Montesquieu, Baron de."

[11]"I have since found that in the constitutions of some of the States there are much stronger restrictions on the Executive authority in this particular than I was aware of. In others the restriction only extends to prosecutions carried on by the General Assembly, or the most numerous branch of legislature, or a contrary provision by law; Virginia is in the latter class. But when we consider how necessary it is in many cases to make use of accomplices to convict their associates, and what little regard ought in general to be paid to a guilty man swearing to save his own life, we shall probably think that the jealousies which (by prohibiting

pardons before convictions) even disabled the Executive authority from procuring unexceptionable testimony of this sort, may more fairly be ascribed to the natural irritation of the public mind at the time when the constitutions were formed, than to an enlarged and full consideration of the whole subject. Indeed, it could scarcely be avoided, that when arms were first taken up in the cause of liberty, to save us from the immediate crush of arbitrary power, we should lean too much rather to the extreme of weakening than of strengthening the Executive power in our own government. In England, the only restriction upon this power in the King, in case of Crown prosecutions (one or two slight cases excepted) is, that his pardon is not pleadable in bar of an impeachment. But he may pardon after conviction, even on an impeachment; which is an authority not given to our President, who in case of impeachments has no power either of pardoning or reprieving." McRee, *Life and Correspondence*, 2:200-201.

[12]John Byng (1704-1757), a British admiral, was assigned to defend Minorca, an island in the Mediterranean, against a French attack in 1755. Because of Byng's bungling, a portion of his squadron suffered heavy damage from the French fleet, while the rest remained unengaged. The admiral and what remained of his force then retreated to Gibraltar, leaving Minorca to the French. British government officials and the public roundly criticized him. In a court-martial Byng was found guilty of neglecting his duty and sentenced to death, as required by law. The court asked the king to show mercy, but he refused. On March 14, 1757, Byng was shot. *DNB*, s.v. "Byng, John."

[13]"The evidence of a man confessing himself guilty of the same crime is undoubtedly admissible, but it is generally and ought to be always received with great suspicion, and other circumstances should be required to corroborate it." McRee, *Life and Correspondence*, 2:202.

[14]"One of the powers given to Congress is, 'To promote the progress of science and useful arts, by securing for limited times to authors and inventors the exclusive right to their respective writings and discoveries.' I am convinced Mr. Mason did not mean to refer to this clause. He is a gentleman of too much taste and knowledge himself to wish to have our government established upon such principles of barbarism as to be able to afford no encouragement to genius." McRee, *Life and Correspondence*, 2:205.

[15]Here McRee uses a cross instead of an asterisk for JI's note. "Some might apprehend, that in this case as New England would at first have the greatest share of the carrying trade, the vessels of that country might demand an unreasonable freight. But no attempt could be more injurious to them as it would immediately set the Southern States to building, which they could easily do, and thus a temporary loss would be compensated with a lasting advantage to us; the very reverse would be the case with them. Besides, that from that country alone there would probably be competition enough for freight to keep it on reasonable terms." McRee, *Life and Correspondence*, 2:205.

[16]"If this provision had not been made in the new constitution no author could have enjoyed such an advantage in all the United States, unless a similar law had constantly subsisted in each of the States separately." McRee, *Life and Correspondence*, 2:208.

[17]Alexander Hamilton addressed the issue of a standing army in the *Federalist* numbers twenty-four through twenty-eight. Alexander Hamilton, John Jay, and James Madison, *The Federalist* (Washington: Robert B. Luce, 1976), 141-175.

[18]"Those gentlemen who gravely tell us that the militia will be sufficient for this purpose, do not recollect that they themselves do not desire we should rely solely on a militia in case of actual war, and therefore in the case I have supposed they cannot be deemed sufficient even by themselves, for when the enemy landed it would undoubtedly be a time of war, but the misfortune would be, that they would be prepared; we not. Certainly all possible encouragement should be given to the training of our militia, but no man can really believe that they will be sufficient, without the aid of any regular troops, in a time of foreign hostility. A powerful militia may make fewer regulars necessary, but will not make it safe to dispense with them altogether." McRee, *Life and Correspondence*, 2:211.

[19]Item seventeen in the North Carolina Declaration of Rights of 1776 states that "as standing armies, in time of peace, are dangerous to liberty, they ought not to be kept up." The act to which JI refers was actually passed on January 6, 1787, during the 1786-1787 session, and the quotation is from section four. The Davidson County to which the law applied is now part of Tennessee. Cheney, *North Carolina Government*, 810; Clark, *State Records*, 24:783-786; Corbitt, *North Carolina Counties*, 85-86.

[20]"I presume we are not to be deemed in a state of war whenever any Indian hostilities are committed on our frontiers. If that is the case, I don't suppose we have had six years of peace since the first settlement of the country, or shall have for fifty years to come. A distinction between peace and war would be idle indeed, if it can be frittered away by such pretences as those." McRee, *Life and Correspondence*, 2:212.

From William R. Davie

Halifax Jany. 11h. 178[*8*][1]

My Dear Sir,

I am happy to find your Election was secured at all events, however I am very sure there will be no danger with in the Town or County for you—and I hope <will> Mr. Johnston will not think himself at liberty to refuse should his Country call upon him at this important crisis.[2]

Mr. Jones continues perfectly anti federal, and is inducing the people here to Doubt very generally of its adoption in the present form.[3]

I am much obliged to you for the inclosures, the letters for Hillsboro shall be forwarded by the first opportunity.—you have seen the Freeman. This piece exceeds in meanness any thing I ever saw, but I believe it is a true picture of the persons, whose image it really bears—These fellows must be scourged—I hope you will do your share of this business, you observe it is a part of a fixed Design to raise a general jealousy and Dis[*trust*] against every member of the pro-fession—

I am very happy the Governor was received in a proper manner at the Assembly a number of Gentlemen came to meet him on his coming to town, and Caswell must have felt some mortification at this Attention to Mr. Johnston, as no notice had been taken of him. I was happy in having an opportunity of shewing <u>them</u> what homage even Freemen would pay to a <u>virtuous man</u> in office

My Compliments to your brother and believe me with the

most sincere friendship yours mo. obd.

William R Davie

RC, Iredell Papers, Duke. Printed, McRee, 2:215-216. Addressed "James Iredell, Esqr. Edenton Favd. by Mr. Amis."

---

[1]The original letter is dated 1787, but the contents indicate that it was written in 1788.

[2]This refers to the election of delegates to the state ratification convention.

[3]Willie Jones was the acknowledged leader of the Antifederalists in the state. He had been chosen as a delegate to the constitutional convention in Philadelphia but had refused the position. At the 1788 state ratification convention, Jones represented Halifax County, while the Federalist Davie represented the town of Halifax. Robinson, *William R. Davie*, 178, 196; Massengill, *North Carolina Votes*, 15, 34.

From Charles Johnson

Strawberry-Hill, January 14th, 1788.[1]

Dear Sir:

I return you the papers containing the Federalist, and am much obliged to you for communicating them to me.[2] I observe that No. 13 of the papers, containing No. 6 of the Federalist, is wanting, and cannot be certain whether it came with the rest or not, as I was at the time of receiving them in too much pain to look them over. Although it has already been looked for, yet if it was sent—which please let me know—I will cause another search to be made for it.

The Federalist appears to me to be elegantly written; the author displays a most comprehensive imagination, and great extent of political knowledge. But I am surprised that he should have thought it necessary to take so much pains to establish, what appears at the first glance, at least to me, an incontrovertible truth, which is—that the States, united under one efficient government, properly balanced, will be much more powerful, have much fewer causes either of internal or external quarrel, and will be able to procure greater commercial advantages, more respectability and credit, than the States disunited into distinct, independent governments, or separate confederacies. Either of these ideas seem so absurd that I must believe they can have few partisans; and had not the Federalist taken so much pains to refute them, I could scarce imagine they could have been at all entertained.

If he means to exhaust the subject, and is equally copious upon each article, he will undoubtedly afford a great fund of entertainment. I shall be particularly desirous to see those numbers that treat of the additional security which the adoption of the new Constitution will afford to the republican form of government, to liberty and property; and that will satisfactorily answer all the objections of importance that shall have made their appearance against it. This is part of the task he has set himself in his first number, and it will afford great room for the exertion of his excursive genius and reasoning powers, as some very weighty objections have already arisen, and still more may possibly arise when the subject comes to be more fully and unprejudicedly investigated. For certainly there are few men acquainted with the great, respected, I may almost say adored, characters who formed the late convention, who did not view the new Constitution with an eye strongly prejudiced in its favor. There are, nevertheless, great defects found in it: ought they not to be more attended to even on that account?

For my part I will candidly, and in confidence, declare to you that it is a doubtful point with me, and which I cannot yet bring to a decision, whether it will be better to receive the new Constitution, with all its seeming imperfections on its head, or run the risk of obtaining another Convention, which may revise and amend, expunge those articles that seem repugnant to the liberties of the people—secure our political liberty by separating the executive, legislative, and judicial powers—affix responsibility to every office—and explicitly secure the trial by jury, according to former usage—the liberty of the press, with all the other rights of the individual which are not necessary to be given up to government, and which ought not and cannot be required for any good purpose. Surely, if there is no immediate, impending danger to prevent the adoption of the measure, it is most devoutly to be wished. This requisite information might easily, as I conceive, be obtained from Congress, as they must be acquainted, by the communications of their ambassadors, with the general aspect of affairs in Europe. I have already said that I have formed no decided opinion; the subject I conceive of too great magnitude, and above me. I only venture my doubts without any apprehension of your placing me in any of our friend Dr. W.'s classes, the burden of each verse of which, if I remember rightly, is, "the government is not for him."[3]

The gout still continues a kind of desultory skirmishing, sometimes forcing one or the other of my outworks; but soon leaving them. This makes me imagine that only its advance, composed of light troops and hussars, have yet made their appearance; and induces me to believe that I have still a heavy, serious attack from the main army to sustain. But as the citadel is in pretty good order, the garrison in tolerable spirits, no scarcity of provision or ammunition, and the assistance of able engineers to be had if requisite, I am determined to hold out to the last extremity, and dispute the ground inch by inch; and I flatter myself that, by a vigorous defence, I shall compel the enemy to raise the siege. When, if they do no considerable damage to the body of the place, I am in hopes speedily to repair the outworks, and put the whole fort in a proper state of defence against the next attack.

I would apologize for taking up so much of your time, but know your good nature will excuse greater intrusions. The truth is, I am quite fatigued with reading, and having taken up the pen, found some relief from weariness, and even pain, by having my attention taken off from it,—so, though the tedious length of this letter may tire you, yet your humanity will be gratified by the consideration that you have been the means of administering relief to the weary and heavy laden. Mrs. Johnson still continues indisposed. Tom, the night before last, had a return of the fever and ague, but is now again pretty well; the rest of the family are in good health. with real regard, I am, dear sir,

Your most obt. and obliged serv't,

Chas. Johnson.

Printed, McRee, 2:598-600.

---

[1]Charles Johnson bought the house in Chowan County that he named Strawberry Hill sometime after 1779. Elizabeth Vann Moore, *Guide Book to Edenton and Chowan County* (Edenton: Edenton's Woman's Club, 1989), 62.

[2]*The Federalist* was a series published under the pen name "Publius" in New York newspapers between October 27, 1787, and May 28, 1788. The essays, written by Alexander Hamilton, James Madison, and John Jay, were issued in a bound volume in June 1788 in an attempt to sway delegates to the New York ratification convention. Morris, *Forging of the Union*, 308.

[3]"Dr. W" is Hugh Williamson. McRee, *Life and Correspondence*, 2:600.

From Archibald Maclaine

Wilmington 15h. Jany. 1788

Dear Sir

I had the pleasure of receiving yours of the 3d. Instant this day, covering a letter for Mr. Moore, whom I expect to see tomorrow, as he is yet in this neighborhood. From the purport of yours, I find you had not recd. mine on the same subject. Mr. Moore had recollected the objection you make with respect to the seat of government, and consequently had abandoned the idea of proposing you for Brunswick—He has however offered his own services, & I make no doubt will be elected.[1]

I am happy to hear that Mr. Johnston's elevation has been received in a manner suitable to his merit—I had no doubt but this would be acknowledged at a future day, whether he was living or dead. I shall always endeavor to pay a proper deference to every man in office, but I request you will present to Mr. Johnston, my sincere respects as a man.

The new constitution we are informed has been received and ratified in three States, and I have not a doubt but it will be received by nine, exclusive of our own[2]—once the new government is set a-going, I am convinced that any state which may be refractory, will be obliged to comply. Indeed from all the information I have had, there is little, or no doubt of our State. In New Hanover county, the people if left to themselves, are in favor of a change. Some demagogues /of the people/, a few <people> persons who are in debt, and every public officer, except the clerk of the county court, are decidedly against any change;—at least against any that will answer the purpose—Our friend Huske is the loudest man in Wilmington against the new constitution[3]—Whether ambition, or avarice, or a compound of both, may be the cause, I leave you to judge.

Parson Tate has picked up all the arguments, good and bad, that have been published against the new form of government.[4] The only original objection he had, was the want of a mint in each state. This he alleges is a never-failing mark of sovereignty, & is to keep the money with us—He appears to be greatly distressed, that we shall be obliged to send our <u>bullion</u> to the seat of government. It is indeed truly distressing.

I am very happy to hear that Mr. Barker has made a proper provision for his daughter & her family, a circumstance of which I had some doubt.[5]

Why do you pay the postage of your private correspondence? when the expense is chargeable to others in the way of business, it is well enough—otherwise, I expect you will not do so in future.

I am with great truth very respectfully & sincerely yours

A. Maclaine

RC, Iredell Papers, Duke. Printed, McRee, 2:216-217. Addressed "James Iredell esquire Edenton." Endorsed "Wilmington 15 Jan. 1788 A. Maclaine. Ansd."

---

[1]Delegates to the constitutional ratification convention were to select a site for the state capital. Residents of the Cape Fear region favored Fayetteville, while most of those living elsewhere supported a central location. The delegates decided that rather than name a specific site, they would choose a location and then allow the General Assembly to select the precise spot within a ten-mile radius. At the convention, JI nominated Isaac Hunter's home in Wake County. McRee, *Life and Correspondence*, 2:216n; Clark, *State Records*, 20:vi; 22:29.

JI was elected to represent the town of Edenton at the convention. Alfred Moore either chose not to run or was defeated. Massengill, *North Carolina Votes*, 30.

[2]Delaware, Pennsylvania, and New Jersey ratified the Constitution in December 1787. Though Maclaine had yet to receive the news, Georgia and Connecticut had also approved ratification in early January 1788. Edmund S. Morgan, *The Birth of the Republic, 1763-89*, rev. ed., Chicago History of American Civilization, ed. Daniel J. Boorstin (Chicago: University of Chicago Press, 1977), 193.

[3]John Huske was an Antifederalist delegate who represented New Hanover County in the 1788 and 1789 ratification conventions. In 1789 he led protesting Antifederalist delegates in a walkout of the convention. Massengill, *North Carolina Votes*, 30.

[4]James Tate, an outspoken Antifederalist, did not serve as a delegate to either of the state ratification conventions. *DNCB*, s.v. "Tate, James."

[5]Thomas Barker made provisions in his will for his daughter, Elizabeth, from an earlier marriage. Betsy Barker, as she was known, had married Col. William Tunstall, a prominent planter in Pittsylvania County, Va. Barker specified that Betsy's inheritance was to be at "her sole ordering and disposal without the interference of her Husband." Will of Thomas Barker, 1787, Chowan County Wills, State Archives; *DNCB*, s.v. "Barker, Thomas."

From William R. Davie

Halifax Jany. 22d. 178[*8*][1]

My Dear Sir

We have nothing worth remarking here, but the dissimination of the Anti-federal principles. Mr. Jones continues to asail the Constitution, and the Virginia communications have strengthened his party;[2] you know his opinion has great weight here, and that it is much easier to alarm people than to inform them.

Col Geddy who is a late convert, has announced himself a Candidate for the Convention and is a most furious zealot for what he calls W. Jones's system, which is indeed all he knows about it; but he has raised the old cant that "the poor are to be ruined by taxes, and no security for freedom of conscience &c"[3]—

I have not yet heard what the N. Jersey Convention have done, however I think there is little doubt, but they will adopt the Government proposed—as its consequences are so highly favorable to the non-importing States. The great deference this State has been accustomd to pay to the political opinions of the Old Dominion will I believe have a very bad effect on the Determination of this great question. This circumstance added to the opposition already formed, in my opinion renders its adoption in this State extremely doubtful.

The Governor writes me there have been 25 numbers of the Federalist printed. I will be obliged to you, to forward me as many as you can; especially as we are in greater want of its assistance here than you are at Edenton.

My Compts. to your Brother and believe me with the most sincere friendship

yours &c

William R Davie

RC, Iredell Papers, Duke. Printed, McRee, 2:217-218. Addressed "James Iredell, Esquire Edenton. Hond. by Mr. Dawson." Endorsed "Jan. 22. 1788. W. R. Davie. Ansd."

---

[1]The date on the original letter is 1787, but the contents indicate that it was written in 1788.

[2]The "Virginia communications" were *The Letters from the Federal Farmer*, the Antifederalist counterpart to *The Federalist*. Published in December 1787 by Richard Henry Lee, the volume cites the Constitution's hazards and omissions, including threats to freedom posed by a centralized government, unfair representation in Congress, and the absence of a bill of rights. Rather than advocate outright rejection of the Constitution, Lee urged readers to withhold support for ratification until these problems had been addressed. Kelly and Harbison, *American Constitution*, 146.

[3]John Geddy of Halifax was a gold and silversmith and a repairer of clocks and watches. In 1778, he became a lieutenant colonel in the county militia. His brother, James, was a noted silversmith in Williamsburg, Va. John Geddy, despite his enthusiasm, was not elected to the ratification convention. *DNCB*, s.v. "Geddy, John."

The "Jones system" included an independent and self-sufficient state; a democratic system adhering to the 1776 state constitution and its accompanying declaration of rights; and a commitment to improving educational opportunities. Robinson, "Willie Jones," pt. 2, 149; William E. Dodd, *The Life of Nathaniel Macon* (Raleigh: Edwards and Broughton, 1903), 51-52.

Hannah Iredell to Margaret Iredell

[January 31st]

. . . Your sons, you may well believe, are in good health, as they are now at a ball; they are both fond of dancing, the eldest full as much so as the youngest, though were you to see the gravity of his countenance, when he sits biting his nails over a law book, you would hardly think it possible he could be so delighted with a country-dance.

. . . Have you seen Mr. Trail, a gentleman who went hence about eighteen months ago? He was very intimate in our family, and carried a letter from Mr. Iredell to his brother. You will find him a very entertaining acquaintance. Ask him for the history of his own and Mr. T. Iredell's passion for Miss Dawson; he will relate it to you with great humor. . . .

Printed, McRee, 2:218.

From Nathaniel Dukinfield

[Sulham, 13th. Feb. 1788.]

Dear Iredell

In a very few days after the receipt of your Letter of the 7h. Sepr., I went with Lady D. to visit my Relations in Cheshire & Lancashire, & soon after my return I received Mr. Johnston's Letter which I am answering this morning—In Cheshire I attended a County-Meeting for the nomination of a Coroner. Mr. Crewe was there. I am not acquainted with him but had engaged a Gentleman to introduce me to him, as I wished to enquire about your Brother—but unluckily he left the Meeting abruptly & I had the mortification of a Disappointment—I am much obliged to you & Mr. Johnston for considering a proper Method of making me a Remittance.[1] I was in London last week. Mr. Lowther had left it & gone to Scotland, but returns in May & I mean to go to Town again to see him—he thinks Tobacco (but it must be good) a very proper Commodity & that or any other sent to any British Port, would suit me. the Sales &c must be done by an Agent, & I shod. find little difficulty in getting one at any Port who would be glad to execute the Commission. Mr. Johnston expresses doubts of the Goodness <of> or Value of the Virginia Dollar Bills in my Mother's possession, if he shod. not be mistaken, I shall be much disappointed—but it is of no Use to fret. I am well convinced Mr. Johnston will do what is best & I shall be perfectly satisfied. The mode of

Government which may be adopted by your Convention will, I hope, tend to your happiness & /be/ of advantage to Britain—At present this Country seems alive in forming Petitions to Parliament for the abolition of the Slave Trade.[2] I hope they will consider /well/ what they do, before they determine in favor of those petitions—I think some<th> regulations might be made in respect to the Conduct towards them on Ship-board, but if carried for a total abolition, I have doubts how we shall work our West India Islands.

I am glad to hear such good accounts of your Wife's & Daughter's health. I wish your own was as good—We have certainly great advantage over you in point of Climate—I don't believe I have had <the> an Head-Ach since 1772 when I had one ague-fit. My Wife & three Boys are very well—the youngest was inoculated in Octr. & was weaned yesterday. 'tis great Pity you have so much inconvenience about the Small Pox—but unless the whole Province would at once consent, the introduction (by Inoculation) into a single or a few plantations might be very distressing—one Comfort is, you are not liable to catch it, while you stay at home & shod. you go Northward, you wod. of course inoculate—As Mr. Lowther has, I understand been lately in Carolina, I shall be desirous of seeing him & making particular Enquiries after every of my Acquaintance. I saw Mr. Mc.Culloh, Mr. Brimage, & Mr. Palmer last week. they seem'd pretty well. I beg my comps. to Mrs. Iredell & all my Friends believe me,

Yours very sincerely

N. Dukinfield—

RC, Iredell Papers, Duke. Addressed "James Iredell Esqr. Edenton North Carolina." Endorsed "Feb. 13 1788 Sir N. Dukinfield. Ansd."

---

[1]The "Remittance" refers to money received from the sale of Dukinfield's mother's estate. Margaret Dukinfield Pearson had died in Bertie County in December 1784. *DNCB*, s.v. "Duckenfield, Nathaniel."

[2]Slavery was a key element in the economy of the British West Indies, but after the American Revolution, West Indian influence in England declined because of low sugar prices, large debts incurred by planters, and a lack of rejuvenating capital. Simultaneously, anti-slavery sentiment in England was on the rise, due largely to a religious revival in the country. While abolitionists had become politically active by the end of the 1780s, slavery would not be abolished in the empire until 1833. Michael Craton, *Sinews of Empire: A Short History of British Slavery* (Garden City, N.Y.: Anchor Books, 1974), 243; Edith F. Hurwitz, *Politics and the Public Conscience: Slave Emancipation and the Abolitionist Movement in Britain* (London: George Allen and Unwin, 1973), 17-18.

From John McLean[1]

Norfolk Febry. 15th 1788

Good Sir

About two days ago Mr. Ferguson favord me with a lengthy piece containing Mr. Mason's Objections to the Federal System and also refutations to each accompanied with an half Joe for four Books of the Federalist.[2] the remainder, as a small recompense for publishing the above Manuscript. since which I this moment receivd by Capt Meredith some material omissions respecting it, which shall be strictly attended to and inserted in their proper place. at the same time I must trespass on your goodness to inform the Author that every possible Attention shall be paid the composition thereof tho' it will all lie on myself having no Assistance but a boy to whom I cannot confide Manuscripts.

I beg leave, (thro your kind Channel) to observe that the Publication of the above will be attended with some material disadvantages with respect to Advertisements which I must omit in the Course of this publication Several other political pieces have been also sent for Appearance in my next, but defective of Marcus' Merit and Argument, I shall take the liberty of laying them on the Shelf of "Old Maids." These considerations, I flatter myself, will have their due Weight with the Author, who, I make no doubt, is possessed of that liberal Spirit which his Writings enforce, and will at a proper time, make a suitable return, for the Attention and pecuniary disadvantages which must arise therefrom to

his most Obedt. Servant

John Mc.Lean

By the letter favord me by Capt Meredith I am instructed to address this to your Care which will apologize (I presume) for this liberty taken by

J M

RC, Iredell Papers, Duke. Addressed "James Iredell Esq Edenton N Carolina." Endorsed "Norfolk Feb. 15th. 1788. John Mc.Lain. Ansd."

---

[1]John and Archibald McLean of New York began publishing the *Norfolk and Portsmouth Chronicle* in 1788. This weekly journal was the first newspaper published in the Borough of Norfolk, Va., after the Revolution. Its history was brief, however. Publication stopped upon the death of John McLean, who died sometime prior to July 22, 1789. William S. Forrest, *Historical and Descriptive Sketches of Norfolk and Vicinity. . . .* (Philadelphia: Lindsay and Blakiston, 1853), 99-100; Brent Tarter, ed.,

The Order Book and Related Papers of the Common Hall of the Borough of Norfolk, Virginia, 1736-1798 (Richmond: Virginia State Library, 1979), 277-278.

[2]A "joe" is a Portuguese gold coin. *OED*, s.v. "joe."

From Baron de Poellnitz

New York The 20 Feb*y*. 1788

Dear Sir

Your favour I received /and/ its enclosed Acct. I paid the 4th. Decbr. to Messrs. Scott /but/ that I did not answer the former til now was Owing to Want of Health and the Acct. I Thought had been paid by Ly anne, because about Two days before my going to England I received One Similar Acct. which I gave to Ly anne To pay as well as Your Letter to Answer. Tho She did not write to me that She had paid nevertheless I presumed it to be So as She had cherfully Agreed to it, and Knowing that Ladies are Seldom exact in their Correspondence I fancied her only in Want of recording the Subject to me: A Silance of about 4 Years on Your part not repeating this Debt confirmed me in the Error, and I did cease to write to you Sir, because I must of Cours have ackwainted You of Ly annes behaviour who being as She told me a relation of Yours, I wished not to bring (without good reasons) a heap of Shocking Events to your notice but as to enter in to This matter is now requisit I proceede to it.[1]

The Duke of Northumberland had instigated the Creditors of Ly anne to Arrest my Property Consisting in ready Money (in hands of Joseph and Herman Berens Two Merchants in the Citty) for Debts She had made before her Devorce with the Duke, but as now Law could in my Absence from England enforce Such an Arrest (The Case having not been previously pleaded) The Duke persuaded my Correspondents Messrs. Berens to Yield to the Arrest. This was the Cause of my Sudden Departure from America.

I wish not Extend in to remarks but must Observe that out of the number of 15 Creditors only One attaquet me for £562.10*s*. stg*s*. and that was Andrw. Corbet Esqr. Ly annes Brother in Law.[2] The Others (Tho Powrefully invited by self intrest as the whole Sum of Debts was Said to be £18,000. Stg*s*. by The Credit of The Duke, and by the connivance of Messrs. Berens) could not be persuaded that I was their Debtor, This Honnesty I Think worth recording, To <a> Contrast <th> This I must add, that Messrs. /Berens/ were not So As the Creditors Strangers to me but Friends full of Professions Transacting my Concerns this 20 Years and (This Case exepted) with integrity

Those Debts became the Subject of a Letter intercourse between the Duke and me; and Tho I was aqwainted with the particulars of the

Collusion in his Devorce, and that one Speciffic Term had been that he Should pay the Debts, <and> Tho also the Duks Conduct was Ungentleman like This notwithstanding I wrote to him politely but finaly I was Obliged to call Things by their True name and resuming All I made him Known, That Ly anne and I would petition to Parliamt. for to Show that The Annuity of £1600 Stg a year had been Settled in the Act of Devorce as an Alimentary Pension for Life, This Devorce was a Collusion, promise had been made by the Husband to pay /The/ Debts yet They were Still unpaid therefore the petitioners prayer was that The House would explain his Sovrign intentions /To Know/ if the Annuity by them granted was Subject to The paymt. of Debts Contracted before the Devorce or not.

The Duks Credit made this Contest pretty public in London There were Respectable Authorities of Opinion, that if Such an Affair came in to Evidence Parliamt. might perhaps revoque The Devorce as having been Obtained by fraude and Collusion. I only will mention this Single Opinion because it would have Operated upon All parties in a most Extraordinary manner, if by chance Such had been the Issue of this Affair. Accordingly I wrote to Ly anne to come to England but by all means in the Brittish Paquet. Two Such Paquets Arrived in England Since I could Calculate that She had received this Letter of myne without any News of her by the Thirde Mr Sayre Wrote giving me Notice that Ly anne had quitted New York and Ordered him to provide Boards for my childern &.&. but /of/ the Date of her departure /of/ The Name of the Vessel and were it was bound to <he did not mention> /no mention was made of/: This was perplexing News! but willing to give the best Explanation to this Unsatisfactory Intelligence, I fancied that Ly anne prompted by impatience had Sligthed my Advice and Stept in Some Marchand Vessel ready for Sail as for to have put our Concerns /in Such hands/ as those of Mr Sayre, Tho indeed it displeased me and that I had Cautioned her About his Caracter, But as this Same Man had onse Allmost persuaded this State to put Money and Lands in Consequence of a Swindling Banck Scheme of his invention in his hands, I made Also Allowance for this Step of Ly anne and put it to the Acct. of hurrie and imprudence, as I had no right to Suspect foul play from her, because her hatered to The Northumberland Family was well Known, and all her Letters to me were full of friendship: But even had I been Able to mistrust female Candour in those Proffessions /as Soon As borne/ the Thought would have vannished, Considering that recently She had Wrote to the Countess Bute her Mother, to the Countess Lonsdale and Ly macartney her Sisters, in Terms of high regard for me, Enlarging on the Subject of her happiness and of my Partiality, Who even She Said had gone So far, as to leave her full powers, and my All in her hands, When lately I went to England.[3]

However Seeing that She did not Arive I Thought her Shipwrekt and perished, in this Dilemma I was Kept by the public Accts of Such Disasters who had happened about that Time; Even her family was persuaded that Such had been her Fate, but just when we were About to fixe the Day for Mourning we got Some Intelligence of her Life by means of the Enquiries made to Know the Name and fate of all Vessels who Since 6 months had been bound from New York to English Ports a Gentleman Charged with that Commission by the Earl of Lonsdale Spoke with Captn Coupar Just Arrived from New York who had Seen Ly anne handed by Mr Sayre on board of a french Paket bound for L'Oriant. upon this Sir Robt. Herries a Bancker in London Wrote to france and received proofs that Ly anne had landed Sevral Months before at LOriant.[4] I must also mention that in his Time I had been acqwainted that my Calling Ly anne to London had given great uneaseniss to the Duke, but that after the News of her Death had been Spread he Seemed to be cured of his former Anxiety, But no Sooner had I received the News of her Life when I Sent So as Usually my Receipt for £400 stgs. due to me for a quarter of her Annuity, and as the rapport of her Death had been Circulated by myself I joined to it a Copy of the Letter received from France as a Testimony of her Life. The Duks answer was that when ever I did produce a receipt jointly Signed by her and me that Than he would Pay. In that Moment I did not Understand the True Intend of this Answer, but after I had followed Ly annes Track upon the Continant I got proofs that when I asked paymt. of the £400 stg. that better than 2 months before my Application the Duke had paid the Said Sum to Ly Anne beeing than At Paris; this made me Thinck that <Ly anne> /The Duke/ had taken an Actif part in Ly annes Expedition, and I found but too Soon my Suspicions grounded.

However to go in to All the Windings of This Affair of Deceit exeeds the Bounds of a Letter Thus I limmit myself to a few facts Sufficient to give (Tho but a feeble Idea) of my Embarassements, of The Plan laid to my ruine, and of the Consequences the Whole has had.

That The Duke had entered in to a Correspondence with Ly anne Since I calld her to come to England, the Concert of hers and his Conduct, and my Ruine are proofs of; But as a Woman will not Execute nor Undertake Such Violant Measures without The Special aide of a Man, So also She to be in Caracter pitched upon Mr Sayre, who was, So as I before have remarket, well fitted for Any plan of Deceit <notwithstanding>. They Agreed Thus, Ly anne was to remain 6 months in Cognito in france, Mr Sayre had this Time to Settle his Affairs and to Sell my Property in New York to Effect This Latter Object he was Empowred by her; in his Turne to Europe he was to provide in Spain a retired place where they intended to Live, The Duke Agreed to pay the Annuity were ever She did choose to live and to let her family and me in the Idea of her Death, further as Ly anne had found among my Peapers the proofs of our Marriage it was resolved that in case that the Place of her residence was by me Discovred to deny Those Ties and so She did til I was Able to proove their reality.

Since This it is regulated that Ly anne is nothing more to me in This Woreld. Mr Sayre sits for Debts in Kings Bench[5] Ly anne has Voluntary followed him to This Place, By ruining my fortune The Duke is freed from what he Dreaded Viz. to Account in Parliamt. for his Conduct of Deceiving the House, and as Ly anne is now deserted by evry one of her relations The Duke has also dropt her no longer Usefull ackwaintance.

In this my Situation I intended to publish The proofs of Those Arts by which my ruine had been promoted, this was near ready for the Press when the following Considerations Occured to me.

Of Sevral persons of Ly annes family, and other People of Credit I must of Cours, in a compleat narative have laid open the behaviour, and <as> Some of Those Caracters could not be Shown in a favourable Light, it would have raised me a Host of Ennemies; and it is an Axiome in Europe that a ruined Man in Oposition both to riches and Credit can't but fare worse by an Apeal to The Public whatsoever may be the Justice of his Claime; nay the Public himself will Grant Oblivion to the Unjustice of the Powrefull or at most give but a<n> Momentary pitty to the Unfortunate . . . however I would have Scorned Consequences But The Duties I owed to my Childern who were in America and in Want of my Care made me give up The Project of an Apeal. A Noble friend of myne Lieut. Genrl Clerss. was of Opinion that I Should Publish my Case but The Moment I left England, <but> /Tho I have both Respect and Defference for his Person and Supiriour <It> abilities/ my Pride would not Alowe me to Stoop to This Vengeance of the feable, and to Stand the Storm it would have probably raised was Keeping myself in London (who could tel for how long) from evry endearemt family, rest, and Liberty at home.

To Enjoy Those to nothing Comparable <Advantages> /Blessings/ of Liberty Allone <was> /had been/ from the Year 1776 my chief Wish, Than allready I begun to range my Affairs in Europe Tho only in 1782 I could come Over to America, Several and great Sacrifices I have made to gain that point, I was a Chamberlain of The King of Prusia, by Sevral Letters from him <in my Possession> /even/ Not the last to in 1781 when he Granted me my Demission I can Show that I was in favour, I had no Debts and possessed a good fortune, who was Strengthned by my Marriage with Ly anne, who did not take place til She Consented to go to America, no Compulsion, no Thought of Amelioration of fortune, but I Say Boldly The noble Ambition to be a Citizen of Collumbia was the /only/ Motive of my Expatriation, of This Citizenship I had formed (according to the Exertions of Spirit Shown in the begin of The Revolution) a Grand Notion, and the federal Plan now likly to be Adopted leaves me no Room to repent of my Choice.

By the last Combination of Malevolence I have lost £2000 stgs. a Year, besides moevables of Worth, and in peapers to an Amount I can not Value. This I may Say with Frances The first Tout est perdu Sauf l'honeur:[6] but as my Wealth was great by Sweeping the Chips together, I have Secured enough for the necessities of Life, The Honble Alexdr. Hamilton a Gentleman of Shining habilities, in Law in State business and as a Soldier in the field, has Obliged me for ever by preserving for me in this Town from The Devouring Teath of Ly anne and Associates, a fine four Store Brisl. House with 21 Acres of Ground which I Thought lost.

But what so ever have been my Looses I am Content with my present Situation and I leave the Destroyers of my former fortune over to The Enjoyment of Their fellony and to the Punishment of Their Conciences.

If Sir you Consent to renew Our Corespondence it will be honouring me and an Addition to the Contentement of

your most obdt. humble Servant

Poellnitz

RC, Iredell Papers, Duke. Addressed "To J. Iredell Esqr. Edenton, Nord Caroline." Endorsed "New York 20th. Feb. 1788. Baron De Poellnitz. Ansd."[7]

---

[1]Lady Anne Stuart's sister Jane married JI's cousin George Macartney. *PJI*, 2:349n, 413n.

For more information on the "heap of Shocking Events," see Baron de Poellnitz to JI, April 22, 1784, n. 2, and JI to Hannah Iredell, November 22, 1787, in this volume.

[2]Capt. Andrew Corbet was the husband of Lady Anne Stuart's late sister, Augusta (d. 1778). *DNB*, s.v. "Stuart, John."

[3]Countess Bute is Mary Montagu (1718-1794), wife of John Stuart, 3d Earl of Bute. They had five sons and six daughters. Countess Lonsdale is Lady Anne's sister Mary, wife of James Lowther, Earl of Lonsdale. Lady Macartney is the sister mentioned in n. 1 above. *DNB*, s.v. "Stuart, John."

[4]L'Orient is a seaport located on the Bay of Biscay in northwestern France. *Webster's New Geographical Dictionary*, 687.

[5]King's Bench Prison was located in St. George's Fields on the south bank of the Thames. Most of the inmates were debtors. The prison had been burned by rioters in 1780 but was soon rebuilt. Ben Weinreb and Christopher Hibbert, eds., *The London Encyclopedia* (Bethesda, Md.: Adler and Adler, 1986), 433-444, 709.

[6]The French phrase "tout est perdu Sauf l'honeur" means all is lost except honor.

[7]See JI to Baron de Poellnitz, April 15, 1788, in this volume.

To Maurice Murphy[1]

Edenton Feb. 25th. 1788.

Sir,

Since you spoke to me on the subject of printing the Laws, which I am appointed to have done, I have seen the Act of Assembly constituting my appointment, and after duly considering the nature of the Trust I am invested with, I am truly concerned in finding myself under the necessity of informing you, that I cannot think myself warranted in employing you in the execution of it.[2] I have received another application, which, with every disposition to give you the preference, in case my duty had admitted of it, it appears to me much more proper I should accept, if the conditions I have stated are complied with. I hope you will believe, that I feel great pain in being under the necessity of being thus explicit, and am,

Sir, Your obedient Servant,

Ja. Iredell.

FC, Iredell Papers, Duke. Addressed "Mr. Maurice Murphy."

---

[1]Maurice Murphy was the publisher of the *Edenton Intelligencer*. Watson, *Index to North Carolina Newspapers*, xii.

[2]In 1787, the General Assembly directed JI to compile the laws of the "late province and present State of North Carolina" for publication. The book was also to include other documents, such as the Carolina Charter, the state constitution, and the peace treaty between the United States and Great Britain. Iredell was to contract with a printer who would have the exclusive right to print and sell the compilation for seven years. The contract went to the firm of Hodge and Wills, who published the book, known as *Iredell's Revisal*, in 1791. Whichard, *Justice James Iredell*, 23; Clark, *State Records*, 24:888-889.

From Archibald Maclaine

Wilmington, March 4th, 1788.

Dear Sir:

. . . You have no doubt seen that in New York there was very nearly one half of the Assembly against calling a convention; yet I am informed by a letter from that place, it is the general opinion that the new constitution will be adopted.[1] This opinion is probably founded on the belief that it will be ratified by nine States, in which case, it will be certainly embraced by the remaining four. That this is the idea of those in the opposition, I have no doubt, for a number of their emissaries were at Boston, during the deliberation of the convention, endeavoring to scatter their poison among the members. It is, however, extraordinary, that though there were in the convention a majority, and that considerable, against the proposed government, it should have been ratified by a majority of nineteen.[2] This is attributed to the Good Genius of America. A rejection in Massachusetts would probably have proved fatal. As the convention of New Hampshire have been sitting now near three weeks, and are said to be unanimous, we may conclude that seven States have come into the measure; South Carolina is certain. Among the other four we shall probably have a ninth. My principal reliance is on Maryland.[3]

I expect in a few weeks the Federalist in a volume. He is certainly a judicious and ingenious writer, though not well calculated for the common people.

Your old friend Huske, and Col. Read, have joined all the low scoundrels in the county, and by every underhand means, are prejudicing the common people against the new constitution. The former is a candidate for the county; but although in the beginning he was ridiculously loud, and even clamorous, he has been taught prudence by his associates. As a proof that he is not actuated by principle, he condemned the whole, after having a slight view of one half only over the shoulders of another person. In truth his objections are a disgrace to his understanding as well as his principles, &c., &c.

A. Maclaine.

Printed, McRee, 2:219-220.

---

[1]When the New York convention met on June 17, more than two-thirds of the delegates were Antifederalists. Nevertheless, the delegates ratified the Constitution on July 26. The Federalists, led by Alexander Hamilton and John Jay, persuaded their opponents that continued resistance would be unproductive when ten states, including Virginia, had already ratified the Constitution. In addition, Jay appeased the Antifederalists by joining them in circulating a letter among the other states calling for a convention to consider amendments to the Constitution. Morris, *Forging the Union*, 312-313; *The Constitution of the United States of America with a Summary of the Actions by the States in Ratification of the Provisions Thereof*, 3d ed. (Richmond: Virginia Commission of Constitutional Government, 1965), 16.

[2]Opposition to the Constitution in Massachusetts came primarily from residents of what would become Maine, because they feared that ratification would diminish their chances for statehood, and delegates from the rural areas that had spawned the recently suppressed Shays' Rebellion. The Federalists prevailed because of their persuasive oratory and the impressive prominence of their leaders, and because of the conciliatory efforts of the Federalist convention president, John Hancock. The

Constitution was approved by the Massachusetts convention on February 6, 187 to 168. Morris, *Forging of the Union*, 303-305; *Constitution*, 16.

[3]By March 4, six states had ratified the Constitution. Maryland followed on April 28, South Carolina on May 23, and New Hampshire on June 21. *Constitution*, 16.

To the Freemen of the Town of Edenton[1]

Gentlemen:

The distinguished honor of having been unanimously elected your Representative in the ensuing convention, without the least solicitation on my part, has made an impression on my heart which no time or circumstances can efface. My gratitude for it is inexpressible, but I am sensible will be shown in the most proper manner, by the zeal and fidelity with which it will be equally my duty and pleasure to execute this important trust. I shall have nothing to lament, but that my abilities will fall so far short of my ardent ambition to serve you. Under the conviction of my present sentiments, that the security of every thing dear to us depends on our adoption of the proposed constitution, I consider it one of the most awful subjects that was ever proposed for the consideration of a free people, and in giving it my utmost support (as I probably shall do), I shall have occasion for all the strength I can derive from the pleasing consciousness that in so doing I shall truly speak the respectable sense of my constituents. This will animate me beyond every thing in what I conceive the cause of Truth and Liberty. God forbid, indeed, that I should, by a blind admiration, imitate the conduct of those who indulge themselves in a blind rejection of it. The one would be as unworthy of the dignity of a free people, as the other is derogatory of those sentiments of respect and deference which we owe the great characters who formed it; and owe certainly as much for our own sakes, whose welfare they took so much pains to consult, as from the sentiments of gratitude with which every mind of sensibility must remember their former eminent services to their country. But I am convinced the more narrowly the constitution is examined by impartial minds, the more highly it must be approved; and from the consideration of our present critical situation, it will, perhaps, be deemed the only probable means of safety we have left.

I am, gentlemen, with the greatest respect and attachment,

Your faithful and obedient servant,

Jas. Iredell.

Printed, McRee, 2:220.

[1]This address was written ca. March 30, 1788, after the election, which, according to the resolution of December 6, 1787, was to occur "on the last Friday & Saturday in March" (March 28 and 29, 1788). Clark, *State Records*, 20:371.

This address appears in McRee between letters dated March 4 and April 2, 1788.

From Archibald Maclaine

Wilmington 2d. April 1788

Dear Sir

I deferred answering your favor of the 11h. past until the election should determine who were to be our members. Below you will find a list of them in such /of the/ counties as from which we have had any intelligence. From Sampson, Moore & Robeson, we have not heard. Our old friend Huske, who very early set his face against the new constitution, has discovered an inordinate ambition, which his friends for some time past, have observed to /be/ growing very rapidly. When I mention this, you will not be surprised to hear that he descends to such humiliating methods of attaining his purpose, as you could not formerly have believed. The Sheriff has declared him duly elected with 97 votes against T. Devane, who had 172. There are three men of the same name, the two youngest of them magistrates. The eldest of these two was the candidate, and in above 80 of the tickets was distinguished as T. Devane senr. esqr. The others were simply T. Devane, but it is known that every voter meant the same person. It is remarkable that Mr. Huske not only depended upon the interest of this man, but that in all his own tickets, many of them written by himself, the name T. Devane is not mentioned without any additions.[1] Mr. Wright sent to request my advice, and whether he should not make a special return, and though I advised him to this as the safest method, he thought proper to decide in favor of Mr. Huske.[2] The jest is, that this gentleman dare not avow his motives, for his opponent is as much determined as himself in favor of the <new> /seat of/ government at Fayetteville, and against the new constitution. Ambition frequently is blind to it's own interest, for it is not impossible but a vote may be lost for Fayetteville, and Mr. Hogg's family are deeply interested in the fate of that place.[3]

I perceive that Hodge has published in a pamphlet your answers to Mr. Mason's objections, to which he has appended the piece I sent him[4]

Make my respectful compliments to the Governor and let him know I have just received his obliging letter and thank him for his attention to my recommendations. I have not now time to write him, which I hope he will excuse. I still hope he will be a member of the convention We are all well, and rejoicing at the long-expected appearance of Spring

Dear Sir truely yours

A Maclaine

New Hanover county[5]

A. J. A. Campbell

A. Tim. Bloodworth

J Pugh Williams

F. James Bloodworth

A. John Huske

Wilmington F. A Maclaine

Brunswick[7]

A. Jacob Leonard

A. Alexius M. Forster

F. Lewis Du Pre

John Cains

F. Benja. Smith

Bladen[9]

F. Thomas Owen

A. Thomas Brown

Saml. Cain

F. Gooden Elletson

F. Joseph Gautier

Cumberland[6]

F. Thomas Armstrong

F. Wm. Barry Grove

F. Alex. Mc.Alester

F. Eliot

James Porterfield

Duplin[8]

F. James Kenan

William Dickson

James Gillespie

Oliver

A. Charles Ward

Onslow[10]

Robt. W. Snead

Danl. Yates

Thos. Johnston

John Spicer

A. Edwd. Starkey

F. Federalist

A. Antifederalist. Those not marked, are doubtful, moderate antifederalists, or such as I cannot form an opinion of. I am inclined to believe from circumstances that we shall have a decided majority, as most of those without any mark of distinction are honest dis interested men. Several of them positively refused to receive instructions

The people of Fayetteville have elected Doctor Ingram on a presumption that under the old charter they have a right to a member.[11] I think they are clearly mistaken

RC, Iredell Papers, Duke. Printed, McRee, 220-221. Addressed "Mr. Iredell."

---

[1]The committee on elections ruled that the votes cast for Thomas Devane Sr. and Thomas Devane were intended for the same person. As a result, Devane (before 1755-1805) was elected as an Antifederalist delegate. Devane also served in the house of commons (1787, 1788, 1792-1793). Massengill, *North Carolina Votes*, 15; Clark, *State Records*, 22:13.

[2]Thomas Wright (d. 1813) was the sheriff of New Hanover County from 1782 to 1798. Mitchell, *North Carolina Wills*, 578; Waddell, *New Hanover County*, 227.

[3]John Huske was James Hogg's son-in-law. Hogg had extensive business and property interests in Fayetteville. *Life and Times of James Hogg*, 55.

[4]Abraham Hodge (1755-1805), a native of New York, moved to Halifax County in the mid-1780s and became state printer in 1785. He was an ardent Federalist and expressed his views in several newspapers that he published. *DNCB*, s.v. "Hodge, Abraham." For JI's answers to George Mason, see JI to Mr. Mason, January 8, 1788, in this volume.

[5]John Pugh Williams (1750-1803), an Antifederalist delegate to the convention, served five terms in the house of commons. James Bloodworth (d. 1799), who served ten terms in the General Assembly, was the brother of Timothy Bloodworth. Massengill, *North Carolina Votes*, 6, 63; *DNCB*, s.v. "Bloodworth, Timothy."

[6]Thomas Armstrong (before 1755-ca. 1802) owned a large amount of land, including thousands of acres in the western part of the state, and served five terms in the General Assembly. George Elliott (1747-1807) owned sawmills and a farm. James Porterfield (d. ca. 1795) was named state commissioner for purchasing tobacco in 1788 and represented Fayetteville in the house of commons during the 1791-1792 session. He was a Federalist delegate to the 1788 convention. Massengill, *North Carolina Votes*, 3, 19, 49; Pool, "Economic Interpretation," 1:131, 132; 2:293.

[7]John Cains (before 1755-ca. 1804) was an Antifederalist delegate to the 1788 ratification convention and served one term in the house of commons (1788). Massengill, *North Carolina Votes*, 11.

[8]James Gillespie (1747-1805) served in the house of commons (1779-1780, 1782-1784) and the state senate (1784-1786, 1789, 1792). He attended both the 1788 and 1789 ratification conventions as an Antifederalist. Gillespie was later a member of the U.S. House of Representatives (1793-1799, 1803-1805). Francis Oliver (ca. 1740-1807) was an Antifederalist delegate to the 1788 state ratification convention. Charles Ward (before 1755-1812) represented Duplin County in the house of commons in 1788. *DNCB*, s.v. "Gillespie, James"; Massengill, *North Carolina Votes*, 22, 45, 61.

[9]Goodwin Elleston (d. ca. 1790) owned more than five thousand acres of land and had not been politically active prior to the convention. Joseph Gautier (after 1755-1807) was a delegate to the 1788 and 1789 ratification conventions. He later served in the house of commons (1790) and the senate (1791-1792). Massengill, *North Carolina Votes*, 19, 22; Pool, "Economic Interpretation," 1:128.

[10]Daniel Yates (d. 1795) was an Antifederalist delegate. He served in the house of commons (1784-1785, 1786-1788) and in the senate (1789). Thomas Johnston (before 1755-ca. 1805), an Antifederalist, served in the house of commons (1782), the senate (1784-1785, 1788), and as county sheriff. John Spicer Jr. (d. 1800) voted as

an Antifederalist at the 1788 convention and as a Federalist in 1789. He subsequently served in the house of commons (1789-1790) and the senate (1794-1796, 1799). Massengill, *North Carolina Votes*, 32, 56, 66; Alan D. Watson, *Onslow County: A Brief History* (Raleigh: Division of Archives and History, North Carolina Department of Cultural Resources, 1995), 8, 29; Joseph Parsons Brown, *The Commonwealth of Onslow: A History* (New Bern, N.C.: Owen G. Dunn, 1960), 35-36.

Two of the delegates elected from Onslow County did not attend the convention, Robert Whitehurst Snead and Edward Starkey. Snead did attend the 1789 convention as a Federalist. The reasons for their absence in 1788 have not been found. Massengill, *North Carolina Votes*, 55, 56.

[11]John Ingram (d. 1797) was elected to represent the town of Fayetteville at the convention. On July 25, the committee on elections unseated Ingram, however, by ruling that Fayetteville was not entitled to representation. Massengill, *North Carolina Votes*, 30; Clark, *State Records*, 22:13.

From D[avid] *Witherspoon*

New Bern 3. april 1788

Dear Sir,

I have read with very great pleasure your answers to Mr. Masons objections, and surely every man who reads them & on whom Mr. Masons observations or indeed the arguments of those in opposition in general have had any effect, must be convinced that the objections to the Constitution are without foundation

If we expect a Constitution the principles of which <u>cannot</u> be violated, we had better, instead of amending that which is proposed, amend the hearts of men

I am affraid there will be a powerful opposition in this State but am happy in observing that the proportion of well informed men on that side will be very small

In Dobbs county, the federal men, finding that they were in danger of losing their election, raised a riot, put out the candles, knocked to pieces the boxes which contained the votes & destroyed the books.[1]

From this county /& Town/ we have four federal men, Spaight, Leech, Neale, Sitgreaves, and on the other side Ben Williams & Nixon[2]

Your publication has been /made/ I believe very correctly by Mr. Hodge I was sorry that my business called me out of Town while it was in hand. You were very soon known to be the author by what means I do not know

For some months after last Superior Court I was in very ill health <am> but am now perfectly well. With very great regard I am

Dear Sir your most obedt. servant

D. Witherspoon

RC, Iredell Papers, Duke. Printed, McRee, 2:221-222. Addressed "James Iredell esquire Edenton."

---

[1]Following this fracas, the Dobbs County Federalists asked Gov. Samuel Johnston, also a Federalist, to call a new election. The governor, unsure of his authority in this unprecedented situation, "recommended" to the sheriff that another election be held but stopped short of ordering one. The Antifederalists boycotted the second election, and the Federalists won easily. The Antifederalists then petitioned the convention not to seat the Federalist delegates. The committee on elections reviewed the request and related testimony, and decided not to seat either delegation, leaving Dobbs County without representation. Trenholme, *Ratification*, 111-115; Clark, *State Records*, 22:10-11.

[2]Abner Neale (after 1755-1800) was a member of the house of commons (1785-1787) and an admiralty court judge. Benjamin Williams (1751-1814) commanded a regiment of North Carolina soldiers during the Revolutionary War. He later became governor and served eleven terms in the General Assembly and one in the U.S. Congress. Richard Nixon (d. 1799) served in the house of commons (1787-1789) and was a member of the Council of State (1793). *DNCB*, s.v. "Williams, Benjamin"; Massengill, *North Carolina Votes*, 44, 45.

From William Hooper

[*Hillsboro. 15 April*]

My dear Sir

Very much do I thank you for your kind letter by Mr. Hunt and the papers which accompanied it. I have read the latter with the greatest pleasure and flatter myself that they will not fail to work conversions amongst the many political Infidels who have hitherto Shut their eyes to the means of Salvation held forth to them by the Convention. I am heartily in Sentiment with you but alas! I fear those who favour the new constitution will be far outnumbered by their Adversaries. The Western country in general are devotedly opposed to it. Mr. Moore and myself essayed in vain for a Seat in the convention, our Sentiments had transpired previous to the Election.

I must beg you to attend to any little business of mine which may remain unfinished on the Halifax Docquet. The few papers which respect it Mr. Moore has. I enclose you Some papers which belong to Howell pray hand them to him[1]

We have had a very Severe Winter but are now blessed with a most delightful Spring. This country presents the most beautiful piece of rural Scenery that I was ever witness to. My daughter has had a long and dangerous attack of the malignant ulcerous Sore throat, but I thank God is perfectly recovered

I shall have the happiness of Seeing you at Edenton 'til then Adieu

Ys.

Will Hooper

RC, Iredell Papers, Duke. Printed, McRee, 2:222. Addressed "James Iredell Esqr. By favour of The Attorney General." Endorsed "Hillsborough April 15th. 1788 Wm. Hooper."

---

[1]Howell is probably Joseph Howell, a plaintiff in a suit against Barbara and John Hill. Minutes of the Halifax District Superior Court, April-October 1789, State Archives.

To Baron de Poellnitz

[*April 15, 1788*]

Dear Sir

I received your obliging letter of the 20th. Feb.[1] At the time I wrote you, & troubled you with my Account, I had no suspicion of any misfortune or distress having happened to you. Sometime afterwards I heard a story concerning Lady Anne, which gave me infinite pain as the account appeared too probable to be doubted, and I have read your affecting confirmation of it with a mixture of concern & i[*n*]dignation it would be difficult for me to express. Your condesending to give me so many particulars is a proof of regard which I highly value. Permit me to assure you Sir, that as I have /uniformly/ entertained the utmost respect for your character, I still retain it with as much warmth as ever, & consider the generous offer of your correspondence as doing me a particular honour—I shall not fail to cultivate it on my part by the best means in my power & shall <indeed> think myself highly obliged by your accepting so poor an equivalent for the <pleas> satisfaction I shall be sure to derive from it. I had indeed flattered myself, that your situation in America would have been much more comformable to your wishes; that the accomplishments of Lady Anne would have added to the happiness of your life, and <the situation of but> her sense of your merit /been/ a pledge for future respectability and satisfaction to herself. But tho' these pleasing prospects are blasted, it is a consolation which must greatly mitigate the pain, that you have nothing to reproach yourself with, that your conduct was not only <ge> kind but generous indeed to a degree that greatly aggravates the guilt of her departure. Good God! What must her situation be? The stings of conscience, the reproaches of ingratitude, perhaps the misery of neglect must 'ere now have made her bitterly repent a conduct so cruel & so unprovoked. The complication of Villainy by which you have suffered is <*illegible* indeed> /<truly> indeed/ astonishing: To be deserted & betrayed in a moment as it were by those in whom you had reason to have confidence & to meet Justice and humanity only from Strangers! Such a fate, bad as the world is <truly uncommon> <extremely> /truly/ uncommon. It <will> certainly requires all the dignity & fortitude of mind you can command. Fortunately, a mind really great can always find recovery in itself for the most extraordinary calamities.

I am very glad to hear the new Constitution is so agreeable to your Principles. It is perfectly so to mine, so much so that I have become an Author on the subject, having undertaken to answer Mr. Mason's Objections, <under the signature of Marcus> a publication which has appeared in <some Virginia> /some Norfolk/ & North Carolina news papers.[2] <There is a great division of sentiment in this State, but I think most Men of abilities & consequence are in its favour—Our Convention is not to meet till the 21 July.> I am very impatient to see the whole of Colo. Hamilton's Federalist, which is a work that will immortalize him and I rejoice to find that a Gentleman whose character I admire so much has been your particular Friend. Mr. Samuel Johnston, whom you knew here, & who is now our Governor, desired me to present you his most respectful Compliments, & to assure you he feels the strongest sympathy for your misfortunes. We are both Members of our Convention, that is to meet the 21st. July. There are great divisions on the subject, but I flatter myself we shall have a maj[*ori*]ty, especially if 9 States agree before us—Mrs. Iredell joins in the most earnest wishes for you & your Family's happiness with,

Dear Sir, Your very respectful and obed. Ser

Ja. Iredell.

FC, Johnson Collection, NCSA. Endorsed "Copy of a Letter to the Baron de Poellnitz, April 15th. 1788."

---

[1]See Baron de Poellnitz to JI, February 20, 1788, in this volume.

[2]See JI to Mr. Mason, January 8, 1788, in this volume.

To Hannah Iredell

Halifax April 26th. 1788

My dear Hannah,

I am very much obliged to you for your kind letters. Thank God my dear Annie continues so well, but I trembled when I read the account of her accident in your room. I feel greatly for what you must have felt at the time. I hope you have talked to her a great deal about being more careful. Your Brother and I are perfectly well. I am sorry I am too poor to send you more than the enclosed. I have however paid Mr. Amis, which is a great relief to me. Billy Dawson is quite well. Your Brother & he leave Town this morning. I shall not be able to get away till some time on Tuesday. I have indeed a vast deal of business to attend to, so that I can't hope to see you sooner than Thursday night or Friday. But you may be assured I shall make no unnecesary delay. Tell my dear Nelly I lament I can't write to her now. Give my love to her & Peggy, your Sister &c not forgetting my Friend Sam, whose safe arrival makes me very happy. Adieu! my tenderest love to Annie, & believe me

Most affectionately yours

Ja. Iredell.

RC, Johnson Collection, NCSA. Addressed "Mrs. Iredell."

From Archibald Maclaine

Wilmington 29h. April 1788

Dear Sir

I cannot suffer Mr. John Hogg to leave this without dropping you a line.[1] I believe his business at Edenton is to know whether Mr. T. Davis is to have the appointment of Master in chancery at Wilmington, as in that case, he is to be the deputy.[2] My own opinion is, that he is of the two, much more proper for the principal, though he has no hopes of succeeding against a man who is connected with one of their Honors.[3] Not being restricted in the appointments by the letter of the act, these very honorable gentlemen look upon it that they are at liberty to bestow sinecures upon their friends, who will be obliged to employ others to do the business.

Martin's paper, which teems with anti-federalism, made General Washington lose his election for Fairfax county; but we since hear that he declined being a member, that Federalists are chosen, and that Mr. Mason was rejected.[4] We have also heard that many of the people in that State, are changing in favor of the new constitution. This is said to be the case with several in this part of the country. It is however no very good sign that in some counties so many have been left out for their attachment to a form of government so well calculated to make the people happy—General Jones, W. Blount, Mr. Hooper, Mr. Moore, Governor Martin, and even Judge Williams (who was mistakingly supposed to conceal his sentiments) have been rejected. I suppose you have heard of the doings in Dobbs[5]—Thank God, we have had nothing like it in any other county—It is said there are several of both parties killed.

We hear that Spencer is returned, so that we shall have the honor of one of the Judges among us. His honor Judge Ashe, who had by his friends as well as himself anounced his inclination to serve the people on this important occasion, and who seemed so secure of being chosen, that he told one of his friends to whom it was inconvenient to attend the election, that he need not go, as he, the Judge, was certain of <his election> /succeeding/—had only Eight votes. This was the more remarkable, as the bulk of the people, were, like himself, anti-federalists.

Poor Mrs. Huske has been ill some time and within a few days past has miscarried. She appears to have an inflammatory sore throat, & Dr. Claypoole, who was called so late as yesterday, has very little hopes of her. She was so ill last night, that Mrs. George Hooper, who is far from being well, thought it necessary to stay with her. Mr. Hogg will inform you how she is this morning[6]

Mr. Hay at last went over the bar on the 29d.[7] my respectful compliments to Mrs. Iredell the Governor & both your families.

I am very sincerely yours

A Maclaine

RC, Library of Congress. Printed, McRee, 2:222-223. Addressed "James Iredell esquire Edenton By favor of Mr. John Hogg."

---

[1]John Hogg was James Hogg's cousin and a partner in the family mercantile business. Kemp P. Battle, *Letters of Nathaniel Macon, John Steele, and William Barry Grove, with Sketches and Notes*, James Sprunt Historical Monograph No. 3 (Chapel Hill: University of North Carolina, 1902), 93 n. 2.

[2]Thomas F. Davis was clerk of court in New Hanover County. *DNCB*, s.v. "Davis, Thomas Frederick."

[3]This is a reference to Judge Samuel Ashe. McRee, *Life and Correspondence*, 2:223.

[4]François-Xavier Martin (1762-1846), a native of France, published *Martin's North Carolina Gazette* in New Bern. He became an attorney in 1789 and was appointed as a judge in the Mississippi Territory in 1809. *DNCB*, s.v. "Martin, François-Xavier."

Elections for the Virginia assembly and the state ratification convention were held concurrently. Fairfax County was a Federalist stronghold, and George Mason, a leading Antifederalist, lost the race for an assembly seat to Roger West. Mason was elected as a convention delegate from Stafford County, where the Federalist vote was divided between two candidates. Miller, *George Mason*, 270, 284.

George Washington refused to be considered as a delegate to the ratification convention. He believed that his support of ratification would appear self-serving, since he was the obvious choice for president should the Constitution be approved. Merrill Jensen et al., eds., *The Documentary History of the Ratification of the Constitution*, 18 vols. to date (Madison: State Historical Society of Wisconsin, 1976-), 9:585.

[5]See D[*avid*] Witherspoon to JI, April 3, 1788, n. 1, in this volume.

[6]Elizabeth "Betsy" Hogg Huske died in May 1788. *Life and Times of James Hogg*, 21.

[7]This is probably a reference to John Hay's visit to his native Ireland. Ashe, Weeks, and Van Noppen, *Biographical History*, 6:272.

From William R. Davie

Halifax May 10h. 1788.

My Dear Sir

Yesterday I got home from Tarboro where I have been this week past, and have to day finished 25 pages of our little collection on the subject of the federal government[1]—I was so constantly interupted by people on business last week, that I am sure what is done is extremely imperfect. you will therefore have much to add, if on consulting the you find there should be room in the compass of such a pamphlet as we propose.

On the subject of a religious test I have struck out a part of what we had written <on that subject>, you can however reinstate it if you think proper.

The Judiciary I have left entirely to <u>you</u>, as you have already wrote on that subject, and in possession of all the objections against it—

You will find many of the popular objections still omitted, which should be answered, if it can be done without swelling the publication to too great a size. I do not know whether the order and manner we have adopted will meet your approbation, if it should not, I hope you will make no scruple to alter it in any manner you think proper—

In the hurry this business has been done I am apprehensive it may want considerable correction. I must therefore beg you and Mr. Moore to attend to this matter.

Mr. Sitgreaves who will hand you this with the papers will also assist in attending and correcting the press &c, and is extremely anxious for the success of our little publication—He brings with him Mr. Hawkins's subscription and his own and has promised me to have it considerably enlarged so that I am in hopes five or Six rheam may be printed.

I congratulate you on the adoption of the constitution in Maryland by so respectable and decided a majority.[2] I have some hopes, I think well grounded too, that So. Carolina and Virginia will put the government in motion before we meet in Convention.[3]

It will be necessary to preface our pamphlet with a note, that it is not offered as an original production, but as a compilation from several fugitive pieces &c. which will excuse us to the author of Marcus and others for the liberties we have taken with them

The Address and title page you will [*observe*] I have left altogether to you. [*Torn*] letter to Mr. Moore on the other particulars.

Make my Compliments to Mr. Hooper and believe me with great respect and regard

your mo obd

William R. Davie

RC, Iredell Papers, Duke. Printed, McRee, 2:223-224. Addressed "James Iredell Esqr. at Newbern Court By Mr. Sitgreaves."

---

[1]The "little collection" was to be a series of essays written in support of ratification by JI, Davie, and Alfred Moore. Little is known about this project; in fact, there is doubt as to whether the collection was ever published. Robinson, *William R. Davie*, 197-198.

[2]The Maryland convention ratified the Constitution on April 28 by a vote of 63 to 11. *Constitution*, 16.

[3]South Carolina and Virginia ratified the Constitution on May 23 and June 25, respectively. *Constitution*, 16.

From Thomas Iredell Jr.

Edenton, May 22d, '88.

My Dear Brother:

. . . Mr. Allen this morning read to me part of a letter he received from a gentleman of his acquaintance, who mentions a conversation he had with General Parsons, the substance of which was, "that General Washington was a damned rascal, and traitor to his country, for putting his hand to such an infamous paper as the new Constitution."[1] Mr. Allen's correspondent desires him to have it published; and, at the same time, to have it inserted "that any person who may be desirous to know his name, may be informed of it by the printer," &c.

T. Iredell.

Printed, McRee, 2:224-225.

[1]Albert Ray Newsome and Louise Irby Trenholme identify General Parsons as Thomas Person, a general during the Revolutionary War and a leading Antifederalist. McRee inserted "S. Person" in parentheses after General Parsons in the version of the letter published in *Life and Correspondence*. To confuse matters further, there was a Samuel Parsons of Montgomery County who was a brigadier general in the militia during the Revolution and a state senator (1784-1785). Albert Ray Newsome, "North Carolina's Ratification of the Federal Constitution," *North Carolina Historical Review* 17 (October 1940): 291; Trenholme, *Ratification*, 107; *PJI*, 2:341; Cheney, *North Carolina Government*, 214, 216.

To Hannah Iredell

Newbern May 27th. 1788.

My dear Hannah,

I was very much mortified and uneasy at not receiving any letter by the last Post, and again at not getting any letter from yourself by Egan. General accounts of you and Annie being well do not satisfy me—I long for a thousand particulars. Mr. Hooper & myself are lodged very agreeably in the same house, & such has been the hospitality of the Town that we have had occasion to dine but twice in a Tavern. Parker who lived in Edenton was yesterday convicted of passing Counterfeit money, knowing it to be so, for which he will lose his Ears &c. the money not being of the last Emission, in which case he would have lost his life.[1] I preserve my health perfectly well. I believe I shall go to Tuckahoe, if not New River, before I return as I hear some accounts of the Tenants that do not please me, and it is necessary to shew that they are not left entirely to do as they think proper. I have received very little money here, tho' with a full share of business. The scarcity of money I believe is really great, notwithstanding the Paper is of so little value. I hope to have the happiness of receiving a letter, and hearing well from you to day. Say every thing kind & tender for me to my dear Annie, and remember me in a proper manner to our Family & your Brothers, & Mrs. Blair, who I am sorry cannot now be included in the former description.[2] I do not forget Nelly & Mr. Tredwell, and hope the pain of their parting will be of short duration. Tell your Brother, we have not heard with certainty of the ratification of South Carolina, but that the account is every day expected—Adieu! my dear Hannah, and believe me ever,

Most affectionately yours

Ja. Iredell

RC, Johnson Collection, NCSA. Addressed "Mrs. Iredell Edenton."

---

[1]William Parker was indicted for "uttering counterfeit money knowing it to be such." A 1779 law provided that a convicted counterfeiter "shall for the first offense stand in the pillory for three hours, and have his right ear nailed to the pillory and cut off, and receive on his or their bare back thirty-nine lashes, and be branded with a red hot iron on the right cheek with the letter C, and on the left cheek with the letter M (which brands shall be at least one inch in length, and three quarters of an inch in breadth) and be imprisoned at the discretion of the court before whom it shall be tried, not exceeding one year, and forfeit one half of all his or their goods and chattels, lands and tenements, whereof he or she was seized or possessed at the time the offence was committed, to the State." Those convicted a second time were put to death. The act for an emission of paper money passed in 1785 made counterfeiting of that currency punishable by death for the first offense. Minutes of the New Bern District Superior Court, May 26, 1788, State Archives; Clark, *State Records*, 24:277, 723.

[2]The following note to Annie Iredell was written at the end of this letter: My dear Annie, I continue to love you very much, and every moment think of you. I hope you are a good Girl, and will be glad to see me when I return. Love and obey your Mamma, and every body will love you. I am, Your loving Papa, Ja. Iredell.

From Archibald Maclaine

Wilmington 4 June 1788

Dear Sir

I had scarcely reached this before I received the pleasing intelligence that South Carolina had adopted the new constitution, by a majority of 77.[1] Though I have not [*seen a line*] on the subject, yet it is past all doubt, as there is a hand-bill in town, directing the procession which is to take place, at the celebration of this happy event. It is said to exceed that of Massachusets, and, and was ordered by the Convention, being drawn up by a committee appointed for that purpose. I understand it is to be in a very few days.—I suppose on the anniversary of a fortunate one.

By a letter which I found on my return, dated the day after the convention met, it was expected that the majority would be small as great pains had been [*taken*] in [*the back-country*] to [*poison the minds*] of the people; yet it was carried by above two to one. Though I could not be more particular in my information, I would not omit communicating what I know will give you heartfelt satisfaction.

Dear Sir Yours very sincerely

A Maclaine

Yanky Doodle, keep it up!

RC, Iredell Papers, NCSA. Printed, McRee, 2:225-226. Addressed "James Iredell esquire Edenton."

---

[1]The vote in South Carolina was 149 to 73. *Constitution*, 16.

From Hugh Williamson

New York 11th June 1788

Dear Sir

The public Papers have not for many days afforded us any News, all Expectation is turned towards Virginia, We take for granted, I do at least, that N Carolina will follow Virginia in adopting or rejecting. I confess that my Hopes are not sanguine, but of this I do not consider myself bound to say all that I think. Congress have before them sundry matters of considerable Import which have been eventing in the Course of Seven month, for there have been nine States on the floor for a few days last past only. Having come on here with a Resolution to indulge myself in as much Leisure as any other of my fellow Labourers, the Start I have some <H> how been constrained to take has not fully accorded with my Plan, but I shall try to mend after a few Land Questions are determined. Those Questions are extremely weighty as the national Funds are concerned.[1] At present I have not Leisure even to return Visits.

Will you be pleased to forward a Line to Mrs. Templeman who probably is anxious to hear the Fate of her Son.[2] You may inform her that he was inoculated on Thursday Week in the morning that on Saturday morning last the Pock had made their appearance two or three on his Face & Severals on his Limbs. On Sunday a few more appeared. on that Night he indulged on a feather Bead, which for Several nights I had caused to be removed, and on Monday he had Some 20 or 30 Pocks on his Face, the whole is Still a Bagatelle, he continues to walk about & has done so every day. He would now attend in Congress was it not that the Place on his Arm in which he was inoculated being not quite free from Inflammation renders it inconvenient for him to put on a Coat with tight Sleeves. His

Servt. who as usual for Africans had the eruption 24 Hours before the Master was first relieved from his Suspicions.

I was yesterday surprised by a message of the Spanish Minister, who sent one of his Family to our lodging to apologise for his not visiting us in Person for he has not had the Small Pox. He had left his Card at the door without coming in.[3]

Mrs. Dawson whom I saw two Evenings Since, also her daughter & grand daughter were well, but she complains of hearing very Seldom from her Edenton Friends. I know that writing Paper is Scarce in Edenton & therefore was able to make one good Excuse, I presume that no other good one could be made.

Be so good as give my Respects to Mrs. Iredell & the other Ladies of your Family

I am Dr. Sir Your obedt. Servt.

Hugh Williamson

RC, Iredell Papers, Duke. Printed, McRee, 2:226-228. Addressed "James Iredell Esqr. Edenton." Endorsed "New York 11th. June 1788 Hugh Williamson. Ansd. June 25th. 1788."

---

[1]On June 6, Congress considered a committee report on a resolution authorizing the establishment of the boundary between land ceded to the United States and the states of New York and Massachusetts. The resolution also sanctioned the surveying of land west of a "line between lake Erie and the state of Pensylvania [*sic*]" and the selling of property in that area for seventy-five cents an acre. *Journals of the Continental Congress*, 34:202-203.

[2]Mary Templeman (d. 1797) of Pasquotank County was the mother of John Swann (1760-1793), a planter who had been appointed to the Continental Congress on December 14, 1787. Mary Templeman had been married to John Swann Sr., who died ca. 1761. She subsequently wed Frederick Blount, and after his death, she married Richard Templeman. *DNCB*, s.v. "Swan (or Swann), John"; Estate of Mary Templeman, 1797, Pasquotank County Estates, State Archives; Sarah McCulloh Lemmon, ed., *The Pettigrew Papers*, vol. 1, *1685-1818* (Raleigh: State Department of Archives and History, 1971), 14n.

[3]Special minister Diego de Gardoqui arrived in New York in 1785 to negotiate a commercial treaty with the United States. The talks were long and unsuccessful, with the pivotal issue being U.S. navigation rights on the Spanish-controlled lower Mississippi River. Gardoqui returned to Spain in 1789. Morris, *Forging of the Union*, 235; Bailey, *Diplomatic History*, 61-62.

To John G. Blount

Edenton June 29th. 1788.[1]

Dear Sir,

I have great pleasure in acquainting you, that on Wednesday last the question as to the ratification of the Constitution was put in a Committee of the whole house (for they do business in that way) of the Virginia Convention, when the numbers were, 89 for the ratification, 79 against it. They afterwards appointed a Committee, to consider of amendments.[2]

I beg my best respects to Mrs. Blount & your Brother,

and am, Dear Sir, Yours very respectfully

Ja. Iredell.

RC, Blount Papers, NCSA. Printed, *John Gray Blount Papers*, 1:404. Addressed "John Gray Blount Esq Washington."

---

[1]This letter is erroneously dated June 19, 1788, in the *John Gray Blount Papers*, 1:404.

[2]For more information on the amendments proposed by the Virginia convention, see William R. Davie to JI, July 9, 1788, in this volume.

From William Hooper

July 2d. Hillsboro[1]

My dear Sir

We are kept in a State of anxious ignorance and suspence as to what may be the final result of the Virginia deliberations upon the New Constitution. To day we are flattered with a report of its being embraced by a large majority, to morrow we may possibly be mortified with accounts of its fate being in doubt or that it is utterly rejected.

People in this Western Country have become much more moderate [*and*] many who were zealously opposed to it have changed their tones.[2] It is Said that the Mebanes advocate it unreservedly and endeavour to make converts.[3] The quakers are for it & Oneals brother bullies in its favour.[4] I have not a little of doub[*t*] but that our Convention will have a favourable issue.

Mr. Moore and I after attending the Court at Fayette three days and being two days from thence on our way hither found our families in good health & Spirits. Not so with Mr. Hoggs. family. The Shock of Mrs. Huskes. death has been almost too much for them all.[5] He bears it with much Seeming firmness when in company, but when Surprized [*o*]n his retirement the big tear Steals from his eye. Mrs. Hogg is reduced to a Ske[*leton*] [*& is*] worn down with anxiety & deep distress.[6] Poor Nelly has almost wept herself blind. A family most deeply to be commiserated! Huske is a walking Ghost—And what has added to their affliction Mr. Huskes daughter has been ill & continues So & Mr. Hogg had nearly died of <a> dysentery at Fayette about ten days ago

While we we were at Wilmington and Soon after Mrs. Huske died, Mrs. Lyon, Mrs. Fowke & Mrs. Wilkinson were buried. the latter a very fine young lady the Wife of Jack Wilkinson.[7] The Town was generally healthy when we left it.

I hope in God that your dear little Girl is perfectly recovered and that Mr. Johnstons family are restored to health. Pray present him and them with my most affectionate regards

Remember me kindly to Mrs. Iredell & the rest of your worthy family—and if Helen the fair who Sojourneth within thine house Should have taken unto herself a help mate pray salute her in my behalf with a holy Kiss of congratulation.

My Wife and daughter & Tom tender their best respects & anxiously express their wishes to See you and Mr. Johnston.

Adieu My dear friend, Ys.

Will Hooper

RC, Johnson Collection, NCSA. Printed, McRee, 2:229-230. Addressed "James Iredell Esq. in Edenton By favr. of Mr. Mc.Kerrell."

---

[1]This document is erroneously dated July 8, 1788, in McRee.

[2]Farmers in the western part of the state were suspicious of a government created and supported by their economic and political foes—the prosperous planters and merchants of the east. Westerners feared that a stronger central government would levy taxes, threaten individual freedoms, and further eastern economic interests. Despite Hooper's statement, support for the Constitution at the 1788 ratification convention came largely, though not exclusively, from easterners. Newsome, "North Carolina's Ratification," 295; Trenholme, *Ratification*, 163-165.

[3]William and Alexander Mebane were Antifederalists who were elected to represent Orange County in the 1788 convention. They, along with the rest of the Orange County delegation, voted against ratification. Massengill, *North Carolina Votes*, 42; Trenholme, *Ratification*, 163.

[4]Louise Irby Trenholme found a correlation between religious denomination and support for the Constitution. Episcopalians and Quakers tended to favor ratification, while Presbyterians and Baptists were more likely to oppose it. Trenholme, *Ratification*, 155.

Oneal is possibly William O'Neal, a prosperous planter of Orange County. Lefler and Wager, *Orange County*, 56, 96.

[5]In a letter of May 23, 1788, to Hannah Iredell, JI wrote in regard to the death of Elizabeth "Betsy" Hogg Huske: "I am truly concerned to communicate the melancholy catastrophe of Mrs. Huske. She is unfortunately no more, and there is reason to fear, owing to a mistake of her case. Her father was with her. You may imagine the dreadful condition of him, and her husband. Poor Huske is in very great distress. She is universally lamented, and none certainly ever better deserved it, &c." McRee, *Life and Correspondence*, 2:225.

[6]Elizabeth (or Ann) McDowell Alves (d. 1801) married James Hogg on July 7, 1765. They were the parents of Elizabeth "Betsy" Hogg Huske. There is conflicting information about Mrs. Hogg's first name. *Life and Times of James Hogg*, 4, 22, 53.

[7]Mildred Rowan Lyon was the wife of John Lyon (d. 1782), a merchant in the firm of Merrick and Lyon. He also held several local public offices, including county sheriff (1768-1771). Lennon and Kellam, *Wilmington Town Book*, 37 n. 54; Walker, *New Hanover County Court Minutes*, pt. 3, 32; Ida Brooks Kellam and Elizabeth Francenia McKoy, *St. James Church, Wilmington, North Carolina, Historical Records, 1737-1852* (Wilmington: n.p., 1965), 15; Will of John Lyon, 1782, New Hanover County Wills, State Archives.

Mrs. Fowke was probably Ann Wright Fowke, the daughter of Thomas Wright, a seaman in Wilmington, and the wife of Yelverton Fowke. Elizabeth F. McKoy, *Early New Hanover County Records* (Wilmington, N.C.: Elizabeth F. McKoy, 1973), 113.

Frances Wilkinson (b. 1770), wife of John Wilkinson, died on July 4, 1788. Kellam and McKoy, *St. James Church*, 114.

From Hugh Williamson

New York 7th. July 1788

Dear Sir

Virginia having confederated N Carolina in Opposition, should she be disposed to Stand out, can only expect countenance from Rh. Island or N York. Let me state in a few Words the politics of Rh Island. You have heard of the Effects of the Know Ye Law by which every Creditor is enabled to wipe off a Debt by paying 2/6 in the Pound, for their Paper is now at 8 for 1, & the mony being paid into the Hands of a Majistrate remains there for some Time for the Use of the Creditor and if he neglects taking it The State Treasury becomes Heir general.[1] Thus private Debts by this Time are nearly discharged in that State. The State Certificate Debt is also nearly paid off by similar means. The domestic or private Debts of the State were to the best of my Recollection about 566 Thousand Dlrs. A Law was made for paying one fourth of this Debt & all holders of Securities were called to bring in their Claims and receive 1/4th of the Amount. Every man who neglected tendering his Claims forfeited the Amount that was offerd that is one fourth. But the Creditors in general neglected. A Second & a third Payment was offered and made in the Same manner and now they have advertised for paying the fourth and last Portion of the Debt Thus the whole of the State Debt is Soon to be expunged by a kind of Legerdemain.[2] For little or no mony has issued during this Process out of the Treasury. It is thought that Rh Island will pretty Soon be ready to confederate, but a was told some days since by a Leader of the Know Ye men that the good People in that State have two capital Objections against the new Constitution; first, they think that every Slave Should be taxed as a white man & not represented. Second, they think that the Ratio for taxing is not proper, the States should not be taxed according to the number of Inhabitants but according to the amount of the Produce exported from each State or grown in it and exported from any other State.[3] I asked him what did Rh Island grow & export. he answered nothing except a little Cheese & Pot Ash. You see how reasonable a Plan his would be, Maryland Virga. So. Cara. would be delighted with it.

The Politics of N York are not So villanous in their Face, but not much more honourable considering them as part of the same Nation. They during the War agreed to give Congress the Power of collecting the 5 per Ct. Import, as Soon as they got Possession of this City they refused to let Congress have such Power because the find the Selfish advantage of imposing a duty on Imports for their own Use. Half the goods consumed in Connecticut or rather 3/4ths of them, half the goods consumed in New Jersey or 2/3rds of them, all the goods consumed in Vermont and no Small Part of them consumed in the Western Part of Massachusets are bought in New York and pay an Import Duty of 5 per Ct. for the Use of this State I say nothing of what the good Citizens of N Carolina import from N York whereas they pay Part of the New Yorkers Taxes.[4] Tis easy to discover why New York does not like the new Govt. But this very Argument must be a very good one with the Citizens of N Carolina why they should like that Govt. Consequently it is to be hoped that they will neither copy N York nor Rh. Island.

I am with great Regard Dr. Sir Your obedt. Sert.

Hu Williamson

RC, Iredell Papers, Duke. Printed, McRee, 2:227-228. Addressed "James Iredell Esqr."

---

[1]For information on Rhode Island's "Know Ye Law," see Richard D. Spaight to JI, July 3, 1787, n. 5, in this volume.

[2]Rhode Island's state debt was paid by the end of 1789. See Polishook, *Rhode Island and the Union*, 155.

[3]Article 1, section 2, of the U.S. Constitution states: "Representatives and direct Taxes shall be apportioned among the several States which may be included within this Union, according to their respective Numbers, which shall be determined by adding to the whole Number of free Persons, including those bound to Service for a Term of years, and excluding Indians not taxed, three fifths of all other Persons."

Some leaders in Rhode Island favored a federal tax system based on wealth rather than population. At Rhode Island's ratification convention, held in March 1790, delegates rejected a proposal for an amendment that would have created such a system. Polishook, *Rhode Island and the Union*, 215, 219.

[4]Under the Articles of Confederation, states could levy tariffs on imported goods. Merchants in states without harbor facilities had to bring foreign goods through the ports of neighboring states and pay that state's tariff. For example, because New Jersey importers used New York's harbors they had to pay the New York tax. North Carolina was in a similar situation since it lacked ports comparable to those in Virginia and South Carolina. Under Article 1, Section 8, of the Constitution, the central government rather than the states has power to impose tariffs. Morris, *Forging of the Union*, 148-152.

From John Swann

New York. July. 7. 1788

Dear Sir

I received your favor some time since & shou'd have acknowledged it before this, but was at that time in the height of the small pox. You will give me leave now, Sir to thank you for your polite engagement in the business on which I wrote you.

From the slow & irregular conveyance which sometimes attends Letters you may possibly hear of the decision of this State on the New Constitution before this reaches you, however as there are Chances against I shall take the liberty to mention their extreme indecision on that Subject an indecision the more astonishing since they are apprised of it's ratification by ten States.[1] The Constitution is ably supported by Gentlemen of great literary Merit, but the Opposition who are by no means contemptible, seem determined to dispute the ground intch by intch. What they propose to themselves from their inflexibility, is hard to discover; since it is certain, if we are to judge from their situation & the disposition of a great part of the State, that they will find their concurrence sooner or later not only expedient but unavoidable. however shou'd their determination be contrary to the general Sense of the Union, I hope it will not be made an Example to influence the deliberations & Conduct of our State. We are, Sir, in the most painful Suspence for Carolina. I confess I shou'd be most sensibly mortified were Carolina to reject the Constitution however unavailing her dissent might be with regard to it's Establishment and doubly so when I reflect that in such a determination they wou'd have the Countenance of Rhode Island alone, who in all probability may veer about when a certain State System of business is gone thro' with.

The Arrangements for putting the new Government into Action have been committed for some days & in all probability will be reported on this Week—

I shou'd, Sir most certainly beg the favor of a line now and then, but knowing that you are so variously employed you are seldom allowed leisure.

I am Dr. Sir with great Respect your obedient Servant

J Swann

RC, Emmet Collection, NYPL. TSS, Thomas Addison Emmet Collection, NCSA. Printed, McRee, 2:228-229. Addressed "James Iredell Esquire No. Carolina Edenton." Endorsed "New York 7 July 1788 John Swann Ansd. August 1[*4t*]h."

---

[1]New York ratified the Constitution on July 26, 1788, by a vote of 30 to 27. *Constitution*, 16.

From William R. Davie

Halifax, July 9h. 1788—

My Dear Sir

I have the pleasure of acknowledging your letter of the <23> 30th. of last month with the Pensylvania debates and the 2d. Volume of the Federalist, for which you will please to accept my thanks—

The decision of Virginia has altered the tone of the Antis in this quarter very much—Mr. Jones says his object will now be to get the Constitution rejected in order to give weight to the proposed amendments, and talks in high commendation of those made by Virginia—they have reached you no doubt before this time—those that are of any consequence by affecting the op<p>eration of the principles of the Constitution are in my opinion quite inadmissible, particularly the 3d. and the Amendment to the Judiciary.[1]

Yesterday I saw a Mr. Lambert from Richmond who say'd Govr. Randolph informed him the day before he sat out that New Hampshire had ratified the Constitution[2]—We spent the 4h. of July here in great good humor, notwithstanding our diffusions about the new Government—Please to have the enclosed inserted in your Gazette for us, and make my request to your brother to correct the press in this Article for us, or your Printer will make an entire different story of it[3]—

A Mr. Lamb as Chairman of a Committee in New York, which he stiles the "Federal Committee" has written to Mr. Jones, Thos. Persons and Tim. Bloodworth recommending to them to be steadfast in the opposition, and inclosing a large Packet of Antifederal pamphlets to each of them[4]—It is astonishing the pains these people have taken—Willie felt some mortification in finding himself in the company of Bloodworth and Persons—

Adieu My Compt. to your Brother. We shall see you I suppose about Tuesday.

I am with much esteem yours &c

W. R. Davie

RC, Iredell Papers, Duke. Printed, McRee, 2:230-231. Addressed "James Iredell Esquire Edenton."

---

[1]For the text of the amendments proposed by the Virginia convention, see Jensen et al., *Documentary History of the Ratification*, 10:1551-1556.

[2]David Lambert (ca. 1750-1817) was a merchant in Richmond. "A List of the Inhabitants and Property in the city of Richmond, 1782," in *Heads of Families at the First Census of the United States taken in the Year 1790, Virginia, Records of State Enumerations: 1782-1785* (Baltimore: Genealogical Publishing Company, 1986), 115; *Marriages and Deaths from Richmond, Virginia, Newspapers, 1780-1820* (Richmond: Virginia Genealogical Society, 1983), 86.

[3]The printer was Abraham Hodge, who by this time had moved to Edenton. His current business partner was Henry Wills. McRee, *Life and Correspondence*, 2:231n; *DNCB*, s.v. "Hodge, Abraham."

[4]John Lamb (1735-1800) was an officer during the Revolutionary War and after the war became customs collector for the port of New York. As leader of an Antifederalist group called the "Federal Republicans," he corresponded with like-minded individuals in other states. His outspoken manner so offended his Federalist opponents that he had to convert his home into a fortress after threats of physical attack. *DAB*, s.v. "Lamb, John."

To Hannah Iredell

Judge Williams's July 18th. 1788.

My dear Hannah,

I did not require the date of my letter to remind me that this is the anniversary of our wedding, a day that united me to one of the best of Wives and most excellent of Women.[1] May God be praised for his goodness in preserving us so long together, and giving us so lovely a daughter, with the prospect of another additional charm to our connexion.

I trust, my dearest Hannah, every hour of my future life will be devoted to make yours as happy as possible, and God in his mercy grant that the blessed opportunity of doing so may be extended to a very late period. Tell my lovely Annie she is ever in my thoughts, and I hope she often thinks of me. Surely a greater blessing was never bestowed upon any Parents than that sweet little Angel.—I found Colo. Davie at Halifax just setting off with his Family, & promised to overtake him here this morning, which I did, and we are to set off together to morrow—His Family stay here. I have been lucky in my fine weather, & am in excellent health—I overtook Payne & Cabarrus at Somerville's last night, from whence they went this morning.[2] Mr. Littlejohn's Children & Tom Johnson are here perfectly well; they are fixed at Colo. Barton's house, close to the School.[3] I heard of your Brother John on a different road. We were very unlucky in missing each other. Pray remember me with the utmost kindness to our Family & your Brother's &c—Kiss my dear little Girl in my name & by my authority, & believe me, my dear Hannah, ever

Most affecly. yours

Ja. Iredell.

RC, Johnson Collection, NCSA. Addressed "Mrs. Iredell Edenton."

---

[1]James and Hannah Iredell were married on July 18, 1773. McRee, *Life and Correspondence*, 1:174.

[2]John Somerville (d. 1807) lived in the Island Creek District in northeastern Granville County. He was a tax collector, commissioner, and coroner. Ray, *Colonial Granville*, 295; Powell, *Gazetteer*, 247; Mitchell, *North Carolina Wills*, 483; Zae Hargett Gwynn, *Court Minutes of Granville County, North Carolina, 1746-1820* (Rocky Mount, N.C.: Joseph W. Watson, 1977), 21, 65, 112, 220.

[3]At the time of this letter, William and Sarah Littlejohn had nine living children, ranging in age from one month to fifteen years. Two others had died within a year of their birth. The Littlejohns would later have three more children. Littlejohn and Littlejohn, *William Littlejohn*, 1.

William Barton lived in the Tabb's Creek District in eastern Granville County. Ray, *Colonial Granville*, 295; Powell, *Gazetteer*, 486.

To Hannah Iredell

[*Hillsborough, July 25, 1788*]

[*My dear Hannah,*]

. . . the prospect at present is rather against us, but I do not despair. The opposition attempt to disconcert us by entering into no debate. However, we notice all material objections which we know have been made, and answer them. . . .[1]

[Ja. Iredell]

Printed, McRee, quoted in "The Convention," 2:234.

---

[1]Historian Louise Irby Trenholme described JI as being "outstanding in debate" and well informed on issues related to the ratification of the Constitution. At the state convention in Hillsborough, JI was joined by other Federalist delegates, such as William R. Davie and Richard D. Spaight, who were also skilled and knowledgeable orators. The Antifederalists, on the other hand, lacked comparable speakers but did enjoy overwhelming numerical superiority. Consequently, they had nothing to gain by engaging in debate. Trenholme, *Ratification*, 147-151.

For more details on JI's contributions to the debate at the 1788 convention, see Jonathan Elliot, ed., *The Debates in the Several State Conventions on the Adoption of the Federal Constitution*, . . . , 2d ed., 5 vols. (Philadelphia: J. B. Lippincott; Washington: Taylor and Murray, 1861-1863), 4:1-252 passim, hereafter cited as *Elliot's Debates*.

From Hugh Williamson

New York 26th July 1788.

Dear Sir

You may be assured that the delegates from North Carolina have not been inattentive to the Respect they owe the State whatever may be their private Sentiments respecting the new Constitution. When a Committee had reported and the Question was taken up for putting the new Govt. into motion and a Time was proposed for chusing Electors and Representatives & for the members entering on Business we stated fully the Situation of our State and <a motion> it was immediately agreed that the Time should be put off as far as we should alledge was absolutely necessary.[1] But no final Question is yet taken & we believe that we shall be able to obtain such Delay that N Carolina may in the interim take her Measures. Every thing on this Head is at present Stationary.

Some days ago there was a large Procession here on 10 States having confederated and Congress were invited to dine with the Company some thousands of them under a particular Pavilion in the Fields.[2] The other States attended but the N Carolina Delegates staid at Home. We conceived it was a Respect we owed the State not to celebrate an Event in our public Characters which the State we represent has not hitherto Sanctioned by her approbation.

Hitherto the State of N York in Convention has not taken its Measures it is thought they will be curious and a Species of Delphic Oracle, neither an Adoption nor Rejection or both as parties may be disposed to construe it.[3]

I am Dr. Sir Your obedt. Servt.

Hu Williamson

RC, Iredell Papers, Duke. Printed, McRee, 2:235-236. Addressed "James Iredell Esqr. Edenton favourd by Capt. Clarke."

---

[1]On the date of this letter, New York became the eleventh state to ratify the Constitution, leaving only North Carolina and Rhode Island. Congress postponed establishing a schedule for instituting the new government until September. *Constitution*, 16. See JI to [*unknown*], September 10, 1788, n. 2, in this volume.

[2]The text of a broadside giving the order of the seventy-six units in this procession can be seen on the Library of Congress's "American Memory Project" website: *http://memory.loc.gov/cgi-bin/query/D?bdsbib:2:./temp/~ammem_Ldsz.* (May 10, 2002).

[3]The term "Delphic Oracle" refers to an enigmatic proclamation, as one might have heard from the seer at Delphi in ancient Greece. *OED*, s.v. "delphically."

From Hugh Williamson

New York 26th July 1788

Dear Sir

We give bad proofs of our Knowledge whatever we may give of our Candour while we go on making mistakes & confessing that we have made them. After the inclosed was written the information contained in the inclosed Paper came to Hand by which it would Seem that the New York Ratification is not like to prove a Hermaphrodite as had been apprehended.[1] Such have been the Effects of the weighty reasoning of the minority and other very <u>weighty</u> considerations. By the Way the antifeds were conscious that they have in many Cases carryed their Elections by imposing false Representations on their Constituents and propogating impudent Lyes. We take for granted that N Carolina will not be the only associate of Rhode Island.

I am Dr. Sir Your obed. Servt.

Hu Williamson

RC, Emmet Collection, NYPL. Printed, McRee, 2:236. Addressed "James Iredell Esqr. at Hillsbro or at Edenton."

[1]Williamson enclosed a second letter dated July 26th with this document. It immediately precedes this one in this volume.

Hermaphrodite refers to something consisting of traits that are opposites. *OED*, s.v. "hermaphrodite."

To Hannah Iredell

Hillsborough August 3d. 1788

My dear Hannah,

As the Convention is to rise today, and I shall not set off immediately with the immense crowd ready to pour from here; I write to give you the satisfaction of knowing that I am perfectly well, as are your Brothers, Mr. Mackenzie, & Mr. Dawson. Mr. Mackenzie is to set off to day but will stop a day or two at Skewawky. Your Brother John is to set off to morrow, and I had resolved to do so too, but Mr. Hooper swears I shall not, for that they will at least have me one day to themselves. Your Brother Sam is detained to finish Copies of the Business here, and it is uncertain when he may be able to leave this. The Majority of the Convention, under the guidance of Willie Jones, were obstinate to an astonishing degree. They have not absolutely rejected the Constitution, but proposed previous Amendments.[1] We are however for the present out of the Union, and God knows when we shall get in to it again.—I had the pleasure of receiving your letters of the 20 July last Saturday. God grant I may find you all well. Say every thing tender for me to my lovely Annie. God knows how impatient to see you all. Remember me very affectionately to your Sister & the Girls, & to the Family at Hayes.

I am, my dear Hannah, Most affectionately yours

Ja. Iredell.

RC, Iredell Papers, Duke. Addressed "Mrs. Iredell Edenton."

[1]The North Carolina ratification convention chose neither to ratify nor reject the Constitution. Instead the delegates passed, by a vote of 184 to 83, the following resolution: "Resolved, That a declaration of rights, asserting and securing from encroachment the great principles of civil and religious liberty, and the unalienable rights of the people, together with amendments to the most ambiguous and exceptionable parts of the said Constitution of government, ought to be laid before Congress, and the convention of the states that shall or may be called for the purpose of amending the said Constitution, for their consideration, previous to the ratification of the Constitution aforesaid on the part of the state of North Carolina." JI had introduced a resolution calling for ratification with a recommendation for amendments, but it was rejected 184 to 84. Trenholme, *Ratification*, 183-188; Clark, *State Records*, 22:23-26, 30-31.

From Arthur Iredell

Guildford Augt. 5th. 88

My dear Brother

Since I last wrote to You I have undertaken the Curacy of this Place, which is very laborious, & occupies by far the greater Part of my Time, for I write my own Sermons. Tom's old Friend Lord Onslow is the great Man of the Place, & has been very civil to me; but my greatest Comfort, & the chief Inducement I had for coming here, is my good Friend Captn. Wilson whom Tom likewise knows.[1] I live almost entirely in his Family, & am more obliged to him than I can tell you. All this sounds as if I had taken root in Surry; but the fact is not so. I shall leave this Place, I believe, very soon & remove into Sussex, where I can get, at least, as good an Income, with less to do—& be in the neighborhood of Malling, to which I am greatly attached.[2]

My Circumstances, you will observe, are not materially changed for the better. I am still one of the Slaves to Hope, & shall be for some time to come—however the Tide will turn, & I will follow Shakespeare's Advice & take it at the full[3]—

Pray have you never received a small deal Box, that left this Country last October in the Friendship Captn. Samuel Milford, bound for Virginia?—It was directed to the Care of Mr. Diack, & a Receipt for It signed by Peter Smith is now before me. It contained a few Law Books which, tho of very little Value, I would yet wish you to receive.

There is no very Material News circulating at home, I mean on this Island—A very violent Contest for Westminster has just terminated in favour of Lord John Townshend the popular Candidate[4]—The King is drinking the Cheltenham Waters.[5] The Russians have just obtained a signal Naval Victory over the Turks[6]—The French are still at loggerheads among themselves, & Your American General the Marquis de la Fayette, is cooped up for taking too forward a Part[7]—These are all the Topics I can think of—for my being lately elected with the D of Richmond's Nephew & some others a Freeman of Seaford, tho it did get into the Papers has not, I think, made such a Noise over the Island as might reasonably have been expected[8]—But, to be more domestick, My Mother's Health is of late much restored, & She is now tolerably well—Would to God She were comfortably settled with you; but it is not, & God only knows when it will be in my Power to furnish her with the Means of getting to You—She has desired me to mention her most affecttely to you all, for She feels too lazy at present to write herself. My dear Fanny is just exerting all Sisterly Attention upon Mrs. Bayley who last Week presented a very fine Boy to her Husband—I wish Mrs. I. would follow her Example. Apropos to that (& in your Ear) Fanny is [*seal*] a little hurt at having received no Answer from my Sister to the Letter She sent—I wish you would w/h/isper this into her Ear—In a louder Key assure her & Tom of my Love—tell the little prattler who makes so free with my Name, that her Uncle Arthur would go a great Way to romp with her—& confirm the Truth of this with a Kiss. Adieu! my dearest James—believe me

always & most affectionately Your's

A I

Give my Comps. to Mr. Dawson—I think I used to send them to Mrs. Blair's Family &ca if so by no means fail when I have so much Resp[*ect*]

Mc.Culloh, I imagine, has got some thing from Govermt. for I saw his Name together with that of the other Agents affixed to an Address of Thanks to the King—Write to me very soon & beg Tom to do so too[9]—

RC, Johnson Collection, NCSA. Addressed "James Iredell Esqre. Edenton North Carolina America."

---

[1]George Onslow (1731-1814), 1st Earl of Onslow, was the son of Arthur Onslow, for whom Onslow County, N.C., is named. George Onslow served in the House of Commons, House of Lords, and on the Privy Council. He is sometimes confused with his cousin George Onslow (1731-1792), who represented the borough of Guildford in the House of Commons from 1760 to 1784. *DNB*, s.v. "Onslow, George"; Watson, *Onslow County*, 5.

[2]Arthur did not leave Guildford for Sussex until 1791. Arthur Iredell to JI, December 6, 1791, and March 5, 1792, Charles E. Johnson Collection, State Archives; McRee, *Life and Correspondence*, 2:343-344.

[3]"There is a tide in the affairs of men/Which taken at the flood, leads on to fortune;/Omitted, all the voyage of their life/Is bound in shallows and in miseries." These words are spoken by Brutus in Shakespeare's *Julius Caesar*, act 4, scene 3.

[4]John Townshend (1757-1833), a supporter of Charles James Fox, served in the House of Commons for Westminster from 1788 to 1790. He had previously represented Cambridge University (1780-1784) and would later serve for Knaresborough (1793-1818). Namier and Brooke, *House of Commons*, 3:553.

[5]In 1788, George III, Queen Charlotte, and three of their daughters spent five weeks at Cheltenham, located northeast of Gloucester. The king, on the advice of his doctors, went to the fashionable spa to take the waters. Gwen Hart, *A History of Cheltenham* (Gloucester: Alan Sutton, 1981), 129-135.

[6]A war between Russia and the Ottoman Empire began in August 1787. Arthur Iredell is referring to the Second Battle of the Liman fought on June 16, 1789, on the Liman River, which is actually an estuary of the Dnieper River, near Ochakov. The Russians destroyed fifteen Turkish vessels and killed more than

three thousand sailors, while suffering the loss of only one ship and the deaths of eighteen men. Simon Sebag Montefiore, *Prince of Princes: The Life of Potemkin* (London: Weidenfeld and Nicolson, 2000), 385, 399-402.

[7]During the summer of 1788, Louis XVI's unwillingness to convene the Estates-General was the narrow focus of widespread discontent born of myriad sources. Dissidents banished from Paris inspired violent protests in provincial cities against the king's obstinance. In August, Louis relented and agreed to a meeting of the Estates-General to be held in May 1789. Owen Connelly and Fred Hembree, *The French Revolution*, The European History Series, ed. Keith Eubank (Arlington Heights, Ill.: Harlan Davidson, 1993), 21-25.

The Marquis de Lafayette (1757-1834), after fighting for American independence, returned to France with ideas of bringing liberty to his own country. In a tangential endeavor, he lent his support to a group of Breton noblemen who wished to reclaim local prerogatives that had been usurped by the monarch. After Louis XVI rejected their petitions, the Bretons escalated their campaign. Lafayette attended one of their meetings and, according to some, spoke seditiously. The king had a dozen of the Bretons imprisoned in the Bastille, and Lafayette, though not arrested, lost his military command. In addition, his perilous circumstances forced him to curtail his activities. *DAB*, s.v. "Lafayette, Marie Joseph Paul Yves Roch Gilbert Du Motier"; Louis Gottschalk, *Lafayette between the American and French Revolution, 1783-1789* (Chicago: University of Chicago Press, 1950), 387-392.

[8]Charles Lennox (1735-1806), 3d Duke of Richmond, was politically active throughout his life. At the time of this letter, he was master general of ordnance in Pitt's cabinet. The nephew referred to in the letter may be Charles (1764-1819), son of George Henry Lennox, the duke's brother. Charles became the 4th Duke of Richmond upon the death of his uncle. *DNB*, s.v. "Lennox, Charles"; Gregory and Stevenson, *Longman Companion to Britain in the Eighteenth Century*, 58, 59, 60; *Burke's Peerage*, 76th ed., 1648-1649.

A freeman is someone who has been given the freedom of the city, which is the supreme honor a town can bestow. Seaford, Sussex, is located sixty miles south-southeast of London. P. H. Collin, *Dictionary of Government and Politics* (Tiddington, Middlesex: Peter Collin Publishing, 1988), 90; *Topographical Dictionary of England*, 3d ed., s.v. "Seaford."

[9]On the original document, this paragraph appears at the top of the first page above the date.

To the Electors of Edenton

[*Edenton Aug. 15th. 1788*]

Gentlemen,

<Having had the honour to be applied to by several Gentlemen to know if permit myself to be offered as a Candidate at the present Election>

<As several Gentlemen have been pleased to ask me if I would offer myself as a Candidate for the honour of being chosen your Representative at the present Election,>

Having had the honour to be applied to by several Gentlemen, to know if I should offer myself as a Candidate at the present Election, <which is a mark of distinction I reserve with all possible gratitude and respect,> and being under the unfortunate necessity of declining to <avail myself of so great a mark of distinction,> I am <nevertheless /at the same time/ so deeply impressed with respect & gratitude for it that I> do so, I think it my duty to acquaint you with the reason<s> which forbids my aspiring to so great & flattering a mark of distinction.

I trust no Person who knows me will believe that I should be capable, from any views merely interested, of declining any public service it was in my power to perform, but from a late Act of Assembly which imposes a severe penalty on Members who do not attend punctually it is probable the Assembly will now meet on the very day appointed, instead (as it has usually been) of nearly a fortnight later, and that being the case I could not attend in Time to be of any service, without being /absent/ the whole of Newbern Superior Court, if not of Edenton, and I could not neglect both or either without prejudicing very materially many Clients who have entrusted with me concerns of the utmost consequence to them.[1] And I sincerely assure you that I can think of no expedient which would prevent my absence being the cause of great injustice to them, as also perhaps to other Persons, /to whom I am opposed &/ whose causes might be prejudiced, if delayed owing to my absence At the same time I have the best reason to believe no indulgence would be granted /by the Court/ to any Lawyers Business on account of his being a Member of Assembly.

I hope this reason will be satisfactory to all who are pleased to wish I should have the honour to represent them. I <can not only decline> feel <in> indeed great reluctance in parting with the satisfaction I lately enjoyed /(tho' on another occasion)/ in representing a Town to which I am attached by the strongest possible ties, and whose recent proof of confidence & regard I shall <face> reflect upon with gratitude & pleasure to the last moment of my life.

I am Gent. with the greatest respect Your faithful & obed. Sert.

J. I.

FC, Johnson Collection, NCSA. Endorsed "Copy of a Letter to the Electors of Edenton Aug. 15th. 1788."

---

[1]"An Act to Compel the Attendance of all Such Persons as are or shall be Elected to Represent any County or Town in the General Assembly of this State, at such time and place as may be appointed" was enacted in 1787. The penalty for missing the first day of the session was five pounds. Twenty shillings was charged for each additional day. Clark, *State Records*, 24:906-907.

To the People of the State of North Carolina[1]

August 18, 1788.

Friends and Fellow Citizens

The situation in which you are left by the proceedings of your late Convention, is such as requires your most serious attention. Perhaps at no period since your ancestors first settled in this country has your condition been more awful and affecting. You are for the first time separated from your sister states, the early and late companions of all your difficulties and dangers, with whom you have hitherto on all occasions run the race of freedom and glory, with whom but very lately you resolved to conquer or to die. Little was it to be apprehended, that in less than six years after the peace, a peace acquired by your and their joint efforts, and which to the astonishment of all mankind gave glory as well as security to the weaker party, those states who had been the willing and the generous sharers of a common danger, should have become separate! weakened the common cause, still in full force, though not in equal apparent danger subsisting! and thus afforded a triumph to our common enemies, who are watching, if not planning for our destruction! Heaven forbid that this disunion should last long! Happy would it have been, if it had not for a moment existed!

But Regret, with whatever poignancy it may be felt, is now useless. The danger is incurred. Eleven other states have a common united government: We have no share in it. If we can derive pride from the consideration, our independence is increased. We are now not only independent of all other nations in the world, but entirely independent of the other states, except for our share of the debt hitherto incurred, which we are now utterly unable to pay. We may form alliances at our pleasure with Great-Britain, France, Spain, Turkey, the Dey of Algiers, or Rhode-Island. We may make what acts of Assembly we please concerning war, peace, negociation, commerce or finance. While the other United States are fettered by the necessity of pursuing a common interest, there is no check upon our separate wisdom, or the free course of our own noble exertions.

There are some men possibly, inflated with ridiculous ideas of our own importance, to whom this prospect may be pleasing. There are many weak men perhaps who think danger never exists but when evils are actually and immediately felt. There may be a few (I trust in God they are a very few) to whom confusion and disorder may be the most acceptable objects. But among the great majority, including both parties, those who are averse to the new constitution, as well as those who are friends to it, I believe the idea of an entire disunion is reprobated with horror. I have had the pleasure to hear that was the case with by far the greatest part of the majority in our late Convention, who unfortunately did not scruple to rush into a temporary one.

Taking it for granted therefore, that all rational friends of their country consider a union with the other states as indispensable to their liberty and safety, I shall beg leave to make a few observations on the policy which has brought us into our present extraordinary situation. It is a situation so new, as well as important, that no pains necessary to its investigation can be considered ill bestowed. I shall hope therefore for the honour of your attention, while we examine it together.

The old articles of confederation were framed and executed in the very midst of the war. The necessity of a general opposition to the arbitrary designs of Great-Britain had been felt by every generous mind from one end of the continent to another. A common danger pointed out the propriety of common exertions: common exertions required common counsels. The different states were therefore represented in Congress, who were entrusted with the common protection of the whole. The necessity of a general co-operation in measures of defence in which we are all interested, in the midst of a danger which none could doubt, occasioned a ready obedience to every recommendation made by that representative body, and their recommendations accordingly had all the force of laws. Warmed with such noble principles, in pursuit of one great object, when the same men framed the articles of confederation, they relied perhaps too much on a continuation of the same ardour, and their system was formed on the basis of requisitions, which at that time had never been known to fail. Possibly they might have foreseen its defects, but provided those articles as the only ones likely to be adopted at that period, when some kind of confederation was absolutely indispensable. Whatever might be the cause of it, it's defects have been long acknowledged by all enlightened minds, and felt by the most ignorant. None can doubt, that a government must be radically defective, which in a country full of resources and affording the greatest commercial advantages, has not been able to pay the interest of a moderate debt incurred to preserve us from slavery, to keep alive even a passive commerce disgraceful to a great degree, to preserve foreigners and citizens from the operation of fraudulent and dishonest laws, to compel the execution of a treaty of peace most honourable and advantageous to us, and humiliating to our enemies, nor consequently to obtain possession of our full share of the advantages of that treaty, perfidy on one part naturally affording an excuse for perfidy on the other. Our national honour, as well as our national safety was wounded, and every friend of this country felt for the degraded reputation, as well as the diminished importance of a people lately high in the estimation of all mankind.

In this situation, the universal voice of America almost called out for a remedy. After one or two ineffectual attempts, at length twelve states met in Convention. Among the members of that Convention, I need not particularly point out the illustrious ones entitled to the utmost confidence of their country. That country must be dead to every sensation of virtue, to every emotion of sensibility, to every impulse of gratitude, before that confidence can be withdrawn. The members of that Convention added to their high character before by the generous readiness with which all local objects were sacrificed to the general good. The sacrifice was noble, and does the highest honour to these states, whose members in the first instance, and who themselves in the latter, have thus added an immortal seal to their patriotism and wisdom. Wisdom it undoubtedly was, but a wisdom to which narrow souls could never reach, and which required a high sense of national honour, and an inflexible attachment to the true interests of the union at large, abstracted from immediate tempting advantages, to bring it forth.

Those respectable men that formed the late General Convention (I shall call them so, notwithstanding the gross abuse so ungratefully and illiberally bestowed upon them) had not only local difficulties to struggle with, but the extreme difficulty itself of forming a wise system of government, combining a proper share of energy in the formation and administration of laws, with that degree of liberty which each state and individual ought unalienably to enjoy. To declaimers who have never thought or read on the subject this may appear an easy task, but to sober considerate men who are forming a constitution that ought not to be lightly changed, and which therefore ought to provide for every contingent case, as well such as are likely to happen seldom, as those which may frequently occur, it must always wear a very formidable appearance. This would be the case in forming a single government. In forming a confederate one, such as our situation required, the utmost attention, moderation, and forbearance were requisite. And as the subject required to be viewed in all possible lights, the mutual aid of a number of sensible men was indispensably necessary, together with the utmost freedom of discussion. What must we therefore think of the modesty of any individual who shall rashly, perhaps without any thought at all, condemn a system, grounded on such worthy motives, and produced by the joint effort of such wise and deliberate counsel! Yet how many instances are there of such individuals who condemn it with the most outrageous abuse!

I mean not in the course of this letter to enter into the particulars of a constitution, the merits of which have been so amply discussed. I shall only observe, that it's leading principle is, that in all cases where the peace and interest of the union at large are concerned we should, as one people united in a common object, be governed by common counsels, and it provides for the execution of these in a regular and peaceable manner by the instrumentality of courts of justice, not leaving us in the condition to which we were exposed under the old confederation, under which, though Congress had great nominal powers (very near equal to those proposed to be given to the new Congress, though the people were not directly represented in it) yet there was no method of enforcing their most material acts of authority but by force of arms, if they possessed this right of enforcing, which is questionable. If they did not, the confederation ridiculously gave an authority, without the means of carrying it into effect. If they did, then every act of disobedience, whether wilful, excusable or unavoidable, might have drawn on a civil war, in which the innocent must have suffered with the guilty. In the one case, the confederation was an absurdity: In the other, the horror and injustice attending it's execution, and the danger upon every such extremity of the union being entirely destroyed, were unanswerable objections against it with every friend to the peace and prosperity of his country.

But whatever may be the defects of the new system, it certainly has one material advantage over the old. By the old confederation no amendments could be made but by the consent of all the states. The necessity of an unanimous consent in any country is a never failing source of weakness and usurpation. It has been found so a thousand times in the seven United Provinces in Europe, where an unanimous consent even of the towns, as well as of the States-General, is necessary for certain objects. This has arisen from an extreme jealousy, and has at critical periods nearly caused their destruction, because some of the towns being very inconsiderable, foreign powers have found it convenient and practical to bribe them to prevent their concurring in measures their common safety required. On such occasions the stronger party have found it necessary to over power the weaker, and rather usurp an unconstitutional power than suffer their country to be ruined. Rhode-Island at length has reduced America to a similar situation. Her forbearing for years to join in any federal measures, and by her example inducing other states to adopt a separate and selfish policy, reduced America to this alternative, either to suffer in form all the evils of a weak impracticable government unable to correct itself, or by one bold and manly effort to strike into a new road of safety which would not only answer our purpose for the present, but suit us to the end of our journey. The confederation could scarcely be said to subsist but in form, as it had been violated in a hundred instances, or if it had not the salus populi, justly called the supreme law, required a new and nobler course.[2] The Convention therefore, did not require an unanimous consent, which was impracticable, but in a manly manner declared, nine states should govern themselves, if the other four did not choose to yield to so large a majority. On such great occasions none but narrow minds will adhere to form; this alternative, or absolute ruin the whole, seemed the inevitable consequence. Which ought they to have preferred?—Upon a similar principle, future amendments to this system may be made, by three-fourths of the whole, and as this article is very important and generally much misrepresented, I will transcribe it at large, in order that it may be seen, that whether the Congress itself shall choose to propose amendments or not, yet if the legislatures of two-thirds of the states do, a Convention must be called for the purpose of consulting on the subject. The article is as follows, viz.

"The Congress, whenever two-thirds of both houses shall deem it necessary, shall propose amendments to this constitution, or, on the application of the legislatures of two-thirds of the several states, shall call a Convention for proposing amendments, which in either case, shall be valid to all intents and purposes, as part of this constitution, when ratified by the legislature of three-fourths of the several states, or by Conventions in three-fourths thereof, as the one or the other mode of ratification may be proposed by the Congress; provided, that no amendments which may be made prior to the year one thousand eight hundred and eight shall in any manner affect the first and fourth clauses in the ninth section of the first article; and that no state, without its consent, shall be deprived of it's equal suffrage in the Senate."

The first and fourth clauses in the ninth section of the first article (which are referred to in the above clause) are as follows, viz.

"1st. The migration or importation of such persons as any of the states now existing shall think proper to admit, shall not be prohibited by the Congress prior to the year one thousand eight hundred and eight, but a tax or duty may be imposed on such importation, not exceeding ten dollars for each person.

4th. No capitation, or other direct tax shall be laid, unless in proportion to the census or enumeration herein before directed to be taken."

This article as to amendments places the subject on a footing altogether new, and is an honour to the constitution proposed which no other in the world can boast. In every other country revolutions of government can only be expected to take place by means of a civil war. The glorious principle of a majority in a fair Convention of the people deciding peaceably for the whole has not yet reached them. The extension of this principle, which formerly existed in the separate states, to the states in their united capacity, at the same time requiring more than a bare majority, to prevent hasty and partial alterations, in my opinion, is entitled to the highest praise. As mankind increase in knowledge, the contemptible vanity of self-perfection gives way to the more enlightened and more just diffidence of any human capacity, however great. The foresight of the greatest minds is nothing, compared to the instructions of experience. Any system therefore that could now be formed would possibly upon trial be found to want alterations, and if such alterations could not be made in a regular and orderly manner, it would be a just exception to any system whatever, let it's merit otherwise be ever so great. Thank God no such exception lies to the system before us. It guards wisely against the two dangerous extremes of too much facility or too much difficulty in obtaining amendments. They certainly ought not to be made but when the necessity or utility is very apparent, and when that is the case it ought not to be in the power of one or two weak or wicked members in the union to defeat the real interest of the whole.

This article has justly been deemed so important, that it has been the means in a most happy manner of facilitating the adoption of the constitution in several of the states. The respectable states of Massachusetts-Bay, South-Carolina, New-Hampshire, Virginia and New-York, though approving of the general principles of the constitution, had objections to particular parts of it, and therefore wished for amendments. But they were at the same time sensible of the necessity of a more intimate union of the states, they dreaded above all things a separation of interests and pursuits, they deemed the present situation critical to a most alarming degree, and as no man could insure us against foreign hostility or domestic dissentions till all the different amendments were adjusted, they generously and discreetly said, "We will not break the union; we will unite with you for the present on the terms proposed, that we may have a national government in existence, and we refer to your equity and good sense afterwards in the constitutional mode the amendments we wish to have adopted." This was the language of patriotism, prudence and affection, and none can doubt it will have it's fullest effect, in respect to all those amendments which are really essential, and which relate as well to the security and prosperity of one state as to those of another. If there are any of a more local nature, and they should not prevail, we ought not to regret that in this instance as well as others three-fourths of America shall speak for the whole, since all the states individually cannot be expected in every instance to agree.

Would to God that a similar principle of conciliation had governed the decisions of our Convention! Why should we not have followed such respectable examples? If Massachusetts, though I believe the fifth only that agreed, thought the condition of previous amendments dangerous or impracticable, surely our state after the certain agreement of ten, and when it was evident the new government would be put in motion, had much more reason for not insisting upon it at that time.[3] The subsequent examples of four other states (three of which were known to have decided when our Convention met) have added great weight to the propriety of the conduct of Massachusetts. Two illustrious examples of highly respectable individuals in two of those states deserve particular mention, as well in honour to those gentlemen, as to sanction the decisions of the majorities in their respective states. The one is Governor Randolph of Virginia. This gentleman, who has long been esteemed for his many virtues as well as for his abilities, was one of the Delegates from Virginia in the General Convention at Philadelphia. He had objections to the constitution which made him forbear to sign it. So far as pride could be concerned, his wishes must have been opposed to the general adoption of the constitution without previous amendments, and it is believed if a few only of the states had agreed he would have persisted in this purpose. But when so many as eight states had agreed, and he saw the difficulty and danger of requiring so many states to tread back the ground they had passed, he nobly declared (I had not the pleasure to hear his words—I judge only of the substance from report) that it was now too late to require previous amendments, and that though he still thought amendments necessary, he would not endanger the union by insisting on them as a condition of adoption.[4] He accordingly, with all the warmth of patriotic virtue, maintained the adoption of the constitution in the then situation of affairs as indispensably necessary perhaps to the existence of the union, certainly to its peace and security; and to the exertion of his great abilities it is not improbable Virginia may be in a great measure indebted for her present station in the union, and America at large for the subsequent adoption by New-York in consequence of her illustrious example. In that state, resides the other gentleman whose conduct I beg leave to state. Being at greater distance, I can only speak of him generally as a distinguished character by name, and who had been remarkable for his opposition to the new consitution. I mean Mr. Melancton Smith, who was a member of the late New-York Convention, and is said, in a debate on the subject of a conditional ratification, to have spoke to the following effect.[5] Having declared his determination to vote against a condition, he urged "That however it might be otherwise presumed, he was consistent in his principles and conduct. He was as thoroughly convinced then as he ever had been, that the constitution was radically defective; amendments to it had always been the object of his pursuit, and until Virginia came in, he had reason to believe they might have been obtained previous to the operation of the government. He was now satisfied they could not, and it as equally the dictate of reason and of duty to quit his first ground, and advance so far as that they might be received into the union. He should hereafter pursue his important and favorite object of amendments with equal zeal as before, but in a practicable way, which was only in the mode prescribed by the constitution. On the first suggestion of the plan then under consideration, he thought it might have answered the purpose; but from the reasonings of gentlemen in opposition to it, and whose opinions alone would deservedly have vast weight in the national counsels, as well as from the sentiments of persons abroad, he was now persuaded the proposition would not be received, however doubtful it might appear, considered merely as an abstract and speculative question. The thing must now be abandoned, as fallacious, for if persisted in, it would certainly prove in the event, only a dreadful deception to those who were serious for joining the union. He then placed in a striking and affecting light, the situation of that state in case they should not be received by Congress, convulsions in the northern part, factions and discord in the rest. The strength of his own party who were seriously anxious for amending the government would be dissipated, their union lost, their object probably defeated, and they would, to use the simple figurative language of scripture, be dispersed like sheep on a mountain. He therefore concluded it was no more than a proper discharge of his public duty as well as the most adviseable way of obtaining the great end of his opposition to vote against any proposition which would not be received as a ratification of the constitution."

I cite with the greater pleasure these two respectable instances, not only as a striking proof of the justice of those sentiments which induced two such men to abandon a cause they were warmly attached to, but that in the midst of the party violence to which we have been unhappily witnesses, we may dwell a few moments with delight on the magnanimous virtue which produced such distinguished instances of candour.

If these considerations have no effect, but it is still asked, Shall we consent to a system destructive to our liberties, without taking proper precautions to secure them? Let us calmly ask ourselves, Can we believe not only that the members of the General Convention at Philadelphia, but that eleven State Conventions meeting separately since, could either be so ignorant of the proper principles of liberty, or so indifferent about them, as to consent to any system by which it could be in reality endangered? Is the vital spark of freedom, which so lately set all America in a flame, existing no where but in the breasts of the majorities of North-Carolina and Rhode-Island, and of the minorities of the other states? Surely it is much more probable that those who have taken so much pains to inflame you, condescending to use very little reason with a great deal of passion, are mistaken in entertaining such high ideas of their own superior wisdom, than that North-Carolina and Rhode-Island now remain the only American bulwarks of liberty. I trust in God the other states are not in so desperate a condition, and hope I shall not offend you in supposing that with equal virtue the eleven United States are not inferior to the late majority of our Convention in wisdom and discernment. The business of government is a very complicated thing. It requires other talents, besides good wishes, to undertake it with success. It requires far superior qualities to those of a mere slave of popularity, to frame a system calculated not merely to flatter the passions of the people it is intended for, but to fix it on a basis of justice which can conciliate the regard, the confidence, the respect of other nations, and give it a fame calculated for duration. Such a system when framed is to be tried by the test of reason, not passion. It is not to be rejected, because plausible objections can be made to it: Plausible objections may be made to anything, and objections of any kind, before they prevail, ought to be found solid, and not plausible merely. Nothing would be more easy than to detect the sophistry with which many parts of this constitution have been attacked: Nothing more easy, than to shew the improper distrust, and the groundless jealousy with which many well meaning men apprehend that the moment this government is set in motion, the very men whom the people and the legislatures themselves have chosen will conspire against their own liberty, and that of their constitutents. But as I before observed to you, I shall not in this letter enter into particulars, but refer you to numerous respectable publications calculated to quiet your fears on this subject. In my opinion, the coolest and most deliberate reason, as well as the most respectable authorities, is on the side of the constitution, and so I am persuaded it will be generally acknowledged when the mist of passion, which has blinded many able, as well as many weak men, is taken off.

In our present situation, what are we reduced to? Have we any national character? Is the state of North-Carolina known to any nation in Europe? No. The United States of America are known. But alas! We are to be no longer one of them. We have no alliance with any power on earth. We have no right, if attacked, to call on the other states for assistance. Our own prowess and resources must defend us against all mankind, or we must sink in a conflict, unless assisted by the charity of others. Can we much longer bear so humiliating, so dangerous a condition? What must our feelings be when we see the prosperity of the other states derived from the energy of their new government, while we are deriving additional weakness from the dissolution of the old, without partaking of any of the benefits of the new? Can we blame our sister states? Certainly no. A cruel necessity dictated a change. Certain ruin, or an alteration, because the unavoidable alternatives. We have had our option allowed us. We have unfortunately chosen for the present a path leading to misery and ruin, if we continue to pursue it. But God forbid that we should not instantly stop short, and do every thing to recover the false step we have taken which our situation will admit of. Is there left us any method of relief?

Our situation is certainly bad, but perhaps not entirely desperate. The majority of the Convention seem not to have considered what they did as a rejection. But it may undoubtedly be considered so by the other states. After not accepting when the opportunity was allowed us, we have no right to chuse our own time at any period hereafter. All the states ought certainly to start upon equal terms. But it is to be hoped they would judge with liberality, and that if we early should agree by means of another Convention, we might immediately be admitted on equal terms with the other states. We have reason to fear however, that the earliest step of this kind that could be taken, might be too late for us to have a share in the first formation of laws. What an opportunity we have lost! Should North-Carolina have no votes in the first Congress, the first system of laws, which will be the most important of any for many years, may be formed much more injuriously for the southern states than otherwise might have been the case, and the supporters of amendments may be deprived of powerful assistance.*[6] Whether or not we can possibly be early enough for this no man can say. But let us get into the union as soon as we can. One Convention can repair the mischief of another. Let all therefore who think with me promote so far as his influence shall extend the measure of petitioning the Assembly for a new Convention. Let the people on this occasion (it certainly is great enough for their exertion) speak their own sentiments. Let them say whether they wish for an immediate adoption, that we may be a member of the union, or not. They have had an opportunity of much reflexion since the first libels were dispersed among them. I am much mistaken if their native good sense is not beginning to break through a cloud of prejudice. Let them call on all who attempt to dictate to them, for reason, instead of abuse. Let them tell them plainly, calumny of the most respectable characters shall no longer impose either on their passions or their understanding: that they consider it not only grossly unjust in itself, but an attack on their integrity as well as on their judgment, and that it is now too late to persuade them that the great majority of America is composed of men who want either virtue or understanding: That it is much more certain that we ought to be a united people, than that their objections to any union at all are founded on any rational principles. This language I trust will be found congenial with the general sentiments of my countrymen, I have seen many symptoms of a change which give me the greatest hopes. I rely on that public virtue which has so often conspicuously shewn itself in this state; on that good sense which though it may for a time be overborne, is sure in the end to rise superior to prejudice. God grant that this fatal disunion, fatal I should have termed it had I been sure it would exist but a day, may last a very short time longer! May we return and embrace with affection those sister states, with whom we have hitherto shared in adversity and prosperity, and with whom alone, whatever vain ideas we may form, we can enjoy security, freedom and glory! And may those respectable states, with a moderation, and forbearance which will do them honour, be willing to receive us with as much cordiality as if we had never strayed!

A Citizen of North-Carolina.

Printed, *A Plea for Federal Union*. Printed, *State Gazette of North Carolina*.

---

[1]This letter appeared in the *State Gazette of North Carolina*, September 15, 1788, and was printed as a pamphlet. Louise Irby Trenholme wrote of this document, "Though the author is not known, judging from the style it might have been written by Iredell." Trenholme, *Ratification*, 199n. See also *A Plea for Federal Union, 1788* (Charlottesville, Va.: Tracy W. McGregor Library, University of Virginia, 1947).

[2]*Salus populi* means public welfare.

[3]Massachusetts was actually the sixth state to ratify. Connecticut was the fifth. *Constitution*, 16.

[4]Edmund Randolph, in a lengthy speech, stated: "I believe gentlemen are sincere in their opposition, and actuated by pure motives; but, when I maturely weigh the advantages of the Union, and dreadful consequences of its dissolution; when I see safety on my right, and destruction on my left; when I behold respectability and happiness acquired by the one, but annihilated by the other,—I cannot hesitate to decide in favor of the former." *Elliot's Debates*, 3:65-86.

[5]Melancton Smith (1744-1798) was a veteran of the Revolutionary War and a merchant in New York City. He served in the Continental Congress (1785-1787) and was a delegate to New York's ratification convention. *BDC*, s.v. "Smith, Melancton."

[6]JI included the following note: "*There are two ways in which amendments may be proposed. 1. The Congress, if two-thirds of both houses concur, may propose amendments. 2. On the application of the legislatures of two-thirds of the states, the Congress must call a Convention for proposing them. And such amendments as either Congress, or such Convention shall propose, will be valid, and for the future form a part of the constitution 'when ratified by the legislatures of three-fourths of the several states, or by Conventions in three-fourths thereof, as the one or the other mode of ratification may be proposed by Congress.' No amendments therefore can be proposed, but through the medium of Congress, or on the application of the legislatures of two-thirds of the states. Those states must be states in the union, because the constitution can refer to no states but such as are bound by it. By our not adopting the constitution, the general party through America in favour of amendments lose the benefit of the votes which our Senators and Representatives might have in Congress, and also of that recommendation by the legislature of this state, which might be of great moment towards making up

the requisite number of two-thirds of the several legislatures in the union. And if a general Convention should be called, we can have no pretence to form a part of it, unless we are in the union, because the general Convention spoken of in the constitution, must mean a Convention of those states which are members of the union; it can never be understood to refer to any state which thought the constitution unworthy of its acceptance, and therefore was in no respect bound by the system which was to be amended. People may rationally correct their own government, but it would certainly be impertinent in others to interfere with it."

From Hugh Williamson

New York [*August*] 23rd 1788

Dear Sir

By Letters from sundry Correspondents it appears that North Carolina has at length thrown herself out of the Union, but she happily is not alone. The large upright and respectable State of Rhode Island is her associate. This circumstance however does not, I hope, render it necessary that the Delegates from N C should profess a particular affection for the Delegates from R. I. That State was some days ago represented by a Mr. Arnold who keeps a little Tavern 10 miles out of Providence & a Mr. Hazard the illiterate quondam Skipper of a small Coasting Vessel & now the very leader of I Know Ye Justices who officiates at County Courts & receives small Fees not as a Lawyer but Agent for Suitors.[1] These two respectable Delegates with the innate Desire of promoting a bad measure lately voted on several Questions respecting the Organisation of the new Govt. in order to fix it in New York, a Corner of the Union, but before the final Question was taken on the Ordinance they caused a Member to move in Congress for a Vote That nothing which the Delegates from Rh Is. or N C had done or might do in voting on this Subject should be construed as in any measure affecting the Rights &c of their Constituents. This was to be a Bull or Absolution. On this Motion the Delegates from N. C. moved that the Word North Carolina should be struck out of the Vote of Absolution. And thereon we called for the Yeas & Nays to prove that we did not wish to have N C associated in any Vote with Rh I. that we did not <did not> wish for Absolution being conscious of having pursued our Duty. That with Respect to the final Vote which was to be taken on the Ordinance we proposed never to assist in such Vote unless N C should confederate for we would not be guilty of paracide by throwing our State out of the Union. On this the Motion was withdrawn, the Rh. I. Gentlemen missed the promised Pleasure of doing wrong & on the next morning they set out Homeward.[2]

I wrote the Governor a Letter concerning the Conduct of some Members when the Business referred to was first moved in Congress and with my usual want of prudent Dissimulation I expressed an honest Indignation by calling Spade a Spade This Letter it seems has been read in the Convention & a Correspondent up the Country writes me that he fears it has hurt me greatly. As I did not consider that Letter as official & one that should be communicated to a public Assembly I took no Copy of it and do not know what it contained but as I am conscious that I never write in the most careless mood any thing but what I think and as I am also conscious that since I have been honoured with a commission from the State I have not in a single Instance preferred my private Interest to the Benefit of the State, that I never have through private Indulgence or inattention omitted a single opportunity of serving the State. Being conscious of no corrupt motive my zeal on a late occasion to serve the State has not been abated at an Hour when I had reason to suppose that the Action would not be popular. Had I supported what I conceive to be a dishonest measure in pursuit of Popularity I should for the first Time, as a pu<p>blic man, had occasion to condemn myself. Doing what I conceive to be the Dictate of Honesty & true Patriotism I mean to abide Consequences, my friends know that I do not depend for a Support on public favour.

The 22nd Amendment so called was certainly a very important one for N C. If an East India Company or a Mediterranian Company should be erected it would greatly interfere with her Trade to those Regions. What could have put foreign Troops into their Head? They should have excepted particularly against the Japanese who are Heathen. The 12th Amendment I take for an Original. Others have talked about a Rebellion in a State but the N Ca. Convention speaks of the State being in Rebellion.[3] Are these the same thing according to the conceptions of Tom Person & Tim Bloodworth? not forgetting the banned Judge Spencer! Is it like the various Expression of an old turned hat & a turned old Hat? Perhaps they conceived that the federal Congress might undertake to declare that a State out of the Union was in Rebellion. To obviate this it would have been safer to have required thirteen Elevenths. The other Amendments or Pejorations I fully understand but this one I do not.

Be pleased present my Respects to Mrs. Iredell & believe me to be with great Regard

Dr. Sir Your obedt. Servt.

Hu Williamson

RC, Iredell Papers, Duke. Printed, McRee, 2:236-238, and *Letters of Delegates to Congress*, 25:317-318. Addressed "James Iredell Esqr. Edenton." Endorsed "New York 23d. Aug. 1788 Hugh Williamson Ansd."

[1]Peleg Arnold (1751-1820), who operated a tavern in Smithfield, R.I., served in the Continental Congress from 1787 to 1788. He was later chief justice of the Rhode Island Supreme Court (1795-1809, 1810-1812) and president of the Smithfield Union Bank. Jonathan J. Hazard (ca. 1744-after 1824) served in the Continental Congress (1788) and the Rhode Island legislature. He was a leading advocate of Rhode Island's paper money policy. *BDC*, s.v. "Arnold, Peleg," "Hazard, Jonathan J."; *DAB*, s.v. "Hazard, Jonathan J."

[2]See *Journals of the Continental Congress*, 34:403-404.

[3]The delegates to the North Carolina ratification convention suggested twenty-seven amendments to the proposed Constitution as well as a twenty-part declaration of rights. The twenty-second amendment would have prohibited Congress from creating a "company of merchants with exclusive advantages of commerce." The twenty-seventh would have prevented Congress from bringing foreign soldiers into the country without the approval of two-thirds of those present in both houses. Two-thirds consent would also have been required under the twelfth amendment to declare a state "to be in rebellion." Clark, *State Records*, 22:16-23.

From William Hooper

[*2 Sept. 1788*]

My dear Sir

I render you many thanks for your kind favour from Halifax & Sincerely congratulate you upon the authentick accounts which we have Since had from New York of the new Constitut[*ion*] having been adopted by that State. North C[*aro*]lina will become [*a by*]word am[*ong*] the nat[*ions. We have*] been a[*mused here with a story that Wilie and Person have been burnt in effigy. Is it true?*][1]

[*The elections to the westward are al*]most all in favour of fe[*deralism. T*]he Surry members who were all anti after experiencing much abuse are all left out & three federalists elected. Lock & Rutherfurd left out, Feds in their Stead. Alex Martin is elected.[2]

This will be handed you by a Mr. Hunter who drives a Waggon. I must request the favour Of you to apply to Edmund Blount in my behalf for a barrel of Clover Seed & if it is ready Send it by this Oppy. as I know not when another will offer. If you could Send us two pounds of tolerable tea you would much oblige us & I will reimburse with thanks when we meet.

If you or the Governour should have any papers which you could spare they will be very acceptable to us.

My Wife Daughter & Son offer their best respects to yourself Mrs. Iredell & the family. I beg you to present our kind regards to the Governour & his family. to Mr. Dawson Complim[*torn*] Mr Pollok. Remember [*torn*][3]

[*Wi*]ll Hooper

RC, Iredell Papers, Duke. Printed, McRee, 2:238-239. Addressed "James [*Iredell*] Esq [*Ed*]enton." Endorsed "Hillsborough Sept. 2d. 1788 Wm. Hooper. Ansd."

---

[1]In a letter of October 23, 1788, William Hooper reported that the two were "publicly exhibited" and paraded in a "negro short coat and proper appendages." Trenholme, *Ratification*, 201.

[2]In Surry County, Federalists John Armstrong, George Houser, and William T. Lewis Jr. were elected to the General Assembly to replace Antifederalists Joseph Winston, Seth Coffin, and James Gains. Gains attended the 1788 ratification convention, while Houser served in 1789. Winston attended both conventions, the first as an Antifederalist and the second as a Federalist. Cheney, *North Carolina Government*, 219-221; Massengill, *North Carolina Votes*, 21, 29, 65.

Matthew Locke, Griffith Rutherford, and George H. Berger of Rowan County were Antifederalist incumbents who were not returned to the General Assembly. All three had been Antifederalist delegates to the 1788 ratification convention. Locke and Berger also attended the 1789 convention, where they continued to oppose ratification. Basil Gaither, David Caldwell, and Thomas Carson were Federalists who were elected to the General Assembly from Rowan County in 1788. Carson was a delegate to the 1788 convention. Gaither attended in 1789. Cheney, *North Carolina Government*, 219-221; Massengill, *North Carolina Votes*, 5, 12, 21, 37, 52.

Alexander Martin was re-elected to the senate for Guilford County. Cheney, *North Carolina Government*, 219, 220.

[3]The original document is in tatters. Missing words, indicated here in brackets, were obtained from the printed version of this letter in McRee. The last paragraph is not included in McRee.

From William R. Davie

Halifax. Sep. 8th. 1788.

My dear Sir

As the publication came by some unknown hand in my absence I had no opportunity of returning it to the printer in the manner you requested.[1] it is very well received here, and I shall disperse it all the way to Salisbury, and cannot help hoping that it will give a determination to the public mind, at present strangely unsettled and wavering—Persons and Mr. Jones are both holding out the doctrine of opposition for five or Six years at least, Mr. Jones says we must have that time at least, before their Judiciary are let in upon us. he is continually haranguing the people on the terrors of the Judicial power, and the certainty of their ruin, if they are obliged now to pay their debts.[2] We are almost lead to believe there is some thing more than a mere mistake in point of principle in his conduct.

I set out for Salisbury the day after tomorrow in but an ill state of health. I am however in expectation that the change of air will be of service to me

Make my respectful Compliments to the Governor and believe me with much esteem

yours very sincerely

William R. D[*avie*]

I think the Governor is right with respect to the uniformity of Petitions, the measure must however be promoted and I wish you would correspond with the Gentlemen at Newbern on this subject. I will take care of this business to the Westward[3]—

RC, Iredell Papers, Duke. Printed, McRee, 2:239. Addressed "James Iredell, Esquire Edenton. To the care of Mr. Bond."

---

[1]See "To the People of the State of North Carolina," August 18, 1788, in this volume.

[2]Antifederalists feared the subordination of state courts to the federal judiciary. They were concerned about the need to travel great distances to federal courts, the absence of a constitutional provision for jury trials in civil suits, and the impact of the federal judiciary on economic matters, such as debts to British creditors, confiscated property, and above all, paper money. Trenholme, *Ratification*, 173-174.

[3]Federalists conducted petition drives for a second ratification convention. Davie led the campaign in the western counties, JI in the northeastern part of the state, and Archibald Maclaine, "the Gentleman at New Bern," in the southeast. Trenholme, *Ratification*, 199.

To [unknown][1]

Edenton Sept. 10th. 1788

Dear Sir,

I inclose you two Blank Writs in case you should have occasion for them. If not, I beg the favour of you to return them to me. I think it safest, as I know not what agreement you may make with Taylor, to ask the favour of Colo. Davie to fill up either or both as there may be occasion. Be pleased to tell him I took the liberty to request it. Though either of the other Gentlemen would readily do it, I mention Colo. Davie because the others might possibly be employed on the other side. If any accident should prevent your seeing him, be pleased to ask Mr. Hooper or Mr. Moore.

Our latest news, such as it is, you will find in the inclosed Papers. They are Edenton Papers, mind. Congress have not yet passed a definitive vote on the time and place of the new Congress meeting. The times mentioned in some votes for the different purposes (and which were not objected to) were: the first Wednesday in January for chusing the Electors of the President: the first Wednesday in February for the choice of the President: the first Wednesday in March for the new Congress to meet. Upon the last Vote New York had the Majority for the place. But it seems one Vote is not sufficient. Baltimore came very near.[2]

I inclose you some Copies of a late Publication, which you may suppose came from the Clouds, or any where but from Edenton. Designing to conceal its origination from here, it has been sent to different places, but not appeared publickly here yet. The Author wishes to be concealed because a knowledge of the Author generally lessens the effect of any publication.[3]

People in general have had their health here much better than usual. I beg the favour of you to present my best respects to Mr. Bennehan and to Mr. and Mrs. Allen and Mrs. Cooper if still with you. I hope their looks on their return will shew that they have come from the back Country.

I am, Dear Sir with very sincere regard, Your obedient Servant

Ja. Iredell.

FC, Iredell Papers, NCSA.

---

[1]The recipient of this letter has not been identified.

[2]On September 13, the Continental Congress passed the following: "RESOLVED, That the first Wednesday in January next, be the day for appointing Electors in the several States, which before the said day shall have ratified the said Constitution, that the first Wednesday in February next, be the day for the Electors to assemble in their respective States, and vote for a President; and that the first Wednesday in March next, be the time, and the present Seat of Congress the place for commencing Proceedings under the said Constitution." *Journals of the Continental Congress,* 34:522-523.

[3]JI may be cryptically referring to his own publication. See "To the People of the State of North Carolina," August 18, 1788, in this volume.

From James Glasgow

12 Septr. 1788.

Dear Sir

Agreeable to yours by Mr. Mc.Culloh I send in all the Acts of Assembly in the Secretary's Office between the Years 1751 and 1774 both inclusive amounting in all to 410 for which you will be pleased send me a Receipt those I should have sent in according to promise but believe me the Season has been so wet for this fortnight or three weeks that th[*ere has*] /not/ been two fair days together.

[*Torn*]t where th[*torn*] no other conveyance than on horseback

with the greatest regard I am Dear Sir Your most Obedt.

J Glasgow

No. Acts sent in by Jno. Holliday to wit[1]

16 passed in 1751 & 1752		
12 do.	1753	1754
10 do.	1755	
22 do.	1756	
30 do.	1757	
27 do.	1758	1759
40 do.	1760	
19 do.	1761	
9 do.		1762
36 do.	1764	1765
29 do.	1766	
[*torn*]		1768
[*torn*]		1769
66 do.	1771	
33 do.	1773	
10 do.	1774	
410		

RC, Iredell Papers, Duke. Addressed "James Iredell esquire Edenton per Cap[*torn*]."

[1]A John Holliday represented Glasgow County in the house of commons (1794-1796). Glasgow County was created from Dobbs County in 1791 and became Greene County in 1799. Cheney, *North Carolina Government*, 231, 233, 234; Corbitt, *North Carolina Counties*, 107.

From Archibald Maclaine

Wilmington 13h. Sept 1788

Dear Sir

I thank you for the address, which however I had from Hodge the post before I received yours.[1] I had no doubt of the author the moment I had given it a reading. I wish you could get the printer to forward a few of them here. Papers of that kind come by the post without charge, and he is to send forward a parcel of his proposals for the laws. Let him know, if you please that I received his letter &c and that I and my friends in this quarter will procure him subscriptions

I expect to see part of the address in our next paper. Some of the subscribers will make a point of having it inserted. Howard is a rank antifederalist, and what is, if possible, much worse for himself; for he is a fool. on my return, I found that he had published a very stupid and scurrilous piece, by way of answer to my address (which you saw at Hillsborough) to the electors of Wilmington. This publication had the signature of William Tatham who had left the place on his way to Europe.[2] I expostulated with Howard, not without bitterness, and sent him an apology, requiring him to insert either that or my letter. After promising upon his honor, to insert the apology as his own, he altered his mind, wrote to me, and wanted some alteration in it, respecting Mr. Jones—I wrote him again, desiring him to return the apology if he did not choose to adopt it, when he informed me, that he should publish in his next paper not only the apology but our correspondence, and they appeared accordingly, but the former, as what I dictated, not as his own. I have with a few others, withdrawn my subscription, and intend to procure another printer, as this man is entirely under the influence of Walker and two other fools and scoundrels, and Bowan his partner, and the man whom we engaged, is God knows where, having purchased some figures in wax-work, with which is going about as an exhibiter of shows[3]

We have in this quarter a very indifferent representation in every respect. Yet I think we shall have another convention called. The people in general cannot bear the idea of being out of the union—Mr. Jones's opponents declined the poll, but a new one started up without effect. He had a majority of 50 votes Mr. Grove assures me that Steele is returned for Salisbury, and that Rutherfurd and Locke are left out, though I do not know who are chosen for Rowan county.[4] Your friends here are well, but the country as well as the town has been and still is sickly. my friends join me in best respects to you and all friends at Edenton

very sincerely Yours

A Maclaine

	Senator			
New Hanr.	Tim. Bloodworth	J P. Williams	T. Devane	
Brunswk.	Lewis Du Pré	Jas. Leonard[5]	J Cains	
Bladen	Thos. Brown	S. Cain	John Brown	
Robeson[6]	John Willis			all good men
Cumberland	A. McCalister	W B. Grove	John Mackay	
Duplin[7]	James Kenan	Dickson		
Sampson	Hardy Holmes	D Dodd[8]	Lewis Holmes	
Onslow[9]		R W Snead		

RC, Iredell Papers, Duke. Printed, McRee, 2:239-240. Addressed "James Iredell esquire Edenton." Endorsed "Wilmington 13th. Sept. 1788 A. Maclaine. Ansd."

---

[1]See "To the People of the State of North Carolina," August 18, 1788, in this volume.

[2]Caleb D. Howard (fl. 1788-1794) and Daniel Bowen began publishing the *Wilmington Centinel, and General Advertiser* in March 1788, but the partnership was short-lived. By August 1789, Howard had moved to Fayetteville and, with John Sibley, was publishing the *Fayetteville Gazette*. *DNCB*, s.v. "Howard, Caleb D."

Maclaine's address was an endorsement of Edward Jones (1762-1841) to become Wilmington's representative in the General Assembly. Jones was born in Ireland, came to Philadelphia in 1783, and then moved to Wilmington in 1786. He became Maclaine's protégé and was admitted to the bar in 1788. Maclaine's endorsement first appeared in the *Wilmington Centinel, and General Advertiser* on July 16 and ran again a week later. The response was published in two parts, August 6 and 13, and was signed by William Tatham, a leading citizen of the recently established town of Lumberton in Robeson County. The author, supposedly Tatham, emphasized Jones's status as a relative newcomer and suggested that he was a potential tool for the British to use to introduce "their power into our civil system under the flimsy mask of two years purification." Jones defended himself in the August 13 issue of the newspaper. He claimed that Tatham did not write the piece, though he did not name the true author. Jones was elected and represented Wilmington in the house until 1792. He then became state solicitor general and served in that capacity until 1827. *Wilmington Centinel, and General Advertiser*, July 16, 23, August 6, 13, 1788; *DNCB*, s.v. "Jones, Edward"; Alice Barnwell Keith, ed., *The John Gray Blount Papers*, vol. 1, *1764-1789* (Raleigh: State Department of Archives and History, 1952), 379n; Cheney, *North Carolina Government*, 182, 222, 223, 225, 227.

[3]Maclaine's endorsement of Jones included criticism of John "Jack" Walker, previously identified. "I look upon him altogether as improper for a member of the assembly, as a collector of public money, or a clerk of court," Maclaine wrote. A large, uncouth man, but also one of wealth and influence, Walker was almost

legendary for his feats of physical strength. One story involves Walker subduing a wild bull rampaging through the streets of Wilmington. A variation of this anecdote has Walker leaping upon the bull's back and riding him. Maclaine, on the other hand, was known for his erudition and eloquence. Their enmity may have stemmed from the Loyalist disputes following the Revolution. Walker despised the Loyalists and their advocates. Maclaine represented them in court. *Wilmington Centinel, and General Advertiser*, July 23, 1788; Waddell, *New Hanover County*, 69-70; Howell, *Book of Wilmington*, 173. See also Archibald Maclaine to JI, August 29, 1787, in this volume.

Bowen and his waxworks had returned to Wilmington by late October 1788. An advertisement for the exhibition appeared in the local newspaper on October 26. The wax figures, which included George Washington, the king and queen of England, and Herod's wife, were exhibited at Major Kingsbury's home, "opposite the market," every evening but Sunday from six o'clock until nine. Tickets, at 10s for adults and 5s for children, were sold at the print shop. *Wilmington Centinel, and General Advertiser*, October 26, December 10, 1788; Archibald Maclaine to JI, October 27, 1788, in this volume.

[4]Willie Jones was elected to represent Halifax County in the state senate. John Steele was chosen as Salisbury's representative in the house. William Barry Grove was elected to the house of commons for Cumberland County. In Rowan County, Basil Gaither was elected to the senate and David Caldwell and Thomas Carson to the house. Cheney, *North Carolina Government*, 220-223.

[5]Leonard's given name was Jacob rather than James.

[6]Elias Barnes and Neill Brown were elected to the house of commons from Robeson County. Cheney, *North Carolina Government*, 221.

[7]Robert Dickson (d. 1790) and Charles Ward represented Duplin County in the house of commons. Cheney, *North Carolina Government*, 221.

[8]William King rather than David Dodd was elected to the house from Robeson County. Cheney, *North Carolina Government*, 221.

[9]Thomas Johnston was elected senator for Onslow County. R. W. Snead was not elected to the General Assembly. Reuben Grant and Daniel Yates were elected to the house of commons from Onslow County. Cheney, *North Carolina Government*, 220-221.

From John Swann

New York, Sept. 21st, '88.

Dear Sir:

I received your favor of the 27th of August, inclosing a copy of an Address to the good people of North Carolina.[1] You will now give me leave to thank you for that inclosure. I do hope and flatter myself that there is too much good sense, candor, and personal independence among the majority of that State, not to do justice to the merit of that publication. I mean that they will, at least, allow it a cool, liberal, and dispassionate reading; a claim which the author has an undoubted right to expect.

North Carolina, you know, sir, has been generally considered to depend, in some measure, on her neighbors for her politics; at least it is affirmed that she discovers on all occasions an attentive disposition: an opinion which has been so unexpectedly contravened by her late conduct, that you will find no difficulty in figuring to yourself the extreme astonishment manifested on all hands at the news of her rejecting the Constitution. The thorough investigation which that subject has undergone, the late period at which it was taken up by our State, added to the example of so many respectable States, had induced a kind of repose in the public mind with regard to the event of her deliberations, from which the transition was not very difficult to censure and crimination. Hence the reason, probably, that all were so ready to impute her conduct to the very virtuous motive of preserving paper money and tender laws; indeed, some, taking a retrospective view of her conduct since the Revolution, and finding her delinquent in complying with requisitions, &c., have not hesitated to pronounce her of little importance to the Union.[2] However, this, like all other violent gusts, was too impetuous to last long; and I now have the pleasure to assure you that her conduct is considered in a much less censorious light. The resolutions passed by the Convention were too evincive of a federal disposition at least, not to have had considerable influence in changing the public opinion.

Congress have at length finished the preparations necessary to give the new Government effect, after a great deal of debate, and perhaps some warmth, occasioned by the indecision, or rather decision of the members, about a place the most proper for the first meeting, &c.[3] This question, sir, had the power to collect all the delegations from the different parts of the Union, so that there has not been a fuller Congress since the declaration of independence. However, this business being settled, Congress, I fear, like all other bodies about to expire, will scarcely have a witness of its dissolution, &c., &c.

Jno. Swann.

Printed, McRee, 2:240-241.

---

[1]See "To the People of the State of North Carolina," August 18, 1788, in this volume.

[2]Leaders in Rhode Island, the only state other than North Carolina that had not voted for ratification by this time, feared that the new central government would eliminate the paper money issued by individual states and thus aid creditors. The "requisitions" refer to the Continental Congress's call to the states in 1782 and 1783 to help pay military expenses. Morris, *Forging of the Union*, 257; Paul H. Smith and Ronald M. Gephart, eds., *Letters of Delegates to Congress, 1774-1789*, vol. 25

(Washington: Library of Congress, 1998), 384. See also Richard D. Spaight to JI, July 3, 1787, n. 5, and Hugh Williamson to JI, July 7, 1788, in this volume.

[3]See JI to [*unknown*], September 10, 1788, n. 2, in this volume.

From Hugh Williamson

New York 22nd Septr. 1788

Dear Sir

Before this Time you must have heard that the new Govt. is to originate on March next before which Time Virginia could not have made all her Elections, with Time for the Members, say from Kentucke, to attend. The new Congress is to meet in New York a Place very eccentric. Eastern Members will be able to attend with too much Ease, this will give them a legislative Advantage, an improper one. Had N Car. been in the Union her five Members in the House of Represent. would have readily turned the Scale in favour of a more Southerly Position. My Patience and Temper have been tryed by this Question and the more so perhaps because for Some Time past I have not considered it proper to vote on the Subject. I think that all Attempts to induce our Assembly to call another Convention immediately will be to little Purpose, for whatever we may publicly say I do privately think that a Want of honesty is at the Bottom with many of our Oppositionists If they seriously have alterations at Heart I think they had best adopt in order the sooner to secure them by legal compulsion. Be pleased to calculate N Hampshire, Massachusets N York Virga. N Car & S Car. call for Amendments & a Strong Body in Maryland and Pensylvania. The Representatives from the Six States requiring Amendments will be 37 while those from the other Seven States are only 28. To say nothing of the Help the amending Corps may get from Pensylvana, and from Maryland. In this Case they may compell Amendments by refusing to vote Supplies except for a very limited Time until the Amendments are made. That our State might not be universally abused abroad I have written the best Apologie I could make for it which you will See in the N York daily Advertiser for 17th. Inst. a Copy of which I have inclosed to Mr. Collins.[1]

Be assured that I am with the utmost Regard

Dr. Sir Your most obedt. Servt.

Hu Williamson

RC, Iredell Papers, Duke. Printed, McRee, 2:241-242. Addressed "James Iredell Esqr. Edenton." Endorsed "New York 22d. Sept. 1788 Hugh Williamson. Ansd."

[1]Williamson's article, written September 16, 1788, and signed "A Republican," appeared in the September 17 issue of the New York *Daily Advertiser.* In it he explained that North Carolina's reluctance to ratify the Constitution was attributable to nothing more than a desire to have certain amendments added. Williamson dismissed accusations that the state's Antifederalists wanted to protect paper money. He also reminded those who questioned North Carolina's contributions to the nation of the state's role in the war effort and its assumption of federal debts to state citizens. For the text of Williamson's "Apologie," see Smith and Gephart, *Letters,* 25:384-386.

From W. Falkener[1]

Warrenton 15th. Octor. 1788.—

Sr,

To a Man of less Philanthropy than yourself it might be necessary to make a formal Introduction to the present Letter, but when I contemplate the Benevolence of your Mind exemplified on every Occasion I have been witness to, I conjecture you will when acquainted with the Cause of this Address readily comply with my Request, and deem the Subject a sufficient Apology for my venturing to trouble you.—It will not I suppose be new to you that a Report has been circulating in Edenton (under the most specious Appearance of Truth) that may, if uncontradicted, be productive of very serious Consequences, as it is evidently calculated to injure me in the Esteem of the People of this Country, and render me an Object of general <Dest> Detestation.

That there are Characters in the united States similar to the One so insidiously manufactured for me, may be known to the Author, nor would it be a Matter of Information to the World I suppose, to say that all Empires & Kingdoms have thought it necessary to have such in their Employ, but I fancy you will agree with me, that none, even from the meanest Electorate of Germany ever moved in So humble a Situation as myself—In Fine, I am sure your Good Sense and general Knowledge of the World will make it unnecessary for me to offer to you any Arguments to obviate the Report; but as all Persons cannot see the Probability or Improbability of Stories invented for private Gratification, so I have thought proper to accompany this with a Letter from a great political and literary Character of England;*[2] by which you will be able to judge of my Correspondence as also of my sincere Attachments to the United States of America—I Shall only add on this Subject (besides shortly stating the Story propagated against me) that after having been One of the First at great Risque and personal Hazard, to set on Foot and carry into Effect a Subscription for the Relief of the American Prisoners confined in the different Goals of England during the last unnatural (though I thank God glorious for the Interests of America) War and becoming a Citizen in Consequence of my Affection to this Country, I Should think myself deserving of the severest Reprobation could I even think of acting with so much Duplicity.

I suggested (the same Hour I received the Information) to our mutual Friend Mr. Ben. Hawkins my Intention of writing to you on this Subject, shewing him at the same Time the enclosed Letter and reading a Copy of the One <he> /it/ answer'd. He instantly concur'd with me as to the Propriety of doing So, adding some Observations which I forbear to repeat lest you should think me adulatory, but which determined my Conduct—I intreat therefore such a Portion of your Service as your Desire to rescue an injured Character from further Mischief may direct: that you will go to the Gentleman hereafter described who lives in Edenton, and making use of the enclosed Evidence in such Way as you think most proper, shew him the Impossibility of his Information being true. Pray Sir believe that I feel myself sensibly affected for the Liberty I have taken by intruding on the Time of One with whom I have So little Acquaintance; <and> that I have the most confident Reliance that your Feelings will prompt your Exertions and obtain me ample Justice, by causing an immediate Contradiction of a Report in which you must be convinced there cannot be the least Semblance of Truth. Please to return by the first Conveyance that conveniently offers the Letter and News-Paper here enclosed, the latter of which I have sent you that you may see the Manner in which I declined the only Office public or private I ever held.[3] It is at the Bottom of the first Column. Mr. B Hawkins desir'd me to present his respectful Compts.—

I am with great Regard Yr. obedient & very hble Servt.

W. Falkener

P.S. As I shall be at FayetteVille the first Day of the Meeting of the General Assembly and continue there throughout the Sitting, pray favor me with your Reply and inclose the News-Paper & Letter by first Opportunity to that Place.

P.S. I have transcribed Dr. Jebbs' Letter as many of his Words to a Person unused to his Hand-Writing appear unintelligible—

Copy of the Story propagated at Edenton concerning Wm. Falkener

"That Mr. Robt. Lemon (or Leeming) a Merchant in Edenton has a Letter or Letters from England, or Some other Place describing my Character and Person; together with an Account of the an/n/ual Stipend I receive from the Court of Great Britain for acting as a Spy in this Country and communicating to them Information"—Wm. Falkener.[4]

Note. I remember to have Seen some time ago in a British News-Paper an Account of a W. Falkner being promoted to Some <Office> Appointment (I think in the Post-Office) probably this Circumstance may have given Rise to this incautious Report. I mention this Sir for your Information.—

RC, Johnson Collection, NCSA. Printed, McRee, 2:242-243. Addressed "James Iredell Esqr." Endorsed "Warrenton 15th. Oct. 1788. W. Falkener Ansd."[5]

---

[1]William Falkener owned six town lots in Warrenton in 1788. As told in this letter, rumors were circulating that he was a British spy, this at a time when British agents were believed to be working as provocateurs among Native Americans to the west. These stories about Falkener apparently did not permanently damage his reputation for he was named as a justice on the Warren County Court of Pleas and Quarter Sessions in 1794 and as a county commissioner in 1796. David B. Gammon, *Tax Lists, Warren County, North Carolina, 1779-1790*, vol. 1 (Raleigh: David B. Gammon, 1994), 85; McRee, *Life and Correspondence*, 2:243; Ginger L. Christmas-Beattie, *Warren County, North Carolina, Court of Pleas and Quarter Sessions*, vol. 3, *1793-1796* (Forest Grove, Ore.: Ancestral Tracks, 2000), 71, 92, 121.

[2]The letter was from John Jebb (1736-1786), who was a lecturer at Cambridge, a physician, a fellow of the Royal Society, and a prolific writer. Falkener's own note in the margin of this letter states: "*Dr. John Jebb of Parliament Street Westminster. A steady and constant Assertor of the Rights of Mankind, the firm Opposer of ministerial Tyranny and abitrary Power; an avowed & warm Advocate for the American Cause during the late Controversy; and a cheerful Subscriber towards the Maintenance of their Officers & Men whilst in Confinement. To whose Memory greater Attention was paid <for> by the Citizens of London & Westminster than upon any other similar Occasion except at the Interment of the late illustrious Earl of Chatham." *DNB*, s.v. "Jebb, John, M.D." See also McRee, *Life and Correspondence*, 2:242n.

[3]Enclosures not found.

[4]A John Leming lived in Edenton in 1790, but no other information has been found. *Heads of Families, 1790 Census*, 19.

[5]McRee reports that JI "thought the charge against him not only false but preposterous." McRee, *Life and Correspondence*, 2:243.

To Hannah Iredell

Halifax Oct. 18th. 1788

My dear Hannah,

A waggon is just going by, by which I have a moment to tell you I arrived here perfectly well yesterday. All our Friends above are pretty well.

I shall be most anxious to hear from you. Give my tenderest love to Annie, & remember me affectionately to the rest of the Family. I expect another opportunity to write to you soon. Adieu! my dear Hannah. God grant your health may continue to recruit, & believe me

Most affectionately yours

Ja. Iredell

RC, Johnson Collection, NCSA. Addressed "Mrs. Iredell Edenton."

From Archibald Maclaine

Wilmington 27h. Octr 1788

Dear Sir

I have had both your favors of the 8h. & 15th. and sympathize with you in the distress occasioned by the sickness of your family. I believe we have been nearly in the same situation in this town, and for a considerable distance up the rivers; though I find that Newbern & Fayetteville have been generally healthy. I am not yet well (having had a slight relapse) and except two superannuated servants, who are /in/capable of any-thing active, every person in my family has been ill at times; so that I have sometimes found it difficult to procure a little water when it was wanted— Mr. Hooper's children and servants have [*torn*] their turn, and my brother is now just recovered <by> of an indispos[*ition*] occasioned I believe by some very wet weather in the co[*torn*]k of his county. I had seen an account of Mr. Bl[*torn*]'s [*death in t*]he paper, and though I did not know him, felt very sens[*torn*] his family. Independent of his sudden death, his loss to the[*m m*]ust be great.[1]

It would be in vain to attempt pet[*itions*] in this and the neighbouring counties, unless persons of some degr[*ee of*] popularity would undertake to forward the business—/In most of them,/ There are none that will stir afoot, and I have no communication with the press. Bowen, indeed, is at last returned, after an absence of several months, and appears very unhappy at the disputes with his partner, who has been dangerously ill, as well their journey-man. He has been told by myself and my friends, (who not only pratronized but <was> presented him with a liberal donation to defray the expense of removing here) that we would not have any-thing to say to a press conducted by Mr. Howard without an explicit and satisfactory apology for his conduct. Bowen agrees that he shall either do this, or relinquish the business; but nothing is yet done.[2]

There has been a county meeting of Onslow, and a petition agreed on.[3] On saturday evening, we had one for this town.[4] It had been proposed for the preceding Tuesday, when the meeting was too small. At that time however Read & Huske attended, and endeavored to throw cold water on the business—The former with much cunning, the latter with bare- faced impudence—He went so far as to reprobate meetings of that kind, for this memorable reason—that something might be [*prop*]osed, which if adopted, would disgrace the town. When it was s[*hown*] that his argument proved too much, and would operate as [*forcibly ag*]ainst all assemblies of what ever kind, he still pertinac[*iously*] maintained his proposition, until I told him it was stupid [*non-s*]ense, and an insult to the understanding of every man to [*whom*] it was addressed—On saturday Read absented himself a[*ltoge*]ther, & Huske after informing the Chairman, with as much importance as he could assume, that he did not think any instructions were necessary, sneaked off, without hearing any thing that might be <said> offered

An instruction to our member to promote the recommendation of the convention for sinking the paper-money, and the passing of a law for ascertaining the value of contracts, passed unanimously.[5] That for calling a new convention, was carried against one dissenting voice. This will be further supported by the signatures of most of those who were absent[6]

As you did not in your letter of the 8th. say any thing of a publication, I thought myself indebted to the printer for half a dozen copies. Pray who is the author of this curious performance? Is he in earnest in his proposed seperation? or is it held out only as a scare-crow? I take it to be a young lawyer in your town, with a dash of the Edenton member. I understand Mr. Jones has published an answer, but I have not seen it[7]

Dear Sir Yours very sincerely

A Maclaine

The sheriff, as is usual with him, neglected to [*torn*] the execution. Monk & wife vs. the Exr. of Wilkinson till it was too late [*torn*]ll. He has enclosed it to Mr. Moore, in order to prevent an amerceme[*nt*] but he tells me that it is not returnable to any day or month[8]—I wish the sale to be delayed at any rate until after our court, as some other legatees will then apply, and I wish to have the matter reheard, merely for my own satisfaction; for as to young Wilkinson, he is such a fool & Scoundrel, I care nothing about him. I am also in doubt whether there is personal property to pay the debts & legacies upon the principal of Monks decree, tho' I believe I admitted assets, but the loan office certificates are of little value

RC, Iredell Papers, Duke. Printed, McRee, 2:243–244. Addressed "James Iredell esquire Edenton."

[1]The late "Mr. Bl" may be either Francis Black of Edenton or Benjamin Blount, a planter of Tyrrell County. Will of Francis Black, 1788, Chowan County Wills, State Archives; Will of Benjamin Blount, 1788, Tyrrell County Wills, State Archives.

[2]See Archibald Maclaine to JI, September 13, 1788, in this volume.

[3]The petition from Onslow County, calling for a new ratification convention, had reached the General Assembly by November 11, 1788. Clark, *State Records*, 21:31.

[4]The meeting in Wilmington was held on Saturday, October 25, 1788.

[5]An amendment proposed at the 1788 state ratification convention would have granted states the exclusive right to redeem existing paper money and liquidate public securities. Trenholme, *Ratification*, 185. For information on the contract law, see Samuel Johnston to JI, November 20, 1788, in this volume.

[6]For more information on the General Assembly's authorization of a second ratification convention, see Samuel Johnston to JI, November 14, 1788, n. 2, and November 20, 1788, n. 1, in this volume.

[7]Maclaine is probably referring to a pamphlet published in August and signed "A Citizen and a Soldier." No copy has been found, but a section of it was reprinted in the September 22, 1788, issue of the *State Gazette of North Carolina*. The essayist attacked Willie Jones without mentioning the Antifederalist leader by name. He accused Jones and his followers of "blow[*ing*] up an idle Fandango about Bills of Rights and Amendments." Then the writer, exasperated at the convention's failure to ratify, posed the question, "Was this a time to smoak a pipe, & suck the paw like a surly Bear, when your house was on fire?" Willie Jones offered his response in the October 20 issue of the *State Gazette*. Trenholme, *Ratification*, 201-202.

[8]An amercement is a fine or other penalty imposed at the discretion of the court. Garner, *Black's Law Dictionary*, 7th ed., 81.

For more information on this case, see Archibald Maclaine to JI, October 24, 1785, and October 10, 1787, in this volume.

From Samuel Johnston

Fayette [*Ville*] 8th. Novembr. 1788

Dear Sir

The Assembly met here the f[*irs*]t day and chose their Speakers,[1] since that I cannot hear that any material Question has been agitated in either House, at first a great number of our Friends were very warm for a New Convention and were very sanguine in their Expectations within these few days. they begin to have apprehensions that they are at present too weak especially in the Senate many of the Members who are in favor of that measure being absent.[2] I understand that there will be a strong opposition to the appointment of Commissioners to fix the Seat of Government.[3] The Western Affairs and disputes with the Indians, seem more particularly to occupy the Attention of the Members at present, an Indian War seems almost inevitable and never were a people worse prepared than we are for a thing <of thing> of that kind while the Indians are supplied and supported with every thing necessary for their purpose by the British on [*one*] hand and the Spania[*rds o*]n the other, at the same ti[*me*] that there appears to a general Confederacy of all the Indian [*N*]ations between the River St. Lawrence and Mexico, the Western inhabitants appear very much alarmed and some of the Members from Cumberland have very strongly expressed their wishes to me, to be under the protectection of Congress and that the Act repealing the Law ceding that Country to Congress might be repealed. I encouraged them with hopes that it might possibly be brought about, but dont know whether the Assembly will take it up[4]—

I keep my health very well so does Billy Dawson and indeed I have heard of no one being sick in this place—I shall be very happy to hear from you, pray present my best respects to our Friends Mr. Moore, Mr. Hooper and Mr. Mc.Laine, and communicate this Letter to them if you think any thing in it interesting. I am with the most perfect Affection and esteem,

Dr. Sir, Yours,

Sam Johnston

RC, Johnson Collection, NCSA. Printed, McRee, 2:244-245. Addressed "James Iredell Esquire at New Bern."

---

[1]The General Assembly convened in Fayetteville on November 3, 1788, and elected as Speakers Alexander Martin in the senate and John Sitgreaves in the house. Cheney, *North Carolina Government*, 220-221.

[2]Fifteen senators were absent on the first day. Clark, *State Records*, 20:475-476.

[3]The ratification convention had endorsed JI's recommendation, Isaac Hunter's home in Wake County, as the point from which to select, within a ten-mile radius, the site of the state capital. There had been other suggestions, however. Fayetteville, in particular, had strong support. Because of this division, the General Assembly could not reach a decision and postponed further action until the next session. Clark, *State Records*, 21:73-74; 22:26, 28-29, 33, 34-35. See Archibald Maclaine to JI, January 15, 1788, n. 1, in this volume.

[4]Residents of the western part of the state petitioned the General Assembly to stop the increasing number of violent clashes between Native Americans and settlers. Petitioners from Greene County, south of the French Broad River, told legislators that "many of our people [*have been*] Barbarously Massacred." Another petition from the same area declared, "We are obliged to Raise arms in our defense or otherwise submit to the Bloody Hatchet." Governor Johnston, however, understood that the responsibility for the violence did not rest solely with the Indians. In a message to the assembly, he referred to the "outrages and hostilities

which have been mutually committed." To reduce the violence, Johnston prohibited inhabitants of Washington County (now in Tennessee) from entering Indian Territory without permission from the district commanding officer. In 1789, the General Assembly ceded the western territory to Congress, with the actual transfer of the land occurring the following year. Papers of the Committee on Indian Affairs, November-December 1788, General Assembly Session Records, State Archives; Clark, *State Records*, 21:10; 25:4-6.

From Samuel Johnston

Fayette Ville 14th. Novr. 1788

My dear Sir

I had the pleasure of receiving your Letter by Mr. Hodge and very heartily Congratulate you on the Birth of your Son.[1] no event could have given me more satisfaction. I hope to hear that Mrs. Iredell and the young Gentleman continue well

I have had my health very well since I came to this place and am very comfortably lodged indeed the people here are generally well and very well provided for in every respect. The Question with respect to a New convention is to be taken up in the House of Commons to morrow.[2] the event in my Opinion doubtfull. The Assembly seem very much at a loss what measures to pursue respecting the Indians there is a strong party for an Indian War others wish if possible to avoid it[3]

There is a great variety of Bills talked of and some have been already before the House.[4] I fear it will be a long Session[5]

Be pleased to present my best respects to Mr. Moore, Mr. Hooper and Mr. Mc.Laine, and to their Honors the Judges. I received Judge Ashe's Letter respecting Colo. Lutterloh.[6] as there is a post from Wilmington I shall hope to hear from you

Inclosed are the Titles of some of the Bills reported by the Grand Committee beside a number of others from private hands[7]

Be pleased to present my most affectionate Respects to Mrs. Iredell and pray omit no opportunity of letting me hear how she and the Children have their health

I am my dear Sir, with the most sincere affection and esteem

Your most obedient Servant

Sam Johnston

RC, Samuel Johnston Papers, NCSA. Addressed "James Iredell Esquire."

[1]James Iredell Jr. (d. 1853) was born in Edenton on November 2, 1788. He became a member of the General Assembly and the U.S. Senate, and served briefly as governor. *DNCB*, s.v. "Iredell, James, Jr."

[2]Governor Johnston asked the General Assembly to call a second ratification convention. The senate invited the house to meet in a joint session to consider the issue. The house refused to meet with the senate, and on November 15 passed a resolution, 55 to 47, stating that to call a convention at that time was not "expedient." Trenholme, *Ratification*, 203-204; Clark, *State Records*, 21:51-52.

[3]See Samuel Johnston to JI, November 8, 1788, n. 4, in this volume.

[4]For information on bills before the house, see Clark, *State Records*, 21:19-25, 29-30, 32-33, 35-50.

[5]Contrary to Johnston's prediction, the session was short. It began on November 3 and ended on December 6. Cheney, *North Carolina Government*, 220.

[6]Henry Emanuel Lutterloh (b. 1743 in Germany) of Fayetteville was a colonel in the Continental Army. In 1790, the General Assembly authorized Lutterloh to conduct a lottery to raise money to bring skilled foreigners into the state. Clark, *State Records*, 20:546; 21:72, 1000; *DAR Patriot Index, Centennial Edition*, vol. 2 (Washington, D.C.: National Society of the Daughters of the American Revolution, 1994), 1862; Oates, *Story of Fayetteville*, 187, 760.

[7]Enclosures not found.

From Charles Johnson

Fayetteville, 14th Nov., 1788.

Dear Sir:

Expecting this will find you at Newbern, I cannot deny myself the pleasure of writing you. And in the first place permit me to congratulate you on the birth of your son, and to assure you that I participate the pleasure you so feelingly describe your family to have felt on that joyful event. You will perceive, by what I have said, that the Governor was kind enough to show me your letter. In it I recognize the genuine, parental affection, which every person of sensibility must feel on a similar occasion. Long, very long, may you continue to enjoy the blessings of domestic felicity.

I shall now recur to the present scene, though nothing of any consequence has yet occurred. On the day appointed a House was formed. We have since chosen our officers of State, a list of whom is inclosed.[1] An attempt has been made to bring on the business of a new Convention. <u>It was introduced in our House by General Caswell</u>, as we counted upon carrying the resolution there, and expected that the question being carried in the Senate would add greater weight to it in the Commons, where we were most dubious of our strength. But Wilie Jones, with his usual adroitness in the finesse of the House, set forth the necessity of a conference, and moved the previous question, which he carried by a very great majority indeed—at least four to one—so few were there that could understand the nature, meaning and extent of the previous question. To evince clearly how much that party excels ours in all the mysteries of political manoeuvre, I need only mention that the very measure proposed by Wilie Jones (that of a conference of both Houses) after he had defeated the resolution introduced by Gen. Caswell, was rejected by the Antifederal party, with Parsons at their head. You will perceive that this afforded no great cause for triumph, though they exult extremely; nor do I think it by any means a fair trial of strength. The business will again be brought on, and I hope with more success—at least we must endeavor to have fairer play. A great number of petitions have been presented, many from counties formerly anti-constitutional.[2] Another circumstance will operate for a new convention; many want to reconsider the seat of government—even this must be risked.[3] Many bills of a public nature are introduced, but their fate being uncertain, I shall not trouble you with their titles.[4] I declined being nominated to my former honorable office, lest another Assembly may be called the present year, and Chowan deprived of a representation.[5] All your friends here are well. We live in the same house, and have a great plenty of venison, turkeys, and every thing else. The town of Fayette has converted your old friend C. into a Fayette-villian; it operates like the charms of Circe.[6]

I am, dear sir, yours sincerely,

Chas. Johnson.

Printed, McRee, 2:600-601.

---

[1]The enclosed list has not been found. The Council of State members elected on November 11, 1788, were John Skinner, James Iredell, John Kinchen, James Armstrong, Josiah Collins, Whitmell Hill, and Dempsey Conner. In a letter written from Skewawky, dated November 19, 1788, JI told Hannah: "Your brother has been re-elected Governor; and the Council are W. Hill, John Skinner, Jo. Collins, D. Connor, Armstrong of Pitt, and myself. Poor Martin, I dare say, will be much mortified. He should be very welcome to my place if I could give it to him, &c." Martin is probably Alexander Martin. Clark, *State Records*, 20:500; Cheney, *North Carolina Government*, 164; McRee, *Life and Correspondence*, 2:246.

[2]The town of Halifax and the following counties submitted petitions to the General Assembly calling for a second convention: Camden, Hertford, Randolph, Johnston, Tyrrell, Hyde, Richmond, Carteret, Dobbs, Chowan, Lincoln, Onslow, Rowan, Surry, Mecklenburg, Martin, Chatham, Currituck, Edgecombe, Sampson, Richmond, and Hertford. Clark, *State Records*, 20:494; 21:31-33, 42, 48, 51.

[3]See Samuel Johnston to JI, November 8, 1788, n. 3, in this volume.

[4]For information on bills before the house, see Clark, *State Records*, 21:19-25, 29-30, 32-33, 35-50.

[5]Charles Johnson was at this time a state senator representing Chowan County. In 1787, he had been a member of the Council of State. Cheney, *North Carolina Government*, 165, 220.

[6]In the *Odyssey,* Circe was a sorceress who transformed Odysseus's men into swine. The term applies to something that lures one into danger. Howatson, *Classical Literature*, 135; Alexander Eliot, *Myths* (New York: McGraw-Hill, 1976), 249.

From Archibald Maclaine

Wilmington 17 November 1788

Dear Sir

Had I been well, I purposed setting off this day for Newbern; but I have been confined a long time with a complication of complaints, principally proceeding from want of exercise after the removal of the intermittant, with which I was first attacked—It is only within two days that I have been able to take up a pen; for my complaint still continues, and dreadfully affects my head. It is an obstructed perspiration /(or rather this is the effect of it)/ to so great a degree, that notwithstanding repeated remedies, I have not been sensible of any moisture on my skin for a fortnight.

In my last, which was written with no little confusion of ideas I mistook what you mentioned about <u>a certain publication</u>, as referring to Aetticus [*torn*] said at this folly, that had I not be[*torn*] I should have wrote you the following post[1]

I have sent my papers, [*torn*] to Mr. Hooper upon the subject, which is intended for you[*torn*] him. I know I need not solicit your assistance in [*torn*] [*c*]an do for me. Much of my business for Newber[*n*] [*torn*] [*C*]ourts will be left undone, and I must now content myself if I am well enough to attend the latter.

Mr. Hogg's son had a letter from his father last night, mentioning that Mr. Johnston is re-elected—There is nothing said of any competitor, though Martin had been much talked of.[2] Mr. Hogg also mentions, first that there is no prospect of a convention, and finally that there will not be one. He adds, that by private information from Virginia, of which it is expected will be authenticated, that the Assembly of that State, have been prevailed upon by Mr. Henry, to refuse doing any thing towards the organization of the new government.[3] Though a man of sense, Mr. Hogg is, I think, a very bad politician, and so credulous that he is /as/ ready to swallow what he fears as what he hopes. I have had no letter from Jones by the boat which brought Mr. Hogg's (perhaps he did not know of it) but there was, I am told by Mr. G Hooper, a sensible man, a passenger, who knows nothing of Mr. Hogg's news, but the election of a governor, and yet seems well acquainted with what is doing, as well as what is said, at Fayetteville. I should have told you that in Jones's last letter of the 9th. he says that there had, on the preceding evening, been a secret meeting of federalists, in consequence of previous notice, when it appeared that they thought they had a majority, though a small one.[4]

I am Dear Sir Faithfully yours

A Maclaine

I have had a letter from Mr. Hay, dated from Belfast the 6h. of Augt. wherein he mentions "the many kind inquiries after Mr. Iredell, although when here but a boy of fourteen, is remembered with pleasure." He was in some hopes of leaving Ireland the 1st. of September, but as he mentions [*torn*] doubtfully, we may allow him two or three weeks longer

Since I w[*rote the above, I*] have had a letter from Mr. Jones of the 13th. w[*herein he mentions*] his doubts of a convention, which was to be trie[*d the next day.*] That there would not be more than four or f[*ive either way*] Some are for again ceding the back country [*and that others,*] /who/ are against it, <who> wish to send troops to suport th[*e inhabitants aga*]inst the Indians.[5] Amazing great quantities [*of*] tobacco, which is now at 40/.

Mr. Jones makes no mention of Mr. Hogg's news from Virginia I lose my ideas as fast as they rise, and my memory is good for nothing—I should have told you, that a scale of depreciation is much talked of, and that Willie Jones has promised to bring it forward, and it is said that T. Person concurs in this, and even says, that /he/ intends the paper-money not to be any longer a tender, but with this condition, that £70,000 more be emitted.[6] I have as small an opinion of one of these gentlemen as I have of the other; and therefore would not trust either of them. W Jones would in my opinion sacrifice any thing rather than give up the party which he has so scandalously patronized. The inflexibility of his pride will soar above every other consideration. [*&c., &c.*][7]

RC, Iredell Papers, Duke. Printed, McRee, 2:245-246. Addressed "James [*Iredell*] [*Ne*]wbern."

---

[1]See Archibald Maclaine to JI, October 27, 1788, in this volume.

[2]Samuel Johnston was reelected governor "by a Majority of votes," according to legislative records, which would imply a contest with more than one candidate. No record of other nominations has been found, however. Clark, *State Records*, 500.

[3]In a letter to Edmund Randolph, dated November 2, 1788, James Madison wrote: "The views of the greater part of the opposition to the federal Government, and particularly of its principal leader, have ever since the Convention, been

regarded by me as permanently hostile, and likely to produce every effort that might endanger or embarrass it. The defects which drew forth objections from many quarters, were evidently of little consequence in the eye of Mr. H—ry. His own arguments proved it. His enmity was levelled, as he did not scruple to insinuate agst the *whole System*; and the destruction of the whole System, I take to be still the secret wish of his heart, and the real object of his pursuit." Smith and Gephart, *Letters*, 25:452.

Patrick Henry, former governor and current member of the Virginia legislature, declared after the state's ratification convention that he would "oppose every measure tending to the organization of the Government, unless accompanied with measures for the amendment of the Constitution." Henry held immense power in the Virginia house and was able to engineer the election of Antifederalists to the U.S. Senate and the passage of a resolution supporting a second constitutional convention. Norine Dickson Campbell, *Patrick Henry: Patriot and Statesman* (New York: Devin-Adair, 1969), 370-375.

[4]See Trenholme, *Ratification*, 203.

[5]Some residents in the western part of the state had long wanted to secede from North Carolina. The state's failure to ratify the Constitution and provide adequate protection against the Indians intensified these sentiments. On November 17, Willie Jones introduced a bill ceding parts of western North Carolina to Congress. The bill was carried over to the next session and was then approved. Trenholme, *Ratification*, 213; Clark, *State Records*, 20:513; 21:106; 25:4-6.

[6]On November 17, Willie Jones introduced a bill in the senate to levy a tax for revenue to redeem "the old Paper Currency, Continental Money, and Specie and other Certificates and for sinking the State Currency." Clark, *State Records*, 20:513.

[7]The original letter is torn so that phrases are missing. The words inserted in brackets are from the version of the letter in McRee. Only the latter part of the document appears in that volume, however.

William J. Dawson to Nelly Blair

Fayette Ville November 17th. 1788

My Dear Cousin,

I am now set down to fulfill my promise and in the first place will tell you what I am sure will be the most agreeable tydings you could receive, that your Uncle with the assistance of some excellent Porter Venison & wild turkey all of which are to be found in abundance in this Town is perfectly recovered & that your humble servant notwithstanding the great scarcity of Cash will I fear be reduced to the necessity of having all his waistcoats considerably enlarged, for at certain times in the day they become very irksome & inconvenient.

Notwithstanding all which has been said against Fayette I think it by far one of the most agreeable Towns in this State I am sure it abounds more in all the good things of this World than the whole of the others put together.

We have plays performed by the most eminent Actors for "tragedy comedy &c" on an elegant Theatre. The wonders of the Magic Art are displayed in a most masterly manner by a little crooked leged fellow to the utter amazement of the gaping Yahoos, but the most wonderfull of all & indeed tis scarcely credible is that Genl. Washington George 3d. The Royal Family with 40 other great personages are at this moment stowed a way in a Tobacco flatt. Yes my Cousin in a Tobacco flatt. so great is their desire to shew their respect for the Honorable Legislature of Carolina that they have even submitted to this indignity to gratify their inclinations. Nor are the people here ungrateful they are making great preparations. Lodgings are prepared for them & they mean to receive Company the last of this Week.

I have seen all the Ladies of this place at the Races these two days but have not had the honor of passing a word with any of them, and from the sample I do not think I shall be in any danger of breaking my heart <about it> if I never should have that honor, for never in all my travel<l>s did my eyes behold such a collection of Hags. 'twas a matter of astonishment to me to see how well the horses kept the path, for I expected they would every one fly the way especially those from our quarter, the others I suppose are accustomed to such hidious sights.

I would earnestly recommed to all the belles in Edenton District who are in want of husbands to come to this place. I will insure them at a very moderate rate that they shall not remain on hand more than three weeks the chance is excellent. there are several Rich old Batchelors who have very much of a Consumptive appearance. Our Land lady is a good smart little woman enough but nothing uncommon she speaks Scotch Irish most divinely /scolds like the devil/ is 25 Years of Age has dispatched two husbands already & is ready & looking out for a third.

Remember me in the kindest manner to every body, & assure your self that a letter from You would be greatly esteemed

by Your Ladyships friend & humble Servt.

Wm. Johnston Dawson

RC, Iredell Papers, Duke. Addressed "Miss H. Blair. Edenton."

From Samuel Johnston

Fayette Ville 20th. November 1788

Dear Sir

I have had the pleasure of receiving your Letter by Mr. Humphrey's and am happy to hear that Mrs. Iredell and your Family continue well. I am very impatient to see your fine Boy.

There is no probability of a Convention till about the time of the meeting of the next Assembly in the Fall,[1] there is no <business> /Bill/ compleated except the division of Rowan County they have complimented you with naming the new County Iredell.[2] Commissioners are appointed to attend the General Convention whenever appointed by Congress.[3] The Western people are very pressing for an Indian War which is strongly opposed by the Eastern Members, who have introduced a Bill to cede all the Country west of the Mountains to Congress.[4] T. Person had Judge Spencer's Court Bill taken up, which after one or two readings was laid aside, the Bill for compelling Debtors to pay agreeable to their Contract, is lost.[5] upon the whole I fear the [*Co*]de of Laws for this State will receive very little additional honor from the Acts of this Session. Judge Spencer is spoke of as a Commissioner to attend the General Convention

People here have their health remarkably well. I am in much better health than when I left home, but have not been able to recover my flesh & Strength tho I am very well accommodated and we have an excellent Table. I am uncertain when I shall be able to leave this place, indeed were I not very anxious to be at home and my presence very necessary there, I should be altogether indifferent about the matter as in other respects I am perfectly at my ease here.

I shall hope to hear from you, be pleased to present my best respects to Mr. Moore and the other Gentlemen of the Bar—and to the Bench or such of them as you think proper. Adieu, My dear friend, and beleive me

Yours sincerely

Sam Johnston

P.S. The Bill for carrying into execution the Ordinance for Seat of Government is laid over to the next Assembly[6]

RC, Johnson Collection, NCSA. Printed, McRee, 2:246-247. Addressed James Iredell Esquire Newbern Forward[*ed by*] Sir Kinston [*torn*] Your most Obt. Servt. S. W. Arnett.[7]

---

[1]Two days after the house voted 55 to 47 against calling a second ratification convention, the senate passed a resolution in favor of a convention by a two-to-one margin. The date proposed for the convention to begin was the last Monday in October 1789. The Antifederalists, sensing momentum building for the Federalists, tried to at least delay the convention. They proposed that it be held in November to coincide with the next session of the General Assembly. They argued that since the convention delegates were also likely to be assembly members, this would reduce their expenses. The recommendation was approved, and the second convention was scheduled to begin on the third Monday in

November 1789. Trenholme, *Ratification*, 204-205; Clark, *State Records*, 20:514-516, 526-527; 21:67-68.

[2]On November 18, 1788, the senate concurred with the house on dividing Rowan County. Clark, *State Records*, 20:520; 21:47; 24:980-982.

[3]Support existed in a number of states for a second national constitutional convention to consider amendments. In anticipation of this meeting, the North Carolina General Assembly named five delegates, all of whom were Antifederalists: Thomas Person, Timothy Bloodworth, Matthew Locke, Joseph McDowell, and William Lenoir. Samuel Johnston and JI were nominated but withdrew their names. This convention was never held. Trenholme, *Ratification*, 205. See also William R. Davie to JI, November 1788, in this volume.

[4]See Archibald Maclaine to JI, November 17, 1788, n. 5, in this volume.

[5]On November 18, Thomas Person introduced two bills in the house related to the judiciary: a "Bill for amending an Act for establishing Courts of Law, and for regulating the proceedings therein," and an "Act for giving Equity Jurisdiction to the Superior Courts." These were carried over to the next session and eventually became law in 1790. A bill for the recovery of debts according to contract was presented in the senate on November 19, 1788, but evidently never become a law. Clark, *State Records*, 20:523; 21:63, 69; 25:65-67.

[6]See Samuel Johnston to JI, November 8, 1788, n. 3, in this volume.

[7]Silas White Arnett (after 1755-1806) was a partner in the printing firm of Arnett and Hodge in New Bern until 1787. He was also an attorney and a delegate to the 1789 state ratification convention. Massengill, *North Carolina Votes*, 3; *DNCB*, s.v. "Arnett, Silas W."

To Hannah Iredell

Newbern Nov. 23d. 1788

My dear Hannah,

I wrote to you a few lines in a very great hurry yesterday evening, Mr. Amis having called to let me know he was just going to leave town in the Stage, which he had not expected would go till the morning.[1] They have however, in consideration of the very warm weather, postponed going till the morning, which gives me an opportunity to write a little more. Besides the great delight I received in hearing of you and my lovely Children being so well, I was very happy in finding you had had such late accounts from Mrs. Dawson and Mr. Tredwell, about whom tho' I concealed it I really had some apprehensions, and in hearing of the arrival of George, which would be such a consolation and relief to his Mother & Sisters. It also gave me great pleasure to find your Brother John continued much better. I flatter myself all will soon be entirely well, and happy in each other. My greatest apprehension is now about your Sister, whose health really requires exercise, and I wish she could be induced to take it.

You must have received long before you get this a letter I wrote you from Mr. Mackenzie's. My health has been since I left you at times very indifferent, but I am now better than when I left home, the particular complaint I had then having left me, and my cold being quite gone. But we have had weather enough to make every body sick. Fortunately however it seems now going to change. Mr. Hooper has had one of his usual attacks, but he is now a good deal better. We are very comfortably lodged and boarded in the same house. We could not wish for better accomodations. I will endeavour to write a line to my dear Annie.[2] Give her however, as well as our fine little Son, a few kisses notwithstanding. Heaven grant I may find you all well.

I am ever, my dear Hannah, Most affectionately yours

Ja. Iredell.

RC, Johnson Collection, NCSA. Addressed "Mrs. Iredell."

---

[1]JI had written a hurried letter to Hannah on November 22, 1788. Its contents were similar to this one.

[2]The following letter from JI to Annie was enclosed with the letter to Hannah: "My dear Annie, I promised to write to you, and for that reason should do so, but I love you so very much I do it with great pleasure. Your Mamma and your Cousin Nelly were so kind as to write me that you were well, and I hope you are a very good Girl. You must be so now for your dear Brother's sake as well as your own. That fine little Boy will want you to teach him to read, and to tell him pretty stories that may improve him. If he be as good as you we shall all love him very much, but I never can love any body better than I do you. Pray give your Brother two or three sweet kisses for me, and tell him to be a good Boy, and I shall love him greatly. I am, my dearest Annie, Your most affectionate Papa Ja. Iredell." Charles E. Johnson Collection, State Archives.

From William R. Davie

[*November 1788*][1]

My dear Sir

accept of my congratulations on the birth of your son, an event naturally the most agreeable and interesting that could have happened. Mrs. Davie has brought me a stout boy, a match for 1/2 dozen Edenton lads of the same eye.

I recd. the papers by Mr. Bond—and I'm glad you had an opportunity of receiving those sheets for we have entirely been grossly used in this business. I have not heard from R—n by either of the two last posts, and begin to conclude he has given over the idea of engaging to print them.[2]—On considering this matter, which is of some importance to the Country, as well as ourselves, & as we stand pledged in some measure to the subscribers, I think it will be necessary to look about for a Printer, and I submit to you whether it would not be well to write to Williamson, who I believe stays this winter in New-York, and who could have it done there or in Philadelphia on the best terms and in the neatest manner, any of their printers would be glad of the job on the terms we offered it to Robinson

As to the matter of transmitting the copy, I suppose that might be done by some opportunity from Edenton or at any time from Norfolk by the packet, and could be returned in the same manner—Now Sir, if this plan meets your approbation, I hope you will write immediately to Williamson on the subject. I think you may assure him they would meet with a very extensive and immediate sale, especially as the question /is undecided/ and the public mind is still in great agitation—

The House of Delegates in Virginia /have passed resolutions/ to the following effect, one "that application be made to the Congress of the United States, so soon as they shall assemble under the new Constitution to call a Convention for proposing amendments according to the mode therein directed—" another, "that a writing shall be drawn up expressing the reasons which induce them to urge their application so early." A third—"That a letter be sent in answer to Govr. Clinton circular letter—and a circular letter on the same subject to the other States in the Union."[3]

R. H. Lee and Grayson are chosen for their Senators, both Anties.[4] This shews that this denomination of politicians prevails at present at least in the Assembly—Madison lost the election by 5 votes only[5]—

It appears to me that the States should immediately concur in calling another Convention, it would satisfy the Honest part of the opposition—and stop the mouths of the rest. recommend me to my friend Alfred—and believe me with the most sincere regard

yours &

William R. Davie

P.S. write me by the bearer if you can.

RC, Iredell Papers, Duke. Addressed "James Iredell, Esquire at Newbern Superior Court."

---

[1]The original letter is undated, but the contents suggest that it was written in November 1788.

[2]Davie and JI planned to publish the debates from the 1788 state ratification convention. A stenographer named Robinson recorded the debates at the convention, and a Mr. Lorimer of Edenton was employed to make fair copies for

the printer. A thousand copies were printed in June 1789 by Hodge and Wills of Edenton. An advertisement for the sale of the publication, at ten shillings a copy, appeared in the June 18, 1789, issue of the *State Gazette of North-Carolina*, which was also published by Hodge and Wills. Robinson, *William R. Davie*, 208; McRee, *Life and Correspondence*, 2:235n.

[3]George Clinton (1739-1812), an attorney and former brigadier general, served as governor of New York (1777-1795, 1801-1804) and vice president of the United States (1805-1812). He was president of the constitutional ratification convention in New York. *BDC*, s.v. "Clinton, George."

The circular letter, which called for a second national convention to consider constitutional amendments, was drafted by John Jay and signed by Clinton as convention president. Jay, who previously had denounced a second convention, was party to this letter to appease the Antifederalists, who were in the majority at the beginning of the New York convention. Morris, *Forging of the Union*, 313.

[4]Richard Henry Lee (1732-1794), a signer of the Declaration of Independence, served in the Virginia house of delegates (1777, 1780, 1785) and the Continental Congress (1774-1779, 1784-1785). He was an Antifederalist delegate to the 1788 state ratification convention. Lee was also a member of the U.S. Senate from March 4, 1789, until his resignation on October 8, 1792. *BDC*, s.v. "Lee, Richard Henry."

William Grayson (ca. 1740-1790) was an attorney who had served as an aide-de-camp to George Washington during the Revolution. He was a member of the Virginia house of delegates (1784-1785, 1788), the Continental Congress (1785-1787), and the U.S. Senate (1789-1790). Grayson was an Antifederalist delegate to the 1788 state ratification convention. *BDC*, s.v. "Grayson, William."

[5]The results of the Virginia election for the U.S. Senate were: Richard Henry Lee, 98; William Grayson, 86; and James Madison, 77. Other votes were scattered among those who had not been nominated. Though Madison was defeated in the Senate race, he was elected to the U.S. House of Representatives. Campbell, *Patrick Henry*, 374-375.

From Arthur Iredell

Guildford Decr. 2nd. 1788

My dear James

I had the inexpressible Happiness of a Letter from You some few Days ago. I have not Time to refer to it, and indeed scarcely enough to felicitate you upon an Event, which it foretold, & which has by this Time taken Place. I pray Heaven my dear Sister is happily recovered from It and that another James will repay the Pangs She has sufferrd for him!

I had intended to write you at large by this Packet, and had set part a Morning for the Purpose, but it is wrested out of my Hands; and you must be good enough to take the meagre Food I set before you. Our poor Mother has had a very serious Attack, from which, I at one time, feared She would not have recovered; but I thank God! She is out of Danger, and gains Strength, tho by slow Degrees. Ld. M. & some other Relations have employed me lately in the paying off all her Debts including the remaing ones of our Friend Tom's[1]—I have done so, and in future I hope She will be a total Stranger to all Want.

I will write you a very long Letter by the next Packet, and perhaps Tom. I ought, for I Am greatly in his Debt, and wish much to pay him—My best Love to Your domestic Party. May every Happiness & Comfort attend you all! And, in particular May Tom's Green Bag be full of Briefs. I rejoice you received the Box safe, such as it was. & I am ever

most Affecttely Your's

A I

I am very properly ashamed of this Scrawl; but I judge of your Feelings by my own, which would be much more gratified by Pot hooks & hangers from You than regular Epistles from any one but yourself. I say nothing of Politicks for you will hear more than I could retail in a Letter, from the publick Voice.

Adieu! once more—

Tell Tom I know a great many of [*his Militia*] Acquaintance here. Dr. We[*seal*] [*torn*]old Cu[*nningh*]am &ca. & ca.

RC, Johnson Collection, NCSA. Addressed "James Iredell Esqre. Edenton North Carolina America."

---

[1]"Ld. M." is Lord George Macartney. Tom is Thomas Iredell, brother of James and Arthur.

To Hannah Iredell

Nixonton Dec. 19th. 1788.

My dear Hannah,

My Brother would tell you it was utterly impossible for me to write by him, being then extremely engaged with a troublesome cause in Court. I shall be detained here, I am afraid all this day at least. I am perfectly well & God grant I may find you [*and the*] Children so. Kiss them most tenderly for me, and tell An[*nie*] [*torn*] very much indeed. I hope to find your Sister much better [*torn*] quite well. There are no plains to be got here.

Adieu! my dear Hannah. Yours most affectionately

Ja. Iredell.

RC, Johnson Collection, NCSA.

From William R. Davie

Halifax Decr. 19h. 1788

My Dear Sir

I had the pleasure to receive your letter of the 7h. this evening; which relieved me from some apprehensions that you might not have got the letter I addressed to you at Newbern.[1] I am sensible of the delicacy of our situation with respect to the correction and publication of the debates, and I really begin to feel no small pain on the subject of geting them printed; enclosed are Robinsons and Turnbulls letters to me on this subject, from which you will be convinced that the business is altogether inpracticable in Virginia.[2] you know best whether it could be done at Edenton—At Newbern the Printer is not equal to such a task <of business,> at Wilmington I suppose the foolish quarrel between M—ne and the Printer would probably embarrass the business, perhaps prevent it altogether.[3] thus situated I think it cannot be done on this side Philadelphia, unless <Arnett> /Wills/ and Hodge would undertake it—We are pledged in some measure to the proprietors of the copy to see this matter affected, and the difficulty of the business has given me infinite concern; I have written to Williamson on the subject, and expect some answer by the next or following post. Supposing from Robinsons silence he did not mean to undertake it himself; I would much rather they had been printed under his direction than our own, as it would have precluded all possibility of reflection with respect to corrections or alterations; I have had some of my speeches which were most defectively taken or rather copied (for I believe it was in the copying we were injured) copied over again in a fair Hand, making no alterations except where /the/ sense was entirely perverted; in this I hold myself perfectly justifiable; with respect to the sanction of Mr. Robinson, I wish most sincerely he would give us a fair copy, compared and corrected by his short-hand manuscript; but this I know we need not hope—The whole of the pages we have except a few are copied by a <u>little boy</u> the son of Mr. Turnbull: this is the reason that the copy is so blotched and incorrect, and he would not take the trouble to copy it again himself—you will perceive by a note at the bottom of his letter respecting a speech of Spencers that the delicacy he pretended on the subject of the copy and corrections appearing in his Hand writing was all <u>effectation</u>—nuller fides fronte say'd poor Strap[4]—There was nothing Sir in all this appearance—The money was all he was concerned in—As to the curiosity of the Public on this subject; I am well convinced nobody will trouble their heads in this about the correction of the press or the copy, and every body will expect to see it grammatical English at least, taking it for granted that this much was the business of the Stenographer—

I have not yet received the remainder, but shall forward them to you immediately as /soon as/ they come to Hand. for Gods sake My dear Sir get us out of this hobble about the printing; this is our principal embarrassment; as to procuring a fair copy, it seems to me also necessary if they are sent to the Northward; I Have thought on that subject, and find it cannot be done at this place. I wish you would therefore see whe[*ther*] it can be done if necessary [*at Edent*]on— The whole may be printed [*torn*] about as large as the first volume of the Virginia Debates, and I think Hodge might soon execute it, and make a considerable sum by it, especially as the political ball is to be kept up untill November next.

R—n sent me 2 Vols. of the Viga. Debts. one of which I forward wih this—Adieu, let me hear from you on this interesting business as soon as you come to a conclusion— Make our best respects to Mrs Iredel. I am glad to hear your boy is a stout thiving fellow. Mrs. Iredell must bring him up next Court. I hope your daughter is entirely recovered, you don't mention her now

Adieu, believe me most sincerely

yours &c &c

William R. Davie

P.S. pray consult Gov. J—n on this business he can advise us.

A merry Xmass.

RC, Iredell Papers, Duke. Addressed "James Iredell, Esquire Edenton." Endorsed "Halifax Dec. 19th. 1788. W. R. Davie Ansd."

---

[1]See William R. Davie to JI, November 1788, in this volume.

[2]For information on the publication of the debates, see William R. Davie to JI, November 1788, n. 2, in this volume.

[3]Archibald Maclaine and other Federalists had helped Daniel Bowen and his partner, Caleb D. Howard, establish the *Wilmington Centinel, and General Advertiser* with the belief that the newspaper would serve their political interests. Howard, however, became an Antifederalist, and Maclaine and his associates were unforgiving. Watson, *Index to North Carolina Newspapers*, xiii; *DNCB*, s.v. "Howard, Caleb D."; Archibald Maclaine to JI, September 13, 1788, in this volume.

[4]Strap is a character in Tobias Smollett's first novel, *The Adventures of Roderick Random* (1748). Drabble, *Oxford Companion to English Literature*, 831, 938.

From Samuel Johnston

Edenton 23d. December 1788—

Sir

I have just received several important dispatches which require an immediate answer.[1] they are of such a nature that I cannot, with propriety, decide upon them without the advice of Council of State.[2]

I have therefore thought proper to order a Council to meet at this place on Saturday the 27th. Instant, at ten o'Clock in the Morning to take the said Dispatches under their Consideration, and to assist me with their Advice on the Subject matter contained in them. I do most earnestly request your Attendance on this emergency, as I am apprehensive there will not be a sufficient number to form a Council unless you are present.

I am with the greatest Consideration & Respect

Sir Your most Obedient Servant

Sam Johnston

RC, Johnson Collection, NCSA. Addressed "The Honorable James Iredell Esquire Edenton." Endorsed "Edenton Dec. 23d. 1788. The Governor Ansd."

---

[1]Abishai Thomas was appointed as an agent for the state of North Carolina on December 4, 1788. He was to seek reimbursement from the U.S. government for expenses incurred by the state during the Revolutionary War. On December 15, Thomas wrote Governor Johnston that the U.S. commissioner, with whom he was to negotiate, would soon leave Hillsborough for Richmond, Va. Thomas told Johnston of his need to accompany the commissioner and to collect documents from around the state to support North Carolina's claims. To do this, Thomas added, he needed money quickly. Johnston advised the Council of State of the situation, and they approved giving Thomas £100 immediately and more later if necessary. Clark, *State Records*, 21:160; Abishai Thomas to Samuel Johnston, December 15, 178[*8*], Samuel Johnston to Abishai Thomas, December 28, 1788, Governors Letter Book, State Archives. The December 15 letter is erroneously dated 1789 in the letter book.

Abishai Thomas, as a young man, lived with John Gray Blount and worked in the Blounts' mercantile business. He later became principal clerk in the Navy Department. Keith, *John Gray Blount Papers*, 1:391n.

[2]JI was elected to the Council of State on November 11, 1788. Cheney, *North Carolina Government*, 165.

List of Taxable Property of James Iredell, 1788

Lands.

750 acres,

viz: A Moiety of a Tract of Land estimated at 1500 acres at Tuckahoe on Trent River in the County of Jones (being the remaining quantity of a Tract of 2000 acres by Patent, the other 500 having been sometime since alienated

<160 Acres, viz: A Moiety of 320 Acres (by estimation) on Reedy Branch near the above>

1060 Acres, viz: A Moiety of 2130 acres (by estimation) in the County of Onslow, on the North East and North West Branches of New River

200 Acres, viz: A Moiety of an Island (estimated at 400 acres, by Patent dated 21 March 1742) lying in Chowan River.

2170 Acres in all.

Town Lots. A House and Lot in the Town of Edenton.

Free Males. Two.

1500
320 Heritage
1180
276 Brown
904

1500 Tuckahoe - excluding that conveyed to Heritage
320 new Patent
1820
320 Deduct Heritage
1500
276 Deduct Brown's (I think this was the number)
1224

Lands as before.

Free Males—Two

Slaves from 12 to 50—Dundee, Sall, Peter, Andrew, Edy, Sukey, Sarah, Ann. (These two last in my employ, tho' not <in> my <employ> property)

Carriage Wheels. Two.

FC, Chowan County Tax Records, NCSA. FC, Johnson Collection, NCSA.

1789

From Hugh Williamson

New York, 5th January, '89.

Dear Sir:

Your favor of the 11th ult. came to hand three days ago. The post in cold weather seems to move slowly. I am very glad that the subject of the new Constitution is to be again before the citizens of North Carolina. Presuming that the same cause that prevented your attendance at the last meeting of the Assembly will prevent you from attending at the next Convention and Assembly, I shall, in such case only, assure the inhabitants of Edenton of my readiness to serve them; but if you can make it convenient to attend as the representative of that town, which I heartily wish, I shall offer to serve some of the counties as delegate in the Convention only.[1] I have, as you may believe, the business much at heart, and wish to add my small mite to the endeavors of our friends.

Mrs. Williamson, who has at this instant been inquiring to whom I am writing, and been informed that I am writing to an inhabitant of Edenton, who is a particular friend, and one of the best men, as well as best lawyers in America, says that either of these circumstances would induce her to present you with her compliments, but all of them united engage her to request that I would present you with a tender of her esteem, &c.[2]

Hu. Williamson.

Printed, McRee, 2:248, and *Letters of Delegates to Congress*, 25:467-468.

---

[1]For JI's response, see JI to Hugh Williamson, January 22, 1789, in this volume. Williamson represented Tyrrell County in the 1789 state ratification convention. Massengill, *North Carolina Votes*, 64.

[2]Williamson married Maria Apthorpe (d. 1790) on January 3, 1789. She was the daughter of Charles Ward Apthorpe, a wealthy New York merchant. *DNCB*, s.v. "Williamson, Hugh"; McRee, *Life and Correspondence*, 2:248.

To William Cumming

[*Edenton Jan. 6th. 1789.*]

Dear Sir,

I return you your Bills you were pleased to leave with me.[1] I suppose, with regard to that concerning Executions, you will think it proper to wait to see the Maryland Act.[2] But I have great doubts about its propriety in many respects. I think it would militate with the principles of the New Constitution, and I am so sure of <its> /that/ being adopted in November /next/ that I don't think it is worth while to prepare a Bill which would be useless if it <does> /is/, or immediately cause a quarrel between our Legislature and the General Government. I think however there <is an> /are/ objections still more formidable. It may operate in many instances very injuriously. /As for example:/ A. obtains a Judgment against B. for £100. B. obtains a Judgment at the same Court against C. for the same sum. C. is a Man of consequence, & can obtain security; B. is poor, & can obtain none. B's goods must be immediately sold, whereas if he could levy immediately on C. he could get the money without this necessity. <I think also Debtors have at present full Advantage enough in the delay of business, and the depreciation of money, and in my opinion the principal difficulties about Executions may be considered in a great measure over, or will be before November, so that I should be unwilling to have any further indulgence in contemplation, and if the payment of debts was too easy it would be a great encouragement to Idleness and Dishonesty, the two most pernicious things to be sure that can subsist in any Country.> /This reason alone would be with me a decisive one since it proves that the poorer sort of People, who are in general the greatest objects of compassion upon Executions would scarcely ever be protected, & would be placed on a worse footing than they are now. I could enumerate other objections that occur to me, but really I have not leisure sufficient, and it is unnecessary./

In regard to your Bill concerning Promissory Notes, I confess myself very reluctant to innovate upon a Law that /by great experience/ has been found very beneficial in England <for a long time>, and given rise to a series of excellent decisions calculated to avoid injustice as much as possible. I think your proposition of a Protest unnecessary, and that it would create a great many difficulties in practice without doing any good, since now the Law is clear that if an Indorsee of a Promissory Note does not give due notice of non-payment &c the Indorser is not liable. What due notice is must depend on the Circumstances of the case, and I am satisfied in this County no one uniform rule could properly be laid down. If all Parties for instance lived in Edenton, <less notice would do (in point of time, I mean)> /earlier notice would be required/ than if one lived in Edenton, another in Hillsborough, & the third in Wilmington. I thought a regulation might be useful in regard to sealed Notes, but that can't be done /properly/ without altering the whole /law/ as to single Bills, and for my part <it> /that/ is an Undertaking I should by no means venture to engage in. I think it would be very dangerous to mention a particular form in the Act, since an innocent Man unacquainted with or not remembering it might lose a debt by an immaterial variation. /Neither should I approve of the method of proposing questions to a Plaintiff on oath, since the blending of Common Law & Equity Proceedings together would, I am persuaded, in practice produce great confusion; and if an example was once set it would probably be followed in other cases, to the entire destruction possibly in the end of the regular principles of both Systems. In one respect I agree with you in opinion, and that is, that Bonds ought not to be assignable upon the same principles as Promissory Notes; but though the legal Interest might be permitted to be in the Assignee yet it should be subject to every kind of defence which the Obligor might have had against the original Obligee./ No form is in the Act concerning Promissory Notes in England /of which our own Act is almost an exact Copy/.[3] <I think however one object of this Bill, in some measure, might be a good one, and that is, that though Bonds may be legally assignable, yet they shall be in the hands of the Assignee subject to all the Equity against the original Obligee. I think this would obviate every mischief as to Assignments.>

I make no apology for the freedom of my remarks. I know you love <freedom of communication> /Sincerity/ better than flattery. At the same time I cannot help saying that many of your propositions appear to me very ingenious, though they do not altogether suit my notions of public policy. And I beg leave to add that I should not chuse to have any share in framing a law which I could not be present to support. I well know how Bills are garbled <in the House> /after they are introduced/, and all the blame of the whole is laid on the Persons originally concerned in drawing them. I have frequently felt this in regard to the Law giving the Equity Jurisdiction, & do not chuse to expose myself to the same mortification again.[4]

I am, Dear Sir Yours very sincerely

Ja. Iredell.

P.S. I inclose you a Copy of an interesting case on the subject of notice where a third Person is concerned.[5]

FC, Johnson Collection, NCSA. Printed, McRee, 2:249-250. Addressed "William Cumming Esq."

---

[1]William Cumming represented Edenton in the house of commons in 1788 and served on the Committee on the State and Condition of the Public Revenue. Since that session ended on December 6, the bills that Cumming left with JI may have been legislation that he was planning to introduce in the following session. Cumming, however, was not returned to the assembly in 1789. *DNCB*, s.v. "Cumming, William"; Cheney, *North Carolina Government*, 220, 222, 223.

[2]The "Maryland Act" refers to a bill passed by the Maryland legislature in December 1790 that allowed wardens of the Port of Baltimore to levy and collect tonnage duties on ships entering the port. A clause in the statute specified that the measure would not take effect until approved by the U.S. Congress. In February 1791, Congress sanctioned the Maryland statute "until the tenth day of January next, and from thence until the end of the then next Session of Congress and no longer." Linda Grant De Pauw et al., eds., *Documentary History of the First Federal Congress of the United States of America*, 14 vols. to date (Baltimore: Johns Hopkins Press, 1972-), 5:1257-1260.

[3]"An Act for the more easy recovery of Money due upon Promissory Notes, and to render such Notes negotiable" became law in 1762. Clark, *State Records*, 23:586-588.

[4]See Samuel Johnston to JI, November 20, 1788, n. 5, in this volume.

[5]Enclosure not found.

From Archibald Maclaine

Wilmington 20th. Jany. 1789

Dear Sir

I was but just beginning to recover when the superior court commenced here, and so weak that I could not attend till the last three or four days—Mr. Hooper, who was apparently well when he arrived, was taken ill, and kept his chamber during the whole term; so that we had only two inquiries executed, two or three appeals from the court merchant tried, and a few of the injunctions dissolved.[1]

My papers are perfectly safe in your possession, and perhaps will be as little trouble to you to bring to Newbern in May, as to send them during the vacation, and will more certainly come to my hands. Is the paper I sent you from Boyd with his letter of any consequence? It appeared to me to be a trifling matter as I cannot conceive that it /will/ enable Mr. Allen to recover from DeRosset's estate.[2]

What has become of the debates of our convention?[3] Mr. Hooper was so much indisposed, and when he was able to see company, had so many people about him, that I forgot to mention the subject

I do suppose with you, that we shall have a hard struggle for the seat of government, notwithstanding the new counties, from which I am doubtful whether we shall derive any strength—Those over the mountains will not vote from local views; for they cannot have any; but unfortunately for us, their private interest is somehow connected with /that of/ a set of people who are strongly opposed to us. Upon the whole, however, I believe we shall succeed. There are a considerable number of people who are not materially interested in the dispute, who cannot shut their eyes to the manifest advantages <offer> which will accrue to the public at large from the encouragement which the seat of government will give to a great commercial town, merely because that town is a few miles distant from the center of the state—As for you, I know you are an obstinate infidel, and argument would only tend to confirm you in error. You would maintain your opinion at the stake. But I will appeal to Governor Johnston, who I know is opposed to Fayetteville, whether it does not in every respect come up to the representations given of it.[4]

Judge Spencer neither read his argument from print nor from manuscript. He gave us something to the same purpose, but much worse—Judge Ashe notwithstanding he had declined interfering, was obliged to decide—He however, took time to consider; that was to rake up all the mouldy authorities which he could collect; or rather to have it believed that he had been searching for law; for I am persuaded he had prepared them <since> in the vacation—He even cited Junius;—very little, as I thought to the purpose. As a favor, Bradley was admitted to bail till next court He struggled hard to put off the trial till December, that he might go to England, or to come to trial immediately; but the attorney General wanted Mr. Tabb as a witness—This Mr. Tabb <was> is the person, between whom & Bradley [*the*] dispute originally was, and knows no more of the duel and the circumstances attending it, than you do—He was /however/ privy to the paper which Bradley signed and published, in which Mr. Swann's name was not mentioned, nor even alluded to. It contained a contradiction in very offensive terms /of an assertion/, which it seems Mr. Swann was the author of; but of that circumstance, Bradley was ignorant.[5]

I am happy to hear that you and your family are so well recovered. Here we are all well, and those whom I call of my family, though in different houses, desire their compliments.

Yours very sincerely

A Maclaine

What progress has Hodge made in the laws?[6] Mr. Hooper, some time ago, wrote me that he had inclosed me a specimen; but forgot it. Can you by any means get me a copy of the amendatory act for our academy?[7] I want it much, that we may have a meeting while Rutherfurd is here, in order to settle and receive Col. Innes's legacy.[8] It is of importance to receive it soon.

Mr. Hooper told me of one Ringrose, formerly of this place, who at Edenton said he wanted to purchase a wench of mine that went off with

Lord Cornwallis.[9] As I cannot hear of her at Philada. where she was, and from Ringrose's letters to me believe he intended to get her for a trifle, I suspect that she is with him, & believe that he is now either at Edenton or Washington. If he is in your town, it may easily /be/ known whether <u>such</u> a negroe is with him—Her real name is Molly—She is very black, short and well set, walks with her toes inward; has a short snub nose, a projecting underlip and a bold and intelligent look—She had a mulatto child now about 6 or 7 yeards old—If such a one is with Ringrose, I could send a person to identify her, though I believe Mr. Hooper, and am certain his man Sam, knows her.

Mr. Hay, who arrived at Fayetteville by land from Philada. has been here—He left this yesterday morning, so fat, that he is as round as a ball

RC, Johnson Collection, NCSA. Printed, McRee, 2:250-251. Addressed "James Iredell esquire." Edenton Endorsed "Wilmington Jan. 20th. 1789. A. Maclaine. Ansd."

---

[1]William Hooper, whose health deteriorated during the last years of his life, died on October 14, 1790, at age 48. A few days before Hooper's death, JI wrote to Hannah, "Poor Hooper has been at times and is now some part of every day I believe a raving Madman, but fortunately his health declines so fast that he cannot probably live much longer, and in his present situation the best thing that can be wished him is Death." *DNCB*, s.v. "Hooper, William"; McRee, *Life and Correspondence*, 298.

[2]The dispute involving Nathaniel Allen and Lewis Henry De Rosset's (d. 1786) estate probably stemmed from a business relationship, though nothing specific has been found. Allen was an entrepreneur with investments in land and shipping. De Rosset was a colonial official and Loyalist. When the General Assembly banished De Rosset in 1779, he left in a ship loaded with tobacco, indigo, and slaves. This vessel was seized by the British, then retaken by an American privateer. The Americans charged De Rosset a salvage fee equivalent to one-third of the value of the ship and cargo. After De Rosset again departed, his ship was once more captured by an American privateer. This time he lost the ship itself. It is possible, though not confirmed, that Allen had some financial interest in this vessel. Palmer, *Biographical Sketches*, 217-218. For more information on Allen's shipping interests and related legal matters, see JI to Mess. Conyngham, Nesbitt, &c, September 6, 1784, n. 1, in this volume.

[3]See William R. Davie to JI, November 1788, n. 2, in this volume.

[4]Maclaine favored Fayetteville as the state capital because it was well established and thriving, while JI supported a site in Wake County because of its central location. For a description of Fayetteville at this time, see William J. Dawson to Nelly Blair, November 17, 1788, in this volume.

[5]For more information on the duel between John Bradley and Samuel Swann, see Archibald Maclaine to JI, July 11, 1787, n. 5, in this volume.

[6]See JI to Maurice Murphy, February 25, 1788, n. 2, in this volume.

[7]In 1783, the General Assembly passed "An Act for the promotion of learning in the district of Wilmington." This statute authorized the establishment of a "public seminary of learning" to be known as "Innis [*sic*] Academy" and named nine trustees for the school, including Archibald Maclaine. In 1788, however, the assembly amended the act. Because several of the trustees had died or moved out of the state, the original act could not be implemented. The amendment increased the number of trustees to between twenty and thirty, and named new trustees to join those who remained. Clark, *State Records*, 24:511-513, 984-985.

[8]James Innes (ca. 1700-1759) was a colonial military officer and a member of the Colonial Council (1750-1759). He lived on a plantation called Point Pleasant on the Cape Fear River near Wilmington. He and his wife were childless, and in his will Innes specified that after his wife's death his library and much of his property were to be used to establish a free school. This was the first private educational endowment in the state's history. *DNCB*, s.v. "Innes, James."

[9]Records indicate that a John Ringrose owned property in Wilmington in 1778. No other information has been found. Lennon and Kellam, *Wilmington Town Book*, 235, 236.

British troops under Maj. James Craig occupied Wilmington on January 9, 1781. Cornwallis, following the battle of Guilford Courthouse, retreated to Wilmington and entered the town on April 12. He departed on April 25 to invade Virginia. Lawrence Lee, *New Hanover County: A Brief History* (Raleigh: State Department of Archives and History, 1971), 27-28.

To Hugh Williamson

Edenton Jan. 22d. 1789.

Dear Sir,

I had yesterday the pleasure to receive your very obliging letter of the 5th. Inst., and sincerely congratulate you on the happy event of your marriage.[1] You have done me a great kindness in representing me in so partial a manner to a Lady, whose own /highly/ respectable qualities will make me very ambitious of the honour of her good opinion. Mrs. Iredell & the other Ladies of my Family and my Brother desire to express their cordial congratulations, and we all anticipate with much pleasure the happiness of <her> /Mrs. Ws/ society in Edenton—which we hope will be the principal seat of your residence.

I am extremely glad you propose offering yourself for Edenton. It was what I much wished, and had in <prospect> /view/, for I never have been reconciled to our suffering you so easily to be out of our last Convention. I cannot at any rate be a Member of Assembly, as being a Counsellor, and it would be a means of my losing Edenton Court, which nothing but such an extraordinary & important business as that of the Constitution could permit me to think of. Possibly I may aim to be in the Convention, tho' I must sacrifice Newbern Court to it, but if I should it must be for some County, as I never could consent to interfere with the election of any Gentleman who might be chosen <as> /the/ Member of Assembly for our Member in the Convention also. One certainly ought to be chosen for both stations. I am therefore very happy in thinking you in all probability will be that Person and I am sure I should go to the Convention with infinitely higher spirits were you to be a Member of it.[2]

I sometime ago received the favour of your letter on the subject of our Debates. I had an opportunity of sending it instantly to Colo. Davie, but have not heard from him since. I should have wrote sooner, but have been from home, & we have been very unhappy about Mrs. Blair, whose life seemed in most imminent danger, but thank God she is now in a fair way of recovery. Davie & myself are in a critical situation. We were <employed> /engaged/ to get the Debates printed having no doubt we could sell the Copy, which we were empowered to do, upon condition to receive gratis about 100 Copies for the Subscribers. We can't dispose of the Copy here or in Virginia, & I dare say he has not much more Cash to advance than I have for the publication. So that we know not what to do, & a number of People who think everything can be done <Exactly> /Just/ as they wish it are very impatient about it.[3]

I heard <lately from Dawson,> sometime ago from Mr. Dawson, who was frolicking at Black's wedding, he being married on the 8 Jan to Miss Lucas, a young lady that possibly you may remember, who lived at Austin Willis's.[4] You may be so kind as to assure Mrs. D. her Son was then very well. He is now I believe at Warrenton.[5] Mr. L. is at Eden house as well as can be expected for a Man who has been 1 year & a half from so charming a Wife.

You will particularly oblige me in remembering me to that Family, and I take the liberty to desire my most respectful Compliments to Mrs. W., whose early notice <tho> /owing to/ your kind <representation> /partiality/ has flattered me highly.

FC, Johnson Collection, NCSA. Endorsed "Copy of a Letter to Dr. Williamson Jan. 22d. 1789."

---

[1]See Hugh Williamson to JI, January 5, 1789, n. 2, in this volume.

[2]Williamson was not elected to the General Assembly but did represent Tyrrell County in the 1789 ratification convention. In 1789, Charles Johnson, Stephen Cabarrus, and Lemuel Creecy represented Chowan County in the General Assembly and at the ratification convention. In the same year, John Hamilton was elected to represent Edenton in the house of commons. Cheney, *North Carolina Government*, 222-223; Massengill, *North Carolina Votes*, 71.

[3]For information on the publication of the 1788 ratification convention debates, see William R. Davie to JI, November 1788, n. 2, in this volume.

[4]Alexander Black married Sarah Lucas on January 8, 1789. Austin Willis was actually Augustine Willis (d. 1799) of Halifax County. Fouts, *State Gazette of North-Carolina*, 1:14; *State Gazette* of *North Carolina* (Edenton), January 22, 1789; Mitchell, *North Carolina Wills*, 565.

[5]"Mrs. D" is Penelope Johnston Dawson, and her son was William Johnston Dawson.

From William R. Davie

Halifax Jany. 23d. 1789

My Dear Sir

Yesterday I reced. the remaining speeches of the debates, amounting to nineteen, nearly as rough as the former, accompanied by a long letter from Robertson, apologising for the delay and the imperfection of the copy.

Inclosed is the letter you sent by our friend Mr. Dawson of which Williamson had sent me a duplicate. I also inclose to you his letter to me of the 24th. of December.[1] It is as he says Hobsons choice with us[2]—it must be printed under his direction—and we must be the guarantee—This renders it still more necessary, that it should be printed immediately—I could get a young man here to copy it instantly, for 20/ a day—but as Governor Johnston desires to correct his speeches, it will be impossible, and if done, you must have it done at Edenton, it would take too much time, trouble & expence, which I see must all fall on you and myself to be sending them backwards and forwards, such a distance. I shall forward the whole by Mr. Black who goes down in a few days, Mr. Granberry who carries this being without any servant.

I shall write you again in a few days by Mr. Black. My compliments to your good family and the Governor and believe me with the most sincere friendship and esteem

yours

William R. Davie

RC, Emmet Collection, NYPL. TSS, Thomas Addison Emmet Collection, NCSA.

---

[1]Enclosed letters not found.

[2]To have Hobson's choice is to have no choice. The term derives from Thomas Hobson (ca. 1544-1631), a stable keeper in Cambridge, England, who let his horses in a specific order. A customer, seeing all of Hobson's animals, might think that he had many options, but in fact, he had to take the one Hobson offered or none at all. *Brewer's Dictionary of Phrase and Fable*, 522.

From Hugh Williamson

New York 24th Jany. 1789

Dear Sir

Having read the inclosed more than once as you may conclude from its Dress I verily thought that I had forwarded it to you long since for it contains some good Funnical Remarks. If it has not hitherto appeared in Edenton be so good as hand it to the Govr. after you have had your Laugh.

The Genl. Assembly of this State after spending near 2 months in pure wrangling, during which Time many of them have had the felicity to make a clear Saving of one Dlr. per day, have at length agreed to divide the State into Six Election Districts for the choice of Representatives in the new Congress. They cannot yet agree about the mode of chusing Senators. The House of commons want to have all Antis & the Senate wish to have at least one of the Congress Senators a federal Man.[1]

Some Time ago I wrote you that in Case our State should agree to try the Effects of a new Convention I should be glad to take a Seat in the same if chosen.[2] There can be no great Harm in saying that Edenton may be more effectively represented both in Convention & Assembly than by its present Member.[3] To the best of my Recollection the Convention Sits very near the Time when the Superiour Court of Newbern sits. I have nevertheless Some Hope that there is not an absolute Interference and that you will be able to represent our Town in the Convention though probably not in the Assembly. I am very indifferent about whether I am in the Assembly or not, my Object is the Convention but I would also of choice serve in the Assembly also, for if the Constitution is adopted some interesting Business comes on before the Assembly. If you can Serve Edenton in both Capacities, so much the better for the public & in that Case I shall offer for one of the Counties in Convention only and I think the competition for that particular Office will not be very great. If you can serve for the Convention only, I shall be glad to Serve the Town <fr> in the Assembly & shall offer to serve one of the Counties, as in the other Case, in Convention. I have not yet determined for which of the Counties I should offer with greatest Prospect of Success. If Captn. Collins should not be disposed to Serve for Tyrrell or if his Business should make it inconvenient for him to attend I presume that with the Interest of the Lake Company I might secure an Election for the Convention in that County. In our own County of Chowan the double Representation will doubtless engage the chief competition but there will probably be sundry Candidates even for the two additional Seats in the Convention. I shall thank you for your advice on the whole of this Business.[4]

Be pleased present Mrs. Iredell & the other Ladies in your Family with my Respects & believe me to be with great Esteem Dr. Sir

Your obed Servt.

Hu Williamson

RC, Iredell Papers, Duke. Printed, McRee, 2:252, and *Letters of Delegates to Congress*, 25:475-476. Addressed "James Iredell Esq Edenton." Endorsed "New York 24 Jan. 1789. Hugh Williamson Ansd."

---

[1]Williamson is referring to New York. He was a member of the Continental Congress, which was meeting in New York at this time.

[2]See Hugh Williamson to JI, January 5, 1789, in this volume.

[3]William Cumming represented Edenton in the house of commons during the 1788 session. In 1789, John Hamilton replaced him. Cheney, *North Carolina Government*, 222-223.

[4]For information on the candidates elected to the General Assembly and the 1789 convention, see JI to Hugh Williamson, January 22, 1789, n. 2, in this volume.

From Nathaniel Dukinfield

Sulham, 4th Feb. '89.

Dear Iredell

. . . Mr. Johnston's last letter gives me sad accounts of the universal sickness that had prevailed among you; and that Mr. Pollok had prudently withdrawn to the Westward, possessing the great advantage of no business to confine him, and finances to defray the expense of rambling. I hope both he and Mrs. Pollok, by so doing, avoided the sickness they might have expected by remaining at Edenton.

Mr. Johnston's appointment to the Government is more honorary than otherwise advantageous, I fear. I flatter myself, however, it has enabled him to give you some good appointment, and yet allow you to pursue your profession. If you have written to me since Sept., 1787, your letter has miscarried.

We have lately been in a pitiable state by the indisposition of our King, whose mental faculties have been these three months so entirely deranged as to deprive him of every power of business, and God only knows when his senses will be restored. Some of his physicians are more and others less sanguine in their expectations of his recovery. But I fear even in this situation their judgments may, in some degree, be biassed by party politics. O tempora, O mores! but such is the land I live in. The Prince of Wales will be appointed Regent, during his father's indisposition, under some restrictions. The ministry will be changed, and Mr. Fox at the head of the new one. Mr. Pitt's resignation I regret.[1]

The commissioners of American claims have allowed me £3,000 for my confiscated property, which will be paid by half yearly instalments in eight years, with interest at 3 1/2 per cent.[2] 'Tis lucky, as you observed in one of your letters, that the confiscation did not lay hold of my negroes, which I had lent to my mother.[3] I think I wrote to you last year soon after the death of my youngest son[4]—Mr. Johnston does not mention any increase to your family—I am in daily expectation of an addition to mine. I was introduced to Mr. Crewe last spring in London, and inquired after your brother. He told me he had left his family some time, and was settled in Suffolk, but he could not give me the least information further about him. I have long wished to see him, but do not at present think there is any probable chance of such an event.

Mr. Lowther is now in London, and I hope to see him, as I must go there as soon as Lady D. is safe in her bed and I can leave her.

I don't know at all what allowances have been made to Mr. McCulloch, but have been told they are very considerable: though (by what I've heard him say) I conclude much short of his expectations.[5] I saw Palmer in November last, and he told me the commissioners had allowed him an annuity of £300; whether this allowance or any part of it is to be continued to his wife in case of widowhood, I don't know.[6] Brimmage I fear has not been very greatly considered; I'm sorry for him. I think I never saw a man more dotingly fond of a child than he is of his son, and very much does he lament his unfortunate separation from his family.[7] McGuire seems very happy, though I'm told he was most terribly afflicted when his Nancy (the mulatto girl he brought over) died last year, and was quite inconsolable for a long time. Colonel Hamilton I have seen sometimes but know little of him. I do not immediately recollect any other Carolinians of your acquaintance.

Lady D. is as well as her situation will admit, my two boys and I perfectly well, and I hope you are all long ago recovered.

I beg my best respects to Mrs. Iredell, Mrs. Dawson, Mrs. Blair, Mr. and Mrs. Pollok, and am yours,

Very sincerely,

N. Dukinfield.

P.S. Feb. 7th. Lady D. was safely delivered of a daughter, about four o'clock this morning.

21st. As I mentioned the King's illness with little prospect of recovery, I am happy to tell you that the accounts we now receive of him are very favorable, and we are in hopes of an immediate and perfect recovery.

Printed, McRee, 2:252-253.

---

[1]The king's breakdown was the second of five episodes of mental illness he experienced during his life. During these periods his behavior was erratic, and he suffered illusions. For example, he believed that London was underwater, he wrote dispatches to foreign rulers about nonexistent issues, and he would on occasion expose his buttocks to court retainers. His inability to rule had far-reaching political ramifications. The king supported William Pitt, while the Prince of Wales was an ardent follower of Charles James Fox, Pitt's leading opponent. To further complicate matters, the prince was a notorious profligate. The change in government did not occur, however, because of the king's recovery during February. John W. Derry, *The Regency Crisis and the Whigs, 1788-1789* (Cambridge: University Press, 1963), 7-9, 187-191.

[2]Dukinfield had filed a claim for £8,762 in losses from the confiscation of his property. Loyalist Claim of Nathaniel Dukinfield, State Archives.

[3]See Nathaniel Dukinfield to JI, January 11, 1784, and the postscript to that letter dated January 25, in this volume.

[4]See Nathaniel Dukinfield to JI, February 13, 1788, in this volume. At the time of that letter, Dukinfield's youngest son was still alive.

[5]Mr. McCulloch is Henry Eustace McCulloh.

[6]Loyalist Robert Palmer filed a claim with the British government for compensation for £8,103 for property lost during the war; the government gave him £112. He also claimed a loss in annual income of £800. The government granted him £650 per annum, plus a £300 pension. Loyalist Claim of Robert Palmer, English Records, Audit Office Papers, State Archives; Palmer, *Biographical Sketches*, 667.

[7]Before the Revolution, William Brimage had been a royal prosecutor and a vice-admiralty court judge in North Carolina. In 1783, the Loyalist Claims Commission granted him £100 per year, but in 1787, he asked for a review. He claimed a loss of £600 in annual income, 640 acres of land, and £1,180 in unpaid debts. The commission increased his pension to £120 and gave him payments of £43 and £240. Loyalist Claim of William Brimage, English Records, Audit Office Papers, State Archives; Palmer, *Biographical Sketches*, 91-92.

From Hugh Williamson

New York 12th Feby. 1789

Dear Sir

Yours of 22nd ult came to hand by yesterdays Post.[1] Mrs. Dawson & her Daughter, whom I have just Seen & to whom I delivered the message you sent, are in good Health and request me to present you and Family with their Respects. Mrs. Williamson says she considers herself flattered by the Wish that you and two or three other respectable Gentlemen have expressed of seeing her an Inhabitant of Edenton which by the way is the Place she has marked for her Residence but she says she is afraid that your Expectations may be founded on some Descriptions of her Qualities that are the Children of Flattery. I have written to Sundry Friends that I shall offer for Edenton both in Assembly & Convention if you cannot Serve but if you can Serve the Town in Assembly then I will offer for some County in Convention only. Your Letter states a fact of which I was afraid viz that the courts will prevent you from Serving in the Assembly. I think it probable that I may be at Home at or before the Election, Some farther Evidence as I take it respecting the Object of my late Appointmt. must be collected in the State which may require the attendance of Col. Thomas or myself. Should this be the Case I shall try to come as I wish at the Same Time to make Some Arrangements for the Settlement of my Family. By the Way I wish my growing attachment to domestic Life may not become too Strong. I do not wish ever to possess that absolute Apathy and want of concern for the Interest of the Nation which I have often blamed in others on whose Services their Country had a Claim.

Be So good as give furtherance to the inclosed & believe me to be with the most perfect Esteem

Dr. Sir Your obedt. Servt.

Hu Williamson

RC, Johnson Collection, NCSA. Addressed "James Iredell Esqr. Edenton."

---

[1]See JI to Hugh Williamson, January 22, 1789, in this volume.

To James Glasgow

Edenton Feb. 16. 1789.

Dear Sir,

I never saw till 3 or 4 days ago the inclosed Resolution.[1] I must intreat the favour of you to give me the earliest information you can, in order that I may proceed with the laws, which I am very anxious to do—I would be obliged to you if you would send me the information in official form.

I am, Dear Sir, with great regard, Your obed. Serv

Ja. Iredell.

RC, Secretary of State Records, Correspondence, NCSA. Addressed "James Glasgow Esqr., Dobbs County."

---

[1]In 1787, the General Assembly appointed JI to compile the state's laws for publication and authorized him to contract with a printer for the project. During the 1788 session, the assembly repealed the section of the statute permitting a £500 loan to the printer. Clark, *State Records*, 24:888-889, 957. See also JI to Maurice Murphy, February 25, 1788, n. 2, in this volume.

To John Steele[1]

Edenton Feb. 17th. 1789.

Dear Sir,

Few things that ever happened to me in my life affected me with greater surprize and pleasure, than the distinguished and I am sure most unexpected honour of having the new County that has been formed out of Rowan called by my name.[2] I have reason to believe, Sir, that this has been in a great measure owing to your kind partiality, and I feel not a little pride in thinking that I have been able to recommend myself so strongly to your esteem.[3] Permit me to return you my sincere thanks for so flattering a proof of it, and <also to make></express/> </I beg the favor of you/> /to request that you will be pleased to express/ my acknowledgments in the warmest manner to the other Gentlemen from your part of the Country who concurred in conferring upon me so great a distinction. My opportunities of rendering any public service have been very few, but no Man's heart is more warmly disposed to the public Interest than mine. I think neither you nor myself could give stronger proofs of it, than in supporting with all the earnestness in our power a Constitution which in my opinion gave us the only chance of being rescued from the dreadful evil of universal Anarchy, which is as far removed from true liberty, as Despotism itself. <I trust in God> But unfortunately few can <in general see this danger in> be sufficiently sensible of this danger, tho' all are deeply impressed with the other.

The manuscript of our Debates came to my hands very lately. We were afraid we should have no other resource but getting them printed at New York, and had wrote to Dr. Williamson accordingly, who engaged to see the work well done. Finding however that Hodge and Wills would have an interval in the publication of the Laws, owing to circumstances that were unavoidable, I have made an agreement with them, and hope the whole will be printed by the beginning of May.[4] They would not purchase the Copy, but agreed to give credit for the expence, and I think there can be no doubt but that will be reimbursed by the sale. I think to have 1000 Copies struck off, & you shall have a large share of them

I enclose you our two latest Newspapers, and sincerely assure you that I am,

with very great respect & esteem, Dear Sir, Your faithful & obliged Ser

Ja. Iredell.

FC, Iredell Papers, Duke. RC, Steele Papers, NCSA. Printed, McRee, 2:254, and *Papers of John Steele*, 1:32-33. Endorsed "Copy of a Letter to Mr. Steele Feb 18th. 1789."

---

[1]John Steele (1764-1815), a Salisbury merchant, served in the house of commons and as a Federalist delegate to the 1788 and 1789 ratification conventions. He was also a member of the U.S. House of Representatives (1790- 1793) and comptroller of the U.S. Treasury (1796-1802). *DNCB*, s.v. "Steele, John"; *BDC*, s.v. "Steele, John."

[2]See Samuel Johnston to JI, November 20, 1788, in this volume.

[3]Iredell County was created in 1788 from Rowan County, and at John Steele's suggestion named for JI. H. M. Wagstaff, ed., *The Papers of John Steele*, 2 vols. (Raleigh: North Carolina Historical Commission, 1924), 1:32.

[4]The 1788 ratification convention debates were published in June 1789. See William R. Davie to JI, November 1788, n. 2, in this volume.

From Henry E. McCulloh

Newman street, London, 18th. feby. 1789.

Dear sir

I am to acknowledge the rect. of your two favors of the 12h. July, & 23d. Sept. last, & am very sensible to the affectionate manner in wch. you express yourself, & your kind Intentions in the papers you sent, & intended sending me, but I have reason to know nothing sent, has availed me, one penny.

I have recd. the bill you drew on me for 31.16.3 Stg. & expect the particulars wch. you promised.—I hope you will excuse the mention I made as to your Mother, to whom I mean to be of some certain assistance, & in which I am sure, I shall recommend myself to You in my earnest request that You will assist & forward George in business, & obtain him a License for the Supr. Cot. as soon as possible.

I have wrote him fully, what my directions & Intentions are, of this date, inclosed, and directed him to beg of You to take the trouble of perusing said letter, which will save me repeating the Contents here.

I am much concerned to find that your State has not acceeded to the Federation.—I have many & definitive things to write you relative to BMC. HM. & T.F. but I think it may be as well, not to go into these

Subjects at present, in hopes, agt. I write again, I may have happier accots. from you to guide me.[1]—

The inclosed <copy> /paragraphs/ of my letter to H Montfort of this date will give you great Concern to hear of the heavy addl. loss hanging over me on his Acct.—In my next, I shall write you more fully on this Subject.—Pray continue to urge Montfort to assist me, as he ought, & take care to keep the Claim as to the protested Bill, alive.

I write BMC. from whom notwithstanding his repeated & solemn Assurances, I neither receive letters, or remittances. As soon as ever your Courts are Stablished, I am determined to proceed agt. him, Montfort, & Frohock.—

You may please to recollect I write you to get sundry Securities of mine from Mr. Donaldson. Shod. you have done so, and got among them a Bond from the Rev. Mr. Agnew to Child, assigned by him to Montfort, & by Montforts order to me, pray send it back to Mr. Donaldson to get proved togr. with the Assignmts. & transmitted to me here, and I beg you to send me the vouchers I have requested, as to payments made to H Mc.C's children.[2]

I beg my best respects to Mrs. Iredell, & best wishes for the happiness of you & yours, & am ever & most affectionately

Dear Sir Yr. assd. friend & obedt. Sert.

Henry E. Mc.Culloh.

P.S. I beg my respects to Mr. Johnston & beg his favor to George.—

(Paragraphs of a letter from H E McCulloh to H. Montfort dat. 18. feb. 89.

"What I have long apprehended, has lately taken place. Cornell's Exors have lately brot. an action agt. me here, for the bond given him in March 1773 by your father, & Cousin Al. Mc.Culloch & myself as his Secs. for 1783. proc. & Int. & on which according to a late decision in our Courts here, they will certainly recover agt. me here, unless I can shew, as your father assured Mr. Iredell, was the real Case, that there was an Accot. Currt. bet. him & Mr. Cornell, in which this bond was, or wod. be settled:—<u>or</u>—unless you can procure & send me as much old proc. issued before the year 1773, as will enable me to pay the very proc. money here, for wch. the Bond was given, and which I am advised, they wod. in that case be obliged to take.—I hope you will write me fully by the first opperty. care of Mr. Stott of Suffolk, giving me all the Information you can on this Subject, and Stating All you know or can find as to the Accot. Currt. bet. Cornell & yr. father, as they stand in your father's books & papers.—Most especially, I intreat you to procure & send to Mr. Stott, for him to send me, (and which I suppose you may readily do, at very little charge, as it is no longer of value with you, as much of the old proc. passed before the year 1773, as you can get to the amot. of abt. 2500 /£/ of it, which with some little, I beleive I may be able to get here, will enable me to pay off the bond with it here, & discharge Us all from this heavy demand agt. me in the first place, & yourself & A. Mc.C. in the 2d.[3]

Cousin BMc.C. whom I wish to, I make no doubt will do every thing to assist in this business. I am &c.")

P.S. to H.E.M's aforegoing Letter to Mr. Iredell

I pray your kind attention to the business mentd. in the above, and that you will write me what old proc. you can pick up, & on what terms:—Further that you will send me an Attested Copy of the late Act of your last Assembly but one, declaring that the Treaty of Peac, shod. be considered as your Superior Law:[4]—also whether in Case N Carolina accedes to the federal Convention, the bond in questn. might not be recoverable in Carolina by Cornell's represents—and pray write your answer by the first opporty—In two or 3 weeks I shall write you what proceedings I am advised to here—(and which must be in our Chancery) to defend myself from the Matter, & wch. if I am <advised> obliged to pay in Sterl. will be most heavy indeed.

Pray excuse the trouble of this long letter, and let me value myself as I do, on your friendship & assistance. God bless You & Yours!

RC, Iredell Papers, Duke. Addressed "Jas. Iredell Esqr."

---

[1]McCulloh is referring to Benjamin McCulloch, Henry Montfort, and Thomas Frohock.

[2]See Henry M. McCulloh to JI, February 25, 1784, which is included with the letter dated February 20, 1784, in this volume.

[3]See Henry M. McCulloh to JI, February 25, 1784, which is included with the letter dated February 20, 1784, in this volume.

[4]The General Assembly passed "An Act declaring the Treaty of Peace between the United States of America and the King of Great Britain to be part of the law of the Land" on December 22, 1787. Clark, *State Records*, 24:885.

From Archibald Maclaine

Wilmington 22d. Feby. 1789

Dear Sir

As Mr. Carmichael is going directly to Edenton, I would not omit thanking you for the copy of the bill which you were so obliging as to inclose in yours of the 15ht.

From the information you give me about the publication of our debates, I suppose we may possibly have them by the time the next convention meets, at which I shall not be present I hope however you will be a member, and that you will be able so to dispose your business at Newbern, as to attend. Notwithstanding I am of opinion that a great majority are already prepared to adopt the new government next fall, it will be proper there should be in the convention a few men who may have it in their power to prevent the majority from running into absurdity.

Inform me what further sum will be necessary to publish the debates, and let me know what you think will be my proportion I think you once mentioned some other publication which would require the aid of your friends—I will very clearly contribute

British politics seem to engage our attention here as much as the new government, in which we have no immediate interest. The indisposition of the sovereign of that country, appears from the papers to be very extraordinary.[1] It is not simply mental, for frequent mention is made of his fever, and in one place of a discharge from his leg; but it does not appear whether this may not been procured by the advice of his physicians. The system of government will probably undergo some alteration, or at least some of the opposition be called to office. If what is mentioned in Martin's paper be true, that Mr. Fox is a member of the upper house, by the death of his nephew Lord Holland, a title and a great estate, added to such abilities, must give great weight to the party.[2] Many people here appear to be pleased that confusion is likely to be introduced into a government which is not friendly to us; others from mere curiosity are anxious to know the event, and I suppose some of the british merchants sympathize with their fellow subjects. It is not a little strange (if true) that a king who has foolishly and wickedly thrown away thirteen provinces, should be so much beloved—No reason can be assigned for this infatuation, but that he has, by chance, appointed a minister of abilities, who has made a reform in the commerce and finances of the nation.[3] History will speak more impartially of him than his subjects do at present

We have had more vessels here this fall and winter than have been known at any one time since 1775, the greatest part of them for West India cargoes; so that saw-mill lumber, slaves & shingles are in great demand[4]

Your friends /here,/ except my brother who is complaining, are all well—I am much pleased to hear that your family & Mr. Johnston's are generally so. I did not know that Mr. Blair had continued ill, which is certainly a very unfavorable /circumstance/ at this season of the year

I am Dear Sir very truely yours

A Maclaine

RC, Iredell Papers, Duke. Printed, McRee, 2:254-255. Addressed "James Iredell esquire Edenton." Endorsed "Wilmington 22 Feb 1789. A. Maclaine. Ansd."

---

[1]See Nathaniel Dukinfield to JI, February 4, 1789, n. 1, in this volume.

[2]"Martin's paper" is *Martin's North Carolina Gazette* (New Bern).

Charles James Fox's nephew, Henry Richard Fox, 3d Baron Holland, lived until 1840. John Burke, *Genealogical and Heraldic Dictionary of the Peerage and Baronetage of the British Empire*, 7th ed. (London: Henry Colburn, 1841), 528; *DNB*, s.v. "Fox, Richard Henry Vassall."

[3]The "minister of abilities" was William Pitt the younger.

[4]In 1783, the British government issued an Order in Council prohibiting American vessels from trading in the British West Indies. This interdiction was officially in effect at the time of this letter, but an illegal trade had developed. West Indian planters, who were forced to pay higher prices under the embargo, were eager to buy cheaper American goods. Morris, *Forging of the Union*, 139.

To Robert Hudson

Edenton North Carolina, Feb. 25th. 1789.

Sir,

I received your favour of the 4th. August, and have felt a strong disposition to serve you in the business that you wrote to me about in the best manner in my power. The Captain of the Vessel in which Mr. Hudson was lost (Capt. Dennison) I am well acquainted with, and I had an opportunity of seeing and conversing with him lately at Newbern, and questioned him very particularly as to the time of <his being> Mr. Hudson's being drowned from on board his Vessel.[1] He was positive that it was on his Return Voyage, & as nearly as he could remember then in the month of Sept., & he mentioned many circumstances to me, which convinced me of the truth of it. I endeavoured to find out other proof but could hear of none. If the taking of the Depositions can be deferred until about the 20th. of May I could attend personally at the taking of them, otherwise <I cant> it will not be in my power. I did not receive the Papers in time to get them taken <in November or early in Dec> when I was last there, though if I had I am sure Mr. Blount would have endeavoured to consult my convenience. I so entirely despair of any success on your part that it would be wrong in me to put you to the unnecessary expence of my taking a Journey there on purpose, tho' if I had any prospect of success by it I would have endeavoured to do so rather than you should run the risque of <any> an Injury. But if they are to be taken there in my absence I will at all events try to get some Gentleman I can depend upon to attend and prepare cross-questions.

I am Sir very respectfully Your obed. Sert,

J. I.

FC, Johnson Collection, NCSA. Endorsed "Copy of a Letter Feb. 25. 1789. To Mr. Robert Hudson About Hudson's Business, in regard to Depositions at Newbern."

---

[1]In April 1776, the assembly gave George Dennison of New Bern £10 for sailing to the French West Indies to obtain ammunition, and on June 27 of the same year, he was commissioned as a privateer. In June 1789, Dennison commanded the *Maria*. He was listed as a resident of Hyde County in the 1790 census. Charles E. Claghorn, *Naval Officers of the American Revolution: A Concise Bibliographical Dictionary* (Metuchen, N.J.: Scarecrow Press, 1988), 89; Clark, *State Records*, 10:552, 636; 21:408; *Heads of Families, 1790 Census*, 139.

From Hugh Williamson

New York, March 2d, 1789.

Dear Sir:

It has not been because I have any thing to write that I have taken up my pen; but to tell you, that my not writing frequently in future must be passed to account of not having the privilege of franking letters, after the 4th instant: and I am conscious that very few of them are worth the trouble of reading, much less the expense of postage.[1]

There has been a considerable debate among the citizens of New York whether a Lawyer or Merchant, both Federalists, shall represent this District in the new Congress. The election comes on soon: it seems to be at length agreed to support the Lawyer.[2] Gov. Clinton will be hard run: a moderate Antifed is started against him, &c.[3]

Hugh Williamson.

Printed, McRee, 2:255, and *Letters of Delegates to Congress*, 25:507-508.

---

[1]Hugh Williamson represented North Carolina in the Continental Congress, but neither he nor any other representative from the state would serve in the new Congress when it convened on March 4, 1789, because North Carolina had yet to ratify the Constitution. Thus, Williamson would lose his franking privilege.

[2]John Laurance (1750-1810) was elected from New York's second congressional district, which included New York City and part of Westchester County. Laurance not only served in the House of Representatives (1789-1793), but also as a federal judge (1794-1796) and a U.S. senator (1796-1800). His opponent

was John Broome, a prosperous merchant and importer. Broome held numerous public offices during his life, including New York City alderman, state assemblyman, and lieutenant governor. Smith and Gephart, *Letters*, 25:508n; *BDC*, s.v. "Laurance, John"; Barrett, *Old Merchants*, 3:213-214.

[3]George Clinton defeated Robert Yates, a justice on the state supreme court from Albany, by a narrow margin in the 1789 New York gubernatorial race. Milton M. Klein, ed., *The Empire State: A History of New York* (Ithaca: Cornell University Press, with the New York Historical Association, Cooperstown, N.Y., 2001), 251-252.

To the Misses Blair

March 15th, 1789.

My Dear Girls;

It is with the greatest concern and reluctance that I find myself obliged to leave home at this affecting period; but I can truly assure you that I shall sympathize with you every moment during my absence on the dreadful loss you have sustained.[1] We have great reason to regret it, for certainly never was there a more affectionate friend as well as tender mother. Would to God it had been possible to preserve her! But, since Heaven has been pleased to decree otherwise, our greatest consolation must be in cherishing her dear memory by the fondest recollections, and endeavoring to imitate her virtues. Long, long will they be remembered by all who knew her. My heart bleeds at the recollection of many happy hours, now for ever past. I beg of you, my dear girls, to consider me as one of your sincerest commiserators, one of your tenderest friends, whose whole life will be employed, as opportunity shall be afforded, in rendering yours as easy and comfortable as possible. Your poor aunt feels exquisitely for you as well as herself. She longs, yet dreads, to meet you again. Regard us, so far as we can become so, as your Father and Mother. We shall anxiously endeavor, by every means in our power, to evince the tenderness and reality of the strongest attachment. Adieu! for the present, my dear girls, and believe me ever,

Your most affectionate Uncle,

Jas. Iredell.

Printed, McRee, 2:255-256.

---

[1]Jean Johnston Blair, sister of Hannah Iredell, died on March 12, 1789. When her husband, George Blair, died in 1772, she was left with five children. JI helped to educate the daughters. He and one of the daughters, Helen "Nelly" Blair Tredwell, corresponded frequently. *PJI*, 1:100n.

To Hannah Iredell

Halifax March 29th. 1789.

My dear Hannah,

I am just arrived here in perfect health. I staid at Mrs. Brickell's all day yesterday, on account of the rain.[1] Be good enough to remind my Brother when Mr. Black comes, or any one else that can be depended on, so that I may receive it the first or second day of Halifax Court, to send me a little Blue book I shall want in Mr. Baker's suit, & unluckily left behind me.[2] God [*grant*] on my return here I may hear happily from you. Give my love in the tendere[*st*] manner to our dear Girls, and assure my dear Annie, & James, with a thousand kisses, that I love them inexpressibly. My heart is constantly with you, though my body is moving so far from you. Adieu! my dear Hannah. Heaven bless you.

I am ever Most affectionately yours

Ja. Iredell

P.S. Respects to Mr. Tredwell, & over the Creek.

RC, Johnson Collection, NCSA. Addressed "Mrs. Iredell Edenton."

---

[1]Mrs. Brickell is probably Nancy Brickell, wife of John Brickell (d. 1789), a planter in Halifax County. Hofmann, *Wills, 1758-1824, Halifax County*, 79.

[2]For information on the Baker case, see JI to Hannah Iredell, April 14, 1787, n. 1, in this volume.

From John Hamilton

[*Wednesday Evening*]

Dear Sir

The Subject of the Judgt. & Executs. of Pitts, I have hitherto considered as a matter between you & myself, as Lawyers. I feel for your Situation & would, with all my soul, be desirous of doing every thing to relieve your Anxiety as a Lawyer—Upon Consideration however I am afraid that were I to suspend the Executs. or countermand it, bad consequences might follow—The property w. either Pitts or Smith have now, may before /a/ 2d. Judgt. be made away <it> with—

My Client is not here, & I do clearly take upon me an act for which I am obligated personally—a Judgt. is had, say erroneously, & executs. is out,—My official duty as a Lawyer is terminated—But this is not all—My Client is oppressed with Debts & weighty excuts. agt. him at this instant—Several wherein I am concerned agt. him & have at this instant an order upon the Sheriff by Garvey for this Money in favour of Batemans executs., which order has been a preventative to the sale of Garveys own property ever Since the Sup. Court.[1]

My Mind upon reflection is agitated to a greater degree than I can express—at first I easily gave way to your request without consideration—The obligation that I am under to you & my reverence for you as a Lawyer would induce me almost to do any thing to return with liberal gratitude the favours received But this is a Stroke of a tender and delicate Nature & my duty to my Clients must outweigh in the present instance the Sentiments of Obligation [*illegible*] I owe to you as a friend or the frank condescension of a young Man such as myself to his Superior—

If I am wrong My Dr. Sir blame the weakness of my mind, for I cannot reconcile a contrary conduct to the Dictates of propriety.

I can only say further, that if my fee upon the Execut. can be any relief ags. poor Man, I must request that it be not levied—

Wishing you all health & happiness & a pleasant journey allow me to assure you how much I am with the greatest esteem & respect

D Sir Your much obliged most obed & very hubl. sert.

J Hamilton

RC, Johnson Collection, NCSA. Addressed "Mr. Iredell." Endorsed "March 1789. John Hamilton."

---

[1]Hamilton and JI appear to have both represented the executors of the estate of Nehemiah Bateman of Edenton. Hamilton was also the attorney for Patrick Garvey of Hertford County in a suit against Wyatt Hawkins, who was represented by JI. *Nehemiah Bateman's Executors v. Henry Montfort* and *Patrick Garvey v. Wyatt Hawkins*, May 1788, Edenton District Superior Court, Trial, Reference, and New Docket Action, 1783-1793, State Archives; Legal Fee Books, vol. 6, James Iredell Papers, Southern Historical Collection.

To Hannah Iredell

Hillsborough April 11th. 1789.

My dear Hannah,

I was highly rejoiced at the sight of Mr. Wills, and the receipt of your agreeable letter by him, and those of my other Friends. Thank God, that you were all so well, and that our dear little Boy had cut two of his teeth so easily. I congratulate you upon it with my whole soul, and hope we may now flatter ourselves that he will in general cut the remainder easily too. I hope by this time Mrs. Johnston is a great deal better, It would have made me very unhappy to have known of her being so ill, without knowing at the same time that she was getting better. I never had my health better in my life than I have had it ever since I left home, and have now great reason to be pleased that I came up here, for I have tried both Mr. Pollok's suit and Mr. Moore's, and gained them both, so that this will be the last time of my attending the Court.[1] Mr. Hooper has been in such indifferent health, that he could not attend the Court but a day or two, so that had I not been here Mr. Moore's suit would certainly not have been tried, & perhaps Mr. Pollok's, which would have mortified and embarrassed me extremely. Mrs. Hooper and Miss Betsey are quite well. Tom is with a Gentleman at Fayette, and the eldest Son William is with his Uncle George at Wilmington.[2] I intend to leave this on Monday. Mrs. and Miss Hooper are not to be down this Spring. A day or two before I came up the Phaeton met with an accident by which it was broke all to pieces. Miss Hooper and Miss Hogg were in it, but fortunately escaped without any hurt.[3] This unavoidably prevents it, tho' otherwise I believe Mr. H. had not intended to go, notwithstanding he himself was I believe anxious about it. Tell my dear Annie, I am very happy to hear she is so well and so good, and that I long greatly to see her. Kiss her and her lovely Brother most tenderly for me. Heaven grant I may find you all well. Adieu, my dear Hannah, and be assured

I am ever Your most affectionate

Ja. Iredell.

RC, Johnson Collection, NCSA. Addressed "Mrs. Iredell Edenton."

---

[1]Cullen Pollock won an ejectment suit against Jesse Thomas and Peter Mallett on April 3. Hillsborough District Superior Court, Minute Docket, 1789-1793, State Archives.

No record of a case involving a Mr. Moore has been found.

[2]William (b. 1768), Elizabeth "Betsy" (b. 1770), and Thomas (b. ca. 1772) were the children of William and Anne Clark Hooper. George Hooper was William's brother. *DNCB*, s.v. "Hooper, William," "Hooper, George."

[3]A phaeton is a four-wheeled carriage usually with a retractable roof and no doors. The design was introduced about 1735. *19th Century American Carriages: Their Manufacture, Decoration and Use* (Stony Brook, N.Y.: Museums of Stony Brook, 1987), 16, 113.

Miss Hogg was either Helen or Robina, both daughters of James Hogg of Hillsborough. *Life and Times of James Hogg*, 21.

To Hannah Iredell

Halifax April 20. 1789.

My dear Hannah,

I thank you for your agreeable letter by Mr. Black, which gave me great satisfaction. Happy indeed I was to hear that you and my lovely Children, and the rest were so well. I continue quite well myself. A few days I was a little indisposed, but not much, & am now perfectly well. Don't distrust my sincerity, for I assure you it was not so at any time I mentioned my being in good health. Tomorrow Baker's Cause is to come on, and I dread it much. I inclose you a trifle of money. I wish I could send more, & am extremely sorry you were left so bare. Tell my dear Annie & James how I long to see them. Give each of them a few kisses for me, and believe me ever,

my dear Hannah, Most affectionately yours

Ja. Iredell.

RC, Johnson Collection, NCSA.

From John Rutherford

Wilmington 22d. April 1789

Sir

I take the liberty upon the acquaintance you have honored me with to beg <you> /the/ favor of you to use your interest in a business which will probably come before the Governor in Council.—The case is that of Mr. John Bradley who unfortunately killed Mr. Swann.[1]—He means to make application to the Governor for a pardon.—And, though I esteemed Mr. Swann; yet I cannot help feeling for the distressed situation of this young man, who is not only a peaceable and well disposed citizen, but has really had a great deal of merit, in supporting a Mother & Brother & Several Sisters, in ease and comfort, by his industry.—Mr. Bradley has sent testimonials of his conduct in that affair to His Excellency, which you will no doubt see. I would willingly hope the case may appear to you such as will merit the clemency of Government, and that you would use that confidence, which you so justly possess, to relieve a distressed family—

I am sensible the liberty I have taken, in obtruding myself upon you in this business, is beyond what I have any right to do—But as your opinion may materially affect Mr. Bradley, and the private traits in a mans character in a case of this kind, I should suppose, in a great measure guide the decision—these circumstances, which appear to me to do honor to the unfortunate party, may have some weight with you—

I must however beg the favor of you not to let this go any further, as it may procure me enemies in this quarter, who may very materially injure me—

With best respects to Mrs. Iredell believe me with very great esteem

Sir Your Most Obedient humble Servant

Jn Rutherfurd

RC, Iredell Papers, Duke. Printed, McRee, 2:256-257. Addressed "James Iredell Esquire Edenton." Endorsed "Wilmington 22 April 1789. John Rutherfurd. Ansd."

[1]For more information on this case, see Archibald Maclaine to JI, July 11, 1787, n. 5, and January 20, 1789, in this volume.

To Hannah Iredell

Halifax April 28. 1789.

My dear Hannah,

Thank God this is the last day of the Court, though I am hurried to death. I am in the fashion of almost every body, have got a bad Cold, but it is much better to day. I don't expect I can leave this till tomorrow afternoon, so don't expect me till Friday.[1] Give my tenderest love to my dear Children, and remember me very affectionately to the Girls & my Brother &c &c Pardon my hurry. It is unavoidable. On Friday I hope to assure you personally how much I am,

My dear Hannah, Ardently & affectionately yours

Ja. Iredell.

P.S. Your Brother & Mr. Dawson are just gone, the latter quite well, your Brother tolerably so. But I shall be home first, I believe.

RC, Johnson Collection, NCSA. Addressed "Mrs. Iredell Edenton By favor of Mr. Mc.Culloh."

[1]Friday would have been May 1, indicating an expected travel time from Halifax to Edenton of approximately two days.

From Samuel Johnston[1]

Edenton 5th. May. 1789.

Sir

Colo. Thomas informs me that he has received all the Accounts and Vouchers of this State against the United States which were not taken by Mr. Winder, and that he is now waiting in this Town to receive instructions relative to their transportation to New York, and money to defray the Expence of such Transportation.[2]

It therefore becomes my duty to call the Council to meet at [*torn*] as possible. I have accordingly appointed [*torn*] 7th. of this Instant for the Council to take this business under their Consideration and hope it will be conveinent for you to Attend.

I am with great Consideration & Regard

Sir Your most Obedient Servant.

Sam Johnston

RC, Iredell Papers, Duke. Addressed "Honorable James Iredell Esquire Edenton."

---

[1]This letter is not in Samuel Johnston's handwriting.

[2]Abishai Thomas was the state's representative in negotiations to settle North Carolina's accounts with the U.S. government. William Winder, an agent appointed by Congress, represented the U.S. government. Clark, *State Records*, 21:440. See also Samuel Johnston to JI, December 23, 1788, n. 1, in this volume.

From Arthur Iredell

Guildford May 5th. 1789.[1]

My dear James

I have to thank you for a Letter dated the 2nd. Feby. The Accounts it brought were in general good ones, and tho I felt much for Mrs. Blair's & Tom's Indispositions, I was heartily thankfull that you, and your more immediate Connections were so perfectly well. Annie I have long been in Love with; but my little James is a greater Favourite, if possible, because I anticipate in him all the merit and Virtues of his Father; which, believe me, tho contrary to the established Mode of wishing, will be a very sufficient Share for him—I would compound for it, as his Uncle & Godfather, aye tho he were, what he may be, my adopted Son.

The Accounts you had of our King were both founded—His Death was reported & believed within an Inch of the Palace where he was confined;

and his Insanity was at last avowed. He has had, however, a most surprizing Escape, and is now, as to his Mind, as well as ever he was in his Life—nay Lord Onslow told me Yesterday he thought it in a better State than he ever knew it in; for that, before his Indisposition, he was too much agitated in his Manner, and used to speak in a very hurrying way, for ever repeating, "what what what &c" but that, since that Time, he has been perfectly calm & collected. He was with him two Days ago, and he then talked both in a jocose & serious Way, and /in/ each with the strictest Propriety. However, he says, his Health is by no means so strong as he could wish it to be, which he attributes to the Anxiety he has for ever on his Mind on account of his Son's Opposition to him in Politicks.[2] You will hear a thousand Reports of his being to go this Summer to Hanover, but not one of them will be true, tho they are generally believed here. Ld. Onslow assured me that it was quite certain he would not go this year.[3]

Your Friend Burke has been getting into another of his Scrapes—His Imagination for ever gets the better of his Judgement, or rather, he has no Judgement at all, out of his Closet. In one of his late Speeches to the H of Lords, as leading Manager of Hastings's Prosecution, he ran riot in Abuse; Hastings petitioned the House, & Pitt, with the Indian Squad (which he dare not disoblige) is now pursuing him to Censure—Some People think they will succeed; and, if they should, that the Managers will throw up their Briefs in disgust, and the Prosecution terminate prematurely. In that Case, I for one shall know what to think of Mr. Hastings; but I own I am of a different Opinion.[4]

I laughed immoderately at the Expence of Iredellshire—and I beg you will send Me a very particular account of that respectable District, to which I feel nearly allied.[5] To be serious, it was a most flattering Testimony of publick regard to you, my dear Brother; and it gives me (who have not the meanest Opinion of you) a very high one indeed of the People who have conferred It. For my Part, I feel [*torn*] to you for giving an Eclat to our Na[*torn*] knows how it might otherwise have acquired—My Mother, I fancy, will write for herself by this Packet. She has got into a better Situation by far than She had before, where She lodges & boards; her Health too is better than it was. I am, I thank God, in every Respect better than I was when I last wrote to You, and with my most Affectionate Regards to all your dear Connections, & in particular to my Sister & Tom,

I am ever Your's

A I

Tell Tom that Hunter has got a Company in the Surry Militia.

RC, Johnson Collection, NCSA. Printed, McRee, 2:257-258. Addressed "James Iredell Esqre. Edenton North Carolina America."

---

[1]McRee erroneously dates this letter May 30, 1789. McRee, *Life and Correspondence*, 2:257.

[2]For more information on the king's breakdown, see Nathaniel Dukinfield to JI, February 4, 1789, n. 1, in this volume.

[3]George III did not go to Hanover during the summer of 1789. Instead he traveled to his brother's seaside home in Weymouth. Christopher Hibbert, *George III: A Personal History* (London: Viking, 1998), 304.

[4]For more information on Edmund Burke and the Hastings case, see Arthur Iredell to JI, February 21, 1786, n. 4, in this volume.

[5]Arthur is referring to the creation of Iredell County, N.C.

From Tristrim Lowther

New York 9th. May 1789

Dear Sir

I arrived here on saturday last after a very tedious & disagreable passage of fourteen days which was so contrary to my expectations that it required some exertion of patience to support & was more particularly to be regretted as it deprived me of an oppy: of seeing the ceremony of administring the oath to the President of the United States which took place amidst the acclamations of thousands the day before my arrival.[1] since which time I have constantly attended the debates of the House of Representatives & have received great pleasure from observing the great liberality of sentiment & spirit of mutual concession which appears from their debates to actuate every member of the House & I have not observed the least attempt to create a party or to divide the house by setting up the southern in opposition to the eastern interest except in <the> a Mr. Jackson from Georgia the violence of whose passions sometimes hurries him into expressions which have or appear to have such a tendency.[2] the members all appear to be very able able men particularly a Mr. Ames from Massachusetts who notwithstanding he is a very young man appears in my humble opinion to deliver his sentiments with the greatest ease the most propriety & in the most elegant language of any man in the House of Representatives[3] as for Mr. Madison of whom I had formed the highest expectations I have had very little oppy of forming an opinion for whenever he has spoke while I have been attending it has been in so low a tone of voice that I cou'd not well distinguish what he said his voice appears to be too defective to appear to advantage [*in*] so large a room however I shall be better able [*to judge*] when he brings forward his motion for considering that article of the constitution respecting amendments which he intends doing on the fourth monday of this month[4] this has excited general expectation tho it appears to be the general opinion of people out of doors that nothing will be done in it & is the more probable from the debates which took place when Col Bland <der> presented the application of the Virginia Legislature when it was strongly contended by Mr. Boudinott late President of Congress & supported by a number of other Members that the application shou'd be laid on the table & that the Congress ought not to take notice of any such applications untill they were made by the number of States required by the Constitution[5]—It is still uncertain & will remain so untill the 17th. who will be Governor of this State but it is imagined that the present one will be continued for his friends have /found/ means to persuade the people of the southern District that he was always opposed to the confiscation Laws & to the partial tax which has procured [*torn*] him a number of partizans & the popularity [*torn*] of Col. Hamilton has been hurt by his declining to represent this District in Congress[6] it is supposed he looks up to be financier general for which he has been preparing himself or to /be/ appointed a forreign ambassador for either of which he /is/ extremely well qualified. he is said & believed to be a man of such extraordinary powers as to be able to render himself master of any subject in a week Remember me Dear Sir in the most respectful manner to Mrs. Iredell & the rest of your amiable family & believe me to be with sentiments of the highest respect & regard

Your much obliged & humble Servt.

T. Lowther

RC, Johnson Collection, NCSA. Printed, McRee, 2:258-259. Addressed "The Honble. James Iredell Esqr. Edenton."

---

[1]Washington's inauguration took place on April 30, 1789.

[2]James Jackson (1757-1806) was a planter, lawyer, and veteran of the Revolutionary War. He served in the U.S. House of Representatives (1789-1791), the U.S. Senate (1793-1795, 1801-1806), and as governor of Georgia (1798-1801). Jackson had a volatile personality. He fought a number of duels, including one in which he killed the lieutenant governor of Georgia. *DAB*, s.v. "Jackson, James"; *BDC*, s.v. "Jackson, James."

[3]Fisher Ames (1758-1808), a Harvard-trained lawyer, was a Federalist delegate to the Massachusetts ratification convention in 1788. In his first bid for Congress, he defeated Samuel Adams and began a congressional career that would last from 1789 to 1797. Even before entering Congress, he had established a reputation as a skilled writer and orator. *DAB*, s.v. "Ames, Fisher"; *BDC*, s.v. "Ames, Fisher."

[4]Since February 1788, James Madison had been promising that he would advocate the addition of a bill of rights to the Constitution. The absence of specific guarantees of individual rights had been the primary objection to the Constitution for many Antifederalists. On May 4, 1789, Madison announced that once the more urgent matters before Congress were resolved, he would introduce a list of amendments. He did so on June 8, rather than the fourth Monday in May. By the end of the first session in September 1789, two-thirds of both houses supported twelve amendments. Ralph Ketcham, *James Madison: A Biography* (New York: Macmillan Company, 1971), 289-291. For the text of Madison's resolution, including the amendments, see De Pauw et al., *Documentary History of the First Federal Congress,* 4:9-12.

[5]Theodorick Bland (1742-1790) was a physician trained in Edinburgh, an officer during the Revolution, and a member of the Continental Congress (1780-1783). In addition, Bland served as an Antifederalist delegate to the Virginia ratification convention and as a member of the U.S. House of Representatives (1789-1790). Bland presented the Virginia application to Congress on May 5, 1789. *BDC*, s.v. "Bland, Theodorick." For the text of the Virginia proposal, see De Pauw et al., *Documentary History of the First Federal Congress*, 4:15-19.

Elias Boudinot (1740-1821), a New Jersey attorney, served in the Continental Congress (1778, 1781-1783) and as president of the Congress (1782-1783). He was also a member of the U.S. House of Representatives (1789-1795) and later director of the U.S. mint (1795-1805). *BDC*, s.v. "Boudinot, Elias."

[6]For information on the New York gubernatorial election, see Hugh Williamson to JI, March 2, 1789, n. 3, in this volume.

To Hannah Iredell

Newbern Sunday Evening May 24.

My dear Hannah,

After waiting most impatiently for the Post, which ought to have arrived yesterday evening and did not till this, I have just received your kind letter, for which I am much obliged to you—I am very sorry to hear Mrs. Pollok is so ill, & greatly distrest that Mr. Hooper continues so much dejected. Give my love most tenderly to my dear Children, & remember me very affectionately to all the rest of the Family, & Mr. Johnston's. And please to give my best respects to D. Williamson—I hope earnestly to meet you at Skewawky. I am much better than when I left home. Adieu! my dear Hannah, & be assured I am ever

Most affectionately yours

Ja. Iredell

RC, Johnson Collection, NCSA. Addressed "Mrs. Iredell Edenton." Endorsed "Newbern 24th. May 1789. Ja. Iredell."

From Anne Hooper

Hillsborough, June 2d, '89.

Dear Sir:

With your usual humanity and goodness, which interest you in the distresses of your friends, you communicated to us in the tenderest manner Mr. Hooper's indisposition. I dreaded it when he left us; but he gave us such flattering accounts from Edenton that we began to be quite easy. I sent Billy to assist his father in his return, which, by this time we hope, he will be enabled to effect. How shall I express my gratitude to you, sir, for your assiduous attention to him, and your tenderness to the whole family? Be assured we all feel it in the most sensible manner; and pray that you and yours may find at all times, but particularly in the hour of distress, so cordial, benevolent, and disinterested a friend, whose heart entering into your suffering, will mitigate it with so lenient a hand. I rely upon your information, convinced that as you are aware that a deception in so interesting a situation as ours would be only increasing our affliction at a future period, you would not beguile us. I hope for the best; and that his present illness may make him more attentive to his health, as well in consideration to his friends as on his own account, in which case, sir, I will still flatter myself that some event will enable us to spend many more agreeable and happy hours in your society and that of your virtuous and amiable family. My best respects wait on Mrs. Iredell. Believe me ever, dear sir, with the greatest esteem and respect,

Your obliged and grateful servant,

Anne Hooper.

Printed, McRee, 2:259-260.

From William R. Davie

[*Halifax June 4h. 1789.*]

Dear Sir,

I have not heard from you since you left this place, and as I shall leave this place for Newbern about the 12h. of this Month, it becomes necessary that the debates, should be here if possible before that time. You are sensible as well as myself how important the sale is to <u>us</u> as the expence will ultimately & entirely fall upon us—The books can't be sold, and the money collected in time to fulfill your engagement with the Printer, so that we shall have the money to advance with out any doubt.[1]

The Anties here were remarking with great triumph the fulfilment of their [*pro*]fecies with respect to Congress never taking up the subject of Amendments; when we critically received an Account of Mr. Madisons notification that he would move this subject, nothing ever gave me so much pleasure—and this coming from a Federalist has Confounded the Anties exceedingly.[2]

My Compts. to the Govr. and my friends I hope you had a healthy and lucrative exercise and believe me as usual

yours very sincerely

W R Davie

RC, Iredell Papers, Duke. Printed, McRee, 2:260. Addressed "The Honle. James Iredell Esqr. Edenton By Mr. Smith."

---

[1]See William R. Davie to JI, November 1788, n. 2, in this volume.

[2]See Tristrim Lowther to JI, May 9, 1789, n. 4, in this volume.

To John G. Blount[1]

Edenton June 6. 1789.

Dear Sir,

I received your favour of the 4th. Inst. I was aware of some difficulties in an application in McConnell's Case to the Court of Admiralty, and at length advised him to sue only on the Bond, which secures the payment of treble costs. I accordingly issued a Writ against Pearson. The Penalty of the Bond is £500. but as it is only to secure a prosecution of the Appeal & treble Costs in case of condemnation I don't imagine more than treble Costs can be recovered, and those I presume taxed Costs according to the Law in that particular governing the Courts. I am very much concerned that Mr. Scott should understand me that the whole Penalty at all events might be recovered, which I never thought, the Penalty being now to be considered as Security for the treble Costs only. And that must have been what I intended, however my expression might have been misunderstood.

I was very glad to finish the business of the commission, and the additional trouble of staying half a day was of little consequence compared to the importance of that which I should have been sorry to have been the cause of delaying, especially when you and your Brother had so obligingly consulted my convenience.

I am, Dear Sir, with great regard, Your obedient Servant

Ja. Iredell.

RC, Blount Papers, NCSA. Printed, *John Gray Blount Papers*, 1:484-485.

[1]John Gray Blount (1752-1833), along with his brothers, Thomas and William, had diverse business interests, including a mercantile company and vast landholdings. Blount represented Beaufort County in the house of commons (1782-1789, 1793-1794) and the senate (1794-1796). As a delegate to the 1788 and 1789 conventions, he supported ratification. In his later years he served on the Council of State (1830-1831). *DNCB*, s.v. "Blount, John Gray"; Cheney, *North Carolina Government*, 175, 209-234 passim; Massengill, *North Carolina Votes*, 6.

From William R. Davie

Newbern July 1t. 1789

My dear Sir,

I have been here and in Beaufort thence three weeks past, having w[*aited*] with anxiety, before I left Halifax s[*everal*] days for the Arrival of the debates. I perceive by your letter to Mr. Sitgreaves you have forwarded 40 [*co*]pies to my care—supposing they w[*ill*] probably be sent in my absence [*I*] mentioned the matter to Mr. Kinchen authorising him to open your let[*ter*] to me, and do whatever you re[*com*]mended—and in order to affect [*it I*] left with him £5 to hire an ex[*port*] to carry those destined for the upper [*dis*]tricts—All which he assured Me [*to*] be punctually executed, and those [*in*] Halifax District immediately [*ini*]tiated for sale—I am [*torn*] the proportion allotted for this District and Wilm[*ington*] cannot be immediately sent on, as the sale [*has*] become more and more dull, and the cri[*torn*] of election being the moment for sale. [*I*] hope you will devise some means that [*torn*] Gentlemen here and Mr. Jno. G. Blount [*torn*] Washington to have them sent forward I know my friend you are already weary of this let[*ter*] and the trouble you have already had—but [*torn*] is an important matter <u>to us</u>.

[*I s*]pent eight days very agreeably at Beaufort [*torn*] some benefit in point of health. I have been a week here—you know Newbern is [*torn*] very temple of dulness—and will expect the [*illegible*] is growing fast [*illegible*] however [*torn*] out tomorrow and hope to leave it all be[*torn*]

My most respectful Compliments to the Gove[*rnor*] and your family and believe me [*with*] the most sincere esteem

Your hum Ser[*vt.*]

<u>William R. D[*avie*]</u>

RC, Iredell Papers, Duke. Addressed "The Honble. James Iredell, Esqr. Edenton." Endorsed "Newbern July 1st. 1789. W. R. Davie. Ansd."

To John G. Blount

Edenton July 1st. 1789.

Dear Sir,

I have received your favour of the 26th., and hope to avail of the opportunity you have been so obliging as to acquaint me with by forwarding you about 100 Copies.[1] Of those you will please to retain what you think proper for Washington, and transmit the remainder when you can to Mr. Sitgreaves. He is entitled to ten more for the Newbern Subscribers, and Mr. Maclaine to fourteen more for those at Wilmington. The rest are for sale. Colo. Davie and myself proposed allowing a Commission for <allowing> the trouble of selling &c. The management of this at Washington I beg leave to submit to you, as you shall think proper. If any are sold at Washington, I will be much obliged to you if out of the sales you will give such a gratuity for the trouble of conveying them there as you shall think sufficient.

Your Brother Jacob returned in perfect health a few days ago.[2] Steele had returned, having done nothing, the Indians saying we were no People, having no head, and that they would not treat with us.[3] Such was the report your Brother heard.

I am, Dear Sir, Yours very respectfully

Ja. Iredell

RC, Blount Papers, NCSA. Printed, *John Gray Blount Papers*, 1:490-491.

---

[1]JI is referring to copies of the debates that had been printed by Hodge and Wills in June 1789.

[2]Jacob Blount (1760-1801) as a young man was employed in the Blount family mercantile business. After marrying Nancy Collins, daughter of Josiah Collins, on February 22, 1789, he moved to Edenton and worked for his father-in-law. Keith, *Blount Papers*, 1:xxvii-xxviii; *State Gazette of North-Carolina* (Edenton), February 26, 1789.

[3]On November 29, 1788, the General Assembly appointed John Steele to lead a commission to negotiate with Native Americans in the western part of the state. In June 1789, the commissioners waited for twelve days along the French Broad River to rendezvous with Cherokee leaders, but they failed to appear. Clark, *State Records*, 20:568; Wagstaff, *Papers of John Steele*, 1:50.

From Tristrim Lowther

New York 1st. July 1789

Dear Sir

I had the pleasure of receiving your favor by Capt. Swift & the debates by Mr. Black who arrived here three days ago for which I beg leave to return you my acknowledgments. it gives me great satisfaction to hear that the Judges are becoming more liberal in their determinations, as I am well convinced it will have the most beneficial effects on our trade a few more such judgments wou'd tend to reestablish the credit of our country for the merchants wou'd not be averse to giving the same credit to the Carolinians which they give to the other states if they were assur'd of recovering the value of their debts in our Courts of justice. I am sure my Father will very much approve of <t>his suit being continued.[1] I hope & trust that your fears respecting the return of Mrs. Dawson & Penny are without foundation & that you will very soon see them return in good spirits & better health than they have enjoyed for many years you wou'd certainly have seen them a month ago but they were strongly disswaded by the Dr. from carrying the child to that warm climate immediately on it's recovery from the hooping cought as it might be attended with the worst consequences.[2] at the same time we are truly sensible of your goodness in so anxiously wishing their return & your generous profers to come for them was the distance no further than Maryland. Inclosed is the draft of a bill for /the/ establishment of the judicial sistem now before the senate it was principally drawn up by a Mr. Elsworth from Connecticut but it is supposed considerable alterations will be made in the bill before it passes both houses[3]

there are not many lawyers in the senate but they compose three fourths of the representatives Present me Dear Sir in the most respectful manner to Mrs. Iredell the Young Ladies & your Brother at whose recovery I very much rejoice & beleive me to be with the greatest sincerity

Your much obliged friend & humble Servt.

T. Lowther

RC, Johnson Collection, NCSA. Printed, McRee, 2:260. Addressed "James Iredell Esqr. Edenton North Carolina." Endorsed "New York 1st. July 1789. T. Lowther. Ansd."

---

[1]In 1787, William Lowther traveled to North Carolina from his home in England to seek, unsuccessfully as it turned out, compensation for his confiscated property. The suit mentioned in this letter was probably a continuation of these

efforts. Loyalist Claim of William Lowther, English Records, Audit Office Papers, State Archives. See also Tristrim Lowther to JI, July 4, 1785, n. 1, in this volume.

[2]Penny Dawson was the wife of Tristrim Lowther.

[3]This refers to the Judiciary Act of 1789. Sen. Oliver Ellsworth headed the Senate committee responsible for writing the bill, and he is credited with being the primary author. While Article 3 of the Constitution states that "the judicial Power of the United States, shall be vested in one supreme Court, and in such inferior Courts as the Congress may from time to time ordain and establish," few details are offered. The Judiciary Act of 1789 provided many of the missing particulars, such as the number of Supreme Court justices and the organization and jurisdiction of district and circuit courts. The law also did much to establish the supremacy of the federal judiciary over state courts. Kelly and Harbison, *American Constitution*, 162-163; William Garrett Brown, *The Life of Oliver Ellsworth* (New York: Macmillan, 1905), 184-186. For the legislative history of the Judiciary Act of 1789, see De Pauw et al., *Documentary History of the First Federal Congress*, 5:1150-1212.

From Baron de Poellnitz

New York 8th. of July 1789

Dear Sir.

Great as there is, and Always will be the Satisfaction of myne to Keep up a Corespondance with You Sir, I do not wish to be troublesome, So as to divert you to often by it from that Time which you employe So Usefully for to promote the Satisfaction and felicity of Your Countrymen—But as this very instant I have had at my House Mr. Scott who informes me that he has to Day an opportunity of a Vessel going to Nd. Ca. I can not resist the Temptation to beg the favour to Send me those of Your performances upon the federal Govr'mt. who are printed, and of which you /make/ Mention in your last, in returne to which I beg to accept <g> a Exampl<es>r. of Hamlt*s*. federalist, which even, Tho no doubt you have, may be Usefull /in duplo/ to be put in hands of Some of the Unbelievers[1]—

We are /put/ in heigh Spirits <from> /by/ the Expectations that Your State will Soon joine Our happy Union, and I Think the most Sanguine Hopes of Success may be rationally entretained, in Consequence of the enlightened Exertions of His Exelley. Johnson and his, and your friends; to the former Honble—Gentlemn. I beg my most humble respects, and pray Assure His Exellcy; that I Shall for ever greatefully acknowledge the Gracious reception given to me whils't I was at Edentons; I beg also my Humble Compliments to Mistrs. Iredell and to Excuse this Scrawl wrote for want of Time in great haste, believe me

Dear Sir respectfully, your most Obdt. humbl. Servt.

F. C. H. B. Poellnitz

RC, Iredell Papers, Duke. Addressed "To J. Iredell Esqr. Edentons North Carolina." Endorsed "New York 8th. July 1789. Baron De Poellnitz. <Ansd. But still to be attended to.> Ansd."[2]

---

[1]See JI to Baron de Poellnitz, April 15, 1788, in this volume. The baron is referring to JI's "Answers to Mr. Mason's Objections."

[2]See JI to Baron de Poellnitz, July 25, 1789, in this volume.

To Henry E. McCulloh

[*Edenton*] July 11.

Dear Sir,

I recd. your favour of the 18th. Feb. <in the midst of my Circuit, at the conclusion of which I intended answering it particularly>, but being then upon my Circuit could not conveniently answer it.[1] I intended doing so <but> however soon after the conclusion of it, but my poor Children have been lately at the point of death, and the youngest (a very fine Boy about 8 months /old/) is still extremely ill, so that you must excuse my <writing now a very short letter> deferring a particular answer to another oppertunity, I <am> now draw on you by Mr. Stott's desire for your Son George. The particulars of this and other accounts I will give you when my mind is more composed than it is at present Mr. Stott informed G. of the sum he is limited to. He principally regretted it on account of the retrospect having /(besides other little expences)/ in particular been obliged to purchase another horse, his <tho> /former/ unfortunately having died owing to an accident. I desired him to acquaint you of this circumstance, believing that you would make him an allowance /at least/ for this article of expence, which I believe was merely owing to a misfortune. As you limit him to a certain sum I don't see the necessity of my drawing for it. The prospect of the Law here is at present very gloomy indeed, & extremely discouraging to young Men, only one Lawyer being allowed to speak of a side. Neither G. nor my Brother are at present defraying their expences of attending Courts. <& observance of expences is extremely high.> This has sometimes induced George to think of trying his fortune in the new County to the Westward, if you approved of it and thought proper to give him something sufficient to set him up there.[2] It is a county where many are now pushing their fortunes, and I am told a very advantageous one for a Lawyer. and really here his situation is discouraging, his unavoidable expences being heavy & his prospects /of the future/ not flattering enough to <encourage him with any considerable hope> atone for present disappointments—I am very sorry the Certificates did not answer nor can conceive why they should not be of the least avail. I intend sending you by a Capt. Clark from here going immediately to Scotland & from thence to England the Vouchers of the payments to H. M. Children &c[3] In fear of an accident I have got the originals registered; tho' our Law concerning R. does not seem to respect cases of this kind. I brought a Suit against Montfort to last Halifax April Court, and he has put in all the dilatory pleas he could.[4] One is, with respect to the capacity of suing, notwithstanding the T. of P., and an act of Assembly made expressly to confirm it as to its operation in our Courts.[5] The suit is in the names of N. M. &C <have not yet recd. the securities from> <recd. the papers from Mr. D. though I requested they might be forwarded to me thro' Mr. Stott as Mr. D. should think best.[6] /I am very sorry you are likely to be /so/ involved <in> /with/ that Debt of Montfort's/ I have not yet been able to find out if any old proc is to be had.> As it was of no other use, the whole or the greatest part of it has probably been paid in Taxes. The Cash value here was 800 per £, and now <it is no Tender at all, so that> /I imagine/ if such a Bond was sued in this Country such money would be no discharge of it. <Our present Current money </in point of law/> is deemed equal to the former Proclamation> Money <it is equal value> (I will endeavour as soon as I can to get you an attested Copy of the Act you wish for, tho' Mr. S. lives so inconveniently it is difficult to get <things> papers from him without an express.) <In case of our accession to the new Constitution I should suppose Mr. Cornell's Rep. might sue for the Bond in this Country, either in one of our own State Courts, or such Federal Judiciary Court as we might be subject to. The nature & number of these is not yet ascertained. I <may> mean if they have not already obtained a Judgment & Satisfaction against you. In case of joint Obligers in this respect, our Case is exactly the same with that of England.>[7]

Mentioned I thought I had wrote to D. but possibly had omitted it. Would, & mention about Agnew's Bond &c.

Mistook the meaning, I believe about Cornell's Bond. In my letter wrote in respect to the Confiscation Subject principally, which I suppose was intended.

FC, Johnson Collection, NCSA. Endorsed "Substance of the material parts of a Letter wrote to Mr. Mc.Culloh July 11th. 1789."

---

[1]See Henry E. McCulloh to JI, February 18, 1789, in this volume.

[2]JI is probably referring to Iredell County, which had been created in 1788.

[3]"H M" is Henry McCulloch. See Henry E. McCulloh to JI, February 20, 1784, n. 17, in this volume.

[4]For more information on the financial and legal relationship between Henry Montfort and Henry E. McCulloh, see Henry E. McCulloh to JI, February 20, 1784, and February 18, 1789, in this volume.

[5]"T. of P." is the treaty of peace.

[6]"Mr. D" is probably Alexander Diack.

[7]For information on the Cornell case, see Henry E. McCulloh to JI, February 18, 1789, in this volume.

To George Macartney

[*Edenton*] July 15th, '89.

My Lord:

Since your lordship's arrival in England, of which I heard with very great pleasure, I have several times had an inclination to take the liberty of writing you, being persuaded that the same goodness which formerly induced such extreme kindness to me, would still influence you to hear with some satisfaction of my present situation, which, though not free from some embarrassments, is on the whole respectable and happy. I was the more desirous of acquainting you of this, because it was owing to your generous influence that I was originally fixed here; and I can assure your lordship that the uncommon obligations I owe you, not only for your frequent and kind applications in my behalf, but more particularly for your obliging personal attention to myself, have never been absent from my memory. Never shall I forget the readiness with which your lordship, though only in London to stay two days took the trouble to devote a considerable part of that valuable time to me and my concerns! and even to call upon me personally on the subject! But, my lord, great as these obligations were, and little as I thought they could be enhanced, how much have they been increased by your noble bounty to my mother, and kindness to my brother since. Permit me to assure you that I never have regretted my poverty on my own account so much as that I could not devote annually a sufficient sum for the support of my excellent mother, or even offer her any occasional relief, but such as must have appeared paltry indeed. God, who sees my heart, knows with what cheerfulness I would have done more, had it been in my power. Unhappy in being able to do so little! accustomed to find little more in my power than to sympathize, with the strongest feelings of my soul, in every emotion of gratitude to you and other generous friends, for every assistance she received. Among these, with what sincerity, what gratitude, and what respect, shall I not ever remember your truly noble relation, Miss Catharine Macartney, of whose death I heard with the most poignant grief. And permit me, my lord, to say that I feel infinitely more strongly than I can express, that greatness and goodness of mind with which Lady Macartney has seconded your generous and extraordinary exertions in my mother's favor. May Heaven for ever bless you both! and long preserve you for the mutual comfort of each other! Rejoiced I indeed am, that, amidst the great honors and universal applause you so deservedly have acquired, you have been so happy as to be allied to a lady whose soul seems so well fitted to your own.

Before I conclude, I think it my duty to mention one thing to your lordship, lest you should suppose I had acted in any manner unworthy of the recommendation your lordship was pleased to give me. In the course of the American war, I took the American side of the question, and I confess, warmly; but I took no active part until long after all exercise of my office was rendered absolutely impracticable, and independence had been in fact declared. Being then at liberty, I chose my side according to the best of my judgment, and I certainly did so very disinterestedly, as no man could suffer more by the war than I did. I knew your lordship's sentiments on the subject and mine totally differed; but I am also assured your lordship has too much dignity of mind to condemn any man for the part he takes in a civil war, if he selects his side honestly, and upon due deliberation; and in no instance of his conduct afterwards violates those principles of honor and humanity, which are indispensable in every situation in life.

I shall esteem it as a particular favor if you will do me the honor to present me to Lady Macartney, as a man who feels the utmost gratitude for her extreme goodness to my mother, and who will be ever deeply interested in hers, as well as your lordship's happiness. I am, &c.,

Jas. Iredell.

Printed, McRee, 2:261-262.

From Samuel Johnston

Edenton 22d. July 1789—

Sir

A person is now attending from New York with a Credit from the Commissioners of the Treasury, desirous of purchasing the whole of the public Tobacco.[1] he refuses to give the price to which I am limited by the Council, and is to lay his proposals before me to morrow, which I think it my duty to communicate to the Council, whom I have appointed to meet on Wednesday the 29th. Instant.

As this is a Business of great importance to the State, I hope it will be convenient to you to attend.

I am with great Consideration & Respect

Sir Your most Obedient Servant

Sam Johnston

RC, Iredell Papers, Duke. Addressed "The Honorable James Iredell Esquire Edenton."

---

[1]In 1785, the General Assembly authorized the state to buy tobacco and then resell it to raise funds to pay the state's debts. An amendment added more specific language to the measure in 1786. According to that amendment, the original legislation was "expressed in terms altogether uncertain and insufficient to answer the purpose thereby intended." Clark, *State Records*, 24:724, 812-813. See also Archibald Maclaine to Samuel Johnston, December 24, 1785, n. 2, in this volume.

To Pierce Butler

[*July 25, 1789*]

Dear Sir,

I had very great concern in observing sometime ago that you had met with an accident in riding out, but I have had the satisfaction to hear since you were pretty well /recovered/ & that Mr. Hayes, who appears to have been much worse hurt, was likely to recover also. I do assure you, Sir, I still recollect with as much pleasure as ever the happiness & honour of your acquaintance, though I am afraid the miscarriage of one or two letters I wrote you may have induced you to think <me more inattentive to it> /me less sensible of the value of it/ than I am ever capable of being. I rejoice, not only that the new government is in motion, but that you have a share in conducting it, flattering myself it is a situation personally agreeable to you as well as highly useful to your Country.[1] I can scarcely permit myself to doubt that the extreme obstinacy of our People will last longer than Nov. next, when our new Convention is to meet, especially should capital amendments be proposed, which I think would have a most happy effect upon them. I do not mean amendments that would weaken any essential power (for in my opinion your strength is not an atom too much), but such /principally/ as shall tend to obviate their fears of abuse by a misconstruction of the powers granted. Besides these, possibly 2 or 3 obnoxious powers may be modified without much injury. God grant the proposition may come in time for us. Possibly the adoption or non adoption of this State may depend upon that very measure, & if we do not adopt then God Almighty knows what will become of us, or whether we shall be ever in the Union. The degree of anarchy we shall be thrown into may be attended with irremediable Evil, I dread to think of.

I am so happy now as to have two lovely Children, one a Daughter between 3 & 4 years old, the other /a/ Son about 8 months. But both have been lately at the point of death, & we dreaded at one time the loss of both of them together. Thank God, however, they are now pretty well recovered, & our fears for this time are over. We have been very unfortunate

/lately/ in the loss of Mrs. Blair & a very promising Son of hers but 22, whose death I believe principally occasioned his poor Mothers.[2] Mrs. Iredell & /the/ Miss Blairs always remember you with very great pleasure, & desire their most respectful Comps. and I sincerely assure you that

I am ever, my dear Sir with the truest respect, Your faithful & obed. Servt.

J. I.

P.S. I beg the favour of your acceptance of a Copy of the Debates of our Convention.

FC, Johnson Collection, NCSA. Endorsed "Copy of a Letter to Pierce Butler Esqr. July 25th. 1789."

---

[1]Congress convened March 4, 1789. Butler represented South Carolina in the U.S. Senate (1789-1796, 1802-1804). *BDC*, s.v. "Butler, Pierce."

[2]Samuel Blair died in Nixonton in September 1788 after a brief illness. Fouts, *State Gazette of North-Carolina*, 1:7; *State Gazette of North-Carolina* (Edenton), September 22, 1788.

To Baron de Poellnitz

[*July 25, 1789*]

Dear Sir

I had very great pleasure in /receiving/ the letter you did me the honour to write me on the 8th. Inst., and am extremely obliged to you for the Copy of the Federalist which you were so kind as to inclose, a work indeed which I had long seen & read with infinite delight, but I think you have done me a great favour in enabling me to impart the satisfaction of perusing it to some person to whom, its merit strange as it may seem, is hitherto unknown![1] In my opinion, it is <the greatest publicat> /one of the greatest political/ publications which have ever yet appeared in the world, and I am sure it will be read with admiration by every Country in Europe.

What I mentioned in my letter as a <little composition> /publication/ of my own was I believe "Answers to Mr. Mason's Objections," a Copy of which, as you are pleased to desire it, I now inclose you. I wrote one or two other little things on the subject, but have no copies of them by me[2] <and the publication of this in a Pamphlet was entirely the work of the Printer.> My zeal I fear far outran my discretion, for I was fully convinced in my own mind that the fate of America depended on the adoption of the Constitution at that <immediate> /particular/ period, and I had long been ashamed of the disgraceful light in which we appeared, not only to every /other/ Country in the world, but even to ourselves. So that I confess my heart & soul was in the subject, & still is. <I beg your acceptance of a Copy of our Debates>. Every effort will be made to procure the adoption <of> /by/ this State in Nov. next. I think myself unfortunate in not being able to be a Member <myself> but the interests of a great many Clients for whom I am employed render my attendence at some Courts about that time absolutely indispensible. For mere private Interests of my own should prevent me. The governor I believe tho' will be a Member & he is as zealous as myself.[3] He is very much pleased with your kind remembrance of him, and desires me to assure you he <even> ever thinks of you with the greatest respect, & will at all times be happy in hearing of your prosperity.

I shall write immediately to a Gent. at Cape Fear for the particulars you wish to know about Gen Howe's Estate, & <let you know> /inform you/ as soon I can. I can only tell you /<as for> how/ that he was always considered as a Man deeply in debt, & I think it very probable (though I do not know it) that he left his Estate greatly encumbered.[4]

Mrs. Iredell desires me to present you <with> her <most> /very/ respectful Compliments. We are so happy as to have two Children living, a Daughter between 3 & 4 years old, & a Son about 8 months, <but very> both equal to our fondest wishes, but very lately they have been so ill as to be at the point of death. Thank God however, they are now considered quite out of danger. We had the misfortune to lose one, a Son older than either, who tho' a very promising Child died when he was only 3 days old. A most affecting distress when we had been married so long with out any children at all! Presuming your Children, or some of them are with you, I beg to be humbly remembered to them. I recollect the promising qualities of Miss P. with very great pleasure. Be assured, Sir, that at all times I shall receive the highest satisfaction in the honour of a correspondence, <& that conveyed by you I shall esteem myself> /with you,/ <that I shall find the enjoyment of this> which I shall consider <me> a most agreeable relief to the general dullness in which I am deemed to pass my time here, and I sincerely assure you that,

I am, with very great respect, Dear Sir, Your faithful & obed. Ser

J. I.

P.S. I beg the favour of your acceptance of <the> /a/ copy of the Debates of our Convention.

FC, Iredell Papers, Duke. Endorsed "Copy of a Letter to the Baron De Poellnitz July 25th. 1789."

[1]See Baron De Poellnitz to JI, July 8, 1789, in this volume.

[2]JI may be referring to his letter, "To the People of the State of North Carolina," August 18, 1788, in this volume.

[3]Samuel Johnston, who owned property in Perquimans County, represented that county in both state ratification conventions. Massengill, *North Carolina Votes*, 32.

[4]For information on the Howe estate, see Archibald Maclaine to JI, August 11, 1789, in this volume.

From William R. Davie

Tarboro Court. Aug 4h. 1789.

My Dear Sir,

It is to be lamented <in> that in the system of things the very causes of our pleasure, from necessity become the very causes of all our pain & anxiety, but thank God your Children have recovered, and you are not as wretched as I am. my youngest son, on whom I had found many flattering hopes, was snatched from me about a fortnight ago—you have <have> felt the pangs of a parent—and will give me the sympathy of friend—Hyder has also been ill but is now considerably better, and I hope entirely out of danger.[1]

The debates were forwarded immediately by Mr. Kinchin to Hillsboro; the sale is but slow here I hope they will find a greater demand among the Western politicians

I have distributed the few copies of the Address you sent me and I believe they will have a good effect[2]—the politicks of this district begin to assume a federal aspect, & I have some hopes there will be a majority returned in favor of the Constitution

My Compts. to your family and the Governor and believe me with the

most sincere friendship yours & &

W R Davie

RC, Iredell Papers, Duke. Addressed "James Iredell Esqr. Edenton Favd. by Mr. Bond." Endorsed "Tarborough Aug. 4. 1789. W. R. Davie Recd. Aug. 13th."

[1]The name of Davie's youngest son has not been found. Hyder Ali was his second oldest son. *DNCB*, s.v. "Davie, William Richardson."

[2]This probably refers to the address written "To the People of the State of North Carolina," August 18, 1788, in this volume.

From Pierce Butler

New York, August 11, 1789.

My Dear Sir:

I was on Friday last honored with your very kind and very acceptable letter of the 25th of July.[1] I am indeed much gratified by your friendly remembrance of me. I do with truth assure you, that neither time nor a long separation have weakened those strong impressions that the goodness of your heart and the fineness of your feelings made on me in our early acquaintance; but on the contrary, convince me daily of your inestimable worth. I have long considered North Carolina fortunate in claiming you to aid in her councils, and promote her welfare. I am sure, if she is sensible of the justness of your opinions, she will be led to true honor and substantial happiness.

I am unfortunate in the miscarriage of your letters, as the one above referred to is the only one I have received since last February twelve-months. I wrote you then a pretty long letter from Charleston, which I hope got to your hand—I wish to know if it did.

I am truly concerned at the loss your family have sustained in the death of Mrs. Blair and her son. "In every friend we lose, we die."[2] How just the observation! You inform me that your two dear children have been at the point of death. I am only surprised that they have lived so long; and still more so, that you, so attached to a domestic scene, can think of keeping your children in Edenton, where, if I do not greatly mistake, I was assured scarce ever a child was raised to manhood. Why not retire to a more healthy situation? Assuredly Edenton has full seeds of putrefaction in her river and many stagnate ponds.

Am I to hope for the satisfaction of seeing my friend on the floor of the Senate? The Southern interest calls aloud for some such men as Mr. Iredell to represent it—to do it justice. I am almost afraid to enter on the subject of the Constitution, yet I will confess to you, from whom I can conceal nothing, that I am materially disappointed. I find locality and partiality reign as much in our Supreme Legislature as they could in a county court or State legislature. Never was man more egregiously disappointed than I am. I came here full of hopes that the greatest liberality would be exercised; that the consideration of the whole, and the general good, would take place of every other object; but here I find men scrambling for partial advantages, State interests, and in short, a train of those narrow, impolitic measures that must, after a while, shake the Union to its very foundation. I once fondly thought that we should by our example contradict the assertion of Mr. Gillies, the Grecian historian, and evince to the monarchies of the East, and mankind in general, that there can exist such a thing as a free, tranquil, and happy Republic, securing to the individual his dearest rights.[3] But, indeed, I am more than short-sighted if we shall do so, unless we very soon turn from the recent error of our ways, and determine to feel for all alike. I write freely to you, but my opinions are only for you. Perhaps I am something like the fox in the fable, having lost my own tail, I wish North Carolina to do likewise.[4] I confess I wish you to come into the confederacy, as the only chance the Southern interest has to preserve a balance of power. Col. Davie and Mr. Williamson can witness for me that I was strongly federal; and that I conceded many points for the purpose of bringing about the Union, and a form of government less exceptionable than that of the old Confederation, where every power was centred in one set of men; but I could not suppose that those concessions would be so soon abused and taken advantage of. Yet so it is; the acts of Congress will speak for themselves. I inclose you some of them.[5] Pray give me your opinion of the Judiciary, Tonnage, and Impost bills. Some gentry proposed in the Impost and Tonnage bills some regulations with a view of forcing North Carolina into the Confederacy; I opposed it; I told the House you might be led, but not forced.[6] If you wait for substantial amendments, you will wait longer than I wish you to do, speaking interestedly. A few milk-and-water amendments have been proposed by Mr. M., such as liberty of conscience, a free press, and one or two general things already well secured.[7] I suppose it was done to keep his promise with his constituents, to move for alterations; but, if I am not greatly mistaken he is not hearty in the cause of amendments.

It is at the moment I write as warm as I have felt it in South Carolina. Will you be able to decipher this? I write in much hurry, without being able to look over what I have wrote. You will be pleased to recollect it is for yourself, and not the public. With best respects, &c., I beg to subscribe myself, as in truth I am,

Your affectionate friend,

P. Butler.

Printed, McRee, 2:263-265.

---

[1]See JI to Pierce Butler, July 25, 1789, in this volume.

[2]A variation of "A man dies as often as he loses friends" from Francis Bacon's *Ornamenta Rationalia*, no. 17.

[3]John Gillies (1747-1836) of Scotland was a historian, whose works include *History of Greece* (1786), *A View of the Reign of Frederick II of Prussia* (1789), and *History of the World* (1807). *DAB*, s.v. "Gillies, John."

[4]In one of Aesop's fables, a fox, who is self-conscious because he has lost his tail in a trap, tries to convince other foxes to cut off their tails. John Vernon Lord and James Michie, *Aesop's Fables* (London: Jonathan Cape, 1989), 149.

[5]Enclosures not found.

[6]For information on the Judiciary Act of 1789, see Tristrim Lowther to JI, July 1, 1789, n. 3, in this volume.

President Washington signed the Impost Act, a law imposing duties on imported goods, on July 4, 1789. The statute specified the duties on a wide variety of products, including liquor, tea, clothing, coal, sugar, coffee, candles, saddles, brushes, and anchors. The president signed the Tonnage Act on July 20, 1789. This statute imposed duties of six cents per ton on U.S. vessels; thirty cents on ships built in the U.S. after July 20, 1789, but owned in part or in whole by foreigners; and fifty cents on all other vessels. Because North Carolina had not ratified the Constitution, the state would be subject to the duties imposed on foreign imports and ships. Hugh Williamson presented a petition to Congress on August 31 asking that duties against North Carolina be suspended. On November 21, 1789, the problem was resolved when North Carolina ratified the Constitution. De Pauw et al., *Documentary History of the First Federal Congress*, 5:940-979; 6:1947-1956, 1958-1960.

[7]For information on Madison's proposal of amendments, see Tristrim Lowther to JI, May 9, 1789, n. 4, in this volume.

From Archibald Maclaine

Wilmington 11h. August 1789[1]

Dear Sir

For above a month past I have been tortured with the rheumatism, so that I have been incapable of all business, and at times unable to turn or raise myself in bed—It is in my arm shoulder and neck, and I now write with difficulty, and at intervals.

I have heard nothing of the debates since I received yours with seven copies. This is the more mortifying, as I believe some of them would sell here and at Fayetteville. Exclusive of some palpable errors, they are in many places defective. No notice is taken of my calling upon Spencer to declare whether the Judges had enforced [*the*] treaty of peace. This must have been <u>intentional</u>, and is the more provoking, as in some places I have no reason to be pleased with the figure I make in the group. How we shall get a few copies forward I do not know, & I am incapable of exerting myself. At all events, you must not suffer by the publication

I perceive that Mc.Calester, who is now at New York, has been offering Genl. Howe's plantation for sale. He purchased it from the heir at law upon credit, for some trifle above £1200, dollars then as I recollect at 16/. But a small part of the purchase money has been paid, and no title yet made, & I think young Howe is still in possession. I do not know whether there is much above 300 acres, all cleared land; but with a privilege of cutting firewood and fencing timber on Mr. T. Hooper's land adjoining There is a pretty good house, though I beleive the inside will want some repairs; and there were convenient offices. The valuable part of the land is about 180 acres of very excellent Marsh, about half of which was once well banked, and Genl. Howe did a good deal towards the repairs; but I do not know that they are complete, and I believe not. Brice had a mortgage on this property, which has been paid off; The buildings and other improvements are worth more than Mc.Calester was to give. He says he has paid a small part of the debt, and he has importuned me with no little earnestness to take the bargain off his hands, on account of some demands I have against the estate, but as those demands are not on my own account, I declined having any thing to do with lands which however valuable to the possessor who can cultivate it, is instead money as an article of sale He purchased upon speculation, & now finds he cannot get rid of his bargain[2]

If the Baron wishes to become a Carolina planter, he cannot purchase in a better time; nor can he get a better bargain if he has it on the terms of Mc.Calester's purchase, but he must be careful how he parts with his money until Howe makes a title[3]

Mr. & Mrs. G Hooper with their family are well, and desire their respects to you, in which my brother, who is slowly recovering from a long indisposition, joins them. Permit me to join in the happiness which you must experience on the recovery of your children and those of Mr. Johnston. Your little boy must have had a severe trial, and I hope and believe that his greatest danger is over

I am very much pleased with the address of the Govr. & Council and the President's answer.[4] Among such as mean well, it must have a powerful effect, but we have a set of mean swindling scoundrels, who with all their bellowing for liberty are fit only to be the slaves of a tyrant.

Jones will be opposed in his election by W Hill, whose merit (from a foolish publication which I have not seen) consists in being a native, and having sucked in the laws of the country with his <country with his> mother's milk. If he imbibed any wisdom that way, it could be nothing but the arts of a huckster, and the dexterity of purchasing poultry and other stolen goods from slaves. He is supported by some of the scotch merchants, by major Walker, and by Mr. John Huske, who though upon terms of intimacy with Jones, declared openly, that he would vote for any one who opposed him. Huske is again a candidate in the county for the convention.[5]

Bradley the postmaster is particularly acquainted with Mrs. Dewey and I suppose has sent your letter to Col. Brown, whose near neighbour she is

I am Dear Sir with much respect & sincerity yours

A Maclaine

RC, Iredell Papers, Duke. Printed, McRee, 2:262-263. Addressed "James Iredell esquire Edenton." Endorsed "Wilmington 11 Aug. 1789. A. Maclaine. Ansd."

---

[1]This letter is erroneously dated August 1, 1789, in McRee.

[2]An auction was held on June 12, 1788, to sell the late Robert Howe's (d. 1786) plantation called Kendale. His son, Robert, was the administrator of the estate. In 1794, James McAlister, son and heir of Archibald McAlister, paid Robert Howe Jr. £1,200 for Kendale. Brice is probably Francis Brice. Fouts, *Abstracts from Newspapers of Wilmington*, 1:23; Brunswick County Record of Deeds, vol. C, 1790-1798, State Archives.

[3]Baron de Poellnitz had expressed interest in the property to JI. Baron de Poellnitz to JI, July 25, 1789, in this volume.

[4]The address from the governor and council has not been located. In a reply to the address, Washington welcomed the message as an indication "of the good dispositions of the citizens of your State towards their Sister States, and of the probability of their speedy acceding to the new general Government." George Washington to the Governor and Council of the State of North Carolina, June 19, 1789, photocopy, Samuel Johnston, Governors Papers, State Archives.

[5]Edward Jones was elected to represent Wilmington in the house of commons, while William Henry Hill, a Federalist, was chosen to represent the town in the 1789 state ratification convention. John Huske, an Antifederalist, served in the 1788 and 1789 conventions for New Hanover County. Cheney, *North Carolina Government*, 223; Massengill, *North Carolina Votes*, 28, 30.

From Hugh Williamson

New York 12th. Augt. 1789

Dear Sir

Major Butler has just Sent me two Packages to be forwarded by the first Vessel & these contain the Articles of public Note so fully that I shall not Send a Single Paper. The N. C. Debates are considerably read in this Place especially by congress Members. some of whom, who formerly had little Knowledge of the Citizens of N. C, have lately been very minute in their Enquiries concerning Mr. Iredell. By the Way I have lately been asked by a Senator whether I thought you would accept of a Judges Place under the new Govt. if it required your moving out of the State as we are not in the Union.[1] To this as you may Suppose I reply'd that I was not prepared to answer, the Question being so complicated. As. How far the Removal. What the Allowance &c.

I am So often asked what I think our State will do that I have left off answering except that we will probably do right if Congress set us the Example. The Board of Commissioners is now filled up by a Mr. Kean from South Carolina & we shall presently See where is the weak Place in our Code of Accounts.[2]

Be pleased present my Respects to Mrs. Iredell & the Miss Blairs as also those of Mrs. Williamson & believe me to be with the utmost Regard

Dr. sir Your obedt. Servt.

Hu Williamson

RC, Johnson Collection, NCSA. Printed, McRee, 2:265-266. Addressed "Honble James Iredell Edenton." Endorsed "New York 12 Aug. 1789. Hugh Williamson. Ansd. Aug. 29th. 1789."[3]

---

[1]The inquiry may have come from Pierce Butler of South Carolina, who supported JI's confirmation as a justice of the U.S. Supreme Court in 1790. It was Williamson, however, who wrote to President Washington on September 19, 1789, suggesting JI for office. Whichard, *Justice James Iredell*, 91; W. W. Abbot and Dorothy Twohig, eds., *The Papers of George Washington, Presidential Series*, vol. 4 (Charlottesville: University of Virginia Press, 1987), 58.

[2]John Kean (ca. 1756-1795) served on a commission to settle accounts between the U.S. government and individual states. He was a veteran of the Revolutionary War and the Continental Congress (1785-1787). Kean was subsequently appointed as a cashier in the U.S. bank in Philadelphia. *Appletons' Cyclopædia of American Biography*, s.v. "Kean, John."

[3]See JI to Hugh Williamson, August 29, 1789, in this volume.

To Hugh Williamson

[*August 29, 1789*]

Dear Sir,

I had the pleasure to receive your obliging favour of the 12 Aug., together with the Packets from Major Butler which you were so kind as to forward. I consider myself deeply indebted to the Gentlemen who did me the honour to propose the question as to my being /one/ of the Judges, & doubt not I am principally to attribute any favorable opinion entertained of me in this respect to your partial & friendly representation of me. I cannot but say, if it should be possible that I could be appointed tho' not now living under the Union, that it is a situation which would be very agreeable to me <as to> <but I doubt not the Salary will> provided the salary was such (as I doubt not it will be) as would be a sufficient compensation for my devoting my whole time to the duties of the appointment, which I could with pleasure do as my inclination from long habit would direct me sooner to <that kind of life than any other, & I believe I should be better qualified for it than for any other employment> such a kind of employment than any other. The necessity of my removing out of the State (tho' extremely painful to me) I should not consider as an insuferable objection, <provided> /if/ it was not required of me to remove <[*further*] to South Carolina or Georgia, for I should not chuse to carry my Family further to the Southward.> /any where to the Southward of this State or very far to the Northward./ I take the liberty, in consequence of your very kind intimation, to mention this, though I can by no means flatter myself that when I am so little personally known so high & dignified an appointment could take place in my favour.[1]

I had great <pleasure> satisfaction in your being returned from Tyrrell by so large a majority.[2] 229 out of 233. There was so violent a contest in this Town that I did not think it was prudent to risque your election here, as many objected to their being 2 Members instead of one, & there was no knowing how to be sure of votes in such a contest as this was.[3] Hamilton was elected only by 41 to 37, against Borritz:[4] I was in the <Majority> /Minority/. A foolish speech of Payne's gave Hamilton success. "That the Mechanics should vote as the Gent. bid them." This was exaggerated to the utmost, & no explanation afterwards would do it away.[5] I inclose our last Papers containing <some> an account of some of the Members. Gregory, Sawyers <Bagge>, Dauge, Abbot, & Charles Grandy, are for Camden.[6] In Currituck, Etheridge & /Major/ Ferebee[7]—<In Pasquotank> John Blount is in for Beaufort, Reading Blount lost his election for Hyde, by not being on the spot. having been suddenly called away[8]

FC, Johnson Collection, NCSA. Endorsed "Copy of a Letter to Dr. Williamson Aug. 29th. 1789."

---

[1]See Hugh Williamson to JI, August 12, 1789, in this volume.

[2]Tyrrell County voters elected Williamson to serve in the 1789 state ratification convention. Massengill, *North Carolina Votes*, 64.

[3]John Mare (1739-1803), a Federalist, defeated JI in the election of Edenton's borough representative to the ratification convention. Mare (1739-1803), a native of New York, was a portrait painter and a prosperous merchant engaged in trade with the West Indies. Massengill, *North Carolina Votes*, 40; *DNCB*, s.v. "Mare, John."

[4]John Hamilton defeated William Borritz to represent Edenton in the house of commons. Some Borritz supporters had suggested that Hamilton should not be elected because he was a lawyer. Hamilton defended attorneys by saying, "It is said they are a dangerous tribe, and a political evil—but if so, it should at the same time be remembered, that they are a <u>necessary evil</u>, and the firm barrier to the people

against the encroachment of power." Cheney, *North Carolina Government*, 223; *State Gazette of North-Carolina* (Edenton), August 13, 1789.

[5]No record of Michael Payne's speech has been found.

[6]Isaac Gregory and Enoch Sawyer, previously identified. Peter Dauge (1739-1801), Henry Abbot (ca. 1740-1791), and Charles Grandy (before 1755-ca. 1803) were Federalist delegates to the 1788 and 1789 ratification conventions. Dauge also served eight terms in the General Assembly. Charles Grandy was a member of the house of commons for three terms. Massengill, *North Carolina Votes*, 15, 1, 23.

[7]Willis Etheridge served in the General Assembly from 1785 to 1787, but neither he nor anyone else named Etheridge represented Currituck County in the assembly or in the 1789 ratification convention. Samuel (1761-1845) and William Ferebee (d. 1791) were Federalist delegates to the 1789 state ratification convention. Samuel was a member of the house of commons (1794-1795) and the senate (1804-1806). William also served in the house (1778, 1782) and the senate (1783). Cheney, *North Carolina Government*, 215, 217; Massengill, *North Carolina Votes*, 20.

[8]Reading Blount (1757-1807) served with distinction as an officer in the Continental army during the Revolutionary War. He was a member of the house of commons (1786-1787) and in 1800 became major-general of the first division of the North Carolina militia. Ashe, Weeks, and Van Noppen, *Biographical History*, 1:161-163.

From William R. Davie

Halifax September 7h. 1789.

Dear Sir

I have the pleasure of acknowledging your friendly letter by Mr. Black. there is something in the sympathy of a friend which can be gotten from no other source. Your Town election Mr. Black informs me has been attended with some disagreeable circumstances—I think this rather ill policy in Mr. Hamilton in his present situation—when the conciliation of every mans regard appeared necessary to his interest.[1]

The elections in this district are generally federal—The members as follow. Halifax, Ashe Qualls Long, Whitaker, Norfleet, myself for the town[2]—Warren P. Hawkins B. Hawkins. W. Hawkins X, Green, & Christmas[3] Franklin—Hill. H. X Hill. J., Lancaster, Sherrod, Christmas[4]—Nash—Griffin, Bonds X Vick, Marens, Ellen[5] Martin—Williams, Hunter, Bryant Mayo. & Stewart,[6] Edgecomb Phillips, Blount, Grey, Hilliard & Fort.[7] Northampton, Bentford, Peete, Pride X, Peebles X, Tarver.[8] the most of these are also members of Assembly and those marked thus X are the only avowed Anties at present. the others are all staunch federalists as such as say they will now vote for the Constitution on the principle of Union.

The Western elections are of the same complection as far as we have heard—even Orange has a federal representation, thus we may safely hope that <that> our accession to the confederacy will not be postponed beyond November next.[9] I set out in 3 days for Salisbury, and when I meet you here will be able to give you a satisfactory Account of our prospects in the back Counties.

My Compts. to your family and the Governor and believe me wt. the most sincere

regard your mo obt.

William R. Davie

RC, Iredell Papers, Duke. Addressed "The Honble. James Iredell Esqr. Edenton."

---

[1]Trenholme describes the race for borough representative in the house of commons between John Hamilton and William Borritz as a "violent contest." Trenholme, *Ratification*, 215. See also JI to Hugh Williamson, August 29, 1789, in this volume.

[2]The Halifax County delegates to the 1789 ratification convention were John Baptista Ashe, Peter Qualls, John Whitaker, and Marmaduke Norfleet. Norfleet did not vote at the convention; the others supported ratification. No one in the group had attended the 1788 convention. Massengill, *North Carolina Votes*, 3, 49, 37, 62, 45.

[3]The Warren County delegates to the 1789 ratification convention were Philemon Hawkins, Benjamin Hawkins, Wyatt Hawkins, Solomon Green, and Thomas Christmas. Wyatt Hawkins and Christmas had attended the 1788 convention as Antifederalists. In 1789, Hawkins continued to oppose the Constitution, but Christmas joined the rest of his Warren County colleagues in supporting ratification. Massengill, *North Carolina Votes*, 27, 23, 13; Clark, *State Records*, 22:49.

[4]The Franklin County delegates to the 1789 ratification convention were Henry Hill, Jordan Hill, William Lancaster, Thomas Sherrod, and William Christmas. Henry Hill, Lancaster, and Sherrod had also been delegates to the 1788 convention and had opposed ratification. Henry Hill remained an Antifederalist in 1789, but Lancaster and Sherrod, along with Christmas, supported ratification at the second convention. Jordan Hill did not vote. Massengill, *North Carolina Votes*, 28, 35, 53, 13.

[5]Nash County's delegation to the 1789 convention consisted of Hardy Griffin, John Bonds, Wilson Vick, William Skipwith Marnes, and Howell Ellen. Bonds, Marnes, and Howell had attended the 1788 convention as Antifederalists. In 1789, Bonds and Marnes supported ratification, while Howell did not vote. Griffin and Vick were Federalists. Massengill, *North Carolina Votes*, 19, 7, 61, 41, 19.

[6]The Martin County delegates to the 1789 convention were William Williams, Thomas Hunter, Nathan Mayo, and John Stewart. Hunter and Mayo

were delegates to the 1788 convention. The former was an Antifederalist and the latter a Federalist. In 1789, the entire Martin County delegation supported ratification. Davie listed Joseph Bryan among the delegates. Bryan, who had represented Martin County in the General Assembly, may have been elected to the convention, but he did not serve. Massengill, *North Carolina Votes*, 64, 30, 42, 57.

[7]The delegates from Edgecombe County to the 1789 convention were Etheldred Phillips, Thomas Blount, Etheldred Gray, Jeremiah Hilliard, and William Fort. Gray and Fort were Antifederalist delegates to the 1788 convention. Gray, though elected to the 1789 convention, did not attend because of illness. Fort and the other Edgecombe County delegates supported ratification in 1789. Massengill, *North Carolina Votes*, 48, 6, 23, 28, 20.

[8]The Northampton County delegation to the 1789 ratification convention consisted of John Manley Binford, Samuel Peete, Halcott Briggs Pride, Robert Peebles, and Samuel Tarver. Binford and Peebles had opposed ratification as delegates to the 1788 convention. Peebles continued to do so in 1789 and was joined by Pride. Binford, Peete, and Tarver supported ratification in 1789. Massengill, *North Carolina Votes*, 5, 47, 49, 58.

[9]In 1788, the Orange County delegation had been solidly Antifederalist. Contrary to Davie's assertion, four of the five Orange County delegates in 1789—Joseph Hodge, Alexander Mebane, Thomas Harden Perkins, and William Francis Strudwick—opposed ratification. Only James Christmas supported ratification. Massengill, *North Carolina Votes*, 73; Clark, *State Records*, 22:48-49.

To John G. Blount

Edenton Sept. 9th. 1789.

Dear Sir,

As it is of consequence that the inclosed letter should reach Mr. Glasgow safely, I take the liberty to recommend it to your obliging care. It concerns the Revisal of the Laws, which I am now busily employed in. We had lately an unfortunate delay for want of Paper, but that want being now pretty well supplied I hope the work will proceed rapidly.

I am, Dear Sir, with sincere respect, Your faithful & obedient Servant

Ja. Iredell.

P.S. A Vote on the subject of Amendments (nearly agreeing with the Report) passed the House of Representatives the 24th. Aug. They proposed adjourning on the 22 of this month.[1]

RC, Blount Papers, NCSA. Printed, *John Gray Blount Papers*, 1:505. Addressed "John Gray Blount Esq. Washington."

[1]For the text of the House resolution, see De Pauw et al., eds., *Documentary History of the First Federal Congress*, 4:35-39.

From John Williams

Montpelier[1] 11th. Septr. 1789—

your favor of the 9th. ult came to hand a few days ago after Mr. & Mrs. Pollok /had/ left this a few days, she came here very Sick & continued very low for near three weeks, but for the last fortnight mended very much and left this <about> a bout a fortnight ago in better health & Spirits than I have Seen her for a twelvemonth past. the letter inclosed to her I Expect to deliver myself at Hillsborough the day after tomorrow when I Shall have to apologize for having broken the Seal which I inadvertantly did before I discovered it, tho' the contents I am as much a Stranger to as if the Seal had never have been broken. I am very Sorry to hear that your two little lovely Babes have been so ill as it must have distressed both Mrs. Iredell & your Self as well as all the family but am happy to hear that they as well as his Excellencys Children are geting again well as I hope to find them at Edenton Supr. Court. your Self I Expect to have the pleasure of Seeing at Halifax and of then hearing that Mrs. Iredell Children & family are perfectly well & that the Governor Lady & family have recovered their healths & well also

I thank you for the few copies of the address of the Governor Council & answer.[2] I wish there had have been more of them, as I intend to take them to the back Country, and to dispose of them in a manner in which I doubt not but they will have the desired Effect. Col Davie had a Short time before favored me with about the Same number which I had disposed of up & down my own county & which had been particularly pleasing, an met the approbation of all I heard Speak of them; Except our friend (if he is within yr. number) Genl. Person

you say you think that I Should be pleased with the answer. I was very much So, but I assure you Sir not more than I was with the address it Self, which in my opinion was a well advised thing, at a proper time, and Will I am purswaded answer very Salutary purposes as well with the Presedent and congress of the united States, as with the Citizens of this State I am also very much pleased with what you Inform me Mr. Madison wrote the Governor & Shall make use of that paragraph in you letter to Evince to them to whome I shew it the probable Effect which the address may have &c.[3]

I have not heard who is Ellected to the convention in many Counties, in this they will be divided on the constitution as they will I am told in Orange Rowan & Several of the upper Counties,[4] in Mecklenburg all for it, & none could be Elected who were agt it,[5] in Randolph all against it, but have heard of no other county where they were all so.[6] I hope there will at least be a majority found for it.

Mrs. Williams in a very particular manner Joines in our best respects good wishes & Compliments to yr. Self Mrs. Iredell & the two Miss Blairs &c. and beg the favor of you to present our respectfull compliments to his Excellency Lady & family and

am Dear Sir with Sincear respect & /and/ Esteem Yr. most Obedt. & very Hble Servt

Jno. Williams

RC, Iredell Papers, Duke. Printed, McRee, 2:266. Addressed "The Honble. James Iredell Esqr. Edenton."

---

[1]Montpelier, the plantation home of John Williams, was located near Williamsboro in Granville County. *DNCB*, s.v. "Williams, John."

[2]See Archibald Maclaine to JI, August 11, 1789, n. 4, in this volume.

[3]James Madison, who at this time was a member of the U.S. House of Representatives, wrote two letters to Samuel Johnston regarding his message to the president. The first on June 21, 1789, and the second on July 31. For the text of these letters, see Clark, *State Records*, 22:634-636.

[4]For information on the Orange County delegates, see William R. Davie to JI, September 7, 1789, n. 9, in this volume. The Rowan County delegation was divided, as Williams indicated. George Henry Berger and Matthew Lock, who had also attended the 1788 convention, opposed ratification, while Maxwell Chambers, Basil Gaither, and John Stokes supported it. Massengill, *North Carolina Votes*, 5, 37, 12, 21, 57, 74; Clark, *State Records*, 22:48-49.

[5]Williams was mistaken in his assessment of the Mecklenburg County delegation. Only one member, Joseph Graham, voted for ratification. The other four—Joseph Douglas, Caleb Phifer, James Porter, and Zaccheus Wilson—voted no. Graham, Douglas, Phifer, and Wilson had attended the 1788 convention as Antifederalists. Massengill, *North Carolina Votes*, 23, 17, 48, 64, 73; Clark, *State Records*, 22:48-49.

[6]The Randolph County delegation comprised three Federalists—William Bailey, Nathan Stedman, and Reuben Wood—and one Antifederalist, Zebedee Wood, who had also opposed ratification at the 1788 convention. Massengill, *North Carolina Votes*, 3, 56, 65, 73; Clark, *State Records*, 22:48-49.

From Archibald Maclaine

Wilmington 15th. Septr. 1789

Dear Sir

Until I received your letter of the 2d. I did not know that you had been a candidate for the convention, and I am extremely sorry you were not returned, as I am fully persuaded you would have had considerable weight[1]

I think the elections, as far as I know any thing of them, are more favorable than last year. Phil & Ben Hawkins are both in the convention. Rutherfurd is not, though Locke is. I have not heard from Halifax.[2] In New Hanover, we have Tim. Bloodworth, Pugh Williams John Huske, J A Campbell and John Gambier Scull—I do not know that there is one federal member among them, tho' possibly the last may[3]—W. H. Hill for the town. He opposed Jones, who is returned for the Assembly.[4] I do not well know who are all for Brunswick, as I am told they have five for the convention, none of whom are in the Assembly—among them are, John Hall, whom perhaps you may remember with my brother, and Will. Lord[5]—Of these two I have hopes. In Bladen, there are two new members, both Young men, but I do not know their political principles, so that excepting Col. Owen, I am uncertain as to that county[6] Robeson members are I believe sure[7]—Hay, Grove, Ingram and a Mr. Adam a merchant are for Cumberland, and all sure. I forget the other.[8] For Rowan county & Salisbury, I think we have three votes, Steele, Stokes & Chambers.[9] Surry, it is said is federal, Lincoln was so last year, & I believe sends nearly the same members[10]—That fool Spencer is again chosen for Anson—Spiller is a member for Sampson, and Clinton who is returned again, is a convert to federalism[11]—

I am persuaded we might have carried our point last year but for Willie Jones; and therefore I am anxious to know whether he is a member.[12] As I do not however believe that he acted from principle, and as he was convinced last Session of Assembly that he had not acquired popularity sufficient to insure the passing of a single bill into a law, I am in hopes he will now take the other side, for which the amendments will furnish him with a sufficient justification. Should I be mistaken, however, there is one thing pretty certain, that he will find a great number of well-meaning members who, ashamed of being led by the nose last year, will prove very restiff. Upon the whole, I think we shall succeed; but I am apprehensive that our success will be accompanied with an evil of a very pernicious tendency,—namely, paper money—Those who wish to defraud their creditors, and those (a still greater number) who think we cannot pay taxes without bills of credit, will be clamorous for another emission of paper

To whom was Payne's expression, "the mechanics must do as the gentlemen bid them" applied—I thought Hamilton was the first gentleman among you;[13] I am sure Cumming frequently boasted of his <u>noble</u> birth

Strudwick, a strong anti, was a candidate for the convention, & within three votes of Col. Campbell[14]—I see his son is chosen for Orange.[15] Strudwick had all Judge Ashe's family & connexions. The Judges not only wish to keep their seats, but to keep them uncontrolled

Mrs. Hooper & her children are gone to stay a month or 6 weeks at Fayette Mr. Hooper is well, but my brother still in a very precarious state of health my rheumatism had abated very considerably, but some unfavorable weather made me very uneasy—I question whether I shall ever be well, though I have been taking guiacum near three months, and mean to continue it.[16] I do not know what effect it has had upon others, but I am persuaded from two trials that with me it has increased the pain to a great degree for some time. Had it anything like that effect upon the Governor?

I can hear of no conveyance for the debates

yours very truly

A Maclaine

not a line from Hillsborough, even to Billy Hooper.

RC, Iredell Papers, Duke. Printed, McRee, 2:266-267. Addressed "James Iredell esquire Edenton." Endorsed "Wilmington 15 Sept. 1789. A. Maclaine. Ansd."

---

[1]For information on the election, see JI to Hugh Williamson, August 29, 1789, n. 3, in this volume.

[2]For information on the Halifax delegation, see William R. Davie to JI, September 7, 1789, n. 2, in this volume.

[3]The New Hanover delegation opposed ratification. Massengill, *North Carolina Votes*, 73; Clark, *State Records*, 22:48-49.

[4]William Henry Hill, who was the delegate for Wilmington at the convention, supported ratification. Edward Jones represented Wilmington in the house of commons. Massengill, *North Carolina Votes*, 75; Clark, *State Records*, 22:49; Cheney, *North Carolina Government*, 223.

[5]In addition to John Hall and William Espy Lord, the Brunswick County delegation included William Gause, Dennis Hankins, and Benjamin Smith. Of the group, only Lord opposed ratification. Smith had attended the 1788 convention and, as in 1789, supported ratification. Massengill, *North Carolina Votes*, 25, 37, 21, 26, 55, 71; Clark, *State Records*, 48-49.

[6]John Cowan, a Federalist, and Duncan Stewart, an Antifederalist, were the new Bladen County delegates. The rest of the delegation—Thomas Brown, Joseph Gautier, and Thomas Owen—had attended the 1788 convention. At both conventions, Brown and Gautier opposed ratification, while Owen supported it. Massengill, *North Carolina Votes*, 14, 57, 9, 22, 46.

[7]Sion Alford, Elias Barnes, Neill Brown, John Cade, and John Willis, all Federalists, represented Robeson County. Barnes, Brown, Cade, and Willis had also attended the 1788 convention and supported ratification. Massengill, *North Carolina Votes*, 1, 4, 9, 10, 64.

[8]The delegates from Cumberland County to the 1789 ratification convention were John Hay, William Barry Grove, John Ingram, Robert Adam, and James Moore. Grove, who had attended the 1788 convention, was a Federalist, as were Ingram, Adam, and Hay. Moore was the lone Antifederalist. Ingram had been elected to the 1788 convention but was unseated when Fayetteville was denied borough representation. Massengill, *North Carolina Votes*, 27, 24, 30, 1, 72.

[9]For information on the Rowan County delegation, see John Williams to JI, September 11, 1789, n. 4, in this volume. John Steele, a Federalist, represented Salisbury in the 1788 and 1789 conventions. Massengill, *North Carolina Votes*, 57.

[10]The Surry County delegation consisted of Absalom Bostick, Gideon Edwards, George Houser, Edward Lovell, and Joseph Winston. Bostick and Winston had been Antifederalist delegates to the 1788 convention. In 1789, Winston joined Houser and Lovell in supporting ratification, while Bostick and Edwards voted against it. Massengill, *North Carolina Votes*, 7, 18, 29, 38, 65.

The delegates from Lincoln County were Robert Alexander, John Caruth, Joseph Dickson, William Maclaine, and John Moore. Moore and Maclaine, who were Federalists, and Alexander, an Antifederalist, had been delegates to the 1788 convention. Caruth and Dickson were Federalists. Massengill, *North Carolina Votes*, 1, 12, 16, 40, 43.

[11]Samuel Spencer, an Antifederalist, was a delegate to the 1788 and 1789 conventions. Massengill, *North Carolina Votes*, 56. For more information on Spencer, see William Hooper to JI, March 15, 1784, n. 6, in this volume.

James Spiller was a Federalist. Massengill, *North Carolina Votes*, 56. For more information on Spiller, see William Hooper to JI, February 7, 1784, n. 7, in this volume.

Richard Clinton (1721-1795) opposed ratification at the 1788 and 1789 conventions. He served in the Revolutionary War and was elected to sixteen terms in the General Assembly. The county seat of Sampson County was named in his honor. Massengill, *North Carolina Votes*, 13; *DNCB*, s.v. "Clinton, Richard."

[12]Willie Jones, leader of the Antifederalists in the 1788 convention, did not run for election as a delegate to the 1789 convention. The delegates from his home county, Halifax, supported ratification. Whichard, *Justice James Iredell*, 84; Trenholme, *Ratification*, 237.

[13]Michael Payne and John Hamilton. See JI to Hugh Williamson, August 29, 1789, in this volume.

[14]Samuel Strudwick and John Ablen Campbell were candidates in New Hanover County.

[15]William Francis Strudwick (1770-1810), an Antifederalist, represented Orange County at the 1789 ratification convention. Massengill, *North Carolina Votes*, 58.

[16]Guaiacum is a type of tree found in the warmer sections of North America. Resin from the tree had been used to treat gout and other maladies since the sixteenth century. *OED*, s.v. "guaiacum."

To Hannah Iredell

Nixonton, Friday Sept. 25.

My dear Hannah,

I am very much mortified at being detained here so long, and receiving so little money, so that after sending you the inclosed trifle, which I am almost ashamed to do, I have scarcely enough left to pay my expences. I shall be with you as soon as possible, but when is now uncertain. Give my tenderest love to my dear Children, & remember me very affectionately to Nelly & Peggy.

God grant I may you quite recovered, & the rest in good health.

I am ever, My dear Hannah, Your most affectionate

Ja. Iredell.

RC, Johnson Collection, NCSA. Addressed "Mrs. Iredell Edenton." Endorsed "Nixonton Sept. 25th. 1789. Ja. Iredell."

From John Steele

Salisbury Septemr. 26th. 1789

My dear Sir,

Your very polite letter by Colonel Davie, and One dated in Feby. last I have had the honor to recieve.[1]—

Since I recied. your first I have been generally from home—which I trust will operate as an apology with you for not answering it Sooner

I have communicated the Contents to Such gentlemen as had a share in proposeing that name to our new County, and they recieve your acknowledgements with Sentiments of very high respect.—

We regret extreemly that you are not of the ensuing Assembly or convention—because no man has done more for our common cause on a former occasion, and there is no man from whom we might expect So much at the ensuing Struggle.—A Struggle I fear it will be, because the State (except your district) Seems much divided—If an adoption Shou'd take place, we will rejoice, but if it shou'd be rejected, we must like Good Christians mourn for the Sins of our Country men—

I have the honor to be My dear Sir Your Obt. Huml. Servt.

Jno. Steele

RC, Iredell Papers, Duke. Printed, McRee, 2:267. Addressed "James Iredell Edenton." Endorsed "Salisbury Sept. 26. 1789. John Steele. Ansd."

---

[1]See JI to John Steele, February 17, 1789, in this volume.

From Arthur Iredell

Guildford Octr. 6th. 1789

I received a few Days ago, my dear Brother, Your most wellcome Packet by Captn. Clark. It was well that it proved really valuable to me, for, sending it as a Letter by the Post, & not as a Parcel by the Coach, from Liverpool to London, the Postage came to one pound six Shillings! However I was so well satisfied to receive It, upon any terms, that I have only laughed a little at the Captain's Expence.

Baffled as You were in the Convention by a Majority, whose Heads were no otherwise of Value than as they might be counted, & whose Hearts were, in general, I fancy, of no Value whatever,—the Struggles made by You & Your Party reflect the brightest Lustre upon your Characters. Your Abilities & Patriotism have been fully established; and in the Event I doubt not they will be crowned with the Success they deserve. I could say much of the Part you took on that memorable Occasion, if I did not fear to offend Your Delicacy. Allow me, however, to say thus much, that I feel a considerable Degree of Pride in being so nearly related to a Man, whose Eloquence is only exceeded by the unvarying Rectitude of his public & private Conduct—It was impossible that you could add any thing to my Affection; but you have taught me to respect Your Talents, & to venerate Your Principles, even more than I have been accustomed to do. The Country & the Times You live in open a fine Field for the Exertion of both, and I anticipate with no inconsiderable Delight the Good it is likely You will do, & the Rewards You are likely to receive. Such Talents as Your's, my dear Bror., are rarely to be met with, & there is no object of laudable Ambition to which You may not reasonably aspire. I perceive You are now at the Head of the Council—When did that Event take Place? & by whose Appointment.[1] You cannot do me a greater Favor than by communicating to me as much Information about Yourself & the State you live in as possible—I am at present as ignorant about your Governmt. as the Face of your Country—& a Pamphlet, from the Journals of a Convention down to a Provincial Kalendar must have It's Charms for me.

Your Account of your Children affected me most sensibly, tho I observed with Pleasure that Annie had recovered, & James was out of Danger. May they in future thrive to Your utmost Wish, & repay with abundant Usury the Anxious Tenderness of their Parents! Your Apprehensions about our poor Mother have been such as I should have expected from You. She is, I thank God, alive, and likely I hope to live; but, in spight of all my Endeavours to the contrary, She continues to live in a Way, & with People that disgrace & impose upon her. She has for almost a Year lived solely at my Charge, & I have strained every Nerve to advance her Money, upon which She might have subsisted very reputably but it has not answered the good Purpose I wished. The only Hope I now have is that of her going to America, if I could raise a sufficient Sum to defray such an Expence, and a favorable Opportunity should present itself. At present I am not able to bring it to bear. Captn. Cotton called upon her lately & proposed, having an Acquaintance with, & a thorough Reliance upon You to advance a Sum for her Passage, & I undertook to find all that should beside be wanting for her Equipment &ca but he has since written to my Mother to say that he could meet with no Virginia Ship that had female Passengers, without which She could not go. However I shall myself look out for one, & bear the whole Expence, if my Uncle shd. keep his Word & send me a Remittance, as I am fully persuaded the being with You is the only Happiness She is now capable of enjoying.

I thank you most gratefully, my dear Brother, for your kind Concern about my Affairs. My Separation from Miss F. was a cruel one, at the first, tho I had long been in some Measure prepared for it, and Time has entirely reconciled me to an Event so much for her Advantage.[2] Will you be surprized to hear that I have since formed another Attachment to one no less amiable, and with the further Recommendation of a handsome Fortune? /about 9,000 £/ It is even so—I met with her, while upon a Visit to her Uncle who lives here, & a very great Similarity in our Dispositions, as well as the most engaging Manners in her, soon made her more & more interesting to me. In a more unaccountable Way (for She has Charms & I have none) She became partial to me. You may imagine all the rest; except indeed the Opposition that has been made by her Uncle (with whom nevertheless I am a great Favourite) on the Score of Fortune.—I have written to my Uncle—I am bustling, as well as I can, for Preferment—and there the Matter rests—You desired to be in my Confidence—I have now given you a Proof that you are; but were I to attempt to tell you how much I confide in, & regard You, I should fall infinitely short of the Truth. My Life hitherto has been an eventfull, but not a fortunate one—I have had little Time, & less Inclination to trouble you with Histories that could afford you no Pleasure—To avoid doing so I have seldom written at all. Should the Tide turn in my Favour, You will then learn the true Cause of my Apparent Neglect—You will feel, my most honoured Friend, that my Esteem & Affection for You are unbounded.

I must now bid you Adieu! You may depend upon hearing from me by the next Packet. Give my Love to Tom—I rejoice his Health is established—& I please myself with the hope that, under Your Eye; he will emulate all Your Virtues. S[*ay*] every thing that is Affectionate for me to my Sister & the Children. May the Time not be far removed when I may see both You & them! & may I have frequent Opportunities of proving how entirely & warmly I am Your's & their's—

Adieu!

A I—

Tom will be good enough to excuse my Writing at present

RC, Johnson Collection, NCSA. Printed, McRee, 2:267-268.

[1]The General Assembly elected JI to the Council of State on November 11, 1788, and for a year he was president of the council. Cheney, *North Carolina Government*, 165.

[2]"Miss F" refers to Amanda Felton, who had been Arthur Iredell's fiancée.

To the Speakers of the Senate and the House of Commons

[*October 16, 1789*]

Gentlemen,

In pursuance of the trust with which I have the honour to be invested, & the importance <as well as distinction> of which I am deeply sensible of, I have since the last Session of Assembly applied myself with all the industry in my power, considering the unavoidable avocations of my profession, to prepare a Revisal of the Acts of Assembly of this State, in the manner in which I have been directed to do so.[1] A Copy of so much as has been published will be /ready to be/ laid before the honorable the General Assembly by Mr. Hodge. It is far short of what I <was in hopes> <expected> /hoped/ would have been published by this time, but an unfortunate disappointment as to a large quantity of Paper which had been bespoke occasioned a delay that I have greatly regretted. This disappointment induced Mr. Hodge to take a voyage to the northward on purpose, & a large supply is <every hour> /daily/ expected. The business <then> /afterwards/ I hope will proceed with great expedition, <though it may necessarily receive a little delay> at least [*as soon as*] my Circuit is over, though I will endeavour to make that as small an impediment as possible. I hope the Members of the General Assembly will be pleased to examine as much as has been already published, and that if there be any thing exceptionable in the manner of the publication it will be pointed out to me that I may avoid a repetition of the like error. I take the liberty to suggest that in the original Act /constituting my appointment/ there is an expression which appears to me, with great deference, to admit of too great a latitude. I am directed to leave out "all acts on which no question of property can arise." <It is extremely> I apprehend it to be extremely difficult, if not impossible, to foresee in almost any case of an existing Act whether a question of property <can> /may/ arise upon it or not. If therefore I am not too presuming, /I beg leave to say that/ I think this part of the Act, if not thought proper to be entirely repealed, might at least admit of an amendment. It will be observed that I have retained all these Acts, or parts of them, by which new Counties have been made. I had some doubts whether strictly in point of law they might not be deemed rather private than public Acts (tho' I <had> thought strong reasons might be urged in <favor of> support of their being public ones), but at the same time they appeared to me of so much public importance that I <thought> /considered/ it was proper to retain them.

I inclose you, Gentlemen, an exact List of the Original Acts I received from Mr. Glasgow.[2] That Gentleman was pleased to send me /on my application/ all that were in his office from the period of Mr. <Swann's> Moseley & Mr. Swann's Edition (the only authentic <one> /general/ collection of the Acts that was ever published) until the Revolution, since which /all/ the Acts published by authority are in being and in my possession, <before which period I have been able to find very few that were published by authority> but I had been able to find very few before that period that had been published by authority <some> </after/> </subsequent to/> /later than/ the Edition I mention above.[3] I had great concern in finding that the collection Mr. Glasgow /sent me/ (though I doubt not all that were in his Office) was not complete. In <an annexed> /the inclosed/ Paper I have stated the particulars, and pray the directions of the General Assembly thereupon.

I have only to add, that it is my earnest wish to discharge this high trust, the honour of which I feel with the greatest gratitude, <with the utmost care & fidelity, and that I> in the best manner it is possibly in my power to execute it, and that I consider myself greatly obliged by the generous advance the Genl. Assembly was pleased to make me at the last Session.[4]

I am &—

FC, Johnson Collection, NCSA. Endorsed "Copy of a Letter to the Speakers of the Senate and the House of Commons. October 16th. 1789."

---

[1]See JI to Maurice Murphy, February 25, 1788, n. 2, in this volume.

[2]See James Glasgow to JI, September 12, 1788, in this volume.

[3]Samuel Swann (1704-1774) of Perquimans Precinct and Onslow County was a member of the Colonial Assembly for approximately thirty-five years. For about a third of that time he was Speaker. Edward Moseley (1682-1749), who was the uncle of Swann's wife, lived in Chowan Precinct, later Chowan County. He held

numerous public offices, including royal councilor, chief justice of the General Court, and Speaker of the assembly. During the 1738-1739 session, the assembly appointed Swann, Moseley, and Swann's brother John to codify the colony's laws. Their work, known as *Swann's Revisal*, was published in 1752 and was the first book printed in North Carolina. *DNCB*, s.v. "Swann, Samuel," "Moseley, Edward."

[4]The General Assembly granted JI an advance of £250 during the 1788 session. Clark, *State Records*, 21:139.

To Hannah Iredell

Halifax Oct. 22. 1789.

My dear Hannah,

I still continue quite well, but have scarcely a moment to tell you so, as I am preparing for Baker's suit to day.—Give my tenderest love to my dear Children, & remember me affectionately to Nelly & my Brother, & the Family over the Creek. Prospects from the back Country as to the Constitution excellent.

Adieu! God grant I may find you all well. I am ever my dear Hannah,
Most affectionately yours

Ja. Iredell.

RC, Johnson Collection, NCSA. Addressed "Mrs. Iredell Edenton."

To Hannah Iredell

Halifax Oct. 25. 1789.

My dear Hannah,

I still continue perfectly well, but am extremely anxious to hear from you. I can't imagine what has detained Hamilton. Mrs. Mc.Coy had entirely recovered her health, and intended writing to Nelly, but Judge Williams was called suddenly and unexpectedly away by the death of Mrs. Satterwhite, a Daughter of his Wife's.[1] Judge Williams tells me Mrs. Pollok is pretty well recovered and in good spirits, though she has been in very imminent danger. They are every day expected. Baker lost his cause against Montfort, which we had great reason to apprehend as the Court gave an opinion against his title last Term[2]—I get very little money, but have had more than enough to replace Mr. Hill's.[3] Strudwick only sent me £19.[4]—I only want to hear of you & my dear Children and my Friends in general being well to be in excellent spirits. As it is, I indulge my hopes much more than my fears. But it would make me extremely happy to have my mind entirely relieved. Give my tenderest love to my lovely Children, and as many kisses as will not be too troublesome for you, and remember me very affectionately to Nelly and my Brother &c.

Adieu! my dear Hannah. I am ever Most anxiously and most affectionately yours

Ja. Iredell.

P.S. Just going to that melancholy house Colo. Mc.Culloch's.[5]

RC, Iredell Papers, Duke. Addressed "Mrs. Iredell Edenton By favor of Mr. Black."

---

[1]Ann Keeling (before 1759-1789) and Thomas Satterwhite were married on October 15, 1772. Her mother, Agnes Keeling, and John Williams were married on November 12, 1759. Agnes Keeling had been married previously. Holcomb, *Marriages of Granville County*, 296, 355.

[2]For more information on the Baker case, see JI to Hannah Iredell, April 14, 1787, in this volume.

[3]Mr. Hill may be Whitmel Hill. JI represented him in a suit in the Halifax District Superior Court. See Whitmel Hill to Samuel Johnston and JI, May 11, 1787, in this volume

[4]For more on JI's financial dealings with Samuel Strudwick, see JI to Hannah Iredell, April 18, 1786, n. 2, in this volume.

[5]See JI to Hannah Iredell, October 27, 1789, in this volume.

To Hannah Iredell

Halifax Oct. 27th. 1789.

My dear Hannah,

Soon after I wrote to you on Sunday I went to Colo. Mc.Culloch's, where I was greatly affected indeed, poor Ben the moment he saw me bursting into tears and the whole time continuing dejected with the deepest melancholy. His Wife was delivered of a fine Boy, now living and in good health, which she herself immediately named "Henry Eustace." He went into her room a very little time after, when she told him unless she had immediate assistance she was gone, and almost instantly expired.[1] I can imagine no event more dreadful, especially as I believe they were as happy a Couple as any in the State. I could not bear to come away that night, and hearing Hamilton was come I sent Peter to enquire for letters, & had the satisfaction to receive these he so obligingly brought me. I think Hamilton behaved very kindly, & shall remember it. My happiness in hearing that our dear Children were so well would have been much more complete could I have had the pleasure to hear that you were so too. But I indulge the hope that you are by this time nearly if not quite recovered, and that I shall be happy enough to find you all quite well.—It gave me very great concern indeed to hear of Mrs. Johnston's misfortune, and your Brother's and James's sickness. God grant they may all soon be entirely recovered.

I had the pleasure on Sunday of seeing Gen. Lincoln and Colo. Humphrys two of the Commissioners for holding a Treaty with the Indians. They came to town on Saturday evening, but none of us knew it. On Sunday morning they called on Colo. Davie, who did not know before that they were in Town, and I luckily happened to call at his house while they were there. They said they had had a great mind to have called on him the evening before, but the weather was bad. We greatly regretted they did not, as we could have spent an agreeable evening with them, the Judges & Mr. Moore & myself having that day dined with him. They went out of town almost immediately. Gen. Lincoln seems a very plain Man, but Humphrys is a lively agreeable Fellow. They made no Treaty with the Indians, but concluded a truce.[2]

I must answer Annie's letter.[3] Tell her and her dear Brother how much I love them, and remember me affectionately to Nelly & my Brother and Billy, the continuance of whose indisposition I hear of with much concern. Present my affectionate remembrance to the Family over the Creek and to Peggy when there is opportunity. I congratulate them all on the sight of George, & beg to be remembered most kindly to him—I hope my Brother will excuse my not writing to him. I rejoice to hear he is better, & that he takes proper care of himself.

Adieu! my dear Hannah. I am ever Most affectionately yours

Ja. Iredell.

RC, Iredell Papers, Duke. Printed, McRee, 2:269.

---

[1]Sarah and Benjamin McCulloch were married in 1778. David B. Gammon and William L. Murphy Jr., *Marriage Records of Halifax County, North Carolina, 1758-1872* (n.p.: David B. Gammon and William L. Murphy Jr, 1983), 169.

[2]Congress established a commission to negotiate a treaty with the Creek Indians in 1789. The delegation included Benjamin Lincoln (1733-1810) of Massachusetts, who had been a major-general in the Continental army. In 1784 and 1786, he had represented Massachusetts in negotiations with the Penobscott Indians. Lincoln's fellow commissioners were David Humphreys, who had been an aide to George Washington, and Cyrus Griffin (1748-1810) of Virginia, who had been president of the Continental Congress (1788) and later became a federal district judge. The commission left New York for Georgia on August 21, 1789, and met with the Creeks in September. The Creeks rejected the proposed treaty but did agree to a truce. Clark, *State Records*, 21:562, 563; *DAB*, s.v. "Lincoln, Benjamin"; *BDC*, s.v. "Griffin, Cyrus"; David B. Mattern, *Benjamin Lincoln and the American Revolution* (Columbia: University of South Carolina Press, 1995), 190-193.

[3]The following note was written at the bottom of this letter: "My dearest Annie, I thank you for your kind & pretty letter. It made me happy to hear that you and your dear Brother were well, and that you had both been so good. I hope you will always be so, and then every body will love you. I wish very much to see you, and will be at home as soon as I can. I am sorry that little Rogue your Brother would not take all the kisses you offered him. I will take the remainder myself when I return. I am, my dear Annie, Your affectionate Papa, Ja. Iredell."

From Arthur Iredell

Guildford Novr. 3d. 89—

I wrote to You, my dear James, by the last New York Packet, and I believe promised to write by this; but to avoid Repetitions, and to be as malicious as possible, I will do more now, I will engage to write to You a few Lines, at least, by every Packet; provided You will, on Your Part engage to follow my Example[1]—If you shall do so, in any Degree, I shall think myself a great Gainer by the Compact; probably in the same Proportion that you have convinced me N Carolina would gain by acceding to the Federal Union. The Priviledge of comparing great Things with small, & Vice versa, is You know of great Antiquity; and therefore you will not wonder at the Effect of Your Eloquence upon me, tho you little dreamt, when you were making your fine Speeches, of the Comparison they have thus provoked—I have read them over & over, and decies repetita placebunt. I would say more if I did not fear to offend the Modesty of a trans-Atlantic Lawyer—Did you practice in Westminster Hall, I should have much less reserve. Bashfullness is with us a tender Plant that will not thrive; and they do not cultivate It therefore in Our Courts of Justice. But I must venture to compliment You upon one Talent, Which I wish, in your Charity, You could communicate to me—It is what I think may be called the Art of Compression. There is no Waste of Language in Your Speeches—You say more in five Words than is commonly expressed in fifty.—I don't know whether you meant to feed the Appetite Your Pamphlet has given me for American Politicks, but I must tell you that I expect you to do so, by continuing to transmit every thing of the kind in which You are at all interested, & as many others as you shall think proper to add: Remembering always to give the Bearer of them a broad hint that we have such things as Stage Coaches in England, which have the Art of conveying a Parcel as well as the Post[2]—Our Politicks are at this Moment very uninteresting. We are, I thank God, idle Spectators of intestine Wars upon the Continent which every Day spread wider & wider, & will probably deluge It with Blood. The last Accounts from Brabant informs us that the Insurgents in that Country had possessed themselves of Antwerp

& Lille. One Report is that the King of Prussia is to join them, & that the P of Orange is to be declared D of Brabant. The Emperor has taken Belgrade, but he would like to keep Brabant for all that.[3] Your European Intelligence is, I suppose, very good—so good that you may laugh at my Information Which, to say truth, is shabby enough.—I have as little to say of myself. The Affair, so interesting to me, of Which I informed You in my last Letter, continues as it was then. I have not received any Answer from my Uncle, but I expect one every Day, a Packet having been long due. The Nature of It, & the Consequences to which it may lead, You shall hear of by the earliest Opportunity—I have little to tell you of my Mother. She is tol[*erably*] well in hea[*lth*] and I supply her with such sca[*nt*] Assistance as She wants; others I have not to give [*her. I*] have not seen her a great while, indeed I have confined Myself very closely to my Cure, partly from Principle, & partly from an Eye to Oconomy. You would think there was no harm in this, if you knew the Popularity it has occasioned—In short, I make my own Sermons, & preach them—to <u>a very good humoured Audience</u>. As I mean to write so frequently, I shall make no Scruple of taking a french leave[4]—I trust you are all well. My most Affectnte. Remembrances to my Sister, Tom, & the Children.

I am yours & theirs most entirely.

A I—

I hope Tom's Patience & good Nature are not exhausted.

I have attempted to persuade my Mother to live in Bath or Bristol, where She must have some Friends left, & might pass her Time more happily, but I have not succeeded. My best hope is of being able to Defray the Expence of an American Voyage in the Spring. She cannot be happy, at least will not be so in this Country.

RC, Johnson Collection, NCSA. Printed, McRee, 2:269-270. Addressed "James Iredell Esqre. Edenton North Carolina America." Endorsed "Guildford Nov. 3. 1789. Arthur Iredell Ansd."

---

[1]See Arthur Iredell to JI, October 6, 1789, in this volume.

[2]In a previous letter to JI, Arthur reported that a packet that JI had sent to him had been delivered by post, a more expensive method than coach. See Arthur Iredell to JI, October 6, 1789, in this volume.

[3]The Duchy of Brabant, located in what is now northern Belgium and the southern section of the Netherlands, was at the time of this letter part of the Austrian Netherlands. Inspired by events in France, the residents of the Austrian Netherlands rebelled and unexpectedly overthrew Austrian rule. Walter W. Davis,

Joseph II: An Imperial Reformer for the Austrian Netherlands (The Hague: Martinus Nijhoff, 1974), 259-264.

[4]"French leave" means to exit without notice. The term refers to the practice, fashionable in France and to a lesser degree England in the eighteenth century, of leaving a social gathering without bidding the host adieu. *OED*, s.v. "French leave."

From Samuel Johnston

Fayette Ville 13th. November 1789

My dear Sir

I am here among a great number of busy people without being able to form a Conjecture with respect to what will be the result of the mighty Bustle. The Principle business which I have heard mentioned, relates to an alteration in the Court System, some mode /of/ calling in the Specie Certificates, altering the Land Tax so as to make it more equal, incorporating the Towns of Newbern Edenton Halifax & Wilmington a great variety of other matter is talked of but very little brought forward in form[1]

There is still a violent & virulent Opposition kept up to the new Constitution but the Friends of that measure count upon its being adopted by a considerable Majority, my particular Situation prevents my mixing much among the people,[2] indeed were it otherwise my health would not, admit of it, for we have been all laid up with violent colds & fevers Mr. Dawson and myself were confined only a day or two, my Brother was dangerously /ill/ for several days but is now in a fair way of doing well. Mr. Dawson and myself are almost quite well we take no other Medicine at present but Porter and Hoar-Hound Tea.[3] I have not been able to recover my Appetite

I hope soon to have agreeable Accounts of you and your Family and remain Affectionately Yours

Sam Johnston

RC, Johnson Collection, NCSA. Printed, McRee, 2:271. Addressed "James Iredell Esquire New Bern by favr. of Doctr. Smallwood." Endorsed "Fayette Ville 13 Nov. 1789. Sam. Johnston. Ansd."

---

[1]The General Assembly, meeting in Fayetteville from November 2 to December 22, considered two proposals to increase the efficiency of the state superior courts: an amendment to "An act for establishing courts of law, and for regulating the proceedings therein," and another measure called "An act for giving an equity jurisdiction to the Superior Courts." Both became law in 1790. The statutes divided the superior court districts into an eastern and western circuit,

established dates and places for the courts to meet, and increased the number of superior court judges by one. Cheney, *North Carolina Government*, 222; Clark, *State Records*, 21:593; 25:65-67.

During the 1789 session the General Assembly passed "An Act Providing Means for the Payment of the Domestic Debt, for Appropriating Certain Monies Therein Mentioned; and to Amend an Act passed the Last Session of the General Assembly, Entitled 'An Act for Levying a Tax for the Support of Government, and for the Redemption of the Old Paper Currency, Continental Money, Specie and Other Certificates.' " This measure prescribed various taxes, including a land tax, to be levied beginning in 1790 and continuing until the domestic debt was paid. The taxes could be paid with "specie certificates of every kind." Clark, *State Records*, 25:7-9.

The General Assembly established a joint committee on November 6-7 to write a bill to equalize land taxes. On November 26, the committee's work was presented to both houses and passed on first reading. No further action was taken, however. Clark, *State Records*, 21:209, 268, 584, 624.

Legislators introduced a bill that would have permitted tradesmen and manufacturers in Edenton, New Bern, Wilmington, Halifax, and Washington to incorporate, that is to elect members to a board that would serve to protect their interests. The senate rejected the proposal on its second reading. House Bills, November 12-December 17, 1789, General Assembly Session Records, State Archives.

[2]Johnston's "particular Situation" was that he was governor and had been president of the 1788 ratification convention. He was reelected governor by the state legislature on November 14, 1789, and chosen as president of the 1789 convention. Cheney, *North Carolina Government*, 160; Massengill, *North Carolina Votes*, 67, 71.

[3]Porter is a dark beer that acquired its name because of its popularity among porters and other laborers. Horehound (*marrubium vulgare*) is an herb that has been used since ancient times to treat coughs, sore throats, and lung ailments. It is administered in tea form as a laxative. *OED*, s.v. "porter," "horehound"; Mildred Fielder, *Plant Medicine and Folklore* (New York: Winchester Press, 1975), 77, 100, 191.

From William R. Davie

Fayetteville Nov. 16h. 1789.

My Dear Sir

We have gone on smoothly as yet—The Superior Court bill seems to meet the General approbation[1]—The University bill will certainly pass[2]—Govr. Johnston is unanimously reelected—He was also elected President of the Convention to day—'tho too unwell to attend the House—C. Johnston V. President.[3] The Anties attempted to put S—r upon us—but the business was better managed[4]—

The calculations are greatly in favor of the Constitution its friends say there is no doubt, of this however I am not so confident.

I have been in very ill health ever since I came here—our present business will not help me much—excuse this scrawl, it is now near 12 O clock at night—I hope to have leisure enough, and better news to send you in a few days—

Adieu am wt. sincere regard yours

W R Davie

If my bill passes wt. salary suppt. you must be a J—

RC, Iredell Papers, Duke. Printed, McRee, 2:271. Addressed "The Honble. James Iredell Esq. at Newbern." Endorsed "Fayette. Ville Nov. 16. 1789. W R. Davie. Ansd."

---

[1]See Samuel Johnston to JI, November 13, 1789, n. 1, in this volume.

[2]On November 12, Davie introduced "An Act to Establish a University in this State," and on December 11, the bill became law. JI was among those named in the act as university trustees. Robinson, *William R. Davie*, 227-228; Clark, *State Records*, 25:21-24.

[3]C. Johnston is Charles Johnson, who was chosen unanimously as vice president of the convention. Clark, *State Records*, 39.

[4]"S—r" is Samuel Spencer.

From Moses Coleman

November 20—1789

Dear Sir

this is to Let you know that the Soot you are inploid for me is Settled the same to be Dismised from Court Mr. Theophalus pearce paying all Cost there unto[1] Sir no more at present But you Well wishes untill Death.

Moses Coleman

FC, New Bern District Superior Court Records, Civil Action Papers, NCSA. Addressed "To Mr. Iredell /Esqur./ attorney."

---

[1]Moses Coleman of Edgecombe County sued Theophalus Pearce and Arthur Jernegan, both of Johnston County, in the New Bern District Superior Court. Details of the case have not been found. *Heads of Families, 1790 Census*, 54; *Coleman v. Pearce and Jernegan*, November 1788, May and November 1789, New Bern District Superior Court, Argument, Reference, and Appearance Docket, 1786-1791, State Archives; New Bern District Superior Court, Civil Action Papers, 1785-1788, State Archives.

From William J. Dawson

Fayette Ville 22d. November 89

Dear Sir

Permit me to congratulate you on the happy decision of the important Question which has So long and So violently agitated [*the*] State.[1] the business has been conducted th[*rough*]out with great moderation. Some of the Gen[*tlemen*] of the opposition to be Sure, have been unr[*easona*]bly tedious trifling and I might add absurd in their objections, which was Submitted to /by the majority/ with a deg[*ree*] of patience that astonished every body. on taking the question for its adoption, there appeared Yeas 193 Nays 75.[2] The minority appear to be perfectly Satisfied Since the dicision, not, because their doubts and fears have been fully removed, but because they have determined chearfully to acquiesce in every measure which meets the approbation of the Majority of their Country men.

The Mr. Johnstons have quite recoverd from their late indisposition.

This is a Sudden and unexpected oppertunity or else I Should have given you a more particular account of the discussion of the constitution, but, I ha[*ve n*]o more time to write in, than the [*faded*] Consul will take to eat his break[*fast Mr.*] Johnston would have written but he is not yet awake

With the Sincerest respect & esteem I am My dear Sir Your Most Obedient Servt.

W. J. Dawson.

The Convention meet on monday to consider of the amendments necessary to be recommended.[3]

RC, Iredell Papers, Duke. Printed, McRee, 2:272. Addressed "James Iredell Esquire Newbern Honored by Monsd. Ducher." Endorsed "Fayette Ville 22 Nov. 1789 W. J. Dawson Ansd."

---

[1]On November 21, 1789, the convention delegates ratified the Constitution. Dawson represented Bertie County at the convention. Clark, *State Records*, 22:48-49.

[2]The total vote count given in Clark's *State Records* is 195 to 77, but, as Trenholme points out, there are only 194 names listed as yes votes in Clark. Trenholme, *Ratification*, 238n; Clark, *State Records*, 22:48-49.

[3]The convention appointed a committee consisting of four Federalists and three Antifederalists to prepare a list of suggested amendments to submit to Congress. A resolution accepting the committee's recommendations was approved on November 23, 1789. Trenholme, *Ratification*, 239; Clark, *State Records*, 22:51-52.

From William R. Davie

Fayetteville, Nov. 22d. 1789.

My dear Sir

Before this reaches you, the news of our accession to the Union will I am sure have received your congratulations—The circumstance of so respectable a majority as 193 to 75 will give great satisfaction to the friends of the new Government, and weight to its operation in this State. —

The Governor has recovered perfectly as well as his brother who has been dangerously ill.

Our legislative business will now begin to move again, and the business of the Convention has terminated with so much moderation—that I hope every thing will go on smoothly.

I must refer to Mr. Moore for a list of the public bills and believe me with great sincerity and Friendship

yours &c

William R Davie

RC, Iredell Papers, Duke. Addressed "James Iredell Esqr. at Newbern. Hond. by Col. Leach."

From Samuel Johnston

Fayette Ville 23d. November 1789

Dear Sir

As I expect Judge Spencer will set out as soon as the Convention rises, I take that opportunity to congratulate you on the Adoption of the new Constitution by a Majority of 118. The Anties behave with great good humor on the Occasion, a few amendments will be recommended which I expect will finish the business of the Convention this day. Fayette Ville is to have a Member[1]

I have been very earnestly sollicited by a Number of the Members and particularly the Antifederal party to take a seat in the Senate, which I have agreed to.[2] Chas. Johnson is talked of as Govr. Billy Blount will be opposed to him[3]

I was not able to attend the Convention till the two last days of last Week. I now find myself much recovered and better than when I left home.

There has been very little done in the Assembly hitherto so that it is probable they will continue at this place some time longer. I will leave them as soon as I can with decency.

2 O'Clock in the afternoon

I understand Spencer will not go in two or three days
The Convention is adjourned sine die
Be pleased to put the enclosed Letter into the Post Office if no immediate opportunity by Water

Yours affectionately

Sam Johnston

RC, Iredell Papers, Duke. Printed, McRee, 2:272. Addressed "James Iredell Esqr."

---

[1]The convention passed an ordinance allowing Fayetteville representation in the General Assembly. Clark, *State Records*, 22:52-53.

[2]The General Assembly elected Samuel Johnston to the U.S. Senate on November 27, 1789. Johnston resigned as governor to accept the post. The term lengths in this initial election were staggered, and Johnston was elected for the shorter term, which ended March 3, 1793. Clark, *State Records*, 21:628; *DNCB*, s.v. "Johnston, Samuel"; *BDC*, s.v. "Johnston, Samuel."

[3]Alexander Martin defeated Charles Johnson and John Williams in the governor's race. Benjamin Hawkins was elected to the Senate from a field that included William Blount and William Lenoir. Clark, *State Records*, 21:630, 661, 666. For a list of all the nominees for senator, see Charles Johnson to JI, November 23, 1789, n. 3, in this volume.

From Charles Johnson

Fayette Ville 23d. Novr. 1789

Dear Sir

Your much esteemed favor of the 8th I received by Mr. Mare, and agreable to your request I have the pleasure of informing you that on saturday the Constitution was finally adopted & ratified. On the Question the votes were 193, for it, 76 against it Majority 117. Permit me to congratulate you upon this glorious event, which I know <y> will give you the most singular satisfaction, as I believe nobody had it more at heart than you; nor <I believ> has any person contributed more to bring about the amazing change in the sentiments of the people, that is evident from the great Majority in favr. of the Constitution; even <my> exceeding that at Hilsboro' against it.

We have lost General Caswell who died <It was on> the 10th.[1] Governor Johnston has been reelected, but will I suppose resign; as he has given his assent to be a Senator in compliance with the general wish of the legislature, who are and will be unanimous in voting him into that office.[2] Several Gentlemen are mentioned & are Candidates for the other Senator viz Mr. W Blount, Hawkins Williamson, Parsons, D White, Bloodworth, Stokes, Osborn, McDowel Mr. Lenoir, B. Smith, Galway &c &c.[3] It seems to be settled & understood that one is to go from the Western Country, but who I can not tell

Upon the Governors resignation, Judge Williams, Mr. Martin & Mr. Blount are spoke of as Candidates, but it is generally supposed that Judge Williams will have the appointment.[4]

I wish the whole Offices were once disposed of & the place for holding the next Assembly fixed, for untill then interesting objects are settled.[5] I'm afraid little business will be done—& I begin already to be tired of this place, to which a severe cough may perhaps contribute.

Believe me sir I am infinitely obliged to you for your information of my Charlie's health;[6] the first account I had of him since I left him. Mr. Cabarrus who lives in the same room & Col. Davie in the next to us, are <both> well—<both> the Governor & Mr. J. Johnston have been both very ill but are now perfectly recovered. Mr. Cabarrus desires his Compts to you & intended to have written to you, but various businesses in which he is engaged have prevented him.

With true esteem & respects I am Dr. Sir Your most obt sert.

Chas. Johnson

RC, Johnson Collection, NCSA. Printed, McRee, 2:273. Addressed "James Iredell Esqr. New bern."

---

[1]Richard Caswell died on November 10. Two days earlier he had suffered a paralyzing stroke while presiding over the state senate. Charles Johnson, who was Speaker pro tempore, replaced Caswell as Speaker. *DNCB*, s.v. "Caswell, Richard"; Clark, *State Records*, 21:588-589.

[2]See Samuel Johnston to JI, November 23, 1789, n. 3, in this volume.

[3]Timothy Bloodworth, William Blount, Benjamin Hawkins, William Lenoir, Joseph McDowell, Thomas Person, John Stokes, James White, John Williams, Richard Dobbs Spaight, and William Polk were nominees for the U.S Senate. Johnson mistakenly lists Williams as Williamson and James White as D. White. James Galloway was nominated as a councilor. Clark, *State Records*, 21:614, 703.

[4]See Samuel Johnston to JI, November 23, 1789, n. 3, in this volume.

[5]On November 14 and 26, the General Assembly voted on the location of the next session of the assembly, but no town received a majority of votes. In both instances, Tarboro received the largest number of votes, with Fayetteville following in second. On December 3, the assembly again cast ballots, and this time Fayetteville received a majority. General Assembly Session Records, November-December 1789, Joint Papers, State Archives.

[6]Charles Earl Johnson was the son of Charles and Ann Earl Johnson. He became a planter and served in the state senate (1817-1820). *DNCB*, s.v. "Johnson, Charles"; Ashe, Weeks, and Van Noppen, *Biographical History*, 2:205.

From Richard D. Spaight

Dear Sir:

Clermont,[1] November 26th, '89.

I return you my thanks for the agreeable information you sent me yesterday, "the adoption of the Constitution by our Convention." I am very happy to hear that wisdom has at last presided in our councils, and enabled the Convention to break through that cloud of ignorance, and villainy, which has so long obscured our political horizon. I am much obliged to you for sympathizing with me in my sore afflictions: I have, indeed, suffered severely. Since the Convention at Hillsborough in July '88, I have never enjoyed one day's perfect health; and, except two or three months last summer, which enabled me to crawl about a little, I have been very ill, and at present see very little prospect of a speedy recovery, &c.

R. D. Spaight.

Printed, McRee, 2:273.

---

[1]Cleremont plantation, Spaight's home, was located near New Bern. *DNCB*, s.v. "Spaight, Richard Dobbs."

To Hannah Iredell

Newbern Nov. 26. 1789.

My dear Hannah,

I have the greatest pleasure in thinking that before this letter reaches you, you will have the delightful satisfaction to hear not only that the Constitution has been adopted by 193 against 75, (which was on Saturday) but that both your Brothers had quite recovered, of both which charming events Mr. Dawson was so kind as to write me, though in a great hurry, on the 22d., and he mentioned your Brother would have wrote too but that he was not awake. It gave me no little Joy to hear that your Brother was able to take the chair that day as President.[1] If my health had not mended before, this would have quite restored it, but thank God my cold has been better every day since I came and now I have scarcely a symptom of it—Mr. Duchane the French Consul was kind enough to notify to me his going to Edenton, & he brought us this excellent news, so that you must be civil to him—

I wait anxiously for Blount & his Wife, who have not arrived. Give my tenderest love to Annie & James, & remember me to all the rest at home & at Hayes, including my Nephew Tredwell.[2] My heart is now as light as a feather, and I shall be most happy on my return if I find you all well.

God bless you! my dear Hannah! and be assured I am ever

Most affectionately yours

Ja. Iredell.

Friday.

P.S. I have just had the pleasure of a letter from your Brother. He is quite recovered, & will undoubtedly be a Senator

RC, Johnson Collection, NCSA. Addressed "Mrs. Iredell Edenton."

[1]Samuel Johnston had been unable to attend the convention because of illness, but on November 22, 1789, he assumed his role as president.

[2]The following message was written to "My dear Annie" at the end of this letter: "I thank you for intending to write to me, and am very desirous to see you and your Brother. God bless you both. I hope you and he behave well, and that your Mamma will have the pleasure to tell me so when I return."

From Archibald Maclaine

Wilmington 26th. Nov 1789

My dear Sir

As you may not have had a direct conveyance from Fayetteville, I cannot deny myself the pleasure of informing you, that last night a letter from Mr. Adam a merchant there, and a member of the convention, assures us that the grand question was decided on Saturday the 21st. by <a major> 193 votes for the constitution, to 75 against it; <a> majority 118, which is considerably more than were against us last year.

We are told that Mr. Huske, to appear the more conspicuous, walked out at the head of the minority—I suppose Judge Spencer was too much mortified to push himself forward From the various intelligence we have received, I am very apprehensive of an instalment or valuation law; but as the Assembly are determined to have all the money out of the treasury, even if they purchase certificates with it, I am not altogether without hopes that the evil may be avoided—It seems to be the general opinion of the members that there is no danger of a new emission, though Person, the B[l]ounts &c are very earnest for it—These last are however unpopular and we are told have been petitioned against, as holders of public money—They have besides lost a principal prop, by the death of Caswell. Unfortunately I have received no letters by the last conveyance, otherwise I could have given you a number of particulars which would at least have been amusing

Your representative Mr. Hamilton distinguished himself by supporting Jones's election against Hill's petition—On the question on the concurrence with the report of the committee, which was altogether in favor of the election, the vote was unanimous[1]

I should not omit to mention, that this assembly is said to be the most moderate one that we have had since the revolution, and that there are nearly one half new members

Oblige me with some information about my affairs in Edenton court.

I congratulate you and my federal friends on the happy change in our situation,

& am very sincerely Yours

A Maclaine

Last post I sent my papers and told the rider to bring me a line from you Mr. H or Mr. Moore—but I have not seen him

RC, Johnson Collection, NCSA. Printed, McRee, 2:273-274. Addressed "James Iredell esquire Newbern." Endorsed "Wilmington 26 Nov. 1789. A. Maclaine. Ansd."

---

[1]On November 3, 1789, William Henry Hill sent a memorial to the house charging that the election of Wilmington's representative had been conducted illegally. His concerns were referred to the Committee of Privileges and Elections, of which John Hamilton of Edenton was a member. On Friday, November 6, 1789, committee member Thomas Person reported that there was insufficient testimony to support the allegations, thus Edward Jones was allowed to represent Wilmington. Clark, *State Records*, 21:200, 210.

To Hannah Iredell

Newbern Nov. 29. 1789.

My dear Hannah,

I received your agreeable letters by Mr. Blount & Mr. Carthy only a day or two ago. The latter Mr. Carthy inclosed me in a very obliging letter from Washington.[1] I was happy indeed in hearing you were all so well, and I assure you not [*at*] all displeased at your endeavour to awake me to a proper sense of attention to the inter[*est*] of our dear lovely Children, whose future situation I know ought to be the invariable o[*bject*] of my thoughts. I hope I shall have discretion enough to correct a fault I know I a[*m*] liable to, & my mind being now easy about public affairs I think, instead of my atte[*ntion*] being relaxed it will be greatly increased towards my private ones, since I confess I have too long indulged despairing apprehensions which, thank God, are now dissipated—[*I*] have so much business here to attend to, that tho' I employ every minute of my time al[*torn*] & shall use every exertion to get away I fear I shall not be able to leave Newbern [*torn*] till Thursday. The rejoicings here are put off till Tuesday, which will interfere in some measure tho' it shall as little as possible with my business.[2] Unfortunately I do not receive money here in proportion to the business I do, & this time Mr. Moore makes the same complaint. None of the Tenants from Tuckahoe have yet paid, tho' they promised to be here the latter end of the Court. I have yet only seen Mrs. Williams in the street, for tho' she has been every day at Hunts with her Sister I can't visit there. I am going to her own house to day. She expressed great gratitude for your letter.[3] Tho' the Convention adjourned on Monday Williams has not yet arrived, nor Spencer, tho' I suppose he wi[*ll*] come to day to get £50. for two days attendance.[4] My health is now excellent God grant I may find yours and all the Family's and your Brother's so on my return. [*torn*] Tell my dear Annie & James I am very impatient to see them, & love them dearly. Remember me affectionately to all the rest, & desire Nelly to have her sixpence ready to pay me. I always include Tredwell tho' I use general words. My Brother must excuse my not writing to him now. I flatter myself long before this Peggy's face [*is a*]s handsome as ever. The Post last night brought no mail, otherwise I should have [*been*] uneasy in not getting any letter from you—I imagine the wind prevented its [*com*]ing. How came you to think of not writing by the Post again? To be sure you must have made a mistake as to the day.

Adieu! my dear Hannah. I am ever Most affectionately yours

Ja. Iredell.

I have not heard from Fayette since I wrote [*y*]ou I believe I omitted mentioning to you that your Brother <he> wrote me he had been much pressed to serve as a Senator & had consented, & that C. Johnson was proposed for Governor, but would be opposed by Mr. Blount. The v[*ote*] for Senators had not however been given.[5]

RC, Johnson Collection, NCSA. Addressed "Mrs. Iredell Edenton."

---

[1]Attorney Daniel Carthy (d. 1817) of New Bern served as an officer in the Revolutionary War, was elected to the Council of State in 1792 and 1795, and represented New Bern in the house of commons (1794-1795, 1810-1811). Neal, *Abstracts of Vital Records*, 1:86; *The Star and North-Carolina State Gazette* (Raleigh), June 27, 1817; Cheney, *North Carolina Government*, 166, 167, 232, 259, 261.

[2]The citizens of New Bern celebrated North Carolina's ratification of the Constitution on December 2, with parades and a banquet at the former governors palace. At the latter, twelve toasts were made, and a twelve-gun salute was fired in honor of the twelve states in the Union. Watson, *History of New Bern and Craven County*, 102.

[3]Elizabeth Williams of Craven County was the wife of Thomas Williams (d. before 1805), who was a delegate to the 1789 state ratification convention. In her letter of November 27, 1789, to JI, which was written in response to his letter of November 26, she wrote, "[I] have no commands at present to Edenton but my ever grateful thanks to Mrs. Iredell for her truely kind letter and my sincere good wishes for her happiness." Massengill, *North Carolina Votes*, 63; Iredell Papers, Rare Book, Manuscript, and Special Collections Library, Duke University.

[4]The Williams in this case is Judge John Williams.

[5]See Samuel Johnston to JI, November 23, 1789, n. 3, in this volume.

From Samuel Johnston

Fayette 29th. November 1789

Dear Sir

I had the pleasure of receiving your Letter by Capt. Daves, that which you sent by express is not yet come to hand You will hear that I am elected a Senator and have resigned the Government for the ensuing year. it is not yet known who will be my Collegue. Lenoir, Blount & Hawkins are in nomination. I should be ready to leave this on Tuesday but am uncertain whether the Assembly will agree to my going before they have elected a Governor which is postponed till Wednesday. there is a great deal of Business before the Assembly, but nothing of consequence done, it is thought they will not rise before Christmass

I have been pretty well for some days till last night I was much disturbed with a Cough, but as it is not attended with any fever I have no apprehensions.

I wrote to Mrs. Johnston very lately and it being uncertain whether this will find you at Newbern I do not now write to her. I wish you well home remember me affectionately to all our Friends

Present my best respects to Mr. Moore & Judge Williams.

I am Dear Sir, Yours Affectionately

Sam Johnston

RC, Johnson Collection, NCSA. Addressed "James Iredell Esquire New Bern by favr. of Thos. Williams Esqr."

From Arthur Iredell

Guil[*d*]ford, December 1st, '89.

My Dear James:

. . . You are all doubtless interested about these continental disturbances. You will hear of the Duke of Orleans coming over to this country, and many curious conjectures about the cause.[1] The fact is this: he was sent over to be out the way of mischief. He is an ambitious fool, and has paid for all the horrors you have read of, with a view of being seated upon the throne, or becoming regent. De Lafayette told him so in express terms before the king: he did not deny it; but agreed to come over here, where he could do no harm. I was told this by a lord of the bed-chamber, and I tell it to you, because it is only privately known as yet, &c.

A. Iredell.

Printed, McRee, 2:274.

---

[1]Louis-Philippe-Joseph (1747-1793), Duke of Orléans, was Louis XVI's cousin and one of the wealthiest men in France. The king's supporters believed that the duke was encouraging public hostility toward Louis so that he might one day claim the throne for himself. As a result, they made arrangements for the duke to be sent on an assignment to England in order to reduce his influence in France. Samuel F. Scott and Barry Rothaus, eds., *Historical Dictionary of the French Revolution*, 2 vols. (Westport, Conn.: Greenwood Press, 1985), 2:734-737.

From Samuel Johnston

Fayette 1st. December 1789

Dear Sir

I wrote a few lines to you on Sunday, which I expected would find you at Newbern, by T. Williams[1] things here remain as they were at that time.

I expected then to leave this place on <that> /this/ day but the Assembly have put off the Election of a Governor till to morrow which will detain me some days longer

I had a conversation yesterday evening with Colo. Davie who seems to think that on account of some difficulties that occur no change will be made in the Court System this Session[2]

Spencer <has been> /is/ here solliciting some further compensation to himself and Brethren for their faithfull Service but is not like to succeed and so dissatisfied with the Conduct of the Assembly that he has expressed a wish to offer his Services to the United States and would condescend to accept an Appointment in their Courts, whether as a Judge of the Supreme Court or of the District Court I have not heard. it is said that neither Cushing nor Rutledge will accept their Appointments and he has no doubt of his being equal to either of them in point of Abilities & Reputation.[3] he has asked Colo. Davie to recommend him to Mr. Elsworth & Doctor Johnson,[4] he is to apply to me on the same Subject but has not yet done it

My Brother is recovering his strength by using exercise on horse back every day, Mr. Dawson is quite well and so am I <app> except that I am frequently subject to take cold and am a little troubled with a Cough

Present my most affectionate Respects to my Sister and the Girls. kiss your dear little ones for me and believe ever, my dear Sir

Your most affectionate & Obedt. Servant

Sam Johnston

RC, Johnson Collection, NCSA. Printed, McRee, 2:274-275. Addressed "James Iredell Esquire Edenton <Be so /good/ as forward the inclosed Letters> Be so good as to forward the inclosed Letters."

---

[1]Samuel Johnston to JI, November 29, 1789, in this volume.

[2]See Samuel Johnston to JI, November 13, 1789, n. 1, in this volume.

[3]William Cushing (1732-1810) was chief justice of the Massachusetts Supreme Court from 1777 to 1789. He then became the first justice appointed to the U.S. Supreme Court and remained on the high court for twenty-one years. When appointed in September 1789, Cushing insisted on first riding the state court circuit in Massachusetts in order to provide a quorum of judges before accepting his seat on the U.S. Supreme Court. *DAB* s.v. "Cushing, William"; Leon Friedman and Fred L. Israel, eds., *The Justices of the United States Supreme Court, 1789-1969: Their Lives and Major Opinions*, vol. 1 (New York: Chelsea House Publishers, in association with R. R. Bowker Company, 1969), 65.

John Rutledge (1739-1800) served in the Continental Congress (1774-1775, 1782-1783), as governor of South Carolina (1779-1782), and as a delegate to the 1787 constitutional convention. Rutledge was appointed as a U.S. Supreme Court justice in 1789 but resigned in 1791 to become chief justice of the South Carolina Supreme Court. In 1795, President Washington nominated Rutledge to be chief justice of the U.S. Supreme Court, but the Senate failed to confirm him. *DAB*, s.v. "Rutledge, John"; *BDC*, s.v. "Rutledge, John."

[4]Oliver Ellsworth, previously identified, and William Samuel Johnson (1727-1819) of Connecticut. Johnson served in the Continental Congress (1785-1787), as a delegate to the 1787 constitutional convention, and in the U.S. Senate (1789-1791). He was also the first president of Columbia College in New York (1787-1800). *BDC*, s.v. "Johnson, William Samuel."

From Archibald Maclaine

Wilmington 9th. December 1789

Dear Sir

I lament that I have it not in my power to inform you who is our Governor; who the second Senator to the United States, and at what time we shall have an election for representatives. The last information we had was, that Martin was within one vote of being elected Governor, and that the senator would be either Blount or Hawkins;—Lenoir losing ground every day[1]

I suppose you will have Mr. Johnston with you before this gets to your hands—I find he will have numberless applications for the few offices to be distributed in North Carolina—Present my compliments to him, and let him know that I have nothing to ask for myself, unless he could procure me a rich sinecure, for I am not fit for anything else, and I dispair of any such being established in my time, though I believe the Anties /with all their patriotism/ would lick their lips, if such a prospect should be held out to them.

What would you think of being the district Judge? Or could you make more by practicing in the federal courts? We have a great lack of men to fill law departments. As Mr. Hay is a young man, and capable of great application, I have thought it might be for his advantage, if he could procure the appointment, to be the Attorney for the district; though I do not find that there is any salary annexed to the office—What I am particularly anxious about is the Judge, and I wish to hear from you on the subject

I have seen the Choice, which I have read over very lightly—The hero of the piece is represented in a detestable as well as /in/ a ludicrous light—The allusions are sometimes happy, and the author has in a few instances expressed himself in a pleasing manner In one or two places he is disgusting, and the lines do not deserve the name of poetry It is upon the whole a miserable hotch-pot, and has nothing to support it but the contemptible character of[2]—

I received your favor from Newbern for which I thank you. Mr. Hooper, is so far at Fayetteville, where was taken sick, as he thought with something like a pleurisy

In haste, I bid you adieu

A Maclaine

RC, Iredell Papers, Duke. Printed, McRee, 2:275. Addressed "James Iredell esquire Edenton." Endorsed "Wilmington 9 Dec. 1789. A. Maclaine. Ansd."

---

[1]Maclaine must have composed this letter prior to attending the assembly because on the day it was written Martin was elected governor and Hawkins was chosen as senator. Clark, *State Records*, 21:666, 669.

[2]*The Choice*, a play by Arthur Murphy (1727-1805), was first performed in March 1765 in London. Howard Hunter Dunbar, *The Dramatic Career of Arthur Murphy* (New York: Modern Language Association; Oxford: Oxford University Press, 1946), 172-176.

From William R. Davie

Fayetteville, Decr. 21st. 1789

My Dear Sir,

We are now in expectation of rising tomorrow, the public business being generally finished and the patience of the members entirely exhausted—I must refer you to our friend Cabarrus for the history of the electioneering business—The varied fenesse and entrigue displayed on that occasion, particularly about the Senators exceeded any thing I ever saw—

I inclose you a list of the bills, you will perceive that some objects of considerable consequence have been <carried> obtained.[1] The University business succeeded to my outmost wish.

As to the business of the Debates, I could not wash my feelings up to the application you requested me to make—This matter I suppose will fall on us at last; we must see what can be collected from the sales; after that, we can with some propriety try the purses of the federal state—The Debates expected from Wilmington have never reached this place—if they had I am sure they would all have sold—Mr. Maclain has certainly neglected that matter or they might have been sent in The course of Two months—

I am out on this business for the expence of sending the debates to the Westward and Tarboro, but as I never expected to be reimbursed I kept no account.

I shall set about making preparation to assist you in this business which has fallen so disagreeably on us, if we are not rewarded Here we must trust as the saints do to an everlasting reward Hereafter. at all event the loss is to be pocketted by us; "profit" no man will suspect you of—

Farewell and believe me with The most sincere regard and Attachment your mo obt.

William R Davie

RC, Iredell Papers, Duke. Addressed "James Iredell Esqr. Edenton. Hond. by Mr. Cabarrus."

[1]For the bills passed during the 1789 session, see Clark, *State Records*, 25:1-63.

From Archibald Maclaine

Wilmington 22d. December 1789

Dear Sir

During the sitting of our court, I wrote you a few lines relative to public matters.[1] I suppose Mr. Johnston is preparing for New York, where I hope he and his colleague may arrive soon, that we may have at least a partial representation in Congress.

It was expected that the assembly would adjourn last Saturday but I suppose they could not then finish. The cession of the western territory to Congress is at last completed, so that we are <at last> rid of a people who were a pest and a burthen to us.[2] The election for representatives, it is said, will be some time next month, and over the mountains in February. The five districts are, Newbern & Edenton, Halifax & Hillsborough, Salisbury & Morgan, Fayetteville & Edenton, and the two districts west of the mountains[3]—Who we shall have here, is very doubtful—Mr. B Smith & Bloodworth are candidates. The former has no popularity, & the latter very little out of New Hanover—Perhaps some other may start up[4]—I understand that Dr. Williamson will be one of the candidates with you.[5]

We do not know here what is done about sinking the certificates; but we hope some method will be fallen upon to set the money now in the treasury into circulation. Never was such a scarcity known, and the paper is now in /an/ actual state of appreciation; but whether that may continue, is questionable not having heard from Fayetteville for some time. I do not know what is become of Col. Davie's reform of the court system—I expect however that it will fall to the ground.[6]

At our court, we tried exactly ten Jury causes, dissolved four injunctions, and left near four times that number where we found them.

I have mentioned to your brother the reason why your injunction bill was not sooner returned, and that the Judges declined ordering the writ without an addition to the formal prayer of the bill, though in the body of it, you had expressly requested that the defendant might be injoined. Judge Ashe once served me in the same manner, which I thought and still think, is being contemptibly minute; and a refusal without a repetition of the same thing, foolish as well as unwarrantable.

When you are at leisure, I shall be glad to hear from you, and to know when Mr. Johnston sets off for Congress.

I am with very sincere regard Dear Sir Truely yours

A Maclaine

Mr. Hooper on his way to Wilmington found himself too much indisposed at Fayetteville to proceed, and returned without waiting for the court at the latter place

23d. Decr.
Doctor Williamson (who will be with you before this) gave me a call on his way through Wilmington—I did not get any information from him, but that a bill is past for buying the certificates at 4/ in the pound, & that the assembly would rise today[7]

RC, Iredell Papers, Duke. Printed, McRee, 2:275-276. Addressed "James Iredell esquire Edenton." Endorsed "Wilmington 22 Dec. 1789. A. Maclaine. Ansd."

---

[1]See Archibald Maclaine to JI, November 26, 1789, in this volume.

[2]"An Act for the Purpose of Ceding to the United States of America, Certain Western Lands Therein Described" passed in the house of commons on December 11, 1789, and in the senate on December 12. General Assembly Session Records, November-December 1789, House Bills, November 12-December 17, State Archives.

[3]In "An Act Directing the Manner of Electing Representatives to represent this State in Congress," the five districts were designated as Edenton and New Bern, Roanoke, Cape Fear, Yadkin, and Western. Each congressional district consisted of two superior court districts. Clark, *State Records*, 25:1-3.

[4]Timothy Bloodworth was elected to represent the Cape Fear district in Congress. Cheney, *North Carolina Government*, 661.

[5]Hugh Williamson was elected to represent the Edenton and New Bern district. Cheney, *North Carolina Government*, 661.

[6]See Samuel Johnston to JI, November 13, 1789, n. 1, in this volume.

[7]See Clark, *State Records*, 25:7-9.

From John Haywood[1]

Fayetteville, Dec. 22d, '89.

Dear Sir:

From being much busied, it has too long been my custom to defer almost every thing, although ever so agreeable in itself, to the last moment: this custom, from being very imprudently indulged, has grown into habit, and it is to that cause I attribute my very unjustifiable and impolite behavior, in failing hitherto to acknowledge the receipt of your highly esteemed and truly friendly letters of June last: I beg you to be assured, my conduct in that particular has not by any means comported with my feelings; and that, even at this moment, the reflection on your goodness in writing them, and on the obligations they laid me under, affects me not only with the most tender and lively sentiments of gratitude, but calls into action every better sensation of my soul.

The Assembly have this evening closed their session: I intended to write you of their acts, but it is all hurry and bustle here, and my office is filled with men who are importunate for their money: Mr. Cabarrus, too, who obligingly takes charge of this, leaves town early on the morrow, so that of necessity I am compelled to forego the pleasure; however, you will permit me to send you here inclosed, such of the laws of this session as have been printed. . . . Suffer me to request that you will be pleased to offer, in the most acceptable manner my best respects to your lady, and to the Miss Blairs: enhance the obligation by accepting them yourself, and believe me, with every friendly and respectful sentiment,

Very much and very truly yours,

John Haywood.

Printed, McRee, 2:276-277.

---

[1]John Haywood (1755-1827), a native of Edgecombe County, was state treasurer from 1787 to 1827. Haywood County was named in his honor. *DNCB*, s.v. "Haywood, John"; McRee, *Life and Correspondence*, 2:277n.

List of Taxable Property of James Iredell, 1789

Lands.

612 Acres, viz. A Moiety of two Tracts of Land in the County of Jones, supposed to contain (according to the nominal acres in the Patents), after deducting what has been conveyed away, 1224 acres. In this, for want of a Copy of one of the Deeds I cannot be perfectly exact, but I believe it is right.

1065 Acres, viz. A Moiety of 2130 Acres (by estimation, according to the best information I have) in the County of Onslow, on the North East & North West Branches of New River.

200 Acres, viz. A Moiety of an Island, estimated at 400 Acres, by Patent dated 21 March 1742, lying in Chowan River.

Town Lots. A House and Lot in the Town of Edenton.

Free Males. Two.

Negroe Slaves, from 12 to 60 years of age} Dundee, Peter, Andrew, Sall, Edy, Sukey, Sarah, Ann. (These two last in my employ, tho' not my property.)

Carriage Wheels. Two.

FC, Johnson Collection, NCSA.

Index

C

D

H

K

L

M

N

Y